W9-BIR-247

SCHOOLING, TEACHING, AND LEARNING
AMERICAN EDUCATION

SCHOOLING, TEACHING, AND LEARNING
AMERICAN EDUCATION

C. M. Charles, Ph.D.
David K. Gast, Ed.D.
Richard E. Servey, Ph.D.
Houston M. Burnside, Ph.D.
of San Diego State University

with 132 illustrations,
including photographs by Houston M. Burnside

THE C. V. MOSBY COMPANY
Saint Louis   1978

Cover art courtesy of The St. Louis Art Museum
Winslow Homer, *The Country School,* 1871

The C. V. Mosby Company
11830 Westline Industrial Drive, St. Louis, Missouri 63141

Library of Congress Cataloging in Publication Data

Main entry under title:

Schooling, teaching, and learning: American education.

    Bibliography: p.
    Includes index.
    1. Education—Curricula. 2. Teaching.
3. Teachers assistants. I. Charles, C. M.
LB1570.S347   371.1'02   77-13496
ISBN 0-8016-0966-6

GW/CB/B 9 8 7 6 5 4 3 2

PREFACE

Schooling, Teaching, and Learning: American Education is presented to you as a basic book in education. The word "basic" often means old, tried, true, steadfast—and sometimes tired and out of date. We have done our best to avoid the latter traits. We have included facts and theories about education that are, indeed, tried, reliable, steadfast, and perhaps even true. We have capped them with exciting educational techniques developed and validated in the last few years, giving balance and practicality to the book. We believe you will find the contents enlightening, interesting, and eminently useful.

This book was prepared for neophytes and experienced hands alike. It provides basic, current information for paraprofessionals, beginning students in teacher education, student teachers, and experienced teachers and administrators. The contents are equally applicable to elementary and secondary teaching. The style of writing aims at being clear, explicit, and readable for both beginners and advanced professionals. Much of the material is original. We believe this material, combined with the latest from recognized authorities, reveals a plausible, optimistic picture of the state of the art in schooling, teaching, and learning.

You will find the book comprehensive. The materials included apply equally to private school, preschool, adult, and university teaching and learning. In truth, we believe that this book provides valuable insights and assistance to teachers in all schools at all levels.

The contents are arranged into five parts. The first part, entitled Education: Purpose, Promise, and Paradox, traces the historical and philosophical antecedents of present-day education, first in Western Europe and then in the United States. Present realities of American education are then compared against these historical dreams.

The second part, entitled The Contemporary Setting: Myths and Manifests, presents detailed examinations of communities, learners, schools, school personnel, and laws that pertain to students and teachers. A unique feature of this section is the specific techniques for studying learners and the communities in which they live.

Part three is entitled Instructional Designs and Strategies: State of the Art. It goes into the nitty-gritty of teaching, including curriculum, principles of instruction, methods of teaching, strategies of teaching, environments that nurture learning, and the skill of asking questions. It draws from the most current ideas and techniques, stressing their application in realistic educational settings.

Part four, entitled The Management of Learning, focuses on diagnosis, instructional planning, accountability, the positive control and guidance of student behavior, and the skills of effective communication between teacher and students. The detailed techniques explained enable teachers to provide their students with the finest in educational guidance and human relations.

Finally, Part five, entitled Professionalism: Skills, Ethics, and Style, charts a course for professional development. The first chapter is directed to paraprofessionals. It provides a multitude of practical suggestions to help them do their work effectively. The final chapter begins with the college student just entering teacher education and outlines programs, plans, and steps that lead to the ultimate level of professionalism: self-actualization in teaching.

You can see from this listing of contents that the

book provides knowledge, skills, and understanding in the following areas:

Historical, philosophical, sociological, and psychological foundations of education
Legal considerations
Human growth and development
Skills for conducting case studies
Principles of learning and teaching
Curriculum, planning, and accountability
Methods and strategies of teaching
Learning environments
Control and guidance of behavior
Skills of effective communication
Uses and functions of paraprofessionals
Professionalism and growth of the professional

These contents make the book at once comprehensive and useful for all who work with school students. A detailed list of contents and a glossary of "teacher talk" assist readers who use this book.

The authors have diligently attempted to avoid all language that might suggest racism or sexism. The latter has proved troublesome. Continued use of the plural, "the individual," "he/she," etc. disrupts the flow of words and ideas. For this reason, you will occasionally see the word "he" used to refer to individual persons, both male and female. This word is used in the universal sense and should not be construed as sexist.

C. M. Charles
David K. Gast
Richard E. Servey
Houston M. Burnside

CONTENTS

5 Learners
the principal clients, 75

6 Skills for studying learners, 95

7 Schools and school personnel
the menagerie, 114

8 The law and schooling
toes and hot waters, 134

PART THREE

INSTRUCTIONAL DESIGNS AND STRATEGIES
STATE OF THE ART

9 Curriculum development
everybody's act, 153

10 Principles of instruction
their application, 171

11 Methods of teaching, 198

12 Strategies of teaching, 225

SCHOOLING, TEACHING, AND LEARNING
AMERICAN EDUCATION

EDUCATION
PURPOSE, PROMISE, AND PARADOX

PART ONE

We begin our journey into schooling, teaching, and learning by taking a look backward. There we find the dreams that humans have held for education. We see plans for what education should be, what it should do, how it should be done, and who should receive it. We see these things first in Athens, whose philosophers built educational dreams that held sway for centuries and whose impact we still feel. Then we proceed through Western European thought into the Age of Reason.

Our attention shifts to the American colonies as they begin their struggles to survive and prosper and later to become independent. We see how education developed first to "delude Satan" and then turned to other ends that were peculiarly American, for example, education for democracy, for the common bond, and for economic efficiency.

Finally, we take stock of present realities of American education. We see that some of our dreams have been realized despite conditions that frustrate teachers and students alike.

The chapter titles are as follows:

1 **Formative dreams**
  fiddlers on the roof

2 **The American dream**
  keeping the faith

3 **Realities of American education**
  beauty marks and warts

FORMATIVE DREAMS

FIDDLERS ON THE ROOF

1

Since the dawn of recorded history man has wrestled with the issues of schooling, teaching, and learning. Over the centuries there has been great change in the purpose and nature of schooling. There have been tremendous innovations in teaching. Related to this is a wealth of scientific discovery about how people learn. That's why the American school as we know it today, with its technological approach to learning, bears little resemblance to schools of 1,000 or even 50 years ago.

But the knowledge and practice of education have strong historical roots. We stand on the shoulders of educational giants who, through past centuries, focused their intellects on the problems of education. Those thinkers planned ideal models for schools, suggested new methods of teaching, and shed light on the eternal question of how people learn.

To understand the present we must have some perspective on this past. As the saying goes, "the past is the greater part of the present." Unless past contributions to education are recognized, we will overlook significant foundations on which the theory and practice of today's education are built. We will also be ignorant of the fact that current practice has deep historical roots, and we will fail to realize that many educational issues and practices that masquerade as the latest innovation are, for better or worse, old notions revisited and reapplied.

Not everything new is good, and not everything old is bad. Some ideas have stood the test of time, and they continue to inspire thought and action. This is why we now examine the work of the grand masters of educational thought.

Our examination will be done in three parts, three dreams, as it were. These three dreams, the keys to the history of educational thought, are

(1) the classical dream, (2) the scientific dream, and (3) the practical dream.

THE CLASSICAL DREAM

The classical dream embodies the remarkable thoughts and insights of those two Greek giants Plato and Aristotle. These thoughts were first set forth in Hellenic times, the golden age of Greece. They were to be resurrected 1,700 years later to form the heart of the educational thrust of the Renaissance.

Let us examine the thoughts of those fabulous minds and get a glimpse of how they have influenced education across the past twenty-four centuries.

Plato and the ideal state

Plato was born in Athens in 427 BC. His natural parents and his stepfather came from prominent Athenian families with political connections. Through his stepfather, Plato was related to Pericles, whose 30-year domination of Athenian affairs had ended in death a year before Plato's birth. Pericles was a democrat, but Plato's relatives on his mother's side were oligarchs, who believed in rule by a wealthy power elite.

Plato grew up during the Peloponnesian War, which had begun in 430 BC as a struggle between Athens and Corinth for commercial supremacy. At the age of 12 years Plato saw the Athenian navy set sail on a disastrous mission against Syracuse in Sicily. Things went from bad to worse for Athens. By the time Plato was 25 years old, Athens had capitulated and lost her empire to Sparta.

During this war, Athenian politics were marked by revolutions, party infighting, and political purges. Following the disaster of the expedition against Syracuse, Athens went through a series of briefly established governments: the Council of Four Hundred, the Government of Five Thousand, a 6-year restoration of the democratic constitution, and the infamous Commission of Thirty who came to power with the aid of Spartan arms.

As a teenager and young adult, Plato was witness to the savage measures taken against political opponents after each change of government. Democrats and oligarchs alike took part in self-righteous purges. And the democracy that followed the reign of the Commission of Thirty did something that Plato could never forgive. Socrates,

Plato's beloved friend and teacher, was condemned to death in 399 BC on the charge of impiety. Socrates had resisted an attempt by the Thirty to be forced into political intrigue. He was eventually charged by the democrats with corrupting the young through his unorthodox teaching, which focused on honesty, wisdom, ethics, and self-examination.

The death of Socrates profoundly affected Plato. He became disillusioned with politics, opportunism, and compromise. He was repulsed by the fact that greed, ambition, and fear dominated politics and served as the springboard of wars. The Athens of Plato's time was not a democracy in the sense that we know it today. Underprivileged slaves outnumbered citizens four to one. Real equality did not exist among the citizens. Class struggles continued between the old aristocracy and the common citizens. Plato saw the common man exploited when the oligarchs were in power. He saw incompetents hold public offices when the democrats were in power.

After the death of Socrates, Plato spent 10 years in self-imposed exile, traveling and studying. He rejected his family tradition of politics. He returned to Athens as a reformer. The rest of his life was devoted to writing and teaching with two major aims: The first aim was to perpetuate the work of Socrates, who left no writing of his own. The second aim was to develop plans for the ideal state and the ideal statesman.

Out of Plato's efforts came the world's first university, Plato's Academy, founded in 386 BC. Its purpose was to train a new form of enlightened politician, a philosopher-statesman. The Academy was not a university as we know it now. It was just a peaceful grove of trees where scholars could stroll and engage in discussion.

It was obvious to Plato that the good life could only be achieved within a good society and that a good society depended on social order and a unified state system of education. These ideas were presented in Plato's great utopian work, *The Republic*. In the form of a dramatized discussion, the book set a model for political governance, social organization, and education that can still be seen today.

The good society proposed in *The Republic* was based on permanent ideals, plus a few assumptions about human nature. Plato realized that every society requires a division of labor and that this division is best achieved when an individual's talents and abilities are matched to the job he is asked to perform. Citizens were stratified in the Republic according to Plato's "Myth of the Metals." This metaphor held that there are four classes of people who correspond to four qualities of metal. The People of Iron are the laborers, men of brawn and little intelligence who do unskilled labor. The People of Brass are the farmers, traders, and artisans who serve the state by skilled labor. The People of Silver are the guardians of the state concerned with protecting the Republic from its enemies. The People of Gold are the statesmen concerned with governing the state.

In Plato's *Republic* all citizens were given a basic, or elementary, education. It began with an emphasis on folktales for the pre–6-year-old children. Children 6 to 13 years of age received instruction in reading, language arts, mathematics, morals, music, and physical education.

After age 13 years, the children of Iron and Brass, destined to be workers and artisans, would receive no further education and would go out to the workaday world of service to the society. The children of Silver and Gold would continue on to Middle School (13 to 16 year olds) for instrumental music, poetry, physical education, and mathematics theory and then on to Gymnastic School (16 to 20 year olds), where boys would receive strenuous physical training and study formal military science.

The People of Silver, with their quality of courage, would at this point be prepared to serve the Republic in a career of law enforcement and military duty. Higher education was reserved for the better students, the more intellectual People of Gold. They were destined to be statesmen. The Republic's leaders-to-be would study science, dialectics, philosophy, and education for a period of 10 to 15 years. At about age 35 years the leaders would begin a 15-year career in public service. Retirement from public duties at age 50 would enable a statesman to devote himself to the study of philosophy to become a "philosopher-king."

Some aspects of the Republic's social organization are not attractive to the modern reader. Plato would abolish family life for all but the laboring class, so as to avoid conflicts in loyalty to family and state. The state would control human relationships to keep the "metals" pure. Plato did con-sider that it might occasionally be possible for "Brass parents" to produce a "Silver child" and that opportunities should be open to such a child. Private property and material possessions would be outlawed because of their corruptive influences. There would also be censorship in teaching materials. Strange ideas? Perhaps. But these very ideas are being practiced in the religious and political lives of millions of people today in various parts of the world.

Plato's educational model may seem familiar. It roughly approximates the traditional educational attainment of the social classes in Western cultures. In the past, more than today, social status by birth tended to govern educational opportunity, although we can't blame Plato for that.

On the positive side, Plato may have realized a fact that many moderns are just discovering. That is that there is a wide range of natural endowment among the people of any community. This endowment encompasses many possible talents. The best thing a society can do for itself and its people is to educate children commensurate with their natural gifts.

In sum, what did Plato leave us? Plato's legacy to education includes the notion of compulsory and basic education for all and state-supported education at all levels for the gifted. Plato is important to educational thought because he was the first to speak comprehensively about the aims of education and to link schooling, teaching, and learning to the needs of society. He saw the development of personal virtues and service to the community as imperative educational goals. *But the major lesson the world learned from Plato is that a society is only as good and as strong as its educational system.*

Aristotle and the rational learner

Plato's most famous student was Aristotle. Aristotle has also had a profound intellectual influence on the Western world. In fact, most of the philosophical terms and classifications we use today were coined by Aristotle. Like his teacher, Aristotle raised many philosophical problems that are still being wrestled with today.

Aristotle lived from 384 to 322 BC. He differed greatly in personality from his teacher. Plato was an artistic visionary, with poetic and mystical talent for social planning. Aristotle was a coldly analytical scientist concerned with collecting and classifying data. Plato, with his great sense of humor and tragedy, would often step out of the academic role to joke, laugh, and cry about human foibles. Aristotle, on the other hand, was the prototype of the dry, always serious scholar who cracked many a book but never a smile.

Aristotle was born in the Macedonian city of Stagira, 200 miles north of Athens. He came from a medical family. His father was physician to King Amyntas, grandfather of Alexander the Great. There is some difference of opinion as to when Aristotle came to Athens to study under Plato. The best evidence suggests that he was about 18 years old and settled down after a particularly wild adolescence (Durant, 1954). The accounts vary, but it is said that Aristotle studied at the Academy with Plato for 20 years. He was Plato's best student. It was a case of genius teaching genius, one 50 years older than the other.

By all accounts they didn't get along. It was more than a problem of age. As a student, Aristotle spent great amounts of money building a large library of manuscripts. Plato criticized his young follower for being a bookworm. Aristotle, in turn, was brash enough to suggest that his scholarship would eclipse the work of his mentor.

After Plato died at age 80 years, Aristotle left Athens, traveled extensively, and married a rich woman. Then he fell on an opportunity that was later to prove invaluable. King Philip II of Macedonia called Aristotle to the court of Pella. His duty was to educate Alexander, Philip's son, who was being groomed as a world ruler. The lad lived up to expectations and became known as Alexander the Great.

Aristotle taught Alexander from his thirteenth to his sixteenth year. Alexander, in keeping with his barbarian forebears, was a wild and passionate young man. He claimed that he learned "the art of living" from Aristotle. At any rate, Aristotle was probably responsible for helping unify and focus Alexander's unruly talents. When Alexander came to power after his father's assassination, he became Aristotle's generous benefactor.

Aristotle returned to Athens in 335 BC and founded the Lyceum, a university dedicated to the study of biology and natural science. The Lyceum was a exciting place because it contained botanical and zoological gardens equipped with specimens from all the known world. It was made possible by Alexander, who put hundreds of "researchers" in the wake of his conquering armies to gather natural specimens and social and political information for Aristotle. Alexander even endowed Aristotle with a great sum of money to buy equipment and hire large numbers of research assistants. For 12 years Aristotle worked and taught under the protection of Alexander. When Alexander died in 322 BC, the Macedonian Party in Athens was overthrown, and Aristotle chose exile. The only alternative was to face trumped-up charges by Athenian patriots. He died a sick and broken man a few months later.

Our intellectual debt to Aristotle is great. We owe to him the basis of scientific classification in the natural sciences. We owe to him the study of logic. We owe to him a concept of the universe. We owe to him a theory of the nature of man that continues as a basic assumption of many religious beliefs. We owe to him the foundations of a psychology and purpose of education. In fact, Aristotelean educational practice formed the basis for the classical humanist tradition in education that endures today.

Aristotle's concept of the universe was known as the form-matter hypothesis. Without a microscope or telescope, Aristotle pondered on his vast collection of plants and animals. He speculated on the ethereal world above him. He studied the parts of animals and experimented with genetics. He finally reasoned that the universe is an organism which has two major causes: *The Material Cause,* the raw material from which all things of the earth are made, and *The Formal Cause,* the form or reality of a thing as it appears in nature. For Aristotle, matter is potentiality in the hands of a "Prime Mover" who gives form and purpose to things in the world. This concept of the universe reentered Western thought after the Dark Ages. It was used in the thirteenth century by Thomas Aquinas to build a metaphysical foundation for orthodox Christianity. Moses Maimonides, the great Jewish scholar of the same period, utilized the form-matter hypothesis in constructing a scientific foundation for the metaphysics of Judaism.

Aristotle's concept of human nature grew out of his idea of the nature of the universe and is important in understanding the classical humanist approach to education. Here it is: For Aristotle life and soul are one and the same. Man's body is matter, and man's life is soul. There are three levels of soul: *The Vegetable Soul* is in all living things and represents the basis and cause of growth, decay, nutrition, and regeneration. *The Animal Soul,* a characteristic of man and animals, is the basis and cause of sense perception; co-ordination and movement (the function of the central nervous system); and the physical fears, appetites, and desires of man and animal. *The Human Soul* is found only in man and sets him apart from the rest of nature.

This higher form of soul represents man's rationality, his ability to make judgments and reason. It is composed of two parts: The first part, commonly called "wisdom," deals with man's capacity for practical judgment, his ability to chose and act wisely. The second aspect may be called "higher reason." This part of the Human Soul deals with man's ability and capacity for making theoretical and intellectual judgments. In this realm the Human Soul elevates man to an intellectual mastery of the world and gives him the power and responsibility to make proper moral and ethical choices.

The education of man in the Aristotelean tradition basically concerns itself with strengthening the qualities of the Human Soul. If man is to rise above animal existence, he must develop the wisdom and reason that can control the appetites and passions of his Animal Soul. The life of true happiness is found in what Aristotle called *The Golden Mean,* which is keeping a sensible balance between need gratification and intellectual reasoning.

In practice, classical humanism has always seen education as a strictly intellectual and academic pursuit. Schooling, teaching, and learning deal with subject matter "disciplines." These disciplines have traditionally formed a curriculum of the seven liberal arts: *Grammar* (the study of language), *Dialectics* (the art of logical argumentation and investigation), *Rhetoric* (the art of speaking and writing), *Music, Arithmetic, Geometry,* and *Astronomy.* The first three were the classical trivium of the Middle Ages; the last four formed the quadrivium (Ulich, 1968).

The seven liberal arts have been expanded to include most subjects in the areas known as the humanities, the natural sciences, and the social sciences. In fact, many colleges and universities require their students to take a balanced selection from these academic areas. College students typically groan about the abstract nature of such courses and their lack of relevance to the "real world." But to do so is to miss the Aristotelean boat. Classical humanists believe the mastery of hard subjects is necessary for sharpening the intellect. It will produce a wise, virtuous, rational person. The practical, everyday, mundane concerns of life are of secondary importance and should not dictate the aims of education.

Indeed it was Aristotle who started a controversy that still blazes in education, the controversy between the servile (or practical) arts and the liberal arts. In schools and colleges, the "servile arts" include home economics, industrial arts, business, physical education, and most professional curricula aimed at producing teachers, nurses, social workers, farmers, craftsmen, technicians, and businessmen. For classical humanists such subjects are not worthy of the name "education" and certainly don't merit university status. In fact, outside of America, schools for these "servile" studies are not connected with university education and have far less status. Even in America the so-called servile arts have gained university status only within the past century. To the practical-minded American the distinction between the servile arts and the liberal arts is hard to make. However, for the traditional scholar there is no comparison between intellectual subject matter and the "nuts and bolts" of courses for job preparation. An academic pecking order still exists. In elementary schools, teachers of the gifted quite often believe themselves superior to teachers who work with slow learners. In high schools, teachers of English literature may look down their noses at automobile shop teachers. At the university level, some professors of liberal arts won't even sit over coffee with their colleagues in the practical arts.

The Aristotelean tradition in education is conservative and aristocratic. It assumes that leisure is the basis of culture (Pieper, 1963). It requires that the school be separate from the home and marketplace. It also requires that students be free from the concerns of hand-to-mouth living so as to be able to concentrate on intellectual pursuits. Strict discipline, separate subjects, rigorous study habits, and separation of the sexes are desirable concomitants of education in the classical tradition.

The light of Aristotle's educational thought was lost to Europe in the Dark Ages. It was preserved by Arab scholars and then rekindled in Europe with the advance of Islamic culture in Spain. Under the hand of Thomas Aquinas and Moses Maimonides, classical humanism flowered and prospered, giving structure to schooling, teaching, and learning throughout the world. Even in today's America, Aristotle's shadow falls heavily on the schoolhouse.

The spirit of the Renaissance

The rediscovery of Aristotle spawned a period of humanism in Western Europe that lasted for 3 centuries, from 1300 through 1500 AD. Known as the Renaissance, this was a time of glorification of the human spirit and powers. It fed a dynamic revival of learning. Cultural diffusion fueled this revival. Diverse peoples and cultures came together through wars, trade, pilgrimages, and the Crusades. Novel ideas and goods stirred man's mind and fired his imagination. The invention of the compass encouraged exploration of the seas, which resulted in the discovery of the New World. The invention of the printing press and the availability of paper from Egypt replaced laborious hand copying of manuscripts on parchment. Printing not only made knowledge more available; it broke the monopoly that the priests had on learning. Information could be disseminated without the Church's censorship or slant.

Important social changes also occurred. Rulers and the monied elite displayed their wealth by becoming enthusiastic patrons of art and intellect. Courts filled with artists and scholars as powerful men sought to surround themselves with talent. With this came a romantic age, an age of chivalry. Wandering troubadours strolled about Europe spreading songs of romantic emotion, passion, tenderness, and gallantry. It was the age of knighthood. Concepts of sex and sex roles changed. The concepts of "lady" and "gentleman" were born. Earlier religious notions that had viewed the body as "the prison house of the soul" were rejected in favor of the cultivation of physical sensitivity. Attitudes toward women changed. Belief in the value and beauty of man's physical nature eventually brought changes in religious attitudes.

During the Renaissance, the university took hold. Great universities were founded throughout Europe, giving scholars a base of operation beyond the courts of noblemen and the homes of merchant princes. Great libraries were assembled, and much wealth was spent in searching for old manuscripts in the thirst for classical Greek knowledge. The study of Latin became a badge of the scholar.

Despite interest in scholarship, education in this age of classical humanism was still the preserve of the wealthy, the nobility, and the clergy. Knowledge of the nature of the learner scarcely advanced beyond Aristotle's time. The child was still seen as a miniature adult. Childlike interests and behaviors were not tolerated by teachers. The mastery of learning was demonstrated by memorization. Strict obedience and study habits were stressed. Motivation came from punishment and rivalry.

The spirit of the Renaissance was classical rather than scientific. But it did bring about a quality of human enlightenment that precipitated an age of science.

The spirit of the Reformation

The Church did not escape this great new focus on man. Its officials, too, became fascinated with man's here-and-now possibilities. Much too fascinated, many churchmen thought. Dissident voices grew within the church, decrying hedonism and demanding a return to eternal verities and preparation for life after death.

Finally such notables as Martin Luther and John Calvin declared their separation from the church. This separation highlighted the growing concern for redirecting the church, and it marked the beginning of the Reformation.

The rise of Protestantism in Europe, a period known as the Reformation, had great effect on schooling, teaching, and learning. The impact of Reformation thought was soon seen in the Puritan schools of the American colonies.

The Reformation also assisted an awakening of nation states. The Church owned over one third of all European soil in the thirteenth century. The vast Holy Roman Empire had brought about widespread unity of social, religious, and political thought. But the rediscovery of Aristotle and the Renaissance helped to strike the death knell for the political influence of the Roman Church.

As absolute authority waned, democratic beliefs appeared. The vitality of Protestantism was related to democratic development. Robert Ulich (1968) tells us that "In every country the Protestant movement was accompanied by social revolutions" (p. 120).

In 1517 Martin Luther (1483-1546) declared his separation from the Church with his famous Ninety-five Theses. He sought educational as well as religious reform. Luther believed, with other Protestant reformers, including John Calvin (1509-1564), that everyone should master reading in order to gain salvation. For Protestants, reading the scripture was (and still is) a major path to heaven.

This Protestant belief resulted in a quantum leap in the development of education. This leap was the concept of universal literacy. The rise of the vernacular, the commonly spoken language of the people, went hand in glove with the new literacy. Luther translated the Bible into German. It was soon translated into English, French, and other European tongues, bringing it within reach of the common man. Latin, Greek, and Hebrew were still seen as requisite to advanced education, but the language of the home and marketplace came into its own in elementary education.

In his 1524 letter "To the Councilmen of Cities in Germany That They Establish and Maintain Christian Schools," Luther advocated that schools come under the jurisdiction of civil authorities for control and support. Here we see the beginnings of secularization of education. For Luther and Calvin it became the duty of civil authorities to see that schools were established and that parents sent their children to them. A hundred years later the Massachusetts Bay Colony put similar concepts into law.

The Reformation set the stage for the education of people on a much wider and more democratic scale. In rejecting the control and dogma of the Roman Church, it made the school subject to new religious and political orthodoxies.

THE SCIENTIFIC DREAM

The centuries that embraced the Renaissance and the Reformation were characterized by classical humanism, not scientific thought. But without the intellectual fertility of the Renaissance and the political and religious freedom of the Reformation, the seeds of science could scarcely have grown. Man's rediscovery of faith in himself freed him to explore the physical world. The classical humanist understanding of the world, through literacy and cultural tradition, gave way to an understanding of the world through examination of natural reality.

The spirit of the new science

In 1500 man renewed the venture into the scientific unknown. Partial freedom from superstition and religious dogma allowed this venture. No longer did man seek truth only in classical ideals and religious rationality. The Aristotelean view of the universe and the metaphysics of the great Church father Thomas Aquinas were shouldered aside by a new concept of the world as a machine. This mechanistic world operated according to universal natural law. God was viewed as a "Divine Watchmaker" who built the world machine, set it into motion, and then sat back to watch it run.

Scientific investigation became the key to understanding this machine. The idea that nature might be predictable was an intoxicating stimulant. The new tools of science took their place alongside the classical books. The laboratory and the open field vied with the library as sources of knowledge.

The Age of Science was marked by men of genius and vision. Copernicus (1473-1543) published his theory of heliocentric astronomy in 1543. It was immediately condemned by theologians, but by 1596 they had accepted it. The work of Copernicus served as a springboard for scientists such as Kepler, Galileo, and Newton. Galileo (1564-1642) used a telescope at the University of Padua and determined that the earth revolves around the sun, not vice versa. This was in direct opposition to Church dogma. Galileo, as the well-known story goes, was forced to recant his findings.

Besides the telescope, scientific instruments such as the thermometer, barometer, microscope, micrometer, air pump, and pendulum clock were invented during the sixteenth and seventeenth centuries. Geography was advanced with the invention of the globe in 1492, the year of the discovery of the New World. Mercator (1512-1594) put his genius to work in the development of maps, globes, and astronomical instruments. A year after his death his son published the first atlas. Gilbert (1544-1603) researched magnetism and electricity. Medicine was advanced by Vesalius (1514-1564), who studied human anatomy by dissection of the human body and published drawings of what he found. Harvey (1578-1657) discovered the circulation of the blood in 1616. Armed with more sophisticated knowledge, physicians began a search for the natural causes of disease.

The interrelationship of the new sciences opened further doors. Mathematics, as applied to astronomy, aided Newton (1642-1727) in composing *Principia Mathematica,* published in 1687. This period of history saw the formation of scientific societies and academies. The Royal Society of London and the Académie des Sciences in Paris were both founded in 1660. The Berlin Academy began in 1700. The pervasive spirit of science spread through all intellectual endeavors. Through the gifted writings of men such as Rabelais (1494-1553), Montaigne (1553-1592), and Voltaire (1694-1778), the age was a period of social realism that took a hard and often humorous look at human nature.

Bacon and the scientific method

The spirit of the Age of Science was epitomized by Sir Francis Bacon (1561-1626). Bacon spent his formative years in the exciting milieu of Elizabethan England, which had become a center of trade and culture—a country well on its way to establishing an empire. Bacon came as close as any modern man to becoming a philosopher-king, a far-ranging scholar with great influence in public life. With a total grasp of the sciences, Bacon rejected Aristotelean logic and deductive reasoning. He predicted a utopian future for man in the conquest of nature by science. In his *Novum Organum,* published in 1620, Bacon persuasively argued that man must banish human error, which he figuratively expressed in the form of four "idols." Man must banish the "Idols of the Tribe," human prejudices and preconception.

In general let every student of nature take this as a rule —that whatever his mind seizes and dwells upon with particular satisfaction, is to be held in suspicion; and that so much the more care is to be taken, in dealing with such questions, to keep the understanding even and clear. (Durant, 1954, pp. 130-131)

"The Idols of the Cave" represent individual biases that man gains through social, political, and academic experience. They should be banished. "The Idols of the Marketplace" arise from the world of commerce and the casual and purposeful misuse of words and knowledge. Had Bacon been able to predict the all-pervasive effect of today's Madison Avenue, he might have seen this Idol as most dangerous to man's mind. To dismiss the "Idols of the Marketplace," Bacon carefully delineated the scientific method of inquiry that still guides the scholar of today: the definition of an hypothesis, the careful gathering and analysis of data, and experimental testing. The "Idols of the Theater" were all previous philosophies, which Bacon dismissed as merely stage plays—constructions of the world not as it is but as it has been fabricated in the minds of men.

Comenius and the science of education

The great educational philosopher of the Age of Science was John Amos Comenius (1592-1670). Comenius was a bishop of the Moravian Brethren, a pietist sect who were cruelly persecuted by the Jesuits and the House of Hapsburg at the time of the Thirty Years' War. As a Moravian brother, Comenius had a wide view of nature that did not conflict with the notion of scientific inquiry. His church also was characterized by a democratic spirit, a belief in equal rights. When the Thirty Years' War began in 1620, Comenius became an emigrant for the rest of his life, living in Poland, Sweden, England, and Holland.

In his *Great Didactic,* published in 1632, Comenius expressed his belief that man was unlimited in his potential for learning. He devised a broad educational scheme to teach everyone everything, so as to build a "Christian Republic." He proposed four schools of 6 years each. In his "School of the Mother's Knee," for children from birth to 6 years of age, Comenius was, perhaps, the first educator to speak of the importance of the home as an educational institution. Greatly anticipating psychologists and early childhood educators of today, he pointed to the importance of the early development of the child's senses and the encouragement of the curiosity. The "Vernacular School," compulsory for all children, would be a place where the arts of humanity and science would be taught in the common language. Comenius' concepts of "Latin School" and "University" were not novel except that he, like Mon-

8. He saw her lift her eyes; he felt
    The soft hand's light caressing,
And heard the tremble of her voice,
    As if a fault confessing.

9. "I'm sorry that I spelt the word:
    I hate to go above you,

taigne, believed that travel represented the true completion of one's education.

Comenius, like the educators who were to follow, was a sense empiricist. He believed that learning took place when the senses were applied to reality. His curriculum stressed a developmental progression of concrete to abstract. As simple and obvious as this idea appears today, it was revolutionary at the time. Classical educators had never worried about presenting their students abstract words and concepts. They assumed that learning takes place in an adultlike rational mind that sorts and analyzes with computer efficiency. Comenius was the first person to point out the need for visual aids in teaching. He believed pictures should accompany words in a textbook. His *Orbis Sensualium Pictus* was the first word and picture text. It was the model for the preprimers and picture dictionaries that followed.

Locke and the scientific learner

The English philosopher John Locke (1632-1704) championed the free and critical mind in his publication *Some Thoughts Concerning Education*. Locke, like Montaigne, was basically interested in the education of what Ulich (1968, pp. 200-211) has called the "gentleman ideal."

This concept of a well-bred, educated, independent, self-reliant, open-minded person, devoted to duty and honor, has figured strongly in modern British culture. These qualities have been nurtured by the famous British "public schools" (which are really private) such as Eton, Harrow, and Merchant Taylors. Locke's ideal gentleman reflected the aspirations of a well-to-do middle class, consisting of merchants, artisans, and traders, which had begun to displace the old hereditary nobility in political and economic influence. Locke rejected bookishness and rote memorization in favor of learning by doing and the application of skill. His curriculum favored the sciences and skills of communication. Like Montaigne he believed that a gentleman could learn from the manual arts. He valued mechanical aptitude. Such educational beliefs appealed to a privileged class involved in practical affairs.

Most important to the history of education is Locke's psychological theory. He likened the mind to a blank slate (the tabula rasa). Unlike Plato and Comenius, he did not believe that the mind already held innate ideas. For Locke, all ideas came to the mind through the senses. Man learned from experience, by experiencing. His mind refined experience through the processes of discrimination, analysis, generalization, and concept development.

The tabula rasa theory became the foundation of modern behavioral psychology. It established a theoretical basis for the advocates of strict environmentalism. For years to come there would be a feud between psychologists who believe that individual human potential is determined by heridity (nature) and those who believe that potential is determined by environment (nurture). Moreover, the tabula rasa theory swept aside the theological doctrine of innate depravity and the classical notion of a ready-made rational mind. This housecleaning opened the door for a new psychology of human learning—a developmental psychology. Rousseau would carry the torch into that arena.

THE PRACTICAL DREAM

For 2,000 years, all standards, purposes, and subject matter of education had been dictated by grand plan, right reason, religious dogma, wisdom of the past, and laws of nature. For Plato, the requirements of the state structured education *from the top down*. For Aristotle the reality of self-evident truth and intellectual pursuit structured education *from the top down*. For the Church of the Middle Ages, dogma structured education *from the top down*. For the classical humanists of the Renaissance, wisdom and knowledge in literature of ages past structured education *from the top down*. For the Protestant reformers of the Reformation, the Scriptures structured education *from the top down*. For scholars of the Age of Science, natural law compelled man to "face reality" and "get in tune with nature," thus structuring education *from the top down*.

The source of truth was at the top of an intellectual ladder. Furthermore, the universities and academies were the repositories and dispensers of this knowledge. *From the top down* they dictated what was to be taught at the secondary and elementary levels. The higher the level of education, the more status it carried for its teachers, students, and subject matter.

The *top down* view of education is basically authoritarian. It requires man to measure up to preordained standards. The top down view is also elitist. It operates on the principle that only certain activities are legitimately educational, worthy of inclusion in the curriculum. It also operates on Plato's myth of the metals. Only certain people are cut out for "formal education."

Although we can still see remnants of the top down view in our schools, the notion was, for practical purposes, doomed by 1800. Its death knell was sounded by the archnaturalist Jean Jacques Rousseau. In 1762 Rousseau published his book *Emile,* which will be described later. *Emile* shook education to its very foundations. It has never been the same.

Rousseau launched the modern era of schooling, teaching, and learning. Beginning with his educational insights and following with practices developed by Johann Pestalozzi, education shifted to a whole new set of assumptions. Truly we could say that man began to think of education *from the bottom up.* With the belief that man is basically good, education was no longer seen as an instrument to discipline the will, suppress the animal appetites, or save a worthless soul. With the belief that children do not learn like adults, the content, sequence, and approach to subject matter changed. With a new appreciation for how people learn came a new appreciation for elementary education and the professional training of elementary teachers. With the rise of suffrage and concern for the common man came the notion that practical education could provide social and economic opportunity. Education could also help put man in control of his own destiny. In short, education was seen to begin at the bottom, based on the natural and social realities of the world. Man and his practical concerns were the new starting points in the educational quest.

Rousseau and the noble savage

The modern era in education had its origins on the island of Juan Fernandez, 400 miles off the coast of Chile. Discovered in 1592 by a Spanish navigator who gave it his name, the island with its deep-water ports, mild climate, and lush vegetation became a rendezvous of ships entering the Pacific after sailing around the Horn. Ships of all nationalities used the island as a port of refuge and supply for fresh food and water. Sailors and unsuccessful colonists planted the island with familiar foods and introduced rats, cats, goats, and dogs.

In 1705 a Scottish seaman, Alexander Selkirk, in conflict with his captain volunteered to leave his ship. He was placed with his belongings on Juan Fernandez, which at the time was uninhabited. Selkirk stayed on the well-supplied island 4 years, at times eluding Spanish sailors who sought to kill him. Selkirk's experiences, published in England in 1711, became the basis of the novel *Robinson Crusoe,* which appeared in 1719. The book's author, Daniel Defoe, was a leading English journalist and a realist in the tradition of John Locke. Defoe endowed Robinson Crusoe with all the traits of a self-reliant, middle-class English gentleman. At the time Europe was fascinated by discoveries and developments in the New World. The book was widely read, and it figured directly in the introduction of a new concept of human nature—the Noble Savage.

One interested reader of *Robinson Crusoe* was Jean Jacques Rousseau. Born in Geneva in 1712, Rousseau was raised by his eccentric father, his mother having died in childbirth. Rousseau was bright, but he had an undisciplined childhood, with behavior that we would call juvenile delinquency. After cruel treatment as an apprentice to an engraver, he became, at age 16, a vagabond.

During a long period of adventure and travel, Rousseau's neurotic personality manifested itself in his pursuit of both sensuality and religion. His travels brought him into contact with the miseries of the peasants on the one hand and the power and artificiality of French nobility on the other. Rousseau became idealistic and imbued with the need for social reform. But he came into the intellectual world as an "outsider"—an alienated man. As Ulich (1968) puts it, "Certainly he was one of those uprooted 'marginal men' in whom hypersensitiveness to the ethical defects of society and personal moral laxity are strangely allied" (p. 212). His life was a complex puzzle of genius, emotionality, advocacy, and reprobate living. But through his books *The Social Contract* and *Emile,* the world discovered the gospel of *return to nature.*

In *The Social Contract* Rousseau eloquently expressed his belief that man is *naturally* born noble and free. Society is artificial. Equality and liberty are the natural rights of man.

Man is born free; and everywhere he is in chains . . . liberty results from the nature of man. His first law is to provide for his own preservation, his first cares are those which he owes to himself . . . Since no man has a natural authority over his fellow, and force creates no right, we must conclude that conventions form the basis of all legitimate authority among men. (Ulich, 1958, p. 214)

For Rousseau the proper convention or social contract would be one that would preserve the natural rights to life, liberty, and the pursuit of happiness. A society has the right to overthrow any leader, government, or external power that violates this democratic covenant. Echos of *The Social Contract* are to be found in our *Declaration of Independence,* for Rousseau had great influence on the thinking of Thomas Jefferson.

Emile did for education what *The Social Contract* did for politics. *Emile* was a novel, a fictionalized account of how Rousseau would raise an imaginary son, Emile. To educate the child, Rousseau removed him from corrupt society and sent him with a tutor to a rural environment. There he learned from nature. The first words in *Emile* are as follows: "God makes all things good; man meddles with them and they become evil." According to Rousseau, only by living close to nature can one's natural goodness properly unfold and develop.

Rousseau's revolutionary educational achievement was the formulation of a developmental psychology. Modern theories of developmental psychology differ from Rousseau's original view, but they owe their beginnings to him. Rousseau's psychology of the individual is a *recapitulation theory*. In such a theory, the individual's development from birth to adulthood is pictured as comparable to the developmental epochs of civilization. Each individual, in growing up, passes through the basic developmental stages of mankind. For Rousseau these stages were the *Animal Stage* (birth to age 5 years), a stage marked by the development of sense perception and motor activity; the *Savage Stage* (age 5 to 12 years), a stage marked by the development of self-conscienceness; the *Rational Stage* (age 12 to 15 years), a stage marked by the development of the powers of reason; and the *Social Stage* (age 15 to 20 years), a stage marked by the development of sexual maturity, social relationships, and moral conscience.

Developmental stages that unfold according to a natural plan dictate the method, organization, and content of education. Here Rousseau made a radical break from the past. The child *was no longer* a miniature adult who should learn what adults wanted him to learn. The concerns of society *did not* take precedent over the concerns of the individual. The child's individual nature was the thing of importance. Education should be based on a thorough understanding of the developmental nature of children.

Rousseau's plan of education in *Emile* was as follows:

1. *Infancy (Animal Stage, birth to age 5 years).* The child is not clearly conscious of his own existence during the first year of life. He should not be pampered in infancy. The early years require freedom for the development of big muscle activity. The child must be permitted to act naturally and experience the natural consequences of his actions. His individuality must be respected. Education during this stage should consist of free and unhampered expression. This will permit the child to become self-dependent (in modern terminology, to develop a good self-image).

2. *Childhood (Savage Stage, age 5 to 12 years).* Education must be "negative" at this stage: "do nothing and allow nothing to be done." The child can't reason at this stage, so experience is his best teacher. The child learns through direct experience. He thinks at the concrete level. Natural activities and exploration should be the curriculum. Language ability develops naturally at this stage, as do the powers of the senses. Reading should not be forced on the child.

3. *Preadolescence (Rational Stage, age 12 to 15 years).* Reason emerges at this stage. Only now can directed learning begin. But the method of teaching is *not* the classical humanistic development of reason through authority. The child's unfolding powers of reason are evidenced by, and facilitated through, natural curiosity and concern for the usefulness of knowledge. The child desires learning at this stage and should pursue knowledge through the natural sciences, geography, astronomy, agriculture, manual arts, and crafts. The child learns from direct observation, discovery, and manipulation. He does not learn best from the

authority of the spoken or printed word. Rousseau proposed *Robinson Crusoe* as a suitable first reader because of its content.

4. *Adolescence and early adulthood (Social Stage, age 15 to 20 years).* The emergence of the sex drive brings with it a growing social awareness and concern. The individual begins to develop a sense of morality, an interest in religion, and a concern for beauty. Prior to this stage, moral and religious teaching is at best in vain and at worst detrimental. This is the stage where the "higher virtues" awaken in the person. The person seeks human relationships and is interested in the study of ethics and the social sciences.

Two traditions grew from Rousseau's educational dreams: The first tradition was "practical." The second tradition was "romantic." Both traditions have their roots in naturalistic assumptions about the world and human nature. But they created very different approaches to schooling, teaching, and learning.

The *practical tradition* was formalized by Johann Pestalozzi. He took Rousseau's developmental stages of the learner and built a methodology of education to support them. Herbert Spencer took Rousseau's belief in environmentalism and, with a boost from the theory of evolution, made educators aware of the importance of practical knowledge. The great American philosopher John Dewey tied this tradition to the methods of science and the practice of democracy. With this background, the practical tradition found ready acceptance in the United States. Americans have always wanted their schools to produce practical students with practical skills.

The *romantic tradition* was first promoted by Friedrich Froebel, who built on Rousseau's view of man's natural goodness. Froebel championed the values of natural expression and spontaneous activity. Let nature take its course, he said. The child will instinctively learn, if the teacher and subject matter get out of the way.

Rousseau's dictum of "return to nature" was to be taken literally by the humanist critics of American education in the 1960's and 1970's. With the support of existential philosophy, educational psychologists like Carl Rogers would champion education as an individualistic pursuit. A conformity-producing society would be seen as "dehumanizing" to the individual. "Open education,"

with range for individual expression, would be seen as the answer. In the romantic tradition, education would become therapy for individuals besieged by their culture.

Pestalozzi and the practical learner

Johann Heinrich Pestalozzi was born in Zurich, Switzerland, in 1746. When he was 5 years old, his father, a prominent physician, died. He was then reared in very modest surroundings by his mother and a woman servant.

Little Johann Heinrich didn't like school. His fellow students ridiculed him for his effeminate characteristics, and he did not do well in the elementary school. Perhaps misery seeks company, for early in his life he became keenly aware of the degradation of the poor. He began accompanying his grandfather, who ministered to those in poverty. Later he attended the Zurich Latin School and the Collegium Carolinum, where he became inspired by the liberal ideals of justice and liberty. He decided to devote his life to helping the downtrodden.

Pestalozzi tried the ministry and was unsuccessful. He turned to law and politics, but his deep moral convictions were too radical. His ideas of social reform ran head-on against those of the Mayor of Zurich. That finished him as a politician. He decided to return to nature and devote himself to agriculture. The writings of Rousseau were extremely popular at that time, and Pestalozzi thought he could "become independent of the whole world" through farming. In 1769 he married a good woman and bought some bad farm land. His intention was to make of his property a model farm, where he could teach poor people to become independent and self-supporting.

By this time Pestalozzi had come to the conclusions that the poor needed skills, not charity, and that their lot would be improved by education. However, his farm soon failed because of his naiveté and lack of practical qualities. But Pestalozzi was undaunted. He still had friends, enthusiasm, and his wife's money. Influenced by Rousseau's *Emile,* he developed a school-orphanage on his property. He combined academic and vocational training. This venture lasted for 6 years. Friends, enthusiasm, and money could not save it. It failed in 1780.

Friends then advised Pestalozzi to write books for a living. This new vocation proved to be his road to success. *Leonard and Gertrude,* a novel of social reform, appeared in 1782 and brought Pestalozzi instant fame. He gained great stature as a friend of the underprivileged.

He was 52 years old when the Swiss Revolution occurred. His sympathies went out to the poor people at Stanz, a village that had been the scene of terrible slaughter. In 1798, with financial support from the government, Pestalozzi began management of an orphanage in Stanz. For 2 years, he attempted to awaken the spirit of the small waifs in his charge. He used love and personal attention in unstructured, informal teaching. He was partially successful, but his good work was stopped by political events.

Pestalozzi's success as a teacher was to be proved at Burgdorf where, in 1800, he opened a boarding school for boys. At Burgdorf, in an old

GUST. IGLER.

BUSY FOLKS.

Tell the story which the picture tells you.

Wheeler's Elementary Speller, 1901.

castle, he developed his ABC of Sense-Perception and wrote *How Gertrude Teaches Her Children*. "Father Pestalozzi," as he became known to the children, was so zealous in his development of a new method that he chanted his lessons, boxed ears right and left, and became hoarse and exhausted by 10 o'clock in the morning.

In 1805 he founded his famous Pestalozzi school at Yverdon. There Pestalozzi demonstrated his new methods. The world took note. Following Rousseau's example, Pestalozzi wrote that "all instruction of man is then only the art of helping Nature find her own way." He called schools "stifling machines" that take children out of their happy preschool years and "murder" their natural interest by subjecting them to "artificial" learning (Pestalozzi, 1898, p. 57). The key terms in Pestalozzi's methodology were "Anschauung," meaning "sense-impression," and "Fertigheit," meaning "readiness." For Pestalozzi, all learning began with sense impression, the use of all the senses. Readiness was conceived as a necessary psychological and physical skill requisite to any new step in learning. The purpose of education was to assist the growth and development of the individual as an organic whole. This organic whole consisted of three aspects: "The Head, The Heart, and The Hand." The *Head,* or intellect, develops through experiences with the senses. The *Heart,* or morality and religion, develops through relationships with other human beings and with God. The *Hand,* or motor skills, develops out of human need to cope with environment. Thus Pestalozzi was the first to build a methodology on the revolutionary notions of developmental psychology put forth in *Emile.*

The Pestalozzian approach to teaching was to use "object lessons." He assumed that an active mind builds concepts by feeding on objects perceived by the senses. The curriculum consisted of form, number, and language. The recognition of numbers and letters was developed through kinetic practice in drawing their shapes. Numbers were learned by counting real objects. Words were learned through the following combination of skills: First came the identification of vowel and consonant sounds. Next came alphabet and letter-sound recognition, followed by syllabication. Third came the all-important word meaning. Pestalozzi stressed techniques of word association and vocabulary building by learning the names of things

in the environment. If this approach sounds familiar, it is because Pestalozzi's general method is still the foundation for elementary teaching today, especially at the primary and intermediate levels.

Pestalozzi's contributions to education include the following once radical but now widely practiced beliefs:

1. Education deals with the total development of the person.
2. Learning proceeds from the concrete to the abstract. Teaching materials must be organized and "graded" as to levels of difficulty.
3. Students can't be forced to learn until they are ready.
4. Mastery at one level is necessary before students can be successful at the next.
5. The classroom should be a place rich in resources of real and manipulable objects.
6. Learning is not confined to the classroom. Field trips and workshop experiences are invaluable.
7. Education encourages independent judgment rather than acceptance of authoritative truths.
8. Learning is psychological rather than logical. It is governed by nature and the nature of the learner. Thus the psychology of learning and the methodology of teaching are important requisites for all who teach.

The school at Yverdon attracted scholars and students from all parts of Europe. American education was introduced to the Pestalozzian method by William Maclure (1763-1840), who brought Joseph Neef (1770-1854), one of Pestalozzi's disciples, to Philadelphia to establish a school in 1809. Pestalozzi's greatest American influence came during the 1860's through Edward A. Sheldon (1823-1897), superintendent of schools in Oswego, New York, and principal of the Oswego Normal School. Sheldon and his followers began the "Oswego Movement," which furthered Pestalozzian thought and ensured its strong influence on teacher education in America.

Pestalozzi died a senile and saddened man at 82 years of age in 1827. His school at Yverdon had closed in 1825 due to faculty squabbles and lawsuits. But "Father Pestalozzi" had done what few educational reformers accomplished before or since: He criticized the system, but he produced positive and practical solutions. He devoted his life to the demonstration of their use.

THE SPILLED INK.

Tell the story which the picture tells you.

Wheeler's Elementary Speller, 1901.

Froebel and the angelic learner

One of Pestalozzi's disciples was Friedrich Wilhelm Froebel (1782-1852), a native of southern Germany. Froebel was treated with contempt by his stepmother. From an early age the boy turned inward. As a student he became interested in natural science and religion. After trying various other vocations, he turned to teaching. At age 23 years he took a post at Gruner's Pestalozzian Institute in Frankfurt. By 1816 he had founded his own school. He was critical of some Pestalozzian methods, but he believed that the child's natural activity and play were the keys to education.

As a mystical idealist, Froebel believed that there was a spark of the Divine present in all children. Taking his cue from Rousseau, Froebel saw growth and development as an unfolding of latent abilities according to a natural plan. But Froebel believed that these unfolding powers were the externalization of a spiritual essence. In short, the learner was a little angel.

Froebel viewed child's play as natural and educative. Unlike Rousseau, he believed that early socialization was desirable. In 1837 he opened the first *Kindergarten* ("the child's garden") and gave the world a new form of education. His kindergarten was to be a place of warm environment, stressing self-directed activity. Froebel's teachers would provide guidance rather than instruction, so as not to interfere with the child's natural development.

Froebel's curriculum featured activities and items rich in symbolic and spiritual meaning. For example, the ball was all important as a plaything: its spherical nature represented the world and the unity of mankind.

Modern kindergarten programs retain many of Froebel's ideas. Children still sit in a circle. They are introduced to music through rhythm and pantomime with musical accompaniment. They are stimulated intellectually through educational games, story time, and directed activities.

The kindergarten had wide acceptance in the United States. Elizabeth Palmer Peabody opened the first kindergarten in Boston in 1860. By 1873 William Torrey Harris, an influential educator and Superintendent of Schools, had made kindergarten a part of the public school program in St. Louis, Missouri.

Froebel is recognized as the father of preschool education. There is no doubt that he influenced Maria Montessori and her unique approach to early childhood education. Froebel was also the spiritual progenitor of the "child-centered" progressive education practices of 1930's and 1940's. Even today many early childhood educators speak with glossy-eyed rapture about "spontaneous activity" and "natural self-expression." The concept of the innately good, instinctive learner, unfettered by the demands of teacher and subject mastery, remains alive in the practices of the romantic humanists of today.

Spencer and the practical subject matter

As we have seen, the practical tradition in education began with a new view of man. The childhood of the noble savage was a period of developmental growth characterized by unfolding needs and interests that, in turn, dictated education. But Rousseau's *Emile* was only a dream. It took Pestalozzi to forge Rousseau's general principles into an educational reality. The new view of man had resulted in a new view of education. This practical tradition was still in its infancy when it received a tremendous boost from Herbert Spencer, working from a new view of creation—the Darwinian Theory. With Rousseau and Pestalozzi, the *nature of man* rejected the traditional curriculum as irrelevant to individual needs. But with Spencer, the *nature of nature* rejected the traditional curriculum as not meeting social needs.

Herbert Spencer was born in 1820 to nonconformist parents. His father, paternal grandfather, and an influential uncle were all schoolteachers. Yet he was to receive only 3 years of formal education. Spencer, whom Will Durant called the most famous English philosopher of the century, worked until 30 years of age as a surveyor and engineer, designing railway lines and bridges. But he was not wasting intellectual time. He had a brilliant and absorbent mind. His curiosity was matched by his ability to classify mentally what he had experienced and read. When he turned to writing, he was able to support his theories with an encyclopedic array of data.

In 1852 Spencer wrote an essay entitled "The Theory of Population," in which he suggested that the struggle for existence leads to survival of the fittest. The idea was not new; it came from Malthus, who had written his *Essay on Population* after reflecting on the survival and adaptation of goats and dogs on—you guessed it—Juan Fernandez Island. Spencer's contemporary, Charles Darwin, also influenced by Malthus, published *The Origin of Species* in 1859. Darwin then began a 20-year field study in support of the notion that the natural struggle for survival brings with each generation an adaptation to nature by the fittest.

But it was Spencer who took Darwin's theory of evolution beyond the world of plants and animals. He used it to explain the development of human history and culture. Spencer's health broke at age 40, but despite continuing ill health, he wrote for another 43 years! He produced a huge body of works, including *First Principles* (1862), *The Principles of Psychology* (1873), *Principles of Biology* (1872), *The Study of Sociology* (1873), *The Principles of Sociology* (1876 and 1896), and *The Principles of Ethics* (1893).

Spencer's volumes were the foundation stones for a social theory that came to be known as "social Darwinism." Spencer's thought was extremely influential in late nineteenth century America, where it lent credence to the national tradition of rugged individualism. It justified the "robber baron" captains of industry and their laissez-faire business ethic. It condoned social inequality on the basis of natural selection. According to the thesis of social Darwinism, the rich, the powerful, and the comfortable reach their positions in life because of their superior qualities. Social welfare, unionism, and the governmental forms of socialism and communism tamper with nature's law and doom society to mediocrity or worse.

Most of Spencer's books fostered a highly conservative social and political policy. Surprisingly, his educational views did just the opposite. In 1859 Spencer wrote an essay entitled "What Education is of Most Worth?" A year later he expanded this essay into his book *Education: Intellectual, Physical, Moral*. Spencer's point of view was revolutionary. He attacked the English school curriculum of his day as a system that perpetuated social class distinctions. He claimed that British education did for Englishmen what face painting and body decoration did for the Orinoco Indians of Venezuela, that is, it served mainly to equip the upper classes with the social graces and skills that set them apart from the poor. What is more, the school curriculum did not square with the new

set of priorities inherent in evolutionary theory. Education failed to face up to some practical imperatives for all mankind. Let us examine his point.

In answering *What Knowledge is of Most Worth?* Spencer suggested that the traditional curriculum be turned topsy-turvy. The real priorities of education, he said, fit a natural hierarchy of needs, as follows:

1. *Self-preservation skills*. This need is met through physical education, health education, and self-protection. Survival is the first order of education.
2. *Vocational skills*. This concern, which Spencer called "indirect self-preservation," calls for subjects that would develop skills of earning a living. Such subjects would include agriculture, industrial arts, business education, and vocational training. Man may not live by bread alone, but bread does come before books.
3. *Family life skills*. The skills of parenthood are imperative to the race. Accordingly, the school curriculum should have a strong program of home economics, psychology, physiology, and child care. Spencer was early to realize that the quality of "parenting" and family life was important in the development of the child.
4. *Citizenship skills*. The need to function as effective citizens called for familiar school subjects: history, civics, economics, and politics. These subjects should stress practical application.
5. *Leisure time skills*. The school should provide students with skills and attitudes so that they might enjoy and make constructive use of their leisure time. The school curriculum should respond with music, drama, and the applied and creative arts. The school should also foster avocational interests and hobbies.

Spencer's five categorical imperatives greatly influenced the progressive movement in American education. In 1918 The Commission on the Reorganization of Secondary Education, a policy-making body of the National Education Association, published the now famous "Seven Cardinal Principles of Secondary Education." This report recommended a major redirection in the aims of secondary education. It was to be the major task of the high school to translate the following principles into curricular action: (1) Health, (2) command of fundamental processes,

(3) worthy home membership, (4) vocation, (5) civic education, (6) worthy use of leisure, and (7) ethical character (Gutek, 1970, pp. 81-82, 93-97). Somewhere the ghost of Herbert Spencer stood smiling in the wings.

The "Seven Cardinal Principles" have served as curricular ideals for American education since the day they were written. They have been reflected in school practice at elementary and secondary levels. Yet even today, blind tradition challenges the practical side of education. "Spencer's Five" remain controversial.

SUGGESTED ACTIVITIES FOR FURTHER UNDERSTANDING

1. Make a documented case supporting the notion that educational change has been the result of social and political reform.
2. Make a documented case supporting the notion that educational change has been brought about by scientific discovery.
3. Have an informal debate on the "liberal arts versus the practical arts in education." Identify some class members as "classical humanists" who will argue the values of the liberal arts. Identify another group as "scientific realists" who will argue the values of an education centered around the practical arts.
4. Stage a panel discussion between Plato, John Locke, and Jean Jacques Rousseau on the major purpose of education. Have class members assume the roles of these famous philosophers. The participants can comment on contemporary issues and events from their point of view.
5. Stage a panel discussion between Aristotle, Francis Bacon, and Herbert Spencer on the content and purpose of subject matter. Class members can play the roles of these philosophers. The participants will critique present school practice from their points of view.
6. Critique each of the following views of the learner: (1) Plato's class system of the "Metals," (2) Aristotle's rational man, (3) Locke's scientific learner, (4) Rousseau's noble savage, (5) Froebel's little angels. Relate each to educational situations you have experienced.

REFERENCES

Boyd, W. *Emile for today.* London: Heinemann Educational Books, Ltd., 1956.

Boyd, W. *Plato's Republic for today.* London: Heinemann Educational Books, Ltd., 1962.

Burnet, J. *Aristotle on education.* London: Cambridge University Press, 1967.

Butts, R. *A cultural history of education.* New York: McGraw-Hill Book Co., 1947.

Campayré, G. *The history of pedagogy.* Lexington, Mass.: D. C. Heath & Co., 1884.

Cornford, F. M. (trans.). *The Republic of Plato.* New York: Oxford University Press, Inc., 1945.

Donahue, J. W. *St. Thomas Aquinas and education.* New York: Random House, Inc., 1968.

Durant, W. *The story of philosophy* (Pocket Library Edition). New York: Pocket Books, 1954.

Gutek, G. L. *An historical introduction to American education.* New York: Thomas Y. Crowell Co., Inc., 1970.

Gutek, G. L. *Pestalozzi and education.* New York: Random House, Inc., 1968.

Hofstadter, R. *Social Darwinism in American thought* (rev. ed.). Boston: Beacon Press, 1955.

Nash, P. *Models of man: explorations in the western educational tradition.* New York: John Wiley & Sons, Inc., 1968.

Pestalozzi, J. H. *How Gertrude teaches her children.* (L. E. Holland and F. C. Turner, trans. [2nd. ed.]). New York: C. W. Bardeen, Publisher, 1898.

Pieper, J. *Leisure, the basis of culture.* New York: The New American Library, Inc., 1963.

Rousseau, J. J. *Emile* (B. Foxley, trans.). London: J. M. Dent & Sons, Ltd., 1955.

Spencer, H. *Essays on education, etc., including education: intellectual, moral, and physical.* London: J. M. Dent & Sons, Ltd., 1911.

Ulich, R. *History of educational thought* (rev. ed.). New York: American Book Co., 1968.

Ulich, R. (Ed.) *Three thousand years of educational wisdom.* Cambridge, Mass.: Harvard University Press, 1947.

2 THE AMERICAN DREAM
KEEPING THE FAITH

Americans from all walks of life have put great faith in public schooling. Indeed the American Dream has always been linked to an efficient system of public instruction. Even though the Dream has not been shared by all citizens, it is a powerful motivation for most. When the Dream has been threatened by any cause, the school has been called to answer. For over 250 years American education has developed out of response to cultural need. The response in many cases has been slow and piecemeal, but it has been observable.

Americans have looked on education as "The Great Panacea" for social ills. Such high expectations have been unrealistic, and they have resulted in some disillusionment with public education. The Great Panacea has shown its imperfections. But the faith has not been displaced. Even those who view current practices as "part of the problem" believe that societal improvement ultimately depends on formal and informal education, although perhaps different from what is common today.

If you look at the history of American education, you can identify a number of basic tenets of faith that people have held with regard to public schooling. These beliefs encompass the major aims of education that grew out of the American experience. As our realities change, some of these tenets of faith assume more importance than others. Some have already undergone a process of reinterpretation. But all continue to play a fundamental role, for they represent both the institutionalized foundations and the idealized promises of American education. Let us now turn to an examination of these basic tenets of faith.

EDUCATION FOR DELUDING SATAN

The Puritans were not optimistic about the human condition. They did not believe that people were measuring up to the model God had revealed as His will. Fed up to the gills, "they meant to establish a city upon a hill, a home for saints and a model for the regeneration of Christendom" in the wilderness of New England (Tyack, 1967, p. 1). Sermons of that day give ample illustration of the Puritan belief that men were, as Jonathan Edwards put it in the title of a 1741 address, "sinners in the hands of an angry god." Fallen man could only regain the state of God's grace and avoid eternal damnation through repentance, conversion, adherence to correct belief, and staying on the narrow paths of personal righteousness. How difficult that would be in a world rich in temptation and seductive comforts!

The Puritans considered literacy a major requisite for individual salvation. Every Puritan soul needed to be able to read God's word in the Scriptures. Thus the early Puritans wasted no time in building schools, which had the simple but basic purpose of teaching the "three R's" for religious and dour utilitarian purposes.

The Puritans believed that Christian education, religious socialization, and vocational preparation were first and best a family responsibility. But the educational laws passed by the General Court of the Massachusetts Bay Colony in the 1640's give evidence that the family, even in frontier America, could not handle all these functions without help. Already traditional patterns of family authority were threatened and altered by life in the wilderness. Young people adapted easily to the new environment, and independence from one's elders was facilitated by the abundance of land. Puritan leaders became concerned over youth's growing independence and idleness (Tyack, 1967). Thus laws were made to bolster and extend the educative function of the family.

The law of 1642 required that parents and masters provide education, apprenticeship, and employment "profitable to the common wealty" for children under their care. Negligent parents faced court charges and fines. This act was the first call for compulsory education in America. Civil authority thus demanded "literacy in reading, orthodoxy in religion, and knowledge of the capital laws as the basic essentials of education necessary for all children in order that they might become good citizens of the state and of the established church" (Butts and Cremin, 1953, p. 102).

The law of 1642 did not establish schools. It only set compulsory educational tasks for parents and masters. The famous "Old Deluder Satan Act" of 1647 required townships of more than 50 families to appoint and pay a teacher for their children. Townships of 100 or more families were to establish a "grammar school," supported by local public taxation, that would go beyond the rudiments of reading and writing and prepare boys for higher education. The Massachusetts act became a model for other colonies, and they soon followed suit. In the language of this act, Satan was seen as "an ould deluder" whose chief project was "to keep men from the knowledge of the Scriptures."

The acts of 1642 and 1647, along with a similar law passed in 1648, made it clear that the state could do four things: It could require children to be educated; it could require the establishment of schools; it could require public funds for public educational purposes; and it could control and supervise the schools through civil government and public officials (Butts and Cremin, 1953).

Although the Puritans believed a real Devil had vested interests in ignorance and idleness that education would conquer, the concept of the Old Deluder has been expanded and generalized by Americans since that time. The Puritans could not envision the host of new problems faced by a growing nation. What the Puritans saw as the works of Satan later became devils in themselves. And as American culture has grown, the list of devils has expanded well beyond the Puritan concerns of ignorance of religion, civil law, duty, and vocation.

Public education has been charged with remedying, and protecting against, an ever-increasing list of individual and social ills. Americans, operating on this adversary theory, have viewed the schools as the second line of defense, the family ideally being the first.

The new deluders include the following:

1. *Foreign ideologies.* Foreign ideologies, especially communism, are perceived as a threat to established governmental forms, economic practices, and socioreligious orthodoxy.
2. *Foreign powers.* Since the Revolutionary War, Americans have been wary of foreign powers. Real or imagined threats to American sovereignty and interests at home and abroad have never been taken lightly. The public school has been the major instrument (until perhaps the advent of television) for the building of a nationalistic viewpoint and a unified public opinion. This includes the assimilation and Americanization of immigrants.
3. *Unemployment.* "Idleness" has always been viewed as sinful in the United States. Americans now look to the schools to supply vocational training for the jobless and for those whose jobs have been voided by technology or economic caprice. In addition, high schools and colleges function as holding tanks where the jobless can pursue constructive endeavors.
4. *Caveat emptor economics.* "The buyer beware." Americans generally have believed that man is protected to the degree that he has "common sense" or "mother wit." We have grown slowly, and not yet completely, out of the nineteenth century laissez-faire economics and social Darwinism typified by a disdain for the "sucker born every minute." To a degree, education has sought to enable us to make intelligent choices at the marketplace.
5. *Dangerous drugs.* Since the middle of the nineteenth century, it has been the school's responsibility to teach the evils of tobacco and alcohol. The school has reflected society's *idealistic* religious moralism. But practical matters are different. Since the 1920's, school health education programs have been pygmies against the giants of cultural behavior and massive advertising to push tobacco and alcohol. Now the widespread use of marijuana and addictive drugs has caused the schools to mount a new campaign in an effort to contain these new devils.

EDUCATION FOR THE NATURAL ARISTOCRACY

One of the major tenets of faith in American education—the identification and nurture of a natural aristocracy—is exemplified best in the life and writings of Thomas Jefferson. Jefferson, a scholar and gentleman farmer, provided some notable services to the American public. He drafted the Declaration of Independence and served as Governor of Virginia, Minister to France, Secretary of State, Vice-President, and President of the United States.

Jefferson was deeply imbued with the Renaissance ideals of human freedom and republican citizenship. He was impressed with Rousseau's faith in natural man. He feared political and religious absolutism and "every form of tyranny over the mind of man." He knew the dangers of political power held by "kings, nobles, or priests," and his writings were directed toward ensuring and preserving liberty.

For Jefferson, the ideal republic would be governed by a natural aristocracy, free-born philosopher-kings elected by the people. Like the philosopher-kings in Plato's *Republic,* Jefferson's public leaders were to be enlightened, college-trained scholars endowed with wisdom and virtue. Such leaders were not to be chosen on the basis of "Pseudo-Aristocracy" of wealth, family pedigree, or religious orthodoxy, but rather on the basis of natural talent.

To this end Jefferson proposed a plan for a universal tax-supported state system of public education. He presented this idea in his *Bill for the More General Diffusion of Knowledge* to the legislature of Virginia in 1779. The notion of tax-supported education for all children was so radical that the bill failed. America was to wait 50 years before Massachusetts enacted the precedent legislation.

Jefferson's plan called for the establishment of school districts within the state. They would have elementary schools and "grammar schools" (what we now call high schools) that would provide selective education on the basis of talent. All white children would receive 3 years of free elementary education. Beyond that, a selected few talented boys of poor parents would be chosen to go on to secondary education and possibly college at the taxpayers' expense. Wealthy parents were free to send their children, regardless of talent, to school at their own expense.

Jefferson believed that public education was a requisite of a free and enlightened society. His advocacy of universal schooling was very liberal in its day, although not so by present standards. Compulsory attendance was not a part of the scheme. Girls were not to be educated beyond the elementary grades and Negroes not at all. Although Jefferson sought to remove the stigma of poverty and the mark of class distinction, he had his own ideas as to what were "natural" distinctions among men. Education for Jefferson was essentially class education with a dual function: enlightening the masses with the basic skills for vocational competence and intelligent citizenship and providing an intellectual elite class of leaders.

Jeffersonian notions with respect to the purpose of education can still be seen today. One is the emphasis on grading competition. Another is on college entrance requirements. In short, he has left us an academic, liberal arts–oriented school curriculum favoring the college bound.

Today we witness charges and countercharges over the issues of elitism and lack of opportunity in schools. Controversies continue over high

school dropouts, continuation school programs, and the lowering of college academic standards to permit the entrance of the "educationally deprived." Many contemporary Americans also hold the Jeffersonian concept that the privilege of higher education brings with it the responsibility of gentlemanly service and selfless statesmanship. They are appalled at the numbers of young people who do not "use" their training, or worse yet, use it to promote special interests and political and social activism.

Jefferson's ideals of the gentleman statesman-scholar died a political death 2 years after his own death in 1826 when Andrew Jackson assumed the Presidency. The common man became more directly involved with government. As Greene (1965) puts it: "The forms of the enlightenment seemed finally shattered. The way was open to something rough, romantic, new" (p. 12). The Man of Reason gave way to politicians, patronage, universal suffrage, the workingman, and smoke-filled caucus rooms.

EDUCATION FOR A COMMON BOND

During the 30-year period from 1820 to 1850, America developed a more diversified character. New social conditions of "urbanization, industrialism, immigration, and the democratization of politics—were most visible and painful" (Tyack, 1967, p. 121). The result was an era of intense debate, politicking, and mob action.

Workingmen's associations and craft unions sought to lessen class inequality and to get the "saddles" off their backs. They challenged the banks, the mills, the financiers, and the monopolies that thwarted their equality of opportunity. They railed against child labor and sweatshop conditions, where children as young as 7 years were employed up to 14 hours a day. They decried the scarcity of free schools for the poor. The lower classes believed the threat of their children becoming weak cogs in a mechanical monster with no hope of escape through educational opportunity.

With the depression of 1837, working conditions became even worse. This was accompanied by increasing immigration of Irish Catholics, Welshmen, and Germans, flooding the labor market. Disenchantment with social conditions lead to the formation of the Native American Association in

1837, a group hostile to immigrants and vehemently anti-Catholic.

Although there were numerous schools, formal education was a hodgepodge of public, private, and charity institutions. Public tax–supported schools, rural and urban, were most often unheated, dismal, overcrowded, poorly equipped, and presided over by "neighborhood incompetents" (Greene, 1965, p. 13). Schoolmasters were either males of the Icabod Crane variety (somewhat less than men in the eyes of their contemporaries) or grim spinsters. Often the public school teacher was a semiliterate girl of 16, who was paid with room and board in the homes of her students. Private-venture schools provided better prospects for learning, but they were open only to the more affluent. Humanitarian groups like the Quakers founded "free school societies" in the large East Coast cities. They utilized Joseph Lancaster's plan of cheap mass instruction by means of employing child "monitors"—what we would call teacher aides today.

WILLIE NAUGHTY.

Little Footprints, 1892.

A growing concern about the spotty nature of U.S. education was voiced by reformers like James G. Carter, Horace Mann, Henry Barnard, William McGuffey, and Daniel Webster, who devoted their life energies to a movement known as the *common school crusade*. The development of a public tax-supported "common school" began in Massachusetts, but spread quickly throughout the country. It did have its opponents. Many were opposed to taxation, especially the very rich and the very poor. Strict Protestant sects feared "Godless" schools. Catholics saw the common school as a Protestant plot.

Yet the common school crusade became a cause that diverse political, regional, and social groups could identify with, each for different reasons. The outcome was a loose consensus of purpose for the common school. A new tenet of faith in education was born: the public school was to provide a common bond among Americans.

James Carter (1795-1849), a Harvard graduate and former teacher, initiated the common school crusade. His campaign involved a broad-scale attack on existing educational institutions from primary schools through the academies. As early as 1821 he was publishing accounts of poor teaching and inadequate funding in the public schools of Massachusetts. Six years later, through his efforts, Massachusetts made district tax support compulsory. He advocated a "science of pedagogy" and the creation of state teacher training schools. He challenged the existing forms of high school education, which were for the most part private academies, classical schools, and "grammar schools." He rightly feared that such schools would tend to build and perpetuate distinctions in social class and deny equality of opportunity to all. In 1827 Massachusetts passed a law requiring townships to establish public high schools. In 1839 the state's first normal school opened for the training of teachers. Carter furthered the cause of the public school as a common bond by drafting legislation that created a state board of education.

The name of Horace Mann (1796-1859), a humanitarian Boston lawyer and the first Secretary of the newly created Massachusetts Board of Education, became synonymous with the common school crusade. Mann's vision for the creation of a common bond among Americans, fostered by

public education, was carried in his many public addresses and annual reports. He was imbued with the notion of mass enlightenment, a concern for equality, and an interest in keeping Massachusetts in the foreground of educational improvement. Mann not only spoke as a social and political liberal, he spoke as a moralist. He was confident that a sense of community responsibility and nonsectarian Christian morality would grow out of the common school. Speaking in a time of great social unrest, he believed the public school could prevent alienation and anarchy by teaching children to value civilized behavior and the laws of the land. Greene (1965) reports his message:

If the children of the poor were taught to help themselves, they would possess the skills and the feeling of independence which would enable them to resist the selfishness of other men.

Moreover, if all children went to school together and shared experiences day after day, the gulf between the classes would be narrowed, and hostility would accordingly decrease. In adult life, then, no matter what the differences among them, they would be able to look back upon a common life, a common store of experiences; and this would overcome estrangement and the sense of coming from different worlds.

The school, therefore, would not only equalize opportunity by equipping all young people to compete, it would also serve to overcome the class distinctions so alien to America; it would become the great equalizer of the conditions of men—the balance wheel of the social machinery. Everyone, no matter how humble, would have a chance to rise. (pp. 21-22)

The liberal-thinking Carter and Mann were joined in the crusade by many political conservatives. The common school idea appealed to them because they believed that it would anglicize and possibly covertly Protestantize immigrants. It would provide the children of the lower classes with character training, which they presumably needed. It also would provide some academic training for the masses. This was seen as a safeguard because "natural aristocrats" were not always being chosen as leaders.

The political conservative's faith in the common school did not stem from faith in the common man. It is best summed up in the words of Daniel Webster:

We regard it *(the common school)* as a wise and liberal system of police, by which property, and life, and the peace of society are concerned. We seek to prevent in some measure the extension of the penal code, by inspiring a salutary and conservative principle of virtue and of knowledge at an early age. (Tyack, 1967, p. 126)

Reformers like Calvin Stowe and William McGuffey assumed that America was a beacon light and a promised land that should welcome the oppressed foreigner. Further they believed that a "commingling" of different ethnic groups would improve the "national character." But they feared nonassimilation, the development of ethnic communities, ethnic-oriented politics, and beachheads of foreign interests. Stowe, speaking on the matter of assimilation, stated that foreigners

. . . should cease to be Europeans and become Americans; and as our national language is English, and as our literature, our manners, and our institutions are of English origin, and the whole foundation of our society English, it is necessary that they become substantially Anglo-Americans. (Tyack; 1967, p. 149)

An important aspect of the common school was the development of the textbook industry. Noah Webster's famous "blue-backed speller," the widely adopted *Elementary Spelling Book,* first appeared in 1785 and remained on the market for a century. By 1850 its sales were over 1 million copies a year. The blue-backed speller was highly patriotic and moralistic. Children memorized its short maxims that inculcated thrift, hard work, property rights, and contentment with one's station in life.

Graded textbooks made their first appearance in education in 1836. McGuffey's famous *Readers* were graded by level of difficulty from first to sixth grade. The *Readers* consisted of excerpts from literature and American folklore. They stressed middle-class morality. The textbook industry built a new mythology of the American through moralistic tales of trial, success, and caution. Patriotism, social conservatism, and the Protestant ethic of work-success and the self-made man were stressed. As far as the school was concerned, ". . . the individual was on trial, not the social order" (Tyack, 1967, p. 181).

By the end of the Civil War the common school

Monteith's Manual of Geography, 1868.

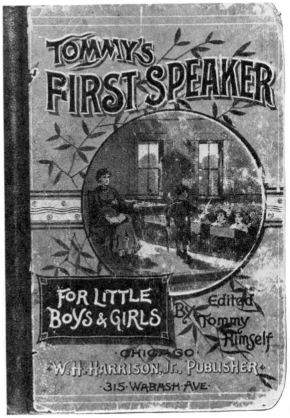

Tommy's First Speaker, 1886.

was an established social institution. Americans began to believe in the ability of public education to provide opportunity and a sense of community. Today both liberal and conservative educators can trace their beliefs to the varied forces that created that unique product of social consensus—the common public school.

EDUCATION FOR ECONOMIC COMPETENCE IN A CAPITALISTIC SOCIETY

Throughout the history of America, social and economic utilitarianism has been a major goal of schooling. Americans have always been an intensely practical people. Unlike the English and the Europeans, Americans have rarely made a great distinction between academic and vocational training. The ancient Greek ideal of intellectualism or "education for its own sake" was viewed with suspicion by Yankees who had serious doubts about the practical value of classical education.

Utilitarianism in American education was a direct outgrowth of middle-class mercantile interests. As trade and commerce increased, the myths of supernaturalism and predestination gave way to new myths of progress and faith in science. Members of the rising American middle class were hungry for practical knowledge that would enable them to become independent tradesmen and artisans who would be better able to control their own destiny.

Benjamin Franklin (1706-1790) best personified this ideal with his far-ranging interests and activities. He was involved in experimental science, improvement of the postal service, practical statesmanship, educational reform, and the dissemination of knowledge via the printing industry and public libraries. The aim of education in Franklin's view was self-improvement. For Franklin that meant learning salable practical skills; examining one's own virtuousness; and becoming socially, economically, and politically versatile. Through his pronouncements and his life-style, Franklin exemplified the personality prototype of the middle-class American entrepreneur: upwardly mobile, self-made, adaptable to novel situations, boldly independent, and financially successful (Rippa, 1967).

Franklin's avowed interest in education can be traced back to 1732, when he began publishing *Poor Richard's Almanack*. For 25 years Franklin dispensed earthy, commonsense wisdom and wit through the mouth of "poor Richard Saunders." The *Almanack* was a means of informal education for farmers and tradesmen. Inherent in the wisdom of Poor Richard was the assumption that the ambitions of an enlightened middle class would result in the improvement of the total society. Unlike Jefferson, Franklin was a self-educated, self-made man who valued the practical arts. He championed the notion that formal secondary and higher education should include the subjects of horticulture, commerce, and mechanical science as opposed to the strictly academic and religious orientation of higher learning in his day.

The beginnings of a middle-class bias in education can be traced to Franklin's articulation of a peculiarly American value orientation. This new view blended the Puritan work-success ethic with the European enlightenment ideal of human progress. It rejected both rigid social structure and dogmatic religion. The validity of this middle-class utilitarian ethos was to go unchallenged for almost 200 years. It seemed particularly suitable in a land of golden opportunity—an open frontier with vast resources and challenges, a land where man's only limitations were personal.

During the later days of the public school movement, America began its growth as an industrial giant. A "Second American Revolution" resulted from a combination of laissez-faire capitalism and mechanical invention. The period from 1865 to 1900 saw rapid growth in railroads, telegraph, and manufacturing, all of which resulted in a highly organized nationwide system of wholesale-retail trade and capital investment. This was the period of the "Captains of Industry": Cornelius Vanderbilt, John D. Rockefeller, Andrew Carnegie, and others who rose from rags to riches by wheeling and dealing in a tax-free, unregulated, free enterprise market. The monopolistic and roughshod business ethics of these robber barons fostered industrial slums and child labor. Such practices were neatly justified by the then popular theory of social Darwinism. Fierce economic competition and its by-product, human suffering, were seen as manifestations of natural law and therefore were morally justifiable.

Andrew Carnegie (1835-1919) best articulated

the industrialist's social theory in his famous *Gospel of Wealth:*

We accept and welcome, therefore, as conditions to which we must accommodate ourselves, great inequality of environment, the concentration of business, industrial and commercial, in the hands of a few, and the law of competition between these, as being not only beneficial but essential for the future progress of the race. (Rippa, 1967, pp. 150-157)

In *Wealth* Carnegie advanced a benign rationale for capitalism with his advocacy of philanthropy, which has left a legacy of privately endowed colleges, libraries, and scholarships. For Carnegie, it was the duty of men of wealth, because of their natural superiority, to provide the community with cultural and educational props for individual self-help and initiative.

Carnegie and his fellow titans of industry were highly critical of education that stressed classical academic subjects. They called for an elementary education that would give workers the basic skills. They sought vocational training in the high schools to prepare skilled workmen for industry. Further they wanted the secondary schools and colleges to provide business and technical education. The powerful National Association of Manufacturers, organized in the decade before the turn of the century, campaigned against the "gross inefficiency" of the public schools and effectively sought the inculcation of the business creed—the values of the business and industrial world—in the public schools.

In the span of 150 years, the preachments of Poor Richard were transformed from a simplistic middle-class ethic to an apology and rationale for the naturally ordained governance of big business. Today most Americans still believe, as a tenet of faith, that the public schools will provide skills that will lead directly to employment. Rightly or wrongly, most Americans view public instruction as the key that unlocks the door to the pleasures of materialism. Critics from the business world point to the surplus of jobless college-educated youth as evidence of the lack of a proper emphasis on voca-

tramp, tramps, tramping, clamp, clamps, cramp, cramps, damp.

    patch, patching, catch, catching.

    rag, rags, bag, bags, drag, drags, dragging, crag, crags.

    wax, flax.

    badge, Madge.

    nap, naps, napping, sap, saps, sapping, gap, gaps, map, maps, mapping, rap, raps, rapping, tap, taps, tapping, trap, traps, trapping, cap, caps, clap, strap, straps, lap, laps, lapping.

    branch, ranch.

TO BE MEMORIZED.

Hearts like doors will ope with ease
    To very, very little keys;
And don't forget that two are these:
    " I thank you, sir," and " If you please."

Politeness is to do or say
The kindest thing in the kindest way.

44

TWENTY-SIXTH AND TWENTY-SEVENTH WEEKS' READING.

air   would

CAMPING OUT.

    Did you ever go camping in the summer time? Frank, Mack, and Will are glad when camping time comes. They like to live in the clear air.

45

New Education Readers, Book Two, 1900.

tional training. Industry itself has tried, although with little success, to move directly into the education business, with the promise of streamlining the unwieldy enterprise of public instruction.

EDUCATION FOR SOCIAL COMPETENCE IN A COMPLEX CULTURE

By the 1890's the second American revolution of industrialism had manufactured sufficient social dynamite to set off a counterrevolution of reform. New Americans who arrived in the large eastern and midwestern cities in search of the good life most often found sweatshops and poverty. The romantic myth of the self-made man operating in a limitless environment of opportunity rang hollow for those victims of a laissez-faire urban-industrial social order. The Puritanical assumption that the individual was on trial in a preordained social order began to be questioned.

Jacob Riis, a crusading journalist, pointed out the appalling conditions of urban ghetto life in *How the Other Half Lives* (1890) and *The Battle With the Slum* (1902). Jane Addams established Hull House in Chicago (1899) and became the most effective American spokesperson for the settlement house concept. Settlement programs spread quickly in the inner cities of the 1890's. Settlement workers sought to combat alienation and disease by providing health care, practical vocational training, playgrounds, day nurseries, and kindergartens. The concept of education for the culturally deprived was born in the settlements. In her influential books, *Democracy and Social Ethics* (1902) and *The Spirit of Youth and the City Streets* (1909), Addams criticized the public schools for stressing an academic curriculum that was not relevant to the realities of the urban poor. She strongly criticized the unspoken social assumption that the underprivileged had little to contribute to community life.

In the 1890's a new tenet of faith in public education appeared: Education could provide social competence in a complex culture. As the historian Lawrence A. Cremin (1961) stated:

To look back on the nineties is to sense an awakening of social conscience, a growing belief that this incredible suffering was neither the fault nor the inevitable lot of the sufferers, that it could certainly be alleviated, and that the road to alleviation was neither charity nor revolution, but in the last analysis, education. (p. 59)

John Dewey and the social learner

It took a Vermont-born professor of philosophy to put together the manifold social concerns of this period and formulate a philosophy of education for the new century. John Dewey (1859-1952) came to the University of Chicago in 1894 to head the departments of philosophy, psychology, and pedagogy. There he met the scholars George H. Mead and Alfred Henry Lloyd, whose work in psychology helped him clarify a theory of interactionism and functional thought. At the same time Dewey became interested in Jane Addams' work with the poor and the exploited. Having witnessed the corruption in city life, he saw the need for philosophical reform that could direct a materialistic industrial civilization "into a distinctive agency for liberating the minds and refining the emotions of all who take part in it" (Wirth, 1966, p. 23).

Dewey clearly saw that industrialism had radically upset the traditional educational functions of the family, neighborhood, and shop. In a simpler agrarian society these agencies had provided wholesome and understandable guidelines for educating children, but in the city they were faltering and failing in purpose. In *The School and Society* (1899) Dewey stated his now famous thesis that the public school must undergo a transformation. The school must compensate for the loss of the important educational functions once performed by family, neighborhood, and shop. Dewey's educational manifesto, *My Pedagogic Creed* (1897) set the philosophical tone for the progressive education movement in the first half of the twentieth century. In it he (Dewey, 1897) stated:

I believe that the school is primarily a social institution. Education being a social process, the school is simply that form of community life in which all those agencies are concentrated that will be most effective in bringing the child to share in the inherited resources of the race, and to use his own powers for social ends.

Education, therefore, is a process of living and not a preparation for future living.

The school must represent life, life as real and vital to the child as that which he carries on in the home, in the neighborhood or on the playground.

That education which does not occur through forms of life, forms that are worth living for their own sake, is always a poor substitute for the genuine reality, and tends to cramp and to deaden. (p. 77)

THE FAMILY TREE OF AMERICAN EDUCATION

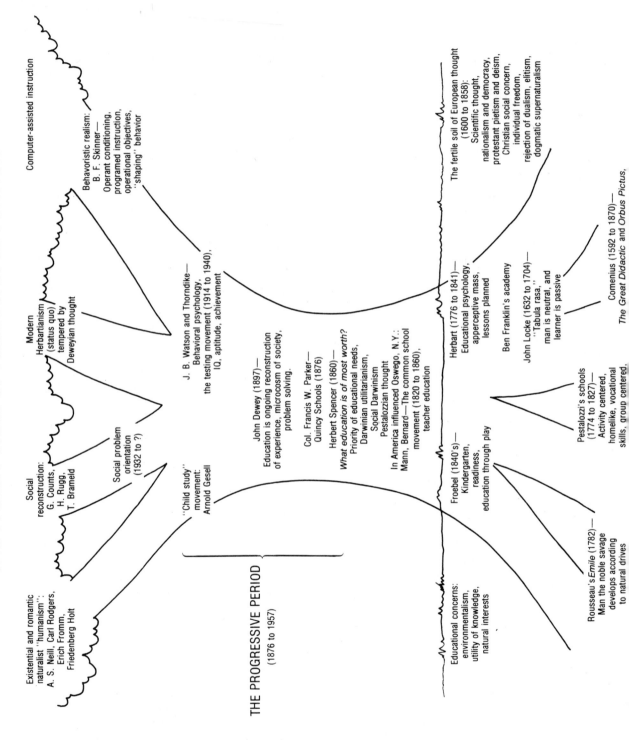

Computer-assisted instruction

Behavoristic realism:
B. F. Skinner—
Operant conditioning,
programed instruction,
operational objectives,
"shaping" behavior

Modern
Herbartianism
(status quo)
tempered by
Deweyian thought

Social
reconstruction:
G. Counts,
H. Rugg,
T. Brameld

Social problem
orientation
(1932 to ?)

J. B. Watson and Thorndike—
Behavioral psychology,
the testing movement (1914 to 1940),
IQ, aptitude, achievement

"Child study"
movement:
Arnold Gesell

Existential and romantic
naturalist "humanism":
A. S. Neill, Carl Rodgers,
Erich Fromm,
Friedenberg Holt

John Dewey (1897)—
Education is ongoing reconstruction
of experience, microcosm of society,
problem solving.

Col. Francis W. Parker—
Quincy Schools (1876)

Herbert Spencer (1860)—
What education is of most worth?
Priority of educational needs,
Darwinian utilitarianism,
Social Darwinism
Pestalozzian thought
In America influenced Oswego, N.Y.:
Mann, Bernard—The common school
movement (1820 to 1860),
teacher education

THE PROGRESSIVE PERIOD
(1876 to 1957)

The fertile soil of European thought
(1600 to 1858):
Scientific thought,
nationalism and democracy,
protestant pietism and deism,
Christian social concern,
individual freedom,
rejection of dualism, elitism,
dogmatic supernaturalism

Herbart (1776 to 1841)—
Educational psychology,
apperceptive mass,
lessons planned

Ben Franklin's academy

John Locke (1632 to 1704)—
"Tabula rasa,"
man is neutral, and
learner is passive

Comenius (1592 to 1870)—
The Great Didactic and Orbus Pictus,

Pestalozzi's schools
(1774 to 1827)—
Activity centered,
homelike, vocational
skills, group centered,

Froebel (1840's)—
Kindergarten,
readiness,
education through play

Educational concerns:
environmentalism,
utility of knowledge,
natural interests

Rousseau's *Emile* (1782)—
Man the noble savage
develops according
to natural drives

As you can see in the "trunk" of the illustration, Dewey's philosophy of education had strong roots in naturalistic environmentalism, as put forth by Rousseau, Pestalozzi, and Spencer. He viewed the learner as a growing organism who lives in, interacts with, and adapts to an environment. This environment is both physical and social. Dewey, however, rejected the Lockean notion of the learner's passive nature. Man was no mere tabula rasa on which nature wrote destiny. Man was more than the sum total of his experiences. Dewey postulated that the learner and the environment act on each other. The environment—life itself—becomes an ever-widening network of experiences and problems for the growing learner. As the learner broadens his experiences and solves problems, he learns. Dewey believed that all human experience was educative. Knowledge was not confined within the walls of the school, nor were teachers the only educators. For Dewey, education and the growth of intelligence involved the following:

1. *Active learning.* As the saying goes, "We learn by doing." Obviously we learn to swim by swimming and not be reading a book about swimming. The same applies to the study of mathematics, science, history, and art. The learner learns best when actively involved in manipulating, questioning, testing, and applying skills and knowledge.

2. *Shared experience.* Human interaction results in learning. Shared experience is important from the standpoint of enculturation (learning one's culture), socialization (learning how to behave in one's society), and vicarious learning (learning from someone else's experience). Man learns best in group situations. Dewey, like Horace Mann, believed that the survival of democracy depended on a democratically oriented school system that encouraged shared experience.

3. *Real problems.* The school should reflect the real concerns of life and living. The curriculum should *not* consist of disciplinary subjects to be mastered. As best as it can, the school must present basic skills and other learnings in lifelike ways. The relationship of learning to practical application must be inherent in all learning situations. Students have to know why they are learning something, and they should feel a need for it. Further Dewey believed that the school should provide, in a controlled manner, ever-increasing experiences with the real world. The school may need to simplify, purify, and balance such experience so that the young learner can comprehend it. For example, the creation of a model grocery store in a second-grade classroom might be a good first step in consumer education.

4. *Problem solving.* The method of instruction most natural to the learner is the scientific method of problem solving. The analytic tools of problem solving equip man to cope with his environment. The steps of problem solving are (a) identification of the problematic situation, (b) definition of the problem, (c) analysis of all aspects and alternatives, (d) testing or trial choice of action, and (e) solution of the problem.

Dewey influenced several generations of educators with his *instrumental* or *experimental* (take your choice of names) philosophy of education. His most influential popularizer was William Heard Kilpatrick. Kilpatrick introduced and championed the *project method* and was largely responsible for making the Teacher's College, at Columbia University in New York, a mecca for educators. Dewey's philosophy also spawned the Progressive Education Association in 1919. That organization folded in 1955 in the heat of pre-Sputnik criticism of the schools. That year marked the end of what had been known as the *progressive movement* in American education.

In *Democracy and Education* (1916) Dewey suggested guidelines for making the schools reflect democratic processes in policy and curriculum. But much of what he sought in the way of reform never came to pass. The social and educational ferment of the 1960's and 1970's attests to the fact that the progressive education movement served largely as an ideal. In Dewey's day sterile and stultifying school policy and curriculum continued, for the most part, to be the manifest reality of American education. The slums and ghettos grew and festered. Segregation of the races and lack of equal opportunity were facts of American life. But the idea of the school as an instrument of social change had been planted.

EDUCATION FOR EQUALITY

Horace Mann's belief that the common school would weld a country of diverse people into a nation of indivisible unity became a partial reality. The common school did Americanize immigrants. During the nineteenth century, approximately 35 million immigrants were assimilated, largely through public education. But the common school did not result in a common bond between all Americans. America did not become a true melting pot.

Most nonwhite Americans had limited access to the avenues of success. For the most part they lacked the educational opportunities of their white counterparts. In most parts of America, blacks and Hispanic-Americans were segregated by law and custom. Blacks were educated in separate public schools. In many cases the schools that minority Americans attended were poorly equipped and poorly financed and had poor teachers. Beliefs about minority Americans' mental capacity and their deserved positions in society created a self-fulfilling prophesy.

Today de jure segregation (segregation deliberately enforced by law) is no longer legal, but de facto segregation (segregation perpetuated in reality without legal basis) is widespread. Especially in American cities, de facto segregation has come to be as great a roadblock to achievement of a common bond as was the legal segregation of years past. White flight from the inner city to the suburbs has resulted in further "ghettoization" of metropolitan areas. Life for the predominately nonwhite dwellers of the inner city has deteriorated. Carl B. Stokes commented on the fact that in the 1950's and early 1960's ". . . whites and blacks in the North at least lived in adjacent neighborhoods. We had contact with one another . . . But not today. The whites are gone . . . the central city has become mostly black and poor-white . . . the outlying areas have become white and affluent. It is America's own version of Apartheid" (Stokes, 1977).

Blacks constitute approximately 15% of the population of the United States. They trace their beginnings in this country to the "Twenty Negers" who were brought in a "dutch man of warre" to Virginia in 1619. Two hundred forty-six years of slavery ended in 1865 with the final defeat of the Confederate Army in the Civil War. In that same year the ratification of the Thirteenth Amendment to the Constitution abolished slavery in the United States. In 1866 the Fourteenth Amendment specified that no state should "deprive any person of

life, liberty or property, without due process of law." But the constitutional amendments did not change custom in the South. The period from the end of the Civil War to the turn of the century was a period of legal disenfranchisement for the Negro. The practice of racial segregation was accelerated by the United States Supreme Court ruling in 1896 in the *Plessey vs Ferguson* case, which legalized the social caste system and "separate but equal" practices. Jim Crow laws were enacted. Black people were forced to use separate seating in transportation and segregated restroom and waiting room facilities. Places of business had the right to refuse service to a person on the basis of color. Some states passed regulations that effectively kept the Negro from becoming a voter. The poll tax and property and literacy tests were required of blacks, but were avoided by whites through grandfather clause statutes. During this period, legalized segregation was reinforced by terrorism in all parts of the country. In the decade from 1889 to 1899 there were an average of 187 lynchings a year (Tyack, 1967).

Social and economic motives have always influenced the white outlook on the education of minorities. This was particularly true in the South, where an early prohibition of formal education for slaves had come about as a result of the Nat Turner Massacre of 1821. In early autumn of that year, a free Negro preacher, Nat Turner, led a number of slaves in Virginia on a bloody massacre of whites—men, women, and children. Turner had identified himself with Moses of the Bible and thought he was leading his people out of bondage. He had been taught to read by his parents and had been educated and freed by his white owner. Rumors of the Nat Turner revolt spread all through the South, giving credence to the long-feared uprising of blacks against whites. It was further believed that Turner had been incited by "incendiary publications" disseminated by Northern abolitionists.

The black man became dangerous because he could read. The result of the Turner revolt, according to Horace Mann Bond (1930), was that "Southern states hastened to adopt laws which would prevent the acquirement, by the slaves, of the accomplishments so 'incompatible with domestic quiet.' Where such laws already existed they were reinforced" (pp. 14-15). This prohibition was extended to free blacks and to any social or religious assemblages in which persons of color could gain instruction from members of their group.

After emancipation, the development of education for blacks was, in part, an effort of Northern missionaries and also of freedmen who, having been armed with political power, saw education as the means to attain equality with the whites. After reconstruction governments were overthrown in the South, blacks generally received the same small amount of public instruction as the "poor whites." But with the rise of the poor whites, blacks lost the equality they had briefly enjoyed.

Competition in the field of labor greatly affected black education in the South. Gunnar Myrdal (1944) has illustrated this period by noting that "... the interests of the white workers against allowing Negroes to acquire skills became stronger. In agriculture and the stagnating crafts, new skilled Negro labor was not welcome: in industry it became a principle that all skilled jobs should be reserved for whites" (p. 898).

Although blacks had successfully been capable of a wide variety of skilled jobs on the plantations before the Civil War, the new economic setting called for "... a redefinition of the Negroes ability to perform such labor" (Bond, 1930, p. 146). The Negro inferiorty myth became popularized, moralized, and entrenched. The *Montgomery* (Alabama) *Advertiser* of August 1, 1900, carried the following article:

The undeniable truth is that the Negro is not fitted to perform any work which requires skill, patience, or mental capacity. There is something lacking in their brain and in their body. Their minds cannot comprehend the intricacies of fine mechanical work and their hands cannot be trained to accomplish it. (Myrdal, 1944, p. 887)

The abilities of the black thus neatly coincided with the needs of industry and the interests of the poor whites in the labor market.

In this bleak era of American history, which Bond has called "The Vale of Tears," an ex-slave stepped forward to become the chief spokesman for his people. Booker T. Washington (1856-1915) was a social and political pragmatist. He accepted the "separate but equal" doctrine, and he championed a quiet, patient development of black skills and middle-class virtues. In a famous speech to white Southerners in 1895, which has been labeled the "Atlanta Compromise," he stated, "In all things that are purely social we can be as separate as the five fingers yet one as the hand in all things essential to mutual progress." Booker T. Washington believed that "industrial" education would be the best avenue of approach for the blacks to use in their attainment of equality. Washington's Tuskegee Institute became a model for black education in the practical arts. Washington's educational aspirations for blacks were grudgingly accepted by the white South and supported by Northern philanthropy. But the Harvard-educated black leader W. E. B. DuBois headed a "radical" element that blamed Washington for accepting the caste system and for neglecting the black's intellect (Tyack, 1967). DuBois favored classical education for blacks. His group held that there should be little difference in education between white and black children. Blacks, they believed, should be taught general history and social sciences, together with black history, black problems, and even special race strategy to help them meet individual and collective problems. The radicals also believed that American blacks should develop pride in their African heritage. They feared that Booker T. Washington's acceptance of separate but equal citizenship and his emphasis on training skilled and semiskilled workers would result in keeping blacks out of higher education and, worse yet, out of the mainstream of American culture.

Public education for black people, as it turned out, did not follow the patterns proposed by either of the two schools of thought. Speaking of the industrial position, Myrdal (1944) remarked: "By and large, in spite of all the talk about it, no effective industrial training was ever given the Negroes in Southern public schools, except training for cooking and menial service" (p. 889). This was because, as Myrdal (1944) stated: "If the white Southerners had to permit the Negroes to get any education at all, they wanted it to be of the sort which would make the Negro a better servant and laborer, not that which would teach him to rise out of his 'place'" (p. 889).

The radicals had some small influence on the improvement of black education during the first part of the twentieth century. Public school implementation of black history and black problem studies was to be 50 years in coming. Race strategy never found its way into the classroom. But the radicals did form the "Niagara Movement" in 1905, which became the National Association for the Advancement of Colored People (NAACP). Under the leadership of DuBois, Moorfield Storey, and Thurgood Marshall, the NAACP rejected the passive approach of Booker T. Washington. To the present day the NAACP has been instrumental in waging a successful, two-pronged legal campaign against de jure segregation in the South and de facto segregation in the rest of the country.

In 1954 the United States Supreme Court ruled unanimously against de jure segregation in public education in the *Brown vs the Board of Education of Topeka*. In the Court's opinion, written by Chief Justice Earl Warren, "We conclude in the field of public education the doctrine of 'separate but equal' has no place. Separate educational facilities are inherently unequal." Warren also stated, "To separate them (Negro students) from others of similar age and qualifications solely because of their race generates a feeling of inferiority as to their status in the community that may affect their hearts and minds in a way unlikely ever to be undone" (Jones, 1974, p. 158).

But the Court did not specify how the transition from segregated to integrated school facilities was to be implemented. A year later in the *Brown II* ruling, the Court placed the primary responsibility for school desegregation on local school authorities. It further admonished local districts to move with "all deliberate speed." Communities in the border states of Missouri, Oklahoma, West Virginia, Kentucky, Maryland, and Delaware took quick positive steps to comply with the law of the land. Baltimore was the first large city to initiate a policy of desegregation.

In the Deep South it was a different story. Resistance to desegregation continued for over a decade. In September, 1957, President Eisenhower had to call in federal troops to protect nine black students attempting to enter the previously all-white Central High School in Little Rock, Arkansas. The following year Governor Faubus closed the public schools for the school year. It was not until 1961 that Little Rock's high schools were desegregated without violence. In 1960 white women attempted to stop four black girls from entering two white elementary schools in New Orleans. This nasty confrontation was carried live on national television. In 1962 President Kennedy

had to deploy federal troops to the University of Mississippi to ensure legal compliance in the case of James Meredith. Meredith, a black, was refused admission to the university, and his case ended in a showdown between "states' rights" advocate Governor Barnett of Mississippi and the federal government.

School desegregation was a highly visible social issue in the civil rights movement of the 1960's. Millions of Americans viewed television coverage of Martin Luther King, Jr. leading nonviolent protest marches in the South. The issues were joined in Alabama; Birmingham, in 1963, and Selma, in 1965, were the sites of campaigns to integrate public facilities and to register black voters. King lead civil rights campaigns until an assassin's bullet cut him down in 1968.

Desegregation of the public schools received a strong push from the Civil Rights Act of 1964. Title IV of the Act, *Desegregation of Public Education,* specified that no U.S. citizen can be denied equal opportunity in education because of race, color, religion, or national origin. Title VI of the Act, *Non-Discrimination in Federally Funded Programs,* put teeth into the law by providing for the withdrawal of federal funds from any program in which discrimination was practiced. Although compliance with the law has been achieved throughout the states, de facto segregation has prevented school desegregation to any great degree. Jones (1974) has observed:

In 1954, only two and one-half million Black students attended segregated schools, while in 1973, the numbers of students attending segregated schools had increased to four and one-quarter million. Thus after desegregation had been operative for nearly 20 years, there were nearly twice as many Black children attending segregated schools as there were when segregation was declared unconstitutional. (p. 170)

Faith in education for equality is not shared by all Americans. It is true that most Americans believe that public education should provide everyone with the basic skills for successful living. But the neighborhood school remains an inseparable part of a given community. Real or imagined threats to that community way of life are taken seriously. Majority Americans who are competing with minorities on the labor market, as well as those who have already achieved comfortable affluence, see the neighborhood school as protecting and reflecting their interests. In many respects the classroom is seen as an extension of the living room. The economic and social threat of integration remains strong.

EDUCATION FOR TECHNOLOGICAL SUPREMACY

Americans have always believed that their schools are a major source of national strength. Federal money and other resources have provided some support to public education almost from the beginning.

In 1787 the Congress enacted the Northwest Ordinance. The ordinance established real estate policies for great areas that were territorial at that time. With the division of land into townships of 36 sections each, one section (640 acres) was to be set aside for the support of public schools. This was the first case of federal aid to education. The ordinance of 1787 stated, "Religion, morality, and knowledge being necessary to good government and the happiness of mankind, schools and the means of education shall forever be encouraged." Over the years the federal government continued to ensure the endowment of public schools by providing grants of land in every state. To date the government has donated over 100 million acres for the support of education (Brodinski, 1967).

In 1862, in the midst of the Civil War, President Lincoln signed the Morrill Land-Grant Act. This ended a long struggle to establish public-supported "peoples colleges" to provide training in agriculture and industrial arts. The Morrill Act made possible the endowment of at least one college in each of what are now the 50 United States and also Puerto Rico, Guam, and the Virgin Islands. A second Morrill Act in 1890 led to the creation of black colleges, which provided the first opportunity for many blacks to gain a higher education. The new land-grant colleges were also among the first to give women an opportunity for a college education.

Land-grant colleges and universities have been instrumental in revolutionizing American technology. Their agricultural experiment stations have produced high-yield foods and fibers. Their laboratories of science and engineering have helped industry develop efficient and innovative manufacturing processes. Their extension courses and services have brought instruction in farming, home economics, and other practical concerns to the doorstep of most Americans. Invention and research carried on in these institutions have had a profound effect on the lives of all Americans. The list of items is impressive: motion pictures, television, food preservation, isolation of the cancer virus, wonder drugs, and atomic research (Brodinsky, 1976).

In 1917 Congress passed the Smith-Hughes Act. With a direct cash appropriation, the federal government began support of vocational education. The act provided the states with matching federal funds for the salaries of industrial arts, agriculture, and home economics teachers and supervisors. It also provided for teacher selection and training in these subjects. In fact, the father of one of the authors of this book began a career of teaching and research in agriculture through the Smith-Hughes Act. He was a city gardener in Los Angeles when he was selected and given the opportunity to teach agricultural subjects in junior high and elementary schools on the basis of his skills and knowledge. In like manner, many thousands of vocational education teachers were identified, recruited, and trained for all levels of public education because of the Smith-Hughes Act. The act ensured the status of the practical arts in American education.

In 1957 the nation was stunned with the Russian launching of Sputnik, the first rocket into space. It was a severe blow to national prestige. Many Americans believed that the Soviet Union's success in space was the result of a superior system of education. Americans began to take a critical look at their schools. In 1958 Congress rushed through the National Defense Education Act (NDEA), providing funds for science, mathematics, and foreign language courses at the secondary and college levels. Monies for NDEA fellowships and student loans were appropriated. In an effort to identify and encourage able students, the NDEA provided funds for guidance counseling and testing.

The stimulus of federal funds provided many developments in education, including the "new mathematics," revised elementary and secondary science curricula, and language laboratories. Additional NDEA funding in 1964 broadened federal support to include social studies and fine arts.

The 1960's became a period of revolution in

educational technology with the extensive use of new media in education. Besides language laboratories, a great movement in programmed instruction began. "Hardware"—teaching machines, computers, and audiovisual machinery—and "software"—programmed textbooks and materials—found their way into the classroom. These materials accompanied educators' quests to make education more efficient. Individualization of learning was promoted, as were special programs for the gifted. Educational research in classroom methods and materials was given new impetus through government regional educational laboratories. Federal funding to school districts throughout the country bought a great deal of innovative teaching materials and hardware.

In 1965 President Johnson signed the Elementary and Secondary Education Act (ESEA). This act launched a new era of massive federal aid to education. By 1975 the ESEA had provided $17 billion to improve schools, school libraries, state departments of education, and educational research. The ESEA has largely focused on the education of the poor and "culturally disadvantaged" through Title I of the act. It has resulted in the improvement of education and educational opportunity for the inner-city poor, the black ghetto dweller, and the poor of Appalachia. It has stimulated additional grants and assistance for the handicapped, the gifted, the non-English speaking, the children of migrant workers, and the native American. Brodinsky reports that the U.S. Office of Education and related agencies operate over 120 programs that aid both public and private education at all levels. This is done at an annual cost of over $12 billion (Brodinsky, 1976).

When the Russians launched Sputnik in 1957 they unwittingly stirred a revolution in American education. They challenged the faith in the American school as a provider of the means, if not the source, of our nation's material well-being. The challenge was answered. Since 1958, education in the United States has been the subject of great and continuing controversy. Public opinion on various educational issues is strongly voiced. Parents and taxpayers clamor over such issues as "why Johnny can't read" or how busing will affect the education of their children. People seek an active voice in education. The challenge of accountability faces teachers and professional educators. Americans have discovered that education is an imperfect panacea. But they still keep the faith in their system of schooling.

SUGGESTED ACTIVITIES FOR FURTHER UNDERSTANDING

1. What parallels might be made in "generation-gap" understanding between (1) Old-World Puritans and their American-born children; (2) Italian, Irish, and Jewish immigrants of the 1890's and their American-born children; (3) depression-reared, World War II veterans and their children of the psychedelic "sixties"? It might be fun and instructional to role-play examples of generation-gap thinking of these three eras.

2. Identify some additional modern "devils" that society expects the schools to conquer, and consider the psychological and sociological reasons why these devils are feared.

3. What evidences of the Jeffersonian concept of education for the natural aristocracy can you find in the school policies and curricula of local elementary schools, high schools, and colleges? How do private high schools and colleges in your area differ from the public institutions?

4. Role-play an argument between Horace Mann and a reluctant businessman in which Mann is trying to persuade the businessman to be willing to support public education with more of his tax dollars.

5. How might Horace Mann have argued with advocates of private education concerning the role of public schools in perpetuating democracy as a way of life?

6. In what ways is, or is not, America a land of "golden opportunity" for (1) an individual's economic advancement and (2) the social advancement of an ethnic minority?

7. Compare and contrast the aspirations of a late nineteenth century American middle-class urban family and a contemporary middle-class urban family.

8. In what ways is Carnegie's concept of the "gospel of wealth" reflected in current attitudes about the support of public education?

9. Why do you think we have been reluctant to put into practice the ideas expressed by John Dewey in *My Pedagogic Creed?*

REFERENCES

Bond, H. M. *Social and economic influences on the public education of Negroes in Alabama, 1865-1930.* Washington, D.C.: The Associated Publishers, 1930.

Brameld, T. Illusions and disillusions in American education. *Phi Delta Kappan,* 1968, *50,* 202-207.

Brodinsky, B. 12 major events that shaped America's schools. *Phi Delta Kappan,* 1976, *58,* 68-77.

Butts, R. F., and Cremin, L. A. *A history of education in American culture.* New York: Henry Holt & Co., 1953.

Cremin, L. A. *The transformation of the school: progressivism in American education 1876-1957.* New York: Vintage Books, 1961.

Dewey, J. My pedagogic creed. *School Journal,* January 1897, *54,* 77-80.

Frazier, E. F. *The Negro in the United States.* New York: Macmillan, Inc., 1949.

Greene, M. *The public school and the private vision: a search* for America in education and literature. New York: Random House, Inc. 1965.

Gutek, G. L. *An historical introduction to American education.* New York: Thomas Y. Crowell Co., Inc., 1970.

Hofstadter, R. *Social Darwinism in American thought* (rev. ed.). Boston: Beacon Press, 1955.

Jones, L. Desegregation and social reform since 1954. *Journal of Negro Education,* Spring 1974, *43,* 155-171.

King, E. J. *Other schools and ours* (3rd ed.). New York: Holt, Rinehart & Winston, Inc., 1967.

Kirkland, E. C. *Dream and thought in the business community, 1860-1900.* Chicago: Quadrangle/The New York Times Book Co., 1964.

Lewis, D. L. *King: A critical biography.* New York: Preager Publishers, Inc., 1970.

Miller, H. L., and Woock, R. R. *Social foundations of urban education.* Hinsdale, Ill.: The Dryden Press, 1973.

Myrdal, G. *An American dilemma: the Negro problem and modern democracy.* New York: Harper & Row, Publishers, 1944.

Phi Delta Kappan, 1976, *58,* entire issue.

Rippa, S. A. (Ed.). *Educational ideals in America: a documentary history.* New York: David McKay Co., Inc., 1969.

Rippa, S. A. (Ed.). *Education in a free society: an American history.* New York: David McKay Co., 1967.

Silberman, C. E. *Crisis in the classroom: the remaking of American education.* New York: Random House, Inc., 1970.

Stokes, C. B. The subject of blacks doesn't qualify as popular any more. *San Diego Union,* February 13, 1977. (Reprinted in full from lecture given at Bowdoin College, Brunswick, Me.)

Tyack, D. B. *Turning points in American educational history.* New York: John Wiley & Sons, Inc., 1967.

Wirth, A. G. *John Dewey as educator: his design for work in education (1894-1904).* New York: John Wiley & Sons, Inc., 1966.

3 REALITIES OF AMERICAN EDUCATION
BEAUTY MARKS AND WARTS

In Chapter 1 you read about the historical development of education. You learned what some of the greatest thinkers believed about education—what it should do, how it should be done, and for whom it should be done. In Chapter 2 you saw how these grand schemes, tempered by Puritanism, democracy, and technology, combined to form the roots of American education, an enterprise unique in the annals of humankind.

In later chapters you will see how the American dream has manifested itself in schools, curricula, and educational personnel and how each of those aspects has been attuned to societal expectations and to the nature of learners.

Before we move into those chapters, however, we will pause for a moment to take stock of present-day realities of American education. Dreams are one thing. Manifestations are another.

THE AMERICAN DREAM, SUMMARIZED

The American dream for education was shown through the basic tenets of faith we hold in education. Those tenets are many. Chief among them are the following:

1. Education makes possible equality of opportunity. Opportunities, although never truly equal for all, become available to the educated. They remain beyond the reach of the uneducated.
2. Education is the golden path to the good life. The finer things of life are available only to the educated. Some of those things cost money. Others require enlightenment and sensitivity. Education provides the wherewithal to acquire them.
3. Education is essential for a democratic society. People cannot govern themselves unless they have learned to read, write, think, cooperate, participate actively and effectively, and abide by the common law.
4. Education begets technology and allows us to use it to best advantage. We live in a society based on technology. Education enables us to advance technology and, at the same time, make productive use of the freedom it affords us.
5. Education is the prime avenue through which people maximize their individual and collective selves. We maximize ourselves as we pursue our aptitudes, sharpen our skills, expand our

horizons, and become able to interact effectively with others.

In short, very few Americans have seriously questioned the value of universal education. We have assumed, and believed, that education is good for everyone, individually and collectively.

But how are these dreams and tenets of faith translated into action? The mechanisms by which education functions almost defy description. If they didn't work so well, you would think them impossible. There are so many parts that mesh, so many people involved, so much money expended, the total package is absurdly improbable. Yet it continues, day after day, year after year.

The factors that produce this immense complication do yet another thing that the great educational philosophers never warned us about. They make it impossible to conduct education exactly in accord with idealized theory. That's why if you were to read educational philosophy, then stack its ideas up against current practice, not only in America but anywhere in the world, you would find that they don't match. They can't. Let us see why.

WHAT PHILOSOPHERS ASSUME

Philosophers, of education or anything else, deal with abstract ideas. Abstractions are marvelous. They can be treated in pure form, uncontaminated by the multitude of factors that interplay in real life. This pure form makes it possible to construct beautiful models, clean of line and lovely in proportion.

If a single builder were given authority, unlimited resources, and students who behaved exactly alike, perhaps an educational reality could be built that would be as precise as the theoretical model. Obviously such could never be. Our society, like all others, has a multitude of cooks spooning and stirring in the educational kitchen. They can't agree on the way to boil water. You could hardly expect their soup to match the recipe. To further complicate matters, there are never enough ingredients, the vegetables are never the same, the broth changes from one day to the next, and the mixture must be served in tureens, saucers, teacups, pans, and mixing bowls. Three fourths of the customers, when served vegetable soup, wish it were chicken. When served chicken, they wish it were split pea.

One can't truly say that the educational soup has

been spoiled by all these cooks. It's just that by the time they all work on it, with ingredients that are never consistent and tastes that continually change, it is no wonder the product doesn't fulfill the promise of the recipe.

The recipes for education are those idealized, pure-form theories that philosophers make. Whatever the theory, you can usually find the following assumptions in it:

1. Everyone for whom education is provided eagerly wants it. They would break their backs to get it.
2. Everyone involved in the enterprise—society, community, parents, students, administrators, law makers—has the same high vision of and commitment to education. They are all on the same wavelength.
3. Unlimited resources are available. You have all the money you need for materials, buildings, libraries, laboratories, playing fields, and so forth, or else you can find it ready at hand in the community, with generous concerned citizens ready to turn it over to education.
4. The ratio of students to teacher is so low that every student receives constant attention from the teacher.
5. All students want to learn. They pant for knowledge—every single one of them.
6. You can always count on everyone to do their level best. Teachers are paragons of technical and personal perfection. Students erase all from their minds save learning. Parents are ever supportive. Administrators are facilitative wizards and impeccable communicators. Everyone cooperates and pulls together.
7. Everyone has a single task to perform. That task is straightforward and uncluttered. Teachers teach. Students learn. Communities support. Legislatures make perfect educational laws.
8. Everyone agrees on what education should do for the learners and for society.
9. Everyone agrees on what the contents of the curriculum should be.
10. Everyone agrees on how teachers should teach and learners should learn.

Those are some of the notions that lie implicit in most philosophies and theories of education. Unfortunately, things don't work out that way in real life. Far from it.

REALITIES OF EDUCATION

Lest you get the wrong idea, be assured that it is perfectly fine for theories to be idealized with components meshing exactly and running smoothly. That condition allows one to see goals clearly, and it helps build smooth, straight paths toward those goals. Once that is done, boulders, thorns, and winds along the paths will not obscure sight of the goal.

But when you add those boulders, thorns, and winds, along with floods, ambushes, rockslides, earthquakes, volcanos, and midsummer snowstorms, your educational journey becomes something other than a pristine romp through grassy meadows. It becomes much, much harder. You never know what surprise lies around the next bend. But that makes the whole affair more interesting, too.

The following sections of this chapter describe some of the realities extant in the American educational dream. There are nine sections: (1) what we expect of schools, (2) schools' programs for learners, (3) school personnel, especially teachers, (4) students, (5) school facilities, (6) materials of instruction, (7) school finance, (8) checks and balances, (9) teaching's devils and ogres, and (10) teacher power. You will find that these realities never received much attention from educational philosophers, great as they were.

What we expect of schools

Put a check mark by each thing you think the schools should teach: reading, writing, arithmetic, spelling, composition, handwriting, typewriting, English grammar, vocabulary, American history, world history, American geography, world geography, map skills, geology, how different cultures live, how humans behave, how humans grow and develop, cooperation, group decision making, critical thinking, health, nutrition, safety, physical education, team games, individual sports, astronomy and space travel, meteorology (weather phenomena), electricity, electronics, biology, chemistry, physiology, physics, algebra, geometry, consumer education, practical mathematics, driver education, home economics, cooking, sewing, automobile mechanics, art appreciation, drawing and painting, music appreciation, instrumental music, vocal music, democratic processes, patriotism, citizenship, American literature, English literature, poetry, drama, world religions. . . . Getting tired? We've only begun. And these are topics that most people agree on.

There are plenty of topics people do not agree on. What do you think about topics such as sex education, alternatives to marriage, birth control, contraception, the Bible as literature, socialism, communism, communal living, sensitivity training, encounter-group therapy, body awareness, the arts of loving, assertiveness training, political activism, radical politics, militancy, alternative lifestyles? These topics have wide appeal among the young. Should the schools deal with them? Some people vehemently say yes. Others vehemently say no.

There's one thing we can be sure of. There is tremendous disagreement within our society as to what we should expect our schools to do.

Very conservative groups say the purpose of schools is to teach reading, English language, and mathematics. You could toss in American history, but you would have to leave out those parts that made us look bad.

Slightly more liberal groups think schools should transmit the factual bodies of knowledge in the "basic" subjects—English, mathematics, natural science, social science, and the classics of literature, art, and music.

Some groups think schools should reflect the great ideals of our society, together with the best that has endured in all areas of human inquiry and knowledge. Some think schools should, above all, offer preparation for effective participation in democratic society. Some think schools should stress diversity, change, and flexibility as preparation for a rapidly changing future. Some think schools should be eminently practical, focusing on knowledge and skills needed for daily living. Some think schools should take the lead in constructing a new social order, one that would stress individuality, cooperation, self-direction, concern for others, and living by the golden rule.

And at least a few think schools as an institution should be done away with altogether. Learning, they believe, could better be done in association with the workaday world of semiskilled and professional people, business people, practicing artists and writers, and so on. People who wanted to learn would seek their own teachers and experiences, in their own way, singly or in groups.

Yet, within this great diversity of expectations, we do find common ground. In the main, schools function within the boundaries of that common ground. There you see a nonending tug-of-war between the "back to basics" factions and the "practical skills" factions. This struggle is determined but relatively mild. It is when schools are persuaded to step over the established boundaries that furor erupts. That is what happened in the past when schools tried to teach about sex education, religion, communism, and evolution.

Schools' programs for learners

What, then, are the common grounds within which schools are allowed to function? To delimit those grounds we can begin with the Seven Cardinal Principles of Education, which you may recall from Chapter 1. First stated in 1918 and then reaffirmed in 1976, these principles are as follows:
1. Health
2. Command of fundamental processes
3. Worthy home membership
4. Vocation
5. Civic responsibility
6. Worthy use of leisure
7. Ethical character

No critic has mounted a serious attack against these principles.

Next we can examine the curricula of the elementary and secondary schools to see how the Seven Cardinal Principles are manifested, as well as what additions to them are commonly accepted.

The elementary schools everywhere lay heavy stress on reading, English language, mathematics, social science, natural science, health and safety, music, art, and physical education. To be sure, disputes contine over content, sequence, focus, and methods of teaching. But few question the basic value of these subjects.

The secondary schools typically stress English grammar, composition, and literature; general science, biology, chemistry, and physics; American history and civics; general mathematics, algebra, geometry, and trigonometry; instrumental and vocal music; art; and physical education. In these areas the secondary schools continue the subject emphases of the elementary schools, taking them on to higher and more sophisticated levels.

In addition, the secondary schools emphasize, through separate courses, topics barely introduced at the elementary level. Typical courses include foreign languages; typing, shorthand, and general business education; home economics; industrial arts; automobile shop and mechanics; vocational education; and speech and drama.

The secondary school also provides widely supported instructional service through its extracurricular activities. Most high schools, and many junior high and middle schools, offer the following activities for elected or interested students: student council or other student governing body; school newspaper; school yearbook; interscholastic athletics; school plays; and a variety of clubs, such as Spanish club, photography club, science club, and writing club. You can see that these menus provide a wide range of nutrients for hungry scholars' minds—surprisingly wide in view of the difficulty we have in agreeing on curricular contents.

But just try and add a new dish to the menu and see what happens. Sure, there are fascinating and worthwhile things to be learned. But what do you take out of the curriculum when you add something new? The pie is only so big, as they say. If you slice it into eight pieces instead of six, each slice is going to be smaller—there's no way around it. Try to drop anything that's already in the curriculum, and you will stir up defensive hornets you never knew existed. This fact makes the curriculum, diverse and valuable as it is, rigid and resistant to change.

Yet curriculum does change. It continually changes, albeit slowly, as new knowledge makes its way into the picture, as we discover more about how students learn, as new media are developed, as national interests change, and as society's outlook on various issues changes. Perhaps you can remember the early 1960's when drastic modifications were made in the foreign language, science, mathematics, and English curricula. Those changes came from a combination of newer knowledge and national urgency (we were highly threatened by the U.S.S.R. at that time). You will see more in Chapter 8 about the processes that come into play as curricular change is pushed.

In summary, different segments of our society, and different individuals among us, have very different ideas about what schools should do and how they should do it. The fuss never ends. It just shifts directions, and different people take up the cry. That is a reality of American education. At the same time, however, we have a paradoxical degree of agreement about the schools. This agreement has resulted in a school curriculum comprised of many courses. The curriculum is set and resistant to change. This, too, is a reality.

School personnel, especially teachers

You may think that schools consist of a number of students, thrown together with some teachers, a few administrators, and an occasional secretary. If so, you are partly right. There surely is a great number of students. But there is an unexpected number of school personnel, as well. The menagerie has many members besides teachers, administrators, and secretaries. They must work together, not in isolation. Unless they continually guard against it, they inevitably squabble. There are disputes, gossip, jealousy, envy, and backbiting to go along with the affection, concern, and camaraderie that can grow among professionals.

Who are some of these school personnel? They include superintendents, associate superintendents, personnel directors, curriculum directors, business managers, principals, vice principals, teachers of all sorts, teacher aides, secretaries, guidance counselors, clerks, librarians, nurses, custodians, and maintenance personnel.

All these people, except for teachers, are expected to be normal, average, typical citizens. That is, they are allowed to have their vices, speak their minds, and conduct themselves the way the rest of us do.

Teachers, however, are in a different boat. We expect the teachers of our children to live above the common mean, to be especially virtuous, to be wise, just, impartial. We expect them to be exemplary in all ways, because they have so much influence on young minds. We especially do not want them to speak their minds on controversial matters, such as politics or religion.

These expectations put teachers in a difficult spot. Although they are, in truth, a cut above the norm in matters of taste, personal habits, and consideration for others, most of them are hardly angels. They do cuss and drink and smoke, albeit out of sight of students. They do have thoughts and preferences. But when around students, they are expected to be neuter and neutral.

As if this were not enough of a bind for teachers,

they are expected to fill different roles while teaching. There is disagreement about what these roles should be. Depending on whom you talk to, you will hear that teachers should be dispensers of information, task masters, facilitators, parent surrogates, ideal models, managers of learning, diagnosticians, personal friends, disciplinarians, inspirational models, or motivators. You will hear they are too easy on kids or too tough, too subject matter centered or too person centered, too structured or too open. In the 1920's there wasn't so much argument. Teachers were supposed to teach. In addition, according to stipulations in their contracts, they were legally admonished to do the following:

1. Attend Sunday school and church regularly.
2. Refrain from consorting with members of the opposite sex.
3. Refrain from marriage.
4. Eschew alcohol, tobacco, and swearing.
5. Contribute generously of time and energy to community activities.

Now we are not so sure.

By and large, teachers are fine people, intelligent, concerned, and hardworking. If they sometimes seem unsure about their roles, it is no wonder. We are unable to decide exactly what we want them to do.

Students

The most shocking reality teachers must face is the reality of students. The great philosophers assumed that students were eager to learn. Modern theorists make the same assumption. Teachers in training are given the idea that since students naturally want to learn, it is solely the teacher's fault when they do not. Textbook writers also seem to assume that students come to school with nothing on their minds except a burning desire to learn algebra and verb conjugation. Is this reality? Your common sense and experience tell you in no uncertain terms that it is not.

Let's list some realities of students to see how different they are from that hypothetical youth who is bright eyed, well fed, eager, perfectly behaved, highly motivated, responsible, and self-directing.

1. Students *do* want to learn. That is an inherent part of their makeup.
2. But they usually prefer to learn things we do not teach in school.

3. They are not all alike. On the contrary, they differ greatly in needs, interests, ability, desire to learn, and ways of behaving.
4. Most students seek attention and acceptance. Younger ones seek attention and acceptance from teachers. Older ones seek these things from teachers, but especially from peers. They use a range of behaviors for seeking attention and acceptance from desirable to undesirable, normal to bizarre.
5. They come from a variety of backgrounds that greatly influence their school behavior. Some come from stable homes; others bounce around from one adult to another. Some are well to do; others live in poverty. Some have caring parents; others are rejected. Some live comfortable lives, whereas others go hungry, live with abuse and hostility, and daily face the seamy side of life. Some have been inculcated with the importance of schooling; others believe that going to school is something like going to jail: they can't wait to break out. Some have been taught courtesy, manners, and concern for others; some believe in an eye for an eye and winning through intimidation.

Don't, however, precast students on the basis of their backgrounds. Some of the have-it-all's seem compelled to delinquency. Some of the beaten and unloved find affection only in school, want to be there, and see education as the way to escape from their worlds. Poor kids have brains, too. Our history is filled with great people who rose out of poverty and misery to power, prestige, creativity, philanthropy, and contributions to humankind.

The point is simply this. Students in school don't always want to learn what we want to teach them. They often misbehave, making teachers' tasks difficult and lives miserable. They are not all of a cloth, but rather vary tremendously, requiring different efforts from the teacher. They will sometimes be uncaring, cruel, hostile, and belligerent. But there will also be many who are kind, caring, affectionate, and concerned, always trying their level best. Those students bring great happiness to teachers' lives.

School facilities

Never in history has any society in the world provided the kinds of physical facilities that we provide for our students. Throughout the land, in communities rich and poor, we have willingly shelled out our hard-earned bucks so that students might learn in comfort, affluence, and even splendor. We have erected magnificient buildings and filled them with the finest furniture, books, materials, and equipment. That generosity has changed during the past few years. We have begun to question the need for "costly palaces," splendiferous stadiums, and manicured playing fields. We have tightened the strings on our purses. Still, American educational facilities are second to none.

Elementary schools. Modern American elementary schools are lovely places, relatively calm, ideally containing about 500 to 600 children. To accommodate those students, the school will consist of about eighteen classrooms, all on ground level, large, airy, and perhaps carpeted. If kindergarten is included, there might be three kindergarten classrooms, larger still, with their own restrooms and playgrounds. There will be a principal's office, reception office, nurse's office, large multipurpose room (cafeteria, auditorium, indoor gym), library, faculty lounge, faculty workroom, and custodians' station. Large playgrounds will be adjacent to the classrooms.

Inside the rooms will contain movable furniture, tables, storage areas, chalk and bulletin boards, and counter-top space. Sometimes there will be a piano and sink. Occasionally the room will have its own library. Typically the classrooms will be self-contained, which means that the same class attends there all day, with the same teacher teaching all or most subjects.

Some of the newer elementary schools are being built in a form called "open space." This means there are no interior walls between the classes. Four or more classes may be conducted simultaneously in one open-space area. This proximity and ease of movement make it possible for teachers to group their students in various ways and do a great deal of team teaching.

Open space has its disadvantages, however. Noise flows from one area to another. Movement can be distracting. Teachers must coordinate their schedules, so that all have noisy and quiet activities at the same time: One group can not be singing while another is trying to do silent reading. This coordination restricts the individual teaching flexibility that many elementary teachers cherish.

Junior schools (junior high and middle schools). Students must make a great transition when they move from elementary school into junior school. Now they are apt to change classrooms for each period of the day, seeing a new teacher each time. Their homework will increase. They will no longer have the security of one teacher and one class. They may begin to dress for physical education and take group showers, an unnerving experience at first. They may have their first gymnasium, their first large library, their first science laboratory, and their first woodworking shop.

Junior schools are usually quite different from elementary schools. Part of this difference is seen in the physical facilities. First, there are many more students present than in the elementary school. This means more classrooms and a much larger school. Then, there are new subjects that require special facilities—physical education, with its gymnasium, courts, fields, lockers, and showers; science, with its special laboratory equipment; homemaking, with its kitchen and serving area; industrial arts, with its shops and tools. There will likely be a large library. There will be a stage and auditorium for plays and concerts.

All these facilities, plus the number and movement of students, make junior schools places of hustle, bustle, and commotion.

High schools. High schools are like junior schools, except on a grander scale yet. Typically they will be much larger, sometimes enrolling 3,000 or more students. Their course offerings run a wide range. Students can now find specialized courses there that were formerly found only in universities and trade schools. Very sophisticated equipment fills laboratories, art rooms, photographic studios, gymnasiums, mathematics areas, business education classrooms, automobile shops, and vocational education facilities. Comprehensive high schools of today have quality facilities that surpass those of most colleges 20 years ago.

These facilities open the world to students. Music, arts, literature (from fine libraries), the sciences—all are there for the taking. Dramatic productions in high schools show astounding quality. Athletic teams annually reach new heights of excellence.

Despite these marvelous facilities, and they are truly magnificent, a large percentage of high school

students do not do well in school. This condition defies explanation. It may be because of compulsory school attendance, overall apathy toward learning, or the feeling that teachers care more for their subject matter and materials than for their students.

Whatever the reason, the reality is this: Our secondary schools offer curricula and facilities second to none—facilities in particular that universities elsewhere in the world would envy. Still many of our students show apathy, even disdain, for secondary education. Instead of taking ad-

vantage of what is offered, they long to be involved in other out-of-school activities. They idly go through the motions, sometimes making life difficult for their teachers.

Fortunately these students are counterbalanced by those who strive for excellence. It is recognized by authorities (although you seldom see it mentioned in the newspapers) that the top 10% to 15% of our high school graduates possess a range of knowledge and skills that exceeds that of the average college graduate earlier in this century.

Materials of instruction

All the laudatory things that can be said for our public school facilities can be said equally for the instructional materials used there. No other school system in the world matches ours when it comes to quantity and quality of instructional materials.

This plethora of materials covers kindergarten on up. If materials are not so evident in higher grades as they are in lower ones, it is because teachers choose not to use them.

We are so inundated with materials that we take them for granted. Travelers to other countries, when they visit schools, report their shock at the barrenness they see in classrooms. They often find only a chalkboard, student notebooks, and pencils. No books, no charts, no maps, no models, no lovely pictures. That's not always the case, of course. Across the world you will occasionally find schools the equal of ours in instructional materials. The astounding thing is that all our schools are well equipped, not just a showpiece here and there.

The following are observations we can make about the instructional materials used in American schools:

1. They are bountiful through all the grades.
2. They are beautiful, colorful, precise, durable, and accurate.
3. They come in great variety for all subject areas.
4. When properly used, they extend and amplify student experiences to a phenomenal degree.
5. Their greatest value lies in their ability to (a) allow manipulation by students, (b) illustrate the unseeable (molecules, microbes, planets, etc.), (c) show what most of us never will see personally (monasteries in Tibet, the Great Wall of China, stone-age Indians in the Amazon, etc.), (d) make precise observations and measurements (most science equipment), (e) give us power to perform mechanical and technological feats (photography, electronics, engine analysis and repair, etc.), and (f) put incredible quantities of information at our fingertips in forms such as print, computer language, and microfiche.

Despite appearances, the instructional materials picture is not all rosy. Teachers don't always use their materials to advantage. They may not know how to use them well, or at all. Or they may rely on them to an undesirable extent. Materials help, but have never yet been able to replace the teacher. Even with the best materials, students can't learn everything on their own.

Moreover, instructional materials have two limitations. First, they are seldom highly instructive by themselves. They can show, exemplify, clarify, even suggest. But they rarely teach by themselves. Thus to be effective they must be used judiciously in an organized program of instruction. Second, materials, like everything else, become counterproductive when used to excess. Too many materials distract learners. Students do best when given only those materials that directly assist specific learning at a specific time.

In summary, American schools use a quantity of excellent instructional materials unequaled elsewhere. Teachers don't always use materials to best advantage. Because of the materials, American students have an unusual opportunity to extend their experiences and have their concepts sharpened.

School finances

There are two remarkable facts about the financial support we give our schools. One is that we spend more money on education, overall and per student, than any other country has ever spent. The other is that many countries spend a far greater proportion of their total revenue on education than we do. We can be justly proud of the financial support we give our schools. However, that support, great as it is, pales in significance when compared to the amount of money we spend on tobacco and cosmetics.

Let's look at some facts and figures about public school expenditures. The figures reported here come from *United States Government Statistical Abstracts*. Through 1974 the figures are accurate. Those reported for 1976 and beyond are projections.

Expenditures. Expenditures for public schools in 1976 totaled a staggering $98 billion, up from $19.7 billion in 1960. These figures include expenditures for higher education. For elementary and secondary schools alone, the 1976 total was $68 billion, up from $16 billion in 1960.

Although the increases seem especially great, they appear more reasonable when seen in comparison to our gross national product. In 1976 they made up 7.5% of the gross national product, as compared to 5% in 1960. Even when you take into account inflation and increased productivity, that is still an increase of 50%.

This increase is what disturbs taxpayers. School enrollments have increased only slightly since 1960, and they are now declining. Growing numbers of citizens are insisting that schools control their spending. They back up their insistence by refusing more and more to increase taxes for school revenue.

Enrollments. You must be convinced by now that schooling is big business. In 1976 there were over 93,000 public elementary and secondary schools in this country. They enrolled 53 million students, almost one fourth of the population. The schools were in session an average of 179 days per year.

Enrollment in public schools increased only 8% between 1960 and 1976, from 49 to 53 million. The number of secondary schools increased very slightly during that period, from 25,800 to just over 26,000. The number of elementary schools decreased from 112,000 in 1960 to just over 67,000 in 1976. This reduction was not caused by shrunken enrollments, but by the consolidation of small elementary schools and the closing of numbers of one- and two-teacher schools in rural areas. Present enrollments, although very large, have begun to decline in elementary schools. They reached their peak in 1970. From that peak they will decline 14% by 1982, the projected low. At that point they may begin to rise once more. Secondary school enrollment reached its peak in 1976. From that peak it is projected to decline 16% by 1984, its projected low.

Other facts and figures. Per capita personal income in 1976 was $6,000. Of that amount, $314 went for school expenditures.

The expenditures per student in 1976 were $1,388 per year.

In 1976 we had 2,181,500 public elementary and secondary teachers. They earned average salaries of $12,500, for a total salary expenditure of $27.3 billion.

Sources of 1976 school monies were as follows:

Federal	$ 5.3 billion
State	$27.4 billion
Local	$35.1 billion

These figures are for all American states, territories, and overseas schools combined. The sources of support varied greatly according to where the schools were located.

Checks and balances

Have you ever wondered how it is that American education stays on such an even keel? You saw earlier in this chapter that groups in our society strongly differ in their views about what education should and should not do and about how the whole process should be carried out. What is it that keeps any one of those groups from grabbing the reins and galloping off to their own particular Valhalla?

What keeps that from happening is an intricate system of checks and balances that affect education. Some of these checks and balances are stipulated in law. Examples are control and finance of public education. Others have grown from custom. Examples are the involvement, interest, and pressures that come from the community. Among these many checks and balances, the following are especially notable:

National and state laws
Societal values, folkways, and mores
Public esteem for and confidence in education
Special interest groups
Textbook publishers
Special national interests
Community pressures
Parental pressures
Accountability
Let us briefly consider each of these forces.

National and state laws. National law requires that free public education through high school be made available for all. It stipulates that students may not be segregated on the basis of race, color, or creed. It makes available federal funds for special assistance to education in areas of national priority. It expressly reserves to the states the right to make educational laws that do not conflict with national law.

State law specifies how schools are to be financed, how they can expend money, who is to be in charge of them, how they can be organized, what they can teach, until what age students must attend, how long the school year must be, how much daily instruction must be provided, and what teachers must do to attain the credentials to teach.

National and state laws are strictly adhered to, overseen, and enforced. Schools and individuals who try to function outside the law will surely be called to account. Our educational laws, their enforcement, and our general desire to live by them contribute greatly to the strengths of our educational system.

Societal values, folkways, and mores. Societal values and customs play a role almost as great as law in influencing American education. You will see schools do relatively little with regard to effective sex education, teaching about religion, or teaching objectively about political systems other than democracy. You almost never hear teachers use profanity in front of their students. Our acceptance of personal equality between rich and poor, bright and dull, female and male, even teacher and student is rare in most of the world, although so normal to us that we take little note of it.

These examples are obvious. Folkways and mores peculiar to certain localities are much more subtle. Some dictate styles of dress and hair; others direct manners, respect for individuals, amount of homework, expectations of teachers, expectations of students' parents, pride in self-sufficiency, and desire to excel in school.

In short, values and customs influence the behavior of students, schools, teachers, and parents. Some values and customs are consistent throughout the land. Others vary from place to place.

Public esteem for and confidence in education. The regard in which education is held influences public support and criticism. This regard waxes and wanes. There have been times in our history when education was generally held in high regard. Such a time occurred in the 1950's. The public opened its purses generously, built thousands on thousands of new schools, raised teacher's salaries, and bought new band uniforms and science laboratories to the heart's content.

The mid-1970's saw education slip in the public's confidence. Beset with an unfamiliar economy of inflation coupled with unemployment, stirred by controversies over desegregation through busing, and stung by accounts of high school graduates who were functionally illiterate, public support for education declined. School districts that had always passed bond issues for building construction suddenly found taxpayer revolt. Public reticence to

support education resulted in the curtailment of athletic programs, salary freezes, and in some cases the temporary closing of entire school systems. All at once, the public seemed to say enough was enough. Schools frantically began to tighten their belts and trim expenditures wherever they could.

Who knows when strong public support for education will rebound. The pendulum will begin to swing the other way sooner or later. But the only thing that would swing it in a hurry would be some matter of national concern, such as we saw after the Russians launched Sputnik. At that time we poured millions of dollars into curriculum development and teacher training for more effective instruction in mathematics, sciences, and foreign languages.

Special interest groups. Among our most effective checks and balances are special interest groups, which seem to spring up like mushrooms after rain. Some of these groups have identity and permanence. One such group is the Council for Basic Education. This group continually pushes for academic rigor and stronger emphasis on "basic" subjects, such as English, mathematics, science, history, and foreign languages. Members of this group rail against "frills" that take time away from basics and that, they believe, could be better taught in the home or community.

Other interest groups grow as concern mounts over what does, or does not, go on in schools. Such groups pull from both sides of the religious question, some bemoaning the satanic godlessness of our schools and others howling when teachers even mention Christmas or Hanukkah. Some groups, such as the Daughters of the American Revolution, are ever vigilant to see that patriotism remains a major thrust of American education. Groups interested in special education, minority group education, bilingual education, and affirmative action make their influence felt strongly in curricular and personnel matters.

The usual pattern is for schools to bend to the concerted push of an interest group, then to move partly back in the other direction as countergroups begin to react.

The reality is this: The educational enterprise is not set in stone. It consists of a great many components. Each component is continually subject to pushes, pulls, twists, bites, hammerings, and caresses from any number of interest groups. Out of all that pushing and shoving comes American education, continually changing bit by bit, but at the same time remaining remarkably stable.

Textbook publishers. Through the years arguments have persisted about whether we should or should not have a national curriculum, one that would be the same in New Orleans as it would in Providence, Boise, or Seattle. Proponents of a national curriculum say our national interests, our mass communication, and our great mobility argue for such a standard curriculum. Opponents say that schools must educate the youth of the local communities and that local control and local curriculum are necessary to attend to local needs.

Irrespective of the arguments, we have in fact moved very close to a national curriculum. That movement has occurred in large part because of textbooks. Texts are very costly to produce. The large companies that produce them cannot make separate books to satisfy hundreds of different communities without having to price the books exorbitantly high. The result is that a given company produces a standard sixth-grade reader, ninth-grade general science text, or eleventh-grade literature book. Wherever that book is adopted for use, the curriculum in that subject will be virtually the same because teachers rely so much on the textbook for organizing instruction.

It is true that the texts produced by various companies vary somewhat one from the other. These differences, however, are mainly superficial. They are most notable in the illustrations and textual wording. The actual contents of various companies' books are quite similar. The companies try to find out what the common expectations are for each subject across the country. Then they have the books written so as to include the topics, information, and activities that will appeal to the largest possible market.

This economic reality has done much to give American education a sameness. The books are made to have the widest possible appeal. This gives them great similarity, regardless of publisher. The books, because teachers use them to organize instruction, give us a fairly standard national curriculum.

Special national interests. Because American society is dynamic, there are always new problems to solve.

Early in this century, we had the special problem of great numbers of immigrants. These groups of people came from all over the world. Their languages, customs, and values differed greatly. Our national interests depended on the integration of these groups into the mainstream of American life to make them productive, functioning members of the national society.

The responsibility for accomplishing this task fell to education. It was our educational system, along with an economy that provided jobs in abundance, that heated the melting pot. Common language drew people together. Mass communication, always our forte, now touched everyone. In this way, diverse groups of people, from dozens of different countries, came to think and act in ways that brought national unity.

But many of these immigrants had never lived in a democracy. They had no tradition of making political decisions or voting. They lacked the traditions of equality and freedom coupled with responsibility. So it was that the schools took on the task of democratizing society. The great psychologist-philosopher-educator John Dewey laid out the guidelines for the role education was to play. These guidelines were specified in his many books, especially *Democracy and Education* (1916), and were exemplified in the public school he directed for many years at the University of Chicago.

In 1941 we made an abrupt entry into World War II. Immediately the schools responded by fostering in the young an immense patriotism, by coordinating drives for scrap materials, by serving as central relief stations (which fortunately were never needed), and by coordinating community mobilization efforts to cope with emergencies that might arise. That national crisis ended in 1945.

Then in 1957 there occurred an event that was to shake American education as no other had done. The Soviets launched the tiny orbiting sphere they called Sputnik. You would have thought they had accosted motherhood, spit out apple pie, and traded their Chevys for ox carts. Our national reaction bordered on the fanatic. Our arch rivals, the Russians, had beaten us into space. Somebody, by gosh, was to blame. Who? Well, it must be the schools.

Now here was a new twist. Schools had been called on many times to resolve national concerns. But they had never been named culprits when problems arose.

They responded anyway. Stung by widespread criticism, they struggled to do what was demanded of them. Just what those demands were was not clear at first. Loud voices soon rose above the din. Rudolf Flesch (1955) said the main problem was that Johnny couldn't read. Admiral Hyman Rickover (1959) said it was that the sciences were so poorly taught in school. Max Rafferty (1963) said it was that we had forgotten the basics and were going soft on communism. The Council for Basic Education (Smith, 1954) said we were wasting our students on frills. The group of academicians who convened in 1959 at Woods Hole, Massachusetts, said we were failing to teach the structure of knowledge within each subject (Bruner, 1960). Given a grasp of structure, even the very young could learn mathematics, science, and language quickly and easily.

All in all, the critics were saying that the Russians beat us because our schools had not turned out scientists and mathematicians with enough on the ball. The schools would have to remedy that lamentable condition and be quick about it.

Immediately the federal government poured millions of dollars of special funds into upgrading science and mathematics programs at all levels. Foreign language received a great push, too, although in retrospect it strains the imagination to see how language was related to national security or prestige. We seemed to be feeling guilty about everything and especially guilty that so few of us could speak the language of countries in the world that didn't speak English.

The federal monies in science, mathematics and language went for curriculum development, instructional materials, and teacher retraining. National Defense Education Act (NDEA) institutes in mathematics, science, and foreign language sprang up all over the country. Tens of thousands of teachers attended them to learn about, and how to teach, the "new" mathematics, science, and language. Much money was also spent in developing new approaches to teaching reading and to teaching English as a second language.

All these efforts must have been thunderously effective, for during a single decade we came from second best (we may have tried harder) to overwhelming superiority in space. We put our famous men on the moon and made the first break, albeit a fleeting one, from the eternal confines of Mother Earth. The technology we developed (based precisely on science and mathematics) was ultra-sophisticated to the point of incredibility.

Yet here is an odd thing. Our great achievements were made without benefit of the new science and new mathematics. The scientists and technicians who did the work had already grown up in the "old" curriculum.

Memories fade fast. The new English, based on transformational grammar, never really caught on. It didn't help students read, speak, or write any better than before. The great foreign language push died out quickly. Students, despite our best efforts, didn't learn to speak foreign languages. They really had little incentive to do so, after all. However, the techniques popularized in the 1960's are still used. The new mathematics, which stirred so much controversy and concern, is no longer recognizable. Its stress on meaning at the expense of computational skills effectively reduced, rather than increased, mathematics achievement. After a trial period of 15 years, it has been remade once again in an attempt to balance comprehension, application, and skills. Only the sciences seem to have proved themselves in their newer guises. The stress that was put on direct observation, recording, hypothesizing, experimenting, and trying to make useful interpretations has persisted. But student interest in science has waned. There are relatively few jobs now available for scientists. Still the science curricula are producing students who are better versed than ever before in the meaning and use of science.

What are the new national interests that schools are supposed to resolve? We are at work on some of them even now—effective desegregation; promulgation of cultural plurality within the greater unified society; equality among races, among ethnic groups, and between the sexes; and individual dignity. Although these thrusts have not sprung from national wounds in the side, they have come from a growing sense of conscience and concern for all members of society. They are pushes in whose resolution the schools are expected to play dominant parts.

And what does the future hold? Who knows. Perhaps the schools will be called on to foster respect, genuine concern for others, and living by the golden rule. Perhaps they will be expected to lead in developing a national conscience for true conservation of resources. One thing you can be sure of: Although public confidence in education may be at a low ebb, when a national concern arises, one that has high priority, the schools will be involved in significant ways.

Community pressures. Communities have ways of bringing great pressure to bear on the schools. Suppose a school system is doing everything with complete legality and the best of intent; even so, the vocally influential members of a community can decide they do not like what is being emphasized in American history, or the way reading is being taught, or the personality of the superintendent, or the record of the football team, or the fact that one of the principals doesn't attend church.

What can they do? You would be surprised. They can harrass individuals, they can complain to the school board, they can write letters to the editor, they can speak out at parent-teacher meetings. Some of these actions are ethical; others are not. But they are all perfectly legal. Even when their outcries have no legal, professional, or ethical basis, these people can make life miserable for their targets, with the result that school personnel change their approach, resign their jobs, or have to experience the trauma of seeing matters through to the end.

The observations made in these pages tend to show pressure groups in a bad light. Let's set the matter straight. Local school boards have legal control over their schools. Their purpose is to see to it that schools have high-quality programs, are run efficiently, and reflect the interests of the community. Boards cannot act contrary to state laws, which provide safeguards for teachers and administrators and which establish curriculum requirements. But they are, since elected by the community, responsive to community desires. They are supposed to be that way.

At their ethical best, communities exert influence through the school board and through reasoned, respectful conferences with teachers and administrators. Parents do have a legal and ethical say in the education of their children.

But pressures are not always brought to bear in ethical ways. The reality is that more often than not, pressures are associated with anger, hostility, and bad manners. Instead of being positively constructive, they put educators on the defensive and make it hard for them to perform their duties.

Parental pressures. Pressures that come from individual parents seldom reflect community concerns. Usually they stem from dissatisfactions about how the particular youngster is being taught or treated. Parents usually will not become hostile or irate unless they think their child is being mistreated. On the contrary, they are overwhelmingly supportive of teachers and schools. This support is usually benign, but it is often active. Some parents want to be involved in their children's education. They help in the classroom, with school projects, on outings, and so forth.

In most ways, parents are a teacher's best ally. They want their children to do well in school, and they will do their part to help. Wise teachers communicate with parents regularly. They relate positive things, not waiting until they have trouble with the students.

Sometimes parents will have real concerns about their child's education, concerns that are legitimate. Teachers can reassure parents by talking with them in professional, friendly terms. They do not put parents on the defensive. They concentrate on positive traits of the student, and where concerns lie, they talk in terms of constructive approaches to rectifying the problem. This approach puts parents' minds at ease and builds confidence in teacher and school.

Accountability. You are aware that in recent years public confidence in education has waned. People generally think that education costs too much and that it is not effective for numbers of students. There is a growing feeling that the curricula don't sufficiently stress basic subjects and basic values, such as honesty, respect, and hard work. There is also a growing feeling that teachers do not perform their tasks well enough. These feelings are kindled by instances of high school graduates who cannot read, spell, write coherent sentences, or balance their checkbooks. They are fueled by student apathy, delinquency, lack of achievement, and dropping out of school.

Because of these concerns about curriculum and teaching, a new pressure on teachers and schools has emerged. This pressure is called "accountability." It simply means that schools and teachers are to be held accountable for their primary function, which is to produce learning.

Complying with community insistence on accountability, schools have begun establishing lists of minimum knowledge, skills, and attitudes they will develop in students. They state these minimums in behavioral (observable) terms so they can be verified by outside appraisers. They then design instruction to focus on the stated knowledge, skills, and attitudes.

This efficiency seems a promising step to most citizens. Teachers, however, view the idea with fear and trepidation. Why? Their reasons are valid.

First, their experience has been that you can beat your brains out teaching, but you will still occasionally have students who won't learn. Anyone who has taught knows they are right. There are some horses we simply can't coax into drinking —not from wells, faucets, buckets, lakes, streams, or crystal goblets.

Second, teachers observe (again, rightly so) that instruction will degenerate into a total focus on the few skills, attitudes, and facts that are specified. Range, diversity, and depth of instruction will be sacrificed. Mediocrity for all will become the hallmark of accountability in teaching.

Whatever the arguments pro and con, the present reality is this: The public is becoming disenchanted with mass education, feeling it is too expensive and inefficient. They are demanding that schools become accountable, that they put it on the line where their expertise is supposed to lie— in promoting steady, observable, acceptable levels of learning in each and every student.

• • •

This concludes our brief examination of some of the checks and balances that keep American education on an even keel. Now we move on to another class of educational realities. These are the problems teachers regularly encounter, within the schools themselves, that render their jobs unduly difficult to perform.

Teaching's devils and ogres

By this time you surely have concluded that education comes with some fine print at the bottom of the contract. Some of the finest print of all—it's virtually microscopic—explains the devils and ogres that beleaguer teachers in their daily work with learners. These devils and ogres are class size, work load, discipline, trivia, meetings, fads, change, and survival. Here is what the fine print says.

Class size. If you think of teaching as working mostly one to one with students, think again. The time you can spend individually, if divided equally among your students, is miniscule. You won't have five or six students at your knee. You will have thirty to forty or more in the class at once. In the elementary school you will have them all day long. In the secondary school you will have at least five classes of different students. Expect the total to reach 150 to 200 students each day.

In trying to give personal attention to each student, teachers more and more are turning to individualized programs of instruction. These programs are no panacea. They work the heck out of you. But that is another story.

This is reality: Your class will be far too large to allow you to teach the way people say you should teach. You will find ways to give individual attention. But the frustration of too many students to deal with will always be present.

Work load. It makes teachers sick to hear other people talk about teachers' soft jobs. "Why, those teachers—they get off at 3 o'clock, never get their hands dirty, have vacations right and left, and don't have to work at all during the summer."

If you have fallen for that line, wake up before it is too late. Conscientious teachers, those who truly give their best to teaching, have a day-and-night job. You may get off at 3 o'clock (if you don't have to attend one of those ubiquitous meetings or an inservice class). But you take your work, your cares, and your pressures with you. They never leave. They stick in the back of your mind during holidays. Only in summer do you find respite, and by that time you need it desperately.

Teaching may look soft. But you can't leave it on the office desk when you close the door at 5 o'clock. You have faced all those kids all day; they go home with you at night, too.

Discipline. We have developed and perpetuated an interesting myth about discipline. We talk about student misbehavior as if it were really the teacher's fault. Maybe the teacher didn't actually initiate the bad behavior, but it is only a simple matter of doing or saying the right thing, and students will snap to like angels.

Why educators persist on that track is understandable. They do want to feel they can control and direct behavior and bring out the very best in every kid. Their intent is laudable. They are partially correct, too. There is much they can say and do that will help students behave. But they are surely deceiving themselves if they believe discipline problems can be solved with wink, frown, understanding, or iron hand.

Some students are truly angelic, most of the time. They are so kind, so concerned, so eager to do well and please. Other students are truly devilish, most of the time. They bully, irritate, harrass. They seem compelled to make life miserable, especially for their teacher. Still other students are sweet part of the time and sour part of the time.

You can say what you like, hear what you like, and believe what you like. But the facts are these: For most teachers, discipline is their biggest headache. Nothing else comes close. Inability to control students is the biggest cause of teacher failure. Nothing else comes close. Good control techniques—positive, productive, and nonpunitive— are the most difficult skills for teachers to learn. Nothing else comes close. In short, discipline is the teacher's toughest problem, and it makes or breaks most teachers.

Here is reality: Students misbehave, sometimes playfully, sometimes maliciously. When that misbehavior significantly interferes with class learning, it must be stopped. But if learning is also to continue for the misbehaving student, positive and productive corrections must be made.

Fortunately, the discipline matter is not hopeless. Chapter 15 reviews the disciplinary techniques presently considered most effective. There are many of these techniques. No single one will work for all students, but at least one of them will be effective for almost every individual. That's why discipline should not be considered a single factor. It is a composite of many factors. Good teachers have learned that you must use a variety of control techniques. They have also learned that good discipline is a nonending series of small acts the teacher carries out every day through the entire year.

Trivia. You would be astounded at how much of teachers' time must be spent on nonteaching tasks. Many of these tasks are trivial. They contribute nothing to teaching and learning. Yet somebody must do them, and teachers are handiest.

What are some of these trivia? The list is very long. In it you will find such things as taking lunch count, collecting meal tickets, collecting money, taking roll, making attendance reports, keeping track of absences, reading bulletins, and sitting through irrelevant meetings. This is not to say that these things are not important. They are. But they are nonteaching tasks that cut into instructional and planning time. Teachers are handy, so they perform them. Each by itself is little enough. But when you put them all together, they take up sizable amounts of time, This frustrates teachers, because time is the most precious commodity they have.

Meetings. How fortunate we are to live in a democratic society, where we have a say about our professional and personal lives. Make no mistake about that. Keep it foremost in your mind whenever you swear at having to attend another meeting.

But democracy does exact its toll. Group input into administrative decisions requires group meetings where give and take can occur. For members of the group—teachers in a school, for example— to be adequately informed about matters important to them, they must meet, hear, and discuss.

The result is that meetings of teachers must occur regularly. But, ask teachers, must they occur so frequently, and must they drag on so interminably?

Increasingly, meetings cut bigger and bigger chunks out of teachers' precious time. Every new program, every curricular change, every new law must be gone through and hashed over. In the past, a faculty meeting held every week or two was the extent of meetings, except when a rare special issue came up. Now, it is not uncommon for teachers to attend meetings two or three times each week, for the entire year. These meetings are tacked on to the end of an exhausting day of teaching. It is no wonder teachers come to resent them so fervently.

Meetings are important. But they can be streamlined. They can be made much more efficient. They can get to the point. They can be scheduled only when necessary.

Nevertheless, if you go into teaching, you can

expect to spend a great deal of time sitting tiredly on hard chairs, daydreaming, wishing you were somewhere else. That's what too many teachers' meetings are like.

Fads. We live in a time of fads. Somebody says open education will solve discipline problems. So we jump on the bandwagon. Then somebody says diagnostic-prescriptive teaching will produce achievement gains. So we jump on that bandwagon.

That "we" is collective. Individual teachers aren't so eager to jump. They have to redo too many things in their teaching organization and routine. But the pressures come, nonetheless. Just as one fad makes its way into teaching, another pops up that cancels it. Seldom is there valid evidence that one is any better, overall, than another. It goes to our credit that we so willingly seek out newer and potentially better ways of teaching. But we are too influenced by new ideas that have not been validated.

Here is an interesting reality: If you teach for 30 or 40 years, you will see the pendulum swing back and forth several times. Every 10 years or so you will suddenly recognize that the newest fad is one you saw before, but in a new disguise.

Change. Whether from fads, national interests, or new knowledge, one thing is certain: Education changes. This means the curricula change, instructional materials change, and methods of teaching change. Teachers are thus caught up in constant change. It becomes part of their professional way of life.

In the 1940's typical elementary schools showed the following picture: totally self-contained classrooms; stationary desks (not chair desks) fixed to the floor in straight rows; one teacher in total charge (no volunteers, aides, or teams teaching); relatively few instructional materials outside of textbooks, workbooks, map, and globe; wooden floor; curriculum that stressed basics, rote learning, reading, memorization, and test taking; teaching method that consisted of assignments, explanations, and activities done by the total group at the same time.

Today the typical elementary school picture is quite different. We see multiple classroom designs —self-contained, open space, flexible partitions; furniture that is easily movable—arranged in circles, clusters, semicircles, etc.; multiple staffing—single teachers, teams of teachers, special teachers (reading, special education, music), teacher aides, parent volunteers, and cross-age tutors all working with students; a plethora of instructional materials—media equipment such as projectors (slide, motion picture, overhead, opaque), record players, tape players, models, collections, and microscopes; floor coverings of vinyl or carpet; a curriculum that stresses a wide range of cognitive (knowledge), psychomotor (movement), affective (feeling, attitude), and aesthetic (beauty, art, music) topics, emphasizing individual work, small-group work, demonstration, discussion, discovery, and creativity; and a teaching method that minimizes lecture and testing and emphasizes diagnosis of needs, prescribed activities related directly to those identified needs, facilitation of student-directed learning, motivation, management of learning (directing and keeping records), and interpersonal relations with students.

The secondary schools have changed almost as much. In the 1940's they resembled two-story elementary schools, except with larger students who changed classrooms every hour. Today they resemble university campuses, replete with special classrooms, laboratories, shops, fine libraries (often called media centers), and what have you. Students often assume great self-direction in planning their programs of study and in carrying them out.

Impressive changes aren't they? Keep in mind that teachers who began their careers in the 1940's are still in their prime. Who knows what further changes they will see before retirement?

If you will be entering the profession in the 1980's, you will, during your career, be partner to unimagined changes in education. We may not be able now to predict what most of those changes will be. But this much is certain: Change there will be. The pace is accelerating.

Survival. Survival is not a devil. It is a necessity, and that is why it is mentioned here. Taking note of the devils and ogres that teachers must confront, perhaps you can see why mere survival on the job becomes such a matter of importance.

It is unfortunate, but beleaguered teachers naturally seek paths of least resistance. You can't blame them for that. Why walk through the viper pit when you can take the smooth path around it?

The trouble is that the easy paths, those that

circumvent devils and ogres, shortchange students. It's not the students' fault that teachers have impossible class sizes, heavy work loads, continual change, and masses of trivia with which to contend.

Teachers are mostly magnificent people. They care about students, they work hard, they have great technical competence, they relate beautifully with students, they are always seeking better ways of teaching. But here, too, is a reality: A few teachers have stopped trying. Tired of fighting the battles, they have given in. They have become lackadaisical, or worse, they have become bitter; they grumble, carp, blame everyone else, and are negative in every way. When you teach, resist to your utmost the influence of this tiny minority. Their negativism is contagious. It spoils a lot of good apples in the barrel.

Teacher power

Through most of the history of American education, teachers and their employers enjoyed a relationship high in respect and mutual admiration. Teachers were quite respected in their communities, and so were administrators. They were pillars, so to speak. But teachers had little legal protection in their work. They could be dismissed for virtually any reason.

That vulnerability led to a push for teacher tenure, which became widespread only a few decades ago. Tenure means that teachers can be dismissed only for "cause." That cause is generally one of three things: incompetence, insubordination, or moral turpitude. Teachers have the right to contest, in courts of law, dismissal proceedings based on any of these counts. The employing (and dismissing) agency must prove incompetence (inability to perform the job at minimal acceptable standard), insubordination (willful refusal to abide by school regulations or directions from administrators), or moral turpitude (commission of illegal acts).

Tenure was a great stride forward for teachers. It protected them against petty aggravations of school board members and administrators, freed them to teach in accord with their professional convictions, and allowed them to enjoy the civil rights available to other citizens. Tenure has been criticized as protecting incompetent "deadwood" within the teaching ranks; incompetence is very

difficult to prove in a court of law. Yet, all in all, tenure has been valuable not only for individual teachers, but for education as a whole.

Since the enactment of tenure laws, teachers have had other group concerns against which to struggle. Although legally entitled to the same constitutional guarantees as everyone else, teachers have faced constant pressure and censure with regard to certain activities. Do you recall the 1920's contractual restrictions on behavior, mentioned earlier in this chapter? Those restrictions may seem laughable now. Yet teachers are still expected to be a group apart, functioning on a higher plane.

For example, Joe Smith, the local haberdasher, can get drunk all he wants so long as he doesn't disturb the peace. It makes no difference who sees him. He can drink on the job if he wishes. People may think it humorous. Let Sally Jones, the local fifth-grade teacher, try that. The wrath descending on her head will be overwhelming.

Or what about all the political rhetoric that goes on in barber shop, beauty parlor, supermarket, or wherever people gather. That's all right for most everyone. But not for teachers. Especially not in their classrooms.

Saddled unjustly with so many restrictions on their behavior, teachers have pushed for public affirmation of their civil rights. The result has been a relaxation (but not a disappearance) of pressures brought on teachers to lead idealized lives.

The efforts in behalf of teachers have not come from concerned groups of citizens, nor from compassionate school boards. They have come from the political (and even economic) clout of groups of teachers, principally through large organizations such as the National Education Association, the various state education associations, and local district or county education associations.

As times have grown more difficult for education and teachers, school personnel have started becoming more militant. Organizations that have espoused this principle have grown accordingly in size and influence. The American Federation of Teachers is one such organization.

As mentioned, the public is becoming ever more reticent to finance building construction and increased teacher salaries. Salaries, for example, grew rapidly in the 1960's and early 1970's, but recently they have lagged well behind the increase in inflation. Faced with irreconcilable decreases in purchasing power, teachers in some areas have gone on strike, withholding their services until acceptable salaries are negotiated. In some cases the strikes were successful; in others they were not. Unlike the standoff in business between labor and management, the public has the whip hand over education. A great percentage of our citizenry doesn't really care whether school remains in session or not. They will go along with things as they are, but if asked for more taxes, they will say no and that's that.

Regardless of your feelings in the matter, here are the realities: Teachers are becoming ever more militant. They have already pushed through collective bargaining in many areas. They have successfully gone on strike. They are joining expensive organizations in increasing numbers, not only for insurance and purchasing benefits, but also for political power to protect themselves economically. Teachers were once apolitical, professionally; this is no longer the case. They officially endorse candidates favorable to education and support them with organization funds. They employ powerful lobbyists. If you want to stay out of politics, don't go into teaching.

A FINAL WORD

The purpose of this chapter has been to show the other side of the coin so beautifully struck by educational philosophers and theoreticians. Their ideas are pure, clean, and streamlined. They assume the best of efforts and noblest of motives of all individuals involved in their educational schemes.

Pure, clean, best, and noblest describe some parts of American educational practice. But these terms don't describe all of it. Events and influences come into play that, when incorporated into the ideal schemes, produce realities that deserve attention.

Our attention to some of these realities may have appeared negative. If they seemed that way to you, let us end on this note: American education is one of the greatest phenomena in human history. It has welded diverse groups into national unity. It has helped resolve national crises. It has fostered democracy as nothing else could. It has helped free us individually to live lives of meaning, to maximize our talents, to explore our interests.

Our ever-changing curricula, practical and meaningful, have helped make American education great. So have our unparalleled physical facilities and instructional materials. But more than anything else, it has been the teacher who has made the difference. We have been singularly blessed with an abundance of caring, competent teachers, the kind that make a true difference in students' lives.

And finally, education still has the support of the American public. True, there has been some disenchantment and not without reason. There has been a tightening of purse strings. That is understandable. But in the final analysis, the basic American belief in education is still there. That belief has been the wellspring from which all else in education has flowed.

SUGGESTED ACTIVITIES FOR FURTHER UNDERSTANDING

1. Interview your next-door neighbors. Find out what they think of schools—how good they are, how valuable they are to society, whether they are worth what they cost, what they are doing well, what they are doing poorly, and what should be changed about them.
2. In class discussions, recall the strengths and weaknesses of your own high school education. What would you change about it, if you could?
3. Interview selected teachers. Find out what their biggest headaches are in teaching and what they think could be done to remedy them.
4. Discuss the pros and cons of allowing community pressure groups affect the schools' programs and ways of teaching.

REFERENCES

Bruner, J. *The process of education*. New York: Vintage Books, 1960.

Dewey, J. *Democracy and education*. New York: Macmillan Publishing Co., Inc., 1916.

Flesch, R. *Why Johnny can't read and what you can do about it*. New York: Harper & Row, Publishers, 1955.

Rafferty, M. *Suffer, little children*. New York, Signet, 1963.

Rickover, H. *Education and freedom*. New York: E. P. Dutton & Co., Inc., 1959.

Smith, M. *The diminished mind*. Chicago, Henry Regnery Co., 1954.

THE CONTEMPORARY SETTING
MYTHS AND MANIFESTS

PART TWO

In this part we take a close look at the communities from which students come and then at the students themselves. We learn what communities and students are like, and we learn how to study both of them. These experiences, and the information that comes from them, enable us to teach much more effectively. We know better what to expect, what we can change, and what we cannot change.

We also examine schools and the people whose work makes them run. We see goals, facilities, and curricula of elementary, junior, and high schools. We discover that schools require more than principal, secretary, teachers, and custodians to operate. Over fifty different types of positions are filled by the personnel who work in the schools.

To conclude, we review the American system of laws and courts as a lead into the legal codes that affect teachers, administrators, and students.

The titles of the chapters are as follows:

4 **Communities**
   a look, a touch, a taste

5 **Learners**
   the principal clients

6 **Skills for studying learners**

7 **Schools and school personnel**
   the menagerie

8 **The law and schooling**
   toes and hot waters

COMMUNITIES
A LOOK, A TOUCH, A TASTE **4**

Paul began his program of teacher education eagerly, and pow! He was hit straight off with a massive assignment—a community study project. His first reactions were bewilderment and frustration. "How do I begin something this big? I have no idea where to start. Anyway, what does this have to do with student teaching? I came here to teach, not play sociologist."

But the assignment didn't go away, so Paul gritted his teeth and plunged in. Following the professor's suggestions, he attended PTA and school board meetings, visited the chamber of commerce and city hall, talked to local shopkeepers and the chief of police. He toured the area around his school, checked records for parents' occupations, asked his fifth graders what kinds of things they

liked to do after school. At every opportunity, he tried to find out more about the environment within which his students lived.

A surprising thing happened as Paul worked on the study. He began to see student identities that went well beyond what showed in the 6 hours spent each day in the classroom. He became more tolerant of their early-morning energy when he realized they had ridden the school bus for an hour. He understood why they didn't bring library books when he asked; the nearest library was 12 miles away. He discovered interesting attitudes toward school held by both students and parents— ideas, opinions, and misconceptions he never imagined.

All in all, Paul began to see his students as people, with problems, special circumstances, and diverse backgrounds. With this new vision, his teaching began to improve. He learned what things would motivate his students, what underlying problems contributed to misbehavior, and thus how to reduce it. His communication with parents improved, and so did his communication with students. Using his new knowledge, he made an effort to teach students in their terms, explore their interests, and delve into areas that were new and exciting to them.

What had started out to be a tedious, boring assignment turned into a fascinating challenge for Paul. It became a real impetus to his professional development as a teacher. "I never stopped to think what happened to these kids the rest of the day. What a difference it is to teach them as total persons, not as 6-hour charges."

Gone are the days (if there ever were such) when being a teacher meant cloistering oneself safely behind ivy-covered walls, rationing out tired bits of stale information to columns of saddle-sore students. Gone are the days (if there ever were such) when going to school meant leaving the "real world" behind. Today teachers know that what goes on in the community is important to the school and to its number-one clients, the students. The reverse is also true: What goes on in school is important to the community.

Teachers, in a democratic society, have a twofold responsibility in the synergic relationships between school and community. On the one hand, teachers need to know what these relationships are and how they affect students. On the other hand, teachers have a responsibility to try to enhance community life for their students.

This chapter focuses on ways you, as a teacher or prospective teacher, can get to know your school's community. It suggests things you can look for; how you can obtain useful information; and how you can put it all together in a logical and meaningful way.

SOME MEANINGS

The term *"community"* is used here as roughly equivalent to *neighborhood*. There is a slight difference in meaning between the two terms—although not even sociologists always make the difference clear. *Neighborhood* usually refers to a *place* where people live in proximity to one another. This place can have ascribed character-istics: an *attractive* neighborhood, and *undesirable* neighborhood, or a *convenient* neighborhood. *Community* can have almost the same meaning in common usage. However, *community,* more accurately, has to do with an identifiable group of people who hold certain aims, aspirations, or beliefs in common. You can talk about a community of people in a broad sense, as a worldwide community of. scholars, or you might have a narrower focus, as the one used in this chapter, and speak of a community of people living in an identifiable neighborhood: an affluent community, an active community, a disadvantaged community.

In this sense you can say that a school is a community in itself—a community of students, faculty, and staff. The nature and function of this school community is important to you as a teacher. A school, as an institution, permits a wide variety of social relationships, which affect its students. For the most part, however, when the term "community" is used in this chapter, it refers to the surrounding community of people who live and work within a given school's service area. Sometimes this is called a "feeder community." What needs to be emphasized is that teachers should not view schools as isolated social institutions. They are part of a larger fabric. To understand schools and students you need to understand parents, shopkeepers, and politicians.

A LOOK (WHAT TO LOOK FOR)
Purposes

You have already seen two important reasons why you should take a careful look at your school community: (1) your responsibility to understand something about synergic relationships within the community that impinge on the learner and (2) your responsibility to do what you can to enhance community life for your students. Under this umbrella of professional responsibility, there are four useful purposes for such an undertaking. A careful look at your school community will help you to (1) identify some of its important instructional resources that can be useful in teaching; (2) recognize environing conditions that may affect your students' intellectual and social development; (3) gain insight into outside pressures that affect school policies and curriculum; and (4) identify some of the intellectual, social, cultural, and physical shortcomings that exist within your school and its feeder community.

Although you should look at your school in the context of its larger community, you will also want to examine it as a separate institution. A careful look at your school and your classroom communities will help you to (1) note patterns of social relationships that directly affect your students; (2) make more relevant decisions about curriculum and teaching; (3) get a clearer picture of the setting within which you must work; and (4) explain your school's programs and needs to the larger community.

Perspectives

The way you look at your school and its feeder community will greatly affect what you see. You will want to find out as much as you can. You'll also want to be as objective as you can about what you find. If your perspective is limited, you won't want to make too many bold generalizations. Of course, you need to generalize, but the challenge is to make well-founded generalizations. They will be well founded if they are based on objective data and if you are able to recognize the limits of your data-gathering techniques and the reliability of your data. A good way to study a community is to look at it from different perspectives.

The wide-angle perspective. The wide-angle perspective will enable you to take in everything—to get the big picture. It's an important perspective for a community study. It lets you see the community as a whole and see just where your school fits into the scene.

It's very easy for teachers to develop narrow views of their schools in relationship to the larger community. Teachers work hard, day after day, at the same site, with the same kids. They are immersed in immediate problems that need immediate solutions. Frequently, teachers lack either time or energy to give thought to the larger community. Because of their involvement in these day-to-day problems, school life appears bigger than it is. The school is seen in isolation from its feeder community. The goals, objectives, and aspirations that teachers hold for their students are seen as paramount.

The wide-angle perspective allows teachers to move beyond their limited view. It takes into account the goals, objectives, and aspirations of parents and other community members for schoolchildren. Teachers aren't the only ones who have ideas about what should go on in schools. Parents

believe their views should be considered because, after all, "who's kids are they?" Local residents and business people believe their voices need to be heard because, after all, "who pays the taxes that keep the schools running?"

The wide-angle perspective encompasses the physical, political, economic, and social relationships that connect the school to its feeder community and its feeder community to the community at large. This perspective reveals a social ecology where total environmental contexts are considered. Within this ecology, a given school is seen as a social institution, functioning within a larger social framework.

But these social institutions, these schools, are not independent. To the contrary, they are economically dependent. They depend on tax dollars. They do not produce a product that gives an immediate return on investments. Any economic returns must be viewed from a long-range point of view. One of Horace Mann's contributions to American education was that he convinced nineteenth century businessmen that the long-range view was the most profitable. He believed that personal wealth was a trust and that education was a natural right. This gave him a rational basis for asking businessmen to support public education.

However, schools are not entirely passive in the economic structure of the community. Economic activity is stimulated by education, both directly and indirectly. Schools make an economic impact on a community by their immediate demands for goods and services. Schooling is a big business—perhaps our largest business enterprise. Americans spend over $100 billion each year on education. Just think of what would happen to our economy if all schools suddenly shut down.

Schools also contribute to the economy indirectly, through their trained graduates. Schools prepare students to participate in the economy. Some people criticize the quality of this preparation. But just imagine what young people would be without schools to prepare them to function economically. In reality, then, a mutually supportive relationship exists between schools and the economy.

The wide-angle perspective shows that schools are politically, as well as economically, dependent. Even here, there is a degree of interdependence. But for the most part, politics have a greater immediate effect on schools than do schools on politics. This relationship is important for teachers to recognize if they want to effect change. When politicians seek endorsements, they approach such groups as labor unions, chambers of commerce, realtors, veterans' organizations, and the American Medical Association. Seldom do they expend much energy in seeking the support of teachers. In the 1976 presidential election the National Education Association came out in support of President Carter. The NEA claims their support was crucial, but the extent to which the NEA spoke for its membership is not clear. On the whole, educators wield very little direct, immediate political power—especially in comparison to other groups.

The wide-angle perspective takes into account the vast array of social relationships that tie the schools to the larger community. Here is a list of the kinds of social relationships of interest to you as a teacher:

1. Chain-of-command relationships. Who is responsible to whom within your school district; within your school; within the various political and public service agencies that impinge on your school and community.
2. Social class relationships. Relationships that are reflected in local residential patterns; types and places of employment; shopping practices; recreational activities; school populations; and so forth.
3. Family patterns. Characteristics that include family size; types of families (single-parent families; nuclear families; extended families); roles of family members; ages of family members; economic status; educational backgrounds; child-rearing practices.
4. School-community relationships. Interactions involving parent-teacher associations; community advisory groups; paraprofessionals; volunteers; communications networks that link school and community; procedures for reporting to parents.

This wide-angle perspective does have some shortcomings. The things you are close to will look unnaturally large, and those things in the background will look small and far away. It's best to stand back and view your school and community as an outsider might. This frame of mind will help you become more objective and keep things in proper perspective.

The wide-angle perspective is useful. But you need more. If all you have is a wide-angle view, your knowledge of school and community will be too general. It will not help you in your classroom. Other perspectives are also needed.

The telephoto perspective. The telephoto perspective is another way to look at your school and community. This perspective allows you to stand off at a distance and focus on one small area at a time. Here, again, you become the objective viewer from without. A telephoto lens brings things at a distance up close, and it blurs objects in the foreground and background. After you get the big picture, you need to zoom in on specific areas of interest and concern.

The telephoto perspective will help you focus on such things as the following:

1. The organizational structure of your school. Its size, composition, and major activities; its physical characteristics; policies, and administrative structure.
2. Unique characteristics of your school's curriculum. Early childhood education; individually guided education; bilingual education, special education, etc.
3. Support components. Staff development; parent participation; parent education; health and safety; library and instructional media; food services; counseling services, etc.
4. Means and routes of school transportation.
5. Types and nature of community resources.
6. Functions of community agencies. Police, fire department, hospital, etc.
7. Impact of specific legislation, ordinances, and school board policies on the school and community.
8. Significance of certain historical events for the school and community.

Taken by itself, the telephoto perspective has some limitations. If you aren't careful, you can end up with disjointed bits of information. It is easy to get caught up in the intricacies of an isolated event, agency, or problem, forgetting the big picture and the main purpose for the study. That's why it's important to take different views.

• • •

In both the wide-angle and the telephoto perspectives you, as the observer, try to get an outsider's view of your school and community. For the most part your information will come from secondary sources and from general observations. As you move in from the general to the more specific, you will gradually shift from assuming the role of a nonparticipant observer to assuming that of a participant observer. This is especially true as you begin looking at your school and community with a close-up perspective.

The close-up perspective. The close-up perspective is the one to use when you want to take a close and careful look at something small or a small part of something big. In the case of a school-community study, it's the view you might take when you want to look at social relationships, habits, attitudes, values, life-styles, and needs of children in specific classrooms. It might also be the view you would take if you wanted to study specific family units or other small social groups. This perspective requires interaction with the individuals or groups to be studied. It involves some firsthand knowledge and experiences.

The close-up perspective will help you see how your students react to their social and physical surroundings. Being a participant observer will enable you to learn something about the culture of your classroom, school, and community. This is the "hidden curriculum." It takes you beyond the facts and into the realm of emotions, values, and attitudes of students, teachers, and others involved.

One shortcoming of this type of study is that the participant observer may become emotionally involved with the people being observed to the point that it will be difficult to remain objective. Two things frequently happen to student teachers as they conduct a school-community study. Some become so overwhelmed with discipline problems in their classrooms that they can hardly see anything else. One student teacher reported, "I can't find out anything about my students' life-styles, attitudes, and values, because there's so much upheaval and chaos in the classroom." Others, who have been able to establish warm relationships with their students and master teachers, make such glowing reports about everything that you would think they were looking for public relations jobs instead of teaching positions.

However, with these shortcomings in mind and with an eye on your main purposes, you will be able to use this close-up perspective to great advantage. You can find out things about people that you can't discover any other way. The secret is to train yourself to be observant as you work with students, parents, and local residents. Pay attention to what people do, when they have free choice, and what they don't do. Look for patterns. Be analytical.

Particulars

Before you launch out on a community study it will be helpful for you to have some particulars in mind, some notions of what to look for. Three points of focus that have been helpful to others who have conducted community studies are (1) site and situation, (2) life-styles, and (3) attitudes and values.

Site and situation. The site is the actual location of the community and school you are studying. Where are the boundaries? What streets? Where is it on a map? Where is it with reference to other geographic points? Is the community on the south side of a large bay? On the east side of a prominent hill? Next to a dry river bed? What's the terrain like? What's the weather like? Where is it with reference to institutions, businesses, municipalities, neighborhoods, transportation systems? Seven miles west of the nearest shopping center? On the east side of the railroad tracks that bisect the town? Is the school in a "bedroom community?" A business district? A rural setting? What does it look like?

In describing the situation of your school community you might pay special attention to the following:

1. Its constituents. Where do the students live? Where do the teachers live?
2. Transportation and communication systems that service the area. How and to what extent are these systems utilized by the constituents?
3. Supportive agencies, such as libraries, museums, schools, education centers, social organizations, and churches.
4. Protective agencies, such as fire department, police, hospitals, and clinics.
5. Business establishments. Where are they? What are they like? How do they affect the school and community?
6. Recreational facilities. What's available? Where are they? How and by whom are they used?

It will also be helpful to find out as much as you

can about the history of the area you are studying. This will help you answer such questions as the following:

1. How did the area and the community get started?
2. Why did people move and build here?
3. What has been the pattern of growth?
4. What still draws people to this area?
5. Why do people leave the area?
6. What are some of the unique problems or needs associated with this community?
7. What natural and human resources are present in the area?
8. How are these resources being utilized?

In studying your school community this way, you will actually be engaging in a piece of human geography. As such you will be interested in (1) physical features of the area, (2) ways in which people have organized space, (3) utilization of resources, and (4) ways in which these elements relate to each other.

As you examine the site and situation, be alert to what goes on below the surface. As an example, several student teachers who conducted community studies reported on the recreational facilities available in a certain area. All of them mentioned a nearby park. Some made it sound like a nice place for children to play after school and on weekends. They described its physical features and the variety of activities provided there for community members. One student, however, checked with the local police and talked with people who lived near by, only to discover that many parents considered the park unsafe for their children. Drugs were being bought and sold there. Older kids reportedly intimidated younger ones. Several muggings had been reported. The police had to increase their patrols in the park area. This same student reported that only a handful of people could be observed using the facilities. Few or no family picnics were being held in the afternoons or on weekends. So, as you can see, merely listing facilities and resources may not give a clear picture of an area.

Life-styles. In general there are three things that influence the ways in which people live their lives: (1) the physical environment, (2) the social environment, and (3) the psychological environment. Some of the influences of the physical environment have already been suggested. One important aspect of the physical environment is the weather. In northeastern Ohio the winters are long and cold. Children arrive at school bundled up in heavy coats, snowcaps, and four-buckle arctic boots. Classrooms have designated places to store this cold-weather gear. Homes and other buildings are equipped with storm windows, storm porches, and storm doors to keep the cold out. People in southern California don't even know what these things are.

The physical environment of a seacoast town, with a large natural harbor, makes a difference in the life-styles of the people who live there. The fishing and shipping industries associated with such a place, as well as the recreational potentials of this kind of area, help create life-styles that are much different from those in the farming communities of the Great Plains or the industrial communities of northeastern Ohio.

The social environment of a community is, likewise, an important determiner of life-styles. The social environment has to do with the ways people react to their physical surroundings: how and why they organize space for housing, transportation, commerce, and recreation and how and why they utilize natural resources. Many decisions related to the physical environment are political decisions. Once these broad political decisions are made and once the environment is arranged in accord with them, these structures become part of the physical environment. Transportation arteries become neighborhood boundaries. Housing developments take on separate identities. Commercial and industrial areas contribute to one kind of life-style for people who live in these areas, but quite another for the executives and junior executives who live farther out in the fashionable suburbs.

The social environment also has to do with the ways in which people relate to one another and how they group themselves. We may not like to admit it, but every city, town, neighborhood, and community has its social class structure. The status associated with each social class influences life-style. Freedom, equality, and every person's right to reach for the top are all part of the Great American Dream. That dream is more easily attained by some than by others. One's chances are often limited by one's station in life. For some the dream becomes a nightmare when they realize they are locked into a social structure.

Like the chicken and the egg (and which came first), life-styles have effect on social status. This is especially true in societies that allow for some degree of social mobility. A blue-collar worker who becomes a white-collar businessman and moves to a "better" neighborhood may find he has a new status. He is now associated with a different class of people. Of course the degree of his acceptance into the new social class will depend on how well he adopts the behavior patterns of the new class.

Two classic sociological studies having to do with social class structures in the United States were done by Davis, Gardner, and Gardner (1941) and Warner, Havighurst, and Loeb (1944). In both the Davis et al. analysis of life in the deep South and the Warner et al. "Yankee City" study, six social classes were identified. The upper upper class consists of people who are the "old aristocracy," the "Hill Streeters," or the "old families." These are the people who live in the best neighborhoods and are the well-established professional people, "big" businessmen, or independently wealthy. They come from the "old families." Many of them have inherited their wealth.

The lower upper-class people are the *nouveaux riches*. They live in large houses in the better neighborhoods. These people may have money (sometimes even more than people in the upper upper class) and prestige, but not quite the status of the "old families." They are the strivers who enjoy displaying their new wealth and position.

Those in the upper middle class are the "good people" who have "made it the hard way." They are the less wealthy professionals, the semiprofessionals, the junior executives, and those who are not "high-hatters," but who would like to be. They belong to the less exclusive country clubs. These are the people who are very active in community affairs. The upper classes often call on them to do the legwork for their charities.

People in the lower middle class are often referred to as "the working class." These are the people who are a mixture of white-collar and blue-collar workers, the "average citizens," neither rich nor poor. This is the social class of "Joe Six-Pack" and Archie Bunker. These are the people who keep the machines running. They are the backbone of the country.

The upper lower class is made up of people who are often referred to as the "poor but honest folks." They are the blue-collar, semiskilled, or unskilled workers. They experience a high rate of unemployment. They live in the poorer sections of town.

Lower lower-class people live in the slums of our large cities and the shacks of our rural areas. They find it difficult to hold steady jobs. These are the people who swell the welfare rolls. They move a great deal and have almost no status outside their own circle of friends.

What does all this have to do with a school-community study? Quite a lot, especially if you are a teacher or student teacher who wants to gain understanding of the "why's and wherefore's" of your constituents' life-styles. The social class structure of your particular school community may not exactly fit the pattern outlined by Davis et al. or Warner et al. Some pattern will be evident, however. If there is a high degree of social class uniformity within your school community, there will be some obvious social class differences when comparisons are made with other communities nearby. Your task is to identify that pattern, whatever it looks like, and to make some meaningful comparisons of life-styles.

What follows is a list of things to look for when you set out to analyze community life-styles. A careful analysis of data like this will help you discover social class patterns.

1. Density, type, and quality of housing. What sort of housing is available for community members? How does housing in this area compare with that of other areas? How do housing and land costs in your school community compare with such costs in other areas? What role have these costs played in the social structuring of this particular community?

2. General standards of living. What are some of the things that appear to be status symbols in this community? How well kept are the homes and businesses? What is the estimated family income of people in this community? What percentage of the children in your classroom and/or school are on free lunch programs? Do your students and other children in the area appear well cared for?

3. Occupations of heads of households. How do people in your school community earn a living? About what percentage of the local families have both parents working? What degrees of

status do various local occupations have in the community?

4. Educational backgrounds of parents. To what extent can it be assumed that most of the adults in the community have a college education? What kind of educational backgrounds are probably required of people in the vocational fields of local residents?

5. Cultural or ancestral backgrounds. What racial and ethnic groups are represented in the local community? In your school? What is the percentage of concentration for each of these groups? To what extent are your community and school racially or culturally integrated? Are there any community or school programs that reflect the needs and interests of any of these groups?

6. Languages spoken in homes. Do any of your students come from families where languages other than English are regularly spoken? Does your school have any kind of bilingual or "English as a second language" (ESL) programs? Can students regularly be heard conversing in languages other than English on the school grounds?

7. Family patterns. How many single-parent families? How large are the families? What are the ordinal positions of your students among their siblings? Do any of your students live in foster homes? Do any of your students come from families you might describe as having unique structures? The nuclear family is the most common pattern today. This is where one set of parents and their children live together. An older pattern, which still exists in some places, is the extended family. This is where two or more generations of parents and children live together or in close proximity to each other. In the nuclear family the full responsibility for child rearing is on the shoulders of the parents. With occupations that take the father out of the home, this often means the mother is most directly responsible. In the extended family, child rearing is often shared by grandparents, aunts, and uncles.

8. Family responsibilities of children. Do your students have regularly assigned chores or responsibilities at home? Are any of the older children expected to take care of their younger siblings?

9. Leisure-time activities. What kinds of vacations do your students' families take? To what extent are local recreational facilities used by local people? How many recreational vehicles, boats, travel trailers, etc. are owned by people in your school community? Where do your students hang out after school and on weekends? What kinds of hobbies do your students have? How much television do they watch each week? Which programs are most popular? How much do they read? What books are most popular? To what extent do your students and their families participate in cultural activities in the community? How many of your students take afterschool music or dance lessons? To what extent do your students participate in sports? How frequently do your students and their parents visit local museums and zoos?

Socioeconomic class structures and patterns of social behavior help define people's life-styles. Answers to the foregoing questions and others like them tell us how people choose to spend (or are compelled to spend) their time, energy, and money. It is possible for an outside observer to judge the quality of another's life by the ways basic needs are satisfied. One might observe that a group of people is adequately clothed and sheltered. They appear to have ample food. They have adequate space to exercise their limbs. However, these objective data, by themselves, do not tell the whole story.

The psychological environment of a group of people is as important to their life-styles as are their physical and social environments. Of course all interrelate. The psychological environment has to do with the way a group of people look at what they have, what they do, and what they are.

Perhaps you remember the riots that occurred in Watts, California. Prior to 1965 an outside observer might have taken a tour through Watts, and come away with the opinion that all was well, based on the standard of basic needs satisfaction. Although many people have called Watts a "ghetto," it certainly did not (nor does it today) resemble the multistoried tenement ghettos in Eastern industrial cities. A drive through the streets of Watts would have revealed a community of single-storied, single-family dwelling units. But to understand the unique problems of this community and to appreciate subsequent changes, one must consider the psychological environment of its residents, along with the physical and social environments. Yes, the people of Watts had greater access to the basic necessities of life than did the starving millions of India. But they were not Indians. They were U.S. citizens who lived just a few miles from Beverly Hills. These were people who, at least in part, felt the sting of social prejudice. These were people who knew the frustrations of trying to believe in the great American dream, while not being able to fully share in its reality.

It is important to remember that people view themselves the way they think other people view them. It's the old "looking-glass self" all over again. It applies to communities just as surely as it applies to individuals. Gerald Suttles (1972) said that community identity is more a function of "foreign relations" than anything else. No group has its identity in isolation. Groups acquire an identity as other groups hold them accountable. The psychological environment, then, has to do with the way people perceive their physical and social environments, which depends greatly on how they think others see them.

In conducting a community study it would be helpful to consider the cognitive map of the area as well as the physical map. A cognitive map of a community can show the ways residents describe their city or community in terms of what it's like and what it ought to be like. A cognitive map can help people make "yes" or "no" decisions about which path to take and where to go. A physical map can point up locations of streets, parks, schools, municipal buildings, etc. It may show the most direct route from one place to another. However, the most direct route may not be the most desired route in terms of physical safety or pleasant scenery. That's where the cognitive map comes in (Suttles, 1972). What parent has not admonished his child to avoid walking on certain streets or playing in certain areas?

A cognitive map of an area can help identify what some sociologists call "the defended neighborhood." The boundaries and nature of defended neighborhoods are pretty clear when you observe the habit patterns and listen to the talk of street gangs in large cities. It may be a bit more subtle in smaller neighborhoods, but it is just as real. Watch how many heads turn and how many curtains part for defensive glances when a stranger

walks down the street of a residential area, especially if that stranger is of a different race or obviously from a different social class. Listen to how people talk about "my neighborhood," "our neighborhood," "the neighborhood," and "that neighborhood." As you note these things, the lines of a cognitive map of the area will begin to emerge.

Attitudes and values. The word *"attitude"* is used rather loosely these days. What some people mean by "a good attitude" or "a bad attitude" is not always clear. Attitudes have to do with a person's predisposition to act in certain ways. The attitude of a group of young men walking toward you on a dark and lonely street will have something to do with your chances of getting home safely.

Whether an attitude is good or bad depends on your evaluation of the anticipated consequences of that attitude. Attitudes aren't values, but they are related to values. They depend on them. If, for instance, you value physical exercise, you'll be inclined to engage in it. The extent of your engagement will be directly related to the strength of your value, to your estimation of its benefits to you.

Values have to do with cultural beliefs or personal judgments about the worth, importance, or desirability of given objects or actions. For most of us, values operate on at least three different levels.

First, we have our secret (or semisecret) values. These relate to the things we enjoy doing repeatedly, but in secret. They are also related to those things we enjoy in select company—not for public consumption, so to speak. An example of the latter is the pleasure some people are said to get from telling or listening to dirty stories with a group of close friends.

Second, we have our public values. These can be either culture-based beliefs and practices or beliefs and practices that are outgrowths of our personal judgments. In either case, they are for public consumption. We do them openly. For instance, Americans spend billions of dollars each year in order to observe, participate in, or have some visible association with competitive sports.

Third, we have our ideal values. Sometimes the ideal is a goal or level of perfection toward which we strive. In this case our ideal value is like the carrot held in front of the racing rabbit or the dream we have of success. In another sense our ideal values have to do with what we say are our preferences, goals, standards, or ambitions. The catch here is that we often say what we think we are expected to say. Very often, in practice, there is a gap between our ideal and our real values. All those people who spend money on competitive sports may not really value competition or sports, as such. Some may be motivated by other desires, such as social acceptance.

In order to understand the value system of a given community it will be necessary to analyze what people say, observe what they do, and try to detect some of the results that follow. This is not an easy job. It demands a multifaceted approach on the part of the investigator. Teachers, of course, cannot be expected to be full-time sociologists or anthropologists. For this reason it will be necessary for teachers to limit the scope of their investigation.

It would certainly be helpful for a teacher to know the attitudes of community members toward education, in general, and specific programs and procedures, in particular. It would also be helpful to know the extent to which the value systems of community members are supportive of or contrary to the purposes and practices of local schools. Here are some things you might look for:

1. The ways and extent to which the school board and other governmental agencies respond to the needs of community children
2. The extent to which local residents support tax initiatives and bond elections for local schools
3. The rate of school absenteeism
4. Attendance at PTA meetings and other school functions
5. The nature of any legal suits or court actions involving local schools
6. The status of racial integration in local schools
7. The degree of teacher turnover in local schools
8. What various individuals and groups think ought to be the goals of the community's schools
9. How parents, teachers, administrators, and others think the schools could be improved
10. What these same people think the schools are doing well

These and similar areas of investigation will yield data that should enable you to identify some of the prevailing attitudes and values of community members with relation to their schools.

You might also be interested in discovering some of the attitudes and values of your own students. Here are some things you might look for:

1. Free-time activities they prefer, both in and out of school
2. School attendance
3. Obvious enthusiasm (or lack of it) for various academic and nonacademic school activities
4. The nature and function of various voluntary social groups of students—how membership is determined; how the group relates to "outsiders"; observable behaviors that tend to reinforce group identity
5. Stated goals and aspirations of students
6. Ideas and experiences students seem eager to share
7. Things students appear to avoid when possible

These are just a few of the things you can look for. The secret is to keep your eyes and ears open. Match what people say with what they do. Now let's consider some sources and techniques for getting information on your school and community's site and situation, life-styles, and attitudes and values.

A TOUCH (WHERE AND HOW TO GET INFORMATION)

What we can offer here are some general suggestions on where and how to get helpful information for a school-community study. You'll have to determine what the best resources are for your particular community. Before you decide how you are going to conduct your study, you should check local administrative policies concerning such activities. Some schools and school districts have strict regulations regarding such things as questionnaires and interviews conducted by teachers or student teachers.

You should also be very careful not to violate your students' or their parents' right to privacy. Teachers are privy to a great deal of confidential information about students and their families. Some of this information is in written records kept by schools. Other information comes from the students themselves, whether you are seeking it or not. Still other information arrives through the local gossip mills. As a teacher, you have a professional and moral responsibility to keep such material in the strictest confidence. Don't let all this deter you, however, from trying to find out all you can about your school and its community.

Sources of general information

County offices. Most county offices can provide you with more information than you can assimilate. This is a good place to start. Most counties have a public information office that can provide you with detailed information on county government and services. The County of San Diego, for example, publishes an attractive booklet entitled *Your Place Under the Sun*. This booklet contains information about the role of county government, county services and programs, human care services, law and justice, land use planning, recreation, county documents and records, animals and agriculture, county administration, budget, taxes, and volunteer opportunities.

City offices. City governmental offices can also provide a great deal of valuable data. Information related to the following is often available: City planning, community development, community resources, city engineering, fire protection, general services, human resources, library facilities, park and recreation facilities and programs, police protection and legal services, solid waste disposal services, street services, tax assessment and collection, public transportation, water and sewage services, and zoning information.

Chambers of commerce. Local chambers of commerce can often provide you with maps, statistics on business and industry, data on population growth, and sometimes a brief history of the area. Information from such sources is usually presented in a public relations format, glossy and better than life. This bias needs to be taken into account when you begin to analyze the data you have collected on your community.

Community libraries. Don't overlook the local library. The librarian may be able to help you locate important historical and statistical information on your community. It is not uncommon for libraries to have documents or books published by local historical societies. Old maps, pictures, and newspapers can also be of help to you.

Community newspapers. Newspapers are an excellent source of current, as well as historical, information. You might check recent and back issues for news and editorials that deal with education. Also check letters to the editor. You can learn a great deal about community attitudes and values regarding schools and education in this way.

School district offices. School districts usually have a community relations and/or public information office. You should be able to obtain from this office maps of school service areas, enrollment data, program and special service information, growth projections, operating costs, district policies, needs assessment data, program review documents, test score reports, and much more.

Real estate offices. Nearby real estate offices can often provide information on the costs of housing in various sections of the community. Realtors might also be able to give you some indication of population shifts and general degrees of transience. For the most part this information will be based on the realtor's own observations and experiences. Not many realtors will have the kind of hard statistical data available from other sources. Input from realtors is of value, however. They are usually in close contact with the local community.

Telephone directories. Area telephone directories can help you locate almost all the important community agencies that you might want or need to contact. Emergency services are normally listed in the front of the directory. You can find the locations of businesses, factories, hospitals, family service centers, schools, and governmental agencies, to mention just a few. The advertisements in the yellow pages can give you additional clues regarding the size and nature of local businesses. Consulting the telephone directory will give you a quick overview of the area you are studying.

Firsthand observations

Take a walking tour. In conducting a community study you will collect a lot of statistical data, historical information, and public relations material. To make sense of all this, to put it in its proper perspective, you need some firsthand experiences. A walking tour is an excellent way to get acquainted with your community. If you have traveled, you know the places you remember best are those where you have taken walking tours on your own.

Secure a map of your school service area from your principal or from the school district office, and start walking. If your school service area is too large, you might drive to one section of the area at a time, park your car, and walk. It will be helpful to have some idea of where your students live before you start. Be sure to take along a pencil and pad so you can record your observations. It might also be a good idea to take along a camera. Record and evaluate what you see, hear, and experience. Your observations may not have statistical validity, but they will go a long way in helping you understand your school's community.

Sit and watch. Another way you can discover many interesting things about your school and community is to simply sit and watch. Locate a comfortable spot on the school playground, a park bench, or at a bus stop. Sit awhile. Notice what goes on around you. What kinds of social interactions do you observe? What can you tell about the school or community from this perspective?

Attend meetings and functions. There are usually many school-related meetings and special functions you can attend. If you have never attended a school board meeting, you might start with this. Some student teachers attend school board meetings only to complain, "The meeting was boring." They missed the whole point. School board members aren't entertainers. What these students should have noticed were such things as the following: What issues were being dealt with? What were some of the concerns of the people who addressed the board? What attitudes and values were evident in what was said and done? What assumptions did board members tend to make in their reports and in their responses?

Other school-related meetings and functions might include PTA meetings, open house, the school carnival, seasonal programs, citizen advisory council meetings, goal-setting conferences, and faculty meetings.

Attendance at some nonschool-related community meetings might also provide you with some additional insights. If your community has an active Urban League or similar organization, check with them about possible community action or planning meetings. Local churches can also be a source of valuable information.

Conduct interviews. You may decide to interview a select group of residents. If you do, you should use a structured approach. Two commonly used tools for conducting interviews are (1) the interview schedule and (2) the interview guide. The interview schedule consists of a set of rather precise questions to which people are asked to respond in face-to-face situations. The interview guide is a bit more general and open ended in nature. It consists of a list of topics to be covered in the face-to-face interview. Either or both of these

devices can be used to great advantage in your efforts to collect data on people's attitudes and values. What follows are some suggestions that will help you in planning for and conducting interviews (Skager and Weinberg, 1971):

1. Make sure your schedule or guide is logically organized and contains a degree of unity.
2. Your lead questions should be noncontroversial, but attention getting.
3. Start with simple questions, then move to the more complex ones.
4. Stick to the point of your original plan.
5. Give subjects opportunities to clarify their meanings when dealing with questions that are difficult or embarrassing.
6. Establish a friendly climate for the interview.
7. Make sure the subject understands the significance and intended use of the interview.
8. Make it clear that no names will be used nor will any person be identified in the reports.
9. Be sure you do not "telegraph your punches" by showing approval or disapproval of responses. Be accepting and as objective as you can.

Use questionnaires. Questionnaires should follow the same principles as interview schedules. Questionnaires can be administered to groups of people at one sitting. They can also be distributed by mail or in person, with instructions (and postage if needed) for returning them to the originator. The boxed material on p. 73 is a sample questionnaire devised by a group of student teachers and approved by their principal and early childhood education coordinator.

Consult cumulative record folders. It is customary for schools to keep cumulative records on each student. These records follow the student throughout the school career. They contain personal data, test scores, grades, teacher comments, some family data, and other information considered important by teachers and administrators. Sometimes a separate health folder is kept for each student as a supplementary document. Some schools include health information in the main folder.

This information should be viewed as confidential. If information is obtained from these documents for the purpose of a school-community study, the reporting of such data should be such that no individual or family group is identifiable.

HOW DO YOU FEEL?

	Strongly disagree	Disagree	Agree	Strongly agree
	1	2	3	4

1. Children should be placed by abilities rather than age.
2. The Elm Street School area has adequate recreational facilities for my child.
3. Elementary schoolchildren should be given homework.
4. My child's work load is appropriate to his or her abilities.

5. Would you appreciate more information concerning combination classes? Yes _____ No _____
6. What subject do you think should receive more emphasis in the classroom? _____
7. Is the school meeting your child's needs? Yes _____ No _____
   a. What is the school doing that you like? _____
   b. What is the school doing that might be improved? _____
8. How should students be disciplined by teachers? _____

This survey is being conducted by members of the POINT VI Student Teaching Program at San Diego State University. Please return it to your child's teacher as soon as possible. Your child will receive a special badge for returning this promptly.

Thank you.

Teachers and student teachers should become familiar with these documents. Much can be learned from them about the long-term interests and needs of students. Student teachers should obtain permission from their master teachers and principals before examining cumulative folders and health records.

A TASTE (WHAT IT ALL MEANS)
Putting it all together

Evaluate. Once you have collected what may seem to be mountains of data, your next job is to evaluate it carefully. Not everything you collect will be important for your report. Try to decide how reliable and valid the various bits of information are. Next try to determine how relevant they are to your study. Keep your main purposes or questions in mind. Ask yourself, "In what way does this shed light on the site and situation, life-styles, and attitudes and values of my school and community?"

Organize. After you have evaluated your col-

lected data, you can start to organize what you consider relevant to your community study. By this time you should have some general categories or even a general outline in mind. One technique that has proved helpful to others is to record each specific fact or idea on a separate 3 × 5 inch card. This will allow you to arrange your information in various ways to see which makes the most sense. Next you can organize your data cards into general categories, or fit them into an outline pattern. You might still add or remove some data cards at this point. Be sure that your sources are clearly identified on each card, where appropriate. Now, after a final evaluation of your categories and your anticipated report format, you should be ready to put it all together.

Make generalizations. It is important to make generalizations. Every time we talk we make generalizations of one kind or another. Scientists are able to contribute to knowledge and understanding as they generalize about their findings. Generalizations have value when they are well founded, that is, when they are based on accurate investigations.

Make sure, then, that the generalizations from your community study are warranted and can be supported. An example of a "bad" generalization is "All the parents of children at George Elementary School believe that the school is meeting the needs of their children." A better generalization would be "From the results of a recent questionnaire, there appears to be substantial belief among parents that the school is meeting the needs of their children. Seventy-five per cent of the 250 respondents indicated that they believed the school was meeting their child's needs."

Identify needs and make suggestions. Conducting a school-community study will help you identify some of the needs of your students and the community. As you evaluate your data, categorize them into physical needs, social needs, and psychological needs. These needs can then be translated into recommended program goals or changes. In this way you cannot only gain valuable insights that will help you in working with children and parents, but you can also make a meaningful contribution to your school and community. The results of your investigation should be shared with other teachers, administrators, and community groups. They will be pleased to have this kind of input.

SUGGESTED ACTIVITIES FOR FURTHER UNDERSTANDING

Select a school. Visit the surrounding community during the hour after school dismisses or on a Saturday afternoon.

1. Take note of where students tend to congregate. Try to determine what it is that draws them there.
2. Check for recreational areas and facilities. How numerous and accessible are they? How many students are using them?
3. Using the six social class levels identified by Davis et al. and Warner et al., characterize the community served by the school. Do you believe the life-styles are consistent with the observations made by Davis et al. and Warner et al.?
4. For a major class project, complete a study of the community following the topics outlined in this chapter.

REFERENCES

Blake, B. F., et al. *Attributes of the community environment and the individual's quality of life.* Paper presented at the Midwestern Psychological Association Convention, Chicago, May, 1975. (ERIC Document Reproduction Service No. ED 126 412)

Brown, M. *Surveying the community.* Glendale, Ariz.: Westside Area Career/Occupation Project, October, 1974. (ERIC Document Reproduction Service No. ED 115 746)

Byrne, R., and Powell, E. *Strengthening school-community relations.* Reston, Va.: National Association of Secondary School Principals, 1976. (ERIC Document Reproduction Service No. ED 126 611)

Davis, A., Gardner, B. B., and Gardner, M. R. *Deep South.* Chicago: The University of Chicago Press, 1941.

Krumbein, E., and Beck, A. City as a center of learning, *Journal of Negro Education,* Summer 1975, *44,* 391-405.

Marsh, C. J. What ever happened to local community studies? *Clearing House,* February 1976, *49,* 260-266. (*Education Digest,* May 1976, *41,* 54-57.)

Milbauer, B. City inside the school, *Teacher,* January 1976, *93,* 57-59.

National Elementary Principals Symposium. Ecology of education: people, places, and things. *National Elementary Principal,* May 1975, *54,* 4-63.

Pellow, D., and Bedger, J. E. *Social ecology of South Commons* (Final report on work completed for the Office of Child Development, Planning Grant OCD-CB-486). Chicago: Council for Community Services in Metropolitan Chicago, 1974.

Skager, R. W., and Weinberg, C. *Fundamentals of educational research: an introductory approach.* Glenview, Ill.: Scott, Foresman & Co., 1971.

Suttles, G. D. *The social constructions of communities.* Chicago: The University of Chicago Press, 1972.

Warner, W. L., Havighurst, R. J., and Loeb, M. B. *Who shall be educated?* New York: Harper & Row, Publishers, 1944.

The art of teaching goes back as far as recorded history. But the foundations of that art were irreparably shaken 200 years ago when Rousseau introduced his novel ideas about child development. For a long time the fledgling science of developmental psychology suffered as an untried and unwelcome theory. It has only been in the past 80 years that theories of human development have left the philosopher's armchair and entered the scientific field. Research in growth and development has had profound effect on teaching, learning, and schooling and has truly revolutionized child care.

The writings of men such as Rousseau and Pestalozzi stirred interest in the scientific study of children. Child study gave way to the science of developmental psychology. In this chapter we will first see what educators have learned from developmental psychology. Then we will look at some specific study skills that readers of this book can use to increase their effectiveness in working with students.

A BRIEF LOOK BACKWARD

The saga of childhood and adolescence from ancient times through the Middle Ages and the Industrial Revolution is not a pleasant one. Infant mortality was high. Life itself was short and often brutal. Because of harsh reality, adults were fatalistic and callous about their young. Children were not considered worthy of much concern until they reached a point where they could assume some adult responsibilities. Until the seventeenth century children were considered to be miniature adults and were treated as such (Aries, 1962). Children were put to work early. We are only a century and half removed from some of the worst practices of child labor in the cities of England and America. Eight-year-old children often toiled 12 hours a day in factories.

Throughout history few boys were formally educated unless they were of the upper class or destined for the clergy. Girls were rarely educated at all. Plato and Aristotle had set the standards for education. The important education was higher education, and that was only for a chosen few. The idea of universal literacy appeared only after the sixteenth century. Even then it had nothing to do with universal suffrage, human rights, or educational opportunity. It was motivated by the Protestant concern that everyone be able to read well enough to read the Scriptures, a concern that grew from the fear of eternal damnation. The concept of original sin was so prevalent in Puritan America that there was little to brighten the life of the young. Children were assumed to be wicked creatures in need of having the Devil knocked out of them.

When the young did receive an education, it was a painful process. Schoolmasters rarely spared the rod. A few great thinkers throughout the centuries spoke about the art of teaching, but most teachers fit the student to the subject rather than the subject to the student. In the rationalistic tradition of Aristotle and orthodox religion, most education began with the presentation of abstract concepts and symbols. The assumptions were that all young people learned alike and that their interests and comprehension were, or should be, like those of adults. The idea of grading material developmentally to suit the age and interests of students did not appear in practice until well after 1800. Subject matter never failed, but many students did.

In previous chapters we followed the development of new thought about the nature of learners. The basic concept of what is now known as developmental psychology was first introduced by Jean Jacques Rousseau in *Emile,* a fictional account of child rearing and education published in 1762. Rousseau dared to say that children were born good and were corrupted by society. Among the many controversial notions that Rousseau suggested were that children develop in stages, that these stages of development dictate the kind of educational experience the child should have, that early education should be exploratory learning from nature, that reading should be introduced at about 12 years of age, and that religious and moralistic education should be saved until adolescence. Rousseau's ideas were based on theory,

not child study, but they were surprisingly close to the empirical findings of the contemporary psychologist Jean Piaget.

From 1774 to 1827 Johann Heinrich Pestalozzi, a Swiss social reformer and educator, operated schools that applied many of Rousseau's notions about education. Pestalozzi and his schools gained worldwide fame and were of great influence in America. Friedrich Froebel developed the Kindergarten as an outgrowth of Pestalozzi's work. Kindergartens were introduced in the United States in the 1850's.

By the 1900's most scientists and educators accepted the theory that the young grow and learn in developmental sequences that dictate the content and methods of instruction. At that point the fledgling science of developmental psychology and its general method of human study came into being.

ORIGINS OF CHILD STUDY METHODS

Child study has taken many forms. Its earliest form was the *baby biography,* which consisted of a detailed account of a child's behavior in the form of a diary-record kept by his parents. Some famous and scientifically minded parents, including Charles Darwin and Jean Piaget, kept such diaries. Darwin's diary of his son's development was published in 1877. The problem with the baby biography lies with the lack of objectivity of the parents and their selectivity in observing and recording (Wright, 1960). Nevertheless, baby biographies are historically important in the development of the systematic study of the young.

Another early form of child study was *intelligence testing,* introduced just after the turn of the century by Alfred Binet of France. The intelligence quotient (IQ) test was further developed in this country by Louis Terman and associates. Intelligence testing was originally devised to provide a quick assessment of a child's ability to benefit from regular instruction. It is still used, and not without controversy, as a predictive measure of academic success and more questionably as an instrument for screening and placement. Intelligence testing assumes developmental knowledge by age level. IQ is determined by how one performs on the test in relation to the average individual of the same age level.

The *questionnaire* was another early device

used in child study. G. Stanley Hall, who founded the American Psychological Association and was an indefatigable researcher, used the questionnaire in studies of elementary and adolescent school students to discover their thinking processes, attitudes, and interests. The questionnaire is still a useful child-study tool for teachers and clinicians.

John B. Watson, the "father of behaviorism" in America, introduced *experiments in behavior shaping* to child study in the years just after the World War I. The legacy of Watson and his followers is the clinical form of child study, wherein individuals and their environments are manipulated, and behavioral reactions are observed. Behaviorists tend to discount the determinism of developmental stages as putting limits on growth, especially mental growth, and believe that learning can be accelerated. The behaviorists have taught students of human development to be objective and to concentrate on observed behaviors as the true evidence of knowledge, attitude, and emotion.

In the 1930's child-study pioneer Arnold Gesell and his colleagues Frances L. Ilg and Louise Bates Ames of the Gesell Clinic of Child Development at Yale University confirmed the theory that the young pass through a series of fixed developmental stages. These stages control growth rate and dictate the success or failure of attempts to train the individual. Gesell's well-known studies of identical twins supported the fact that twins will possess equal physical skills by the age of 2 years, regardless of the fact that one has had training and the other has not. Gesell and his followers benefited child study by documenting a wealth of information on typical behaviors for each age level from birth to age 16 years (Ilg and Ames, 1955). They came to the conclusion that behaviors are "patterned and predictable." The Gesell Institute's findings are subject to some dispute because the data were obtained from Anglo-American, middle-class subjects.

Human study was further promoted through the Institute of Child Welfare at the University of Minnesota during the 1930's. Dorothea McCarthy studied language development by using a *cross-sectional* or *normative method* of child study, wherein age norms were established by studying the responses of many children of different ages. Another researcher, Mildred Parten, used *time*

sampling as a technique to study the social behavior of preschool children.

Long-term or *longitudinal studies* in human development have been pursued by researchers at Fells Research Institute in Yellow Springs, Ohio; at the University of California, Berkley; and at Stanford University. In these studies the growth and development of individuals have been followed and closely documented for as many as 35 years. The longitudinal study provides a comprehensive view of an individual's development and allows for evaluation of IQ, child-parent relationships, and other factors as early predictors of success and failure in adult life. The Terman study at Stanford University discovered that many children who were identified as "geniuses" were, in fact, leading quite ordinary lives by the time they were 35 years old.

Psychiatry has also added much to human study. Jacob Moreno introduced *sociometric techniques* to show the social relationships of individuals in a group. The result is a diagram known as a *sociogram,* a simple and commonly used device. Psychiatry has also introduced various *projective techniques,* such as the Rorschach test, wherein subjects are asked to describe what they see in a series of ink blots; the thematic apperception test, wherein subjects are shown pictures of ordinary and provocative situations, then asked to make up stories about them; and questionnaires, which are designed to probe attitudes and feelings. Erik Erikson, a child psychologist with a background in psychiatry and anthropology, used doll play as a technique to unlock the true thoughts and feelings of children. Erikson has given educators tremendous insight regarding the sociopsychological development of children and adolescents, as we will see later.

Jean Piaget, a giant among researchers in child development, has conducted his studies of the thought processes of children from 1921 to the present day. Piaget started with baby biographies of his own children and simple observations of spontaneous behavior. He was soon convinced that he could learn more about children if he presented "problems" to them. His ideas developed into what he calls the *clinical method.* With the now famous Piagetian tasks, children are presented problems, are asked to solve them, and are asked to explain how they solved them. Piaget's findings support the concept of a developmental sequence of mental maturity by stages. Piaget's findings also support the principle of unified growth with a careful delineation of the factors that influence mental development: (1) Physical maturation; (2) experiences in dealing with things; (3) social interaction; and (4) equilibration, a process of unifying maturation and experience to build mental structures. We will take a closer look at the work of Piaget later in this chapter.

THE LEGACY OF CHILD STUDY

Observation and experimentation are the basic tools of science. Ever since Darwin's voyages to South America on the *H.M.S. Beagle,* natural scientists have used these tools to accumulate a wealth of data about the growth and development of species. These data tell us a great deal about the development and relationships of organisms in nature. Observational study has also given impetus to ecology, the science of the complex balance of natural relationships.

The study of children by psychologists, sociologists, psychiatrists, anthropologists, and educators has shared the empirical methods of the natural sciences. An impressive and ever-expanding body of knowledge about human growth and learning has resulted. Scientific journals and professional organizations articulate research findings from field, clinical, and controlled experimental studies. Such journals include *Child Development,* published since 1930 by the Society for Research in Child Development; *Childhood Education,* the journal of the Association of Childhood Education International, published since 1924; and *Child Development Abstracts and Bibliography,* published since 1927 by the Society for Research in Child Development. A review of the literature of child study will show that most studies rely on careful, detailed, and systematic observation and recording of children's behaviors.

Developmental research continues to explore a number of areas, including the following:

Growth and developmental stages
Intelligence measurement: its uses and abuses
Cultural and subcultural differences in child rearing
Parent-child relationships
Family structure and organization
Socialization and peer group influences
Community and regional influences on youth
The ecology of the classroom
The psychological effects of the learning environments
Self-concept and personality development
The capabilities of exceptional children
Aggression and emotion
Psychologically and emotionally disturbed individuals
Mental growth and maturity
Learning rates and styles
The effects of teaching materials and methods
Language development and learning
Nonverbal communication
Play and playthings
Childhood traits and environmental factors related to success and failure in later life

The data from these studies provide valuable insights for parents in child rearing, for educators in planning instruction, for social workers and counselors in guiding troubled students, and for special educators in gauging the needs of learners who differ from the norm.

Many valuable findings have resulted from the study of human development. These findings give us scientific knowledge about how humans grow, develop, and behave and about their emotions, needs, fears, pleasures, interests, self-concepts, and urgent life problems at various periods of their lives. This scientific knowledge, in turn, guides the efforts of all people who work with children and youth.

Of all these people, none can make better use of this information than teachers. From it they learn two basic things, each extremely important. First, teachers learn what to expect of students at various age or developmental levels—what they are capable of, how they react to situations, what they naturally strive for, and how they normally relate to other people. This knowledge guides matters of curriculum, objectives, activities, materials, physical environments, and psychosocial environments. Second, teachers learn how to influence student behavior—how to motivate, guide, and shape it. This knowledge affects activities, materials, and environments, too, but it has special importance with respect to interactions between teacher and students. The teacher is facilitator, communicator, encourager, motivator, guide, and disciplinarian, roles intended to influence strongly the behavior of students. Scientific knowledge enables us to enact these roles with precision and positive effect.

The following sections describe some of the basic knowledge that researchers have gained in areas of human development. The sections are physical development, intellectual development, and psychosocial development. They present information considered especially helpful to teachers.

Physical development

"Well now, who is this big child? You've grown so much I didn't recognize you!" Everyone remembers their Aunt Martha saying something like this. Children almost grow up before your eyes. They make changes in height, weight, proportion, musculature, sexual maturation, and general appearance. Such changes may be of only passing interest to Aunt Martha, but they are quite important to those who work with children and youth. We are going to take a brief look at three periods of physical growth: early childhood, middle childhood, and adolescence. The age span of each period roughly parallels an education level: preschool or early childhood education, elementary education, and secondary education.

Early childhood (age 3 to 6 years). Candidates for nursery school, kindergarten, and first grade are usually well-proportioned little people. They have lost the disproportionate large head–short legs look of the infant and toddler. By 6 years of age a child's body proportions are more like those of an adult. Except for the fact that girls have a little more fatty tissue, there are no marked sexual differences in children's bodies at this age. The child's skeletal, muscular, and nervous systems are maturing. By 3 years of age, the child usually has a complete set of temporary (baby) teeth. Preschoolers can take falls without a great risk of breaking bones. They have "soft bones," that is, the bone structure contains a great deal of cartilage. But as the child approaches the middle years of childhood, this cartilage is slowly replaced by bone.

The preschooler's muscular development is uneven. The large muscles are more fully developed than the small muscles. This accounts for the fact that most youngsters of this age have trouble with fine coordination. Programs in early childhood ed-

ucation are careful to stress big muscle activity. Eye-hand and small muscle coordination increases as the child approaches the end of the preschool years. The girls begin to outshine the boys in drawing shapes, cutting on the line with scissors, folding papers, stringing beads, pouring liquid into a glass, toileting, and dressing themselves. Because boys have a slight advantage in muscle tone, they tend to be more proficient in ladder climbing, ball throwing, and jumping. When it comes to the coordination involved in hopping and skipping, the girls are better. Some of these sex-related physical differences may be the result of learning that reflects societal attitudes.

Environmental factors affect human growth throughout the years of physical growth. But these factors are particularly important for 3- to 6-year-old children. Nutrition, sleep, hygiene, and the emotional climate of the home environment are often reflected in the growth of the preschooler.

Middle childhood (age 6 to 12 years). Physical growth during the period of middle childhood is less rapid than in the preschool years. At the beginning of this period boys are slightly taller and heavier. By the age of 11 or 12 years, the girls have begun a surge in adolescent growth and have surpassed the boys in height and weight. Development of the organs increases during this period. Near the beginning of the middle-childhood period, eyesight becomes keener, with the coordination of binocular vision. Brain development will increase to adult size. Heart and lung development may not keep pace with skeletal growth near the end of this period. Teachers should be careful not to overtax youngsters with physical exercise, especially those who are large for their age.

Dental development is characterized by the loss of the baby teeth and the acquisition of the permanent teeth. The cycle of losing and acquiring teeth goes on between the ages of 6 and 11 years. It is viewed by the child as an important measure of growing up. The permanent dentition of all twenty-eight teeth will be completed by 13 or 14 years of age.

Toward the end of this period many children enter an awkward age. The taller and larger children may show problems of coordination. Good posture needs to be stressed. The puberty cycle begins before the age of 12 years for some children. Reproductive organs begin to mature. Secondary sex characteristics appear. Girls may be pleased or embarrassed by the development of their breasts and hips. Some girls reach menarche (first menstruation) while still in elementary school. Boys' voices begin to change, and facial hair begins to show. Interest in sex is great during the latter years of this period. Programs of sex education are usually introduced in the fifth and sixth grades to counter fears and misconceptions and create positive attitudes.

Individual differences in physical size and maturity are most pronounced among fifth, sixth, and seventh graders. In a classroom visit to one of these grades, you can often see students who range in size from that of the average 6-year-old child to that of the large adult.

Adolescence (age 12 to 18 years). Adolescence is characterized by great physical change. The growth spurt that begins for boys at about 9 to 10 years of age accelerates when they reach age 13 or 14 years. At around age 15 years it begins to slow once more, but continues to the age of 18 years and beyond. Girls begin their growth spurt earlier and attain adult height and weight 2 years earlier than boys. They also reach sexual maturity earlier than boys. The average age of menarche is 13 years, but it can be reached as early as 9 and as late as 18 years. Most girls are sexually mature, although not necessarily fertile, by age 16 years. Boys reach full sexual maturity about 2 years later than girls. By the end of the adolescent period, facial characteristics and body structure are adult in appearance.

During periods of rapid growth, young people may have problems of coordination. There is danger in requiring physical exercise that necessitates great stamina. Heart and lung size may not be commensurate with skeletal stature. Youngsters in early adolescence may be awkward, but by the later high school years awkwardness has largely disappeared. Coordination becomes highly developed and refined.

Adolescents have heterosexual interests in abundance. But this is usually overshadowed by strong friendship ties with like-sexed peers. Adolescence is an age of identity and growing independence. When sexual and role identification is complete, adolescents move into heterosexual relationships.

Table 1. Average heights and weights of American children*

Age (years)	Males		Females	
	Height (inches)	Weight (pounds)	Height (inches)	Weight (pounds)
3	37.8	32.0	37.5	31.0
4	40.8	37.0	40.6	36.0
5	43.7	42.0	43.8	41.0
6	46.1	47.0	45.7	45.0
7	48.2	54.0	47.9	50.0
8	50.4	60.0	50.3	58.0
9	52.8	66.0	52.1	64.0
10	54.5	73.0	54.6	72.0
11	56.8	82.0	57.1	82.0
12	58.3	87.0	59.6	93.0
13	60.7	99.0	61.4	102.0
14	63.6	113.0	62.8	112.0
15	66.3	128.0	63.4	117.0
16	67.7	137.0	63.9	120.0
17	68.3	148.0	64.1	122.0
18	68.5	149.0	64.1	123.0

*Modified from *Child Growth* by Wilton Marion Krogman. Copyright © 1972, The University of Michigan, The University of Michigan Press, Ann Arbor, Mich. Used by permission of the publisher.

Intellectual development

Intelligence, intellect, brain power. Oh, how glibly we toss the terms. Now here's a little task for you. Let's see you define these terms. Make it easy on yourself—just define one of them. If you say ability to think or ability to reason, you have to go one step further: You have to tell what that means, too.

You may have guessed by now that intelligence is one of those ultravague, hard-to-pin-down concepts that we regularly use in education. We seem to put considerable stock in whatever it stands for. We speak of "her IQ" as 123, rating her intelligence on that basis. We give intelligence tests to everyone, dutifully enter their scores into personal records, and then . . . then what? Nothing. Seldom do we do anything at all, based on those scores. Once in a great while the score is used for an educational purpose. Presently we will take note of such uses.

But first let's stand back and look at this intelligence business. We will take this look through three concepts of intelligence and intellectual development: the IQ concept; the model of intellect concept; and the developmental stages concept.

The IQ concept: an expanding balloon. As the twentieth century burst on us, two gentlemen of France, Messrs. Binet and Simon, were commissioned to perform an interesting task. French teachers were plagued with slow learners, whom they considered unfit for education. They wanted ways to identify these learners early in the game. Binet and Simon were charged with the responsibility for developing devices that would identify these students.

After a time they came up with some tasks that seemed to do the trick. The tasks included tests of attention, memory, and comprehension, and they were successful in weeding out slower learners.

In the United States, Lewis Terman, a psychologist at Stanford University, seized on Binet and Simon's work and used it in his research in human intellectual development. He adapted their tasks, added some of his own, tried them out on hundreds and hundreds of school students across the country, and in 1916 published the granddaddy of all intelligence tests, the Stanford-Binet test.

To this day, the Stanford-Binet test sits atop the heap of intelligence tests. We have dozens and dozens of such tests. A few of them are good, individually administered tests, such as the Wechsler Adult Intelligence Scale (WAIS) and the Wechsler Intelligence Scale for Children (WISC). Most of them are mediocre to good group-administered tests, such as the California Test of Mental Maturity. All such tests have two traits in common: First, they imply that intelligence grows in a continual fashion. Each day we become increasingly capable intellectually, until we reach full intellectual development. This full development is reached as early as age 14 years on some tests (Stanford-Binet) and as late as age 25 years on others (WAIS). Beyond that optimal age, the intellect declines very gradually for the remainder of one's life. (Take heart, those of you over age 25 years. This maximum refers to intellectual efficiency—how easily the wheels and cogs turn—not to wisdom, which continues to grow into old age.) Second, these tests imply that one's level of intelligence, compared to other people, remains virtually the same throughout life. If you are in the middle, you stay there; if you are in the top 5%, you stay there.

Most of these tests incorporate procedures for translating raw scores into intelligence quotient (IQ) scores. IQ is defined as mental age (MA) divided by chronological age (CA) multiplied by 100. Sally may have an MA of 12 years, which means she does as well on the test as an average 12 year old. But she may have a CA of 10 years, which means she was born exactly 10 years ago. Thus her IQ is 120:

$$\frac{MA\ (12)}{CA\ (10)} = 1.2 \times 100 = 120$$

Most of the well-known intelligence tests have a verbal component, which yields a verbal IQ, and a nonverbal component, which yields a performance IQ. Together, they yield an overall IQ.

As to what these tests actually measure, there has been wide discussion, dispute, and confusion. They are said to measure ability to think, to learn, to solve problems, to deal with abstractions, to process and retain information. Since it is almost impossible to define these abilities operationally, many cynics define intelligence as "whatever intelligence tests measure."

Again, one's IQ is thought of as permanent. As it keeps its relative place, intelligence is thought to grow continually, just as a balloon increases in size when blown up to capacity. But in this case there is no way to make the balloon fill faster. The IQ cannot be manipulated.

The model of intellect concept: cells of the cube. The late 1950's saw the emergence of an alternative view of intellectual development. That view was proposed by J. P. Guilford (1959), who used a cube metaphor to consider the intellect. The cube shows three facets: one for incoming data, one for manipulations the intellect performs on those data, and one for the products that result from those manipulations.

The incoming data, called "contents," fall into four categories: figural, symbolic, semantic, and behavioral. The mental manipulations, called "operations," fall into five categories: cognition, memory, divergent production, convergent production, and evaluation. The outcomes, called "products," fall into six categories: units, classes, relations, systems, transformations, and implications. Thus within the cube there are 120 interactions: 4 contents × 5 operations × 6 products. Each interac-

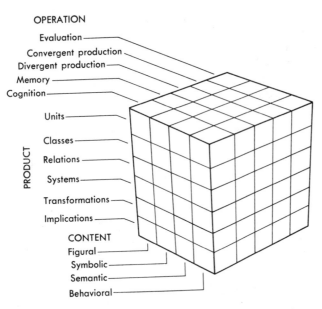

OPERATION
- Evaluation
- Convergent production
- Divergent production
- Memory
- Cognition

PRODUCT
- Units
- Classes
- Relations
- Systems
- Transformations
- Implications

CONTENT
- Figural
- Symbolic
- Semantic
- Behavioral

From Guilford, J. P. *The nature of human intelligence.* New York: McGraw-Hill, Inc., © 1967. Used with permission of McGraw-Hill, Inc.

tion can be considered to occur within a cell, giving 120 cells in the cube. The cube, facets, and cells are shown above.

Unlike IQ conceptions, which suggest one main intelligence, plus perhaps two secondary intelligences (verbal and performance), Guilford sees the intellect as composed of 120 separate entities. Moreover, his work implies that practice strengthens the contents of each cell. Intelligence is therefore changeable, modifiable through education.

Guilford's work has been carried into the practical arena by Mary Meeker (1969). She has devised ways to use existing intelligence tests to identify strong cells and weak cells in the cube, and she has developed procedures for strengthening the weak ones. Her work has yielded gratifying results, especially for minority ethnic students (Meeker and Meeker, 1973).

The developmental stages concept: steps on the stairs. In 1921 there was launched one of the most remarkable careers in the annals of psychology and education. That was the year Jean Piaget, the renowned Swiss psychologist, began his work, which still continues at the Jean Jacques Rousseau Institute in Geneva. From the beginning, Piaget's investigations into the nature of intellectual development were recognized throughout Europe. They were much akin to the ideas of Maria Montessori, the fabulous Italian medical doctor who turned her energies to the education of young children. Their careers overlapped for almost three decades, and while these people did not collaborate, they came to very similar conclusions.

In the United States, however, Piaget's notions received relatively little attention. Before 1950 we were caught up in the intelligence test frenzy, concerned about getting IQ scores for all students. Piaget's work didn't include the IQ. It didn't even provide a test. It just didn't fit in with what was occupying our minds and energies.

After 1950 we began to see the limitations of IQ tests. Mainly we saw that although they did predict school success, they suggested nothing for teaching. Except for their value in identifying students for inclusion in special education programs, they were useless.

At that time interest in Piaget's work grew swiftly in this country. His findings provided different insights into intellectual growth, insights that held promise for guiding teaching and learning.

But this emerging interest in Piaget was short lived. It was smothered by an unexpected development in American education. That development was the "new" mathematics, science, and English that remade educational practice in this country. Stung by Russia's 1957 launching of Sputnik, critics from all walks of life lambasted the schools, scapegoating them because the U.S.S.R. beat us into space. This insistent criticism culminated in the Woods Hole Conference of 1959. There groups of scientists, mathematicians, and other academicians met to consider the public school curricula. Jerome Bruner, the Harvard psychologist, coordinated their efforts, which he published in a small but mighty book entitled *The Process of Education* (1960). One of the key points of this book was that it is possible to teach anything in an intellectually honest way to learners at any stage of development, provided you use appropriate language, activities, and materials. Another of the key points was that education should emphasize the structure of the various disciplines—how the parts fit together and what they meant. Educational moguls bought the two ideas, lock, stock, and barrel.

Overnight, new mathematics, new science, and new English inundated the schools. All of them emphasized student awareness of basic structure. They pushed down into the primary grades, right into kindergarten. Meaningful mathematics, transformational grammar, and discovery science became catch words at all levels of public education.

Fifteen years later, we had all learned our lessons. The new curricula didn't do any better than the old. In some cases, particularly primary grade mathematics, learning suffered significantly.

Why? The explanation lies partly, if not totally, in what Piaget had been saying all along. His message was this: Little children are not adults in miniature. They do not, in fact they cannot, learn in the same ways adults learn. Their minds work differently. They have their own ways of thinking and manipulating the world.

As the advocates of the post-Sputnik curricula folded their tents and stole away, American interest in Piaget resurged. This burst of attention came partly as a companion of the new primary school movement, popularized first in the British infant schools, and partly because Piaget could explain why primary grade students could not perform tasks in their mathematics programs.

Piaget provided a third concept of intellectual growth. His is the most useful, especially in primary education. It is useful because it tells us what we can expect of children intellectually, as well as what we cannot expect. This information enables us to provide instruction suited to individual abilities.

Piaget's investigations convinced him that intellectual growth proceeds through stages. Each stage has its own characteristics, causing people to function differently than when in other stages. Three of the stages overlap the years when individuals are in school. These stages are "intuitive thought," "concrete operations," and "formal operations." The intuitive thought stage typically characterizes children between the ages of 4 and 7 years, the concrete operations stage is typical of children from age 7 to 11 years, and the formal operations stage develops between the ages of 11 and 15 years, at which time intellectual growth is completed.

You must take note of this fact: The ages mentioned for entry into and exit from these three stages are *averages*. Normal students vary in them by as much as 2 or 3 years. Gifted and retarded students vary even more. Thus although you might expect an 8-year-old child to be func-

tioning at the concrete operations level, you cannot be sure that such is the case. That's why it is important to be able to assess levels of development, a skill that will be described later.

What are the characteristics of intuitive, concrete, and formal thought? The following can be expected:

1. *Intuitive thought* (age 4 to 7 years). Preoperational—thought processes are unlike those of adults. Children at this level:

   Reason on the basis of hunches and intuitions. They do not use logical processes, and they do not understand logic.

   Are poor at explaining relationships and remembering the order of events.

   Often do not understand speakers accurately.

   Engage in both communicative and egocentric speech. Egocentric speech is noncommunicative, consisting of monologue and mimicry.

   Argue a great deal, without expectation of persuading the other person.

   Have difficulty remembering rules.

   Prefer games with few rules. "Win" and "lose" have no bearing.

   Can make rudimentary groupings and classifications.

   Cannot adequately conceptualize number or number processes. They cannot learn addition and subtraction processes with comprehension and cannot use them.

   "Lie" commonly, without malicious intent to deceive.

   Accept adult authority almost totally.

   Have few feelings of guilt. Misbehavior is seen as "bad," and punishment is accepted as its just consequence.

   Are highly imitative of each other, to a contagious degree.

2. *Concrete operations* (age 7 to 11 years). Can carry out mental processes. Children at this level:

   Can comprehend number, number processes, and relationships.

   Can carry out operations "in their heads," although while doing so they "see" real, concrete objects.

   Do not adequately comprehend abstract ideas such as love, loyalty, dignity, and freedom.

   Are able to conserve, that is, recognize that a quantity remains the same regardless of changes in shape or arrangement of parts.

Are highly argumentative with each other, although rarely so with adults.

Are sorely hurt by name calling.

Are becoming more reasonable and persuasive in their arguments.

Prefer cooperative win-lose play, with rules.

Can use logical reasoning as long as it does not involve abstract ideas.

Have a sense of honesty, but still lie a great deal, now with intent to deceive. Sense of guilt has become established.

Can remember and follow rules.

Show increasing social behavior, beginning to form cliques, groups, and clubs.

Usually accept adult authority, but often question it behind the adult's back.

3. *Formal operations* (age 11 to 15 years). Full adult thought—can think using abstract ideas. People at this stage:

Enjoy exploring abstract ideas.

Can use mental operations that involve only abstractions.

Have an affinity for idealism and social justice.

Are highly influenced by formal language's concepts, ideas, classifications, relationships, and logical structures.

Use reasoning to explore the possible as much as the actual.

Can learn complex mathematical, linguistic, mechanical, and scientific processes.

Insist on rules that are moral and fairly applied.

Consider wrongdoing as more than mere breaking of rules. Intent and circumstance must be considered.

Delight in considering different customs and points of view.

In summary, we can see that young children think in ways very different from adults. They cannot use logic or cause-effect relationships. They cannot conserve. They cannot carry out mental operations in their heads. They cannot remember rules. They cannot remember steps in a series. They cannot do number operations with understanding.

As they move into the concrete operations stage, they become much more adultlike in their thought processes. They can conserve, remember rules and steps, and use cause-effect relationships. They can carry out mental operations, but these operations always involve concrete objects. They cannot think using abstractions that have no concrete referents.

As they progress on into the formal operations stage, they become fully capable of adult-type thought. They use logic and abstract ideas. They explore the possible as well as the actual. They are sensitive to justice and social equality. They are fascinated by nonconventional ideas and behaviors. They have a respect for adult authority, but often challenge it directly if they think it is being abused.

Piaget's concept of intellectual development can thus be likened to steps on the stairs. As each new step is taken, important changes occur in what one becomes able to do intellectually.

Psychosocial development

You are yourself, are you not? Wise men say, "Know thyself." Having such intimate contact with yourself, you would expect to know it well. And of course you do, to a degree.

Yet how remarkably little most of us know about ourselves. Sure, we know about our likes and dislikes, our interests, what pleases and hurts us, what sorts of people and places we enjoy. It is the deeper part that we know so little about, that important, partially hidden part about which humanists are so concerned. That part includes our needs, our values, our self-concepts, our potentialities, and the crucial tasks with which we must contend at different times in our lives.

These things, say the humanists, are the elements that most tellingly say we are human, that most decisively separate us from the other animals, that most significantly point the way toward development of ourselves. That is why the great humanistic psychologist-educators like Abraham Maslow and Carl Rogers so stress knowledge of these traits, together with procedures for assisting their development to the fullest.

And while self-knowledge and self-development are so greatly important to each of us individually, they are doubly important to teachers. As we each come to know our own self and learn to help it grow, so do we come to learn the selves of our students and learn to help them grow.

If we are to gain insights into psychosocial development, both of ourselves and our students, we should examine the following five areas:

1. Interests
2. Needs
3. Values
4. Self-concepts
5. Crucial tasks

Interests. Our interests are the things that attract and hold our attention and that we seek out repeatedly. These things can be objects, compositions, activities, people, animals—you name it. The key phrase is "seek out repeatedly." Curiosity may draw our attention to something and hold it for a while. But that would not be considered an interest. Interests persist over periods of weeks, months, or years.

But interests do change. The interests you had when you were 5 years old differ from those you have now.

Moreover, certain interests seem to be generally connected with age. We can specify many interests that are common to 6 year olds, or 12 year olds, or 16 year olds. Not all students at a given age will share those predominant interests, but the majority are likely to do so.

Knowing about students' interests can help teachers very much. When class activities can be built around interests or when they can include those interests, student attention and motivation

Table 2. Some predominant interests of students at different age levels

Age level	Interests
5 to 8 years	Stories; dramatic play; pictures; songs; poems; rhythms; painting; animals; organized games; models; dolls; gangs and clubs; class projects; collections; comics; books on adventure, animals, foreign lands and people
9 to 10 years	Competitive games; team games; trips; reading; maps; letters; wrestling; sports; jumping rope; jacks; cooking and sewing
Preadolescent	Group; gang; club; sports; competitive and outdoor games; picnics; hobbies; construction; pets; movies; television; comics; books on science and adventure
Adolescent	Opposite sex; music; dancing; gossip; sports; cars; movies

are assured. Attention and motivation make learning sparkle.

What can we expect students' predominant interests to be at different ages? Of course, these interests will vary somewhat with locale, ethnic group, and the current rage on television. But in the main, Table 2 shows what to expect.

Needs. Needs run deeper than interests. Interests, although very important, are transitory. Mostly they are learned. After a time many of them are forgotten. But needs persist. They underlie most behavior, which in turn can be viewed as an attempt to satisfy these persistent needs. They seem to be consistent across ethnic groups and locales. Some of them change with age. Others remain the same throughout life.

Abraham Maslow (1943) gave us a theory of needs that helps explain human behavior. It also helps us remember to provide school conditions that help students meet needs. Maslow's concept identifies categories of needs. It places these categories into a hierarchy, which is an arrangement of stages or steps, each higher than the preceding one. His concept is commonly referred to as Maslow's hierarchy of needs:

Higher	Aesthetic
	Self-actualization
	Esteem
	Love and belonging
	Safety
Lower	Physiological

Maslow's belief was that lower needs, such as physiological and safety needs, had to be met before higher needs could come into play. That is, if you are hungry or threatened, you will bend your efforts in these directions. You will not be seeking to self-actualize (realize your highest potentialities) while living with great hunger or fear.

In education we aim primarily at ends included in self-actualization and aesthetic needs. But to allow these needs to function, we have to be sure that our students are meeting their lower needs—that they have food, air, and water; feelings of security; a sense of love and belonging; and a sense of esteem from others.

Maslow didn't see people "driven" by these higher and lower needs. Instead, he saw that people took pleasure in attempting to satisfy them. Thus he saw this pleasurable attempt to satisfy

Table 3. Some predominant needs of students at different age levels

Age level	Needs
5 to 8 years	Assurance, physical activity, direct sensory experience, encouragement, praise, warmth, patience, concrete experiences in learning
9 to 10 years	Physical activity, group membership, admiration
Preadolescent	Affection, warmth, greater independence, acceptance by peer group
Adolescent	Sense of identity, acceptance by and conformation to peer group, security with independence

needs as the prime motive that energizes and guides human behavior.

Maslow's ideas are stimulating and helpful, but there is a second way of viewing needs that is more helpful yet for teachers. This view comes from inferences made from observations of student behavior. These inferences describe what students seem to be seeking through the behaviors they exhibit. Whereas Maslow's hierarchy is thought to remain constant throughout life, this second view sees needs varying in relation to age (Table 3).

Values. Values are whatever we consider important and worthwhile in life. As the name indicates, they are those things that have value for us, that we want, that we think right, that we consider good, that we believe just. Unknowingly, we expect others to share and live by the values we ourselves hold.

Often, though, we do not know what our own values are. Students usually cannot, by themselves, describe their values. Yet values are the stars that guide our lives. Since they so strongly influence our behavior, it behooves us to attempt to identify what they are for each of us individually.

The procedures currently used to help people identify their values are grouped into a technique called "values clarification." This is a procedure for helping students identify what is truly important to them in their lives (Raths, Harmin, and Simons, 1966). It begins with the teacher listening attentively to what students say, during both class discussions and informal conversations. The teacher then asks nonjudgmental questions that elicit more

responses from students. Examples of such questions are as follows:

> Is that what you mean?
> Where do you think that idea comes from?
> Have you thought of any other possibilities?
> Should everyone think that way?

Such questions, in the way they cause students to reflect on what they have said, help establish in students' minds those things that have deep importance for them. Evidence for such importance comes when students show they *freely chose,* from among alternatives, the position they have taken; that they *prize* the choice they have made, as shown by their willingness to affirm it publicly; and that they will *act* on the basis of their beliefs.

Raths (1963) suggests that teachers listen for student comments such as "When I get . . . ," "What I like to do . . . ," and "Someday I'm going to. . . ." The teacher can then follow with the clarifying questions listed previously, plus questions such as the following:

For prizing: "Are you glad you feel that way?"
"Do you tell others about it?"
For acting: "Is there anything you can do about that?"
"Will you do it?"
"Have you done it before?"

Self-concepts. A great deal of concern has been voiced in recent years about students' self-concepts. The concern has arisen for two reasons: First, people with good self-concepts live happier, more fulfilling lives. Second, people with good self-concepts do better as students in school. These factors are known to go together. What is not known, however, is which causes the other.

Our self-concept is the totality of what we believe to be true about ourselves, plus the value we place on those beliefs. This totality contains several traits that seem to have special importance for school students. Among them are physical appearance, intelligence, and personality traits. It has been established that primary schoolchildren usually have adequate self-concepts, but that beginning in about third grade, the self-concept begins to slip. It reaches the depths during the junior school years, when students are generally dissatisfied with everything about themselves, and improves again as students move through high school.

There are several scales one can use to assess individual student's self-concepts. In the main, they get at parts of the following factors:

I am unique, although similar to others.
My appearance and personality satisfy me.
People care about me.
People support my ideas, opinions, and activities.
I recognize my need for others.
I belong.
I have a sense of purpose in life.
I have the ability to do.
I am successful.
My efforts are recognized.

Crucial tasks. Some psychologists and educators have identified tasks whose accomplishment is crucial to individuals at given periods in their lives. Chief among these concepts are those of Erik Erikson and Robert Havighurst. Erikson sees humans as progressing through eight stages in their lives. Five of these stages are completed by the time students leave high school. Havighurst has identified several "developmental tasks." He believes that groups of these tasks must be successfully accomplished by school students during early childhood, middle childhood, and adolescence if the students are to live healthy, normal lives.

Let us see what Erikson and Havighurst have to say.*

ERIKSON'S PSYCHOSOCIAL STAGES

Erik Erikson (1950) believes that man has an innate potential for healthy psychological growth. For that growth to lead to health instead of illness, the individual must successfully resolve key conflicts that arise at various stages in life.

Erikson identified eight stages in human development, each of which requires resolution of a key conflict. The first five stages, which cover childhood and youth, are presented here. Suggestions for their successful resolution are made, and the results of successful and unsuccessful resolutions are noted.

---

*Material in this section is modified from Charles, C. M. *Educational psychology: the instructional endeavor.* (2nd ed.). St. Louis: The C. V. Mosby Co., 1976a.

TRUST VERSUS MISTRUST (BIRTH TO AGE 18 MONTHS). The first of the key developmental stages for Erikson occurs during the first 18 months of life. Our tendencies to be trusting or mistrusting greatly influence our attitude toward life and our dealings with others. Erikson considers basic trust "the cornerstone of a healthy personality." He believes that trust facilitates most life encounters, whereas basic mistrust hampers them. Trust grows out of the child's feeling that there is someone whose concern can be counted on at all times.

AUTONOMY VERSUS SHAME AND DOUBT (AGE 18 MONTHS TO 3 YEARS). For the first few months of life we do not recognize ourselves as separate from others. At about the age of 18 months, however, the sense of the self starts to clarify. We begin to see that what we say and do belongs to us and not to others. We show a greatly increased desire to act independently. We want to do things for ourselves instead of having others do them for us.

Autonomy grows out of successful behavior. The key determinant of whether children see their behavior as successful or unsuccessful is the reactions that adults make to it. Behavior that is approved and encouraged leads to a greater sense of ability and confidence in oneself. Behavior that brings on constant disapproval and punishment leads to self-doubt and shame.

INITIATIVE VERSUS GUILT (AGE 3 TO 6 YEARS). By the age of 3 years, the child's sense of autonomy, provided it has been nourished and not thwarted, has reached a high level of development. Along with this sense of autonomy comes a benign aggressiveness, an active reaching out to explore and try out the new and different. This eagerness to try one's own wings is called initiative, and the time of life in which its development is crucial falls between the ages of 3 and 6 years.

If the trait of initiative is to become solidly rooted, children must be encouraged in their active manipulation of the environment. Piaget stressed this activity as necessary for intellectual development. In the same degree it is necessary for psychosocial development. Initiative is a trait that serves us well throughout life. If stifled at this age through reprimand, punishment, or reproof, it may never develop fully, or if so, only through later intensive effort.

When their explorations are harshly controlled and bring punishment, children begin developing a generalized sense of guilt that may plague them throughout life. Initiative aids full functioning; guilt shackles it.

INDUSTRY VERSUS INFERIORITY (AGE 6 TO 12 YEARS). By the age of 6 years the child is virtually bursting with new powers. Language has advanced rapidly. The child is about to enter a new and powerful stage of intellectual ability that will permit operational thought and a new style of reasoning. Bones, muscles, and organs have grown in size and strength. Coordination is improving daily. New modes of interacting with peers are developing that will make possible cooperation and competition.

Here, says Erikson, is where the child must learn to channel those energies and powers in purposeful directions. Mere play, important as it may be, is not enough. The child must become productive and task oriented. The tasks need not be distinguishable from play, except that they often should lead to an end—a product, a solution, a skill, an understanding.

When energies are directed to purposeful tasks, the child develops a sense of industry. This sense of industry brings with it an increased sense of competence and of ability to do and perform.

If this drive for industry is stifled through adult disapproval and punishment, a debilitating sense of inferiority results. Reprimand and reproof for activities, which so often come when the activities are noisy, cause the child to feel guilty. If the products of the activities are frowned on or put down, the child comes to feel inferior. Feelings of inferiority should be vigorously avoided at this stage, for it lies on the borderline of adolescence, an age fraught with self-doubt and feelings of inferiority and incompetence.

IDENTITY VERSUS IDENTITY CONFUSION (AGE 12 TO 18 YEARS). Childhood comes to an end, and the individual begins the roller coaster trip into adulthood. No time in life is so menaced by self-doubt. Nowhere else are the feelings so sensitive. Rarely will one again experience such heights of exhilaration and such depths of despair.

The individual is now on the way to becoming an independent man or woman, leaving behind the dependency of childhood. But what man or woman? What sort, patterned after whom? With what uniqueness?

This stage of life, according to Erikson, is crucial in making the sort of determinations and clarifications that establish personal identity. Early in life the child became aware of selfness. But that was a self seen as distinct from others. This new independent adult self is one apart from others, yet at the same time directed by them. It is a vague amalgamation of one's unique traits, self-perceptions, goals and aspirations, and the expectancies of others.

The individual now struggles with lingering questions, such as Who am I? What will I become? What can I do? What is my relation to others? How do others see me? In this struggle, this search, adolescents mimic many different heroes and try out, mostly in talk but partly in behavior, various life-styles. For adolescents life is a supermarket filled with mannequins, each exemplifying a style of human life. They are to be looked at, tried out, and accepted or rejected, one by one.

This identity shopping spree inevitably produces conflict with adults, especially parents, who have settled into comfortable life-styles and who have forgotten that they themselves had to go through the same experiments. Yet there is no compromising the situation. The young *must* explore. And conflict will result. As painful as this process is, for both adults and adolescents, it is natural and inevitable. Probably it is desirable, although it hardly seems so at times of conflict. Psychological weaning must occur. The young must leave the nest. Continued strong dependency of the young on the parents (or vice versa) forestalls identity development and stifles independent functioning.

DEALING WITH THE THREE I'S. Teachers and nonteachers alike speak of the three R's, which is fine for early academic training. But for in-school development of the personality it would be well if more thought were given to the three I's—Erikson's critical stages in the development of *initiative, industry,* and *identity,* the last three of the five stages just discussed.

The first I requires special attention during preschool and early primary years. Teachers should be ever conscious of the need children have for developing initiative as opposed to feelings of guilt.

The second I requires attention throughout the elementary school years. This is the period during which students have optimal opportunity to develop a lasting sense of industry as opposed to inferiority. Teachers can further this development by providing numerous interesting, worthwhile activities for children to do, activities that lead to a product bringing a sense of pride to children and their parents.

The third I absorbs students during their junior and senior high school years. They experience a continuing struggle for clarification of their sense of identity, a sense that will profoundly influence the remainder of their lives. Teachers can help by being sympathetic and understanding of the dynamisms responsible for much of adolescent behavior that seems disorganized, frenetic, irresponsible, and at times bizarre.

HAVIGHURST'S DEVELOPMENTAL TASKS

We saw how Erik Erikson identified and explained states in life that were critical in the development of key personality traits. Robert Havighurst looked at development from the same point of view. He identified many tasks that individuals must adequately accomplish at different points in life. He used and popularized the term "developmental task," which he defined as a task that "arises at or about a certain period in the life of the individual, successful achievement of which leads to his happiness and to success with later tasks, while failure leads to unhappiness in the individual, disapproval by society, and difficulty with later tasks" (Havighurst, 1953, p. 2).

Havighurst did not consider task accomplishment crucial to adequate personality development, as did Erikson. He saw the tasks as something more akin to rungs on a ladder to be climbed. You might miss two or three of the rungs and still get to the top. But hitting most of them at the right time increases both the ease and the pleasure of climbing the ladder.

Havighurst's stages within which the various tasks fell paralleled the stages that Erikson identified. Infancy to early childhood made up the first stage. Middle childhood made up the second. The third stage was preadolescence and adolescence. Except for the first, these stages coincide with Erikson's initiative versus guilt, industry versus inferiority, and identity versus role confusion. They include the tasks that have special importance for teachers.

INFANCY AND EARLY CHILDHOOD (BIRTH TO AGE 6 YEARS). Developmental tasks that come early in the first period, tasks such as learning to walk and to talk,

do not concern teachers. Tasks that come toward the end of the period, however, are important in the lives of kindergarten and first-grade students and therefore important to teachers. The following are among the tasks Havighurst identified:

1. Learning sex differences and sexual modesty. This task is being accomplished during the early primary school years. Boys and girls still have an unabashed natural tendency to explore each others' bodies. They are uninhibited in their movements and bodily positions, and they take little notice of whether dresses are down or pants are zipped. They are just beginning to notice that boys and girls at school go to different restrooms.

2. Forming simple concepts of social and physical reality. Children's conceptions of reality depend largely on their stages of intellectual development. Children at about age 6 years are just beginning to move from egocentric intuitive conceptions of the world to more detached and logical conceptions. This development will provide them with more accurate concepts of reality. It puts them on an intellectual level somewhat closer to that of teachers, and it permits more adequate interaction with topics commonly taught in school.

3. Learning to relate oneself emotionally to parents, siblings, and other people. This relationship implies a constructive ability to give and take. Previously, the child has been very self-centered. Only now does the realization begin to grow that other people have their own points of view that must be taken into account. Children are becoming able to cooperate and help, but they are still predominantly self-centered.

4. Learning to distinguish right and wrong and developing a conscience. Again, this task requires intellectual progression into the concrete operational stage. Even then, right and wrong are seen as applying mainly (and rigidly) to other people. Development of the conscience is a slow matter.

MIDDLE CHILDHOOD (AGE 6 TO 12 YEARS). Middle childhood was the phase where Erikson saw the opportunity and necessity for developing a sense of industry. Havighurst implies much the same in the tasks he lists for the period. Among them are the following:

1. Learning physical skills necessary for ordinary

games. This task has little importance for children in the primary grades. They come naturally equipped for the unorganized games they prefer. At about the age of 9 years, however, children become fascinated with organized, competitive games, many of which call for special skills in catching, throwing, running, and so forth. These skills then acquire paramount importance in the children's lives.

2. Learning to get along with age mates. Piaget wrote that verbal confrontations aided intellectual development in the young. Although primary teachers are not overly troubled with squabbling, teachers of middle-grade children might suspect that their students were all on the way to becoming geniuses. Verbal squabbles are the bane of their existence. Fusses and fights come as surely as day and night. Through these myriad confrontations, together with much teacher arbitration and counseling, children come slowly to the ability to get along with each other.

3. Developing fundamental skills in reading, writing, and calculating. In the main, this is what elementary school has been about. The three R's still play a dominant role in the curriculum, although far from an exclusive one. All subsequent learning is so dependent on these skills, especially on reading ability, that their importance as a developmental task can hardly be overemphasized.

4. Developing conscience, morality, and a scale of values. Toward the end of this period, the student can recognize and retain varying points of view, can make value judgments about them, and can describe many ideas about right and wrong. Conscience and morality are beginning to play important roles in life. Some of the newer instructional techniques in moral development and values clarification can help children accomplish this task more easily and fully.

5. Developing attitudes toward social groups and institutions. Awareness of other people, places, and conditions grows rapidly toward the end of this period. This awareness, combined with developing values and senses of right and wrong, thrusts students into positions of judging people and institutions. Proper attitudes toward other groups of people and toward organized ways of dealing with life problems require ac-

curate information, tolerance for viewpoints other than one's own, and a willingness to seek the worth inherent in others. Skillful teachers can help students avoid development of prejudice while establishing attitudes that recognize the good and value in all people.

PREADOLESCENCE AND ADOLESCENCE (AGE 12 TO 18 YEARS). Middle childhood was a time of inner calm and outward turmoil. Puberty puts an end to the inner calm. It signals the onset of what has been called the storm and strife of adolescence. Self-identity becomes the primary overlay on behavior. Doubts about the self abound. Relations with others run hot and cold. The feelings are ultrasensitive. Emotionality, rather than rationality, directs much of individuals' behavior. Havighurst's tasks for this period reflect the identity struggle that fills adolescents' lives:

1. Achieving new and more mature relations with age-mates of both sexes. Gone is unisex. Gone is the boy-girl group cleavage of childhood. Heterosexual relations step to the fore. And what a time of uncertainty and misgivings; peer relations assume gigantic proportions. Other-directedness becomes a way of life, as students search simultaneously for group and individual identity.

2. Accepting one's physique and using the body effectively. Almost all teenagers are dissatisfied with their physical appearance. They fervently regret that their nose, skin, hair, eyes, torsos, legs, and fingers do not look straighter, slimmer, brighter. They spend hours agonizing over the images in their mirrors. They want to look almost exactly like everyone else, except that they want to look better than they believe they do. Coming finally to accept one's appearance is a tedious process. Few people achieve it easily; some never do.

3. Achieving emotional independence of parents and other adults. Psychological weaning is a traumatic task to accomplish. One wants to be independent and grown up, yet one may yearn to remain a child at times. Independence is not given and accepted easily. Its achievement is marked with conflict and ill feeling. But the drive toward independence is strong. Without it one cannot move past the line that separates psychological childhood from psychological adulthood.

4. Desiring and achieving socially responsible behavior. The period of adolescence brings with it a rejection of adult authority along with rejection of many social institutions. Out of this pattern of rejection and rebellion must be pieced together a predisposition toward socially responsible behavior—behavior that, although critical, is also constructive. This outlook grows as students see that they do, in fact, have some control over their destinies. It grows as they are given opportunities to direct portions of their own school learning. And it continues growing with the realization that the earth is a finite space, its people and resources lying exposed, to be ravaged by the uncaring or conserved by the caring.

5. Acquiring a set of values and an ethical system as a guide to behavior. Value systems begin their growth in early childhood, but they do not become clearly definable until the later adolescent years. By this time the individuals have become more sure of themselves and of what is important, good, and right in life. Late adolescence can become a time of highest idealism, with individuals rallying around causes they consider necessary and just. Successful achievement of this developmental task gives a sense of direction and stability that will serve well during the coming adult years, when new life-styles, occupations, and personal relationships must be entered into.

PRINCIPLES OF DEVELOPMENTAL PSYCHOLOGY

You have seen how enlightened child rearing and educational practice rest on a foundation of developmental psychology. The information you have considered to this point can be synthesized into a number of commonly agreed-on principles of growth. These principles provide a concise guide to parents and educators.

Principle of environmentalism. *Human behavior is shaped by the environment.* The young learn what they live. They learn from the environment and adapt to it. They bring their inherited qualities, such as physical nature and native intelligence, into the environmental situation. Environmental factors then limit or enhance mental, physical, and emotional growth.

Principle of developmental growth. *Human growth is characterized by stages of development.* Human needs, abilities, and interests manifest themselves at certain stages or age levels. If one is to develop into a healthy person, needs must be satisfied when they are manifested. Mastery of tasks common to a given stage of development is necessary for success at the next level. Human developmental stages are universal, and each culture provides conditions for meeting growth points to the fact that the young are not miniature adults. They do not think like adults. They do not learn like adults. They do not socialize like adults. But they are in the process of becoming adults, by stages.

Principle of unified growth. *Human growth is an interrelated function of mental, physical, and emotional development.* Developmental psychologists believe that the intellect, the body, and the psyche are interdependent. One of them cannot be treated separately from the others. People bring their total beings into any learning experience. "The whole child" may be a cliché in education, but it is an important concept, nonetheless.

Principle of individual differences. *Individual growth and learning rates vary within general developmental norms.* The young grow and learn at different rates. Both heredity and environment affect these rates. Chronological age is not always a valid indicator of a student's ability to perform a given task. Developmental levels often span several years. Normal behavior, including interests and skills, ranges between the upper and lower age limits of a developmental stage.

Principle of readiness. *Optimal learning takes place only when the learner is ready.* Balanced factors of experiential background, mental maturity, physical ability, and emotional interest must be present for effective learning to occur. Havighurst calls this "the teachable moment." It is a waste of time, or even harmful, to try to force performance from individuals who do not have the maturity, interest, or experience for the task.

Principles of developmental psychology in practice

Today the foregoing principles of developmental psychology underlie most educational practice. A careful look at the school and its curricula show how educational practice is related to each of the principles.

Environmentalism applied. The school and classroom are clean and attractive in a functional way. The teacher maintains a warm, open, and accepting social climate. The school provides many learning resources, books, manipulative objects, films, records, real artifacts, and so forth. Field trips are available. The teacher prepares lessons, units, learning centers, and open experience instruction that add richness and variety to learning. The students find the school and the classroom enjoyable places to be. They like to work there. This is quite a change from the past.

Developmental growth applied. The classroom and curriculum reflect the growth levels of students. Short and varied activity periods are made to correspond to known attention span. Large and small muscle activities are stressed. Students begin their learning with manipulatable objects. Abstract thinking is introduced later, in the middle and upper grades. The curriculum is organized developmentally to capitalize on students' interests. Abundant opportunity is given for practice and skill mastery in all subject areas at each grade level. For students with learning problems, remediation is carried out so that later, more difficult tasks can be approached with confidence.

Unified growth applied. The school and classroom provide not only a stimulating environment to engage the intellect, but also a developmental program to foster physical health and growth. Physical skills are taught, not left to chance. Students are guaranteed recesses and lunch periods for exercise, toileting, and nutrition. Federally supported lunch programs provide food for those who can't afford it. It's hard to learn on an empty stomach. The ventilation and seating are checked regularly to be sure they are correct.

The teacher also maintains a healthy emotional climate in the classroom. Concern for values is evidenced through discussions, presentations, and values clarification techniques regarding social, ecological, and ethical subjects. Respect for individual rights, beliefs, and property is a byword. The teacher is a friend and counselor to the student. Most important of all, the school curriculum is designed with active learners in mind. Teachers realize that students learn best when active, when doing. The physical and the mental go hand in hand in learning.

Individual differences applied. Educators

know that individuals learn and grow at different rates. Within any class there will be a wide span of ability, interest, and social and physical maturity. Grouping students by ability is one way teachers have attempted to reduce the range of differences in the classroom. Sometimes this takes the form of "homogeneous grouping," wherein entire classes of students have similar abilities. Homogeneous grouping, however, is not a complete solution. Even within homogeneous classrooms there is sure to be a range of differences. More often, teachers have used "ability grouping" within classes. In many elementary classrooms the teacher will direct three or more reading groups, with each group working at a different level.

Grouped mathematics and spelling are also common.

Recently there has been a strong movement toward individualizing instruction. Commercial and teacher-made programs of individualized reading are in common use. Self-paced, programed teaching materials are available in practically all curriculum areas (Charles, 1976b). Commercially prepared multimedia teaching modules are in use. The learning center concept is widespread. Diagnostic-prescriptive teaching systems have been developed by school districts and industry to guide individual students through a multiplicity of skills in reading and mathematics. The more directed, competency-based, behaviorally oriented approaches to individualization are successful in presenting material in an orderly fashion. This allows students to achieve mastery at their own rates of learning. But because competency-based programs do not always satisfy the interests of learners, "open experience" learning is also provided. Here learners can explore topics free of strict guidelines and formal evaluation. In the final analysis, however, the teacher is the most crucial factor in making sure that the individual needs of the student are met.

Readiness applied. Ideally children begin their schooling with kindergarten. Kindergarten is not just play without purpose. Activities such as cutting, matching, organizing, pasting, and identifying shapes, colors, numbers, and letters are all readiness activities requisite to reading and mathematics. As adults we often lose sight of the fact that these simple, taken-for-granted skills are not second nature to the child but are major and essential items to be mastered. The kindergarten teacher develops listening skills and an interest in the printed page by reading stories to the children. The ability to follow directions is an outcome of directed play activity.

The child's knowledge of the world starts with family and neighborhood. The elementary school curriculum is designed to build on an ever-widening awareness of outside reality. Concepts of time and distance require years of maturity and experience. A second grader cannot really conceptualize history. For all he knows his grandfather and Plato were contemporaries. If the child lives in Los Angeles, a visit to San Diego represents just as great a trip as a visit to New York. The enlightened educator will acknowledge such facts and will not expect a true understanding of history and geography until intermediate school or high school. This does not mean that we do not introduce the telling of time or begin to make maps of our community in the early grades, for these are readiness skills that broaden concepts that can be built on when the student is maturationally ready.

But readiness does not end with young children. It is a factor that influences learning throughout our lives. Neither sixth graders, nor twelfth graders, nor you and I can learn new information unless we are "ready"—in the following sense:

1. We have the level of intellectual development necessary to deal with the concepts involved. Can 8-year-old Mary do logical, abstract reasoning?
2. We have the level of language development necessary to grasp the meanings of the words and other symbols involved. Can 16-year-old Juan, who is just beginning to learn English, learn the symbolism in Shakespearean sonnets?
3. We have the background of experiences necessary to allow us to relate the new information to things we already know. Can 12-year-old Susan grasp the mechanisms of the double helix arrangement in the DNA molecule?
4. We have the skills necessary to perform the new operations we are asked to learn. Can 22-year-old Oscar, who is 5 feet 3 inches tall, learn to play basketball for the New York Knickerbockers?

SUMMARY

These considerations of human development in physical, intellectual, and psychosocial areas have presented information considered important to teachers. You can see how human development influences education and how education in turn influences human development.

This information is vital to success in teaching. Yet, as is always the case, it will not mean very much to you until you have a hand in putting it to use. The next chapter will teach you how to study learners. When you carry out such a study, these ideas will come down out of the sky. They will become part of your way of thinking and doing and will help put the stamp of professionalism on your work.

SUGGESTED ACTIVITIES FOR FURTHER UNDERSTANDING

1. Arrange a visit to a sixth-grade class. Observe the students during recess. Note and record the various levels of physical development evident among them.
2. Invite a psychometrist or other qualified person to demonstrate the administration and interpretation of the Stanford-Binet or Wechsler intelligence test. Discuss possible uses of the test results.
3. Discuss the relative merits, as far as school practice is concerned, of viewing intelligence from the perspectives of Piaget, Guilford, and the traditional intelligence quotient.
4. Working in groups, indicate how specific subject matter can be enhanced by relating it to the known interests of students. Be specific as to subject and grade level.
5. Remembering your own past, identify specific ways you coped with selected developmental tasks that have been identified by Havighurst and Erikson.

REFERENCES

Aries, P. *Centuries of childhood*. New York: Alfred A. Knopf, Inc., 1962.

Bruner, J. *The process of education*. Cambridge, Mass.: Harvard University Press, 1962.

Charles, C. M. *Educational psychology: the instructional endeavor* (2nd ed.). St. Louis: The C. V. Mosby Co., 1976a.

Charles, C. M. *Individualizing instruction*. St. Louis: The C. V. Mosby Co., 1976b.

Compayre, B. *The intellectual and moral development of the child, part I*. New York: D. Appleton & Co., 1896.

Erickson, E. *Childhood and society*. New York: W. W. Norton & Co., Inc., 1950.

Erickson, E. Youth and the life cycle, *Children*, 1960, *7*, 45.

Gordon, I. J. *The teacher as a guidance worker*. New York: Harper & Row, Publishers, 1956.

Guilford, J. Three faces of intellect. *American Psychologist*, 1959, *14*, 469-479.

Havighurst, R. L. *Human development and education*. New York: David McKay Co., Inc., 1953.

Ilg, F. L., and Ames, L. B. *The Gesell Institutes child behavior*. New York: Dell Publishing Co., Inc., 1955.

Maslow, A. A theory of human motivation. *Psychological Review*, 1943, *50*, 370-396.

Meeker, M. *The structure of intellect: its interpretation and uses*. Columbus, Ohio: Charles E. Merrill Publishing Co., 1969.

Meeker, M., and Meeker, R. Strategies for assessing intellectual patterns in black, Anglo, and Mexican-American boys—or any other children—and implication for education. *Journal of School Psychology*, 1973, *11*, 341-350.

Papalia, D. E., and Olds, S. W. *A child's world: infancy through adolescence*. New York: McGraw-Hill Book Co., 1975.

Prescott, D. A. *The child in the educative process*. New York: McGraw-Hill Book Co., 1957.

Raths, L. Clarifying values. In R. Fliming (Ed.), *Curriculum for today's boys and girls*. Columbus, Ohio: Charles E. Merrill Publishing Co., 1966.

Raths, L., Harmin, M., and Simon, S. *Values and teaching*. Columbus, Ohio: Charles E. Merrill Publishing Co., 1966.

Wright, H. F. Observational child study. In P. H. Mussen (Ed.). *Handbook of research methods in child development*. New York: John Wiley & Sons, 1960.

SKILLS FOR STUDYING LEARNERS 6

In Chapter 5 you saw discussions of human development, with attention to aspects that have most importance to teachers and schooling. Emphasis was placed on physical, intellectual, and psychosocial development. Principles of developmental psychology and their applications were examined. The information presented there provided a general understanding of how students grow and develop and what this growth and development imply for education.

If you are to progress in your ability to understand students and work productively with them, you need to take a further step. You need to carry out a detailed study of an individual student in school. By doing such a study, you will gain much more precise knowledge of students as individuals, with their own special abilities and inabilities, interests, ways of working in school, and ways of relating to others. It is one thing to read about humans in general, but quite another to study one of them in particular. It is like the difference between reading about flowers and examining a carnation that you are holding in your hand.

This chapter provides the skills and suggested procedures that will enable you to carry out a study of an individual student.

LEARNER STUDY AS TEACHING TOOL

Learner study skills are practical skills for teachers and others who work with youth. They are, as we will see, easy to learn and apply in the classroom. Teachers who master these skills are more effective in dealing with problems of behavior and learning. Three traditional teaching concerns are (1) guidance and placement; (2) diagnosis of problems in behavior, health, and academics; and (3) evaluation of growth and learning. These are especially difficult to cope with if the teacher doesn't have the necessary tools. Competence in these areas distinguishes the truly professional teacher from the assignment giver or drill sergeant. Applying these skills will not make the job of teaching easier, but it will surely make it more effective and satisfying.

Competent teachers spend a good part of their time finding out about students so they can tailor appropriate learning experiences for each of them. Most teachers spend the first weeks of the school year learning about their students. Typically they learn to identify the student by name and determine prior academic achievement and other background information from cumulative records. They may also give informal inventories to assess academic proficiency and interests. Sometimes teachers just settle for scuttlebutt about their new students, which is passed around the lounge by teachers "who have had them before."

But there is more to learning about new students. For one thing, this learning shouldn't stop at the end of the second week of school. It is a continual process. The most effective teachers have an attitude, a philosophical point of view, that sets the uniqueness of each student above the stereotyped routines and fixed subject matter of teaching. The professional teacher views the school as an environment for learning that identifies and builds on students' talents, potentialities, and special needs.

Learner study is an ecological endeavor that even goes beyond the concept of "the whole person." For teachers to be knowledgeable about "the whole person," they must be aware of backgrounds, interests, needs, behaviors, and self-image. But more than this, the teacher must see the student as one who is both product of and participant in an environmental situation. The student affects the environment (including the teacher), and the environment affects the student. In the classroom environment there is a relationship of group members to one another. There is also a relationship of the individual and the group to things within the environment and to the total environment itself.

Sometimes, as teachers have experienced, the "balance of nature" within a classroom can be tipped by a spit wad, a fire drill, a visiting hamster, a verbal insult, or a new student. The result may

be negative, fistfight, lesson gone astray, wasted time. Or the result may be positive, leading to a good learning experience. In most cases the ecological balance of the classroom is not extremely precarious. But it helps to view the classroom as a habitat comprised of a group of people (adults and youth) who are interactive and interdependent on their environment. With such a viewpoint we may be more sensitive to the subtle effects of interpersonal relationships on the emotional climate of the classroom. We may be more inclined to see how subtle changes in the physical environment can affect attitudes and performance. Hopefully we will be better able to see ourselves as affecting positively or negatively the ecological balance of the classroom.

OBSERVATIONAL STUDY

The study of students by direct observation is a time-honored technique. Since 1890 there have been over 1,500 empirical studies of children and adolescents reported in development periodicals. One of the study techniques most commonly used is *observational study,* a collective name that covers various techniques including diary descriptions; anecdotal records; ecological records (specimen descriptions); checklists and rating scales, including trait ratings; time samplings; normative comparisons; and informal inventories (Wright, 1960). Observational study techniques are based on direct observation, recording, and analysis of student behavior as it naturally occurs. These techniques can be complicated or quite simple. For scientific studies, elaborate recording devices such as multiple movie cameras, video-, and audiotape recorders are used. Analysis may involve complicated rating scales and devices for content evaluation. For the average learner study, simple techniques are preferable.

Observational study skills use two approaches: *open forms* and *closed forms.* In open form observation all behaviors are recorded and analyzed. In closed form observation a research tool such as a checklist limits the observer to making note of specific, predetermined behaviors.

Diary descriptions

A traditional open form is the diary description. Diary studies of children have helped child development specialists determine behavior traits at various stages of development. Diary description is a longitudinal technique whereby a narrative record of a child's behavior is kept over a long period of time, often many years. Diary studies can suffer from biased selection, unreliable recording, inefficient gathering and processing of data, and unwarranted interpretation (Wright, 1960). In general, diary descriptions are not a practical tool for the teacher.

Anecdotal records

A useful technique for teachers is the *topical diary description,* better known as the *anecdotal record.* The anecdotal record is a brief account of student behaviors that are being observed and recorded for a specific purpose. Teachers most often use anecdotal records for noting the nature and frequency of misbehavior. Anecdotal record keeping is often the first step in programs of behavior modification, which will be examined in Chapter 17. In order to plan a strategy for behavior change, it is important to consider the behavior in its context, noting its causes and effects. Anecdotal record keeping may also follow a program of behavior modification or therapy as a means of evaluation. The following anecdotal record was made by a teacher who was trying to determine the reasons why two boys were fighting. She recorded five behavior episodes, each less than 3 minutes in length.

Monday 3/24, 11:40, lunch (outside cafeteria): Jeff and Larry fighting in lunch line. Mr. Markle approaches, and Jeff stops. Jeff initiates intimidation of Larry after Mr. Markle goes into lunchroom. John joins Larry. Soon all three boys appear to be discussing something.

Tuesday 3/25, 10:10, recess (playground): Jeff and John interrupt game in which Larry is playing. Jeff makes karate chop motions at Larry. Larry dodges. John grabs Larry from behind in a bear hug. Jeff resumes threatening gestures. Larry falls to ground, and Jeff threatens to kick him. Larry rolls over, reaches into his pocket, and gives Jeff something. Jeff and John leave.

Wednesday, 3/26, 11:42, lunch (outside cafeteria): Larry cuts in cafeteria line ahead of first graders. Mr. Markle sends him to end of line. Soon he is joined by Jeff who begins jabbing him in the back. This goes on

for a few moments until Larry gives Jeff something from his pocket.

Thursday 3/27, 10:05 (inside classroom): Before recess bell Larry complains to teacher of a stomachache. He asks to be sent to the nurse's office. At 12:00 he tells nurse he would like to go directly to the cafeteria for lunch.

Friday, 3/28, 8:45 (inside classroom): Larry tells teacher that his mother does not want him to play at recess. At 10:05 Jeff and John in corner of room standing over another boy. When teacher approaches, she discovers Larry sobbing quietly. All three boys claim nothing is going on. Teacher notices that Larry's front left pants pocket is reversed.

From this anecdotal record the teacher was able to determine that Larry was being forced to give Jeff his lunch money. Jeff often needed the presence of another boy, John, to carry out the threat. The teacher also discovered after a conference with Jeff that Jeff's mother was leaving for work at 6:30 AM and that Jeff was not getting breakfast at home. His lunch money was being spent on the way to school for candy. A subsequent conference with Jeff's mother solved the problem. Analysis of the problem by means of anecdotal record prevented the teacher from reacting to the outward manifestations of the behavior. The teacher could have punished both Jeff and Larry for fighting, compounding Larry's anguish and not solving Jeff's problem.

Anecdotal reporting is not without its limitations. Anecdotal records suffer from observer subjectivity. Brief and random observations may not provide a sequential relationship of observed behaviors. Observations motivated by spur-of-the-moment concerns may lack proper direction. However, the validity of anecdotal description may be improved by (1) identification of a problem by the observer, (2) objective selection of behavior specimens, (3) suspension of judgment while gathering data, and (4) analysis and interpretation of anecdotal records after all observations are completed.

Ecological records

Case study reports rely heavily on ecological records. This technique is also known as specimen records, on-the-spot running records, and running records (Wright, 1960, 1967; Cohen and Stern, 1958).

Ecological records are narrative descriptions of

student behavior in a natural habitat. The observer is interested in how the student behaves in typical situations of home, school, playground, clubhouse, or neighborhood. The ecological record is deliberately unselective. The observer records everything the student says or does. The technique is ecological in nature because the observer also records everything said or done *to* the student. The student's reaction to the entire situation is important. Careful notation of interaction with others and with various objects in the environment is also made.

Ecological recording is a longitudinal technique. The observer makes observations over a period of time. Eight weeks is about the shortest practical time span for ecological observations supporting a learner study report. Observation over an extended period of time is important because it can (1) show regression, stasis, or growth in social and adaptive behavior; (2) document behavior in a wider range of environmental situations; (3) bridge, rather than focus on, atypical events in the student's life; (4) document patterns of behavior and the conditions that trigger or accompany them; and (5) increase the validity of reporting and the information derived from observations.

Ecological observation sessions are typically 15 to 45 minutes in length. They are usually scheduled randomly. The purpose of the observation is deceptively simple: to see how the student behaves in a particular environmental situation. The observer does not observe with the idea of proving something. The observer does not have a predetermined checklist of behaviors to watch for, but instead faithfully records everything that goes on in strict behavioral terms. Great care is taken not to weave inferences or interpretations into the observations. If an on-the-spot interpretation of behavior is necessary, it must be separated from the factual description by parentheses or a notation at the end of the episode. Like anecdotal records, ecological records should be analyzed and interpreted after they are made. The observer does not generalize from a single episode of behavior. Accurate generalizations about behavior can only be based on the cumulative information contained in a series of behavior episodes.

The following behavior episode was taken from a study report done by a student teacher. It is a good example of ecological reporting.

Social interaction

NOVEMBER 22, 9:10 TO 9:30 IN MS. CALE'S ROOM, REYNOLDS SCHOOL
SELF-SELECTION TIME

(It is 2 days before Thanksgiving, and a group of children are up front with Ms. Cale peeling apples for applesauce; others are choosing their activities for self-selection.)

After being released for self-selection, Keith grabs the plastic dinosaur on his desk and runs across the room and up the steps. He is making growling noises and moving the dinosaur in swimming motions before him. Steven, Stevie, and Jimmy are on the steps playing Mouse Trap, and Keith sits down next to them. The four boys work together setting up the game. . . .

Keith: "Here Stevie, this piece goes here and then this one." Stevie takes the pieces and finishes setting up the game. The boys play with it quietly for about 5 minutes. Then Keith discovers that if you hit the mouse trap lever hard enough, the mouse will shoot up and land several feet away.

Keith: "Hey you guys look!" Keith hits the trap, and the mouse flys down the steps into the room. The boys giggle and scramble over each other and the bookshelf on the floor to get to it. Keith hits the mouse again, runs back up the steps, and then hits it again.

Keith (laughing): "Watch this time . . . look. Hey Stevie, give it back. It's my turn now."

Stevie: "No, I want it."

Keith: "Stevie!" He reaches to grab for the mouse. Stevie pulls away and falls back into the books; all the boys laugh.

This "new development" of the game continues for about 5 minutes. Keith lets the others have a turn hitting the mouse, but will crawl over anyone trying to pick it up first. Then Ms. Cale sees what is going on.

Ms. Cale: "You boys had best find something else to do that you can do quietly."

Jimmy stays to clean up the game, Steven and Stevie go with the first-graders who are building blocks, and Keith begins to hum to himself as he walks around the room. He doesn't touch anything but holds his dinosaur with both hands, shaking it up and down. After about 2½ minutes of this, Keith comes to the group peeling apples.

Keith: "What are you guys doing?"

Ms. Cale: "We're peeling apples for the applesauce, Keith."

Keith: "Applesauce, yuk! I hate applesauce."

Ms. Cale: "Don't you like apples and sugar and cinnamon?"

Keith: "Yes, but I hate applesauce."

Keith stands watching open mouthed for another minute, then drops to his knees and watches. The children neither welcome or reject him from their circle. Then Keith reaches over and grabs an apple peeling off the newspaper to eat. He grins and laughs. Jason and Mike laugh at him also and grab peelings to eat, but the girls yell "Keith" and tell Ms. Cale.

Ms. Cale: "Keith, you're not to eat the peels."

Keith: "Why?"

Ms. Cale: "Because if everyone did, we'd have a big mess all over the floor."

Keith continues to watch the group. He asks Crystal if he can peel her apple. She says no. He doesn't ask anyone else. When Ms. Cale leaves the group to go back to the sink, Keith immediately starts eating apple peels. Jason and Mike are laughing. Keith then drops to his knees and hands and crawls around the group barking like a dog. All the children think this is funny and feed him apple scraps.

Ms. Cale flicks off the lights as a signal to end self-selection. Keith jumps up from the floor, dives underneath the table, and runs across the room to his class with Miss Tison.

Guide for ecological observation and recording.
The episode you just read was structured by an observation guide. Here is a guide you may find helpful when making ecological observations.

PREPARATIONAL CONCERNS

1. Choose a student and identify the general purpose(s) of your study.
2. Plan to make a variety of observations of the student to include independent or quiet work, direct involvement with teacher, classroom (social interaction) activity, and out-of-classroom activity.
3. Have recording materials—pen, pencil, clipboard, paper—handy.
4. Observe and record unobtrusively. Stay within earshot. Do not indicate the purpose of your presence to the students. Be ready to say you are doing "teacher work" or make some noncommittal comment.
5. Arrange the timing of your observation so that you will have a period of free time immediately afterward to go back over your scribbles, abbreviations, and shorthand to clarify and fill in information while it is fresh in your mind.
6. Keep records confidential by using "subject" for student's name (or use fictitious names) and by guarding the records as you would your checkbook.
7. Suspend your prejudgments and knowledge of the student during observation periods. All val-

ue judgments and conjecture, if recorded, should be placed in parentheses.

OBSERVATIONAL CONCERNS:

1. *General situation, setting, environment.* Identify the task or activity the student is engaged in; note what others are doing, number of students, nature of the environment, proximity of the teacher, general noise or activity level, degree of teacher control, and tasks, restrictions, and schedules set by the teacher or inherent in the situation.
2. *Particular stimulus for behavior.* Identify persons with whom the student interacts, materials manipulated, the student's reactions to demands and comments of students and teachers, nonverbal communication, and the subject's reactions to surprises, unplanned changes in routine, and novel situations.
3. *Student's approach to activity.* Note the ability to work independently, self-reliance, and self-confidence. Does the student plunge in or hold back? How is interest in the activity manifested? Is the student concerned about orderliness and neatness; does the student approach the task impulsively, methodically, haphazardly? Note the degree of frustration and fixation. What does the student do when "stuck?" Identify the student's attention span and quality of "stick-to-itiveness." Does the student show an ability to concentrate on the activity? Does the subject see the activity as an end in itself or a means for socialization?
4. *Student's social interaction.* Note ways the student shows leadership, responsibility, self-sufficiency, sociability, personal appeal to others, emotional security and stability, domination over others, and dependability. Also note lacks. Does the child prefer one-to-one, small-group, or large-group situations? What kind of social contact is most comfortable? Most threatening?
5. *Student's energy-movement coordination.* Is work done at an even rate? Is the subject relaxed, tense, listless, lethargic, energetic? Does work begin in a nonpurposeful way and eventually calm down or vice versa? Does the student have coordination problems? Can materials be manipulated? Are body movements rigid?
6. *Student's tempo of work.* Does the subject

work deliberately or rapidly? Does the tempo vary with the type of activity?

7. *Student's attitude.* Does the subject share materials and cooperate? Does the subject prefer to work alone? Does the subject cope with problems in a positive manner? Is the subject aggressive, hostile, or withdrawn?

8. *Student's verbalization.* Does the subject hum or talk to self while working, shout, talk loudly, giggle, communicate in whispers? Is the subject's speech fluent, free of defects? Do the content and tone of speech differ when speaking to objects, imaginary friends, peers, younger students, older students, parents, teachers, or other adults?

Checklists and rating scales

Checklists and rating scales are also commonly used observational study tools. They are considered closed forms because their aim is to document and measure specific behaviors, events, or traits. With a checklist or rating scale, the observer is limited to recording only those things that relate to items defined and listed on the form being used. Checklists and rating scales range from simple teacher-made tally sheets to complex research instruments that produce a profile of behavior or personality traits.

Checklists and rating scales can be designed to serve a variety of purposes. They can do the following:

1. Assess the mastery of educational goals
2. Document the frequency of on-task and off-task behaviors
3. Note the nature and frequency of undesirable behaviors, such as fighting, bullying, hogging equipment, or yelling in the classroom
4. Document cause-effect relationships involving specific behaviors, events, environmental situations, times, activities, and persons
5. Assess emotional characteristics by noting behaviors of acceptance-rejection, liking-disliking, adventuring-withdrawing, independence-dependence, etc.
6. Identify personality traits or characteristics

Checklists differ slightly from rating scales. Checklists provide for a check or brief notation of the listed behavior or event that is being watched for. Checklists can give quantitative information when they provide for tallies of behavior. Rating scales go a step further. They require specified quantitive measures. For instance, a sample checklist item might be "The child begins appropriate work within 2 minutes after entering the classroom." The checklist requires an answer of "yes," "no," or "not observed" or a tally of answers appropriate to the behavior observed. The rating scale would require a quantitative measure, such as "less than 25% of the time," "25% to 50% of the time," "50% to 75% of the time," and so forth.

Rating scales should not be confused with "trait rating," a technique that involves checklisting of positive and negative personality traits, such as jealous, apprehensive, cheerful, conforming, friendly, competitive, respectful of authority, sullen, or independent. The observer uses a trait rating checklist to guide assessment of the individual's personality characteristics.

A perusal of human development materials can provide a wide variety of tried and proved checklists and rating scales that can be used in learner study. Some examples include Hendrick's *Social-Emotional Competence Scale* developed in the Santa Barbara City College Children's Center (Hendrick, 1975) and Stott's *Children's Behavior Checklist* (Stott, 1967).

If made by the teacher, checklists and rating scales must be carefully prepared. They need to cover appropriate developmental behaviors, interests, and needs. They need to list possible behaviors, events, or traits that relate to the purpose of the observation. They need to measure the standards and educational goals of the classroom or school in which they are used. They need to be interpreted with positive statements, such as "John is reluctant to share classroom materials; he often requires teacher attention and guidance in situations that call for cooperative play." The foregoing statement is better than saying: "John invariably hogs materials; he shows no cooperation, he threatens and bullies other children to the point of requiring disciplinary action."

Time samplings

Time sampling is another useful closed observation technique. In time sampling the observer records behaviors as they occur within uniform and short time intervals. The length, spacing, and numbers of intervals are procedural concerns. This technique can assess typical behaviors by means of very brief but scheduled observations. Observations are from 1 to 3 minutes in length. Intervals between observations may range from 15 minutes to 1 hour. Longitudinal studies may only require one observation a day (Wright, 1960).

Usually a checklist is employed with time sampling, but not always. Sometimes sketches of observed behaviors are made. Teachers most often use a variation of time sampling to assess the degree to which a child participates or stays on assigned tasks. One novel form of time sampling is used in an individualized high school reading program to measure involvement as a basis for grading. A student monitor circulates and observes students working in a reading laboratory with programed materials. The monitor occasionally notes each student's behavior in one of four categories: participation, nonparticipation, purposeful transition, or nonpurposeful transition. The students in the laboratory represent a wide range of ability. They are graded not on what they have mastered, but on the degree to which they have participated with purpose.

NORMATIVE COMPARISONS

Normative comparisons provide a single but useful approach to the study of individuals by comparing them with the behavioral and physical norms for their age group. The normative comparison gives the investigator a reliable guide to typical physical (height, weight, physical maturation, and coordination) and behavioral (interests, activities, needs, abilities, and social development) characteristics. This is particularly helpful to those who do not have a thorough professional background in human development. It gives them a frame of reference. But a word of caution is appropriate. So-called normal behavioral and developmental characteristics for a given age cannot be narrowly defined. Remember the principle of individual differences? A normative comparison is used to assess how the student compares with the norms, but cannot be used as a strict measure of normalcy. It functions best when there are considerable differences between the subject's development or behavior and that of the average student of the same age.

The following is a normative comparison of the same third-grade child we met in the ecological report.

Self-concept: Keith

A NORMATIVE COMPARISON
based on Erik Erikson's psychosocial stages (1950)

Keith's self-concept seems very poor. Because of events in his early childhood, he apparently did not resolve the first two key developments of Erikson's cycle: trust versus mistrust and autonomy versus shame and doubt.

According to the cumulative folders and Keith's grandmother, his legal guardian, Keith was kept isolated in his bedroom for 2 years just prior to age 3 years. He was allowed out to eat and watch television occasionally. He played with no other children, and there were no real toys to play with in his room. At that time he was living with his mother and stepfather. After his mother's death (Keith was about 3 years old), his grandmother gained custody.

This period of isolation may have built into Keith a basic mistrust of people. He is fearful of people leaving him, is upset by his constant change of babysitters, and identifies so closely with the one teacher he has had for more than a year (Miss Tison) that it is difficult for anyone else to control him. When he first arrived at Reynolds School as a kindergartner, he was afraid of the dark, closed doors, loud noises, and anything new.

When Keith's "sense of self" began to emerge, he had little chance to develop "successful behavior." The only two adults he had contact with seemed to reject him; it must have seemed to him that he was constantly being punished, whatever his behavior. Keith seems now to expect punishment, and he has difficulty distinguishing which behaviors will, and will not, get him into trouble.

Whenever a teacher pulls him aside to speak with him, his first response is "Am I in trouble?" Yet when he is punished for inappropriate behavior, he's "never done anything. Everyone always picks on me."

At this time Keith is still working at the initiative phase. He is still exploring a world that most of us know and take for granted. He becomes aware of things in his environment that we see everyday. Keith is noticing them for the first time. Just last year he discovered flags. He had been saying the Pledge of Allegiance for 3 years and never fully realized that a flag was behind it. He became very excited about the whole idea, looked up flags in the encyclopedia and drew pictures of them. (This fact was related by Miss Tison, his special education teacher.) Keith needs more time to work out his initiative phase, but this can be trying for teachers in a classroom environment where exploration must be somewhat controlled.

Within the last 2 months, I have noticed Keith becoming more aware of himself and his achievements in relation to his other classmates. He seems to be realizing that he doesn't do as well as others in his English and

Student's name _____ Age _____ Date _____

PROJECT POINT INTEREST INVENTORY

1. When I go home I _____ .
2. The thing I like to do best with my family is _____ .
3. My job at home is _____ .
4. My family goes mostly to _____ .
5. On weekends I usually _____ .
6. The thing I like to do best is _____ .
7. What I don't like to do is _____ .
8. I mostly play with _____ .
9. My best friend is _____ .
10. The person who helps me the most is _____ .
11. The thing my family likes best to do together is _____ .
12. My favorite TV show is _____ .
13. My favorite subject in school is _____ .
14. My least favorite subject in school is _____ .
15. My favorite kind of book is _____ .
16. When I am not in school I like to read _____ .
17. I usually go to bed at _____ .
18. Pets we have at home are _____ .
19. My favorite pet would be _____ .
20. I earn money by _____ .
21. If I could be someone else I'd like to be _____ .
22. My favorite game or sport is _____ .
23. My hobby is _____ .
24. I'm really good at _____ .
25. I'd really like to have _____ .

Here is a list of things that some boys and girls like to do in their spare time. If you *never* do the thing shown, leave the line blank. If you like to do it, make one check on the line. If you like to do it *very much,* tell something about it.

Watch TV _____ Play games inside _____
Draw or paint _____ Play cards _____
Read books _____ Tease _____
Play sports _____ Cook _____
Make things with tools _____ Make models _____
Collect things _____ Fix things _____
Experiment with science _____ Swim _____
Talk _____ Roller skate _____
Play an instrument _____ Ice skate _____
Dance or sing _____ Go to the movies _____
Write letters _____ Walk or ride around _____

history class, and it bothers him; he calls himself "dumb" and "stupid." Miss Tison told me that for the first time Keith is becoming aware of failure. This would indicate that Keith is facing the industry versus inferiority conflict. How well he resolves it depends on how often he is given a chance to succeed and how he is taught to handle his failures.

INFORMAL INVENTORIES

The term "informal inventories" covers a wide range of devices including checklists, rating scales, questionnaires, and simple tests. They are designed to give the investigator some knowledge of the student's abilities, attitudes, and interests. Teachers commonly use informal inventories to determine academic placement. Informal inventories can supplement observational study. In fact, we recommend that they be used to provide supplementary information in case studies. In child study procedure, informal inventories should be given after all observations of the child have been completed. The inventories can be scheduled into regular classroom periods. They should be administered to students other than the subject, so the subject will not feel singled out. If arrangements are carefully made, the subject will not be aware that he is being studied.

Since we have already discussed checklists and rating scales, we will turn to the *attitude and interest inventory*. Attitude and interest inventories are simple questionnaires that can elicit a good deal of information about the subject. Most often they are teacher made, with specific purposes in mind. Usually they consist of a list of questions with a space for the student to provide an answer. Younger children and nonreaders may need to have the questions read to them and their answers recorded. The boxed material on p. 102 is an ex-

---

INFORMAL READING INVENTORY: JOHN V., AGE 13 YEARS

San Diego Quick Assessment

In this test John was presented a series of cards, each of which listed ten words determined to be representative of a given functional grade level. His task was to pronounce and identify the words on each list. Results of this assessment indicate that John should be able to independently read ninth-grade material. Instructional materials should be of a difficulty between ninth and tenth grade, and he may be frustrated with material at the eleventh-grade level. John's word recognition skills appear to be above his actual grade level.

Phonics Skills Assessment

In this test John was asked to pronounce a series of nonsense words categorized to demonstrate the various phonics skills. The only category in which he had any difficulty was in determining whether to pronounce the hard or soft C and G sounds. However, after a brief review of the general rule relating to this pattern, he demonstrated proficiency in this category as well.

Informal Reading Inventory

In this test John was asked to orally read printed paragraphs that corresponded in difficulty to a given functional grade level. Any problems he had in reading the paragraphs were noted, and after reading each paragraph he was asked a series of comprehension questions. The highest level paragraph available in this assessment was rated at the eighth-grade level. At the eighth-grade level John had almost no difficulty with respect to word recognition and scored 100% on the comprehension questions.

Diagnostic Spelling Test

In this test John was orally given a series of words to write that were classified as being representative of given grade levels. John had reported that spelling was an area in which he was having some difficulty. The results of the test placed him at about the seventh-grade instructional level. One must note the rather wide range in his demonstrated ability to read printed words (between ninth- and tenth-grade instructional levels) and his ability to correctly spell words given him orally.

ample of an interest inventory that has been used with success by a great number of teachers.

Two popular informal measures used to determine reading ability are graded word lists and graded paragraphs. Although these inventories can be teacher made, it is easy to find institutionally developed or commercially available assessments. One popular word list is the *San Diego Quick Assessment*. Popular commercial informal reading inventories include materials by Silvaroli and by Sucher-Allred.

The boxed material on p. 103 is an excerpt from a student's report on John V., a 13-year-old seventh grader.

Intellectual assessment

One of the most important things teachers can find out about students, particularly at the elementary level, is the level of intellectual functioning at which they can operate. This information can be obtained by having students respond to a series of tasks, based on Piaget's findings. These tasks correspond to "stages" of intellectual development, which you saw described in Chapter 5.

First- and second-grade teachers can expect several of their students to be at the intuitive thought stage and several of them at the concrete operations stage. A few students in fourth grade are still functioning mainly at the intuitive stage. Fifth-grade teachers can expect several students to be at the concrete operations stage, several at the formal operations stage, and maybe one or two still at the intuitive level.

You can tell by behavior, speech, and academic performance which levels characterize most of your students. Some students will puzzle you. You can't tell whether their failure to perform is an intellectual or an instructional matter. There are some easily made and administered tasks you can use with these students to reveal their levels of intellectual functioning. If you will put together the following sets of task materials and use them with students, you will find the results most enlightening.

Task 1. Right-left

Materials: None
Procedures: Say "Show me your right hand. Good. Show me your left hand. Show me your right leg.

Show me your left leg. Good. Now take your right hand and touch your left leg."
Interpretation: This task is done successfully by most students in the second half of the intuitive thought stage. It requires holding semicontradictory ideas in the mind at the same time.

Task 2. Image reproduction

Materials: One pipe cleaner, pencil, and paper.
Procedures: Say "See this wire?" Hold it straight horizontally. "I'm going to bend it like this, and a little bit more, until it is completely bent like this."

Remove the wire. Give pencil and paper to the child. Say "Now I want you to draw me a picture of what the wire looked like before I started bending it." Wait for the drawing. "Now draw what the wire looked like after I had bent it a little bit." Wait. "Now draw a picture of what the wire looked like after I had finished bending it."
Interpretation: This task reveals whether the student can hold a progressive series of images in the mind. Successful accomplishment is an indicator of movement from intuitive thought into concrete operations.

Task 3. One-to-one correspondence

Materials: Fifteen wooden blocks.
Procedures: Take six blocks and place them in a row. Say "See if you can make a row of blocks that is just like mine. Is yours just like mine? Good." Lengthen or compress your row. "Now where are there more blocks—in your row, in my row, or is there just the same in both rows?"
Interpretation: One-to-one correspondence must be established, or the test is terminated. Look to see whether the correspondence is maintained even when the blocks are rearranged. This maintenance of correspondence is essential to the development of number concepts.

Task 4. Number conservation (snacks)

Materials: Twenty small objects of the same size—tiny blocks, jelly beans, or pieces of breakfast cereal such as Trix. Ten should be of one color and ten of a second color.

Procedure: Place the ten objects of one color on the table in this arrangement: Say "Let's pretend these are your delicious snacks, this many for this morning (top group) and this many for this afternoon (bottom group)."

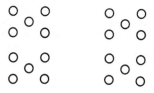

Place the other ten objects beside the first ones: "These are your snacks for tomorrow. This many for tomorrow morning (top) and this many for tomorrow afternoon (bottom)."

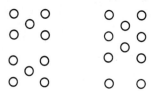

"On which day do you have more snacks to eat—more today, more tomorrow, or just the same for both days?" If student says "same," continue. "Let's pretend a funny thing happens tomorrow. You are *so* hungry in the morning that you eat this many (move three from the bottom group up to the top group, so the groups look like this)."

"Now when do you have more snacks to eat—more today, more tomorrow, or the same both days? Why?"

Interpretation: Children still functioning at the intuitive thought stage will center on the group of eight or the group of two, and say there are either more or fewer to eat tomorrow. If they reply that there's still the same, they are conserving number, a characteristic of the concrete operations stage. If they can conserve number, they are intellectually capable of learning and using basic number operations with understanding. If they cannot conserve number, they should continue instruction in number readiness, manipulation, and, some people believe, rote memorization of addition and subtraction facts, done through singing, clapping, and chanting.

Task 5. Conservation of two-dimensional area (cows and pastures)

Materials: Two rectangles of green felt, 6 x 4 inches, attached with rubber cement to a tag board (make the tag fold so that when closed the edges of the felt match exactly); two tiny cows, or other animals; twenty small blocks, all of one color. (Monopoly houses or hotels are good. These are to be barns, but they needn't be larger than the cows.)

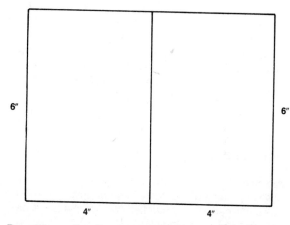

Procedure: Say "Let's pretend these are two pastures of grass, one for you and one for me. Who has more grass—you, or me, or do we have just the same?" Same. Student must be convinced. Help if necessary. "Now, here's a cow for your pasture, and here's a cow for my pasture. Which cow has more grass to eat—your cow, or my cow, or do they have just the same?" Same. "Good. Now let's pretend we want to build some barns for our cows—one for yours, one for mine; another for yours, another for mine; another for yours, another for mine, etc. . . .

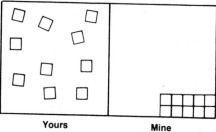

Now which cow has more grass to eat—yours, or mine, or do they have just the same?"

Interpretation: Ability to recognize, despite appearances, that equal amounts of grass remain develops, on the average, about halfway through the concrete operations stage.

Task 6. Floating bodies

Materials: Five objects of approximately the same size, but of different densities, for example, marble, wooden bead, small piece of Styrofoam, metal nut or washer, and pencil eraser.

Procedures: Place the five objects before the student and say "Suppose you were to put these in water. Which of them do you think would float and which do you think would sink? Tell me why in each case."

Interpretation: Look not for correct or incorrect answers, but for the reasoning processes used. Check for responses that relate to the weights of the objects compared to water. These indicate intellectual advances beyond statements such as "metal doesn't float," "wood floats," etc. Such advanced logical thought processes appear toward the end of the concrete operations stage.

Task 7. Conservation of three-dimensional space (hotels)

Materials: Twelve 1-inch cubes (plastic or wooden blocks); piece of tag board with the following rectangles outlined with felt marker. (Do *not* include numerals that show the dimensions.)

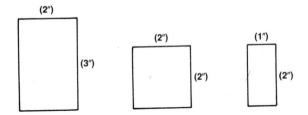

Procedures: Place the twelve cubes on the 2 × 3 inch rectangle. Say "This is a hotel. Each block is one room in the hotel. The owner of this hotel wants to build another hotel on this piece of land (point to 2 × 2 inch outline). He wants it to have just the same number of rooms as this first one. How many stories high do you think it will have to be, so it will have just the same number of rooms?"

Have student predict, then allow to verify by using blocks to build new hotel.

Repeat procedure for 1 × 2 inch plot.

Interpretation: Look for rapid mental calculation of number of stories. Student must coordinate three variables simultaneously. Although this is a conservation task, success indicates movement into the formal operations stage.

Task 8. Word problem (liver)

Materials: Card with the following statement, which you read but do not show to student.

"I am glad that I do not like liver, because if I liked it, I would always be eating it, and I detest eating things I don't like."

Procedure: Read the statement to the student. Ask "What's strange about that statement?" Repeat if necessary.

Interpretation: Look for recognition of verbal absurdity. Recognition plus explanation for absurdity indicates formal operational thought.

Task 9. Word problem (baking)

Materials: Card, one side containing this statement: "A cook wishes to test the effects of baking times and temperatures on a new cake. If he selects the following temperatures: 350°, 375°, and 400°, and the following baking times: 30 minutes, 45 minutes, and 60 minutes, how many different experiments must he conduct?"

The other side contains the pertinent data:

Temperatures: 350° 375° 400°
Times: 30 minutes 45 minutes 60 minutes

Procedure: Read the question to the student. Place the card before the student, so that the temperature and time figures show.

Interpretation: Ask student to verbalize thought processes. Watch for experiments with various combinations, carried out mentally. Correct answer (nine) is not essential, but should result if the operational processes are utilized properly. Success indicates adult-level thought.

Use of these nine tasks should enable you to pinpoint the intellectual stage of students from kindergarten through high school. Throughout, one looks for thought processes that are being used, not for correct or incorrect answers. Technically, all responses that students make are correct for their stage of intellectual development.

The instructional implications are clear: Know what to expect of students; know what they can and cannot do at their stage; and don't expect performances from them that they are intellectually incapable of providing. Too often we expect the impossible. The results are anxiety, frustration, and sense of failure for student and teacher alike.

Affective assessment

To work most effectively with students, we need to know about their feelings, emotions, and relationships with others. Projective writing and sociograms can be helpful in revealing this information.

Projective writing. Projective writing can help the investigator understand the feelings and emotional concerns of the student. One of the most common and useful projective devices is the autobiography. Students can be asked to write an autobiography as a literature assignment. Students reveal a great deal about themselves in autobiographies—their home life, their relationships with others, their fears, their problems of identity, and their internal conflicts over competing values and loyalties.

Preschoolers and primary grade children often express themselves in artwork. The content of a drawing or painting can be a direct statement about the child's feelings. Often it is symbolic (Prescott, 1957). A recent visit to a kindergarten class introduced me to a child who, when given the opportunity to paint, painted only a large single eye. The student teacher in the classroom initially labeled the child as "really weird." Subsequent study revealed that the boy's parents were highly religious people who made frequent references about "the watchful eye of God."

Creative expression can also act as a catharsis for blocked feelings. The creative writing of adolescents is especially fertile soil for study. Young people will often write on themes reflecting personal concerns that they will not freely discuss with adults. Although this writing can be revealing, a word of caution is in order. The average teacher is not trained to make psychological interpretations of projective writing. Therefore most investigators are wise to stick with the obvious and not play the game of amateur psychoanalyst.

Sociograms. A sociogram is a device used to measure social relationships within a group. Basically, it is a diagram that graphically illustrates inter-

personal relationships. By employing a sociogram, an investigator can determine patterns of leadership, friendships, cliques, and rejection.

In order to plot a sociogram, the teacher needs to ask each student at least two confidential questions: "Who would you choose first to be your friend? Who would you choose last to be your friend?" The questioning should be done as a part of planning for group work. The answers, written on cards or pieces of paper, are plotted below.

In our sample sociogram Lance is the "star."

Four classmates have chosen him. In contrast, Janis is an "isolate." She gave no choice of friend and was rejected by two of her classmates. Sue and Mary made "mutual choices" of friendship. Mary was also valued as a friend by Linda and Sally, who have rejected each other. One might suspect that there is some jealousy over Mary between these two. Steve has not chosen a boy as friend, and Dave and Jeff have rejected him. Steve, in turn, has rejected Janis. There is a "chain" of friendship ties beginning with Steve and

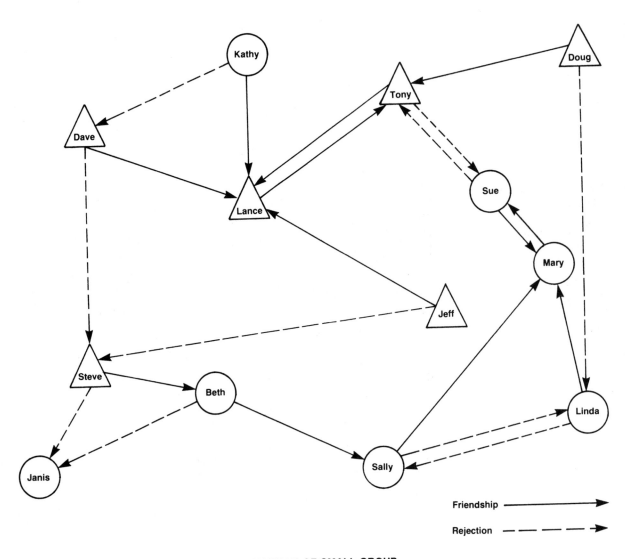

SOCIOGRAM OF SMALL GROUP
Showing patterns of friendship and rejection

ending with Mary. This sociogram of a small group provides us with some useful information. If we want to choose natural group leaders, the sociogram indicates Lance and Mary. If we want to identify youngsters who need a friend and perhaps lack self-esteem, we might begin with Janis and Steve.

Sociograms provide insight into social relationships that may not be apparent on the surface. They are of value in solving problems of an interpersonal nature. But there are some cautions: Sociogram data, like fish, are good only when fresh. Friendships and allegiances can change over a short period of time. Also, sociograms may run the risk of recording a temporary falling out of friends and not give a true picture. Some school districts forbid the administration of sociograms because of parental complaint. Unfortunately, there continue to be instances when the purpose of the sociogram is questionable and its data not protected by professional confidence.

BACKGROUND INFORMATION

Studies of learners usually include the collection and analysis of background information. Case study reports open with a brief description of the subject and a statement of the purpose of the study. But paradoxically, learner study should not begin with a thorough review of a student's background. This comes later, after observational study and perhaps after normative comparisons and informal inventories are completed. The careful student of behavior wants to learn just enough about a subject to guide the study objectively. Bias enters when one is too well acquainted with the perceptions of other people. This does not mean that the sources of background information are entirely subjective. But the fact is that some sources, such as teacher opinion, can be subjective and misleading. In some cases they do more than reflect a student's problem; they contribute to it.

Cumulative records

Cumulative school records are the most widely used source of school-related information about students. Cumulative records, or "cum cards" as they are often called, are started for each child beginning in public school. These records are kept at the school and updated from kindergarten through twelfth grade. When a child moves, his cum record is sent to his new district. Most cum records are in the form of files that can be easily stored in regular office file cabinets. The cum folder is most often a standard form providing for the notation of various kinds of information about the child. Cumulative record data include:

1. *Family data.* Full names of parents; names, ages, and birth order of siblings; names of others who live in the home; parents' occupations; present and previous addresses; language spoken in the home; and some family history.
2. *Health and growth data.* Preschool health history; illnesses, their cause and treatment; absences caused by ill health; referrals to school nurse, doctor, or welfare personnel; results of visual and auditory testing; measurement of height and weight (should be recorded every 6 months); condition of teeth; and need for medication.
3. *Test data.* Dates and scores (and sometimes interpretation) of all tests administered to the student, including intelligence tests, readiness tests, standardized achievement tests, aptitude tests, and diagnostic tests for learning disabilities.
4. *Academic record data.* Brief record of the child's academic performance; present and past teachers and classroom assignments; special scholastic accomplishments in scholarship, athletics, and music; and personal interests and activities.
5. *Teacher comment data.* Brief record of comments made by each of the child's teachers. These comments are sometimes anecdotal in nature. Often they refer to the child's character traits. This section of the cum record can be highly subjective. In recent years it has been the subject of controversy. Teachers are now urged to keep their comments positive, professional, supportable, and nonlibelous. This has come about because parents now have the legal right to see their child's cum records.
6. *Other data.* Correspondence, reports, and other documents that relate to the student's school life and general well-being.

Laws protecting personal privacy have had the effect of restricting access to school records to school personnel and the student's parents or guardians. In most cases, student teachers assigned to the school have access to records, but this depends on district policy. University students and others who are not employed by the school district will most likely be denied access to cum records regardless of the fact that their child study assignment is a bona fide college requirement.

Teacher conferences

One of the first things the investigator should do is consult the teacher of the student. This is especially true if school records will not be available to the observer. The teacher can provide a great deal of information about the student that will be helpful in a case study. Close cooperation between teacher and student teacher (or college student) will pay dividends. Often a classroom teacher can help the student select a likely subject for study. When this is done, both student and teacher can benefit from the study. It is advisable that students doing a study be entirely open about their assignment. The offer of sharing the results of the study with the classroom teacher encourages cooperation from school personnel and mandates professional reporting on the part of the student teacher.

Parent conferences

Parent conferences are not advisable unless the investigator is also the student's teacher or student teacher. Contacts with parents should generally be left to school personnel. Parent conferences should not be called for the purpose of gaining information for a child study. All parent conferences should have a definite purpose, such as grade and progress reporting; review of health or behavior problems; the need for testing, remediation, or special assignments; and academic retention or advancement. Information for a case study should be a by-product of the parent conference.

Home visits by teachers used to be a widespread and beneficial practice. This is unfortunately no longer true. The home visit is a practical reality only in smaller communities. A person doing a child study should not contact parents or make home visits without the consent, encouragement, and cooperation of school personnel.

Community study

Community study data can provide important background information for the child study. In Chapter 4 you learned how to study the community.

PREPARING A CASE STUDY REPORT
Case study report format and content

The case study report is the product of careful observation of student behavior and analysis of all relevant information. The typical case study relies heavily, but not entirely, on ecological records. Other approaches that we have considered provide further detail. For instance, specific information about the family background, academic history, medical history, and level of cognitive development cannot be derived from observational study. The case study worker should consult cumulative records, confer with the teacher, use rating scales, make normative comparisons, and perhaps administer informal assessments in order to get a complete picture of the student. A profile of the student as measured by various techniques gives a stronger base for interpretation of problems and needs.

This brings us to an important point. The case study report should be more than an academic exercise. Every case study should result in recommendations for teachers, and possibly parents. A good case study will provide the teacher with great insight regarding (1) the cause and nature of the student's learning difficulties, (2) the student's social and emotional adjustment, and (3) the student's interests and capabilities. The case study is indeed the professional starting point for an individual program of guidance.

A format and content outline of a case study is as follows:

I. Introduction and identification data section. This section should contain the following:
   A. A brief description of the student you have studied (age, sex, position in family, grade, school, socioeconomic and ethnic background) and the reasons for studying this particular person. It is wise to use fictitious names to protect the subject.
   B. A list of persons (their fictitious names and positions or relationship to the subject) referred to in the observational report. (Actual names should be submitted on a separate card.)
   C. A chronology of your observation (date, amount of time spent, observation environment and locale, situational purpose of observation, and page in section II of the report that contains the ecological records). For example: 11/1/78, 30 minutes; Mrs. Smith's third-grade classroom,

Wilson School, observation of social interaction, pp. 6-7 of field notes (ecological record).

II. Ecological record section. This section should contain the following:

A. Ecological records of the observations in chronological order (each record prefaced by date, amount of time spent in observation, observation environment and local, and situational purpose of observation). A case study should be based on the ecological records of at least eight separate behavior episodes.

B. Interpretations of each ecological record, if necessary. All interpretations and supplementary information related to behavior observed should be kept separate from the straight factual reporting of what is seen and heard. Normally interpretations, conjecture, and related information should be appended at the end of the observation report.

III. Normative comparison section. This section should contain the following:

A. Subject's physical development (height and weight) compared to published norms.

B. Subject's interests and mastery of developmental tasks compared to norms defined by Havighurst, Gesell and Ilg, or other developmental psychologists.

C. Subject's psychosocial development compared to Erikson's stages.

IV. Informal inventory section. This section should contain the following:

A. Attitude and interest inventories.

B. Informal assessments of reading level or readiness for reading.

C. Intellectual development as measured by performance on the Piagetian tasks.

D. Other checklists, rating scales, and measures of the child's social, physical, and intellectual characteristics.

E. Projective measures of the student's self-image.

F. Sociogram data showing patterns of friendship, acceptance, and rejection, if allowed by the school.

V. Background data section. This section should contain the following:

A. Information from cumulative (school) records.

B. Information from conferences with the subject's teachers.

C. Information from conferences with the subject's parents (optional and possibly not advisable for beginning teacher trainees).

D. Information from community study reports that may have a bearing on the case.

E. Analysis of the academic and creative work that the subject produces.

VI. Final conclusions section. This section should contain the summary and analysis of information about the student gained through ecological records, normative comparisons, informal inventories, and background data.

VII. Recommendations section. This section should contain, as a result of the study's findings, the following:

A. A list of behavioral objectives designed to help the teacher foster an improvement in the student's intellectual, physical, social, and/or emotional growth.

B. Necessary recommendations for referrals to appropriate school or community specialists, such as those listed here:

1. School nurse or doctor: for general health problems, injury, physical disability, disease, and personal hygiene; also for suspected visual handicaps.

2. Speech and hearing pathologist: for hearing and speech handicaps.

3. School psychometrist: for learning disabilities, evaluation of mental capacities, interests, testing.

4. School psychologist: for persistent emotional or psychological problems.

5. Social worker: for evidence of physical abuse, malnutrition, desertion, etc.

6. Bilingual or bicultural teacher: for language problems or lack of understanding because of cultural differences.

The foregoing is an ideal format and content for a thorough case study. A briefer form of case study can be done omitting the normative comparisons, informal inventories, and some aspects of the background data section.

ETHICS AND ETIQUETTE OF LEARNER STUDY

If you are going to conduct a study you should have, *and use,* common sense. You should also be courteous and professional. When you undertake a learner study, you assume responsibility for protecting privileged information. You are in a position of trust. A study may reveal information that is personal and private. Nonprofessional handling of such information may hurt the student. It could even result in a charge of libel against you the investigator. You can avoid problems by following some simple rules.

1. *Gain permission to study the student.* Observations in schools will require the permission of the principal and the subject's teacher. Inform school personnel of the purpose and nature of your study. Be prepared to abide by school or district policy, which may impose certain restrictions (for instance, you may not be allowed to see the cumulative record).

2. *Keep the case study school based.* Do not call parents. Many parents are justifiably concerned about personal privacy. They will not always appreciate home inquiries made by college students. Leave parent contact to school personnel. You should avoid observations in the home and interviews with parents unless you are encouraged to do so by both school personnel and parents. If the classroom teacher invites you to sit in on a parent-teacher conference, do so.

3. *Cooperate with school personnel.* Do not pull rank with school personnel or parents. As a student, your opportunity to observe a student is a privilege, not a right. Visiting students and student teachers are guests and should behave like guests. The sincere and courteous student will often be given a great deal of help and latitude in conducting a study.

4. *Focus on observed fact; avoid hearsay.* Record only observed behavior and factual data. Avoid inferences, conjecture, and statements that are value judgments. Do not record hearsay information regardless of source. Do not press the student, the teacher, or the parents for confidential or emotionally charged information. If such information is freely given, its inclusion in a report is up to your good judgment. Great care must be taken not to make statements that are libelous. For example, one might say: "The subject's grandmother cares for him on weeknights until his mother returns from work." This is better than saying, "The subject has to stay with his grandmother on weeknights because his mother usually makes the singles' bar scene after work and does not get home before midnight."

5. *Provide anonymity for your subject.* Unless a case study is being done by a professional, it is best to avoid real names of persons and places involved. It makes sense to protect the subject, teachers, school, and yourself. Fictitious names should be used. The student studied can be referred to as "subject." If the case study is to be submitted to an instructor in fulfillment of professional classwork, a card with actual names may be submitted separately. The same procedure is advised if a report is to be utilized by school personnel.

6. *Keep the report positive.* A case study report should always be constructive in tone and approach. Diagnosis of problems and needs is a valid concern of the case study. But references to the source and nature of problems must be handled with discretion. Blame laying and fault-finding serve no constructive purpose. Explicit criticism of parents, peers, teachers, neighborhood, or school has no place in the study. Recommendations should be based on fact and stated in constructive and positive ways. Not only is a positive, constructive approach professional, it is also practical. The findings of your report are far more likely to be accepted, valued, and acted on by school personnel if you are positive in your remarks.

SUGGESTED ACTIVITIES FOR FURTHER UNDERSTANDING

1. Arrange to observe an individual student at work in the classroom, at play, or in leisure activities with others. Take careful notes, but do not make it evident that you are observing.
   a. Describe the individual's social interaction in terms of leadership, dominance, submissiveness, sociability, and emotional security.
   b. Describe the individual's overall tempo of movement—fast, jerky, lethargic, measured, systematic, etc.
2. Interview a student and complete an interest inventory, following the form presented in this chapter.
3. Select a student of age 6 or 7 years. Administer the first four Piagetian tasks described in this chapter. Interpret the results in terms of the student's readiness for mathematics.
4. Select a student of age 11 years or older. Administer Piagetian tasks 8 and 9 described in this chapter. Interpret the results in terms of the student's readiness for doing highly abstract reasoning.
5. As a major class project, carry out a detailed study of a selected student, following the topics and techniques outlined in this chapter.

REFERENCES

Charles, C. *Teachers petit Piaget.* Belmont, Calif.: Fearon Publishers, 1974.

Cohen, D., and Stern, V. *Observing and recording the behavior of young children.* New York: Teachers College Press, 1958.

Dowley, E. Cues for observing children's behavior. *Childhood Education,* 1969, *45,* 517-521.

Erikson, E. *Childhood and society,* New York: W. W. Norton & Co., Inc., 1950.

Gordon, I. *Studying the child in school.* New York: John Wiley & Sons, Inc., 1966.

Hendrick, J. *The whole child: new trends in early education.* St. Louis: The C. V. Mosby Co., 1975.

Prescott, D. *The child in the educative process.* New York: McGraw-Hill Book Co., 1957.

Stott, L. *Child development: an individual longitudinal approach.* New York: Holt, Rinehart & Winston, Inc., 1967.

Strang, R. *An introduction to child study* (4th ed.). New York: Macmillan Publishing Co., Inc., 1959.

Werry, J., and Quay, H. Observing the behavior of elementary school children, *Exceptional Children,* 1969, *35,* 461-470.

Wills, C. The two-a-day observation plan, *Childhood Education,* 1972, *48,* 370-374.

Wright, H. Observational child study. In P. H. Mussen (Ed.), *Handbook of research methods in child development.* New York: John Wiley & Sons, Inc., 1960.

Wright, H. *Recording and analyzing child behavior.* New York: Harper & Row, Publishers, 1967.

7 SCHOOLS AND SCHOOL PERSONNEL
THE MENAGERIE

The first two chapters of this book described the lofty ideals of education, first through the history of Western civilization and then through 300 years of American history. These ideas, plans, and schemes forecast education in a perfect world, or at least in a perfect setting. They assumed abundant resources, single-mindedness of purpose, and joyful effort by all.

The next three chapters brought us down to earth. First we saw some of the realities of American education, noting significant differences between philosophers' perfect dreams and what really happens in educational practice. Next we examined the community that the school serves, how it influences (and in turn is influenced by) the school, and how teachers can find important information about the community from which their students come. Finally, we examined the natures of

school students, seeing how they are alike and how they are different in physical, intellectual, and social development. There we explored means of identifying educationally important information about school learners.

Now we come to the educational setting that we, the public, provide for youth. The setting we shall consider consists of the schools and the personnel who work there. If you still think of schooling as teacher, classroom, and students, you are in for a surprise. Our schools provide a wealth of physical facilities. They are staffed by a variety of professional, technical, and skilled workers. All this is provided free to students by taxes that almost all Americans pay.

This chapter consists of two major parts. The first part describes the public schools, their levels, makeup, and organization. The second part identifies many of the people who work there, describes their duties, and alludes to the type of training they require.

SCHOOLS: THE MILLS AND HOW THEY WEAVE

In this part we will survey the public schools. We will note typical divisions into elementary, junior, and senior high levels, as well as their chains of command. We will examine each level to see what its primary purposes are and how these purposes are achieved. We will also consider some of the special programs that function in the schools.

Typical school organization

Most school districts organize their schools into three levels: elementary school, junior school, and high school. Some states include kindergarten in the free public system; others do not. The three-level organization usually follows one of these two patterns:

Level	Grades
Elementary school	(k) 1 to 6
Junior school	7 to 8 (9)
High school	(9) 10 to 12
Elementary school	(k) 1 to 4 (5)
Junior school	(5) 6 to 8
High school	9 to 12

Some small school districts organize schools into only two levels. That pattern looks like this:

Level	Grades
Elementary school	(k) 1 to 8
High school	9 to 12

Whatever the organization by levels, each school is administered by a building principal, who is directly responsible for what goes on in the school. Everyone who works in a school is responsible and accountable to the principal. This goes not only for teachers, but also for secretaries, nurses, librarian, custodians, teacher aides, and adult volunteers.

The principal, in turn, is responsible and accountable to the superintendent of schools. Often, larger districts will have an assistant superintendent between the principal and the superintendent.

The superintendent, who is the administrator ultimately in charge of all that goes on in the school

district, is responsible to the board of education.

Thus school districts have an administrative chain of command structured as follows:

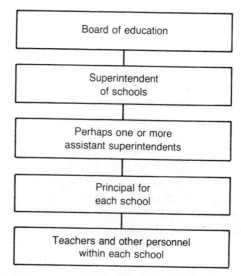

Elementary schools

Elementary schools always include grades one through four. Usually they include grades five and six. Often they include kindergarten, as well.

Goals. The main goals of elementary school education include the following:

1. Basic English language competencies, including correct grammar and spelling, reading fluency, and oral and written expression
2. Basic skills in mathematics, emphasizing the fundamental processes of addition, subtraction, multiplication, and division
3. Interest in, knowledge about, and skills for investigating natural phenomena
4. Knowledge of human activities in meeting basic needs of food, clothing, and shelter; in means of self-governance; and in working cooperatively with others
5. Knowledge of safety and health, including body functions, nutrition, and physiological development
6. Knowledge of and appreciation for aesthetics, emphasizing art and music
7. Skills in locating information and processing it; learning how to learn
8. Ability to participate harmoniously and effectively in group endeavors

Curriculum. To reach these major goals, elementary schools provide a curriculum organized around the following subjects: reading, language arts, mathematics, social studies, science, health and safety, physical education, music, and art.

READING. Reading receives more emphasis than any other topic in elementary schools. It begins in kindergarten and takes up a significant part of each day's work through sixth grade. Instruction focuses on word recognition, skills for pronouncing unrecognized words, word meaning, sentence and paragraph comprehension, and reading for pleasure.

The most common approaches to teaching reading are (1) the basal reader approach, which uses well-organized textbooks from which children read and do exercises; (2) the language experience approach, in which children compose stories that are written on charts by the teacher for the children to reread; and (3) individualized approaches, built on commercial programs and kits, on library books and magazines, or on combinations of materials and activities that work well for the teacher.

The biggest controversies that persist in reading have to do with sight-word emphasis versus phonetic analysis, sequentially developed programs versus those built around students' immediate interests, and developmental skill building versus wide free reading.

LANGUAGE ARTS. The language arts include all aspects of English language instruction other than reading. That covers spelling, grammar, handwriting, oral expression, written expression, and dramatic arts.

Next to reading, language arts receive the greatest emphasis in the elementary school.

MATHEMATICS. In the elementary school, arithmetic comprises most of the mathematics program. Instruction centers on number readiness; facts of addition and subtraction; procedures for adding, subtracting, multiplying, and dividing; and the application of these procedures to the solution of problems stated in words.

Elementary mathematics has shown great fluctuations in the past 20 years. In the early 1960's, the "new math" programs came into vogue. These programs stressed understanding the structures, relationships, and processes of mathematics. In an attempt to foster this understanding, the new programs popularized terminology such as "sets," "union of sets," "greater than," "smaller than," and

"missing addend." Activities using number bases other than the familiar decimal (base 10) system were popular: They were supposed to help youngsters comprehend the nature of number systems in general. Fundamentals of algebra and geometry were also stressed, even into the primary grades.

The new math has now disappeared. We found that students brought up in it were not able to compute as well as they should.

But a new topic has arrived on the mathematics scene: metrics. National conversion to the metric system is in progress. Elementary schools must assume major responsibility for familiarizing the young with metrics.

SOCIAL STUDIES. Social studies is a topic that incorporates the familiar subjects of history, geography, government, economics, sociology, psychology, and anthropology. It blends these traditional disciplines into units of work suitable for young learners. In many schools each grade level has its own particular emphasis in social studies. The sequence of these emphases moves from simple to complex and from close at hand to farther away. Here is an example of grade-level emphases:

Kindergarten	Oneself and one's family
Grade 1	The home and the school
Grade 2	The community and the people who work there
Grade 3	Various states in the union
Grade 4	Regions of the United States
Grade 5	U.S. history and geography
Grade 6	Other nations of the world

These emphases attempt to show how humans relate to each other, why they behave as they do, what their past has been, how they provide for their basic needs, why they live where they do, how they adapt to their environment, and how they govern themselves.

SCIENCE. Historically, science has been the most neglected part of the elementary curriculum. Probably it still is, for elementary teachers have considered it less important (and more worrysome to teach) than the other subjects.

Nevertheless, much progress has been made during the past 20 years in upgrading elementary science. Most of that progress traces directly to the National Defense Education Act of 1958. This act poured millions of dollars of federal money into programs for improving instruction in science and mathematics.

With this NDEA money, the National Science Foundation helped bring about the development of elementary science programs that have been highly influential. Chief among these programs have been Elementary Science Study (ESS) and Science Curriculum Improvement Study (SCIS). These programs developed new approaches and materials for teaching science to children. They emphasized the process of doing science as well as the factual information gleaned from it. Great amounts of money were provided for training teachers in the use of these newer approaches.

Elementary school science is intended to foster student interest in the physical universe as well as to provide for the development of skills necessary for doing science. This helps students explain and predict much of what they observe. For this reason, science programs now not only stress factual information, but also provide many highly interesting, open-ended activities in which students investigate and arrive at their own findings.

At various times in the elementary years, the science program provides activities built around themes such as living things, air and weather, astronomy and space travel, energy, machines, geology, light and sound, archaeology, and microscopic organisms.

HEALTH AND SAFETY. Elementary health education usually includes the study of nutrition, basic foods and vitamins, personal hygiene, care of eyes and ears, care of teeth, appropriate dress for warmth and comfort, adequate sleep and exercise, functions of parts of the body, and avoidance of alcohol, tobacco, and drugs.

Safety education includes proper crossing of streets, playground and corridor regulations, bicycle use, and fire drills.

PHYSICAL EDUCATION. The purpose of physical education is to develop tone in both large and small muscles, develop eye-hand coordination, promote skills in team and individual games, and develop attitudes of teamwork and good sportsmanship.

As is true with music, physical education is either taught well or practically neglected. There is little in between. Some teachers simply send students to the playground. Others use a carefully designed regimen of activities for developing student balance, strength, grace, and coordination.

MUSIC. Music education receives uneven attention in elementary schools. Children are uninhibited about singing, and almost all of them like music. Some of their teachers are talented in music and emphasize it strongly. Others have no musical ability and hence do little with music.

Music education is intended to increase appreciation and enjoyment of music; develop basic skills in rhythms, pitch, and note reading; and provide for the development of special aptitudes that may emerge in children. In accord with the latter, many school systems have special music teachers, as well as school bands, orchestras, and vocal groups.

ART. Art education stresses an appreciation for visual beauty and provides wide opportunity for creative production in various media. Arts and crafts receive much attention throughout the elementary grades, especially at the primary level.

Art media and equipment available in most elementary schools include crayons, tempera paint, clay, construction paper, easels, glue, and scissors. Almost every elementary teacher has favorite art activities, with groups of them linked to seasons and holidays. Projects completed by students decorate the room and bring glows of pleasure to proud parents' hearts.

Levels in elementary school. Even though the elementary school is thought of as an entity, great differences in students, curriculum, and methods exist between kindergarten and sixth grade. These differences, with regard to the learners themselves, are far greater than for any other such age span in life.

Kindergarten children still cry readily, cannot tie shoelaces, tumble about the floor, use baby talk, are uncoordinated, and must work under direct supervision. Intellectually, they cannot conserve number, do operational thought, follow rules well, understand others accurately, or distinguish consistently between right and wrong. By sixth grade, these same students will have doubled or tripled in weight, will be far stronger with much better coordination, and will be able to work well by themselves. Their attention spans will have increased twofold or more. Intellectually, they will be able to do propositional thinking, which permits logical and mathematical reasoning. Many will be able to do high-level abstract thought. They will be able to remember rules and follow them.

Because of these vast differences, elementary schools in reality have three distinct levels within them. These levels are kindergarten, primary, and intermediate.

KINDERGARTEN. Kindergarten is a level unto itself. The children are dependent and insecure. They are often traumatized over the break from home and mother. They have not developed intellectually to the point that they can do many of the school tasks expected of older students. They are just learning the ropes, both socially and educationally.

Their educational program consists of readiness programs for reading and mathematics; experiences with language; much body movement; art and music; and learning to share, cooperate, take turns, raise hands, and stand and move in lines.

PRIMARY. What a difference a year makes, especially if the children have attended kindergarten! At primary level—grades one, two, and three—the children can behave well in groups, can read, are advancing in mathematics, and, all in all, act much more grown up and confident than kindergartners.

Primary grades provide instruction in all the typical subjects of the elementary school. They continue to stress language, art, and music, but mathematics and social studies receive much attention, too.

INTERMEDIATE. By intermediate level—grades four, five, and six—virtually all students are functioning intellectually at the concrete operations stage. Many of them have progressed to formal operations, which means they can use the same thought processes as adults.

Intermediate students can work well individually, and they can cooperate extensively on group projects. Some have special aptitudes, skills, or interests that surpass those of their teachers. They can "study," that is, inquire, define problems, seek out information, and formulate conclusions. Their ability to work on their own frees the teacher to facilitate and manage their learning and to work alongside them.

Special organizational schemes. Much experimentation has occurred in elementary school organization during the past few years. We still see more schools with self-contained classrooms than any other type. The self-contained classroom, where the teacher plans and directs most of the activities, has come to be known as the "tradition-al" classroom, and schools made up of this type classroom are called traditional schools. Don't get the idea that traditional means backward or stilted. This sort of classroom and school has served very well. Indeed, there is no evidence to suggest that any of the newer types of organization are more effective.

Yet we have new organizational schemes appearing regularly. This phenomenon points to a dissatisfaction with traditional organization, and it illustrates education's continuing attempt to find better ways to teach and learn.

The newer, special ways of organizing classrooms and schools include open space, open education, team teaching, and year-round schools.

OPEN SPACE. The open space concept removes interior walls that typically separate one classroom from another. Thus you have a number of classes operating within sight and earshot of each other.

Open space is intended to facilitate flexible grouping of students and team teaching. Often, four classes work together in the same area of the open building. Their teachers plan cooperatively, and the students share some activities in common. For example, they can all view films together and can have physical education and music as a total group. Flexible grouping allows one teacher to work with a large group, while the other teachers work with small groups or individuals.

In many cases, open space has not produced the results that were hoped for. Teachers have had to coordinate their activities more than many would like. All students must have their boisterous activities at the same time, or one group disrupts the activity of the others. Team teaching and flexible grouping have not always panned out either. The amount of planning time for making such arrangements tends to be excessive.

Still, great numbers of new schools being built, both elementary and secondary, are open space. For the time being, school authorities want the flexibility they provide and think that teachers will be able to adjust to them.

OPEN EDUCATION. Many people think that open space and open education are synonymous. They are not. In fact, they can be (but don't have to be) quite opposite.

Open education is carried out in "open classrooms." If a school has several of these classrooms, it may be referred to as an open school, one that provides open education.

Open education refers to organization and management that allow much student choice and self-direction. The teacher helps, but dominates neither the planning nor the learning activities. Instead, the teacher "facilitates" student learning. This facilitation is done through talking, exploring, suggesting options, helping find resources, and deciding on ways of working that suit the group. Emphasis falls continually on maintaining relationships, interacting positively with others, fostering a sense of personal and group worth, and providing for the development of individual potential.

Open education has seemed to improve students' attitudes toward school, especially when the students have been unmotivated and difficult to work with. There is little evidence, however, to support open education on the grounds of academic achievement. It seems to be a fact of human nature that most of us simply will not discipline ourselves sufficiently to become adept in tool subjects such as grammar, written expression, spelling, and mathematics. Most of us have to be continually urged and coerced into sticking with topics for which we don't have a consuming natural interest. Unfortunately, most subjects taught in school don't have the student appeal of automobile racing, rock music, and the affairs of the youth heroes of the moment.

TEAM TEACHING. For years and years, attempts have been made to enable teachers to work more closely and cooperatively. The underlying idea is that all teachers have strengths and weaknesses. By teaming, each can capitalize on strengths while avoiding weaknesses.

Team teaching sounds good, so good, in fact, that the idea never dies out. It must not be easy to implement, however, because it is seldom seen on a significant scale. In practice, it requires too much of that old bugaboo, time for planning. Teachers resent spending precious time in planning sessions. Interpersonal factors of dominance, resentment, and incompatibility enter, too. To team teach well, teachers' personalities must mesh, they must be on the same wavelength philosophically, and they must have similar styles of class control. That's asking a great deal, and it probably explains why so few groups of teachers are able to team teach successfully.

YEAR-ROUND SCHOOLS. Many schools have begun to operate on a year-round basis. That means they don't take the usual 3-month summer vacation. Individual students still attend the same number of days per year as before. But by having four different "tracks" of students that start and stop on a staggered basis, you can increase yearly school attendance by 25%. In purely economical terms, this means a district can get by with one-fourth fewer schools to serve their student population. The tracks typically have 9 weeks of class, followed by a 3-week vacation. This totals to 48 weeks in the year. Many schools close completely for 1 month for maintenance and repair.

Attempts have been made to support year-round operation on the basis of student achievement. The premise is that the normal amount of forgetting that occurs during the summer is reduced in year-round operation. These attempts have not been successful. Students in year-round schools learn as well as, but no better than, students elsewhere. Problems arise for teachers, students, and families over vacation times. Teachers typically have to change classrooms after every break, which is quite inconvenient.

Still, many teachers, parents, and students like year-round operation. It cuts down on building costs, and for that reason alone, school districts are slowly coming to favor year-round operation.

Junior schools

Here we will consider junior high and middle schools together; we will use the term "junior school" to refer to both of them. They cover approximately the same grade levels, although middle schools usually include sixth grade, and sometimes fifth.

There are notable differences between middle school and junior high that we should keep in mind. The principal differences are philosophical. For example, in comparison to junior high schools, middle schools are supposed to be more student oriented, more flexible to student needs, and more likely to individualize instruction; to include more team planning and teaching; and to allow more student independence and freedom. Junior high schools tend to be more subject centered, to exert more teacher control, and to adhere to group learning within a standard six-period instructional day.

Goals. The junior school presents an abrupt, and sometimes traumatic, transition from elementary into secondary education. Subject matter is emphasized. There are different teachers to whom students must adjust. Teachers and classes seem to be more serious, demanding, and efficient. Because they have so many different students during the day, teachers can't get to know each one well.

Junior schools have a difficult task to perform. They are supposed to induct learners into the separate disciplines and prepare and propel them along into high school. Most junior school students, however, are not overly enthralled with the new hurdles they must jump.

Consider the age of the students, and you can understand why. Here they move from the calm of prepuberty into the chaos of puberty. Incredible changes are occurring in their bodies—mysterious, frightening, and exciting. The opposite sex is beginning to look mighty good. Peer pressure has begun to supplant parental suggestion when it comes to dress, grooming, and idols of the popular culture. Music, cars, sports, and cult heroes assume gigantic proportions. In short, this is a time of great physical, physiological, emotional, and social change for students. Is it any wonder they don't get too excited about grammar or history? It's a tough time for students. It's a tough time for their teachers, too.

Curriculum. To meet the educational challenge with which they are confronted, junior schools provide a curriculum of separate subjects not unlike the high school curriculum. In some cases, especially in middle schools, the curriculum is made more flexible by scheduling "core" segments, often English and social science combined, that take up approximately 2 hours of the school day.

Otherwise, the curriculum consists of required courses in English, mathematics, social science, science, health, and physical education. Reading, which so dominated the elementary grades, disappears in many junior schools, except as a remedial course. Art and music, also very important in elementary school, are retained, but usually as elective courses that students may or may not choose. Added to the elective courses are foreign language, industrial arts, and home economics.

The junior school, through this curriculum, attempts to incorporate the suggestions made by the National Commission on the Reform of Secondary Education (1973). These suggestions are divided into content goals and process goals; these are outlined further in the discussion of high school curriculum (p. 123).

Let's note the recommended content for required and elective courses in the junior school.

ENGLISH. Junior school English continues most of the topics that constituted elementary language arts. These topics are grammar, spelling, and written and oral expression. Parts of speech, sentence structure, outlining, and summarizing are emphasized. Handwriting receives little further attention. Literature study is often introduced in grade eight.

MATHEMATICS. Junior school mathematics instruction, in the main, followed the trials and tribulations, innovations and reentrenchments of elementary school mathematics. New math burst on the scene with all its promise in the early 1960's. To avoid repeating the story, let's simply say that new math didn't work out too well. Its stress on meaning was accompanied by declines in computational skills and scores on achievement tests. Recently junior school mathematics programs have moved toward greater emphasis on computation, application, and practical mathematics.

Topics normally covered in junior school mathematics include application of basic skills to the solution of practical problems, plus instruction in fractions, decimals, and percent. More advanced students may be introduced to algebra and geometry. If the junior school includes grade nine, most of the students will receive algebra instruction at that time.

SOCIAL SCIENCE. Social science in the junior school may be presented through separate subjects, such as history, geography, and civics, or through an integrated approach, called social studies.

If done as separate subjects, the most common courses are world geography, U.S. history, history of the state, regional study of some other part of the world, and civics.

If done as social studies, the program may consist of continuing courses that integrate history, geography, economics, sociology, and anthropology, with sustained emphasis on the skills of reading and interpreting charts, maps, globes, graphs, political cartoons, and so forth.

Oftentimes, social studies and English will be offered in a combined core program. The English activities are built around the part of the country and the time period being studied. This core offering is favored because it shows the interrelatedness of knowledge, provides instructional flexibility, and softens the shock of the pell-mell schedule of class and teacher changes.

SCIENCE. Junior schools offer classes that are simply called science or general science. In content they are similar to elementary school science, but they usually include much more information, depth, demonstration, and experimentation. Their quality has improved dramatically since the 1960's because of the new curricula and the training programs financed by the National Defense Education Act.

Earlier mention was made of the contributions of Elementary Science Study and Science Curriculum Improvement Study. Their effects are felt in junior school science, too. In addition, science instruction has profited from work done in the Intermediate Science Curriculum Study (ISCS), Introductory Physical Science (IPS), Biological Science Curriculum Study (BSCS), Earth Science Curriculum Project (ESCP), and Secondary School Science Project (SSSP). These study projects have produced excellent programs for junior schools in earth science, biology, physical science, energy, chemistry, and investigative procedures.

HEALTH. Junior schools usually teach health as a separate subject, not as a part of science, safety, or physical education. However, its focus is not markedly different from what it was in elementary school. Usually it includes attention to nutrition, cleanliness, disease, dental care, organs of the body, and the dangers of alcohol, tobacco, and drugs. The chances are it will also include a unit of instruction on sex education that describes the functions of the sex organs, but not a great deal more.

PHYSICAL EDUCATION. Participation in organized physical education is one of the major adjustments that students must make when they enter junior school. They must now dress in uniforms and (gulp!) take showers in public. If you think youngsters have lost their sense of modesty, you should see them the first time they dress and shower.

For the athletically inclined, physical education, with its emphasis on team and individual competition, is a favorite subject. For the timid, weak, and uncoordinated, physical education can be traumatic. Here there is great need for teachers who are encouraging and understanding and especially for teachers of boys' physical education who know their job is not to make men of all the boys, but to help them exercise their bodies well and enjoy doing so.

• • •

The remaining courses are usually offered as electives in junior schools.

INDUSTRIAL ARTS. Only a few years ago, the only industrial arts course available to junior school students was woodworking. Now facilities, materials, and instruction are provided in woodwork, metalwork, plastics, graphic arts, electronics, and sometimes automobile shop.

Some schools have arranged cooperative teaching between art teachers and industrial arts teachers. This enables them better to assist students in topics such as design, the graphic arts of printing and photography, and the crafts of leather, textiles, and ceramics.

HOME ECONOMICS. Once the sole province of girls, courses in home economics are being elected by increasing numbers of boys, especially courses in cooking and food decorating. Often these elective courses in junior school will be entitled simply "cooking," "sewing," or "home decorating."

FOREIGN LANGUAGES. There was a time in the middle 1960's when American educators had a great vision: All American youth would learn a foreign language. Wide-scale instruction, tons of media, and millions of dollars were brought to bear on language instruction. But the vision turned out to be an impossible dream.

Foreign language programs have disappeared from most elementary schools. They still remain in junior schools, but as electives rather than requirements. They are offered on a much smaller scale than before.

Students may elect to take a foreign language in junior school. Most junior schools offer only one language. The most common offering is Spanish. Some schools offer French or German. Others offer the language spoken by large numbers of community members, such as Italian or Portuguese.

MUSIC. Students with musical talent and interest may involve themselves greatly in music in the junior school. They may elect to explore or specialize in instrumental music, vocal music, and music appreciation. They have the opportunity to participate in band, orchestra, choir, and glee club, and they may be allowed to perform in public concerts and festivals.

ART. Like music, art is not required for junior school students, but it is available in many forms. Students who elect art will receive instruction in art appreciation, drawing, crafts, design, weaving, macramé, modeling, and perhaps painting. Many junior schools have exhibitions where students may present their work to the public and to other students.

High schools

Junior schools are, comparatively speaking, the forgotten relatives in the educational family. They have as much as anyone else, when it comes to money, materials, and buildings. It's just that nobody pays much attention to them. Elementary schools, in contrast, receive continual attention and are the scenes of much ferment and innovation. The same is true for high schools.

High schools have always been in the spotlight in our country. They have drawn much public attention with their athletic teams. Indeed many smaller communities get so caught up in the spirit of competition that mass hysteria pervades the community during football and basketball seasons. High schools also attract attention with their musical and dramatic performances, their gala school proms, and their commencement festivities. In truth, thousands of smaller communities across the land build their social activities around what is going on in the high school. The school is the center of the community.

Goals. Despite the great social interest in the high school, little attention was paid to its curriculum, facilities, teaching effectiveness, or graduates—little, that is, until the famous 1960's. Especially stung by criticisms related to the cold war of the 1950's, the high schools reacted with an immediate frenzy of breast-beating, soul-searching, mea culpa's, and defensiveness. Acid-tongued critics, such as Hyman Rickover (1959), Arthur Bestor (1955), Mortimer Smith (1954), and Paul Goodman (1964), scored the high schools for what they called anti-intellectualism. They shouted for a return to the basics, to the separate disciplines ("social studies" was a favorite target of attack),

and to overall academic rigor. Teachers, however, looked on their suggestions as retreats to earlier emphases that had been abandoned because they were ineffective for so many students.

Schools did pay attention to a more reasoned report prepared by James Conant. A former president of Harvard University, Conant spent considerable time studying what American high schools were really like, then making concrete suggestions to improve areas he considered weak. He reported his findings and recommendations in the widely acclaimed book *The American High School Today* (1959).

Unlike the stinging accusations of Rickover, Goodman, and others, Conant's suggestions made sense to people working in high schools. He urged the development of "comprehensive" high schools, schools large enough, with sufficiently wide offerings, to attend to the needs of all students. These schools would provide three things: a good general education for all, a good program of elective studies that had immediate practicality, and a good program of college-preparatory academic studies. Conant's specific suggestions had to do with counseling, individualizing instruction, stressing composition, strengthening programs of developmental and remedial reading, requiring homework, stressing marketable vocational skills, and giving more attention to the high-achieving students.

Conant's suggestions had an immediate positive effect on high schools, and they still serve, with modification of course, as criteria for judging the overall quality of the school.

More recently, three other reports have received positive attention from secondary school educators. Those reports are (1) *The Reform of Secondary Education* by the National Commission on The Reform of Secondary Education (1973), (2) *The RISE Report* by the California Commission for the Reform of Intermediate and Secondary Education (1975), and (3) "The Seven Cardinal Principles Revisited," an article by the Bicentennial Committee of the National Education Association (1976).

The Reform of Secondary Education grew out of the work of the National Commission on The Reform of Secondary Education. This commission was established under sponsorship of The Charles F. Kettering Foundation. The commission conducted hearings, panels, visits, and discussions in high schools and communities across the country. They concluded that secondary school education should be made more student centered, with more openness and alternatives.

Within this student-centered openness and the alternatives provided, the curriculum should be aimed at two classes of goals: *content goals* and *process goals*. These goals are as follows:

Content goals: Communications skills
Computation skills
Proficiency in critical and objective thinking
Occupational competence
Clear perception of nature and environment
Economic understanding
Responsible citizenship

Process goals: Knowledge of self
Appreciation of others
Adjustment to change
Respect for law and authority
Clarification of values
Appreciation for human achievements

The RISE Report (RISE stands for reform of intermediate and secondary education) was prepared for the California State Department of Education in 1975 by a commission chaired by Leland B. Newcomer. It was the secondary complement of California's Early Childhood Education Commission. Its purpose was to plan programs of intermediate and secondary education that would prepare individuals for the next quarter century through schools that would be effective, enjoyable, and able to develop in students a continued interest in learning.

The RISE Commission aimed its recommendations toward producing educated adults who:

1. Know how to learn
2. Have skills for finding and performing vocational work
3. Understand and value themselves
4. Care for the environment and will work to preserve it
5. Understand and appreciate all peoples and cultures, without prejudice
6. Have command of the skills of speech, writing, mathematics, and productive thinking
7. Understand the rights and responsibilities of citizens in the American form of government

8. Understand the economic system and can manage money
9. Understand human physiology and biology, so as to keep the body healthy
10. Are sensitive to artistic, literary, musical, and other aesthetic experiences

To produce such educated adults, The RISE Commission made many recommendations. A few of them are that intermediate and secondary schools do the following:

1. Recognize the learner as the principal client of the school
2. Rely on demonstrated competencies by students as the mark of learning
3. Provide learning options in terms of time, space, format, and programs
4. Require mastery of essential reading, writing, and computational skills by all students
5. Provide extensive opportunity for career awareness, exploration, and preparation
6. Develop within learners personal responsibility and decision-making skills
7. Promote personalized instruction for all learners
8. Provide aggressive public information programs to keep people informed about the schools' goals and programs

"The Seven Cardinal Principles Revisited" is a report prepared in 1976 by the Bicentennial Committee appointed by the National Education Association (NEA). The committee's purpose was to review the *Seven Cardinal Principles of Secondary Education,* published by the NEA in 1918, and determine whether those principles are still valid today.

The original seven cardinal principles were as follows:

1. Health
2. Command of the fundamental processes
3. Worthy home membership
4. Vocation
5. Citizenship
6. Worthy use of leisure
7. Ethical character

After lengthy deliberations, the Bicentennial Committee left the original seven principles intact. They considered them as valid today as they were in 1918. The committee did, however, make some amplifications and clarifications that brought the principles more closely in line with present reality.

Their comments took the following directions:

1. *Health*. Should be expanded to include attention to environment, dietary needs, food additives, pollution, sanitation, and mental attitudes. Attention should be given to total mental, physical, and emotional health for every individual.

2. *Command of fundamental processes*. Should continue stress on 3 R's. In addition, new emphasis should be put on (a) sources of knowledge and means of information retrieval; (b) skills of objective and critical thinking; (c) knowledge of sources and functions of political power; and (d) skills in humanistic processes such as human relations, group process, and interethnic relationships.

3. *Worthy home membership*. Should be reworded as "worthy family membership." In the face of the changing family, the home's loss of influence, and the increase of "affinity groups," the schools should stress rediscovery of the well-being that comes with rich family membership, ways to make times that parents spend with children "high-quality times," and the overall positive role that the family plays in American society.

4. *Vocation*. Still of paramount importance in the lives of young adults. The schools should direct their focus to the general skills and attitudes necessary for all vocations. They should cultivate problem solving, reason, communication, and skills dealing with others. The specifics of each particular job are best learned outside of school, on the job itself.

5. *Citizenship*. Vastly important to the continuance of our way of life. In addition to knowledge of government and responsibilities of citizens, the schools should emphasize respect and support for leaders of integrity, understanding and respect for the ideals of democracy, and a global viewpoint that sees every person not only as an American citizen, but also as a "citizen of the world."

6. *Worthy use of leisure*. Increasing in importance. Technology and a shortened work week are providing more leisure time than ever before. The schools' task is to teach people how to relax, how to avoid erosion of leisure time, and how to use this time for regeneration and expansion of the mind and personality.

7. *Ethical character*. Again, more important than

ever before. We have great need for ethical models, people who live by the golden rule. We need to cultivate respect for the institutions that give meaning to the democratic way of life, to human conscience, and to individual life. The schools must help the young develop self-direction, responsibility, and a sense of nobility—doing the right thing for the right reason.

Curriculum. The comprehensive American high school provides a curriculum of great breadth and depth. The range of offerings, the abundance of instructional materials and facilities, and the quality of instruction surpass those of the majority of universities in the world. At the same time they provide not just for the intellectually elite, but also for average and below-average learners. Remedial programs are provided for all students needing them in reading, computation, and written expression. Vocational programs of several different types are provided. A plethora of extracurricular activities are available, activities such as school government, intramural athletics, interscholastic athletics, drama, vocal and instrumental music, school newspaper and yearbook production, dances and social events, and a host of clubs, including language, photography, service, literature, and journalism.

Most larger high schools provide course offerings in the areas of English, mathematics, social science, natural science, health, physical education, business education, industrial arts, home economics, vocational education, vocational agriculture, foreign languages, music, and art.

ENGLISH. English has the largest enrollment. It includes courses or emphases in grammar, composition, creative writing, journalism, American literature, English literature, world literature, business English, speech, and dramatics.

MATHEMATICS. High school mathematics courses range from very elementary to very advanced. High schools usually offer courses in general mathematics, algebra I, II, III, and IV, plane and solid geometry, trigonometry, and college or honors mathematics.

SOCIAL SCIENCE. The social studies area contains separate courses in American history, American geography, world history and geography, civics, economics, sociology, psychology, state and regional history and geography, anthropology, and international relations. It may also contain some "social studies" classes that integrate two or more of the separate courses into an area of study.

NATURAL SCIENCE. High school instruction has probably reached its highest sophistication in the programs of natural science. Again, the offerings range from elementary to highly complex, with sophisticated materials and equipment. Courses normally taught include general science, biology, chemistry, and physics. In addition, the offerings may include physiology, geology, aeronautics, botany, zoology, and advanced courses in biology, physics, and chemistry.

As was the case for elementary and junior school science, government-sponsored programs for curriculum development, teacher training, and materials acquisition have contributed greatly to the quality of high school science. Notable among these programs have been Biological Sciences Curriculum Study (BSCS), Chemical Educational Materials Study (CHEM Study), and the Physical Sciences Study Group (PSSG).

HEALTH. Health is usually a one-semester course required for all students. It typically emphasizes hygiene, dental care, nutrition, sex education, and the dangers of tobacco, alcohol, and drugs.

PHYSICAL EDUCATION. Physical education is a required course that is taken for at least 2 years and often for as many as 4 years. The activities most commonly included are team and individual sports, rhythmic activities, aquatics, gymnastics, body building, and total body exercise.

BUSINESS EDUCATION. The area of business education includes courses in business mathematics, general business, typing, shorthand, business English, office management, consumer education, filing, office machines, business law, and record keeping.

INDUSTRIAL ARTS. Course offerings in industrial arts include woodworking, metals, plastics, electronics, automobile mechanics, drafting, mechanical drawing, graphic arts, photography, ceramics, textiles, and crafts in wood, leather, jewelry, and fabrics.

HOME ECONOMICS. Courses offered in this area, many of which are taken by boys as well as girls, include cooking, sewing, interior decorating, food decorating, sex education, marriage, family management, child development, nursing, and consumer education.

VOCATIONAL EDUCATION. Vocational education is intended to provide in-school training combined with work experience outside the school. Courses often included are machine shop, electricity, food services, carpentry, nursing, plumbing, painting, sales, sheetmetal and welding, cosmetology, building construction, and radio and television. Distributive education is an area closely related to vocational education. It, too, provides on-the-job training, focusing mostly on retail selling, advertising, marketing, and salesmanship.

VOCATIONAL AGRICULTURE. A popular offering in many high schools, the vocational agriculture part of the curriculum provides course work in farming, animal husbandry, forestry, landscape gardening, and farm mechanics.

FOREIGN LANGUAGES. The ferment that occurred in foreign language instruction in the 1960's was mentioned earlier. Instruction has been greatly improved through emphasis on conversation and the use of language laboratories.

Course offerings have seen Latin almost disappear in favor of Spanish, French, and German. Many high schools also offer work in Hebrew, Chinese, Portuguese, and Italian.

MUSIC. Music courses are elective at the high school level. Mostly they are designed for students who have shown aptitude for and interest in music. Such courses include band, orchestra, piano, and choir. Courses are also available in general music, music appreciation, and glee club.

Students in the band, orchestra, choir, and glee club are responsible for producing public concerts and the music at athletic contests, commencement, and some social events.

ART. Most high schools offer art courses within an art department. A few offer them within other departments, such as industrial arts and home economics. Whichever the case, the course offerings are generally the same: basic design, art appreciation, drawing, painting, weaving, crafts, ceramics, photography, commercial art, illustrating, and cartooning.

• • •

The preceding fourteen areas make up the curriculum in most larger high schools. Smaller high schools offer fewer courses, but in the same areas. Very large high schools may provide more special attention for students who are gifted intellectually, musically, or artistically.

How does a student select a program from

among these dozens of different courses? That selection is structured largely by graduation and college entrance requirements.

Carnegie units (named after the Carnegie Foundation for the Advancement of Teaching) are used as the basic measure of course work completed in high school. Graduation requirements from high school specify the earning of 16 to 18 Carnegie units, distributed across specified courses, areas, and electives. Courses from ninth through twelfth grade may be counted. One Carnegie unit is earned for successful completion of a course that meets for one school year, with daily classes that average at least 40 minutes in duration. Most high schools require students to earn Carnegie units in English, social science, natural science, and mathematics. Electives are taken in addition to these requirements.

Summary

This concludes our overview of the organization and operation of the public school system. It has not included all programs and levels. Some districts provide free public preschool and adult school. Almost all provide special schools or classes for students who are mentally retarded, educationally handicapped, orthopedically handicapped, blind, or deaf. Almost all provide special instruction in speech therapy, remedial reading, and remedial mathematics. Larger districts provide continuation schools for students who are incorrigible or who run afoul of the law. A few provide special classes where instruction is presented bilingually. Space does not permit our considering each of these schools and programs in detail.

We will now move on to an overview of the people who operate the schools.

PERSONNEL: DIRECTORS, PERSUADERS, AND MAÎTRE D'S

This overview of personnel will be quite brief, consisting, for each type of work, of mention of general duties, lines of responsibility, and type of preparation required. In case you wonder why each description must be kept to a minimum, consider this: There are a startling number of different kinds of work required to operate schools as we do. We can't even touch on all of them here. Even so, we will take note of some *fifty* kinds of jobs that are common in school districts. These jobs are grouped into the following categories: district administrators, building administrators, teachers, academic support personnel, health service personnel, clerical workers, food service personnel, custodial workers, and maintenance personnel.

District administrators

The professionals known as district administrators perform the central administrative tasks that coordinate, direct, and facilitate the work of all other personnel in the district. We will note eleven of their jobs.

Superintendent. The superintendent is the administrator in charge of all that goes on in the district. Each district has one superintendent. The superintendent is responsible for seeing that school board policies are translated into action and that all educational programs and personnel function as they are supposed to. Superintendents may be mildly innovative, but if they try to change things too fast, they stir up hornets' nests of resentment. Similarly, if they stand stock-still, they will be criticized as do-nothings.

Superintendents typically have short stays in a district, usually somewhere around 5 years. By that time enough people are dissatisfied with their work that they are dismissed. They will then usually be hired by a district that has just fired its own superintendent.

The superintendent is responsible to the local board of education. Everyone else who works in the district is ultimately responsible to the superintendent, although in practical terms authority is passed down to other district and building administrators.

The superintendency ordinarily requires a broad background in education, extensive administrative experience, and advanced studies in school administration.

Assistant superintendents. Very small districts do not have assistant superintendents. Medium to large districts have one to several, who are in charge of segments of the schools' operations.

Such districts will often have assistant (or associate or deputy) superintendents for business management, curriculum, and personnel. The assistant superintendent for business oversees the financial affairs of the district. The assistant superintendent for curriculum oversees all matters of teaching, teaching facilities, programs, materials, and equipment. The assistant superintendent for personnel is in charge of employment, assignment, and removal of all employees below the top administrative levels.

Assistant superintendents are directly responsible to the superintendent. In turn, certain employees, but not all, are responsible to them. Their backgrounds should be similar to that of the superintendent, along with a specialization in the type of work they perform.

Curriculum director. The curriculum director sees to curriculum development and implementation in "regular" (not special education) programs and classes. Continual watch is kept on new research and programs across the country. Those that appear promising are brought to the attention of the assistant superintendent and superintendent, who may wish to implement them. That implementation then becomes the duty of the curriculum director.

The curriculum director is responsible to the assistant superintendent for curriculum. Except for a few clerical personnel, curriculum directors have no one directly responsible to them. Their work is mainly monitoring, developing, and advising.

Curriculum directors require broad experience in teaching, knowledge of research and development, and advanced studies in educational curriculum, supervision, and administration.

Special education director. The special education director oversees and directs all district matters having to do with special education—instruction, facilities, in-service training, and program development and implementation. Special education includes programs for the gifted, mentally retarded, educationally handicapped, orthopedically handicapped, autistic, deaf, and blind. Thus special education directors must be well versed in aspects of these areas. In addition, they must keep themselves current with research and development in teaching techniques, programs, facilities, equipment, and materials used in special education.

The special education director is usually responsible directly to the superintendent and in turn is in charge of all programs, personnel, and facilities in special education.

Necessary background for special education directors includes wide special education experience and ability to read and interpret research,

plan programs, and direct personnel. Advanced studies in special education are necessary. Finally, the special education director should be adept at submitting grant proposals for state and federal assistance, since considerable amounts of money are available to support innovative programs.

Pupil personnel services director. The person in the position of pupil personnel services director is in charge of noninstructional matters that have to do with students—matters such as attendance, testing, records, health, and psychometric and psychological services.

This director is responsible to the superintendent and in turn has authority over psychologists, psychometrists, elementary school counselors, school nurse, and clerical personnel in that office.

Desirable background for this job includes teaching experience and advanced studies in psychology, counseling, and testing.

In-service education director. The person in the position of in-service education director oversees the planning, organization, and provision of training programs for teachers and other personnel who are employed in the district. Adequate planning requires that the director keep tabs on innovations in teaching practice and on the expressed desires of district personnel.

The in-service education director is usually responsible to the assistant superintendent for curriculum. Only clerical personnel, plus teachers of in-service classes, are responsible to the director, whose work is mostly organizational, advisory, and facilitative.

Background for this position includes ability to note and assess innovations in educational practice, experience in working closely with teachers and paraprofessionals, and knowledge of practices and procedures in teacher training.

Curriculum specialists. District offices often have one to several specialists in the various curriculum areas. These people monitor national research and development in their specializations, provide direct technical and materials assistance to teachers, and advise on and help conduct in-service education programs. They attend conferences often, and they help organize conferences in their own locales.

They are responsible to the assistant superintendent for curriculum, and they work closely with the in-service education director. They have no personnel, other than clerical, under their direction. Their services are advisory and demonstrative and are provided on request.

Desired background for this position includes extensive teaching experience, in-depth knowledge of practices and materials in the curriculum area, and proved ability to work productively with teachers.

Compensatory education director. Compensatory education refers to all programs that are supported entirely or in part by special state or federal funds. These programs are carefully budgeted, and they are subject to continual monitor and review.

The compensatory education director is usually responsible to the assistant superintendent for curriculum and, in turn, has responsibility over special program directors, teachers, paraprofessionals, and clerical personnel.

Desired background for this work includes successful teaching experience, ability to work with others, and an eye for organization and detail.

Athletic director. The athletic director is in charge of athletic programs in a given district. Duties include scheduling games and meets, budgeting funds, purchasing equipment, and coordinating the work of the various coaches.

The athletic director is responsible to the superintendent and is in charge of the people who work in the athletic program.

Athletic directors have an extensive background in coaching and a proved ability to organize and work with others.

Special program directors. Special program directors head up district programs that are supported largely by outside funds, such as those in compensatory education. Such programs come and go as special monies are available.

These program directors are often responsible to the compensatory education director or to the assistant superintendent for curriculum.

Desirable background includes teaching experience, knowledge of and expertise in the thrust of the special program, and organizational ability. This is often a first administrative job for those who aspire to principalships and other administrative positions.

Project writers. Some districts that depend heavily on state and federal funds to support their programs employ project writers. These people work in the central office, but they have no direct administrative duties. They earn their keep by writing project proposals that seek outside funding.

Project writers are usually responsible to the assistant superintendent for instruction. They work closely with other administrators, but have no one under their direction. They travel a good deal and monitor trends in funding.

Desirable background includes experience in special projects, knowledge of sources of funds, knowledge of proposal preparation, and success in obtaining funding.

Building administrators

Building administrators are those people who direct programs and functions that take place within a single school. Large secondary schools typically have four administrative levels. They are principal, vice principal, dean of students, and department heads. Elementary schools have only a principal, and sometimes a vice principal.

Principal. The principal is the administrator-in-chief of the individual school, responsible for organizing, monitoring, and facilitating the instructional program; providing curricular leadership; managing the work of everyone in the school; interpreting the school's program to parents and community; and handling student problems. The principal is responsible to one of the assistant superintendents or, in very large districts, to an area director. In turn, every person who works in the school is responsible, while in the school, to the principal.

Principals have backgrounds of successful teaching. Usually they have had experience at other administrative levels. In addition, they have completed advanced studies in school curriculum and administration.

Vice principals. People who hold the position of vice principal are often in their first administrative job. They stand in charge when the principal is away from the building. Often they have the onerous, but important, role of school disciplinarian, the person who has to deal with students who engage in chronic or serious misbehavior.

Vice principals, usually one per school, are responsible directly to the principal. Ordinarily they have little if any direction over teachers or department heads. They have the same qualifications as

principals, except this is usually their first administrative position.

Dean of students. The person who fills the position of dean of students is charged with the well-being of individual students in the school and is responsible to the principal. Duties include counseling, advising, informing, scheduling events, solving problems, and arranging student functions.

Elementary schools rarely have this position. In high schools this person may be the head counselor.

Preparation for this position includes several years of teaching and counseling, plus advanced studies in counseling and pupil personnel services.

Department heads. Larger high schools have teachers who are the designated heads of their curriculum departments. These teachers, usually with a reduced teaching load, coordinate the programs, materials, and facilities of their department. They are responsible to the principal. Teachers in the department work through the department head, although they are legally responsible to the principal.

Department heads ordinarily have a background of teaching experience plus advanced studies in their disciplines. Sometimes these positions are bestowed as honors on senior members of the staff.

Teachers

Teachers are the people who organize instruction, carry it out with students, and evaluate the results. There are so many different kinds of teachers and their duties and tasks vary so greatly that several chapters would be needed to depict them adequately. Here let it suffice to say that teachers, whatever their subjects and whomever their students, are responsible for selecting content, organizing it, presenting it, monitoring student progress, evaluating the results, and keeping records. They also maintain discipline in the classroom.

Although the variety of teachers is too great to describe here, three groups deserve mention. These groups are regular elementary and secondary teachers, special teachers, and special education teachers.

Regular elementary and secondary teachers are in charge of their own classes, made up of students who reflect the normal range of abilities (a range that runs from quite high to quite low).

Special teachers, common in elementary but not secondary schools, have a teaching specialty in which they spend most of their teaching day. Examples are special teachers in music, physical education, speech therapy, and remedial reading; these people work with students each day from several other teachers' classrooms. These teachers often travel from one school to another.

Special education teachers are those who work with students who are mentally retarded, orthopedically handicapped, autistic, educationally handicapped, blind, or deaf. They have undergone special training to prepare them for their teaching roles.

All teachers are semiautonomous. Rarely do administrators, other teachers, or parents seriously question their program organization or their methods of teaching. These questions arise only when complaints are made or teachers have continuing difficulties with students.

Teachers, responsible directly to building principals, have prepared for their work by earning a bachelor's degree, completing prescribed work in courses on education and how to teach, and performing successfully in programs of student teaching. Most of them continue to take college classes to upgrade their skills.

Academic support personnel

Many professionals who work in schools do not have direct teaching responsibilities, but perform tasks that require specific expertise. By performing these tasks they support the work of teachers and administrators. Such professionals include counselors, librarians, media specialists, psychometrists, psychologists, and paraprofessionals.

Counselors. Counselors have many duties, ranging from individual work with students with chronic behavior problems to making out class schedules, to advising students on personal, educational, and vocational matters. Ideally, counselors are available to talk with all students. The lion's share of their time, however, goes to work with "problem" students.

Counselors, responsible to the building principal, have backgrounds in successful teaching, plus advanced professional studies in techniques of counseling.

Librarians. Librarians are in charge of school libraries. Increasingly, they have training not only in referencing and cataloging, but also in audiovisual media. Indeed, many schools are calling their materials areas "media centers" instead of libraries. These centers contain both library materials and audiovisual media.

Librarians are responsible to the building admin-

istrator or, if the library is in the central offices, to an assistant superintendent. Many are former teachers. They help teachers by collecting, maintaining, and making available references, books, and other media carefully selected for student use.

Media specialists. Media specialists are in charge of the audiovisual materials and equipment. No longer does that simply mean films, filmstrips, and projectors. Videotape equipment, computer centers, and educational television are all in common use today. Media specialists often keep teachers up to date on the latest techniques of graphics, slide-tape presentations, and videotape and filmmaking in the classroom.

Media specialists may be stationed in very large schools. More commonly they work with many schools from a center in the school district and are responsible to one of the assistant superintendents.

Psychometrists. Psychometrists are specialists in testing, especially in the use of individual tests for assessing intelligence or diagnosing individual difficulties. They usually administer tests that qualify students for gifted, mentally retarded, or educationally handicapped programs. They organize the administration of group achievement and intelligence tests, but these tests are usually administered by classroom teachers.

Psychometrists are often, but not always, former teachers. They have prepared for their work through advanced studies in psychology, educational psychology, and special education. They work out of the office of pupil personnel services, and they are responsible to that director.

Psychologists. Psychologists are more specialized yet than psychometrists. They are qualified to diagnose students' emotional problems and provide therapy for these students.

Many school systems do not have a psychologist. In those that do, the psychologist usually works out of the pupil personnel office and is responsible to the director.

Some psychologists are former teachers, but most are not. They have spent years in advanced study and training for their work and often hold doctoral degrees in psychology.

Paraprofessionals. Paraprofessionals work alongside teachers in the classroom, always under the direction of the teacher. They include instruc-

tional aides, adult volunteers, and cross-age tutors. In a similar, but separate, category are student teachers, who do provide direct instruction to students, but under the supervision of the classroom teacher. See Chapter 18 for a detailed description of the duties of paraprofessionals.

Instructional aides help teachers with tasks such as preparing, distributing, and collecting materials; supervising student activities; keeping records; and taking care of a host of small tasks that eat into instructional time. Aides, while under the direction of the teacher, are legally responsible to the principal. Often they have completed 2 years of college plus some specialized training for their job.

Adult volunteers can provide much help to teachers if they are sensitive to students. They may assist on a regular basis, or they may be invited occasionally to make special presentations. They require no training and receive no pay. They must abide by school regulations and are legally the responsibility of the principal.

Cross-age tutors are older students who work with younger students part of the day. Studies have shown that cross-age tutoring is beneficial to both the younger and the older student.

Student teachers are skilled professionals who are nearing completion of their training programs to become teachers. They work regularly in a given classroom and assume many or most of the teaching functions. They work under the combined direction of the classroom teacher and a university supervisor. They are legally responsible to the principal while in the school. They are academically responsible to the university supervisor of student teaching.

Health service personnel

Schools provide limited health service to students, but leave health care to parents. The schools' service is limited to on-duty nurses who can take temperature, cleanse wounds, and give first aid. They can also check for contagious diseases, give sight and hearing tests, and recommend programs of hygiene. They do not dispense medications except under the direction of a medical doctor. A nurse's station contains beds where ill students may lie down until they recuperate or until they are taken home or to a doctor.

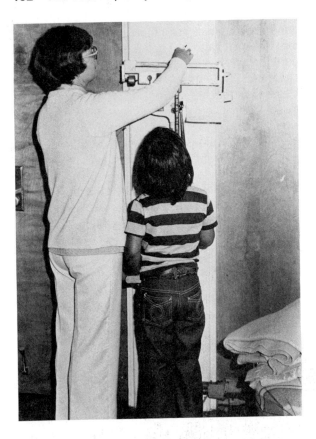

Clerical workers

You would be surprised at how much schools are run by clerical staffs. The principal is in charge of the school, but the receptionist, secretary, and clerk typist implement policy and take care of the nitty-gritty details of communications, arrangements, meeting the public, and directing students.

The principal's secretary is certainly one of the most important people in the school. She manages the other clerical people, takes charge of school records, keeps channels of communication flowing in the school, keeps track of appointments and special events, takes care of the school correspondence, puts in orders for supplies and materials, prepares multitudes of reports, and acts as a buffer between the principal on one side and teachers, students, parents, and community on the other. She is the highest paid clerical worker in school and worth every penny she earns.

Receptionists and clerk typists work under the direction of the principal's secretary. They greet people who enter the office and do much of the necessary record keeping, filing, and typing.

Food service personnel

Many schools make noon meals available to their students. Some do not. Those that do typically provide cafeteria service where students purchase warm, balanced meals at nominal cost.

Meals are planned and ingredients are purchased by a head nutritionist. Foods are prepared and served by cooks and cafeteria workers, who also clean after the meal. At one time most schools with cafeterias prepared the food in the school. Now districts tend to prepare all the food in a central location and then take it to the individual schools to be served.

Custodial workers

The head custodian, like the principal's secretary, is one of the most influential people in the school. Teachers like to be on good terms with the custodian. This seems to ensure careful cleaning and prompt attention to odd jobs and other special requirements. Cantankerous custodians can make things tough for teachers by cleaning poorly and

being unwilling to help with shelves, boxes, and other paraphernalia.

Schools now make wide use of night custodians, in addition to day custodians. They can do much work at night, and their presence cuts down on vandalism.

Some schools also have gardeners. Asphalt and concrete don't surround all schools. Some have beautiful expanses of lawn, trees, shrubs, and flowers, all of which must be sprayed, clipped, pruned, planted, fertilized, and watered. Football fields and other turfed areas require special care. Schools with large areas of plantings may have one or more full-time gardeners. Others, with less needs, may share a gardener with other schools, or one of the custodians may take care of watering, trimming, and mowing.

Maintenance personnel

The maintenance people keep the school buildings and equipment shipshape and working. Larger districts employ a sizable number of such people. They tend to be specialists. The jack of all trades has all but disappeared. Now we have carpenters, cabinetmakers, fencing experts, glaziers, plumbers, electricians, heating and air conditioning experts, and people who repair shop equipment such as lathes and drill presses.

Summary

This concludes our rapid overview of the fifty or so types of positions into which school personnel fit. Had we given separate attention to the vast array of teaching positions, the list would have been much longer yet. Still, the idea should be clear that schools are operated by more than principal, secretary, teachers, and custodian.

Little was said about the legal responsibilities and restrictions that influence the work of these various people. We need a separate chapter for that. And, as luck would have it, that chapter comes up next.

SUGGESTED ACTIVITIES FOR FURTHER UNDERSTANDING

1. Arrange visits to schools that have open space, open education, or team teaching programs in effect. Compare and contrast these approaches with traditional school operations.
2. Arrange interviews with school personnel from various kinds of jobs. Find out what psychologists, nurses, media specialists, and food service personnel do (and are not allowed to do).
3. Pretend that students in your class, plus members of their immediate families, are spared while all other vestiges of civilization unexplainably disappear. You decide you want to educate your young. What will you teach them, how, and why?

REFERENCES

Bestor, A. *The restoration of learning.* New York: Alfred A. Knopf, Inc., 1955.

Bicentennial Committee of the National Education Association. The seven cardinal principles revisited. *Today's Education,* 1976, 65(3), 57-72.

California Commission for the Reform of Intermediate and Secondary Education. *The RISE report.* Sacramento, Calif.: California State Department of Education, 1975.

Conant, J. *The American high school today: a first report to interested citizens.* New York: McGraw-Hill Book Co., 1959.

Goodman, P. *Compulsory mis-education.* New York: Horizon Press, 1964.

National Commission on the Reform of Secondary Education. *The reform of secondary education.* New York: McGraw-Hill Book Co., 1973.

Rickover, H. *Education and freedom.* New York: E. P. Dutton & Co., Inc., 1959.

Smith, M. *The diminished mind.* Chicago: Henry Regnery Co., 1954.

8 THE LAW AND SCHOOLING
TOES AND HOT WATERS

BUS LOADING

This chapter deals with four important topics related to the law and schooling. The first relates to the law and how it works. Under this topic is a discussion of the nature of the law as it exists in the United States and a description of our system of courts and their jurisdictions. The second concerns the law and the student. What follows here is a discussion of selected laws and court cases that affect school-aged children. The third topic is the law and the curriculum. What is considered here is the nature and extent of the court's influence on school curriculum matters. The last topic covers the law and the teacher. Legal responsibilities and liabilities of teachers are discussed here, with special attention given to *tort* liability. Legal codes and court cases are examined as they relate to teacher conduct.

To keep the authors out of hot water, a disclaimer is in order here. The content of this chapter is not intended to be taken as legal advice on any particular problem. The purpose is to provide teachers and prospective teachers with a general overview of our legal system and how it relates to various aspects of schooling. New legislation and court decisions create constant changes in the law. People seeking help with particular problems must seek counsel from qualified legal consultants.

THE LAW AND HOW IT WORKS

Modern law has a great deal in common with aspects of human conduct such as religion, morals, ethics, custom, and science, but it is unique in one important regard: It is an arm of organized political government, and it is applied exclusively by that government. The body politic upholds and enforces its laws through its courts and through the enforcement and correctional agencies related to those courts.

Types and sources of law

Western societies have seen their laws as having come from one or more of the following sources: (1) God—religious or canonical law; (2) nature—"higher law," "natural law," or rational law; or (3) man—man-made law, decrees, legislation, or court precedent. Laws governing most nations today are man-made laws.

When legislative bodies pass laws or ordinances, when these laws or ordinances are codified, and when responsibility for enforcement is delegated, this is what is called *statutory law*. These laws usually have to do with society as a whole more than they have to do with relations between individuals.

Contrasted with statutory law is *common law*. When judges interpret laws as they pertain to cases before them and when they make judicial decisions on the basis of precedents set by previous court decisions, this is what is called common law, case law, or judge-made law. This phenomenon gives the law dynamic and constantly changing qualities.

Yet another category of law is *equity law*. It obtains when, for example, a judge issues an injunction or a restraining order to prevent the highway department from removing a landmark that has sentimental value. This may be done when a person or group of persons lodges a complaint. In their appeals to the courts for equity, they are not interested in having someone sent to jail or in receiving monetary damages. Equity has been called the "conscience of the law." It is sometimes considered a supplement to common law. It takes up where statutory and common law leave off. England had separate equity courts from about 1340 to 1875. Some states in the United States have equity courts. For the most part, however, judges do double duty, serving as law judges and equity judges.

The legal system of the United States is based on English common law. Since the middle of the nineteenth century, however, statutory law has played an increasingly important role in the functions of our courts. It can therefore be said that U.S. law now combines common and statutory law. The old common law was a strong conservative social force. Grounded in *laissez-faire* economics, one of its primary concerns was to protect the freeholder and his property rights. Statutory law gained national importance in the United States during the nineteenth century as a result of a new social consciousness. Statutes and codes were passed to help alleviate social injustices and to protect the natural and civil rights of all citizens. A combined approach to the law has enabled the courts to maintain many of the dynamic and flexible qualities of common and equity law, while having statutes and codes to rely on for the common good. The interplay of the two is such that statutes are extended and reduced as courts interpret them in their conduct of cases.

Here in the United States we have two systems of justice that work side by side. On the one hand we have the federal system, and on the other hand we have the state systems. The sources of law for each of these systems are the following: federal and state constitutions; federal and state legislation (and local ordinances); and the decisions made by federal and state courts. Our courts are of primary importance. They are the backbone of our system of justice. Article III, Section I of the U.S. Constitution states: "The judicial power of the United States shall be vested in one supreme court, and in such inferior courts as congress may from time to time ordain and establish."

Federal court system

The federal court system consists of the U.S. Supreme Court, the circuit courts (officially called the courts of appeal), the district courts, and special courts. Nine justices sit on the bench of the U.S. Supreme Court. In general, the jurisdiction of the Supreme Court extends to conflicts between the federal government and state governments, conflicts between states, and matters pertaining to foreign citizens, aliens, and foreign countries. It has appellate jurisdiction that extends from lower courts in the federal system to state supreme courts. This means that cases tried in lower courts can be appealed to higher level courts and finally to the U.S. Supreme Court. Most of the school-related cases reaching the Supreme Court have to do with human rights, especially as they pertain to racial discrimination, religion, and matters relating to self-incrimination in cases dealing with alleged subversive activities and affiliations (Bolmeier, 1973).

Next in line in the federal court system are the eleven U.S. courts of appeal (or circuit courts).

These serve the various states, territories, and protectorates to which they have been assigned. The ninety-seven judges of this court system have appellate jurisdiction from the U.S. district courts, territorial courts, tax courts, and certain regulatory commissions and administrative agencies. These appellate courts make final decisions in approximately 85% of all federal cases (Abraham, 1975).

Below the circuit courts are the ninety-four U.S. district courts. These courts are served by approximately 400 judges, who have jurisdiction over criminal and civil actions involving federal laws and certain other conflicts where damages are in excess of $10,000. Congress has the authority to assign other areas of jurisdiction to these courts as special needs arise (Abraham, 1975). Each state and territory, along with the District of Columbia, is assigned at least one district court. Where population figures demand it, more than one court is assigned to a state. These are the trial courts of the federal system. The circuit courts and the Supreme Court are responsible for reviewing final decisions made by the district courts and considering appeals from these courts (Bolmeier, 1973).

Other federal courts include legislative courts (for example, the Court of Military Appeals and the territorial courts), the U.S. Court of Claims, the U.S. Court of Customs, and the U.S. Court of Customs and Patent Appeals. These courts serve special functions and only rarely deal with matters directly related to schools. The Court of Claims handles cases brought against the federal government or a government employee who is alleged to have caused injuries to a plaintiff through neglect or wrongful behavior (Abraham, 1975).

State court system

Each state creates its own laws through its legislative bodies and has its own system of courts to administer justice. The state court systems run parallel to the federal system. This does not mean that states are completely autonomous and free from the constraints of federal law—quite the contrary. The U.S. Constitution spells out the subordinate role of state governments to the federal government very clearly. Article I, Section X of the Constitution outlines certain restrictions of the power of the states. The *supremacy clause* of Article VI sets the constitution and the laws of the

United States up as the "supreme law of the land," regardless of the content of state constitutions and laws. Section I of the Fourteenth Amendment imposes on the states the duty to protect certain civil rights of their citizens. In effect, the Fourteenth Amendment makes the First Amendment binding on the states. This is true also of the Fifteenth and Nineteenth Amendments.

State and federal courts, however, are separate entities. Most of the legal business of the nation is conducted in state courts. In certain instances the higher state courts can appeal to the federal courts (and especially to the Supreme Court) for final determinations or interpretations of law.

Although state court systems vary in makeup and function, there are enough similarities for us to sketch their general structures. At the lowest level are the justices of the peace or, as they are designated in some cities, magistrates. These are not necessarily lawyers. They are either elected to specified terms of office by counties, townships, or towns or are appointed to office by local governmental executives. They perform some court work, but usually their duties are of a "quasi-legislative, quasi-judicial, and quasi-administrative" nature (Abraham, 1975, pp. 139-140). One of their more popular duties is the performance of marriage ceremonies. Justices of the peace often handle misdemeanors and civil matters involving less than $200.

Next in line are the municipal courts. These include traffic courts, night courts, small claims courts, and city courts. It is usual for such courts to handle civil cases involving limited judgment and misdemeanors. The municipal courts take cases involving penalties of not more than 1 year in the county jail and/or fines up to $1,000. They also are empowered to hold preliminary hearings for more serious crimes. Once initial determinations are made, people committing the more serious offenses are normally bound over to superior court for trial (Hyink, Brown, and Thacker, 1975).

The county courts are usually considered the general trial courts of the states. Such courts handle criminal cases, civil suits for $5,000 or more, domestic cases, juvenile cases, and probate. They also have appellate jurisdiction over cases originating in lower courts (Hyink et al., 1975).

Beyond the county level are the courts of appeal (or the intermediate courts of appeal). For the most part these are strictly appellate courts. They are responsible for reviewing cases from lower courts. Final decisions are often made at this level; however, it is possible for cases to be sent on from the appellate courts to the state's highest court for final consideration.

The highest courts in the states' systems of courts are called by various names, such as state supreme court, final court of appeals, or supreme judicial court. The major function of these courts is to serve as final court of appeal for lower courts, although certain designated cases may be originated at this level. Decisions of a state supreme court are considered to be final. Only when "all remedies below" have been exhausted will the U.S. Supreme Court consider appeals from the states (Abraham, 1975, pp. 143-144).

Court action

In general there are two types of cases handled by the courts: criminal cases and civil cases. *Criminal cases* involve individuals or groups who have been charged with committing criminal acts. Criminal acts are designated as either misdemeanors or felonies. Misdemeanors are considered to be minor violations of the law. Felonies are of a more serious nature and carry heavier penalties. In certain instances the law gives judges authority to designate whether an infraction of the law is a misdemeanor or a felony. Possession of marijuana is an example (at least in some states). If a person does something that the laws of society forbid, such as murder, rape, or theft, or does not do something that the laws of society demand, such as filing income tax returns or registering for the draft, that person can be charged with having committed a crime. In such cases a prosecuting attorney acts for the state against the accused. A defense attorney (or counsel) is either secured by the accused or appointed by the court, if the accused is indigent. During the formal arraignment proceedings, the accused may enter a plea of guilty, not guilty, or nolo contendere (no contest). Under a plea of nolo contendere the accused, in effect, throws himself on the mercy of the court.

Not all criminal cases go before a jury. Certain cases involving minor offenses such as misdemeanors are automatically tried by a judge or magistrate without a jury. In cases involving pleas of nolo contendere, when there is plea bargaining, or

where the accused waives the right to trial by jury, accused persons may also be tried by a judge. In these cases the judge makes the determination of guilt or innocence and assesses penalties of imprisonment and/or fine, where applicable. In cases tried by jury, the jury determines whether or not the accused is guilty, and the judge assesses penalties.

Teachers, like all other citizens, are subject to criminal action by the courts. If a teacher, in a fit of anger, lunges at a student with obvious intent to do bodily harm, that teacher may be found guilty of *assault*. If a teacher actually strikes a student in a willful and unlawful way, that teacher is guilty of *battery*. Assault and battery are usually classified as misdemeanors. However, if the assault or battery is of an especially dangerous nature, for example, if a deadly weapon is used or intent to murder or do great bodily harm can be demonstrated, the assault or battery would be designated a felony.

Rape and other forms of sexual misconduct involving a teacher with a student who is a minor are criminal offenses. The public might be quick to forgive or even overlook certain acts of misconduct by teachers, but sexual misconduct involving minors is not one of them. The sad fact is that there have been cases in the past where teachers have been fired or pressured to resign their jobs when they were only accused of sexual misconduct and not proved guilty.

Some time ago a male teacher went into the boy's restroom after school to chase out one of his sixth-grade boys. The boy charged the teacher with making improper sexual advances toward him. There were no witnesses. The teacher was immediately relieved of all duties pending an investigation. Although the court did not find him guilty, he was pressured into resigning his position. Naturally he could have resisted the pressures and stayed on, but life would have been very uncomfortable for him had he done so.

Male teachers are especially vulnerable to charges of sexual misconduct. For this reason it is not uncommon for administrators to warn male teachers to avoid being alone with a student in the room and to avoid excessive physical contact with students.

The second type of case handled by the courts is the *civil case*. Although teachers can and sometimes do become involved in criminal action, the most common type of court action involving teachers is *civil action*. A civil case is one wherein an individual or group brings suit against another individual or group for having wronged him or them in some way. The individual or group bringing the suit is called the *plaintiff*. The individual or group against whom the suit is brought is called the *defendant* (or *respondent*). The plaintiff seeks a remedy that involves the defendant. Whereas criminal action involves statutory laws, civil action involves disputes between parties. There is often some overlap, but for our purposes we will view these two separately.

The kinds of remedies made possible by civil action are as follows: (1) an injunction, (2) a mandamus, and (3) monetary damages. An *injunction* involves the court prohibiting a defendant from doing something. For example, a defendant might be prohibited from building a fence that inhibits access to his neighbor's property. A *mandamus,* on the other hand, requires the defendant to do something. For example, the court might require that, as a result of a class action suit, a school district develop a plan to desegregate its schools. *Monetary damages* obtain where a defendant is required to pay a plaintiff a sum of money in compensation for injury or loss. For example, a teacher might be made to pay medical and other damages for injury to a student caused through teacher negligence.

THE LAW AND THE STUDENT
Children may and must go to school

Our country's first laws affecting the establishment of public education were permissive with respect to school attendance. The Massachusetts colony's Olde Deluder Satan Act of 1647 required that each township of fifty families appoint a teacher and that each township of a least 100 families set up a grammar school to prepare young people for the university. These efforts were to be supported by the parents and masters of the children. Whether or not a child actually attended school was left to the discretion of child and parents. Even with the beginning of the common school movement in the 1820's, compulsory education was not the rule. The first order of business for Horace

Mann and his followers was to establish a system of universal, state-supported education. Farther down on the agenda was the notion of compulsory education.

It wasn't long, however, until the idea that all children *may* attend school was followed with the assertion that all children *must* attend school. Again Massachusetts led the way. In 1837 Massachusetts organized the first state board of education, with Horace Mann as its secretary. Fifteen years later (in 1852) its legislative body passed the nation's first compulsory school attendance law. Eventually every state had such a law.

Shortly after the Supreme Court's famous 1954 school desegregation decision (in *Brown* v. *Board of Education*), three Southern states (Mississippi, South Carolina, and Virginia) repealed their compulsory education laws. Since then, South Carolina and Virginia have reinstated theirs, and there is growing pressure in Mississippi to do the same (Goldstein, 1974). So, as it stands today, free, universal, compulsory education is the rule among the states. The mandatory attendance ages for most states range from age 6 or 7 to 16 years. The permissive ages for attendance at a public school range from age 5 to 21 years.

A related issue involves the questions "Shall compulsory school attendance be limited to public schools?" or "Can the law be satisfied by attendance at a private school?" In 1922 the Oregon State Legislature passed a law making it mandatory that parents of children between the ages of 8 and 16 years send their children to public schools. This law was to go into effect in 1926. Two groups that operated private schools in the state—the Society of Sisters and the Hill Military Academy—challenged the act in District Court. The trial court ruled in favor of the plaintiffs and granted a preliminary injunction. In an attempt to secure a reversal, the state appealed the case to the U.S. Supreme Court. The Supreme Court subsequently affirmed the ruling of the trial court, upholding parents' rights to send their children to private schools (Bolmeier, 1973). This means, then, that education is still compulsory for children of designated ages, but parents have a legal option to utilize either public or private schools for their children's education.

Married, school-aged children may attend school

In the past many school districts have adopted rules that excluded married students of school age from public school attendance and from participation in certain extracurricular activities. The courts, however, have tended to uphold the rights of school-aged, married students to obtain an education. What the courts have not tended to uphold is the right of married students to participate in extracurricular activities such as athletics.

In 1964 the Kentucky Court of Appeals ruled on a case tried in a lower court that involved a 16-year-old girl who had married. The school board rules required that she withdraw from school for 1 full year. The trial court issued a permanent injunction against the enforcement of the school board regulation. The board then took the case to the Kentucky Court of Appeals. The court of appeals upheld the lower court's ruling. The court suggested that since there was no element of immorality or misconduct in the case and no evidence that the girl's presence would adversely affect the welfare and discipline of other students, she should be allowed to continue her education (Goldstein, 1974).

In the case of *Kissick* v. *Garland Independent School District*, 330 S.W. 2d 708 (Texas 1959), the father of a married high school student sought an injunction against the enforcement of a board regulation that prohibited married students from participating in athletics and other extracurricular activities. The court in this case ruled in favor of the school board. The married student in question was seen by the court to have vested constitutional rights to pursue his education, but no vested rights to play football.

Student records can be seen

It is customary that schools keep records on their students. Certain records are mandated by law. Most schools have some sort of cumulative record-keeping system. This normally consists of a folder (or folders) for each student, to which new materials are added each semester or year. Cumulative record files contain such information as date of birth; place of residence; parents' names and occupations; family size; student health data; grades; test scores; special assign-ments; and, among other things, teacher comments. Until recently these records were considered to be confidential and only open to school personnel. Parents and students of legal age were not allowed to inspect them, unless permitted to do so under a court order.

Although school pupil personnel records are still not considered public, the courts have ruled that "persons of interest" may inspect them. A "person of interest" is usually considered to be a parent; another person or persons authorized by a parent; a pupil or former pupil of legal age; local, state, and federal authorities; and certain organizations authorized to conduct research for the purpose of developing, validating, or administering tests, improving instruction, or administering student aid programs.

In the case of *Van Allen* v. *McCleary,* 211 N.Y.S. 2d 501 (N.Y. 1961), the courts upheld a parent's right to inspect the school records of a dependent child. The parent in this case was recognized as having an obvious interest in the school records of his child (Nolte, 1971). The opening of school records to parents and other persons of interest should in no way abridge a pupil's right to privacy, as interpreted by law. In general when authorized research is conducted involving pupil personnel records, names of pupils or their parents are not to be used. When the information obtained is no longer needed, it is to be destroyed. Even when information is given to outside sources from a pupil's records by virtue of a court order, the parent and the pupil must be given advance notice.

Not only does the law permit parents to inspect the school's records of their children, but parents and older students have the right, under the law, to challenge school records. Actual procedures for doing this may vary a bit from state to state. In general a file entry that is alleged to be inaccurate or unsubstantiated may be requested to be removed from a student's record. Information in the record that is based on secondhand or thirdhand sources and not on personal observation can be challenged. In addition, conclusions or inferences made by persons not competent to make such judgments are also vulnerable. It almost goes without saying that teachers, support personnel, and administrators would be wise to be very careful about what they include in a student's permanent record. Factual data and objective reports of first-hand observations are not only the safest, legally, but are of most help to those professionals who may need to interpret cumulative data in order to help the student.

There are certain records that are not subject to parental inspection or challenge. These include a teacher's or administrator's private notes, records, and daily grade book. Such documents are usually exempt as long as they are not part of the student's permanent record and are seen only by the teacher, administrator, or a substitute teacher. Furthermore, information in a pupil's cumulative record may not be used to challenge grades that parents or pupils think should be higher (Howlett, 1976 supplement).

To paddle or not to paddle

There is an old Hassidic saying that suggests you punish a child with one hand, but caress him with two. This saying generally reflects the spirit of the law today with respect to corporal punishment. There are two states (Massachusetts and New Jersey) where corporal punishment (spanking) is not allowed. For those states where it is allowed (twenty-one states specifically authorize it in some form), the courts have warned that it should be used only as a last resort and should be administered in kindness. States and school districts have their own rules with respect to corporal punishment. Teachers would be wise to follow these regulations very carefully, even though, for the most part, the courts have been on their side. Let's take a look at some sample cases.

William Glaser was a seventh-grade student in a Pennsylvania junior high school. On several occasions William reportedly had to be warned by his teachers about his apparent hostility toward another student named George Espinosa. On December 3, 1971, William was involved in an altercation with George in a classroom. The teacher took the two boys in to see the assistant principal. On interrogation by the assistant principal it was concluded that William was at fault. As a result, a decision was made to paddle him. William protested that his mother did not want him to be paddled. He was paddled anyway, in the presence of another staff member. His mother subsequently filed suit against the school district. She claimed that (1) the paddling constituted cruel and unusual

punishment and (2) her parental rights were usurped by such an act on her son by another person.

It was not difficult for the court to reach agreement on the first charge. It was noted that school districts have the right to establish standards for student conduct and to use reasonable means for enforcing such standards. The paddling, in this case, was not considered to be cruel or unusual punishment. Parents have the right to correct their children, and schools, standing in loco parentis, have a similar right. Of course, no one has the right to inflict permanent or severe damage on another, whether parent or school official. Federal courts have tended not to rule against corporal punishment. Their main concern seems to be with cruel and unusual forms of punishment as mentioned in the Eighth Amendment of the U.S. Constitution.

The second charge was a bit more sticky. Whether or not the in loco parentis status of the school should be able to override the rights or wishes of parents during school hours is a philosophical issue not easy to resolve. In this case the court decided that the regulations of the school need not be applied uniformly in all situations. What is needed, according to the court, is a selective approach to the administration of such regulations. In other words, each case needs to be considered on its own merits. It was noted that some parents will be found to approve of the administration of corporal punishment, whereas others may disapprove. What is needed, then, is some way of balancing or harmonizing these various desires. The court finally ruled that the district could administer corporal punishment *except* in such cases where parents have notified the school of their desire to have their children exempt from such punishment (Goldstein, 1974).

In another case (*Baker* v. *Owen,* 395 F. Supp. 294 [M.D.N.C. 1975]) the Supreme Court upheld the school's right to administer corporal punishment even in cases where parents have requested it not be used on their children. The court did outline some conditions, however. The force used by a school official on a minor student must be "reasonable." Furthermore, the court ruled that the child is entitled to a certain amount of due process (as per the Eighth Amendment) prior to the administration of punishment. The student's right to due process, according to the court, needs to be balanced against the school's need to maintain order. Four due process principles outlined by the Supreme Court in this case are as follows: (1) A student should be warned ahead of time that a specific behavior may result in a paddling; (2) spanking should be used only as a last resort, after other means of correction have failed; (3) a second staff member, who has been notified beforehand, must act as a witness to the spanking; and (4) on request, parents should be given a written report of the incident and the reasons leading up to it (Flygare, 1976).

To illustrate a point made earlier, that the law constantly changes, on April 19, 1977, the Supreme Court ruled that a hearing is not necessary before a paddling. (See *Ingram* v. *Wright*, 75-6527.) The court's five-to-four decision upheld a federal appeals court's ruling that the cruel and unusual punishment clause of the Eighth Amendment does not apply to school spankings, even if they are severe. It also upheld the ruling that the Fourteenth Amendment's due process clause does not require advance notice or a hearing prior to the administration of corporal punishment by school officials. This should not be taken to mean that teachers now have a free hand to beat children into submission at will. Children, like all other citizens, are still protected under law from criminal assault and battery. How this case will affect school policies on corporal punishment remains to be seen.

Suspensions and expulsions

As indicated earlier, the law clearly states that school-aged children not only have a right to but must attend school. Because of this our courts usually do all they can to ensure children of an education. There are occasions, however, when students are suspended or expelled from school for various infractions of school regulations. As a general rule, a suspension is for a relatively short period of time, such as the balance of the day of the infraction and the day following. Administrators may, however, suspend students for longer periods of time, up to 2 weeks. An expulsion is for a longer duration than a suspension. It may be for the balance of the school year or for an indefinite period of time. Students who have been expelled from school may be required to appear before a county board of education with their parents or guardians for a hearing before being allowed to return to school.

Procedures and policies regarding suspension and expulsion vary from state to state and from district to district. Some states, such as Colorado, may spell out very specific grounds for expulsion or suspension. In such cases all other grounds could be considered illegal by the courts. Other states may define their grounds in more general terms, using such phrases as "for good cause," or may include in their statutes an umbrella category such as "disorderly conduct" or "misconduct." Grounds for suspension in California include such things as the following:

Continued wilful disobedience, open and persistent defiance of the authority of the teacher, habitual profanity or vulgarity . . . Smoking or having tobacco on school premises . . . the pupil has on or near the school premises used, sold, or been in possession of narcotics . . . Membership in secret clubs . . . Misconduct . . . Wilful damage of school property. (California Education Code, Sections 10602-10606)

According to a 1975 Supreme Court decision (*Goss* v. *Lopez*), the due process clause of the Fourteenth Amendment applies to cases of student suspension. This means that a student is entitled to prior notice and a hearing before his removal from school. In instances where a student's continued presence at school is considered to be dangerous to others or disruptive of the academic process, that student may be removed immediately, and the necessary notice and hearing may follow.

Students involved in a school disturbance in 1971 were suspended from school. Subsequently they brought suit against the school district to have such suspensions declared illegal and to have suspension records expunged from their school records. They claimed that they had not been accorded due process, as was their right under the Fourteenth Amendment. Although the school board argued that all local remedies had not been exhausted, that this case was not within the jurisdiction of the court, and that at issue was a moot question, the court ruled in favor of the students (*Lopez* v. *Williams*, 372 F. Supp. 1279 [S.D. Ohio 1973]) ("Recent judicial developments," Oct., 1974). A student's right to due process should be considered in any case of suspension or expulsion.

In general a student may be suspended or expelled if he refuses to obey a "reasonable" rule of the school. Sometimes what constitutes a "reasonable" rule has to be decided in court. A student may also be suspended or expelled even if he does not violate a specific written rule, but his behavior is such that it violates generally accepted standards of good conduct. In most court situations the rule of common sense is applied in cases involving suspension or expulsion (Peterson, Rossmiller, and Volz, 1969).

Pupil dress and grooming

It has been a long-standing practice of schools to establish dress codes for students. Fashions constantly change, and it is becoming increasingly difficult for schools to enforce dress and grooming regulations. The courts have not always agreed on the appropriateness of such rules. Although a survey of court actions involving student dress might indicate that more rulings have been handed down to uphold school regulations, clearly each case must be judged on its own merits.

It appears that students can be forbidden to wear such things as metal heel plates, which can damage floors and create disturbing noises. They may also be forbidden to wear "immodest" clothing. Of course, in a legal proceeding, acceptable standards of modesty would have to be clarified. Girls, on the other hand, may not be required to wear special clothing for physical education classes if such clothing is considered immodest and in violation of religious beliefs. Although in several instances the courts have upheld schools' rights to enforce rules related to boys' hair length, long hair seems to be less offensive to school personnel as time goes by.

In 1923 an Arkansas girl was suspended from high school for insisting on wearing talcum powder. The matter was taken to court in an effort to get the girl reinstated. The court upheld the school action. In a strong dissenting opinion, one of the justices contended that such a decision fails to consider the realities of modern life. He further suggested that if all girls using cosmetics were suspended, most high schools would not have a female student population (*Pugsley* v. *Sellmeyer*, 250 S.W. 538 [Ark. 1923]) (Peterson et al., 1969).

A case that received much attention in the 1960's involved a high school girl in Alabama who was suspended for refusing to participate in the school's physical education program. She and her parents contended that it was contrary to their religious beliefs for her to wear prescribed gym clothing, which they considered immodest, or to be in the presence of others wearing such clothing. They sought court action to have the girl's suspension revoked. Prior to the suspension the school board agreed that the girl could wear alternative clothing for the class and could be excused from doing exercises that she and her parents thought were immodest. Both the trial court and the appellate court agreed that the school board had acted reasonably. They emphasized, however, that the girl should not be required to wear the prescribed gym clothing, nor perform exercises that she and her parents considered to be immodest. On the other hand, the courts agreed that she should be required to attend her assigned physical education class (*Mitchell* v. *McCall,* 143 So.2d 629 (Ala. 1962) (Nolte, 1971).

In *Dunkerson* v. *Russell* 502 S.W. 2d 64 (Ky. 1973), a suit was brought against a school district in an effort to have a high school dress code declared invalid. The code in question regulated the length of boys' hair and prohibited girls from wearing jeans to school. The plaintiffs in this case claimed that these rules were arbitrary and unreasonable in the light of changing customs and violated their First and Fourteenth Amendment rights. The court in this instance ruled in favor of the school's regulations. The court contended that no constitutional First or Fourteenth Amendment issue was involved in such matters ("Recent Judicial Developments," July 1974).

Two other cases are worthy of note. Both have to do with boys' hair length. In the first case a suit was filed against a school district, on behalf of a 12-year-old boy, to have the school's hair code declared void. In this instance the court ruled in favor of the student. The court directed some strong comments toward the school authorities involved. It suggested that they overstepped their authority in making such rules (*Warren* v. *Board of Education Perry Local School Dist.,* 41 Ohio Misc. 87, 322 N.E. 2d 697 [1974]) ("Recent Judicial Developments," July, 1975). The other case involved a high school student's challenge of school grooming standards on the basis that they represented unlawful sexual discrimination. The student claimed that hair style regulations were applied only to male students. The court in this case ruled in favor of the school's standards (*Trent* v. *Perritt,* 391 F. Supp. 171 S.D. Miss. 1975) ("Recent Judicial Developments," Oct., 1975).*

In the 1960's there were two court cases in Mississippi involving black students wearing "freedom buttons" at school. In both instances school officials demanded that the students refrain from wearing such buttons in school. In *Burnside* v. *Byars* the trial court held for the school board, but the circuit court of appeals reversed the decision of the lower court in favor of the students' First Amendment right to free speech. The principal of the all-black high school involved in this case argued that wearing such buttons had nothing to do with the students' education and might cause a commotion. In the case of *Blackwell* v. *Issaquena County Board of Education,* there was a commotion at the school directly related to the "freedom buttons," and both the trial and appellate courts upheld the school's right to suspend the involved students. The school's action in this case was viewed as necessary to maintain order (Nolte, 1971).

Search and seizure

The Fourth Amendment of the U.S. Constitution guarantees the right of citizens to protection against illegal search and seizure. A person subjected to interrogation has the right to remain silent, the right to have counsel present, and the right to waive counsel and his privilege against self-incrimination. The extent to which all this applies to students in public schools has not always been clear to school personnel. Teachers and administrators have the responsibility for maintaining order in schools so that their assigned educational tasks may be accomplished. In order to do this, it often becomes necessary to subject students, their desks, and their lockers to a search for such things as weapons or contraband. In most instances the law will be on the teacher's side as long as the rule of "reasonableness" is applied and as long as certain guidelines are followed, especially when a criminal indictment is anticipated. If there appears to be a likelihood that the student to be searched will be held to a criminal charge or expelled from school, his rights under the Fourth Amendment need to be protected, as mentioned previously. Before conducting a search the teacher should inform the student involved of the reason for the search, if at all possible. Any student who has reached the age of criminal responsibility must be placed under arrest before he can be searched.

School officials may usually conduct searches if they have some reason for thinking that a student's locker, desk, or pockets contain some sort of weapon or contraband. When the search is an in-house activity, not involving the police, the school official is usually considered to be functioning in loco parentis. This means that the official is not acting as an agent of the government and is therefore not necessarily bound by all the restrictions of the Fourth Amendment. This should not be taken to mean, however, that teachers or principals can be arbitrary or cavalier in conducting searches. Not only should searches and seizures be conducted by school officials in a reasonable manner, but they should be conducted only in situations related to official school duties (Younger, 1974).

An example of a case where a school official was not held to account for the Fourth Amendment restrictions on search and seizure, spelled out in the *Miranda* decision, is *State* v. *Stein,* 456 P. 2d 1 (Kans. 1969). In this case a high school student was convicted of robbery by a trial court and subsequently appealed his case to the Kansas Supreme Court on the grounds that his rights under the *Miranda* decision were not read to him at the time the principal searched his locker for evidence of stolen goods. What reportedly happened was that two police officers came to the school to question the suspected student. The officers asked the principal if he would search the boy's locker. The principal, with the boy's permission, did conduct the search, which did lead to evidence of the boy's guilt. The court affirmed the conviction by the lower court. The contention of the court was that the *Miranda* warning was not applicable in the case of a principal searching a school locker. It is not easy (and it may not be wise) to second-guess the courts, but had a policeman, as an agent of the government, searched the locker without proper

---

*See also *Journal of Law and Education,* January 1977, **6** (1), 101, offering a summary of *Independent School District No. 8 of Seiling, Dewey County* v. *Swanson,* 553 P. 2d 496 (Okla. 1976), wherein hair codes were seen as having nothing to do with the proper function of a school.

warrants, the case might have turned out different-ly. The principal, however, was acting not as an agent of government, but as one assuming paren-tal responsibilities (in loco parentis). As Nolte pointed out, this question of the applicability of the *Miranda* decision to school locker searches by school officials is still a matter to be settled by the courts (Nolte, 1971).

THE LAW AND THE CURRICULUM
Federal influence

It may seem strange but the U.S. Constitution does not mention education. There are no articles or amendments that spell out the purposes of edu-cation, what should be taught in the public schools, or how. There is nothing in the Constitution about compulsory education or even a minor child's right to an education. This does not mean, however, that the federal government has no interest in mat-ters related to the education of the young. Even a cursory look at the current educational scene should reveal that the federal government exerts a strong influence on education through the civil rights decisions of its courts. It also exerts a strong influence through its various grant programs. Since the Constitution does not deal specifically with education, Congress is somewhat limited as far as direct control of public education is concerned. Any power not specifically prohibited by federal or state constitutions is usually considered to be with-in the jurisdiction of the states. The states there-fore have historically assumed the primary re-sponsibility for establishing and maintaining schools.

The term "curriculum" has at least three levels of meaning, as it is commonly used today. At the first level it refers to prescribed courses of study. Second, it is often used to mean all activities for which the school has responsibility and over which it has control. An even broader meaning is given to it at the third level. Here it is often taken to mean anything at all that occurs at school, whether or not school authorities consider themselves responsi-ble (Morris, 1974). Courts use the term in all three senses. In terms of federal government influence on education, the broader definitions are probably more applicable.

The interest of the federal government in the ed-ucation of its citizenry can be traced through its legislative acts dating back to the Northwest Ordi-nances of 1785 and 1787. These ordinances man-dated that every new township set aside one sec-tion of land for the support of common schools. The Morrill Acts of 1862 and 1890 made 30,000 acres of land per congressman available to each state for the purpose of establishing and maintain-ing agricultural and mechanical arts colleges. The famous Smith-Hughes Act of 1917 gave federal support to vocational education at the secondary level. Following World War II the federal GI bill gave great impetus to higher education through its support of the education of returning veterans. Since then the pace has quickened. The National Defense Education Act (NDEA) of 1958 provided federal funds for a variety of school-related activi-ties, such as research, mathematics, and science education. Among others, there was the Public Welfare Act of 1962; the Health Professions Assis-tance Act of 1963; the Elementary and Secondary Education Act (ESEA) of 1965, which provided $17 billion for a wide variety of educational programs, especially to enhance the education of the poor; the creation of the National Institute of Education in 1972; and, more recently, Public Law no. 94-142, designed to ensure that each of America's 7.8 mil-lion handicapped children has access to a free, publicly supported education. More than 120 edu-cation-related programs are currently being funded by the federal government through the U.S. Office of Education at an annual cost of some $12 billion. (Brodinsky, 1976).

Legislative acts are not the only evidence of the federal government's influence in the field of edu-cation. Decisions handed down by federal courts have also had significant impact on American edu-cation. These decisions reflect a wide range of is-sues related to the constitutional rights of citizens. It is very rare that the U.S. Supreme Court consid-ers a case dealing with specific curriculum areas. For the most part these types of decisions are left up to the states.

There is one case, however, that has historical interest for educators. This is the case of *Meyer* v. *Nebraska,* 262 U.S. 390, 43S.Ct. 625 (1923). Fol-lowing World War I, in 1919, the Nebraska state legislature enacted a law making it illegal for any public, private, or parochial school to teach a for-eign language to children who have not completed the eighth grade or to teach any subject in a lan-guage other than English. This was at a time when people who spoke German were suspect. Robert T. Meyer, an instructor at Zion Parochial School, was charged with teaching the subject of reading in German to a 10-year-old student named Raymond Parpart, who had not yet finished the eighth grade. Meyer was tried and convicted in Hamilton County's District Court. He was fined $25 for his crime. Subsequently, he appealed his case to the Nebraska State Supreme Court and lost. The case was then appealed to the U.S. Supreme Court, where the decisions of the lower courts were reversed (Bolmeier, 1973; Morris, 1974).

In almost all other cases where the Supreme Court has made rulings in matters of school curriculum, religion has been a factor. This case, however, was decided on the basis of the due process clause of the Fourteenth Amendment. The court contended that under the Fourteenth Amendment, teachers have a right to exercise their professional callings, and parents have a right to engage teachers to instruct their children. It further concluded that the Nebraska law exceeded the normal limitations put on the power of the state and conflicted with the rights of the plaintiff (Bolmeier, 1973).

From the very beginnings of the common school movement in this country, Bible reading and prayer were integral parts of the school curriculum. Many teachers in the 1950's were required by law to read, or have one of the students read, a passage from the King James Version of the Bible and to have the students recite a prayer each day. This was common practice. Some states mandated such activities, and others allowed them. Several suits were filed in the early 1960's challenging this practice in the schools. The establishment of religion clause of the First Amendment was appealed to by both the plaintiffs and the Supreme Court in making final decisions.

The First Amendment states that "Congress shall make no law respecting an establishment of religion, or prohibiting the free exercise thereof. . . ." Being guided by this amendment, the Supreme Court, in 1962, ruled that a state-approved prayer for classroom use was in violation of the Constitution. (See *Engel* v. *Vitale*, 370 U.S. 421 [1962].) Similarly, in 1963, the Supreme Court concluded that required Bible reading and recitation of the Lord's Prayer in public schools were also in conflict with the Constitution. (See *Abington*

School District v. *Schempp*, 374 U.S. 203 [1963].) Naturally the critics of the Supreme Court's decisions cried loud and long. Their voices can still be heard. In some quarters the court was criticized as being antireligious. Nothing could be farther from the facts. The court was careful to spell out and defend its neutral position. What the court opposed was mandated, state-supported religion. The constitution and the courts still recognize every citizen's right to the free exercise of religion. In the *Schempp* case the court even went so far as to suggest that an objective study of the Bible and religion as part of a secular program of education is entirely consistent with the First Amendment (Corwin, 1974). Bible reading in public schools is not permitted as an act of worship, but it is allowed as part of an objective course of study.

School desegregation may be considered under the heading of curriculum only if the broadest definition is used. It is, nevertheless, a crucial and current issue facing public education. The case that laid the groundwork for school policies regarding race relations, that held sway from 1896 until 1954, was a case that had nothing to do with education. Homer Plessy lived in Louisiana. He was one-eighth Negro and could pass for white. One day he decided to travel first-class on the East Louisiana Railway from New Orleans to Covington. In those days there were separate sections on trains for blacks and whites. Plessy was discovered by a conductor and eventually ejected from the train and put in jail. Plessy sought relief through the courts. The case went all the way to the U.S. Supreme Court, but not to Plessy's advantage. What came out of his appeal to the Supreme Court was the acceptance of the doctrine of "separate but equal" facilities for the races. This doctrine was applied to schools and became a justification for segregation (Nolte, 1971).

In 1954 the Supreme Court made a landmark decision that flatly asserted that there is no place for the "separate but equal" doctrine. The court said that "Separate educational facilities are inherently unequal" (Bolmeier, 1973, p. 94). The court's ruling in *Brown* v. *Board of Education* turned the tide of school segregation. Its effects are still being felt as one school district after another is ordered by the courts to formulate a plan for school integration.

State influence

The Tenth Amendment says that, "The powers not delegated to the United States by the Constitution, nor prohibited by it to the States, are reserved to the States respectively, or to the people." This means, in effect then, that the power to establish and control schools falls within the jurisdiction of the various states. State legislators are responsible for establishing the legal base for the operation of schools. Administrative functions are delegated to state superintendents of public instruction and state boards of education. State boards are responsible for determining educational policy, within the limits set by the state legislature. Curriculum is one of the important policy matters dealt with by state boards of education.

State education codes are often very specific in what they require teachers to teach, although instructional method is seldom mentioned. Many state codes prescribe such courses of study for elementary schools as reading, writing, spelling, language, arithmetic, geography, history of the United States and the state, civics, music, art, health, morals and manners, and often additional subjects to be determined by local school boards. Among other things, New York's code lists instruction in patriotism and citizenship; instruction relating to the flag and holidays; instruction regarding the nature of alcoholic beverages; instruction regarding the nature and effects of drugs; and instruction in the humane treatment of animals and birds (Morris, 1974). Illinois' code is specific to the point of requiring instruction on the accomplishments of Leif Erickson (Goldstein, 1974). Oklahoma's code includes agriculture, horticulture, stock raising, and domestic science in its curriculum mandates (Peterson et al., 1969).

Since states have legal control of the school curriculum, many also control textbook selection. In such states as New Mexico, North Carolina, and California, for instance, the state boards of education provide for the selection and adoption of textbooks for their public schools. Formerly California had a single adoption of state-approved texts. More recently the California State Board of Education provides a "multiple adoption." In practice this means that the state adopts a variety of approved texts for a given subject area, and the local school districts and schools make choices from this approved list. Districts can make selections from outside state-approved lists in certain instances.

Of course, once a teacher closes the classroom door, he or she is in charge of the curriculum. The state and the local district may have certain accountability measures, but the teacher has a good deal of freedom, within parameters of the law, to structure the curriculum for his or her specific class. Teachers can get into legal difficulty for failing to teach a mandated subject or for teaching a prohibited subject. The famous Scopes "monkey trial" of the 1920's is a classic example of a teacher being brought before the courts for teaching a forbidden subject, in this case evolution. The *Meyer* v. *Nebraska* case, mentioned previously, is another example.

THE LAW AND THE TEACHER
A duty to protect

Teachers and school administrators have a legal duty to protect students from harm and injury. Districts and boards of education have been afforded a certain amount of immunity from tort liability by the courts. This immunity, however, does not apply to teachers and administrators who have direct charge of minor students and who stand in loco parentis. In order to protect children, teachers must take action to make sure that their charges are kept from harm. They have a further duty to use disciplinary and even criminal processes in dealing with misbehavior (Younger, 1974). Any failure to so act on behalf of their students constitutes negligence on the part of the teacher or administrator.

In tort liability cases involving incidents of alleged teacher negligence, courts apply the criteria of "the reasonable and prudent person," and "reasonable foresight." The court tries to determine whether or not the teacher acted in a manner commensurate with the expected behavior of a reasonably prudent person in like circumstances. The court also tries to determine the extent to which the teacher exercised reasonable foresight in anticipating danger to the student. This means that if a construction crew is digging a deep trench in front of the school, the teacher has a responsibility to warn students of possible danger and to take necessary precautions to route them around the danger area.

Providing adequate supervision. A major responsibility of teachers and principals is to provide adequate supervision of student activities. In *Ziegler* v. *Santa Cruz City High School District,* a student fell from a railing near a stairwell after being pushed by another student. The fall resulted in the student's death. Students had been warned not to sit on the railing, but at the time of the accident there was no teacher on duty to supervise this potentially dangerous area. The school was consequently held by the court to be negligent (Younger, 1974).

In another case (*Dailey* v. *Los Angeles Unified School District*) a teacher who was supposed to be watching the playground sat in his office working on lesson plans and talking on the phone. His back was reportedly turned toward the playground. A "friendly slap fight" by two students resulted in the accidental death of one of the students. The students were breaking the school rules by engaging in such a fight, but this did not relieve the teacher of his duty to protect. The court held that the charge of inadequate supervision was justified (Younger, 1974).

In light of a teacher's duty to protect and to adequately supervise, here is a list of points teachers should remember:

1. Don't punish students by sending them out of the room where you can't see them.
2. When assigned supervision duty, stay at the assigned place and keep alert for potential dangers.
3. Make sure students are warned about hazardous conditions on the playground or near the school.
4. Make sure that students selected for special errands or for such duties as school safety patrol are reliable, competent, and properly instructed in their duties. (Patrol activity must be voluntary and only engaged in with permission of parents.)
5. Be sure your students are instructed on safe and approved ways of using all school equipment.
6. Be careful not to permit pupils of grossly different sizes to compete with each other in contact sports such as football.
7. Make certain you are in your classroom before school starts or the bell rings. If it can at all be avoided, do not leave students in the classroom alone. If something unforeseen happens to make you late for school, be sure to notify your principal. If you are not in class when you are supposed to be and an accident or act of violence occurs, you could be held liable.
8. Make sure shop and other school equipment is in good and safe working order. In 1974 the courts awarded a student $95,000 in damages for an injury received in a shop class. The student charged that the school was negligent in installing and maintaining the bench saw on which he received his injuries (*Scott City School District* v. *Asher,* 312 N.E. 2d 131 [Ia. Ct.App. 1974]) ("Recent Judicial Developments," January 1975).

Field trips. A teacher has the same responsibility and duty to protect on field trips as in the classroom. However, one difference is that more things can go wrong on a field trip. Not only does the teacher have a duty to protect the students, but also a duty to protect others from the students. Don't be scared away from taking your students on field trips. They are a valuable part of the education process. In case of a problem the courts will be on your side if reasonable care has been taken to ensure a safe and profitable trip. Here are some guidelines to follow:

1. Take your students on approved field trips only. Even if it is just a walk around the block to count the trees, get permission from your principal. Your school or district may have a list of approved field trips and guidelines for teachers and students. Read this material carefully.
2. Secure written parental permission for each minor student taken on a field trip. This won't relieve you of liability, but it supports your position of reason and foresight.
3. Plan carefully in advance. This is one of the best ways to convince a court that reasonable care was taken.
4. If at all possible, make a dry run by yourself to check out potential hazards.
5. Alert your students to potential dangers ahead of time. Discuss the trip with them. Let them know what to expect.
6. Make sure there will be adequate adult supervision at all times during the trip. Parents are often recruited for this purpose. If you do have

parents going along, however, be sure to give them advance instructions as well. Make sure they know just what is expected of them.

7. If private cars are used, make certain that your principal approves, and be sure each driver is properly licensed and insured (Richey, 1974).

Medical treatment

What happens when a child is injured or becomes ill at school? Send him to the nurse? But what if a nurse is not available? This is a sticky situation. On the one hand a teacher can be held liable if he does too much, and on the other hand he can be held liable for doing nothing. It should be remembered that, except in dire emergencies, only qualified medical personnel have a legal right to treat students at school or on field trips. It's always best to involve the parents as soon as possible in case of illness or injury. If the parents or authorized medical personnel cannot be reached and the emergency is such that something needs to be done right away, before help can arrive, then the teacher may render aid. Only such aid should be given that a "reasonably prudent person" might give under similar circumstances. If there is no emergency, the teacher has no right to render medical treatment.

In the case of *Guerrieri* v. *Tyson,* 24 A.2d 468 (Pa. 1942), two teachers treated the infected finger of a 10-year-old boy. The teachers thought that if

they soaked the boy's finger in hot water, it would reduce the pain and draw out the infection. No doubt they had good intentions. But what happened was that they boiled a pan of water and held the boy's hand in the hot water for about 10 minutes. As a result of the "treatment," the boy's hand was permanently disfigured. The teachers were sued and held liable for the damage to the boy's hand (Peterson et al., 1969).

Accountability

In recent years states have passed laws aimed at holding teachers and school districts accountable for the academic achievement of students. In the early 1970's California passed into law two acts representative of this trend. The Stull Act requires teachers to write and commit themselves to clearly stated instructional objectives. The intent is to hold teachers accountable for the attainment of these objectives. School districts are expected to adopt standards of expected student progress and to hold local schools accountable for establishing anticipated percentages of achievement. The second law is the Ryan Law, which makes similar demands on teacher training institutions. Anticipated percentages of student achievement are not required, but clearly stated instructional objectives for all education courses are mandated.

With this emphasis on accountability it was inevitable that sooner or later someone would seek relief through the courts for not receiving adequate instruction. In 1976 an 18-year-old high school graduate filed suit against the San Francisco Unified School District, charging the district with negligence and intentional misrepresentation that, he alleged, deprived him of basic academic skills. Because of his limited ability to read and write, the plaintiff contended that he suffered a loss of earning capacity. Needless to say, this case received wide attention. The implications were far reaching. As it turned out, however, the courts dismissed the charges. In the opinion of the court the plaintiff failed to establish a cause of action. The court recognized the multitude of factors that could affect the student's progress. Many of these were beyond the control of the schools. Whether or not this precedent holds for future cases remains to be seen ("Recent Judicial Developments," January 1977).

SUMMARY

The law is very complex, especially as it relates to schooling. It's not enough for a teacher or principal to know something about statutory law—the criminal code, the education code, and so forth. Teachers also need to have some understanding of the principles and practices of case (or common) law as it pertains to their profession. This is important not just to keep the teacher out of hot water, but also for its value as a teaching resource.

SUGGESTED ACTIVITIES FOR FURTHER UNDERSTANDING

1. Invite to your class a principal, a school nurse, and a pupil personnel officer. Ask them to describe legal restrictions that affect their work.
2. Debate your opinions about whether schools should have dress and personal appearance codes. Since noncriminal, are these violations of personal rights?
3. Visit a school playground, a shop, and an athletic field. List the potential dangers teachers should warn students about.
4. Plan an imaginary field trip with a class of students to a real place. What precautions would you need to take before and during the trip to protect students from harm and yourself from liability?

REFERENCES

Abraham, H. J. *The judicial process* (3rd ed.). New York: Oxford University Press, Inc., 1975.

Bolmeier, E. C. *Landmark Supreme Court decisions on public school issues.* Charlottesville, Va.: The Michie Co., Law Publishers, 1973.

Brodinsky, B. 12 major events that shaped America's schools. *Phi Delta Kappan,* September 1976, *58*(1), 68-77.

Corwin, E. S. *The Constitution and what it means today* (1974 ed.) (Revised by H. W. Chase and C. R. Ducat). Princeton, N.J.: Princeton University Press, 1974.

Flygare, T. J. Procedural due process now applies to corporal punishment. *Phi Delta Kappan,* January 1976, *57*(5), 345-346.

Goldstein, S. R. *Law and public education.* Indianapolis: The Bobbs-Merrill Co., Inc., 1974.

Howlett, *Teachers' guide to school law: state mandated and permissive responsibilities and rights of certificated personnel.* Burlingame, Calif.: California Teachers Association, 1974. (With 1974 and 1976 supplements)

Hyink, B. L., Brown, S., & Thacker, E. W. *Politics and government in California* (9th ed.). New York: Thomas Y. Crowell Co., Inc., 1975.

Morris, A. A. *The Constitution and American education.* St. Paul, Minn.: West Publishing Co., 1974.

Nolte, M. C. *School law in action: 101 key decisions with guidelines for school administrators.* West Nyack, N.Y.: Parker Publishing Co., 1971.

Peterson, L. J., Rossmiller, R. A., & Volz, M. M. *The law and public school operation.* New York: Harper & Row, Publishers, 1969.

Recent judicial developments, *Journal of Law and Education,* July 1974, *3*(3), 474.

Recent judicial developments, *Journal of Law and Education,* October 1974, *3*(4) 635.

Recent judicial developments, *Journal of Law and Education,* January 1975, *4*(1) 270.

Recent judicial developments, *Journal of Law and Education,* July 1975, *4*(3) 530.

Recent judicial developments, *Journal of Law and Education,* October 1975, *4*(4) 694.

Recent judicial developments, *Journal of Law and Education,* January 1977, *6*(1) 101.

Richey, R. W. *Preparing for a career in education.* New York: McGraw-Hill Book Co., 1974.

Saye, A. B. *American constitutional law: text and cases.* Columbus, Ohio: Charles E. Merrill Publishing Co., 1975.

Younger, E. J. *Law in the school* (2nd ed.) (Prepared by J. S. Moskowitz). Montclair, N.J.: Patterson Smith Publishing Corporation, 1974.

INSTRUCTIONAL DESIGNS AND STRATEGIES
STATE OF THE ART

Part three takes us where the action is, right into the arena with students. Curriculum development is the first topic. Everybody wants a hand in developing curriculum, which is the school's total program for learners. Following that is a chapter on applying principles of instruction, principles based on what is known about how students learn, remember, and use what they know. These principles, when applied in various ways and combinations, produce many different methods of teaching. Eleven methods receive detailed attention, followed by thirteen specific strategies of teaching. These methods and strategies employ techniques known to make learning occur effectively and efficiently.

Closely allied to methods and strategies of teaching are environments for learning. Two aspects of environment receive attention —the physical environment and the psychosocial environment.

Part three ends with techniques of questioning, considered in the unique perspective of questioning as drama, in which both teacher and students have important roles.

The chapters titles are as follows:

9 **Curriculum development**
everybody's act

10 **Principles of instruction**
their application

11 **Methods of teaching**

12 **Strategies of teaching**

13 **Environments that nurture learning**

14 **Classroom questioning as cooperative drama**

CURRICULUM DEVELOPMENT
EVERYBODY'S ACT

9

"I wish they had to eat it!

As the cartoon shows, curriculum making is everybody's act. The child's comment contains a kernel of truth. Students' reactions to the curriculum stew they are fed may be proving the old adage about what too many cooks do to the broth.

At any rate let us use the cartoon as a way to look into curriculum development. Get a piece of notepaper and jot down the best answers you can give to the following:
1. What is meant by curriculum?
2. Who decides what it should be?
3. How does it change?
4. Who should be responsible for making the changes?

Put your notepaper aside. After you read the chapter, you will be reminded to review what you have written.

We can begin with this idea: Curriculum refers to a group of studies organized for specific purposes. These purposes are usually tied to personal needs, societal needs, or both. For example, you may be interested in photography and want to study it. Your curriculum will consist of all the reading you do; all the courses you complete; all the information you extract from camera dealers, camera buffs, and practicing photographers; and all the photographing you yourself do.

If your purpose were to become a professional photographer, you would follow a curriculum designed by the faculty of a school of photography.

On successful completion of the curriculum, you would receive a diploma or certificate. You might show this, as well as some samples of your work, to anyone interested in hiring a photographer.

In these examples, the purpose of the curriculum is to satisfy a personal need or desire. However, not every curriculum is followed as a matter of choice. Some are followed as a matter of demand. Such is the case for curriculum based on societal needs.

The societal curriculum is the one all of us have followed since the day we were born. The studies include the ideas, skills, and values characteristic of our people or society.

The ideas are notions about our environment— what is alive and what is not, what can be used for this and what can be used for that, what goes with this and what goes with that.

The skills are efficient patterns of behavior involving language, mathematics, problem solving, and creating all kinds of things, including new patterns of behavior.

The values are our beliefs in what is good, truthful, just, appropriate, fair, and so forth. These govern how we act toward ourselves and other people and how we make many choices.

The purpose of this curriculum is to prepare us to become effective members of society. This ensures our existence and promotes our group well-being.

Every society has a curriculum, whether it has schools or not. For example, the Camayura Indians, a small, almost extinct tribe in Brazil, have the following curriculum for their young:

1. *Spoken language,* learned through listening and practice in communication within the family and other members of the tribe. Language also includes mathematics, a simple system consisting of number names through five.
2. *Occupational skills,* learned through imitation and occasional tutelage by members of the family and tribe. Boys learn to wrestle, hunt, fish, farm, build houses and canoes, and make hunting tools; girls learn to harvest, grow cotton and spin it, prepare food and take care of the young.
3. *Social behavior,* learned through imitation, verbal directions, and physical coercion. The mother is responsible for this during the child's early years. She punishes by scolding and slapping. When the children reach puberty, the father is responsible. He counsels, and, when he thinks he must, he punishes by scarifying the recalcitrant learner with a rakelike tool. Aspects of social behavior concerning expectancies for adults are taught by parents and the tribal shaman during the preparation period before initiation into adult status.
4. *Religious beliefs,* learned through observation and participation in tribal ceremonies and taught by direct instruction from the tribal shaman during preparation for initiation. Heavy emphasis is placed on responsibilities and taboos.
5. *Economics and politics,* learned through observation and participation. Individuals own very little. Obedience to the chief, who is also the shaman, is automatic. Subchiefs may conduct planning sessions for certain activities.

In this society without schools, the teachers are parents, adults within the extended family, and the tribal shaman. The curriculum consists of the skills, social behaviors, and ideas central to the Camayuras' existence. Values are interwoven throughout the curriculum.

But there is a big difference between Camayuran curriculum and American curriculum. A society such as ours, because of its vast size, complex organization, intricate technology, heavy reliance on written communication, and occupational specialization, requires a much more extensive, diverse curriculum. The school is delegated a large responsibility by society for preparing the young to become effective adults. However, parents, neighborhood, church, and mass media share the responsibility. The precise responsibility of each is difficult to delineate. This causes problems, which will be mentioned later.

At this point we are concerned mostly with the school. The curriculum it provides is intended to help each person do two things: develop individually and function in and maintain society. From now on we shall refer to the program of the school merely as the curriculum.

In the next sections we will see how curriculum is shaped by forces from society, from increased knowledge in the various subject disciplines, and from increased knowledge about how humans grow, develop, and learn.

Before examining the process, let's take a moment to skim over the subjects usually included in

the elementary, junior school, and high school curricula.

ELEMENTARY SCHOOL CURRICULUM

Reading

Language arts, including spelling, grammar, handwriting, listening, speaking, composing, and creative writing

Mathematics

Social studies

Science

Health and safety

Physical education

Music

Art

JUNIOR SCHOOL CURRICULUM

Required for most students:

English grammar, literature, composition, speech

Mathematics general mathematics, algebra

Social science history, geography

Science

Health

Physical education

Electives from which students must choose:

Music

Art

Industrial arts

Home economics

Foreign languages Spanish, French, or other

HIGH SCHOOL CURRICULUM

English grammar and composition, American literature, English literature, world literature, speech, drama, journalism, and creative writing

Mathematics general mathematics, algebra I through IV, plane geometry, solid geometry, trigonometry, and honors (college) mathematics

Social sciences American history, American geography, world history, world geography, civics, economics, sociology, international relations, psychology, and anthropology

Natural science general science, biology, chemistry, physics, physiology, geology, botany, zoology, aeronautics, and honors (college) science

Health hygiene, dental care, nutrition, sex education, and the dangers of tobacco, alcohol, and drugs

Physical education team and individual sports, rhythmic activities, aquatics, gymnastics, body building, and total body exercise

Business education typing, bookkeeping, shorthand, office management, general business, business English, filing, consumer education, office machines, and business law

Industrial arts wood shop, metals, plastics, electronics, automobile mechanics, photography, ceramics, textiles, and crafts in wood, leather, jewelry, and fabrics

Home economics cooking, sewing, interior decorating, food decorating, sex education, marriage, family management, child development, nursing, and consumer education

Vocational education machine shop, electricity, food services, carpentry, nursing, plumbing, painting, sales, sheetmetals, cosmetology, building construction, and work in radio and television

Vocational agriculture farming, animal husbandry, forestry, landscape gardening, and farm mechanics

Foreign languages Spanish, French, and others in accord with the locale

Music band, orchestra, piano, choir, and music appreciation

Art basic design, art appreciation, drawing, painting, weaving, crafts, ceramics, photography, commercial art, and illustrating

How did the school curricula come to include these courses? Many factors have merged over the years to result in the curriculum. Among these factors are tradition, national and regional interests, practicality, economics, morality, knowledge of human learning, and desire to enable each individual to pursue personal interests.

In the next section we will examine the process that typically occurs when the community exerts pressures for curriculum change.

HOW SOCIETY SHAPES THE CURRICULUM

Where its existence is concerned, society is protective. It wants a life supported by the ideas and ideals it has always held. Whatever occurs that demands a change is a threat. But things do change. Curriculum is no exception. Let us take a look at some of the conditions that bring about curricular change.

Technological innovations

Inventions in transportation, communication, production, and medicine are a mixed blessing. On the one hand they bring us easier ways of life; on the other hand they bring us new problems.

The invention of the automobile, for example, gave us incredible freedom of movement. It also brought traffic problems that threaten both life and property. Curriculum changes made to cope with these new problems include the study of pedestrian safety in the primary grades, bicycle safety in the later elementary grades and the junior high school, and driver's training and automobile shop in the high school.

The invention of the television gave us unimagined access to ideas and events. With it came moral and economic dilemmas. To contend with these dilemmas the curriculum now includes values clarification and critical thinking skills. These skills focus on the use of propaganda in advertising. They are taught from grade four on through the high school. Some high schools include courses in consumer education that deal in part with the ways of coping with advertising.

The invention of the many machines to automate production has given us much more leisure time. But we have not known how to use it. This has resulted in a greater diversity of studies in art, music, physical education, and industrial arts in the junior and senior high schools.

Advances in medicine have been phenomenal, but they have resulted in such high costs that

health education in all grades is emphasized more than ever before.

These examples give you an idea of how technical innovations regularly necessitate changes in the curriculum. Just imagine what may result from widespread use of the laser beam and solar and nuclear energy.

Economic crises

Whenever an economic crisis occurs, society is certain to examine its curriculum to see what needs to be changed.

During the Great Depression of the 1930's the stock market crashed, many banks closed, industrial production dropped, and there was widespread unemployment. One large metropolitan school system responded by starting a thrift education program. The children in grades five and six were taught about how banks operate and were encouraged to open savings accounts with the few pennies they could scrounge or earn.

In many high schools a "seniors' problems" course was added. In this course students were encouraged to think and become informed about the economic problems they would face in the near future. In some high schools almost the entire social science program was devoted to problems of living, in which personal economics played a large role.

Today strong scrutiny is being focused on the relevance of the curriculum to learners' occupational futures. The result is that career education is receiving a new emphasis at all grade levels.

The threatened depletion of our natural resources and the scarcity of energy resources have given a place to environmental studies at all grade levels.

We can look for more changes. Perhaps the concept of a life work, or a single occupation throughout one's life, will be modified to a concept of productive work in a cluster of occupations for different stages of life.

Political crises

Wars, threats of war, instances of corruption in government, and drastic changes in the allocation and use of power all cast tremors of change through the curriculum.

The last war to which the society was totally committed was World War II. Through the curriculum the children in the schools were mobilized to support the war. They were taught the importance of supporting the cost of the war through investing in savings stamps and conserving the materials they used. Some learned how to grow victory gardens. In the later elementary grades and the high school the war itself became a subject of study in social studies, history, geography, and government. When the war was over, these curricular elements disappeared.

During the 1950's the threat of war with Russia pervaded the consciousness of every school student. Bomb drills were held. On signal from the teacher, students scooted under their desks, scrunched themselves into a kneeling ball with hands over the back of the neck and waited for the signal to resume. Students in all grades were instructed on what to do to protect themselves if they were at home or on the street when an atomic bombardment occurred.

One of the greatest changes in curriculum occurred when the Russian government was successful in launching two satellites into space in 1957. The society regarded this as a display of political and technological superiority of the most threatening sort. Many people believed that the curriculum was at fault. In fairly rapid succession, the new math, the new English, the new science, and the new social studies were introduced into the schools at all levels. These studies were supposed to produce an intellectually effective society that would regain technological and political superiority. And to ensure an appropriate container for all the great minds being produced, a new thrust was given to physical education. Calisthenics, strength measurement, and personal improvement programs were instituted at all grade levels.

The Vietnamese war had a divisive effect on the society. Some people believed in it; others did not. As it continued, suspicion of the abuse of power at the highest military and governmental levels grew. When some of the worst suspicions were confirmed, the curriculum felt it. In some schools the societal base for curriculum was all but forgotten. The feeling was that all an individual can really rely on is himself or herself. A new emphasis was given to learning the basic skills. The study of ideas was reduced to whatever could be used in individual inquiry, with little attempt to arrive at group closure.

Whatever the next political crisis, it too will demand a change in curriculum.

Social change

Social changes occur when the social organization and roles within the society take new directions. They may be sparked by any of the crises discussed so far, by technological innovations, or by the decision of any group within the society to generate political power to its own benefit. Let's note a few more obvious social changes that have occurred in recent years.

A remarkable change has occurred in the family. It is no longer the agency of social control that it once was. Because both parents work, some children are not supervised from the moment they leave school in the middle of the afternoon until shortly before the evening meal. The same is true of children in families where there is only one parent who must work. In some instances supervision at home is available, but the children use their bicycles or public transportation to participate in activities several miles from home.

The changes made in the curriculum to cope with these conditions include having children in the elementary grades explore, through role-playing or simulation, alternative behaviors—for coping with temptation, discovering consequences of certain behaviors, and resolving interpersonal conflict. Studies of the family explore individual roles in various kinds of families—families with new parents, one-parent families, and two-parent families. Sometimes high schools offer courses in family living in which the responsibilities of family members and interfamily relationships are explored.

Closely related to the change in the family is the role change of individuals as they interact with other people. Ignorance of suitable roles may lead to delinquency and crime.

Curriculum changes introduced to help children learn their roles are often similar to those used to help them learn about family roles. Much of value clarification is directed toward this need. And whatever is done to teach the uses of reading, music, art, and crafts as leisure activities is meant to help people conduct themselves properly when on their own.

Sex roles are also changing. Have you noticed? Women's rights groups insist that girls be given the same opportunities as boys for self-development.

On these groups' insistence, the curriculum in social studies at both elementary and secondary levels must include studies of the contributions of women. Reading content is to include stories and poems about girls and women in positions of leadership and responsibility. Participation in athletics is to be open to both sexes at all grade levels.

The roles of minorities in the society are changing. In most schools the social studies curriculum includes studies of minority histories, the contributions of minority members to great events in the history of the society, and the customs of various minorities. In some instances English is taught as a second language. In other instances instruction is provided in both English and the language of the minority.

A society feels very deeply about its ideals, organization, and roles. These elements are often in conflict. However, curriculum change is one of the most peaceful ways to enable opposing ideals to coexist within the same social milieu.

Changes in the power base

Traditionally the local school board has been the power base responsible for curriculum decisions. Working within financial and legal requirements imposed by the state government and considering suggestions made by the state department of education, the board was free to base its decisions on local needs. This mode of operation is still followed in some states.

However, in recent years two very strong new forces have emerged. The first of these forces is the Department of Health, Education, and Welfare (HEW), an institution of the federal government. On the basis of national educational needs assessments, this department was instrumental in getting legislation passed to fund programs in early childhood education; compensatory education for disadvantaged children; and special education for the gifted, educationally handicapped, mentally retarded, and physically handicapped. The result has been curriculum change for the students involved.

A second strong force is the department of education within each state. It may work cooperatively with HEW, or it may operate on its own, but in much the same way, to influence curriculum.

Because education is costly, state governors and legislators have also begun to make their influence felt. At one time these individuals were content to be advised by the professionally staffed state department of education. Now they may ask for advice from the department, but they do not necessarily accept its validity. They may pass laws with more attention to interest groups than to professional opinion, regardless of its documentation. In a very real sense, some governors and state legislators have become the power bases for making curriculum decisions that local boards must accept.

Changes in the power base have tended to diversify curriculum. What a student will pursue in school may be determined more by the kind of learner he is than by the school he attends.

• • •

In review, these comments show that cultural, social, political, and economic forces impinge on the curriculum. They cause ideas and attitudes to be reexamined and sometimes changed. The same is true for demands for new skills and the new uses of skills. Because these forces change the roles of people and how they organize to live, work, and play, they are often referred to as *social forces.*

As we consider these social forces and their influences, we might think that curriculum is a fragile structure pushed this way and that by every extreme of human experience. Oddly enough, however, curriculum remains fairly stable.

The ideas portion of curriculum continually changes, bit by bit. But the skills portion changes very slowly. Skills change little except in their organization. New math and new English are prime examples. The skills still have to do with computation and communication. The way they are taught undergoes periodic reorganization.

It is predictable that conflict will occur when so many people are involved in making the curriculum. Despite the conflict, students still learn. They do manage to be proficient members of the society when they are adults. The tugging and yanking that occur in the curriculum do not seem to make too much difference. Perhaps a view of how the society decides on its curriculum will help us to understand why this is so.

The power base and the pro's at work

The power base is the local school board. The pro's are the professional educators—the teachers, the administrators, and the schools of education in the various colleges and universities where teachers are trained and where much of the research in education is conducted. The term "professional educators" is tongue-taxing, and when repeated in discourse it becomes pretentious. We shall just refer to them as the pro's.

Let's listen in on some conversations that regularly occur in thousands of communities across the nation.

Mr. S., the superintendent of schools, and Mr. P., the president of the local school board, are checking the agenda for the next board meeting. They have just finished looking at the list of items when Mr. P. remarks, "I hope we'll be able to consider all these issues. I don't want to overload the agenda, but I'm really concerned about all this flack about high school graduates. Every time I read the newspaper, I see complaints about graduates not being able to spell or write so it makes sense."

"I join you in that concern," says Mr. S. "I was discussing it the other day with Mr. C., the curriculum director. He has begun an assessment of what the district is doing."

"Will he have anything ready to report at this meeting?"

"No, he won't, but I'm sure he'll have something for us at the following meeting."

"All right. I'll just make an announcement that the matter is under study."

"Fine. I'll see you at the board meeting."

What we see here is the impact of the press, the voice of society, on those who must make decisions. The president and his associates on the board, all elected officials, must cope with a myriad of problems, not only of learning, but of buildings, instructional materials, personnel, and finances. They cannot be aware of everything at the same time. Besides, the last time the board reviewed the assessment of learning in the district, it appeared that students in the district were learning as much or more than students elsewhere.

Also, we see that Mr. P. has mentioned his concern to Mr. S., the pro in this scene. He knows what he can expect from him—an investigation of the issue, a report on what is discovered, and some recommendations on what might be done about it. This pro is well trained for his position. He was first a teacher and then a principal for several years. He has an advanced degree in educational administration. If he were the superintendent of a smaller district, he would have to make the investi-

gation himself. Perhaps he would have to ask the board to hire an expert to help him. Mr. S. doesn't have to do this in this case. Mr. C., the curriculum director, will do it.

The next day Mr. S. telephones Mr. C.

"Say, Henry," he says, "Yesterday I told Mr. P. that you were checking into the spelling and composition skills of our high school graduates. Could you have anything to report to the board at next month's meeting?"

"Yes, Tom," responds Mr. C. "I think so. I have just had a preliminary survey made of our last achievement tests to see how our students did on those items. From what I can see, about half our students do very well and the rest do poorly."

"Those who did well must have done very well or the total results would not have been so high."

"Right. But ability in these skills tends to vary widely from grade level to level, and a lot of repeated experience from grade to grade appears to be needed for the kind of mastery that's expected."

"Don't we provide for that?"

"Not really. The last curriculum change we made tended to make practical composition an optional subject all through the grades."

"Even in the high school?"

"I'm afraid so."

"Will we have to change the whole thing? When are we scheduled to review that part of the curriculum again?"

"Our next review is scheduled for 2 years from now.

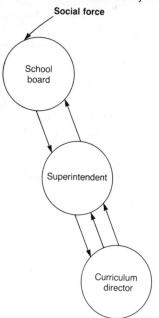

Fig. 1. Initial exploration.

But I don't think we'll have to redo the whole English program. I've been thinking about a practical skills curriculum that includes practical mathematics and practical English. I think it has possibilities."

"Good! Look into it. And find out about the costs involved."

"Will do."

The illustration for this episode shows one force that causes a district to respond to concerns about curriculum. Of course, there are other forces as well. For example, there are concerns that arise from poor student performance on achievement tests. There are concerns that surface during routine curriculum reviews, carried out every 4 or 5 years or so, one or two subjects each year. And there are concerns voiced by the pro whose responsibility it is to check the effectiveness of instruction and to be alert to the need for change.

Let's continue our story that began with Mr. S. and Mr. P. Assume that the curriculum director has looked into programs conducted in several other school districts, and he has decided that the practical skills curriculum offers the best possibilities in meeting the need for improvement of instruction in written composition.

Mr. C. calls Ms. L., the language arts specialist, and Mr. M., the specialist in mathematics, to his office for a conference. He needs the services of both because the new curriculum idea combines the two subject areas. Each specialist knows the research and trends in instruction as well as the most useful instructional materials available. Each also knows which teachers in the district are competent in teaching the subjects in question.

Mr. C. presents his proposal to the specialists. After a few questions Ms. L. asks, "Don't you really think each of us might deal with this problem separately? Good language teachers are not always good math teachers."

"Mixing math and language is like mixing fire with water," adds Mr. M. "Each element has its own uses. Put the two together, and you lose the utility of both."

"But try to cook without one or the other and you end up with some mighty impalatable food," remarks Mr. C. wryly. "I would like for the two of you to try to put your heads together to come up with the skeleton of a program."

"For each grade level?" asks Ms. L.

"No, not for this first go-round. Think in terms of clusters of grades—primary grades, intermediate grades, junior high, and senior high," replies Mr. C.

"Some learning objectives and activities for each cluster?" asks Mr. M.

"Yes," says Mr. C., "And—"

"We know," interrupts Ms. L., "And be sure to survey the instructional materials now in our schools and materials center for possible use."

"And to keep new materials at a minimum," adds Mr. M.

"We are all on the same wavelength," announces Mr. C. with a broad smile. "Do you suppose you can have something ready to show me by a week from today?"

The two specialists look at each other and nod in agreement.

As the two walk down the corridor to their offices, Ms. L. says, "Well, we tried, didn't we?"

"Yeah," agrees Mr. M., "Apparently he doesn't know that you language types drive me up the wall."

"Oh, come now, Alec," jibes Ms. L., "Don't you know that mathematics is just another form of language?"

"Maybe so, but a mathematical sentence says something that any intelligent person can understand. That's more than you can say for most language sentences," Mr. M. retorts good-naturedly.

As we observed this meeting, we discovered that specialists are protective of their areas. This is common among pro's. However, when the need is great enough, the barriers can be struck down.

So the two specialists begin to work together. They easily suggest instructional objectives for their particular areas, but combining the two gives them trouble. One day over lunch they are discussing their problem. A social studies specialist has joined them. After listening to their conversation for a minute or two, she begins making suggestions.

Children in the primary grades might be involved in making simple recipe holders. They could have mathematics practice by keeping track of their materials and determining what they should charge. Then they could work together to compose an advertising brochure to sell their products.

Children in the middle grades could write their own newspaper and compute the cost in materials and their own labor.

Junior high students could study an ecology problem in which recycling is involved. They could compute savings accrued through recycling and use the results in letters to their state assemblymen to recommend a law.

High school students could simulate businessmen computing costs and carrying on the necessary correspondence.

Ms. L. and Mr. M. attack their task with new vigor. They meet with the curriculum director at the appointed time. He is pleased with their work and is delighted to discover that only a few inexpensive materials need to be bought. He asks the specialists to refine their work and have it ready for a presentation to the board within 3 weeks.

So far, Ms. L. and Mr. M. have been armchair planners. They have not as yet submitted their ideas to teachers, the people who will be putting the curriculum change into effect. So now they decide to contact teachers to attend a series of after school meetings at the district office.

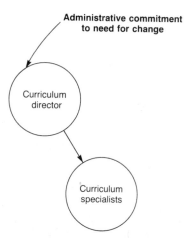

Fig. 2. Preliminary plan.

At the first meeting the curriculum director begins the proceedings by reminding the teachers of the increasing frequency of news items about high school graduates' lack of practical writing and basic mathematics computation skills. He reports his preliminary assessment of the current curriculum and describes the practical skills curriculum currently being followed in another district. After stating that the purpose of this meeting and those following will be to develop a practical skills curriculum for their district, he expresses his confidence in his colleagues by saying that he is certain that the program they develop will be superior to any other. Wishing them well in their endeavor, he turns the meeting over to the specialists.

The specialists present an outline of the program they developed. Then they divide the teachers into small groups as follows:

The primary group, consisting of two kindergarten teachers, three first-grade teachers, a second-grade teacher, and two third-grade teachers.

The middle-grade group, consisting of two fourth-grade teachers, three fifth-grade teachers, and three sixth-grade teachers.

The junior high group, consisting of four English teachers and three mathematics teachers.

The senior high group, consisting of three English teachers and two mathematics teachers.

The groups' first task is to react to the outline consisting of proposed instructional objectives and suggested learning activities as to appropriateness for the grade levels. After 20 minutes of discussion, each group reports its opinions. The general results may be listed as follows:

The proposed objectives and activities are generally appropriate.

A few examples of other objectives and activities that could be included are offered by each group

The elementary teachers who teach in self-contained classrooms are generally most positive toward the proposed program.

The elementary teachers who work in loft schools with some team teaching see difficulties, but none considered insurmountable.

The junior high school teachers are seriously concerned about what the new combination of subjects may do to the social studies–English core (a combination of subjects taught during an extended period of the day in such a way that the skills and content complement each other).

The senior high school teachers have reservations about the combination of subjects in their departmentalized program, because there every teacher teaches one subject at a time during periods of equal length.

The event we have just observed shows that curriculum development includes the advice of classroom teachers. You can see that their concern at this point is not about the feasibility of the program. Perhaps the curriculum director's remarks at the beginning of the series of meetings took care of that. Also, they are aware of what has been reported through the mass media. And it is a safe bet that a few have already made changes in their instructional approaches and plans so as to give greater emphasis to practical composition and mathematics skills.

The teachers' deepest concerns are about the mechanics involved in the change: How can it be fitted into the curriculum? Who is going to assume responsibility for instruction? How can learners, school space, and school time be organized to meet the proposed objectives?

When the series of meetings closed, the specialists' original outline had acquired objectives and suggested activities. The more the teachers worked on the proposal, the more they were convinced that the new curriculum should be tried out in selected schools and classrooms. When they suggested this, the specialists accepted it as continued evidence of anxiety. They knew that this anxiety would be multiplied many times at the classroom level if the change were introduced too quickly. They took the suggestion to the curriculum director. He saw merit in it and presented it to the superintendent. Mr. S. was delighted. He knew the board would like the idea. A pilot program would be evidence of action on a problem. It could also provide a background for future financing based on program effectiveness.

The practices to be tried out included the following:

1. Devising and testing units of instruction on the use of practical skills in daily life situations. These units would be used in selected self-contained classrooms in elementary schools.
2. Coordinating the efforts of language arts and mathematics teachers in selected elementary loft schools in teaching written composition and mathematics organized around daily life situations.
3. Introducing a practical skills core in a selected junior high school to be taught by a team consisting of an English teacher and a mathematics teacher. The classes taking this core will study social studies as a separate subject.
4. Organizing the schedule in a selected senior high school to arrange for pairs of English and mathematics teachers to teach in adjacent classrooms during two periods in succession. This will be for high school juniors only. During the second semester, a practical skills laboratory will be instituted for juniors who are having difficulty in the regular program.

Copies of the outline of the proposed curriculum and a description of the pilot program were distributed to the members of the board a week before its regular meeting.

At the appointed time the board convenes. Very quickly it approves the agenda for the meeting and the minutes of the last meeting. Routine matters receive due attention. Finally the moment comes for presenting the proposed curriculum change and pilot program. At the request of the superintendent, the curriculum director makes the presentation. The curriculum specialists serve as consultants. After the presentation, the board responds with questions and comments.

The following paragraphs introduce each member of the board, summarize the most significant

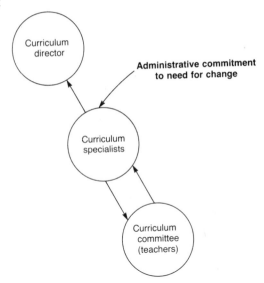

Fig. 3. Plan to be tested (pilot program).

comments or questions, and indicate the responses made to each question.

Mr. P., the president of the board, is a successful store owner whose wife is a teacher and whose four children attend the schools. He is quite satisfied with the schools, and he has a deep respect for the superintendent and the members of his immediate staff.

His comment: I think this is an excellent pilot program for a curriculum change that most of us feel the need for. We should commend Mr. C. and his staff for such a carefully thought-out proposal.

Response: Smiles of pleasure from Mr. S., Mr. C., Ms. L., and Mr. M.

Mr. Q., the member who has served longest, is a successful real estate broker. His two children attended the schools in the district and are now living away from home. He believes that education today is too expensive and that it would be more effective and less costly if the curriculum emphasized only the basic skills.

His comment and question: It's about time our schools are emphasizing the practical needs of students. Is this program going to add to the costs of instruction or is it going to replace something less useful?

Response (as given by Mr. C.): This new program represents a realignment of our resources. It is not really an addition, nor do we see it as a replacement for anything else in the curriculum. Conducting the pilot program will involve some extra expense, but I believe we have the funds to cover it. (Mr. S. nods in the affirmative.)

Ms. R. is well known throughout the community as a leader in support of the arts. She is an officer in a literary society and a concert association.

Her comment and question: I recognize the need for

learning the practical skills, but I also believe the need to learn about music, art, and literature is just as important. Mr. C., because you have said that this program represents a realignment of the district's resources, I am interested in seeing how this realignment will effect instruction in art, music, and literature. Would you please tell me?

Response (Mr. C. directs the question to Ms. L.): I don't think that music and art will be affected in any way. The emphasis in literature will be somewhat reduced, but not drastically. In the instructional guides for teachers we shall include learning activities based on literature. For example, students would reenact the problems of the impecunious but ambitious hero in *Great Expectations* in terms of budgeting and correspondence in modern terms. Greater understanding of the novel and its times as well as practice in practical skills will be the result.

Mr. T., a recently elected member of the board, is a successful young lawyer. His two young children have not entered school. He regards his election to the board as the first stepping-stone toward a political career. During his election campaign he had stressed the need for schools to become laboratories in which children learn how to be responsible citizens in the American democratic system.

His comment: I think this is a splendid idea. If every citizen could compute accurately, I am sure that people would trust each other more, particularly when they enter into transactions involving money. If every citizen could compose courteous, straightforward, and purposeful correspondence, there would be much less social turmoil and conflict because of simple misunderstanding.

Response (by Mr. C.): You have a strong point, Mr. T.

Ms. U. is a concerned mother and housewife who has just been elected to the board. Her three children are in elementary school. In her election campaign she underscored the need for greater parent participation in educational decision making and in school instruction.

Her comment: At last! Something that I know something about and can help my children with!

Response: Gentle laughter by all present at her candor.

The pilot program is ultimately approved. Let us stop now to see what has really happened.

What we have just witnessed is a meeting of minds. Prompted by a need for change originating within the society itself, the pro's have prepared a design for instituting a change in the curriculum, and the board as society's representatives has approved the beginning move toward the change. The process is deliberate and careful. Because it is, it ensures that the curriculum meets the needs of the young. The winds of change, for all the ap-

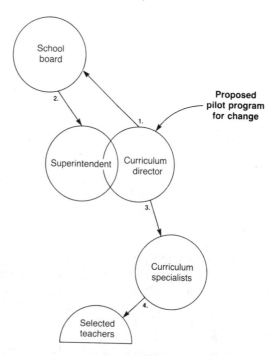

Fig. 4. Pilot program approved and instituted.

parent movement they cause, are neither over- nor underestimated. Conflicts are placed in their proper perspective. How great is the change? Not very. The process of change involving the concerns of so many people keeps it within recognizable bounds.

Now let's see how the previous events eventually influence teachers' work and learners' experiences.

CURRICULUM CHANGE IN THE CLASSROOM

The pilot program has been conducted for a year. At its beginning, the students' skills were assessed. The mathematics specialist worked with a small group of teachers to develop simple tests to determine what the learners knew when the program started. The English specialist and a small group of teachers developed a product-analysis procedure to assess children's original, practical compositions written at the beginning of the school year. Administering and correcting the mathematics test was a simple task. Analyzing the compositions was a time-consuming task, but it was the only way to obtain the desired information.

Because children in kindergarten and grades one and two could not be expected to respond effectively to tests and were not capable of writing compositions independently, observation guides were prepared for use all during the program. On an exchange basis, the primary teachers observed each other's classes every 2 months.

At the end of the pilot year, the children were again tested, and they wrote new compositions to be analyzed. In most cases, considerable growth had occurred.

At the curriculum director's direction, the specialists prepared a report and a new proposal to present to the board. This proposal suggested that the pilot program be continued for another year and that the teachers involved in it prepare instructional guides at each grade level. Satisfied with the results of the program, the board approved the proposal. It also approved the expenditure of funds for some additional instructional materials.

During the following year the pilot program continued. Tentative curriculum guides were prepared. They were tried out in classrooms not involved in the pilot program. At the close of the school year, there was further assessment of results with children in the pilot schools. A follow-up proposal was prepared for the board. It included a report of the results, copies of the tentative instructional guides, and a plan for an in-service training program for teachers. The board approved the proposal, but it modified the in-service training program to reduce its cost.

All the teachers in the district were informed of the curriculum change and how they might receive in-service training during the summer and throughout the following year. The instructional guides were prepared for distribution to all the schools and teachers who would be affected by the change. Here are some of the teachers' reactions when they heard about the new curriculum:

"Another change! We just went through one in science."

"It's about time we emphasize some practical skills."

"And I just finished individualizing my mathematics and language arts programs!"

"I think my kids would really like some of these learning activities."

"I wonder how the principal will ever be able to organize a master schedule with these two studies combined."

"Did you ever see a textbook designed for teaching these two subjects?"

"Something really new and different! I'm going to like this!"

"I've really been doing this for the last couple years. It works, and the children like it."

"I think it will be fun to try this."

Let us see what happens in several classrooms as teachers attempt to institute the change.

The student-oriented teacher

Ms. DeLaCoeur is a first-grade teacher. She is what many would call student oriented. She has an excellent background in how the young child grows and develops, and she believes that children's learning follows the paths of their interests. For this reason, she provides many choices of activities for her learners. Her classroom is replete with what she calls activity centers. There are so many different centers, separated by baffles of various kinds, that a visitor coming to the room for the first time is confused. However, a careful survey of the centers reveals that they provide for learning a variety of language, mathematics, and art skills. When her principal asked her for a copy of her daily instructional schedule, this is what she gave him:

8:30 to 9:00	Free-choice activities
9:00 to 9:20	Sharing (oral language)
9:20 to 10:30	Communications laboratory
10:30 to 10:50	Free play
10:50 to 12:00	Mathematics laboratory
12:00 to 1:00	Lunch
1:00 to 2:00	Investigative and expressive laboratory

Puzzled by the last entry in her schedule, her principal visited her classroom to see what was going on. He learned that this period was devoted to learning health, science, and social studies ideas and that each lesson usually ended with the children involved in an expressive activity based on what they had just studied.

The principal visited Ms. DeLaCoeur's classroom several other times. He observed learners involved in the following activities:

With the guidance of the teacher, writing a group letter to the school gardener asking him to come to the classroom to tell them about how to plant a garden

Using a knotted planting string to decide how many

seeds were needed to plant a section of the garden

Counting the number of cups of water needed to water the plants

Measuring the height of plants

With the guidance of the teacher, filling in a chart telling how much the plants had grown in a week

Individual learners dictating letters to the teacher to be sent to the gardener to thank him for his visit

The principal decided that Ms. DeLaCoeur's instructional program was fulfilling the requirements of the curriculum addition.

The knowledge-oriented teacher

What Mr. Lore, a seventh-grade mathematics teacher, thinks about teaching and learning is summed up in his favorite saying, "If you want chocolate cake, you have to put chocolate in it." In short, learners learn exactly what they are taught.

Ms. Wissen, the seventh-grade English teacher who must team with Mr. Lore in the curriculum change, is much of the same mind. One day, after a textbook salesman had emphasized what fun the students would have going through his product, she remarked to him, "My students come to class already knowing how to have fun. What I want to know is how your textbooks will help them learn to read, write, and speak like civilized human beings."

As you can see, neither Mr. Lore nor Ms. Wissen was pleased with the prospect of trying to combine mathematics and English. Although they had adjacent classrooms with classes scheduled at the same period, they preferred that their team exist on paper only. Their one concession to the change was that they would meet once a week after school to exchange notes on what they were doing about teaching practical skills in mathematics and language. The two agreed on the following:

Both would insist that anything written by students, including numbers, would not be accepted if the writing was messy and illegible.

Both would insist that during discussions the students would speak clearly with an appropriate choice of vocabulary.

Both would introduce a learning activity at least once a week that would give support to the other. For example, Mr. Lore might have his stu-

dents complete a family ledger for weekly expenses, total the expenses, and write a mock check in payment for the expenses. During the same week, Ms. Wissen might have the students write imaginary letters requesting reimbursement for expenses they had incurred as salesmen. These ideas had been suggested in the instructional guide.

Both agreed to report to the other any special needs for learning that either observed.

After a time, this arrangement became cumbersome and meaningless to both. They could see little evidence of learning, so they decided to work more closely as a team. They would work with combined classes one day each week. The following is what occurred during their first effort:

On the day previous to the meeting of the combined classes, Mr. Lore taught the class how to measure a room for area and how to compute the area in square yards. Ms. Wissen taught the class how to write a courteous letter to the owner of a company thanking him for excellent service.

When the combined classes met, albeit crowded in one classroom, Ms. Wissen presented the tasks for the period.

1. Each student would receive a card giving the dimensions of a rectangular living room to be carpeted. Each would compute the area of the room in square yards. The computation would be checked at the calculator by Mr. Lore.

2. The student would choose carpeting from swatches of carpet obtained from a local furniture store. The carpeting was priced differently from swatch to swatch. After making a selection, the student would compute the cost of the carpet and write out a mock check in payment. The computation and check would be verified by Mr. Lore.

3. Then the student would write a courteous letter to the owner of the furniture store thanking him for the prompt delivery of the carpeting and the thoughtfulness of the workmen who laid it. The check would be enclosed in the letter. Ms. Wissen would check the letter.

4. If time remained at the end of the period, the classes would discuss ways of expressing courtesy in a letter.

Despite a few bottlenecks at the calculator, all activities except the last were completed. Ms. Wissen decided she could use the next class period for the discussion.

In time, each teacher became more aware of the responsibilities of the other. Mr. Lore found opportunities for his students to use language skills in mathematics, and Ms. Wissen eventually bought her own calculator to use in class.

Carefully monitoring what their classes were doing and measuring progress frequently, both teachers were satisfied that their learners were learning what they needed to know.

The society-centered teacher

Mr. Tomodachi is truly concerned about the high school seniors in his practical skills laboratory. He wants them to meet societal expectations in practical language and mathematics skills. More importantly, he wants them to be able to function both as independent members of society and as participants in solving problems related to their general welfare. He knows the odds are against him. The students in his class have a defeatist attitude toward learning. After all, they had to enroll in the laboratory because they made so little progress during their junior year.

Using an instructional guide provided by the district, together with his own insights gained from experience in teaching, Mr. Tomodachi devised a series of instructional units. Here is a partial list of the units and a brief description of each:

Studymate. The purpose of this unit is to help students become well acquainted with each other. It begins with a few social games and construction enterprises, leads into values clarification centered on preferred activities, and ends with the forming of teaching-learning groups. The teacher has studied his learners' needs in practical skills. The students who are below level in mathematics skills are tutored by those who are more advanced in the skills. The same is true for students who are below level in language skills.

Write or Else! The purpose of this unit is to improve students' skills in written composition. It begins with students talking with people who have responsible positions in the community. These people include the manager of an automobile repair shop who needs mechanics who can write up repair estimates and prepare statements on completed repairs, a city councilman who tells them about the kinds of letters that prompt him to work toward needed changes, and a personnel manager who will not interview people who are unable to write clear, well-organized, legible letters of application. The discussion is followed by a laboratory in which students prepare letters and statements. Signed with anonymous names, the letters are sent to other members of the class who read and role-play their reactions.

Save the Community. This is a class simulation that the teacher devises from a current community problem, such as having a signal light installed at a dangerous intersection, getting some city land set aside for a park, or protecting small children from molestation on the way to and from school. The final act in the situation has the students presenting a proposition to a governmental body and writing a letter or petition to an assemblyman or councilman.

Compute or Else! The purpose of this unit is to improve everyday computation skills. The students check receipts, statements, and differences in costs of items. Each learner is allotted only so much to spend.

Most of Mr. Tomodachi's students make marked improvement in their practical skills. His greatest satisfaction comes when he learns that one of his students has begun to participate more actively in classroom and school affairs.

· · ·

You have seen that teachers, because they interpret curriculum from different points of view, react in different ways to curriculum changes. In each case we examined, the change was implemented fully.

There are many fiery disputes about whether a teacher should be student oriented, knowledge oriented, or society oriented. None of these orientations is superior, overall, to the others. Often a teacher changes orientation from subject to subject. A fourth-grade teacher may be student oriented when teaching art, music, and physical education, knowledge oriented when teaching work analysis, spelling, and mathematics, and society oriented when teaching social studies, science, and health. A high school mathematics and science teacher may be knowledge oriented when teaching mathematics and society oriented when teaching science. And then there are some teachers who maintain the same orientation no matter what they teach.

These examples may have lead you to some misconceptions. Primary teachers are not always student centered, junior high school teachers are not always knowledge oriented, and senior high school teachers are not always society centered. Our examples were simply for illustration.

Perhaps you have sensed a new definition for curriculum. It may be stated simply in this way: *Curriculum is what teachers and children do in schools*. Ask a pro what curriculum is, and this definition will most likely be the response. However, such a definition has credence only when it is seen in perspective. In perspective it holds sway *after* and *within* the decisions made by society.

Reviewing the process

The curriculum change process we observed reflected a series of checks and interactions. They proceeded in a Rube Goldbergian fashion from the school board to the teachers and learners and back again to the board. The new development will be carefully monitored. Press releases will occur from time to time. The voices of the societal fault-finders will be hushed, for a while.

Curriculum changes may occur in other ways. Occasionally teachers themselves respond to social forces. Let us assume, for example, that five or six teachers have begun to develop and teach social studies units about the role of women in a modern society. They have developed instructional objectives, formulated sequences of learning activities, and collected or devised the necessary instructional materials. They invite the social studies specialist to visit their classrooms to see what they are doing and accomplishing. Favorably impressed, the specialist gathers information about the program, obtains samples of plans and materials, and presents them to the curriculum director. Eventually the new development is presented to the school board. Acting on the advice of the curriculum director and the superintendent, the board may approve it as an optional study to be encouraged in all schools or may set the wheels in motion to include it as a required study.

Sometimes an energetic interest group in the community may bring about a change. In a large city recently there was a series of child molestation crimes, some ending in murder. Angered and concerned about these events, a group of community members met and planned an instructional program for children. They found informed resource persons to help them. A quick review of their intents and plans resulted in approval by the school board. A new study area was added to the curriculum of the schools in neighborhoods where the crimes had been committed.

Another resource of curriculum change is legislation. Without consultation with parents or teachers, at the behest of a strong lobby, or for no better reason than to ensure an exchange of votes on a

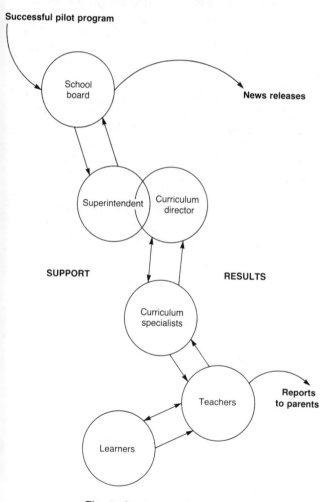

Fig. 5. Curriculum change in effect.

favored bill, legislators pass laws demanding new instruction of one kind or another.

An adoption of state-approved textbooks may also bring about curriculum change. Committees of teachers throughout a state may review textbooks and make recommendations for adoption, but their recommendations may be disregarded. Teachers may find only one set of materials available to them. They must then make accommodations in curriculum to correspond to their instructional materials.

During recent years state departments of education and the federal Department of Health, Education, and Welfare have encouraged changes in curriculum. Successful in getting appropriation laws passed, these state and national agencies inform superintendents about instructional programs they would like to see developed. If interested, the superintendent, with the approval of the board, will prepare a proposal for a new program. If the agency accepts the proposal, the district receives additional funds to explore and implement the new program.

Some of the earlier state and national pushes,

from a teacher's point of view, were ruthless. Neither teachers nor parents were consulted in their development. More recently, proposals are required to show evidence of teacher and parent participation in both the planning and implementation stages. This has given rise to a new idea in curriculum development. Instead of the district serving as the agency for developing curriculum, the individual school serves in this capacity. Of course, the board must still approve proposals before they are submitted, and the services of curriculum specialists are still available to help in the planning. But the school, rather than the district office, is the center where action occurs in developing curriculum.

To ensure that teachers and parents are not limited by their own provincial views, the funding agency restricts the choices of programs for which to submit proposals and provides guidelines that must be followed.

A favorable spin-off from this innovation is that teachers and parents must learn to work together in developing curriculum. If the innovation continues to grow, we may see teachers and parents in every school making important curriculum decisions. Changes will be made in accord with their view of social forces. The curriculum will be different from school to school. To ensure that new children moving into the school's service area are not penalized, the teacher will have to develop effec-

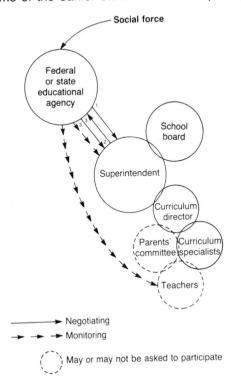

Fig. 6. A social force prompting curriculum change through a federal or state agency.

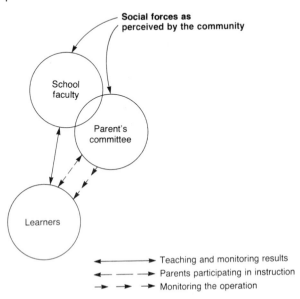

Fig. 7. The school as the main curriculum development center.

tive assessment procedures to determine what each new child's needs are within their curriculum framework. Parents will have to develop ways of introducing new parents to their roles in school.

At this point it is difficult to predict whether this innovation will come into full flower. It may require more time, effort, and energy than many teachers and parents have to expend. We shall have to wait to see what happens.

A final word

We have seen a variety of ways that curriculum is changed and a variety of roles for participants in the process. Before coming to a close, let us consider a parody of an adage: "Society and teachers propose; children dispose." In other words, children have the final say.

Some years ago a devoted elementary curriculum supervisor was hired by a school district to help its teachers improve their instruction. She was instrumental in having certain materials and instructional guides removed from the classrooms. The teachers were frustrated without their familiar materials. Some began to come to her office for advice. "What shall we teach?" they asked. She would toy with a pencil or paper clip for a moment and then say very softly, "Ask your children."

Students have the ultimate role in curriculum development. They "say" what they mean in the ways that they respond to what teachers try to get them to do. And the only desirable response that students can make is to learn.

SUMMARY

The societal curriculum consists of the ideas, skills, and values characteristic of a society or people. This curriculum is taught to the young to ensure their existence as well as the continued existence of the society.

Technological inventions, economic crises, political crises, social change, and changes in the power base of a people are conditions reflecting the work of social forces. These forces, because they change the roles of people and how they organize themselves for living, working, and playing, prompt changes in the curriculum.

Curriculum change is slow.

The school board, or the power base, and the pro's (superintendent, teachers, etc.) work together to develop or change curriculum. When the board becomes aware of a possible need for change, it directs the superintendent to investigate it. The staff of specialists does the actual investigation. They prepare a preliminary plan, which is submitted to a curriculum committee of teachers. Together they formulate an instructional strategy. On the approval of the board, the strategy is tested in a pilot program. If the program is successful, the new development is monitored for effectiveness.

Teachers, whether student oriented, knowledge oriented, or society oriented, accommodate to the change, in accord with their points of view.

As far as the pro's are concerned, the curriculum is what teachers and children do in classrooms. This definition is viable only when seen within the context of the societal definition.

Other ways of developing or changing curriculum include changes instigated by teachers, interest groups, state legislation, textbook adoptions, and proposals for change funded by the state or national government.

An innovation in curriculum development or change identifies the school as the basic developmental unit. Cooperating with parents and involving them sometimes in classroom participation, the faculty of the school develops the curriculum. Both teachers and parents monitor the program.

After all is said and done, the learner has the final say. Successful curriculum development has occurred when teachers and learners are able to work together productively on topics of importance to both society and the individual student.

A glance back. Now it's time to take out the notes you made at the beginning of the chapter. Do you still think the same way you did then? Why?

SUGGESTED ACTIVITIES FOR FURTHER UNDERSTANDING
Remembering what you've read

1. Make a list of the study areas or subjects taught in the public schools. Arrange them in what you believe is the most feasible order of importance. Then decide why you chose that order.
2. Make a list of the different pro's involved in curriculum change or development. Arrange them in what you believe is their order of importance. Then decide why you chose that order.
3. Make a diagram similar to those in the chapter showing how curriculum is changed when a group of teachers starts making innovations.
4. Make a list of the different ways that curriculum may be developed or changed. Choose the one you think is the best and tell why.

Thinking about what you've learned

1. Imagine that someone has invented something new that will improve economic production, transportation, communication, or health care. Whatever it is like is up to you. Then develop logically the conditions it might cause to prevail and how these changes might prompt a need for curriculum change.
2. Imagine that all curriculum change or development was the prerogative solely of the state or national government. Do you think this would be more advantageous to the teachers or the learners? Why?
3. Imagine that all curriculum change or development was the prerogative solely of each teacher. Do you think this would improve or reduce the effectiveness of learning in schools? Why?
4. You are probably thinking about the teacher you are or would like to be. Do you think of yourself as primarily student oriented, knowledge oriented, or society oriented? What would you say to other people to convince them that this is what you really are?

Using what you've learned

1. Arrange to visit a classroom for an hour or an instructional period. Observe the teacher and learners carefully as they do their work to answer these questions:
   a. What is the purpose of the leason?
   b. What does the teacher do to get it started?
   c. What do the learners do to learn?
   d. How does the teacher bring the lesson to a close?
   e. How would you classify the teacher you observed? Student oriented? Knowledge oriented? Society oriented?
2. Obtain an instructional guide or teacher's edition for any subject at any grade level or a state framework for instruction in any subject. Examine it carefully to see whether it offers provisions to meet the needs of teachers having different orientations.
3. Participate in this simulation. Have the class count off in fours: one, two, three, four; one, two, etc. All the one's are a group, all the two's are a group, etc. Have all persons get in their group.
   All odd-numbered groups are school faculties.
   All even-numbered groups are interest groups.
   Situation: The school board has given its approval to a variety of community-based instructional programs developed by the following interest groups:
   The Community Music Association
   The Community Art Association
   The Child-Protection Association
   The Zoo Association
   The Museum Association
   The Historical Society
   The Health Association
   The Wildlife Association

All these groups may institute programs in schools, *but only after negotiating with each school.*

All the groups, with the exception of the Wildlife Association, have managed to get programs in the schools. As a matter of fact, 20% of the instructional time each week in all grades is now devoted to instruction sponsored by the groups. School faculties believe that basic instruction will be reduced in effectiveness if any more programs are instituted in the school.

The Wildlife Association has been slow in generating interest in school-oriented programs.

Phase I (10 minutes)
   Groups representing school faculties meet to decide how they are going to prevent the intrusion of any more instructional programs sponsored by interest groups.
   Groups representing the Wildlife Association as an interest group meet to decide generally how they are going to use a local game refuge and local experts on wildlife to carry on a program in the schools.

Phase II (15 minutes)
   Interest groups convene at the schools with the faculties to try to have their program included in the school.

Phase III (rest of the period)
   Evaluation.
   Discuss: Who was successful? What arguments appeared to be most effective? How did the members of the various groups feel? Why?

4. Interview an elementary teacher or principal or a high school teacher to discover what a pro does and how he or she feels about curriculum development or change.

REFERENCES

Gwynn, J. M., and Chase, J. B. *Curriculum principles and social trends* (4th ed.). New York: Macmillan Publishing Co., Inc., 1969.

Hass, G. *Curriculum planning: a new approach* (2d ed.). Boston: Allyn & Bacon, Inc., 1977.

McNeil, J. D. *Curriculum: a comprehensive introduction*. Boston: Little, Brown & Co., 1976.

Saylor, J. G., and Alexander, W. M. *Planning curriculum for the schools*. New York: Holt, Rinehart & Winston, Inc. 1974.

Shuster, A. H., and Ploghoff, M. E. *The emerging elementary curriculum* (3rd ed.). Columbus, Ohio: Charles E. Merrill Publishing Co., 1977.

Smith, B. O., Stanley, W. O., and Shores, J. H. *Fundamentals of curriculum development* (rev. ed.). New York: Harcourt Brace Jovanovich, Inc., 1957.

Taba, H. T. *Curriculum development: theory and practice*. New York: Harcourt Brace Jovanovich, Inc., 1962.

Zais, R. S. *Curriculum principles and foundations*. New York: Thomas Y. Crowell Co., Inc., 1976.

PRINCIPLES OF INSTRUCTION
THEIR APPLICATION **10**

Education is not exactly a new fad. It's been with us as long as we have any way of knowing. It's part of every society, always has been, and always will be.

Education hasn't always been formal, of course, not always done through schooling, with desks, crayons, and salutes to the flag. It hasn't always tried to promote worthy use of leisure time or develop citizens who can function in democratic milieus. But it has always been done in some form, because any human society must teach its young if the group is to survive. Unlike honeybees or gila monsters, human infants don't have ready-made patterns of behavior that serve the group or the individual self. Our behaviors, necessary to survive and function as humans, must be learned.

But how do you teach the young? What do you do, and how do you do it? What do they do? Within what settings does learning occur best? What materials, if any, are necessary or desirable? How much time should be spent on education? We'll stop the list of questions here. We could fill up all the pages of this chapter with them, and there would be no room left for the answers.

Let's begin with a grateful acknowledgment of the fact that we do know a great deal about schooling, teaching, and learning. Sure, we run into mysterious, fuzzy, and frightening areas. We trip over questions we can't answer. We crack our heads against walls of bureaucratic inflexibility, and we are washed to and fro by changing tides of public sentiment and opinion. Yet despite it all, we have learned many things about teaching each other and about learning from each other.Some of the things we have learned seem to hold true irrespective of time, place, and circumstance. Other things we have learned seem to apply only to specific times, places, learners, and circumstances. If

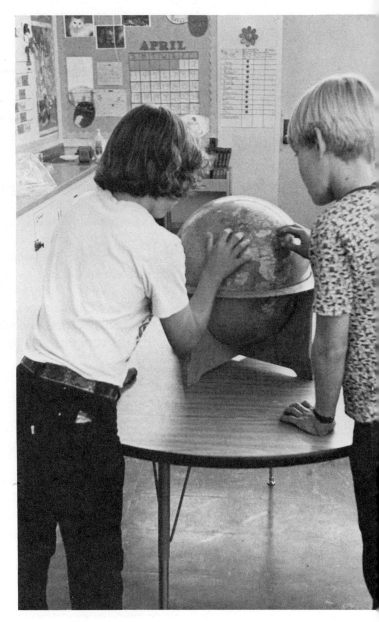

a thing holds true, time after time, we can refer to it as a "principle."

Webster's New Collegiate Dictionary provides several different definitions for the word "principle." The definition that comes closest to the meaning we use in this chapter is "a fundamental truth; a primary or basic law, doctrine or the like." In this chapter on principles of instruction, we need to do two things. First, we need to identify important principles of learning. Second, we need to identify the principles of instruction, some of which are based on principles of learning and some of which do not relate directly to principles of learning.

PRINCIPLES OF LEARNING

Principles of instruction are based on principles of learning. They go beyond the principles of learning, on to matters of arranging learning environments, formulating objectives, selecting materials, initiating and conducting instructional episodes, maintaining productive self-discipline, matching students to instructional tasks, and so on. Yet all these instructional matters turn back to what we knew about the types, processes, procedures, and conditions of learning.

This section presents an outline of established principles of learning. Brief explanations accompany these principles.

I. All humans have a natural potential for learning. This potential is especially great in the young, but it endures strongly throughout life. The potential is effectuated through experience. The most common definition of learning stresses this role of experience: "Learning is the change of behavior that results from experience."

II. Learning occurs in three great domains, each of which is vitally important to all of us. These domains are as follows:
   A. *Cognitive*. Knowledge and ways of knowing.
   B. *Affective*. Feelings, attitudes, and values.
   C. *Psychomotor*. Physical movements and skills.

III. People learn through several different procedures. Chief among these procedures are the following:
   A. *Classical conditioning*. Pavlovian-type automatic learning wherein new stimuli become associated with behaviors. We automatically leave the classroom when the bell rings. We go on the green light and stop on the red.
   B. *Instrumental conditioning*. Skinnerian-type learning in which reinforcement (reward) follows on the heels of a given act, thus increasing the likelihood of one's repeating the act. This is the procedure used to train animals. It works equally well for humans. We sit up straight if the teacher praises us for it. We do whatever we can that brings us positive recognition from our peers.
   C. *Trial and error*. By trying, we do some things right (that lead in helpful directions) and we do some things wrong (that lead to dead ends). We remember both the correct and incorrect responses and thus learn to use the correct ones, while avoiding the incorrect ones.
   D. *Imitation*. Most of our social behavior, very complex in nature, is learned by observing other people and imitating their behaviors that are attractive to us.

E. *Verbal association*. We learn verbal symbols for concrete objects and abstractions. We learn to associate these symbols so as to speak and think, which in turn enables us to progress on to other learnings.

F. *Cognitive reorganization*. We put things together in our minds and in our own classifications and relationships and behave on the basis of this organization. Insightful learning (the aha! type) is of this sort. So is creative, problem-solving learning.

G. *Logic, inductive and deductive*. We learn much through the processes carried out in our own minds. If every book we see has a title, we learn (by inductive logic) that all books have titles, including those millions of books we have not seen. If an authority tells us that all living things contain carbon, we learn (by deductive logic) that the elm tree outside our window contains carbon.

IV. People employ several different intellectual processes in learning. These processes, although different, are interrelated. They include the following:

A. *Perceiving*. Noticing, taking note of. To perceive means to become aware of. We are literally inundated with thousands of visual, auditory, and other sensory data, almost every minute of our waking lives. Most of those data don't even register in our awareness. Yet we have the interesting ability to selectively turn attention to these data if we wish. We can note them, recognize them, point to them, react to them, and so forth. All these acts provide evidence that we are perceiving the data. This perception cannot be stressed too strongly in learning. Without perception, learning cannot proceed.

B. *Discriminating*. Making distinctions; being able to tell one thing from another. Going hand in hand with perception, discrimination allows us to separate items of data from each other. It lets us sort the items out, just as we sort apples from oranges from peaches. Discrimination involves the ability to note both similarities and differences among data items. Without this ability, all incoming data would appear the same. Again, learning could not occur.

C. *Making relationships*. Making intellectual connections between and among items of data. It is very difficult to define the term "relationship." The best the dictionary can do is to tell us relationship is the condition of one thing to another. Not much help there. Still, we have intuitive grasps of the meaning; we use the word with understanding.

The first thing we have to realize is that relationships exist only in the mind. We make them up. Among the many kinds of relationships we can make, four are especially important in learning and teaching. Those four are as follows:

1. *Similarity relationships*. These permit us to group data together on the basis of traits they have in common. Thus we can group all animals that have hair, give milk, and are warm blooded into a single group— mammals.

Continued.

2. *Association relationships*. These are made on the basis of noticing that items of data usually occur together. Thus we group together such diverse items as sand, cactus, heat, dryness, snakes, and lizards; they all fit into the stereotyped notion of desert.

3. *Cause-effect relationships*. These are made on the basis of noting that a particular event always follows on the heels of another particular event. When this happens, we often infer that the first event causes the second. If we heat the air inside a balloon, the balloon gets larger. We say that heating is the cause and expansion is the effect.

4. *Means-end relationships*. These are similar to cause-effect relationships, except that we first focus attention on an end result we desire and then try to decide the "means" that will bring about that end. If we want a fat goose to eat, we can find several means to that end. We can buy one at the market. We can steal one from the neighbor's pen. Or, as a last resort, we can feed our own goose all its little heart desires until it is plump and waddly.

These kinds of relationships lie at the heart of learning. Similarity and association relationships permit us to sort, group, and store masses of data. Cause-effect relationships permit us to predict and control events. Means-end relationships provide us with skill, process, and technical know-how. All learning beyond the most elementary level involves the fabrication and use of these relationships.

D. *Analyzing*. Breaking something—an object, an idea, a composition—down into its component parts. Analysis is an intellectual process that helps us ferret out, from a group of interrelated items of information, those that are key, essential, and desirable. It lets us see how the items fit together. It lets us make better sense out of what we are perceiving. Analysis of a political speech, for example, enables us to clarify the key points that were included, together with obvious, intended, and hidden messages. What was the speaker *really* saying with those words, we ask. Analysis of a chemical permits us to identify the elements it contains. Analysis of a soil sample allows us to determine the plant nutrients it contains and lacks. Analysis of a painting permits us to identify message, effect, and technique of the artist. In essence, analysis is the process we use in attempting to better understand the objects and events around us.

E. *Synthesizing*. The putting together of parts, so as to make a new entity. Synthesis is the reverse of analysis. When we synthesize, we combine and recombine existing parts so as to produce a larger, more complex entity. Using certain chemicals, we synthesize amino acids in the laboratory. Using common words and expressions, we synthesize (compose) a poem, a new entity that has beauty or power far beyond the collective total of its individual parts. The Moog Synthesizer puts together musical notes out of pure tones and allows them to be played as pleasing compositions. Synthesis, which is the prime process within creativity, is the vehicle we use to construct the larger picture, to produce, and to create. It is one of the most advanced of human intellectual abilities, one we all have in lesser or greater degrees, and fortunately one that can be improved with use.

V. People learn best when tasks and materials are appropriate to their individual levels of intellectual, linguistic, and social development; to their backgrounds of experience; to their levels of academic achievement; and to their preferred styles of learning. Let us briefly examine each of these four factors.

  A. *Intellectual, linguistic, and social development.*

    1. *Intellectual development.* This occurs throughout the elementary and secondary school years, usually reaching its full growth by around age 15 or 16 years. This development is not a straight-line progression, like a muscle follows as it increases in strength. Rather it is more akin to climbing stairs. Each stairstep has its own particular abilities and inabilities. The best explanation for this progression has come from the work of the Swiss psychologist Jean Piaget. Piaget has shown that the individual progresses through various intellectual levels, three of which are particularly pertinent to school learning. These three levels (remember, there are earlier levels, too) are as follows:

      a. *Intuitive thought.* A level characteristic of children in kindergarten, first, and second grade. Thinking occurs mostly in terms of visualizations and intuitive hunches. Thought about abstract ideas is not possible. Series of steps and groups of rules cannot be remembered accurately. Logical thinking is not yet possible. Number processes, such as addition and subtraction, cannot be done with understanding.

      b. *Concrete operations.* A level characteristic of children in third through sixth grade. Although still functioning at the intuitive thought level part of the time, the students are now able to carry out logical thought processes, to categorize and conceptualize, and to do logical thinking based on cause-effect and means-end relationships. They can conserve, that is, realize that a given quantity remains the same regardless of changes in shape, size, or arrangement. This ability permits them to carry out number processes with understanding. They can remember rules and series of steps. They cannot, however, adequately deal with highly abstract ideas.

      c. *Formal operations.* A stage of intellectual development characteristic of individuals in junior high school and beyond. At this level students become able to engage mentally with highly abstract ideas, to carry out experimentation in their heads, and to deal with complex social and moral issues. This is the level of adult thought. Although all of us use concrete thought a good deal of

Continued.

the time, we are able, when the occasion demands, to use formal thought. This is an ability that the vast majority of students in the elementary school do not—in fact cannot—possess.

2. *Linguistic development.* This is very important in learning. It is a factor that had not received much attention prior to efforts to improve educational experiences for bilingual students. Bilingual programs provide instructions in the students' native tongues until such time as their linguistic ability in English has developed to the point that they can benefit fully from instruction in English. This point is basic: Most school learning is verbal or at least has a verbal overlay. Students who cannot cope with this verbal aspect cannot learn adequately in school.

3. *Social development.* This refers to one's ability to relate acceptably with other students, cooperate, take turns, show consideration, and so forth. Schooling, both of necessity and design, is social in nature. Groups of individuals must live, work, talk, and play together. The kinds of activities best suited to student learning depend on the extent to which students have developed social skills. If they cannot work together, they must have learning experiences that do not depend on cooperative efforts.

B. *Background of experience.* As was the case with linguistic ability and social development, the experiences students have had in their lives strongly affect the ways in which they learn. Much has been said in recent years about the interrelationship of culture and learning. Culture refers to the conglomerate of objects, values, and lifeways of people. The culture of the Navajo Indians includes the objects, values, and lifeways that characterize that group.

As we are able to identify any subgroup within the larger American society, so are we able to note cultural differences peculiar to that group. This means that school students from that group will bring with them a background of experiences different to some extent from other students in school.

This difference in background of experiences makes a difference in learning because instructional materials and language have to be somewhat standardized. Textbook producers would find impossible the task of making the contents of their books equally familiar to students from such diverse groups as Navajo Indians, inner city blacks, transient farm laborers, and white-collar professionals. The language, the illustrations, the contents, the activities could not be equally suited to all.

Because of this fact, backgrounds of experience, if they are quite different, can have debilitating effects on students' abilities to learn in school.

C. *Levels of academic progress.* Learning occurs best when the instructional activities are difficult enough to challenge the students but not so difficult as to frustrate them. Whether or not an activity is appropriate for

given students depends in large part on their level of academic performance. They cannot profit from reading at a third-grade level. They cannot progress well in trigonometry if they have not yet learned basic arithmetic. By the same token, they will not progress properly if they continue reading fifth-grade material long after they have reached eighth-grade level. Nor will they improve in ability to overhaul an automobile engine by continuing to practice removing the valve covers.

D. *Preferred styles of learning.* It has long been known that different individuals prefer to learn in different ways. Some prefer to learn through reading, some through talking, some through work with their hands. Some prefer to work alone, others with a partner, still others in groups. Some prefer having the teacher organize, direct, and evaluate their learning activities. Others prefer to be on their own, doing things their way.

Students seem to learn best when allowed to work in ways consistent with their preferences. We know that some have analytical minds. They are concerned about details, sequential organization, leaving nothing to chance. Others have global minds. They see the big picture. They are not so concerned about details, the ways parts fit together or the way things work. We are just learning how to determine preferred learning styles and how to adapt instructions to those styles.

VI. Many factors in the learning situation are known to speed, strengthen, or otherwise enhance learning. These factors include the following:

A. *Clarity and organization.* We can learn things that don't make sense to us; we regularly do so. But if we want to progress in meaningful learning, the kind that we can comprehend and consciously use, we will find our paths considerably smoothed by clarity and sequential organization.

Clarity depends on the use of words whose meanings are understood. It depends on specification of who, what, where, when, why, and how. It depends on relationships that tie these elements together into a structure that gives form to the material. It depends on informational episodes short enough to avoid intellectual overload, which comes with too much information given at once without time for sorting and review.

Organization facilitates meaningful learning. Good organization, done by the teacher, the skilled learner, or the material itself, provides a flowing

Continued.

sequence, so that each idea leads smoothly and naturally into the next.

This organization can be logical or psychological. Logical organization puts ideas into sequence according to steps in a process or according to which pieces of information seem to build best on which others. Psychological organization arranges ideas into sequences that have the greatest emotional impact on learners or that provide contrasts, changes of pace, and sidelights that maintain interest.

B. *Progression from known to unknown and concrete to abstract.* Learning occurs best when it is built on top of something already known. By beginning with the known, learners have a secure basis from which to proceed. The new learnings can be hooked to, stacked on, or tucked into nooks and crannies of existing knowledge. This procedure provides meaning, structure, and organization, thus enabling learners to process it quickly and retrieve it easily.

The same principle holds for abstract learning. Abstractions are best learned when they are built out of concrete information. The concept of time, as an abstraction, grows on the basis of concrete clocks and calendars. The concept of love, as an abstraction, grows on the basis of concrete examples of people showing concern and affection for each other.

C. *Appropriate practice.* It is true that learning can occur without learner repetition or reinactment, what we refer to as practice. Such learning occurs continually through the processes of modeling and imitation. Nevertheless, most learning is brought to greater effectiveness, efficiency, permanence, and use ability through practice.

Not all kinds of practice are equally useful. Useful practice consists of repetitive reenactments with a specific purpose in mind. That purpose might be the improvement of a recognized weakness, just as we work on our backhand in tennis or on our ability to pronounce final r's correctly in Spanish. Also, results of these efforts must be discernible. It does no good to practice the tennis backhand if we cannot see the results of our efforts. It can even be harmful, because we may be building in errors that will be hard to erase.

Thus practice should have a purpose, and we must be able to see its results. One of the best ways to practice is through applying what we are learning in realistic settings. We practice the backhand in matches where little is at stake. We practice trilling the r in Spanish conversation. We practice using words we have learned to spell in writing letters, articles, and informative essays.

D. *Reinforcement.* Learning can occur without reinforcement, just as it can occur without practice. Again, however, learning is often speeded, guided, and made more permanent when reinforcement is present. You will recall that reinforcement is the occurrence of a stimulus after an act and increases the likelihood of that act's being repeated. In common parlance, reinforcement is called reward. Reward is given when someone performs a desired act. That reward usually makes the individual more likely to repeat the act.

Reinforcement is a very powerful tool for shaping and controlling behavior. It grew out of behavioristic psychology and was popularized by the great psychologist B. F. Skinner. Reinforcement has been thoroughly validated as a means of facilitating learning and retention.

E. *Corrective feedback.* Corrective feedback is a process of informing learners, as they practice, exactly what they are doing wrong and exactly what they need to do to improve. One of the prime reasons for purposeful practice is to provide for corrective feedback. Often, much of this feedback comes from the observed results of the act. We get feedback about our tennis backhand when we see what the ball does. If it goes ripping over the net and into the opponent's court, we are reinforced, and we try to repeat the act. If it goes thudding into the net or sailing over the backstop, we decide to try something different. The results of our act give us feedback.

The problem is, when the result is no good, we don't know exactly what to do about it. That's where we need corrective feedback—an expert who can tell us precisely what to do to improve. This kind of feedback, given in the right way at the right time, can dramatically improve our rate of learning.

F. *Practicality.* It is a fact of human nature that we learn more quickly and remember longer those things that are useful to us. If a thing is practical, we can use it. If it is impractical, we cannot, and thus it means little to us. Typing and driver training are practical skills that people learn well and quickly, despite the fact that both are comparatively complicated. Learning the various meters of classical poetry is not too practical for most of us. That's why we do a poor job of learning them and why we forget them so soon.

VII. Certain highly transient states within the learner are known to affect learning. These states are easy to manipulate in teaching and among them are the following:

A. *Motivation.* Motivation is a drive or desire to do a particular thing. A very large group of factors is believed to affect motivation. Maslow (1943), the great humanistic psychologist, proposed a "hierarchy of needs" that he thought explained human motivation. Here you see his hierarchy:

Aesthetic	↑
Self-actualization	
Esteem	Higher
Love and belonging	
Safety	Lower
Physiological	
	↓

Maslow believed that every person has an inner drive (motivation) toward personal growth. To realize that growth, each individual seeks to

Continued.

meet important groups of needs. Needs occur in levels, arranged in order. The lowest level, fundamental to all others, is physiological needs. The individual is always motivated to meet these needs, and as they are met, they allow the individual to seek gratification of the next higher level of needs. And so it goes up through the hierarchy to the highest levels.

A second way to look at motivation is to examine interests of students. We all develop interests as we have experiences that prove pleasing to us. We are interested in sports if sports have brought us pleasure. We become interested in reading, hiking, music, photography, motorcycles, etc. in the same way. Students at various age levels are known to have large numbers of interests in common. This enables teachers to relate learning to those interests, thereby ensuring student motivation toward involvement in that learning.

A third way to consider motivation is to examine the phenomenon of curiosity. Curiosity is an inclination to investigate new things. All of us have the trait, some more than others. We see curiosity come into play in relation to objects, ideas, and events that are puzzling, unexpected, incongruous, humorous, novel, colorful, animated, or suspenseful. Skillful teachers continually look for opportunities to weave such traits into instruction. This provides the spice that motivates student involvement.

A fourth way to look at motivation is to examine the powerful effects of reinforcement. When students learn that their good efforts bring rewards, they show far greater inclination toward learning. Teachers use reinforcers—social (praise, recognition), graphic (markers, stars), and tangible (tokens, candy)—to increase student motivation in the learning tasks provided.

B. *Attention*. Attention refers to the focusing of senses and/or mind on the task at hand. We have an uncanny ability to control our own attention. We can home in with our senses and mind, and we can just as easily disengage, not seeing or hearing, while our mind takes off on its own flights of fancy.

In learning and teaching, however, attention is necessary. We can't learn what we don't perceive. Attention affects the quality and quantity of perception.

Several procedures help increase and direct attention. A first procedure is simply intent to pay attention. If we really try our best, we can pay attention to even the dullest, least inspired instruction. We can make ourselves examine a fiber of cotton; we can make ourselves listen to the professor drone on; we can force ourselves to wrestle with considerations of the common good.

Fortunately, there are other procedures for helping learners attend that remove some of the burdens. Teachers can provide advance organization, already discussed as a means of facilitating meaningful learning. They can provide the factors known to attract learner curiosity: suspense, humor, incongruity, novelty, surprise, and so forth. They can use instructional models—live, recorded, graphic, or tangible—that have clarity, prestige, and personal attractiveness. They can provide physical movement, verbal exchange, role playing, and demonstrations. They can provide changes of pace when fatigue begins to set in. Skillful teachers employ as many of these techniques as feasible. Learners have a responsibility to pay attention to task. There are many ways teachers can help them live up to that responsibility.

C. *Active response*. As a rule of thumb, people learn faster when they are actively responding than when they are passively receiving. True, there are many exceptions. Social behavior can be learned without response. So can much factual information. Still, active response sets up some important conditions for learning. Among these conditions are attention, practice, and opportunity for feedback. Responding forces us to pay attention. Responding allows us to practice what it is we are learning, thus increasing speed and permanence. It affords the opportunity for providing corrective feedback, also known to facilitate speed and accuracy of learning.

D. *Sense of purpose*. Again, as a general rule of thumb we learn faster, remember longer, and make better use of what we learn when we have a sense of purpose for what we are learning. Sense of purpose means that we know why we are learning what we are learning, what good it will do us, and how we can use it. Some subjects and topics have a built-in sense of purpose. That's the case for typing, driver training, vocational agriculture, photography, sailing, and other topics directly related to work and avocation. Other topics and subjects have little innate purposeful-

Continued.

ness, as is the case for algebra, geometry, chemistry, and history. It's awfully hard to explain to learners, if they don't feel it already, just why they should spend time on these areas of study.

Whenever possible, and to whatever extent possible, we should attempt to provide a sense of purpose in learning. This purposefulness supplies motivation, focuses attention, and furnishes learners a sense of satisfaction, all of which influence learning.

VIII. Less transient states within the learner are also known to affect learning. These states cannot be manipulated easily, as can motivation, attention, active responding, and sense of purpose. They can, however, be modified slowly. At the same time instruction can be adapted to them. These states include the following:

A. *Intellectual development.* This state was discussed previously. Mention was made of the contributions of Jean Piaget in describing the stages of intellectual development through which individuals progress. There is some evidence that progression through the stages can be speeded. Piaget questions the value of attempting to accelerate progression. He believes it is best to allow this development to occur naturally, in its own good time.

Mary Meeker (1969) does attempt to affect intellectual development. Basing her work on Guilford's (1959) model of the intellect, she has devised means of identifying weak areas of intellectual development within the individual, and she has devised activities that can shore up those weaknesses.

B. *Language ability.* One's ability to make full use of the language of instruction—usually English in this country—greatly affects the ability to learn. This generalization holds true for both native and nonnative speakers of English.

Language ability is a learned skill. It can be developed fairly rapidly, although, of course, it cannot be manipulated from moment to moment. For native English speakers, language ability can be developed most rapidly through word study and wide reading. For nonnative English speakers, language ability can be increased rapidly through specially organized programs in which English is taught as a foreign language, focusing on vocabulary development, phrases, expressions, and extensive practice in listening and speaking.

C. *Background of experience.* As described earlier, learning best proceeds from the known to the unknown. Materials used in schools contain ideas, objects, and values that are assumed to be common to all students. Often, however, students will not have experienced those ideas, objects, and values. They cannot therefore build new learnings on them. When this is the case, teachers are left with two possibilities. Either they can change instruction, using different materials, or they can attempt to provide the experiences that do not exist in the student's life space.

In actual practice, both avenues are used. Teachers adapt instruction to avoid the debilitating effects on learning of lack of requisite experiences. Meanwhile, they begin providing, both inside and outside of class, experiential ideas, objects, and events believed to facilitate future learning.

D. *Preferred styles of learning.* This state, too, was discussed earlier in the chapter. It is well established that individuals have different styles of learning that they ordinarily select when given the opportunity to do so. Learning in general seems to progress more satisfactorily when students are allowed to use their preferred styles.

Evidence is still lacking concerning whether learning style preferences can be changed and whether one can learn to switch easily from one style to another as demanded by the learning situation. We do know that many school tasks require a detailed, analytic approach. Most college and university study requires this approach. Some tasks, however, require global, synthetic, exploratory, or creative approaches. It remains to be determined how well students can learn to use such different styles of learning and whether they can consciously convert from one to the other when necessary.

E. *Sense of personal worthiness.* William Glasser (1969) has identified this sense of worthiness as crucial to successful experience in school. People who do not see themselves as worthy cannot interact to best advantage with other people, and they cannot take best advantage of school learning opportunities.

Sense of worthiness is not something that can be turned on and off like the kitchen light. It can, however, be manipulated, albeit slowly, in the school setting. Sense of worthiness grows out of successful encounters with both subject matter and other people. Both are important; both can be influenced greatly by teachers.

Both behaviorists and humanists stress success experiences in subject matter. Behaviorists strive for virtually 100% accuracy, believing that success breeds success, as they say. Humanists stress success, but also think occasional failure must come as people test their powers. You don't know what you are capable of until you test yourself to the limit, which may bring failure. Such failure, however, is seen as the natural result of growth and striving, not as the result of stupidity or ineptness. Such positive failure is occasionally valuable in the total growth of the person.

Personal relations with others profoundly affect the sense of worth. Teachers now have access to established techniques for bringing about quality relationships with and among students. These techniques are admirably described in the works of Glasser (1969), Rogers (1969), Gordon (1974), and Ginott (1972).

IX. Transfer of learning (application to other situations) is increased through task

Continued.

similarity, understanding, practice, and application. Transfer is one of the two primary purposes of school learning. What we learn now should aid us somehow in the future. The other primary purpose of school learning is the development of the individual self, an idea often discussed in this book. Here let us consider briefly the factors known to increase our ability to apply what we learn in school.

A. *Task similarity*. What we learn now will serve us in the future in proportion to the degree of similarity between learning task and future task. That is, school learnings help us if they are similar to situations we will face later. They do not help us if they are unrelated to anything else we will ever encounter.

To illustrate, consider the development of foreign language instruction. Prior to 1960 most foreign language teaching stressed vocabulary development, verb conjugation, and rules of grammar. As a result, language students had good vocabularies, could conjugate verbs like whizzes, and could tell you where adjectives came in the sentence. What they couldn't do was talk to another person in that language. The ability to understand other speakers and to make oneself understood never developed, because listening and talking were not stressed. So you see that what was learned in school did not transfer well to future communication situations. There was not sufficient similarity between the learning task and the later situation. That fault, by the way, was remedied. Language instruction now places much greater stress on speaking and understanding.

So it is with all aspects of the curriculum. What we learn in English, mathematics, science, art, and group process skills will serve us later if we encounter situations similar to the learning situation. The implication is obvious: school learning should be made as similar as possible to situations students will encounter later.

B. *Understanding of rules and generalizations*. Transfer is further increased when learners understand the basic rules or general principles of what they are learning. These general ideas transfer to a broad spectrum of subsequent tasks. For example, in driver training you learn the general rules of conducting vehicles on public streets. You may learn to drive a Chevrolet. What you learn will enable you to drive not only Chevrolets, but Fords, Plymouths, Triumphs, Rolls Royces, Jaguars, Hondas, and any other automobiles you can name. Much of what you learn will also help you to drive motorcycles, tractors, trucks, and buses. The general principles involved are the same—traffic rules, steering wheels, gear shifts, brakes, accelerators. What you learn will even help you in learning to fly an airplane. There are general principles common to both tasks. There's a bit more you'll have to learn about flying a plane, though.

C. *Practice*. Extensive experience with the material being learned increases its transferability. This is not because of traits inherent in the practice itself, but rather because of the familiarity with basic principles that comes with practice.

D. *Application*. Continued practice in applying learnings greatly promotes transfer. When we are required to apply what we have learned to new problem situations, we are forced to search for similarities in learning task and subsequent task. We are forced to seek out specific items and generalized ideas that can serve. Furthermore, we accustom ourselves to seeking ways of applying what we know. This continued attitude of knowledge application enables us to better deal with situations that occur both inside and outside school.

X. Retention (remembering) of what is learned is increased through intent to remember, sensory involvement, practicality, emotional involvement, use of mnemonics, overlearning, and continued use of the material learned.

Retention is slighted in education. This is hard to justify. Anything truly worth learning is equally worth remembering. Yet in practice we learn for the test, then blithely forget all we learned. The blame for this strange situation must be shared equally by curriculum, teachers, and students.

Curriculum is to blame when it includes material that is useless, impractical, irrelevant, and devoid of meaning. Such material might as well be forgotten. There is no reason to learn it in the first place.

Teachers are to blame when they stress grades and tests, using them as threats to motivate students. They are to blame when they fail to help students see the purpose, meaning, and usefulness of what they are learning. As a result, the students learn for the test, never intending to remember the material beyond test time or to make any use of it.

Once students have attained an ability to reason, they must share in the responsibility for their learning. They cannot justify sitting back in grudging compliance with whatever is asked of them. Their responsibility is to make the most of learning. They must seek learnings that are stimulating and useful. They must attempt to remember and apply those learnings. When they do not, they are to blame.

But, as Glasser says, what has happened in the past has no bearing. The question is, what are all curriculum makers, teachers, and students going to do about it, starting right now?

One thing we are going to do is examine recognized ways of improving retention.

A. *Intent to remember*. Strangely enough, we remember better those things we intend to remember. This intent helps us to focus on the learnings more keenly, run them through our minds, and seek ways to apply them.

B. *Sensory involvement*. Generally speaking, we remember better when we use both eyes and ears than if we use only one of these organs. Retention is further increased when we add the sense of touch and further yet if smell and taste are brought into play.

This sensory involvement gives us more handles on what we learn,

Continued.

more vehicles for retrieving it from storage. Ever notice how an odor will bring back memories from the dim past, not even thought of for years?

C. *Practicality*. We remember better those learnings that are useful to us. Ability to recall seems to be related to the number (and/or strength) of associations we make between the learned material and other objects, ideas, and events. When we see learning as practical, we naturally relate it to other situations in which it might be used. These relationships give us additional means of drawing the learning out of our memory banks.

D. *Emotional involvement*. If you ever have had an automobile accident, you remember it in glowing detail. If you have been associated with grief, you remember all. If you have had peak aesthetic experiences, you remember time, place, people, objects, situation, all. The point is clear. We remember those things that have heavy emotional overlay.

Unfortunately, we cannot often provide peak experiences in school. We would not want to provide despair experiences. But we can provide emotionality in moderation, and students' retention of the learning will increase as a result.

We can provide mystery, suspense, joy, humor, even sadness (fictional, but real enough). We can provide excitement. We can provide music and drama. We can provide the thrill of excellence. We can provide the charm of personal concern. We can weave through teaching and learning the whole range of positive human emotions. At the same time we can avoid those negative emotions that, although they increase retention, bring along a host of other suppressive effects on learning.

E. *Use of mnemonics*. Mnemonics are devices that aid the memory: 30 days hath September; every good boy does fine; spring forward, fall backward. All of us know and use a few of these devices. But we look on them more as tricks than as bona fide learning aids.

What a shame! Mnemonics are fascinating in themselves, and they afford us incredible power of retention. Ever wonder about those folks who perform their feats of memory magic, learning the names of thirty people, say, the first time they meet? Well, here's a funny thing. Their memories work just like yours and mine. The only difference is that they have learned to use their memories well. And the way they do it is by using mnemonics.

How long mnemonics have been with us is not known. We do know they were used extensively and impressively in Hellenic times. Greek orators were said to speak for hours without notes, never missing a point they wanted to stress. They often used a device known as "loci," that is, places. You can use this device by thinking of four rooms in your house, each containing five notable objects: stereo, fireplace, dining table, and so forth. You can use these places to remember a list of twenty items or ideas. You associate the ideas, in order, with the objects in each room. Associations should be outrageous visualizations. Those stick in the mind. Now all you have to do to remember the twenty items is to stroll through your house. You will encounter the items you want to remember right there.

Mnemonics are fascinating, useful, and eminently worth teaching to to students. If you would like to read more about them, refer to pp. 327-348 in *Educational Psychology: The Instructional Endeavor* (Charles, 1976).

F. *Overlearning*. This is the most commonly used technique for aiding retention. Overlearning means continued practice with material after the point that it is fully learned. Suppose, for example, you memorized the capital cities of all the states of the union. You could recall all of them without error. Now if you would continue practicing them, your ability to remember them later would be increased.

Overlearning can stamp in responses so that they become automatic. You may have noticed that after several trips from home to college you automatically make all the correct turns and stop at the right places. You have overlearned these acts to the point that they are habitual. You can think about other things and still do them right.

G. *Continued use*. It is a simple fact that if we continue to use what we have learned, it stays with us. When we don't use it, it slips away. You have seen this happen with your high school Spanish, with your junior high algebra, with the names of your best friends in third grade, with the words of your favorite songs. If we don't use it, it gets away. If we use it, we keep it.

XI. Several factors in the physical environment affect learning. Among them are light, heat, and ventilation; space for movement; instructional materials; and orderliness with flexibility. All these factors can be controlled by the teacher.

A. *Light, heat and ventilation*. These factors are so commonplace that we sometimes forget about them. Direct light must not strike learners' eyes for extended periods of time. It will cause headaches and tension. Heat must be neither too great nor too little. The range for comfortable learning is narrow. Most students become distracted when the temperature falls below 68° F or above 75° F. The most desirable level seems to be about 70° F for most students, although that will seem too cold if the outside temperature is very high. Ventilation must provide a constant supply of oxygen. Stuffiness makes students lethargic.

B. *Space for movement*. Another thing we often let slip our minds is the need for physical movement. Unless you are sick or exhausted, it becomes sheer torture to stay in the same place without moving. If you have ever sat and worked at, say mathematics or an English composition for a long time, you probably have felt an uncontrollable urge to get to your feet and move around. The physical learning environment must make provision for such movement.

C. *Instructional materials*. A vital part of the learning environment, instruc-

Continued.

tional materials make two significant contributions to learning: First, they give learners something to manipulate, to use their hands on. This manipulation focuses attention and ensures more active involvement. Second, they expand tremendously learners' realms of experience. In picture, text, and film, you range from Kilimanjaro to Everest to the Matterhorn. You visit Eskimos, Pygmys, and Australian aborigines. You see moon landings, Mars, and the Milky Way, never leaving the classroom except in your mind.

D. *Orderliness with flexibility*. Order brings tranquility and relaxation. Clutter brings confusion and restlessness. Anywhere there is purposeful activity, so, too, will there be disarray—for a time. But that disarray should be brought back to normalcy every so often. It is important for learners to know where materials belong and to replace those materials at the end of each instructional period. However, order should not become compulsive. When it does, it makes learners uneasy when clutter is necessary; they are unable to work to full capacity. However, it is psychologically calming to have work periods proceed from quiet to purposeful noise and then back to orderly calm. This means that the physical environment must provide sufficient storage for materials—a place for everything. Students must help see that materials are returned to their proper place when no longer needed. Movement about the room should be orderly, with established routines and patterns. Congestion at the pencil sharpener and teacher's desk should particularly be avoided.

XII. Several conditions within the psychosocial environment can improve learning. Among those conditions are responsible participation by learners; student sense of acceptance and worthiness; avoidance of threatening tasks and situations; and a pervasive sense of warmth, openness, and trust.

The psychosocial environment is made up of the attitudes, feelings, and personal relationships that exist within the classroom. This environment is the teacher's responsibility, although students must play responsible roles in maintaining it.

The environment gains quality as each of the four conditions increases. Let us see how the teacher controls these conditions.

A. *Responsible participation by learners*. Humanistic psychologists have continually emphasized that education should teach learners to exercise freedom of choice with attendant responsibility. This freedom and responsibility help them become self-directing people in all aspects of life.

Beyond this, however, we have learned that when students help plan their own instructional activities, they are more likely to engage in them fully. When they help decide on class rules, they are more likely to follow them. This responsible participation by learners cannot be expected of children in the early primary grades. But as they grow older, they should have increasing opportunities to play significant roles in planning and carrying out their own learning.

Students are not experts in curriculum, learning, or instruction. They are not skilled in organizing activities or in obtaining instructional materials. Yet they can assist by indicating which types of activities they prefer, which materials they enjoy, what new topics they might like to explore. They can be responsible, under the direction of the teacher, for obtaining and distributing materials, planning and carrying out individual and group projects, and helping resolve conflicts and other problems that arise during instruction.

At several places in this book you will see mention made of students' responsibilities in the teaching-learning process. Their responsibilities differ from the teacher's, but they are, in the long run, just as important.

B. *Student sense of acceptance and worthiness.* Again we return to this familiar tune. You must know it by heart. Let's keep it short this time.

We can learn better and feel better about schooling if we feel worthwhile personally. Teachers can help all students feel more or less worthwhile, depending on the extent to which they can show genuine concern for their students, accepting them as important individuals. They needn't accept all student behavior. They may reject much of it. When they do, they can differentiate between the behavior and the person, and they can insist on behavior that shows students in their best light.

C. *Avoidance of threatening tasks and situations.* Learning in its widest sense requires much of students. They must pay attention. They have to involve themselves actively, responding and manipulating. They often explore, investigate, create. They are supposed to participate responsibly. They are expected to establish meaningful relationships with "significant others," other people who are especially important in their lives.

To do all these things, individuals must feel secure, accepted, wanted, important, worthwhile. But it is not possible to feel these ways when the psychosocial climate is cold, rejecting, and threatening.

Mental health practitioners long ago identified ways in which people protect themselves psychologically when they feel threatened, unwanted, unimportant. We cannot leave ourselves bare. We cover up in various ways. We may withdraw. We may become defensive, suspicious of others. We may overcompensate, becoming aggressive, boisterous, braggadocian. We may seek to hurt and reject others as a way to cover our own feelings. When we do any of these things, our ability to learn is hampered. We cannot form important relationships with others. We are reluctant to try, afraid of failure. We cannot be properly open to new experiences.

Obviously, threat in the school setting should be reduced to a minimum. We can do this by eliminating sarcasm and abrasive criticism, by showing students we care about them and their learning, and by looking on failure not as a crime, but as an opportunity for growth.

D. *Pervasive sense of warmth, openness, and trust.* Warmth is gentleness

Continued.

with strength, protection with urging, affection with high standards. It is a message of pleasant, good-humored seriousness. It is genuine. It is the condition that puts you at ease, while giving you the feeling that there's something special there for you.

Openness is behavior without facade. No pretense, no affectation, no snow job. It is a genuine communication of attitude, feeling, and reaction. But we can be open, yet cold. That is no good for helping students. If you are open and warm, if you care about others and communicate that care, this is good for helping students—very good indeed.

Don't get the idea that warmth and openness always dictate smiling happiness. Cares, concerns, disappointments, even moments of anger are shared by people who are warmly open. The key ingredients are care, concern for the other person, and desire to help. These ingredients provide warmth.

When this kind of warm openness exists in the classroom, trust begins to grow. The feeling of one for all and all for one slowly takes over. Trust cannot develop overnight. Hurt students, like hurt teachers, are wary. Burnt children continue to dread the fire. But the teacher who continues to say you are competent, you are worth my time, you can learn, you must not be satisfied with less, I will help you however I can—that teacher will nourish trust within students. In the long run, that's what students remember. That's what causes them to say, years later, that was a great teacher.

XIII. Many conditions in the physical and psychosocial environments inhibit learning. Among these conditions are destructive sarcasm, intimidation, boredom, frustration, fatigue, lack of purpose, and sense of failure.

In one place or another, we have already considered most of these conditions, usually as the reverse sides of positive conditions that enhance learning. Let's think about them again, but briefly.

A. *Destructive sarcasm*. Sarcasm can be delightfully funny, especially if you see Don Rickles dishing it out. It's not so funny to be on the receiving end, however, when somebody other than Rickles is laying it on. Until they know their students very, very well, teachers do better to forget sarcasm. Even then handle it with kid gloves. It can hurt, and hurt stifles learning.

B. *Intimidation*. Most of us have faced physical intimidation from bullies. That's pretty scary. Some of us have faced intellectual intimidation. That's just as bad, maybe even worse when it comes to learning.

Intellectual intimidation can come from teachers, parents, and other students. It's the message that says you're stupid, your opinions have no value, your knowledge has no depth, your insights miss the mark. The intimidator picks out your errors, tells how things really are, and talks loud. He is argumentative. He doesn't listen, or if he does, it is to try to pick apart what you say.

Nobody likes an intimidator. If it's a fellow student, you can keep out of the way most of the time and go about your business. If it's the teacher, you're stuck. You will suffer. You will dread school. You will be unable to relate personally to your teacher. Your learning will assuredly suffer.

We avoid being the intimidator not by playing dumb, reacting with wide-eyed amazement to whatever someone says. We don't apologize if we happen to know more than our students. What we do is listen to them, pay attention to what they say. We don't blatantly correct their mistakes or question their opinions. We might gently tell what our opinion is, stressing that it's just an opinion. We might ask whether the student has considered an alternative idea. We might call on other students to express their opinions. In these ways we avoid casting ourselves in aggressively superior roles. We avoid being disdainful. We do not put others down. Our purpose is to help them learn. Intellectual intimidation has precisely the opposite effect.

C. *Boredom.* As interest wanes, boredom waxes. It comes with monotony, with too much of the same. It comes with irrelevance. It comes with blandness.

When bored, we disengage. We no longer pay attention. We daydream. We seek new things to do; sometimes these things are bothersome to others.

This failure to maintain attention throws a damper on learning. What's more, no one likes to be bored, and the result can be a poor attitude toward learning. Fortunately, boredom is easily corrected.

D. *Frustration.* Frustration occurs when we keep trying tasks beyond our abilities, when tasks take too long to complete, and when interferences prevent task completion. The result is increased tension and an intense desire to walk away from the task. Learning cannot proceed well under these conditions.

Frustration is cured through shortening tasks, making them easier to complete, and removing barriers to their completion. Sometimes a short break from the activity will solve everything.

E. *Fatigue.* Tiredness, whether physical or mental, inhibits learning. It reduces attention and motivation, and it depresses active involvement. Fatigue comes as a result of tasks that are too long. Breaks, movements, and changes of pace revitalize learners. Mental fatigue doesn't require sleep. It only requires fresh ideas and a bit of variety.

F. *Lack of purpose.* If you don't see the point of what you are doing, if you can't see any reason for it or any use, it's going to be all the harder for you to learn. Sense of purpose provides direction, helps focus attention, increases motivation, and thus assists learning and retention. Without it, students vacillate, they drift, they resist learning.

G. *Sense of failure.* According to Glasser (1969), the sense of failure comes from an inability to establish caring relationships with others and an

Continued.

inability to develop a personal sense of worthiness. If he is right, and he may well be, errors, even a mountain of them, don't produce a sense of failure. On the other hand, mountains of achievement don't produce a sense of success, not if you don't feel yourself a worthwhile person or if you can't establish caring relationships.

A sense of failure depresses learning. It reduces motivation. It makes things seem not worthwhile. Errors can help us learn, can help us grow as individuals. Failure cannot. The key point is that there is a world of difference between making errors and feeling oneself a failure.

Résumé

To this point we have had a rapid overview of some of the most widely accepted principles of learning. Brief as that overview was, it filled quite a number of pages. It would be well, then, to see the principles in outline form, without the accompanying commentary. Here they are:

I. Humans have a natural, life-long potential for learning.
II. Learning occurs in the following three great domains:
   A. Cognitive
   B. Affective
   C. Psychomotor
III. People learn through different procedures, among which are the following:
   A. Classical conditioning
   B. Instrumental conditioning
   C. Trial and error
   D. Imitation
   E. Verbal association
   F. Cognitive reorganization
   G. Logic, inductive and deductive
IV. People use several different intellectual processes in learning, including the following:
   A. Perceiving
   B. Discriminating
   C. Making relationships
   D. Analyzing
   E. Synthesizing
V. People learn best when tasks and materials are appropriate to the following:
   A. Intellectual, linguistic, and social development
   B. Background of experience
   C. Levels of academic progress
   D. Preferred styles of learning
VI. Factors in the learning situation that speed, strengthen, or otherwise enhance learning include the following:

A. Clarity and organization
B. Progression from known to unknown and concrete to abstract
C. Appropriate practice
D. Reinforcement
E. Corrective feedback
F. Practicality
VII. Transient, maniputable states within the student that affect learning include the following:
   A. Motivation
   B. Attention
   C. Active response
   D. Sense of purpose
VIII. Less transient, but modifiable, states within the student that affect learning include the following:
   A. Intellectual development
   B. Language ability
   C. Background of experience
   D. Preferred styles of learning
   E. Sense of personal worthiness
IX. Transfer of learning (usefulness in other situations) is increased through the following:
   A. Similarity between learning tasks and subsequent tasks
   B. Understanding of rules and generalizations
   C. Practice
   D. Application
X. Retention (remembering) is increased through the following:
   A. Intent to remember
   B. Sensory involvement
   C. Practicality
   D. Emotional involvement
   E. Use of mnemonics
   F. Overlearning
   G. Continued use
XI. Factors in the physical environment that affect learning include the following:
   A. Light, heat, and ventilation
   B. Space for movement

C. Instructional materials
D. Orderliness with flexibility
XII. Conditions within the psychosocial environment that affect learning include the following:
A. Responsible participation by learners
B. Student sense of acceptance and worthiness
C. Avoidance of threatening tasks and situations
D. Pervasive sense of warmth, openness, and trust
XIII. Conditions in the physical and psychosocial environments that inhibit learning include the following:
A. Destructive sarcasm
B. Intimidation
C. Boredom
D. Frustration
E. Fatigue
F. Lack of purpose
G. Sense of failure

PRINCIPLES OF INSTRUCTION

Principles of instruction are those teaching procedures that produce predictable results for most students, most of the time, under most classroom conditions. They are not foolproof. They don't work 100% of the time, with 100% effectiveness. They do, however, have a track record of proved effectiveness. You can rely on them most of the time.

Principles of instruction, in the main, are based directly on principles of learning. Usually the relationship between the two is clear. Take our learning principle VI part A (the effect of clarity and organization on learning) for example. The directly related principle of instruction is to provide clarity and organization in the tasks given to learners. Because these relationships are so evident, they will not be elaborated here.

There are, however, some principles of instruction that go beyond principles of learning. These principles of instruction fall into four main categories: (1) instructional planning, (2) classroom management and discipline, (3) record keeping, and (4) instructional evaluation. Each of these categories will be discussed on the pages that follow.

Instructional planning

Purposes and procedures of instructional planning have received much attention in earlier parts of this book. Therefore only brief commentary will be made here.

To perform their jobs well, teachers must plan in advance. They must have a script that reminds them to provide what their students need. The general needs of learners were spelled out in the section on principles of learning. Specific needs must also be attended to. These needs relate the curriculum to specific knowledge, skills, materials, and experiences that will best promote the personal and academic growth of each student.

Planning is ordinarily done on long-range and short-range bases. Long-range planning lays out the goals and learning activities for units of work, semester courses, and year-long courses. You will see long-range planning described in Chapter 16. Short-range planning itemizes specific objectives, activities, materials, and procedures for lessons that are completed in one period or a group of a few periods. Many different formats are used for this type of planning. Individual teachers have their own preferences. Fig. 8 (Charles, 1976) shows a lesson plan format that has proved useful to student teachers and beginning teachers. It contains many reminders and needs only to be checked and noted, not written out in full. (See p. 194.)

Classroom management and discipline

Classroom management refers to establishing physical and psychosocial environments, to establishing class routines and responsibilities, and to ensuring student conduct that contributes toward an optimum learning opportunity for all students.

The physical environment has been mentioned previously. It should contain comfortable furniture suited to the physical needs of the students; proper heat, light, and ventilation; space for movement; adequate instructional materials, suitably stored, obtainable, and replaceable; a sense of order; and aesthetically pleasing surroundings.

The psychosocial environment has also received prior attention. It should be warm, open, stimulating, supportive, and facilitative. High expectations intermingle with acceptance of errors, while regard for the individual prevails.

Class routines and responsibilities should be established very quickly. Everyone should know what is expected, how things are done, and how each person contributes to the class well-being. These routines and responsibilities run a wide gamut: assignments, movement patterns, material distribution and collection, work procedures, pencil sharpening, hall passes, tardiness, absences, homework, and so on. Students can help decide on rou-

THE QUICK CHECK LESSON PLANNER

subject _____
date _____ time _____

OBJECTIVES

act   object   conditions

general objectives	sample action verbs
perceive	note, point to
relate	group, associate
reproduce	repeat, draw
analyze	divide, separate
apply	use, solve
evaluate	compare, judge
produce	make, write

IMPLEMENTATION-FACILITATION

method
telling
showing
questioning
(student) doing

grouping
large
small
individual

names/responsibilities

motivators
special interests
novelty
problems or puzzles
manipulable objects
competition
other:

sequence/names/acts

student activities
acting out
answering
computing
constructing
discussing
drawing
listening
observing
reading
singing
taking notes
telling
writing
other:

sequence/specifics/management

materials
charts
equipment
filmstrips
games
globe
kit
lab
library books
maps
models
motion pictures
objects
pencil and paper
pictures
programs
recordings
references
supplies
textbooks
workbooks, worksheets
other:

reinforcers
fun
achievement
knowledge of results
praise, approval

marks, stars, etc.
tokens, candy, etc.
special privileges
other:

EVALUATION: MEANS OF APPRAISAL

informal observation
formal observation

student self-appraisal
oral exam

written exam
other:

Fig. 8. The quick check lesson planner. (From Charles, C. M.: *Educational psychology: the instructional endeavor* (2nd ed.). St. Louis: The C. V. Mosby Co., 1976.)

tines and responsibilities, which should be kept clear, brief, definite, and enforceable.

Discipline. Discipline—class control—is the great bugaboo of teachers. It's distressing but true that control makes or breaks the teacher. Without good control, worthwhile learning is doomed. The students will not attend to task, and the teacher's life will be miserable.

Then we need the strong hand, the birch rod, the withering stare, right? Wrong. They may keep students under control, out of fear and dread. But they do not teach self-direction, decision making, or responsibility. Besides that, they are inhumane.

What we need is positive warmth with strength, high expectations with humor, standards with acceptance and helpfulness, sense of purpose with flexibility. How do we get these things? Research and successful practice have shown that there are many things teachers can do to foster purposeful self-discipline in the classroom. These things fall into three categories: preventive control, supportive control, and corrective control.

PREVENTIVE CONTROL

A great percentage of potential discipline problems can be avoided completely through advance preparation, with attention to the following:

Clockwork routines. Everyone knows what to do when. Materials and activities are ready. Transitions are made quickly and easily, without the awkward confusion that feeds misbehavior.

Worthwhile interesting activities. People eagerly engage in learning activities that are useful and interesting. They don't look for devilish things to do to enliven their hours.

Clear sense of purpose and direction. When students know exactly what they are supposed to do and why, they are likely to do it.

Established guidelines and expectations. Set routines and enforceable boundaries on behavior forestall undesired actions.

Anticipation of special events and the unexpected. Students will behave differently at Halloween, on the day of the big game, on the last day of school. This behavior, rather than being struggled against, can be directed positively and built on with discussions, role-playing, values clarification, sessions of good will, and so forth. The unexpected brings predictable student be-

havior, predictable in that it will not continue on track. A dog runs into the room. A student falls and lays open the scalp with a profusion of blood. A student runs in and says the teacher next door has fainted. What do you do now? Advance planning will take care of much of the problem. Plan with the students what they must do if you have to leave the classroom. Arrange with another teacher to cover for you if necessary. Discuss the unexpected event, how it could be made a positive experience. This will allow your students to calm down. Soon they will be able to return to the lesson.

SUPPORTIVE CONTROL

By being ever attentive to your students you can spot misbehavior potential and nip it in the bud. Here are some things you should practice:

Physical presence. Always keep physically near to students. When working with individuals or groups, be sure everyone in the class can see you and you them.

Eye contact. As you talk with the class, look at students' faces. When one seems inclined to mischief, establish direct eye contact. A brief pause will often do the trick.

With-it-ness. Show your class that you are with it. You always know what's going on in the group. Your eagle eye misses nothing.

Immediate problem response. Don't react to trivial matters, but if it looks like something unwarranted is about to develop, respond to it immediately. Use Glasser's reality approach; ask the student what he or she is doing and help to redirect the activity. Or praise students who are behaving correctly. Or shake your head. Or say the behavior is interfering with your work. Or simply say please don't do that.

Overlap. When involved with an individual or group, always pay attention to the rest of the class, too.

Accept and guide. Accept students as persons, but don't accept their disruptive behavior. Rechannel it.

Communicate. Talk regularly with students to stress their responsibilities, the expectations you hold for them, and the things that might be interfering with their class responsibilities.

Stress student responsibility. Students have responsibilities to themselves, to the teacher, and to the class. Without preaching or moralizing, keep drawing attention to these responsibilities.

CORRECTIVE CONTROL

Despite your best planning and your most diligent supportive efforts, students will misbehave. Hopefully, it won't occur too often. But when it does, you have to deal with it. Here are some suggestions:

Use the reality approach. This approach is detailed by Glasser (1969). Ask the misbehaving student what he or she is doing; ask whether the behavior is helping the class; get him or her to decide on a better course of action.

Suppress cruelty. There are times when you say, with fire in your eye, we don't do that in this class.

Use restitution. Restitution means replacing what was ruined; supplying quid for quo; making it up in some way. This is not punishment, it is justice. It is making things right.

Use deprivation. You can face the misbehaving student with "You do something wrong, you lose something you value—a privilege, a chance to be with others, some free time."

Use isolation. Another tactic confronts the student with "Your disruptive behavior makes it impossible for the group to work. You therefore must sit alone, apart from the group."

Call for administrator assistance. Do this only when you cannot handle the situation yourself.

Call for parental assistance. After school, call parents on the phone. Tell them calmly what the problem is. Ask them if they can help. Usually they can and are most willing to do so.

• • •

These suggestions for preventive, supportive, and corrective control, when fully applied, make a tremendous difference. No one of them alone is magic. As Haim Ginott (1972) says, good discipline is a series of little victories. Each of these suggestions can bring a little victory.

Record keeping

Records of student performance serve useful purposes. They help teachers keep track of where each student is, achievementwise. They help in planning instruction. They help in reporting to parents. They are indispensible in evaluating curriculum, teaching, and student performance.

Record keeping can break teachers' backs and spirits if too many records are kept and if the procedures are inefficient. The amount of necessary record keeping depends on the teaching method being used. Various methods are described in the next chapter, and you will see there what they entail.

Basically, enough records should be kept so that the teacher always knows, and can show evidence to others, what the achievement and/or progress level is for each student in the class. These records should be kept on charts that require little more than checks or numbers. The charts should be available only to teacher, administrators, and individual students and their parents.

Instructional evaluation

Evaluation is a process of judging worth or value. It is done by comparing performance against standards. These standards, usually set by the teacher, may be absolute or relative. Absolute standards mean that students are supposed to reach a certain score or a certain objective. Relative standards assign top scores or grades to students who do best and lowest scores or grades to students who do worst, regardless of how high or low the scores are. Absolute standards are used in "criterion-referenced" evaluation. Relative standards are used in "norm-referenced" evaluation. Both types of evaluation have their advantages and disadvantages, supporters and critics.

Evaluation is usually thought of as grading students. Grading is part of the picture, but there is more to it. Evaluation should describe student progress. This progress can be used to judge student effort. Equally important, or more so, student progress tells a great deal about the effectiveness of teaching. If students are not learning up to teacher expectation, the fault may not lie with the students. It may lie with the methods of instruction, materials, or activities. It may lie in the psychosocial climate of the classroom. It may lie in individual problems outside school. Or it may indeed lie with the students themselves, who are not fulfilling their responsibilities.

A final word

This completes our overview of principles of instruction, with some hints about their application.

We considered a number of established principles of learning. We saw how those principles of learning directly suggested principles of instruction.

We then saw that other important principles of instruction fall beyond direct connection with principles of learning. Thus there are more principles of instruction than there are principles of learning.

Throughout we remembered that principles of instruction generally hold true for most teachers, for most students, for most teaching situations. They don't always hold true; there are exceptions. But the odds are in their favor. In teaching, that's the best we can do for now: get as many of the odds as possible in our favor. By "our," we mean teachers and students alike.

The next three chapters show, in detail, how principles of instruction are applied.

SUGGESTED ACTIVITIES FOR FURTHER UNDERSTANDING

1. Explain how principles of teaching are related to principles of learning.
2. Examine principle III (people learn through different procedures). For each of the subcategories, identify at least three things you have learned through these procedures.
3. Select a topic and organize a lesson on it. Make it your best. Analyze it in terms of principle VI (factors in the learning situation that speed, strengthen, or otherwise enhance learning). Present your plan to the class. Let them suggest changes they would make.
4. List six factors that inhibit learning. Explain how you could reduce or eliminate these factors in the classroom.

REFERENCES

Charles, C. *Educational psychology: the instructional endeavor* (2nd ed.). St. Louis: The C. V. Mosby Co., 1976.

Ginott, H. *Teacher and child.* New York: Macmillan Publishing Co., Inc., 1972.

Glasser, W. *Schools without failure.* New York: Harper & Row, Publishers, 1969.

Gordon, T. *Teacher effectiveness training.* New York: Peter H. Wyden/Publisher, 1974.

Guilford, J. Three faces of intellect. *American Psychologist,* 1959, *14,* 469-479.

Maslow, A. A theory of human motivation. *Psychological Review,* 1943, *50,* 370-396.

Meeker, M. *The structure of intellect: its interpretation and uses.* Columbus, Ohio: Charles E. Merrill Publishing Co., 1969.

Rogers, C. *Freedom to learn.* Columbus, Ohio: Charles E. Merrill Publishing Co., 1969.

11 METHODS OF TEACHING

This chapter will show you that there are several different methods of teaching, all of them good ones. It will spell out the details and procedures of eleven of these methods, and it will note the special contributions each method makes to teaching and learning. It will teach you how to select and use methods, or combinations of methods, that best reach the various instructional objectives considered important in education.

Chapter 12 will discuss thirteen strategies of teaching that entertwine with these eleven methods. It will present these strategies in enough detail so you can recognize them when you see them and perhaps begin to use some of them. It will certainly give you a starting place for finding out more about the strategies and how they are used.

Most teachers know and make good use of one teaching method, perhaps two, and three or four strategies. Rarely, however, do you see one who systematically uses a combination of several methods and strategies. Yet if a teacher is to reach effectively the diverse objectives of education, a skillfully selected and applied combination of methods and strategies will be necessary.

Experts have identified a number of important educational objectives. Some of these objectives have to do with knowledge; others have to do with understanding and application, evaluation and creativity, attitudes and values. No one method-strategy combination can reach them all.

GENESIS AND METAMORPHOSIS

My professional development began in a peculiar way. I lived in a small college town, went to high school and on to college there. When I did student teaching for my credential, I was assigned to two master teachers who had been my own teachers in high school. They were Mr. Stapelton, a biology teacher, and Mrs. Gonzales, a Spanish teacher. That assignment gave me massive doses of their teaching methodology. I had taken two courses from each of them in high school, and now I was working closely with them from the other end of the picture, the teaching end.

Their methods were very similar. Each relied heavily on a textbook, made daily reading assignments, gave homework, required students to keep notebooks, and gave many quizzes and examinations. Both stressed knowledge acquisition above all else. Neither gave special emphasis to application, creativity, evaluation, or attitude development. As a result, I think it fair to say that their students acquired high levels of factual information, but were unable to do very much of anything practical with the information they possessed. Mrs. Gonzales's students could conjugate Spanish verbs beautifully, but could not speak Spanish. Mr. Stapelton's students could recite, without error, the classifications of the plant and animal kingdoms, but could make no applications to ecology, to the improvement of plant and animal habitats, or to human nutrition and general health.

Both Mrs. Gonzales and Mr. Stapelton were fine teachers, knowledgeable, humane, and hard working. Students liked them and knew they would learn in their classes. They were excellent models for me. I was very lucky to get to work with them. Partly because they were so good at what they did,

I came away from those experiences with a one-sided view of what teaching was all about.

I thought teaching excellence was exactly synonymous with the way they taught. I rarely thought about why they (and I) taught in that manner, about what it was we were trying to accomplish. The objectives were simply taken for granted. You were supposed to learn facts, mountains of them. You could have a nice time learning those facts. You could work with others, you could laugh a little, you could watch an occasional entertaining film. You could make a beautiful notebook, something you could show your parents, be proud of, and keep. That, to me, was what teaching and learning were supposed to be.

In the years that followed, I marched in step with Mr. Stapelton and Mrs. Gonzales. My own students learned a great deal of factual information, they were reasonably content and active, and they did well on the standardized tests they took at the end of the year. They seemed to like me well enough, and most of them wanted to please.

Yet before long some unsettling observations began to enter my consciousness, observations that made me question my marvelous teaching methodology. I taught Spanish and biology. My students in Spanish were not learning to carry on conversations, and that bothered me. In my college classes I had become able to converse in Spanish, but I couldn't get my own students to do so, even though they made great scores on their tests of vocabulary and verb conjugation. I began to fret about why they didn't learn to converse. (You have to realize that this experience occurred in the dim past, even before the emergence of the audiolingual emphasis that stressed understanding and speaking in foreign language study.)

Then I turned to teaching eighth-grade English, where we spent hour after tedious hour diagraming sentences and memorizing rules of grammar. Again my students worked hard, mainly I think to please me. I just couldn't figure out a way to make grammar interesting, like I could Spanish and biology. We couldn't even make beautifully illustrated notebooks. What, after all, can you do to beautify a diagramed sentence or a dangling participle?

But more than that, I had an embarrassing time trying to answer the occasional timidly put question about *why* it was important to know verb tenses, compound sentences, and parts of speech. What good did it do you? I wanted (and tried) to tell them it would help them speak better, but I couldn't truly see that it did, and neither could they. I wanted to tell them it would help them write better, but they didn't care about doing any writing. You probably know the reasons I resorted to: It's good for you, even though you can't tell it. You have to do it to pass your tests. You have to do it to be ready for ninth grade. And mainly, you have to do it because I say so.

Boy, did we all, students and I alike, look forward to the little bit of time we spent on literature, so we at least could read an interesting story and talk about it. Funny, no one ever asked why we had to do that.

Too bad I didn't know then what is common knowledge now. I could have had my students working at purposeful activities, learning to speak Spanish through dialogues, plays, and conversations. My English students could have been rewriting grammatically incorrect essays and stories about interesting topics, and they could have been applying what they knew in writing club, newspaper, and class journal activities. I could have stressed creativity. I could have included activities on story line, role playing, clarification and discussion of comparative values, inquiry, and simulations. In short, I could have made schooling not only interesting, but worthwhile, productive, and useful for my students.

I don't feel too guilty about the way I taught. It was good for those days and times. We had ideas about better ways of teaching even then. But the ideas were at the theoretical level. No one had yet developed the new methodology and explained it well enough to enable us average teachers to apply it.

You have an enormous advantage over my early situation. Levels and types of educational objectives have been clearly outlined for both the cognitive (knowledge) and the affective (feelings, attitudes) domains. Methods of teaching have been developed that lead to attainment of all these diverse objectives. These methods include detailed descriptions of teacher and student roles, activities, learning environments, materials, and procedures. They have been validated. We know they work. It is easily within your grasp to become adept at using various methods of teaching, so you can effectively help your future students reach various

instructional objectives in ways that are interesting and useful. You can do that by (1) examining categories of educational objectives currently in use; (2) reviewing and then acquiring a firm grasp of the elements of the several methods described in the following sections of this chapter; and (3) planning, evaluating, and, if possible, applying instructional episodes designed to reach different types of objectives in a selected subject area. The remainder of this chapter is designed to help you do these three things.

AIMS, GOALS, ENDS, AND OBJECTIVES

In the pages that follow you will see how the educational goals and objectives one intends to achieve indicate which teaching methods and strategies should be used. Before getting into that, let's take a moment to see what people mean when they use the words "aims," "goals," "ends," and "objectives."

You hear the terms "aims," "goals," "ends," and "objectives" used to refer to the outcomes of education, to the results that one hopes to see accrue at some point in the future. Three of these terms—aims, goals, and ends—are virtually synonymous. They refer to large, broad, general outcomes. Objectives, on the other hand, have come to refer to much more narrow, precise, observable outcomes of teaching and learning.

We first began paying serious attention to the aims, goals, ends, and objectives for American education back in 1918. In that year the National Education Association's Commission on the Reorganization of Secondary Education (*Cardinal Principles,* 1918) issued its report, 5 years in the planning, on what should be the ends and purposes of American secondary education. Within a few years, it had become universally acknowledged that the "Seven Cardinal Principles of Education" described in that report were the broad educational objectives not only for secondary schools, but for all of American public schooling.

The original Seven Cardinal Principles of Education were "intended to help move toward a more ideal democracy by focusing on the development of the individual and on the interrelationship between individual and society." The principles were as follows:
1. Health
2. Command of fundamental processes

3. Worthy home membership
4. Vocation
5. Citizenship
6. Worthy use of leisure
7. Ethical character

As part of its bicentennial activities, the National Education Association (1976) established a committee to reexamine the seven cardinal principles, with an eye to assessing their present-day validity and continued usefulness. The committee, with wide participation, reaffirmed, for the most part, the continued usefulness of the original seven principles. They suggested some changes in the wording that explains each of the principles, so as to bring them more in line with present realities. Also, they stressed that the original principles promised more than the schools could possibly deliver. Still, the committee could not find basic fault with the principles as the current major goals of American education.

Out of these seven cardinal principles come the goals (or aims or ends) of the various parts of the school curricula. For example, you may have seen reference made to the goals of the mathematics curriculum or the English curriculum. Again, these statements are quite general in nature. English curriculum goals, for instance, will include such statements as clarity of written and oral expression or interpretation of intended messages in written materials.

Objectives, much more precise and definite, grow out of goals established in the curricular areas. They home in on small segments of the curriculum. Various terms are used to indicate their functions. For example, "long-range objectives" describe precise outcomes, in terms of learner behaviors, for lessons that require several days or weeks to complete. "Enabling objectives" refer to intermediate accomplishments that mark the way to the attainment of the long-range objectives. "Lesson objectives" refer to short-range, quickly attainable accomplishments that can be reached, usually, in a single lesson.

Whatever their special name, most instructional objectives are behavioral in nature. That is, they specify observable acts that students are to become able to perform. That's why they are so commonly called "behavioral objectives." They focus on ultimate behaviors, not on instructional activities or on unobservable conditions. They tell what the student will become *able to do*. These objectives are stated in terms of observable action verbs, plus the object of those actions, for example:

The student will be able to list the
(verb)

seven cardinal principles.
(object)

Unobservable acts are not acceptable in behavioral objectives. You could not, for example, use verbs such as understand, appreciate, or think. They might sound laudable and important, but if you (the teacher) cannot see or hear the acts, you have no way of knowing whether your students are reaching the objectives. All you can know is what they say and do that you can hear and see.

Most experts in the techniques of preparing behavioral objectives include two other elements in addition to action verbs and objects. These two elements are "givens" and "criteria." The term "givens" refers to the materials and conditions furnished to the student. The term "criteria" refers to acceptable levels of performance. Here's an example:

Given a map of the United States, the student will
(given)

be able to point out the Great Lakes, the Gulf of
(verb)   (object)

Mexico, and the Mississippi River within 2 minutes
(object)   (criteria)

with 100% accuracy.
(criteria)

These carefully detailed, observable behavioral objectives have been of great help in making teaching, learning, and evaluation more effective and efficient. They bend all teaching methods, strategies, materials, and activities directly toward the production of the observable acts they specify. This cuts down on drifting and wheel spinning, and it helps both teacher and student keep on the track.

However, despite their acknowledged value, there are times when behavioral objectives do not help in guiding instruction. Such is often the case with aesthetic experiences. Virtually all primary teachers agree that touching and petting animals such as goats, chicks, and rabbits provide a valuable experience for children. Yet, one must be-labor the point to specify the behavioral outcomes that justify the experience. Just what would you expect the students to become able to do as a result of their experience in petting animals? Professional experience and judgment simply verify the value of the experience. The same thing is true for student visits to art museums and attendance at athletic events and concerts.

When the experience is judged valuable in itself but we can't see clearly what the behavioral outcomes might be, we can use "experience objectives" instead of behavioral objectives to guide teaching. An experience objective focuses on the nature of the experience itself rather than on the observable outcomes of that experience. Examples of experience objectives would be as follows:

The students will listen to selected fairy tales read by the teacher.

The students will watch a televised performance by the Boston Pops Orchestra.

The students will read selected verse written by Ogden Nash.

OBJECTIVES AND DOMAINS

When talk turns to the topic of objectives, you will almost always hear mention made of "domains," especially of the "cognitive domain" and the "affective domain." Occasionally you will also hear mention of the "psychomotor domain." *Cognitive* has to do with knowing, knowledge, and the use of knowledge. *Affective* has to do with feelings, attitudes, and values. *Psychomotor* has to do with physical movements.

Within each of these three domains, which seem to encompass almost all areas of human behavior related to education, concerted attention has been given to the elaboration of educational objectives, that is, to the specification, in observable terms, of desirable outcomes toward which education should be directed.

Beginning in the 1950's, a committee of college and university examiners worked together to produce handbooks of educational objectives in these three domains. The two best known are *Handbook I: Cognitive Domain,* edited by Benjamin S. Bloom (1956), and *Handbook II: Affective Domain,* edited by David R. Krathwohl (1964). These handbooks are taxonomies, with their objectives arranged in ascending order from simplest to most

complex. *Handbook I* was published in 1956, and it has had much influence on education. *Handbook II* was published in 1964, and it has had relatively little influence on education.

The reason for the value of *Handbook I,* commonly called Bloom's *Taxonomy,* is that it specifies objectives that are recognizable, usable, and important to educators. The objectives elaborated in *Handbook II: Affective Domain,* on the other hand, have not been helpful. They are difficult to apply in a systematic way, and they don't match up with what educators attempt to get at in affective areas. Education in the affective domain has been influenced not by behavioral objectives, but rather by the work of humanistic psychologists, such as Carl Rogers and Abraham Maslow, who have not considered behavioral objectives to be worth their salt. Objectives established in the psychomotor domain are rarely heard of at all.

Let's take a brief look at these taxonomies.

Bloom's *Taxonomy:* cognitive domain

The taxonomy in the cognitive domain consists of six levels of objectives. Five of these six levels contain additional sublevels. The levels are as follows:

1. *Knowledge.* Involving the ability to *remember* specifics, universals, methods, processes, settings, and so forth, as shown through ability to repeat the information learned
2. *Comprehension.* Involving *understanding* of what is being communicated, as shown through ability to translate, interpret, and extrapolate the information learned
3. *Application.* Involving ability to *use* information that was learned
4. *Analysis.* Entailing ability to *break down* material so as to identify its parts, their relationships, and its overall organization
5. *Synthesis.* Involving the *putting together* of parts so as to build something new, such as a unique communication, plan, or set of relationships
6. *Evaluation.* Involving *judging* the quality or effectiveness of materials, processes, etc. in terms of internal consistency or external standards

Each of these levels is considered "higher"— more complex, more advanced—than the one that precedes it. Thus knowledge is the lowest level of cognitive objectives when evaluation is the highest.

The taxonomy does not suggest a systematic method or strategy of teaching. It does remind us that there are various areas and levels of intellectual activity that should receive attention in education—that there is much more to focus on than just knowledge. You will see later that various methods and strategies of teaching have the power to get at different levels of objectives listed in the taxonomy.

The Charles variation. C. M. Charles (1976), developed a taxonomy of cognitive/psychomotor acts that has proved useful in guiding teaching. That taxonomy, a spin-off from Bloom's work, is made to parallel the intellectual activities that individuals use in cognitive learning. The cognitive/psychomotor acts, stated as verbs, are as follows:

1. *Perceive.* To *become aware of,* as shown through ability to note, signal, point to, and so forth
2. *Relate.* To *categorize,* as shown through ability to group, note similarities and differences, identify cause-effect and means-end relationships, and so forth
3. *Reproduce.* To *replicate from memory,* as shown by describing, acting out, assembling, and so forth
4. *Analyze.* To *break information and patterns down* into their parts and relationships
5. *Apply.* To *use* what has been learned in a new situation, as in the solution of problems.
6. *Evaluate.* To *determine the worth or value* of something, as shown in the making of comparative judgments
7. *Produce.* To *combine or restructure parts* so as to develop ideas, processes, compositions, or objects new to the learner

The cognitive/psychomotor acts combine knowledge and use of knowledge with intellectual and physical activity. Thus they are helpful in the preparation of behavioral objectives. Like Bloom's *Taxonomy* they remind us to provide instructional activities that make learners use different levels of the intellect.

Krathwohl's *Taxonomy:* affective domain

The handbook of educational objectives in the affective domain, edited by Krathwohl, has not proved nearly so useful in education as has Bloom's *Taxonomy.* It deals with paying attention, responding, and valuing. These areas, although certainly important, make up only a small part of the burgeoning humanistic movement in education, a movement that has vitalized instruction in the affective domain. We will note the contents of Krathwohl's *Taxonomy,* and then we will see the larger affective area that is being dealt with in education. Krathwohl's *Taxonomy* includes the following levels:

1. *Receiving.* Meaning the learner is *paying attention,* is sensitive to stimuli and phenomena, and is controlling that attention
2. *Responding.* Entailing *reacting willingly* to what is being perceived
3. *Valuing.* Involving responses that indicate not mere compliance, but *commitment* to an underlying idea
4. *Organization. Developing a system of values* so that dominant and pervasive ones emerge
5. *Characterization by a value or value complex.* Involving a value system that has been so organized and internalized that individuals *consistently act* in accord with their dominant values

You can see why these objectives have not helped teachers. The first two, receiving and responding, are not ends of education, but are natural conditions that occur within individuals. The third, valuing, also occurs naturally. We may want to develop certain values and not others, but the valuing process occurs naturally. The fourth and fifth can be considered legitimate outcomes of education, ends toward which we might strive. Again, however, the valuing process is only a small part of what teachers attempt to get at in education.

Affective domain for education. The affective domain makes sense to educators, that is, it takes on relevance and helps guide teaching, when it is viewed in the following way:

1. Part of the affective domain relates directly to the cognitive domain, facilitating the attainment of cognitive objectives. Such is the case for those affective conditions that characterize the classroom climate as open, warm, facilitative, trusting, nonthreatening, and nonpunitive. These are conditions that help students move toward humanistic goals of education.
2. Those humanistic goals stressed in education include (a) development of the self to its fullest potential and (b) actualization of the self, which means that individuals are freed to function in

ways dictated by their own rationally developed value systems. Development of the self means bringing to the highest level possible our physical and intellectual abilities, our aesthetic sensibilities, our creative talents, and our skills in communicating and relating with others. Actualization of the self means living our daily lives in accord with what we believe best and right for ourselves, making optimal use of the talents and abilities we have. It requires that we see ourselves as worthwhile and that we see other people and other things as worthwhile, too. It requires that we recognize human emotions for what they are and are able to deal with them. It requires that we have clarified our values, organized them, and used them as the basis for a consistent morality.

When the affective domain is seen in these ways, it is no longer mysterious to educators. They know what to get at and how, because they have at hand teaching methods and strategies known to further human development in the respects just mentioned.

• • •

This concludes our brief examination of aims, goals, ends, and objectives as they are used in education. You can see, or you will later see, that one single method of teaching cannot produce growth in skills, values, morality, concepts, aesthetics, responsibility, attitudes, personal relations, self-direction, etc. These different ends are reached through different avenues—different teaching methods and strategies. Such methods are discussed in the sections that follow.

METHODS

The term "method" refers to an overall way of organizing, approaching, and carrying out instruction. It includes planning, lesson preparation, interaction with students, management of materials, evaluation, and record keeping. Method is large in scope. It can be contrasted with teaching "strategy," which is small in scope, specific, direct, and designed to produce a definite behavior in students. You might use a questioning strategy, for example, to cause students to respond actively. But unless you did all your teaching by asking questions (as Socrates is purported to have done), questioning would not be a method of teaching.

Here we will begin to examine our eleven different methods of teaching. Although these methods have characteristics in common, they are clearly different, one from the other, with regard to the objectives they can efficiently promote, the ways they are organized and conducted, and the roles they require of students and teacher. The methods we will consider are as follows:

1. Diagnostic-prescriptive teaching
2. Competency-based education
3. Read-review-recite
4. Expository teaching
5. Simulations
6. Modeling
7. Projects
8. Group process
9. Inquiry/discovery
10. Facilitation
11. Open experience

Some of these methods are high in structure—teacher planning and control. Examples of methods with high structure are diagnostic-prescriptive teaching and competency-based education. Other methods are low in structure—teacher direction and dominance. Examples are facilitation and open experience. The higher the structure, the more direct and efficient the learning, especially the learning of skills and factual information. This efficiency is gained at the expense of learner self-direction and responsibility, however. The lower the structure and control, the greater the student self-direction and freedom to pursue special interests. Low structure, however, is rarely effective in promoting rapid acquisition of basic skills.

As you read through the descriptions of the various methods of teaching, remember that each method has both strengths and weaknesses in helping learners attain the various objectives of education. Look for those special strengths. The best teachers, and I am sure they interest you, are learning to combine and use several different methods and strategies so as to increase their teaching effectiveness.

Diagnostic-prescriptive teaching

Diagnostic-prescriptive teaching (DPT) is as its name suggests. It is a highly structured method that consists of three essential parts:

1. *Diagnosis* of the strengths and weaknesses of individual learners in given subject areas. The

diagnosis is commonly done through written examinations, although it can be done, and often is with young students, through observation of behavior and analysis of work completed during lessons.

2. *Prescriptions* made for each learner individually to correct or strengthen areas of weakness that were revealed in diagnosis. These prescriptions may be completed individually or in very small groups, and they may be carried out with or without the presence of the teacher.

3. *"Postassessment"* done by the teacher after the students have completed their prescriptions. This assessment, made through examination or observation, determines whether student deficiencies have been corrected. If they have, the student moves on to the next area where diagnosis has revealed a need. If deficiencies have not been corrected, students repeat the prescription or receive an alternative prescription, a process that is repeated as long as necessary.

DPT is used extensively in subject areas where basic skills and knowledge are emphasized, areas such as mathematics, English, reading, language, and spelling. It is also used in combination with other methods for any curricular area where minimal skills are essential as a basis for further work. Such areas include music, art, wood shop, electronics—in fact, virtually every discipline or subject area that has a basic knowledge and skills on which all else rests. DPT has no equal when it comes to promoting rapid learning of the basics.

To prepare for DPT, *teachers* need first to establish a comprehensive list of skill and knowledge objectives they want their students to attain. These objectives must be written in behavioral terms, with action verbs and objects of those verbs, as described earlier.

Then diagnostic procedures must be devised to enable teachers to determine which of the objectives each student can or cannot reach. These devices are usually written tests. The tests are made up of items linked directly to the behavioral objectives.

Next a suitable learning activity must be formulated for each of the objectives. The activities, which will become the prescriptions, are designed expressly to enable students to develop the behaviors described in the behavioral objectives. The activities are coded to the objectives and diagnostic tests. This makes it easy for the teacher, after the diagnosis is completed, to inform the students about which prescriptions they are to complete.

When a student has completed the prescribed activities, the teacher carries out the postassessment to be sure that the areas of weakness have been corrected. Often postassessment is done using the same test or observation that was used during diagnosis.

Finally, the teacher needs to make a master record sheet on which to check student attainment of objectives. This chart can show students' names down the side and various objectives across the top. Check marks or dates can be entered to show that students have demonstrated attainment of the objectives. The record sheet could look like the one shown below.

The *students'* roles are very simple. When directed to do so, they take diagnostic tests and return them to the teacher for checking. The teacher tells them, individually, which prescriptions to complete. Students obtain necessary directions and materials and complete the activities. When finished, they inform the teacher, who administers a criterion test. This test reveals whether students have reached the objectives and are ready to move on to new diagnoses and prescriptions, or

Students	Objectives 1	2	3	4	5	6	7	8	9	10	
Amy											
Bill											
Carl											
Dotty											
Edgar											

DIAGNOSTIC-PRESCRIPTIVE METHOD OF TEACHING LETTER WRITING (SIXTH GRADE)*

3A This card lists the five things a good friendly letter has: It is neatly written, it often begins with a compliment, it is newsy, it sounds conventional, and it does not end abruptly. INSTRUCTIONS: Study this card, then go on to card 3B.

3B This card has an example of a friendly letter that contains the five elements just listed. INSTRUCTIONS: Go on to card 3C.

3C Now you are ready to write your own friendly letter. Remember the *five parts of a letter, punctuation, capitalization,* and the *five elements of a friendly letter.* INSTRUCTIONS: Your letter may be to a real or make-believe friend.

4 This card gives an example of an *invitation.* There is an explanation of the three essential elements of a friendly letter, and these elements are underlined in the example. INSTRUCTIONS: After studying this card, do work sheet 4A.

5A Write a letter inviting your parents to open house at Anza, April 15, 1977, 7:30 PM *or* make up your own letter of invitation. Remember the *five parts of a letter,* the *three essential elements of an invitation,* and appropriate *capitalization, punctuation,* and *closing.*

5B You have been invited to a Halloween party to be held at 510 Goblin Way on October 31. The time is 8:00 PM. INSTRUCTIONS: Write a letter accepting this invitation, still using the three essential elements of an invitation.

---

*Courtesy Penny Morton, San Diego State University.

---

whether they have not reached the objectives and therefore must repeat the prescriptions.

The boxed material above is a small example from a DPT unit on teaching letter writing at the sixth-grade level.

Competency-based education

Competency-based education is a highly structured method useful in developing learner power, or competency, as the name suggests, in a variety of subjects and topics. The method directs all the objectives and activities toward a single, general end. That end is the ability to perform a given activity in a highly competent way.

Like DPT, competency-based education is planned, organized, and controlled by the teacher. The structure is such, however, that it allows flexibility in the instructional activities. This flexibility permits students to select among optional learning activities, each of which leads to the same objective. Given this opportunity to select, students can work through learning activities suited to their own preferred learning styles.

Unlike DPT, whose unparalleled strength lies in the acquisition of basic knowledge, competency-based education ranges effectively into other levels of learning. It is good for learning basic information, although not as good as DPT. It is good for activities in the application of knowledge, such as in controlled (teacher-directed) problem solving, and serves well for structured activities into some of the aesthetic and creative areas.

Nagel and Richman (1972), two of the popularizers of competency-based education, describe the method as consisting essentially of two strategies: mastery learning and individualized instruction. Nagel and Richman suggest organizing instruction through vehicles called "instructional modules." They have designed and implemented both undergraduate and graduate programs of teacher education built entirely on such modules.

Modules are refinements of instructional devices that have been in use for many years, devices commonly known as units of instruction, "unipaks," or learning activity packets. These devices are packaged sets of instructions, materials, and activities developed around a single topic or central theme. They are designed so that students can work through them at their own speed, with minimum assistance from the teacher.

Modules are the most highly refined of these instructional packages. They are prepared in written form by the teacher, one module for each topic to be taught. They contain an *introduction,* which gives a brief overview of what the module contains, what it can accomplish, and what the students must do. Following the introduction comes a statement of one or more *objectives,* couched, of course, in behavioral terms that specify exactly what the student is to become able to perform. The objectives include criteria, which the student's performance must reach before credit is granted. Matched to each behavioral objective is a group of *learning activities.* Each activity leads to the attainment of the objective at criterion, or competency, level. The activities differ. One of them might, for example, consist mainly of reading; a second might consist mainly of viewing slides and films; a third might consist of working through a workbook or laboratory manual. Individual students select the optional learning activity they prefer and complete it according to directions provided.

Once they have read the introduction and the behavioral objectives, students who believe they can already reach competency level may request *preassessment.* This is ordinarily a written test based directly on the behavioral objectives for the module. If the student passes the test, credit is given for the module, and the student moves on to the next module in the series. If preassessment is not requested or if the test is not passed, students *work through* the learning activities they select. They work on their own, at their own pace. They work individually or in very small groups. They confer with the teacher only when clarification or other assistance is needed.

When the learning activity has been completed, a student who is confident of being able to meet the behavioral objective will request *postassessment.* Like preassessment, this phase is usually accomplished by means of a written test, although it is sometimes based on a product completed during the instructional activity. The teacher conducts the postassessment when requested. If the student reaches the criterion level for the module, *credit* is earned.

If the criterion level is not reached, *remediation* is required. This process requires that students repeat at least some portions of the learning activity or complete an alternate learning activity. *Feedback* is given by the instructor to pinpoint areas of weakness and guide the student toward acceptable performance.

Presented in the boxed material on pp. 208 and 209 are portions of a module used in a highly successful upper-grade program in values clarification.

The *teacher's* role in competency-based education consists of the following functions:
1. Selection of the topic, based on curricular requirements or student need.
2. Organization of the instructional package, which, regardless of the form it takes, should include behavioral objectives, optional learning activities, pre- and postassessment devices, and remediation procedures.
3. Obtaining and organizing support materials for the various learning activities. These materials must be placed in an area easily accessible to students.
4. Preparation of the pre- and postassessment devices, which should call on students to perform, at a high level of proficiency, the very same behaviors that are described in the behavioral objectives.
5. Administration of assessment devices, when requested by students.
6. Conferencing with students as necessary to clarify, assist, and provide corrective feedback.
7. Keeping records of student progress.

The *students'* role in competency-based education consists of the following functions:
1. Read the introduction and objectives. Request preassessment if so desired. If not, continue.
2. Work through learning activities.
3. Request postassessment when learning activities have been completed.
4. Follow remediation procedures, if necessary.

Read-review-recite

Most of the teaching methods considered in this chapter are relatively new. One of the exceptions is the read-review-recite method, so-called for want of a more inspiring name. It is a method of long standing that simply grew out of practice and never had a name. The label selected here is not pretty, but it does describe the method.

You may not have had experience as a student

Agent

MODULE FOR VALUES CLARIFICATION

What are my values?*

Introduction

Just imagine what the world would be like if we all valued the same things. How different our lives would be!

First, what is a value anyway? Well, it's something important. Something very special and very important to a particular individual. A good example would be honesty. Some people think that is pretty important. Of course, honesty is something we all value or think is important. Even if we are not honest all the time, we try our best.

Another value could be jogging. Some people jog everyday and believe it is pretty important. This is an example of a value not shared by everyone. Why, just imagine what the world would look like if everyone jogged at 6 AM every morning.

How do we know if something is really a value or just something fun to do, like eating ice cream? Well, you must put your values to a test. But we will talk about that later.

The big question you need to answer now is *"What are my values?"*

This module will teach you to think about your values and will help you discover the answer to that question.

Your mission

Your mission is to pinpoint or locate your own personal values. To accomplish your mission you must follow the directions in this module. When your mission is accomplished you will:

1. Know what a value is
2. Become aware of your own personal values
3. Learn that others have values different from yours
4. Learn that it is best to respect the values of others
5. Learn to see how values affect decision making

---

*Courtesy Bette Osborn, San Diego State University.

---

with some of the newer methods of instruction, such as DPT, inquiry/discovery, or open experience. But you surely have participated in the read-review-recite method. You will recognize it immediately.

Read-review-recite consists of three main parts, all named in the title. The teacher begins the process with a reading assignment. This assignment is usually made in a textbook used in the course, but it can be made within reference materials, magazines, or what have you. Students are often told in advance what to look for in the reading.

After the reading assignment has been completed, students are called on to review the material. This review may be done in several different ways. One way is for students to write out answers to questions about the material read. These questions may be included with the material, or they may be prepared by the teacher. A second way to review the material is to conduct class discussions about it. A third way is to complete written exercises about the material that involve its interpretation, translation into one's own words, or application to problems. A fourth way is to prepare oneself to teach the material to another person. A fifth way is to make up an objective or essay examination on the contents (and of course learn the answers to your own questions!). A sixth way is to think of modifications in the presentation of the information, such as giving it a snake-oil salesman

Student's name _____

MODULE FOR VALUES CLARIFICATION

It's ok for you, it's ok for me*

Introduction

I think we all have a pretty good idea of what values are by now. I think we also realize that values don't come as a gift. That is, we are not born with them. We must think about our values and choose carefully those we can be proud of, are willing to defend, and intend to make part of our life. Remember if we only do it once, it really is not a value. And don't forget the other guy's values may be different from yours and that's *OK!*

Now you will need to get *Think Sheet 3* from the file and choose one of the following jobs. Don't forget to mark ☒

Job 1

1. Watch a really *great* film. The name of the film is *If It's OK For Me, It's OK For Others*. You will find this film in the values center.
2. Sit down and discuss the film with a group of other students. Decide who should be secretary and briefly explain what you discussed. Write your report on *Think Sheet 3*. Include the names of the people in your group.
3. Answer a few questions on *Think Sheet 3*.

Job 2. This job can be done with four or five people. Use the sign-up sheet. This job is about value appreciation. Most of us like to be appreciated for giving gifts, for being thoughtful, and for our special talents. If this is one of your values, you may want to select this job.

1. Get the study print "Hero Of The Game" from the values center. Read the story on the back with the people in your group.
2. Plan a skit that will demonstrate a method of showing appreciation. Remember all must participate. When your skit is ready to perform for the class, let the teacher know.
3. Answer a few questions on *Think Sheet 3*.

*Courtesy Bette Osborn, San Diego State University.

or a propaganda slant. All these ways of reviewing the material will make it more understandable and more easily remembered.

Once the review exercises are completed, students are called on to recite. This recitation, in olden days, was done individually by students, responding orally to questions posed by the teacher. Now it is much more common to use written tests, so as to get response from all students over the entire range of the material. There are, however, excellent alternatives to tests. One is to have students make written reports in which they react in some way to what they have learned. These reports can be done individually or in groups. Oral presentations, such as reports and panel discussions, can be used. Skits and role playing are effective ways for students to demonstrate their understanding of the material. Projects, involving construction, composition, and creativity, can be used. Whatever the vehicle, the purpose of recitation is to show the teacher that students have learned what they were supposed to learn.

The roles of teacher and students are simple and straightforward. The *teacher* selects the reading assignments; plans, prepares, and directs the review activities; and plans, prepares, and directs the recitation. The teacher can be completely in charge of all aspects or can involve the students in helping plan procedures for review and recitation, even to the point of putting them in charge of those activities. *Students* are obliged to read the assignments, complete review activities, and recite the knowledge gained, in whatever manner required.

This method can be deadly boring, or it can be wonderfully lively. Which direction it takes depends almost entirely on the philosophy and personality of the teacher.

The read-review-recite method is a good middle ground between highly structured methods such as DPT and lowly structured methods such as open experience. It can get at bits of most of the goals of education. It is good, but not excellent, for the acquisition of subject matter. The same can be said with regard to interpersonal relations, application of knowledge, and creativity. It can be especially useful for teachers who are teaching subjects in which they feel insecure about their own competence. They can learn right along with the students.

Expository teaching

Much of what was just said about read-review-recite holds true for expository teaching. It is a familiar, tried and true method that has a wide range of usefulness. It fits well into most subject areas and grade levels, and its effectiveness, even excellence in some regards, has been well established.

Exposition means to make clear, and expository teaching is intended for that express purpose—to make information being learned as clear and understandable as possible. For material to be clear and understandable, students must be able to grasp (explain, put into their own words) the concepts, generalizations, and processes being taught. They must also see how those concepts, generalizations, and processes relate to each other and to other concepts, generalizations, and processes. This means that students must perceive relationships of various kinds—similarity relationships, cause-effect relationships, means-end relationships, and so forth.

To ensure that students acquire this clear understanding of the material being presented, the *teacher* plays a central, dominant role in the in-structional process. Lectures and demonstrations are the instructional techniques most commonly used.

Lectures can be very effective for explaining ideas and for dealing with abstractions that cannot be shown through concrete means. At their best, lectures begin with a *preview* of what is to come (advance organization), follow an *orderly sequence,* use *media,* objects, and other props to hold attention and clarify, involve *theatrics* (voice modulation, gestures, dramatic movements) as necessary to hold student attention and clarify, and at the end present a *summary* of points covered. Frequent examples should be given, but anecdotes and jokes should be included with discretion, only insofar as they help illustrate and keep students' attention. When overused, they detract from the message, regardless of how entertaining they might be.

Demonstrations, when they are possible, almost always serve more effectively than lectures in clarifying concepts, generalizations, and processes. Often, of course, demonstrations are not possible. How, for example, could you demonstrate your interpretation of symbolism in Shakespearean sonnets? But when it is possible to demonstrate material, to show the objects and processes, the resultant student learning will almost certainly occur more rapidly, accurately, and lastingly than it will through verbal descriptions.

Demonstrations become even more effective when verbalization accompanies them. If, for example, you are demonstrating the process of making linoleum block prints, your students will learn much better if you explain verbally what you are doing as you complete each step.

Demonstrations are very effective for teaching involved processes, such as making prints, developing color film, and executing a good golf swing. Some of these processes, like the golf swing, can scarcely be taught at all without demonstrations. When you try to learn such procedures through purely verbal descriptions, you end up like one of the blind men describing the elephant.

A good demonstration begins, like a lecture, with an overview of what will be shown. Students are told to watch for certain points. The demonstration is then done in a simplified way, so as to accentuate the essential elements. This simplification assists students by cutting down on the number of elements they must remember. As they become adept at reenacting the process, they can add the nuances that complete the flavor.

You have seen that processes can be taught effectively through direct demonstration. Concepts and generalizations can also be taught through demonstrations, but the demonstrations have to rely on models, drawings, or photographs. For example, you can use models to help students develop concepts of atoms, molecules, and the solar system. You can use photographs to help students develop generalizations about good and poor habitats for deer. You can use drawings to help students understand the movements of the continental plates across the earth's surface.

The *students'* role in expository teaching is to pay attention and retain as much of the information as possible. Often students, especially in higher grades, take notes and make diagrams during the lectures and demonstrations. Later they are expected to show that they have understood and remembered the ideas presented. Examinations are often used for this purpose.

Like the read-review-recite method, expository teaching has an established tradition of practicality and effectiveness across virtually all age levels and subject areas. Its great strength lies in getting subject matter across to students. It is a favorite of many teachers because it allows them to inject personality and performance into instruction. It does nothing, in itself, to further interpersonal relations among students. For that matter it does little toward any of the affective ends of education. But when done well, expository teaching has no equal for making subject matter understandable and few equals for making it exciting.

Simulations

Simulations are in-class activities patterned after real life situations. The method uses simulations as the organizational and instructional vehicle for helping students learn, through active participation, about significant aspects of social and economic life.

Simulations lend themselves very well to instruction in the social sciences. They can bring about a higher degree and a longer duration of student involvement than any other method of teaching. They can provide superior practice in group cooperation, thus fostering interpersonal relations. They can provide controlled controversy, where groups seek, in orderly ways, to resolve conflicts of interest and where students have to reconcile incompatibilities between self-interest and the good of the group.

The simulation method has had its greatest use at the secondary school level. Increasingly, it is being used at the elementary level, especially in intermediate-grade social studies where it permits students to relive pioneer life along the Oregon Trail or visit historical sites all over the country.

Simulations usually involve three main parts: the introduction, playing the simulation, and the evaluation. In the *introduction,* students are briefed on the goals of the simulation, its activities, and its rules. In *playing the simulation,* variations in procedures occur. Most commonly, this phase involves role playing of survival, group endeavor, or conflict situations. In the *evaluation,* learners make judgments about learnings they have acquired, both in cognitive and in affective areas.

The *teacher's* role begins with the selection or preparation of the simulation. Directions for simulations can be purchased, with necessary materials for an entire class, or they can be composed by the teacher. The teacher introduces the objectives, activities, and rules of play. During playing the simulation, the teacher interprets, guides, assists, and referees. The simulation itself ensures the learning of necessary knowledge, skills, and attitudes. The teacher merely facilitates the process for the students. In evaluation the teacher helps students identify what they have learned, organize those learnings, and interpret their overall meaning.

The *students'* role is mainly one of involvement. They work together to carry out the activities of the simulation, following the rules laid down in the introduction. The activities require them to make decisions, follow through on those decisions, solve problems, and analyze their own behavior. Out of this process grow abilities to reason, to use decision-making processes, to participate effectively in groups, and to express ideas clearly and forcefully. Self-concepts improve as students see themselves as important members of groups, contributing and becoming able to deal with realistic situations.

The simulations method is very effective in moving toward goals of education that have to do with interpersonal relations, decision making, and effective group membership. It is not strong in getting at aesthetic objectives, and it is only moderately effective in promoting sequential learning of subject matter.

Modeling

One of the newest methods of teaching, and at the same time one of the oldest, is a method called "modeling." Modeling makes the most of teaching through demonstrated example and learning through imitation. It is an old, old technique of teaching, probably the first ever used. Yet it is very new in that it has only recently come to be used as a comprehensive, sophisticated, validated approach to teaching.

Modeling has been developed out of the work of the Stanford psychologist Albert Bandura. It has long been his contention that humans learn almost all their complex social behavior through seeing others act and then imitating those actions. Individuals add bits of their own personality to their imitations, and this addition helps account for the slight changes that continually occur in social behavior.

Bandura and his colleagues have identified basic processes that seem to be involved in teaching and learning through modeling (Bandura, 1971). They have identified traits of models (the persons or things demonstrating the behavior, concept, or process) that produce the most efficient learning in observers. They have also explored other factors that influence learning through modeling, such as attention focusing, motivation, reenactment, and corrective feedback.

Basically, modeling requires only two things. First, it requires a model to demonstrate the information to be learned. Second, it requires that learners pay attention to what is being demonstrated. With these two aspects in effect, learning occurs. They are both essential to the process.

Modeling can be greatly enhanced, however, by giving attention to traits of the models, to ways of securing and holding learner attention, to making provisions for learner reenactment (repetition) of the information observed, and to giving corrective feedback when learners reenact the information.

Models can be live, televised, filmed, or recorded. They can be real people, graphic presentations (cartoons, pictures, charts, etc.), verbal descriptions, or three-dimensional objects. They are known to be more effective, more likely to be imitated, when they have prestige, power, ability to reward, conviction, and clarity. Peers—other students—can be very effective models. Whatever the model and whatever traits it possesses, it must present very clearly the concept, process, or behavior to be learned.

Students, for their part, must attend closely to what is being presented by the model. Their attention can be directed by advance organization and can be maintained both by attractive traits of the models and by reinforcement supplied by the teacher.

As mentioned, learning will definitely occur, given the modeled event (which, of course, must contain information consonant with the learners' intellectual and linguistic abilities) and the careful attention of the learners.

Learning will be increased, speeded, or taken to higher levels, however, if learners are given techniques and conditions that help them remember what was observed, if they have the opportunity to practice reenactment of what they have observed, and if they receive immediate corrective feedback that tells them specifically what they are doing wrong and what they need to do to improve.

The *teacher's* role in the modeling method is to do the following:

1. Model information for students and/or select other models to present the information. Attention should be given to model traits known to attract and hold attention, to make the presentation very clear and understandable, and otherwise to increase the likelihood of being imitated.
2. Help focus and maintain student attention on what is being modeled.
3. Provide advance organization, mnemonic (memory) devices, and other aids to help students remember what they observe.
4. Provide suitable opportunities for students to practice reenactment of the information they saw modeled.
5. Provide corrective feedback, during student reenactment, so as to speed and improve learning.
6. Provide, when possible, opportunities for students to apply what they have learned.
   Students' roles are quite simple. They have only

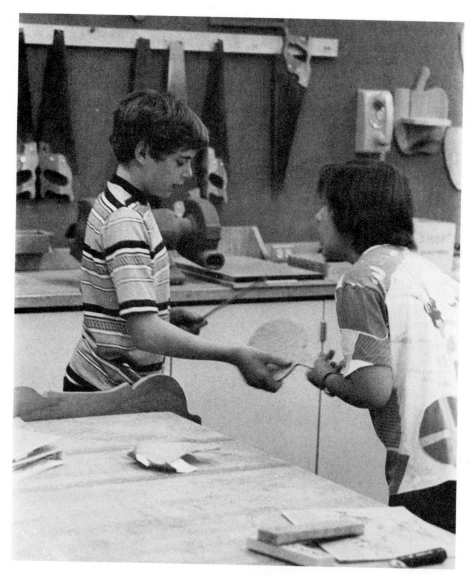

to pay attention to the modeled event, remember as much of it as possible, and practice reenacting the information.

Modeling is the most effective method available for teaching complex social behavior, as well as some of the intellectual skills such as problem-solving processes. It is highly effective, as well, for teaching attitudes and values. It is moderately effective for teaching concepts and processes and is relatively ineffective as a method for teaching items of factual information.

Projects

Next to simulations, no method of teaching brings about more intensive student involvement than does the project method. This involvement is not forced or coerced. To the contrary. Students rally to projects as eagerly as dowagers rally to plumed hats.

Much of projects' appeal comes because the method puts students in charge of their own learning. They get to plan and organize their work. They may work in groups, as most of them prefer, or they may work individually, as a few of them prefer. They get to do the fun part, the legwork, the rummaging around. And in the end they have a tangible product to show off.

The *Merriam-Webster Dictionary* (a fine pocket version, by the way) in its usual terse manner defines "project" as "a specific plan or design:

scheme: a planned undertaking ⟨a research ~⟩." This neat little definition, especially the part about a planned undertaking, gets right at what the project method is all about. It is an undertaking, in a selected part of the curriculum, that students plan and carry out. You can have projects in almost all topics: creative writing, construction, art, research, mapping, measuring, and so on and on.

The actual project, which as you can see is the sine qua non of the project method, almost always aims toward some end product, some tangible thing. This product might be a creatively developed object (such as a learning center), a work of art (such as a tie-dyed fabric), an illustration (such as a class mural), a document (such as a research report), a narrative (such as a photo essay), a creative composition (such as a class literary journal), . . . You get the idea.

Sometimes, projects focus on process rather than product. Examples could include such processes as archaeological digs (skills of), library researches (techniques of), and opinion sampling (procedures of).

You can see how any of these project areas—and only a tiny sampling was mentioned here—brings about very active student involvement. That active involvement is the first of two great strengths of the project method. Teachers don't have to worry about motivation, attention, or cracking the whip.

The second great strength of this method lies in its breadth of effect. This method gets at all levels of educational objectives. Remember Bloom's *Taxonomy* in the cognitive domain—knowledge, comprehension, application, analysis, synthesis, evaluation? Projects bring progress on all these fronts. Students must of necessity acquire knowledge as they work through their projects. They must understand what they are doing, what the knowledge means, and how it interrelates. They must apply what they are learning in order to produce the end product. As they make this application, they analyze information, break it into parts. They synthesize information and put it together in new or more useful ways. They continually evaluate their efforts and results.

And do you remember the affective domain? The climate of free choice tempered with responsibility? Interpersonal skills—they grow in group projects. Self-concept—it rises with competence, accomplishment, and recognition. Attitudes, val-

ues, self-fulfillment—few kinds of instruction provide so fertile a bed for their nourishment as does the project method.

Teachers, when using the project method, must identify or suggest suitable areas and topics for students to explore. They can help by telling about or showing examples of projects other students have completed. As the project work begins they must conference with individuals or groups to help identify goals, procedures, and helpful materials, keeping the overall activity within realistic boundaries of time and resources. They should discuss with students the personal meaning and value accruing during the work. They should, as projects are completed, arrange for them to be displayed or shared with other students.

Students have the responsibility for organizing their work and time so they can show continual progress. They should strive to produce an end product they will be proud of, that they will feel good about sharing with others. As in other approaches, they are to take the matter seriously, but with pleasant attitude and good humor.

The project method can claim only moderate efficiency in helping students acquire basic subject matter knowledge and skills, such as those of fundamental mathematics and English. But it has unusual strength in helping students organize and apply information, show responsibility, follow through, and make sense of what they have learned. It also has exceptional strength in affective areas, because of the cooperative work that, properly guided by the teacher, enhances interpersonal relations and also because of the conditions it provides for the development of personal traits and abilities.

In these pages, justice cannot be done in showing the great range of applicability peculiar to the project method. You can find dozens on dozens of fascinating topics for projects in almost all curricular areas across all grade levels. The boxed material on pp. 215-217 is a brief listing of such project topics. It comes from a section called "activities for the class-lab" in *Educational Psychology: The Instructional Endeavor* (Charles, 1976).

Group process

The project method focused first on subject matter, then drew into the picture interpersonal relations and other affective processes.

The group process method does the reverse. It

in art

modeling and sculpting clay
making collages of various kinds
drawing, coloring, etching with crayons
illustrating talks, sayings, mottoes, stories, etc.
doing macramé
making mobiles and stabiles
making mosaics
painting with tempera, finger paints, acrylics, watercolor

doing origami (paper folding and paper sculpture)
making puppets
sculpting in soap and plaster
making silk screens and prints
making wood cuts and vegetable prints
weaving
making wire and toothpick sculpture
working in leather

in communications

setting up a creative production center for:

writing poems, stories, plays
collecting sayings, mottoes, proverbs
collecting pictures for scrapbooks and illustrations
designing scenery and costumes for plays

designing bulletin boards around current events, personal information, etc.
making flannel board stories
making puppets and giving performances
making box movies

setting up a media center for:

printing and stamping notices, announcements, mottoes
illustrating word origin booklets
illustrating creative writing booklets
illustrating stories, lessons, lectures

making personal tape recordings of poetry, letters, speeches, etc.
producing dioramas and mobiles
assembling multimedia presentations

setting up a publishing center to publish:

creative writing books
who's who books
word origin books
picture scrapbooks

class photo albums
news releases
class newspapers
class magazines

setting up a performing arts center for:

performing skits and plays
dramatizing events
giving speeches

giving book, movie, television reviews and critiques
dramatizing stories and songs

in foreign languages

preparing talks and slide presentations
making costumes
performing skits in the foreign language
acting out scenes from stories

learning typical songs and dances
interviewing and inviting to class people who speak a foreign language or who have lived in a foreign country

Continued.

From Charles, C. M. *Educational psychology: the instructional endeavor* (2nd ed.). St. Louis: The C. V. Mosby Co., 1976.

making collections of things from a foreign country (currency, art, music, artifacts, clothing, utensils, etc.)

subscribing to a foreign newspaper

writing a class newspaper in a foreign language, including news items, stories, poems, riddles, etc.

corresponding with foreign students

keeping a diary in the language

reading librettos of operas in the language

having in-depth study projects about the art, music, literature, politics, sports, schools, religion, costumes, industry, farming, mining, ruins, famous places, etc.

preparing a "Who's Who" of the country

preparing travel maps and itineraries

making greeting cards with foreign language inscriptions and scenes of the country

in mathematics

estimating distances, dimensions, volumes

measuring volumes, weights, dimensions of objects, rooms, etc.

planning and building a scale model house, office building, airport, city, gymnasium, football or baseball field

studying and preparing architectural plans

computing interest rates, commissions, profits, discounts, income tax, property tax

constructing measuring wheels, balances, quadrants, other similar devices

constructing geometrical shapes and forms boards

keeping football, basketball, baseball statistics

making time and distance lines and models

making lists of personal uses for arithmetic

making illustrated reports on the history of numbers

making and using number games, counting devices, charts, graphs, posters, flash cards, meters, speedometer, abacus, fractions

setting up and using an "arithmetic discovery table" with objects and directions

keeping cost records for feeding pets, family budgets, etc.

making scales for barometers, thermometers, rain gauges

making graphs for daily temperature, rainfall, etc.

keeping statistical records for the class

using adding machines and calculators

computing costs for various kinds of historical and present-day trips

practicing making exchanges between United States and foreign currencies

in music

identifying the musical resources of the school (instruments available, musical groups, performers, talented students, teachers)

setting up musical groups in the class (singers and instrumentalists)

identifying music typical of festival days (Christmas, Hannukah, Chinese New Year, Easter, Cinco de Mayo, etc.)

studying the music of a foreign country, learning typical songs and dances, performing them for other classes

making a list of musical programs on AM and FM radio, television, community concerts, etc.

making a study of folk music of any time or place, learning to perform it and presenting performances to other classes

identifying and learning typical songs of Italy, France, Spain, England, Scotland, Ireland, Germany, Switzerland, Russia, Hungary, Greece

learning typical folk songs of ethnic groups in the United States

dramatizing ballads and folk songs such as "Aunt Rhody," "Cockle Shells," "Dublin City," "Ballad of Barberry Ellen"

making appropriate costumes and performing the minuet, gavotte, rondo, jig, modern dances

setting short poems to music

composing and presenting a class opera that dramatizes a contemporary or historical event

in science

setting up and maintaining a "discovery table" with many kinds of objects for observing and experimenting

setting up an electricity lab with cells, wires, bulbs, buzzers, switches, fuses and making electromagnets and telegraphs

setting up an optical lab with lenses, prisms, light sources, colors

setting up an acoustical lab with sound-producing objects, transmission media, amplifiers, insulators

setting up a machine lab with simple machines, weights, spring scales

setting up an air and water pressure lab to check pressures, densities, weights

setting up a power-harnessing lab for using solar, wind, water, steam, muscle power to drive small pieces of equipment

setting up a weather station and keeping daily records

making and using telescopes, microscopes, thermometers, barometers, sundials, compasses

setting up, maintaining, observing aquaria, terraria, ant colonies, etc.

growing and observing cultures of microscopic plants and animals

raising butterflies, silkworms, tadpoles and observing and recording their development

conducting nutrition experiments with plants

developing and using systems for classifying plants, animals, minerals

making collections of insects, rocks, fossils, leaves, seeds

making models of atoms, molecules, solar system, galaxies, watersheds, geological formations, volcanoes, parts of the body, etc.

in social science

maintaining a current events bulletin board

making a time line for students' own lives

making a time line for the school, street, community, country, mankind, etc.

writing a history of the school, street, community with interviews, checks of city documents, etc.

describing the sources of common foods

selecting one food and making lists of all the people who help process it

doing studies of different cultures and comparing them to our own

describing schools in other societies

contrasting primitive and modern means of travel and communication

diagramming latitudes and longitudes and reading these positions on the globe

determining the date and time of day in various parts of the world

making relief, outline, salt and flour, jigsaw puzzle, topographical, product, pictorial, population maps, etc.

drawing political cartoons

interpreting political cartoons

utilizing role-playing to enact such situations as "Meet the Press," "You are There," interviews with historical figures, dramatizations of such historical events as the Scopes Monkey Trial, Constitutional Convention, signing of the Mayflower Compact, court trials, sessions of Congress, a New England town meeting, etc.

keeping actual or imaginary diaries of events, travels, etc.

interviewing students and parents on any issue

interviewing policemen, pilots, farmers, etc.

conducting debates on issues of current interest

comparing authors and newspapers for accuracy and objectivity

keeping track of the stock market during the year and trying to explain its advances and declines

choosing the five greatest ideas, men, women, world events, books, etc. and then defending the choices focuses first and foremost on interactions among group members, on processes related to pursuit of a common goal, on the give-and-take of information and opinion, on conflict resolution, on leadership and followership, and on facilitative procedures within the group.

Joyce and Weil (1972) see the group process method as fitting into two primary areas of concern: (1) the furtherance and enhancement of society and (2) the development of improved interpersonal relations. In this country, group process is directly aimed at the improvement of democratic processes. It helps structure classrooms so they lead toward the following goals (Joyce and Weil, 1972, p. 31):

1. Establishment of social systems, within the classroom, based on democratic procedures
2. Scientific inquiry procedures into the nature of social processes
3. Activities in solving interpersonal and social problems

Group process, far more than other methods of teaching, helps students move toward the goal of citizenship, the fifth of the seven cardinal principles of education. Although critics point to flaws in American democracy, flaws of which most of us are quite aware, there does not exist anywhere in the world, nor has there ever existed, a large society that could boast of greater personal freedom than that you and I enjoy. Although we may decry abuses of this freedom, few Americans would relinquish it in order to live in societies where there are higher levels of governmental control. When you get right down to it, most Americans, once they have adequately sampled the lifestyles possible in other countries, will loudly proclaim that there's no place like home.

But the freedom we enjoy exacts its toll. Not only must we be vigilant, as they say, but we must carry the democracy on our individual and collective backs. That means that each of us, if we are to have some control over how we govern ourselves, must function as responsible decision makers. We must be educated and enlightened. We must keep ourselves current. We must pay attention to government and participate, at least by voting. True, we can afford the luxury of letting many people decide not to participate actively. But if too many of us decide against it, you can be sure there are plenty of people ready to take charge of our lives and make us do it their way.

Ralph Tyler, one of the most respected people in American education, has stressed and re-stressed the unparalleled role the American school plays in perpetuating democratic society. Nowhere else do the schools so reflect a microcosm of society, he says. Teachers here maintain a democratic climate better than anywhere else. Students play larger roles in decision making. The prevailing sense of justice and fair play among students and teachers is unequaled by the schools of any other country (Tyler, quoted in "The Seven Cardinal Principles Revisited," 1976).

But we might as well face facts. No method of teaching is more difficult to implement than group process. It is inefficient for learning subject matter, and most teachers, parents, and administrators still look on subject matter knowledge as the hallmark of educational effectiveness. It seems to involve a great deal of wheel spinning and must waste time in making group decisions, providing for arguing pros and cons, voting, and so forth. Critics point out how much quicker it is for teachers to make these decisions and get down to the business of learning. Advocates counter that group process, however inefficient it may seem, is indispensable if we are to perpetuate a democratic society.

Herbert Thelen (1954) has suggested a group investigation format that gives direction and adds efficiency to group process. His format consists of the following elements:

Consideration of a real personal or social incident or problem that will bring forth strong reactions from the students

Formulation of a stated problem, growing out of these reactions, that can be investigated (identified and shaped with the help of the teacher)

Development of a plan of investigative attack on the problem, including procedures, roles of participants, and organization

Investigation and report of findings by the participants

Evaluation of proposed solutions to the problem

Repetition of the cycle if conflict recurs during the evaluation phase

The *teacher's* role is to function as a participant in the group process, clarifying and counseling, but not providing additional structure. The role includes encouraging students to examine their own roles, their procedures, their contributions, and the meaning for them that grows out of the process.

The *students* play active roles from beginning to end. They may look to the teacher for guidance but not for final answers. Those answers, as well as personal meaning and interpersonal relationships, develop from students' activities.

Similar group process procedures have been developed by Donald Oliver and James Shaver (1966) and by Byron Massialas and Benjamin Cox (1966).

Inquiry/discovery

Here you see very brief summaries of two lessons. One of the lessons is built around the inquiry/discovery method. The other is not. Can you tell which involves inquiry and discovery?

Lesson 1. Capitalization (fifth grade). The teacher introduces the lesson by stating the rules about capitalizing the first word in each sentence, persons' names, and the names of cities and states. Two correct examples illustrating each of these rules are shown, on a chart, to the class. Two incorrect examples are also shown. Students are told that errors are shown, and they are asked to point them out. Students complete work sheets that contain sentences with no capitalized words. They capitalize words according to the rules they have learned.

Lesson 2. Capitalization (fifth grade). The teacher introduces the lesson by presenting written paragraphs to the students. The paragraphs contain sentences with proper names. The students are informed that all the capitalized words are correct in the sentences. They are asked to circle all the capital letters. Then, working alone or in pairs, they are asked to make up rules that tell which words, among those in the paragraphs they have, should be capitalized. They are allowed to look in their language books or other references if they wish.

Now, which lesson best illustrates the inquiry/discovery method of teaching? What is your evidence? What one-sentence statements can you now make to describe inquiry/discovery learning?

The inquiry/discovery method of teaching has one main purpose. That purpose is to develop in learners the ability to learn on their own; to observe information; to organize it; to evaluate it; and to arrive at their own concepts, conclusions, and generalizations. This process helps students learn to use information. It helps them become their own authorities. They begin to think for themselves

without having to turn to other authorities for answers and conclusions.

Inquiry/discovery can teach students to use both inductive and deductive processes of logic, although it emphasizes the inductive. Induction is a process of observing instances of related information, then arriving at some conclusion about them. For example, every day at noon I walk past a large bed of flowering plants. I never see snails on the sidewalk except when it is raining. But every time it rains, there are snails out on the walk. What do I induce from those instances? Many conclusions are possible: Snails fall with the rain; snails are thirsty for water; snails like for the rain to wash their shells; snails can move about more easily when it is damp; snails like to move about when it is dark and cool.

Deduction is quite different from induction. Deduction is a process of reasoning from statements that are known (or believed) to be true. It is the major process used in formal logic. Using the snail example, deductive reasoning might proceed in this way:

Snails move about when it is damp and the sun is not shining.
Rain makes the ground damp and the light dim. Therefore rain is likely to cause snails to move about.

Jerome Bruner (1961) has contributed greatly to the development of inquiry/discovery as a method of teaching. He refers to self-discovered learning, which results from inquiry, as the most uniquely personal learning any of us has. He contends that learning accruing from inquiry has special value, in terms of its usefulness and permanence, and that the process of learning through inquiry increases intellectual potence, while shifting motivation for learning from external rewards and punishments to internal ones.

Few people argue with Bruner's contentions that inquiry and discovery produce learning that is more permanent and more useful, while building ability to learn on one's own. The arguments against inquiry learning center first on its inefficiency. One could not hope to learn nearly so much information through inquiry as through expository teaching. Second, critics contend that teaching through inquiry is inordinately difficult. It cannot be done well by the majority of teachers.

As to the first argument, advocates of inquiry

grant its inefficiency as a means of acquiring vast quantities of information. They defend the method on the grounds that whatever information is learned in this way tends to be more lasting and more usable than information learned through memorization and on the unshakable conviction that there is no alternative to inquiry for teaching people how to learn on their own.

How does Bruner see inquiry/discovery used as a method of teaching? He sees emphasis being put repeatedly on activities that require inquiry, ideally activities involving questions that don't have already-determined answers. Are there such questions? Of course. You can think of dozens of them if you try. Here's an example: Under which colors of light do lima beans grow best? Students can inquire into that unanswered question and discover plausible answers.

Harold and Greta Morine (1973) have written a book entitled *Discovery: a Challenge to Teachers,* in which they suggest procedures and activities for implementing a quality inquiry/discovery program. The procedures they suggest include providing quantities of examples for students to observe in a given topic, then teaching them to ask themselves fruitful questions about their observations, questions such as the following (Morine and Morine, 1973, p. 111):

What do I observe?
Do I see any patterns?
What connections do I see?
What generalizations can I construct?
What hypotheses do I have?

Frank Ryan and Arthur Ellis (1974) have produced a very useful book on inquiry entitled *Instructional Implications of Inquiry.* They suggest many specific instructional activities, complete with useful examples, for teaching the processes of hypothesizing, gathering data, processing data, and making inferences.

The *teacher's* role consists of helping students focus in on a topic, have sufficient material to observe or consider, ask fruitful questions, clarify thoughts, and examine answers.

The *students'* role is to observe data, organize them, ask questions, formulate hypotheses, and test those hypotheses.

The process of teaching through inquiry can be used at all grade levels. It is not an efficient

way of learning basic facts and processes. Nor is it an efficient means of teaching interpersonal relations or democratic processes. Its strength lies in its power to teach processes of thinking, asking questions, formulating hypotheses, observing data, and testing hypotheses. It is an effective method of teaching students to make use of scientific processes of problem solving. And it is one of the few methods we have that causes and helps students to try to make sense of what they see or think about and thus to learn on their own.

Facilitation

No one has expressed the essence of facilitative teaching better than Carl Rogers. Let us turn to the words of that remarkable man, that leader of the humanistic thrust in psychology and education, to see what facilitation is about.

Rogers (1971) made an interesting comparison between facilitation and traditional teaching. He began by describing what he believes good traditional teachers do, as follows:

1. They select the subject matter they think their students should learn.
2. They organize the subject matter in ways known to help students learn, such as breaking it into manageable parts.
3. They design the instructional activities in which students will engage.
4. They select the instructional materials students will use.
5. They direct students through the activities, giving lectures and demonstrations, asking questions, making assignments, and so forth.
6. They evaluate student progress, making judgments that usually lead to a grade or mark.

You have had teachers who taught exactly this way. If they acted kindly toward you, you probably considered them very good teachers. You learned a good deal or at least had the opportunity to do so. This traditional way of teaching is efficient and effective. Why, then, does Rogers disparage it?

Rogers doesn't like this method of teaching for two reasons. First, he thinks it results in learnings that are mostly inconsequential, learnings that have no significant influence in students' lives and behaviors. Second, he believes it stifles qualities and conditions that should emerge in education, qualities such as freedom, self-direction, responsible choice making, fulfillment of personal needs and interests, and establishment of trust and genuine feelings between people.

Rogers calls traditional teaching the "jug and mug" approach. The teacher is the filled jug. The learner is the empty mug. Teaching consists of pouring contents from the filled jug into the empty mug.

Instead of jug and mug teaching, says Rogers, we need facilitation. Here's what facilitation is like, and you can see how it contrasts with traditional teaching:

1. The teacher observes students and talks with them at length. The purpose of this observation and communication is to determine what students, individually and collectively, truly want to learn about and to become able to do. (This determination is crucially important in facilitative teaching. The ultimate goal is twofold: [1] to establish interpersonal relationships that facilitate productive learning and growth of the self and [2] to permit students to engage in learnings that will have personal significance and meaning for each of them.)

2. Following identification of student directions in learning, the teacher talks further with the students, not to direct or suggest, but to help clarify topics of study, procedures for investigating, and resources, such as materials, people, and places, that will make possible the desired learnings.

3. The teacher then assists students, however possible, short of telling answers, giving directions, or making assignments. The teacher helps secure materials, arranges learning space and activities, participates alongside learners, and always remains available for conferencing.

4. As learning activities progress, the teacher interacts with students, helping them explore the significance of what they are learning. This is a way of helping each student become more fully aware of personal meanings. It also helps students change their behavior in ways consonant with their new abilities and insights.

5. Evaluation plays a relatively inconsequential role in facilitative teaching. Ordinarily it would not go beyond an exploration, between teacher and student, of the meaning and value of what was learned, plus a consideration of the effec-tiveness of procedures and resources used in the learning. However, if the student has not made an appropriate attempt to learn, Rogers believes the teacher should candidly say so, again offering help but stressing the student's responsibilities as well.

Very interesting implications can be drawn from Rogers's reflections on traditional and facilitative teaching.

The *teacher's* role differs markedly in the two approaches. Traditional teaching casts the teacher into a role of selector, organizer, planner, director, and evaluator. Facilitative teaching has the teacher working as communicator, clarifier, helper, cog lubricator, and red tape cutter.

The *student's* role in traditional teaching is to pay attention, participate in activities, do the assignments, and perform as well as possible on tests. In facilitation, the students take on many of the duties that belong to the teacher in traditional teaching. They must identify topics for study, work out procedures, identify resources, complete the work to their own satisfaction, and attempt to clarify the significance and meaning that have accrued from their activities.

The *outcomes* of learning from the two approaches are similar in some regards and dissimilar in others. The similarities include serious student involvement with topics, resources, other students, and the teacher. The dissimilarities include specific topics investigated, means of motivation and guidance employed, arrangements of learning environments and activities, and purposes and methods of evaluation.

The facilitative method represents a remarkable advance over other methods in promoting some of the most important ends of humanistic education. For the cognitive domain, those ends are skills and knowledge that have special meaning and usefulness for individual students. For the affective domain, they are self-fulfillment of needs, development of the total person, clarification of values, establishment of moral codes, and development of ability to choose wisely while accepting responsibility for the consequences of those choices. In short, it is a way of putting learners in charge of their own learning, while teaching them how to find, organize, and use material and human resources.

However, the facilitative method, like all others,

draws its share of fire and derision. On a philosophical level, serious questions arise concerning the extent to which learners can identify those areas of learning that, in the total scheme of things, have the greatest importance in their lives. Cannot experienced teachers, who see the larger perspective, better identify educational needs?

On the practical level, three concerns arise. One of these concerns has to do with efficiency. Teachers are trained and skilled in organizing and presenting material to students. The facilitative method is seen as comparatively neanderthalian in its efficiency. It overly wavers, washes, and spins its wheels. A second concern has to do with maturity levels of students. It is laughable to primary teachers to think of attempting to set up a curriculum based on the facilitative method. Students must have reached certain levels of intellectual and social development before they can function in this way. A third concern has to do with the choices students would, in fact, make if given complete freedom. Few would choose to discipline themselves in ways necessary to master fundamentals of mathematics or English.

Enlightened teachers do not swallow any method hook, line, and sinker. They take the best that a method has to offer, use it to achieve appropriate ends, and interweave it with other methods that better reach their objectives. So it is with facilitation. There is much there to help every teacher and every student. It doesn't answer all questions about teaching and learning, but it comes as close as any other single method.

Open experience

If you blanched at the student latitude provided in facilitation, you may twitch and faint as you read about open experience. If, however, you felt a ticklish thrill in your stomach at the idea of student self-direction and search for personal meaning, the open experience method should make your skin tingle with excitement.

Open experience is a method of teaching wherein students are allowed to involve themselves, virtually on their own, in learning activities in the classroom. The *teacher* does not suggest or direct but simply provides materials and activities. *Students* choose to engage in them or not, as they please. They have to follow only two basic ground rules: they are not allowed to do physical damage

to classroom, materials, or fellow students, and they must practice the golden rule in their dealings with others.

Chaos, right? Maelstrom. Plague and pestilence. Slovenliness. Slothfulness. Law of the jungle. *Lord of the Flies.*

Not so. Open experience, odd as it may seem, has often brought about exactly the opposite results.

Consider the case of Herbert Kohl, who more than any other person popularized the open experience method of teaching. His key ideas are presented in his remarkable little book entitled *The Open Classroom* (Kohl, 1969). In this book he recounts his early experiences as a teacher—a traditional teacher in Carl Rogers's words—in an inner city school in New York. Daily he faced recalcitrant students who had virtually no interest in the contents of the prescribed curriculum. The overriding concern in the school was control, how to keep the lid on the kids while they continually threatened to boil over. The overriding teaching technique was the imposition of firm adult authority. Thus the lives of teachers and students in that school were a continual struggle of the one against the other, never working together, never cooperating, never relating to each other as people.

Kohl slowly hit on the idea of putting into full-scale practice some of the ideas long advocated by humanists such as Maslow and Rogers. He did it more than anything else as a way of preserving his own sanity. The students, in showing their hate for school, made his life miserable by yelling, falling out of their seats, and running around the room. But as luck had it, the changes he made turned out wonderfully well for both his students and himself.

He gave up trying to push the formal curriculum down their throats. He talked with them about things important in their lives, things they liked to do, things they wanted to learn about. He tried enriching the environment with materials, and he suggested that they, too, help add to the environment by bringing in things they cared about. At the same time he began believing it was all right for teachers to act like other human beings, relating warmly to students, talking with them about items of interest, and showing the full range of emotions, including both anger and delight.

What resulted was a gradual transformation of

Kohl's classroom from a place of bedlam and hostility to a place of purposeful activity. He became able to relate to his students as individual people, not as a mob of enemies. The students, for their part, stopped making life miserable for Kohl.

Most teachers at first shrink from the notion of using open experience, even for a few minutes. They fear that chaos will result, that they will lose control, that students will learn nothing of consequence. But if they put open experience to the test they often find eye-opening results.

Such as the case for Mr. Johnson, a real teacher who here wears an alias. Mr. Johnson was enrolled in a graduate class on individualizing instruction. One way of individualizing instruction is to use open experience, where the classroom is richly stocked with instructional games, intriguing devices to manipulate and take apart, interesting magazines and books, and so forth. Students are allowed a certain amount of time each day to select whatever they want to engage in, including the option of doing nothing at all. Kohl says to start with 10 minutes a day and increase the amount of time as students learn to handle it. They understand that they cannot be disruptive or physically or emotionally damaging to others.

Mr. Johnson was encouraged to set up an open experience approach in his class. He balked at the idea. He was a thoroughly traditional teacher, a very good one, who carefully selected, organized, and directed his students' learning activities. He could not see his students spending class time, as he put it, with "hammers, wigs, and ducks." But he acquiesced under persuasive pressure and agreed to give it a try. He did his best. He brought in checkers, chess, and other games. He got his students to bring their motorcycle and automotive magazines. He brought a gasoline engine from a lawn mower, along with his own set of tools. He supplied a quantity of popular books, magazines, and arts and crafts materials.

Now to make the story short. After 3 weeks, Mr. Johnson enthusiastically reported these results:

His students showed remarkable new interest in school. Many of them began arriving very early, eager to get in the room before school and mess around with the stuff inside. Many of them stayed after school until he made them leave. Students from other classes joined in.

The number of discipline problems went down, not up as Mr. Johnson had feared.

The students, rather than becoming disorderly, showed unexpected responsibility in caring for the materials. Mr. Johnson did insist on orderliness and consideration.

Mr. Johnson, to his amazement, lost none of his tools, books, magazines, or crafts supplies.

Mr. Johnson avowed that open experience had given him a new perspective on teaching. He intended to continue using it, allowing students to work before and after school, as well as a certain amount of time during school hours.

Summary

This concludes our overview of eleven tried and true methods of teaching. No one of these methods is maximally efficient in promoting all the established goals of education. Each method has its strengths. Used in judicious combination, they provide instructional organization and activities that fit personalities of teachers and students, learning styles of students, and special demands of subject matter. The teacher's professional task is to select and combine the best from each method so as to provide well-rounded instruction for all.

SUGGESTED ACTIVITIES FOR FURTHER UNDERSTANDING

1. Choose two teaching methods you find especially effective and comfortable. Plan a lesson on the same subject, using each of the methods. Note differences they require in involvement of students, teacher preparation, length of lesson, student work, etc. See which you would consider most effective for that subject.
2. Examine the teaching methods listed in this chapter, and discuss the advantages and disadvantages of each. Decide what subjects and types of lessons are best suited to each method. Decide which method or methods best fit your style as a teacher.
3. Choose a method that you like least and use it to teach a lesson to your classmates. Try your very best to make it work. You may be surprised how effective it is, and you will have added a new teaching method to your repertoire.

REFERENCES

Bandura, A. *Social learning theory*. New York: General Learning Corporation, 1971.

Bicentennial Committee of the National Education Association. The seven cardinal principles revisited. *Today's Education*, 1976, *65*(3), 57-72.

Bloom, B. (Ed.). *Taxonomy of educational objectives. Handbook I: cognitive domain*. New York: David McKay Co., Inc., 1956.

Bruner, J. The act of discovery. *Harvard Educational Review,* 1961, *31,* 21-32.

Cardinal principles of secondary education (Bulletin #35): Washington, D.C.: Department of the Interior, Bureau of Education, 1918.

Charles, C. *Educational psychology: the instructional endeavor* (2nd ed.). St. Louis: The C. V. Mosby Co., 1976.

Joyce, B., and Weil, M. *Models of teaching.* Englewood Cliffs, N.J.: Prentice-Hall, Inc., 1972.

Kohl, H. *The open classroom.* New York: Vintage Books, 1969.

Krathwohl, D. (Ed.). *Taxonomy of educational objectives. Handbook II: affective domain.* New York: David McKay Co., Inc., 1964.

Massialas, B., and Cox, B. *Inquiry in social studies.* New York: McGraw-Hill Book Co., 1966.

Morine, H., and Morine, G. *Discovery: a challenge to teachers.* Englewood Cliffs, N.J.: Prentice-Hall, Inc., 1973.

Nagel, T., and Richman, P. *Competency based instruction,* Columbus, Ohio: Charles E. Merrill Publishing Co., 1972.

Oliver, D., and Shaver, J. *Teaching public issues in the high school.* Boston: Houghton Mifflin Co., 1966.

Rogers, C. Forget you are a teacher. *Instructor,* 1971, *85,* 61-66.

Ryan, F., and Ellis, A. *Instructional implications of inquiry.* Englewood Cliffs, N.J.: Prentice-Hall, Inc., 1974.

STRATEGIES OF TEACHING 12

The previous chapter dealt with methods of teaching—those large, overarching, global ways of organizing and presenting instruction. Eleven methods were discussed. They ranged from highly structured to lowly structured, and each had its own strengths in helping students reach important goals of education.

Perhaps you remember that the chapter also mentioned strategies of teaching. Strategies were described as much smaller in scope than methods. They were said to be special techniques useful in affecting small areas of student behavior. Mention was made of the way that strategies could be interwoven with methods and that several strategies could fit comfortably into a single method.

In this chapter we will take a detailed look at some of those strategies, thirteen of them to be exact. You will see how each can be used toward a clear, definite end—how a questioning strategy can produce student involvement and force use of

different levels of mental functioning, how an acceptance strategy can develop emotional security and cement warm personal relations, how a mastery learning strategy can propel students to high levels of knowledge and skills.

Each of these thirteen strategies has its special intents, procedures, and effects. Each has been established as effective, efficient, and worthwhile. As was the case with methods of instruction, teachers who would be true professionals must learn how to use each of these strategies, then select, combine, and incorporate those that best suit their purposes, their students, and their subject matter.

The thirteen strategies of teaching, arranged in order from most structured to least structured, are as follows:

1. Mastery learning
2. Behavior modification
3. Precision teaching

4. Engineered environments
5. Advance organization
6. Individualized instruction
7. Questioning
8. Great expectations
9. Synectics
10. Values clarification
11. Classroom meetings
12. Reality approach
13. Acceptance

We will now proceed to a consideration of these strategies.

Mastery learning

Mastery learning is a teaching strategy used to bring almost all students, not just a few of them, up to high levels of proficiency in the material being learned. It deals solely with cognitive and psychomotor learning, not with affective learning. It is based on the conviction that, given the appropriate conditions, all students can master the material being taught. Considerable experimental evidence supports this contention.

"Mastery" in itself is not a precise term. It refers to a rather high level of proficiency, corresponding roughly to the level ordinarily reached by the top 10% of students. Mastery learning advocates have shown that, generally speaking, 90% of students can be brought up to this level (Block, 1971).

What produces this miraculous achievement? Basically, mastery learning requires two conditions, both of which are significant departures from typical teaching. These conditions are as follows:

1. Time limitations are made flexible, rather than rigid. In typical instruction, all students work at a topic for a fixed amount of time—an hour, a day, 3 weeks, 2 months. At the end of that fixed amount of time we can see that some students have done very well, some have done very poorly, and most are clustered between the two extremes. This occurs even when students try their best. Thus typical teaching holds time constant, while allowing achievement to vary, to fall where it may.

Mastery learning reverses this picture. It holds achievement to an acceptable high level, while varying the amount of time necessary for each individual student to reach that level.

An interesting rationale underlies this strategy. The rationale contends that what we have ordinarily thought of as learning *ability* (often called intelligence) is more accurately learning *rate*. That is, more intelligent people learn more quickly. But less intelligent people can learn just as fully, adequately, and completely, given more time in which to do so. Block (1971) and Block and Anderson (1975) cite growing experimental evidence that lends credence to this notion.

2. The second condition required for mastery learning is a carefully organized system for monitoring student work and providing corrective feedback. This means that teachers must provide ways to note the progress of students. When errors are made, they are pointed out as soon as possible, not 2 or 3 days later. Clear suggestions are provided to help students correct what they have been doing wrong. This continual monitoring can be done by having students check their own work frequently against answer keys or models of quality work. Instructional aides, cross-age tutors, and volunteers are helpful in this function. Programed materials can be useful, also.

Providing corrective feedback quickly does two good things. First, it prevents students' practicing errors, stamping those errors into their minds. Second, it keeps them progressing continually, instead of wasting time when obstacles block their way.

The *teacher's* role in mastery learning is to break the material into sequenced, manageable parts. The teacher decides what level of performance constitutes mastery and places students into tasks at their levels of achievement. Teachers must provide ways to monitor the work of each student and to provide immediate feedback when necessary. One of their most important tasks, easy in theory but difficult in practice, is to provide variations in time allotments that individual students require for reaching mastery level. Finally, they must devise an adequate system of record keeping. Different students will be reaching mastery at different times and will be working at different tasks. Teachers must have a way of keeping track of the work and progress of all students.

The *students'* role is simply to work at assigned tasks. They will come to take seriously the notion of mastery. They can help self-check their progress and help keep records. They ask for help when they reach obstacles they cannot surmount.

The *outcomes* of mastery learning are more than worth the effort involved. Students can, most of them, reach high levels of achievement in important educational matters. This achievement pleases both them and their teachers. Both feel successful and capable. Mastery learning especially promotes achievement in areas of basic knowledge and skills. It is not effective in promoting affective learning.

Behavior modification

Imagine a pigeon enclosed in a glass box. It is hungry, having had little to eat for 2 days. It moves about, stretching wings and neck, looking here and there. No one knows what goes on in its mind; no one cares. Its movements are what's important.

By chance the pigeon happens to peck a white plastic disk embedded in one wall of the enclosure. Immediately a buzzer sounds, and a pellet of food drops into a little bin, open to the pigeon. The bird investigates the pellet and eats it.

Back to pacing, stretching, turning, pecking at random. Again it pecks the disk. Again food drops.

After four or five occurrences, the pigeon wastes no time. It beats a hot path between disk and food. It has learned, through a principle called reinforcement, to peck the disk, a behavior that is not normally a favorite of pigeons.

Now imagine a kindergarten child, Timmy, in school, in a classroom, rolling on the floor, paying no attention to the beautiful story being read. Teacher sees Marilyn, next to Timmy, sitting quietly, paying attention. Teacher says "Oh, I like the way Marilyn is sitting so nicely, paying attention." Timmy immediately sits still and attentive. Teacher says "Thank you, Timmy, for sitting nicely. My, you are a good helper." Timmy sits and pays attention for several minutes.

Do you think it a long leap from pigeon in glass box to boy in kindergarten class? It may seem far-fetched, but the principle that controlled their behavior was exactly the same. If you know about the work of the great psychologist B. F. Skinner, you recognize the principle as the application on contingencies of reinforcement. In sum, applying reinforcement involves catching the organism doing what you want it to do and rewarding it by giving it what it wants. The hungry pigeon wanted food. Timmy wanted the teacher's approval.

When this principle of behavior control is used in the classroom, it is called behavior modification. Behavior modification is a teaching strategy that influences very powerfully what students do, not only in comportment (good and bad behavior) but in academic work as well.

A large number of reinforcers are known to be effective in influencing student behavior. A reinforcer is technically a stimulus supplied after an observed behavior that serves to increase the likelihood of that behavior's being repeated. In more common terms we think of a reinforcer as a reward. We give the students rewards when they do what we want them to do. This makes them repeat the behavior that earned the reward.

Teachers now routinely apply behavior modification in working with learners. The strategy, perfected only within the past 20 years, is just now coming into universal use. Its power is uncontested. There still remain disputes about whether its use is ethical, but no one denies its effect.

Earlier in this book you saw discussions about using behavior modification in working with students. If you would like to find out even more about the strategy, you should read Madeline Hunter's book *Reinforcement* (Hunter, 1968). It provides a snappy summary of principles of reinforcement and how they are applied. Then you should examine a fine work by Naisworth et al. (1969) that gives a useful overview of procedures for using behavior modification in the classroom.

Naisworth's book describes the range of reinforcers available to us all the way from social reinforcers, such as nods and smiles, to graphic reinforcers, such as marks and points, and on to tangible reinforcers, such as tokens and candy. Different reinforcers have different levels of strength. But they are all based on "Grandma's Rule" (Premack, 1965): First you do what I want you to do, then you can do something you want to do or can have something you want to have.

The basic nonpunitive paradigm for behavior modification in the classroom is as follows:

Rules: Clearly stated okay's and no-no's
Ignore: Paying no attention at all to inappropriate behavior
Praise: Rewarding desired behavior

In this paradigm you try to catch 'em being good, then reinforce that behavior.

When students show behavior that is *very* inappropriate, you may not be able to ignore. In this case, you call attention to the behavior, stating calmly that it must stop. In severe cases, you must restrain the undesired behavior, usually by isolating the offender from the remainder of the group.

Here is a list of reinforcers that are useful and available for use by teachers in the classroom (Charles, 1976a, p. 210):

Being right
Being first
Receiving attention
Receiving praise
Receiving privileges
Receiving stars or marks
Receiving tangible tokens
Receiving edibles

Behavior modification is a very useful strategy for shaping student behavior in both cognitive and affective areas. As such, it fits well into methods of teaching that have moderate to high structure. It is not so useful in methods with lower structure, such as facilitation and open experience.

Critics say it is not ethical to use such subterfuge to direct behavior and that behavior modification teaches students to work for external rewards rather than for the pleasure of learning. Teachers eagerly accept it, however, because it is a technique of proved effectiveness, wide range of usefulness, and doubtful ill effect.

Precision teaching

Precision teaching is a special application of behavior modification that has led to remarkable student growth in both academic and social areas. Popularized by Ogden Lindsley (1971), precision teaching allows students to chart their own progress in matters such as subject matter learning, attention to task, nondisruption, and completion of assigned work.

Like other behavioristic strategies, precision teaching relies on Skinnerian principles of reinforcement. It is carried out in the following way:

First, a target behavior is identified. This target behavior can be one toward which the total class is working, or it can be set up differently for individual students. Whichever is the case, each student keeps a record of individual progress. The target behavior could be any one of a number of possibilities: spelling achievement scores, reading rate (number of words per minute), number of mathematics problems completed, consecutive minutes spent on task, consecutive minutes without getting up and walking around the room, and so on.

Second, the target task is quantified in some way. Academic target areas can be quantified in terms of scores made on tests or exercises or in terms of amount of work completed satisfactorily. Psychomotor behavior, such as running, jumping, and lifting, can be quantified in terms of times, frequencies, and amounts. Social behavior can be quantified by counting the number of appropriate or inappropriate acts during a fixed amount of time. For example, records can be kept of the number of minutes that individual students refrain from disruptions, such as talking out during class.

Third, charts are provided, on which students graph their individual performances. Here is one such chart:

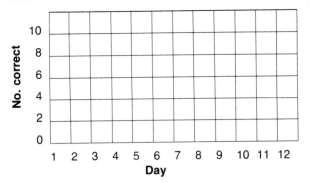

Students are taught how to mark their scores on the chart. They thus show graphic evidence of improvement and progress, or lack thereof.

For example, suppose that Sally is keeping track of the number of correct responses made on daily 10-minute quizzes in her history class. At first she is missing the majority of quiz items, because she has not been reading the assignments carefully. Keeping the chart, however, motivates her to improve, so that over a 2-week period her numbers of correct answers are 3, 3, 4, 7, 6, 8, 10, 9, 10, and 10. Shown on the chart, made up especially for this activity, the picture would be as follows:

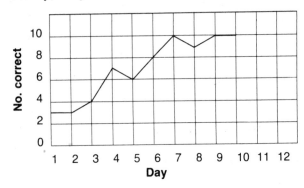

Precision teaching is being used with notable success in both regular and special education classes. The reinforcer used is nothing more than the graphing process itself, where students show records of their progress. The curriculum is arranged so that it lends itself as much as possible to quantifiable student performance. The emphasis is continually put on improvement of each student's performance. Students work to surpass their own previous records; they are in competition with themselves. The charts can be kept in students' folders to provide a record that clearly shows their progress in many different areas of the curriculum.

In using precision teaching, *teachers* must select curricular areas in which student performance can be quantified. They must prepare charts for students to use, introduce the concept and procedures of precision teaching, and instruct students on how to graph their performance on the charts.

Students must learn how to transfer scores they have earned onto their charts. They are responsible for keeping the charts that show graphic evidence of improvement over their past performance.

The outcomes from this strategy can be spectacular. Students, when they take the process seriously, ordinarily strive to outdo themselves. The ceiling on their performance will have to be raised as they reach top levels; they must be continually able to show improvement and not be stuck against the ceiling.

Engineered environments

The engineered environment is a behaviorally structured classroom environment that focuses primarily on growth in academic performance. This strategy is used to focus student attention on small segments of the curriculum and cause students to work at those segments, while reducing diversions and distractions to a minimum.

One of the best examples of the engineered classroom strategy was provided in Project Success Environment, a study carried out in the Atlanta Schools (Sapp, 1973). This project was devised to produce rapid growth in reading and mathematics for continually underachieving students. The strategy consisted of the following three parts:

1. The curricula (mathematics and reading) were broken down into small behavioral segments, sequenced so that one segment led to the next.
2. Students were placed at the working level best suited to each of them individually.
3. A combination of social and tangible reinforcement was used to motivate the students.

Project Success Environment brought about striking improvements in student performance. The increases in both mathematics and reading were more than double what would normally be expected.

The engineered environment strategy brings to bear some of the most effective techniques to come out of the behavioristic camp. Behavioral objectives are used to make precise identification of the desired outcomes. Students are fitted into instruction at levels that allow them to progress easily, yet still encounter challenge. Effective techniques of behavior modification are employed systematically to excite student performance.

Teachers have total responsibility in engineering their classrooms. They must arrange objectives, sequence instruction, secure instructional materials, place students, provide reinforcement, and keep records.

Students have only to engage in the activities that have been assigned to them.

The engineered classroom strategy has been shown to have great effectiveness in producing cognitive gains in academic areas. It is efficiency exemplified, right to the point, without frills, frosting, or funny stuff. It is an excellent strategy for assisting learning in basic skills and knowledge. Its effectiveness in exploratory, aesthetic, and personal relations is questionable. But it is unexcelled for doing well what it is designed to do.

Advance organization

This section explains a teaching strategy called "advance organization." In it you will learn (1) what the term means, (2) why the procedure is important in teaching, (3) which kinds of instructional objectives it promotes, and (4) how it is used in teaching. As you read through the material, check yourself on this what, why, which, and how. You should be able to explain each of these aspects after you complete the section.

The paragraph you have just read is an example of advance organization. The strategy entails giving a brief, clear preview of what is to come. Ordinarily, it makes mention of essential elements in the material to be learned and indicates how those elements relate to each other.

The strategy was formalized by David Ausubel (1960), who advocated its use in helping learners more readily grasp new, meaningful material. Ausubel's view has been supported by research. Advance organization is now accepted as a useful strategy for assisting both learning and remembering. It provides a mental framework onto which items of information can be attached and from which they can be retrieved (remembered) more easily. Although Ausubel built a case for advance organization in connection with meaningful learning, there is reason to believe that the strategy can be even more useful in helping students learn less meaningful material. For material to have meaning, we must be able to see both internal and external relationships, that is, how the parts of the material relate to each other and how it relates to other things in our experience. When material is meaningful, we already perceive such relationships. To say it is not meaningful implies that we do not perceive such relationships. Advance organization, then, provides a framework of relationships that adds meaning to what is being learned.

Let's look at an example. Suppose the first sentence of an article is "A yagroh gheez slet the morrot." This sentence has little meaning, other than English grammatical structure, because we do not see external relationships between the words and items of our experience.

Now suppose you have advance organization before you read the article. "This article is about a yagroh, something it does, and where it does it. Yagroh is another name for an animal familiar to you. Gheez is a verb that tells what it does, and slet the morrot tells where the act takes place. You will find clues in the remainder of the material that will help you make sense of the first sentence."

Advance organization has been especially useful in facilitating cognitive learning. Although it can help in learning discrete items of information, its real strength is its ability to help learners make sense of what they are learning. Thus it leads toward objectives at the comprehension level of Bloom's *Taxonomy*. Probably it can be of value in affective learning as well. Affective learning cannot be separated from language, cause-effect, and means-end relationships. Advance organization enhances one's ability to grasp such relationships.

As to how advance organization is used, you can see an example by looking back to the first paragraph of this section. Whether given orally by the teacher or in writing at the beginning of the material itself, advance organization indicates what's to follow, what it means, and possibly how it's used. In short, advance organization reviews, in advance, the what's, how's, and why's of the material to be learned.

The *teacher's* role in advance organization is a major one. The what's, how's, and why's must be pointed out to students. The teacher later reviews the material to ascertain whether students have grasped those aspects.

The *students'* role is to seek out the what's, how's, and why's identified in the advance organization and be sure that each of these aspects is understood.

Advance organization is a strategy that fits beautifully into the expository method of teaching. Remember that the prime purpose of expository teaching is to make material plain, meaningful, and understandable. Advance organization contributes significantly toward this end.

Individualized instruction

We have some truisms in education that are incredibly persistent. They hang on and on. But when they become a natural part of our language, it seems we almost stop paying attention to what they mean.

One such truism is "We learn by doing." That came out of the work of that giant among educators, philosophers, and psychologists John Dewey. Since his day, countless thousands of lectures have been given on the topic of learning by doing, with the professor droning on endlessly before a class of yawning students whose only involvement is to sit there passively. Get the contradiction? But it needn't be that way.

Such is the case also for another truism "Take the learner where he/she is and take him/her as far as you can." That implies one thing: individualized instruction. Again, how many professors have lectured on that topic to the entire class, making no provisions whatsoever for individual differences among the students? And how many teachers, graduates from those classes, go out, filled with the glamor of individual differences, and proceed to teach as though the idea had never existed?

Let's not be too harsh on ourselves. In truth, we did not have, until recently, clearly defined procedures for individualizing instruction. We talked about it a great deal, but we really didn't know how to handle it in the classroom.

Fortunately, that's not the case anymore. We no longer have any excuse for not individualizing instruction, if we truly think it important. We have the tactics, materials, and procedures. We know, not in idealized terms, but in practical terms, exactly how to individualize in multiple ways, ranging from highly structured to very open (Charles, 1976b).

Individualized instruction is a teaching strategy that helps us give attention to individual differences—differences in ability, interests, needs, and preferred learning styles. It lets us take individual students "where they are" and move them along "as far as we can take them."

The strategy can be employed in any one of the eleven teaching methods described in the previous chapter. Diagnostic-prescriptive teaching, for example, individualizes instruction in terms of student ability and rate of learning. Competency-based instruction individualizes in terms of learning preferences and time. Open experience individualizes in terms of interests and needs.

Does this leave us seeking a definition of individualized instruction? If so, let's have one. Individualizing instruction means doing what you think best for each individual student. This does not always mean individual work. Sometimes what is best is for students to learn to work well in small and large groups. Nevertheless, we must think of individualized instruction in terms of individual students, and oftentimes this does mean individual work.

If we examine all the individualized approaches available to us, we can see that each of them makes variations in one or more of the following four aspects:

Content: The subject matter being learned
Objectives: The desired outcomes of the learning experiences
Activities: What students do while learning
Time: The amounts of time allotted to instruction and learning.

To illustrate, open experience varies content; different students work at different subject matter. Diagnostic-prescriptive teaching varies objectives; different students work toward the attainment of different objectives within the same subject matter. Modularized instruction varies activities; students select activities they prefer from among a variety of options, all of which lead to the same objectives. Mastery learning varies time; different students are allowed different amounts of time for reaching the instructional objectives.

Look closely, and you will see an acronym: COAT (content, objectives, activities, time). When you vary even one of these elements for individual students, you are individualizing instruction. The more of COAT you vary, the more you are individualizing instruction. You can see that individualizing instruction is a "movement toward." We cannot completely vary content, objectives, activities, and time for all the students in our class and still maintain an organized program. But we can move toward that state to the extent allowed by student needs, subject matter, outside pressures, and our own philosophies. We do, in fact, have all the necessary techniques for using the strategy.

The *teacher's* role in individualized instruction varys greatly, in keeping with the COAT variations. If diagnostic-prescriptive teaching is used, the teacher must compile the overall list of objectives, prepare diagnostic devices and prescribed activities, conduct postassessment, and keep records.

You can review this procedure in the previous chapter on the diagnostic-prescriptive method of teaching.

If modularized instruction is used, the teacher must prepare the modules so they specify objectives, pre- and postassessment procedures, optional learning activities for each objective, and very clear instructions so students can work through them on their own.

If learning centers are used, the teacher must construct the centers, provide multiple learning activities with clear directions, introduce students to procedures of working in centers, and manage student movement through the centers.

If open experience is used, the teacher must take primary responsibility for equipping the classroom with a variety of activities and materials of very high interest and must see that students follow the established rules.

If combinations of these approaches are used, or if the teacher composes some other means of varying content, objectives, activities, or time, the teacher is responsible for structure, materials, procedures, facilitation, and record keeping.

Students' roles vary almost as much as the teacher's, according to the individualized approach used. Sometimes they do what is prescribed for them. Sometimes they are allowed to select among options. Whatever the case, individualized instruction ensures that they always play active roles in the process.

In these pages we cannot make a complete examination of the various approaches to individualizing instruction. To see these matters treated in detail, consult *Individualizing Instruction* (Charles, 1976b).

Questioning

Questioning is a teaching teachnique that has been used since the very beginnings of formal education. Socrates purportedly used questioning as a total teaching method, believing that immense knowledge lay unrealized within the mind of every person. By using skillfully put questions, a teacher could bring to conscious awareness the knowledge that already lay fallow within the learners' minds.

In the main, however, questioning has been used not so much to teach as to test. Teachers have long used questions to check whether students completed assignments and grasped their meaning. At first this questioning was done orally, by grilling one student at a time. With the advent of written tests, teachers made still wider use of questioning. This use reached its zenith (where it still remains) following the appearance of objective or short-answer tests, an invention of this century. The objective test permits asking the greatest number of questions of the greatest number of students in the shortest amount of time.

It was not until very recently, however, that questioning developed into what could legitimately be called a strategy of teaching. This development was advanced greatly through the work of Norris Sanders (1966), who showed how to use questions to cause students to think at different cognitive levels.

Sanders devised types of questions that correspond to Bloom's *Taxonomy of Educational Objectives* in the cognitive domain. Some kinds of questions caused students to deal with factual knowledge; others with comprehension; and others with application, analysis, synthesis, and evaluation. Sanders' work helped move questioning from a testing function to a teaching function. It helped teachers remember to help students use higher cognitive processes, such as synthesis and evaluation, instead of forever focusing on lower processes such as knowledge demonstrated solely through memory.

Charles (1976a) carried this work a step further by exploring thirty-five interactions that occur between five sources of information and seven levels of cognitive/psychomotor acts. The five information sources were objects, symbols, meanings, behaviors, and compositions. The seven cognitive/psychomotor acts were perceiving, relating, reproducing, analyzing, applying, evaluating, and producing.

Charles provided an illustrative question for each of these thirty-five interactions. These interactions and sample questions are presented in the boxed material on pp. 233-234 (Charles, 1976a, pp. 297-298).

Questions should be dispersed throughout the material being learned and included in the communications between teacher and students. They may be used as advance organizers. They may be used as study problems. They may be interspersed in written material to arouse and focus at-

35 sample questions *

The seven cognitive/psychomotor acts and the five information categories can be combined in thirty-five different ways. Below you will see a sample question provided for each of these combinations.

perceiving

1. **perceiving objects**
   "Point to the largest red block."
2. **perceiving symbols**
   "Which symbol stands for sodium?"
3. **perceiving meanings**
   "Raise your hand when you hear the colloquialism that expresses surprise."
4. **perceiving behavior**
   "Who noticed what Jack did in the pet shop?"
5. **perceiving compositions**
   "Does the nursery rhyme 'Little Bo Peep' come first, second, or third on the record?"

relating

6. **relating objects**
   "In what ways are a lemon and a grapefruit alike?"
7. **relating symbols**
   "What do you think the following abbreviations stand for?"
8. **relating meanings**
   "How are these sayings alike? How are they different? 'Look before you leap' and 'Strike while the iron is hot'?"
9. **relating behaviors**
   "How does rapid walking affect the heartbeat?"
10. **relating compositions**
    "Which of these paintings fall in the American Primitive group?"

reproducing

11. **reproducing objects**
    "Construct a model of the hydrogen atom."
12. **reproducing symbols**
    "Draw whole, half, quarter, and sixteenth notes."
13. **reproducing meanings**
    "Can you tell the fable of the fox and the grapes in your own words?"
14. **reproducing behaviors**
    "See if you can serve the tennis ball the way I showed you."
15. **reproducing compositions**
    "Who thinks he can recite the Gettysburg Address?"

analyzing

16. **analyzing objects**
    "Where does the spark plug fit in this Wankel engine?"
17. **analyzing symbols**
    "Can you circle the letters in the Spanish alphabet that don't occur in the English alphabet?"
18. **analyzing meanings**
    "What are the word origins from which our word 'neology' is derived?"
19. **analyzing behaviors**
    "Summarize the main things an artist does as he prepares his canvas."
20. **analyzing compositions**
    "In which part of his poem did Frost hint at a possibility of suicide?"

applying

21. **applying objects**
    "How are you supposed to use the grafting compound to seal wounds on the tree?"
22. **applying symbols**
    "See if you can use these pictographs to write a message to a friend."
23. **applying meanings**
    "What trend is the food-population ratio likely to follow in Bolivia?"
24. **applying behaviors**
    "Now see if you can use the scale to play this simple tune."
25. **applying compositions**
    "Use these articles to illustrate Marcuse's point of view."

*From Charles, C. M. *Educational psychology: the instructional endeavor* (2nd ed.). St. Louis: The C. V. Mosby Co., 1976.

Continued.

evaluating

26. **evaluating objects**
"Is this cake sweet enough?"
27. **evaluating symbols**
"Which of these drawings best represents the spirit of ecology? Why?"
28. **evaluating meanings**
"Why do you think the statement 'All change must come in the hearts and minds of men' is valueless for change?"
29. **evaluating behaviors**
"Overall, who has had a greater influence on their respective sports—Bill Russell or Arnold Palmer? Why?"
30. **evaluating compositions**
"Compare Marlowe's and Goethe's delineations of Faust, with emphasis upon his believability as a human being."

producing

31. **producing objects**
"Can you cut a Christmas scene on this linoleum block?"
32. **producing symbols**
"What do you think would be a good code mark to represent happiness? Show us."
33. **producing meanings**
"How could we go about writing our own mottoes?"
34. **producing behavior**
"Show us how you'd react to a surprise birthday party."
35. **producing compositions**
"What melody can you compose to go with this verse?"

tention, to suggest other possibilities, to hint at other avenues to be explored. They should be presented in such a way that students have to respond to them in order to proceed. That response will ensure that students are using the various levels of cognitive functioning.

While learning what kinds of questions to ask, teachers should also learn how to ask the questions. Questions properly phrased don't, in themselves, puzzle students. Instead they help students focus on problems and possible solutions they might not have otherwise considered. Toward this end teachers should practice asking questions so they are clear and to the point. They should make key words a part of their natural way of questioning. Such key words include the familiar who, what, when, and where. These words call for factual information—the knowledge level of Bloom's *Taxonomy*. To get at higher levels, teachers should place equal stress on how and why. These key words can call for comprehension, application, analysis, synthesis, and evaluation.

Also, teachers should learn to phrase questions correctly on their first attempt. It is common to hear teachers reword their questions two or three times before they get them just right. Once asked, the question should not be repeated unless it is evident that the students have not understood.

Finally, teachers should not answer their own questions unless they are doing so to produce a dramatic effect. This point seems self-evident. Yet if you listen to teachers ask questions, you will be surprised at how often they supply the answer before students have time to reply. The real purpose of questioning is to cause students to make considered responses; they must have time to respond.

Great expectations

In 1968 Rosenthal and Jacobson published a book that caught wide attention. Entitled *Pygmalion in the Classroom,* the book delved into the relationship between how teachers expected certain students to perform and how those students did, in fact, perform. The experimental stratagem entailed the random selection of student names. Teachers were then told to expect unusual learning gains for those students, because they were above average in intelligence. In fact, there was no difference between the randomly selected students and the control group against which they were later compared. The authors reported that by the end of the school year, the students believed by their teachers to be advanced showed significantly greater achievement gains than the comparable control group.

This observation led Rosenthal and Jacobson to conclude that teacher expectations greatly influenced student performance. If teachers expected students to be high achievers, they related to them and taught them in ways that produced greater achievement. On the other hand, if they expected students to be low achievers, they related to them and taught them in ways that resulted in lower achievement.

The research reported by Rosenthal and Jacobson has been soundly criticized by Elashoff and Snow (1971), who discounted point by point the evidence presented. Support for Rosenthal and Jacobson, however, has come from other quarters (Baker and Crist, 1971).

Based on the evidence that exists, one can conclude that harmful effects are not likely to occur if teachers consider all their students capable. On the other hand, positive effects can occur. The work done in mastery learning is based on the belief that virtually all students can reach high levels of proficiency when given sufficient time combined with clear directions and corrective feedback.

Teaching in a way consonant with this belief requires great persistence, great willingness to keep working with students when they do not seem to be progressing. But it is probable that such persistence is one of the traits of teachers that is most likely to produce learning (Brophy and Evertson, 1976).

To employ the great expectations strategy, *teachers* must truly anticipate high levels of performance from their students; behave as though they are fully confident that each student will perform well; show examples, if available, or recount anecdotes of work done by other students; make expectations and work activities as clear and understandable as possible; communicate with students as their work continues in process; and show an unending determination to help and help again.

You can see that this strategy is as much one of attitude as it is one of technique.

Synectics

You have to go beyond your Merriam-Webster pocket dictionary to find the definition of the mysterious term "synectics." The gigantic *Random House Dictionary* (unabridged) comes through, however, as it always does. Synectics (singular, it explains) is "the study of creative processes, especially as applied to the solution of problems by a group of diverse individuals." What we know about this process, about how to use it, and about how to develop ability in it we owe mostly to William Gordon (1961), J. P. Guilford (1959), and A. Osborn (1963).

You no doubt want to be more creative in your problem-solving ability, so be like this: intuitive, detached, speculative, and autonomous. How about it, did it work?

No one becomes more creative merely by reading about traits of creative people. But don't despair. Gordon believes that we all have an innate creative ability and that we all can learn to use this ability better than we now use it. So does Osborn, that ultracreative inventor of techniques for improving creative thought—brainstorming is one of them. And so does Guilford, whose fascinating "model of the intellect" includes divergent production as one of our innate mental processes. What Guilford implies and Gordon and Osborn say outright is that certain exercises can increase our ability to do creative, productive thought.

Guilford writes of two elements—fluency and flexibility—that are vitally important in divergent thinking. (Let us contrast divergent and convergent thinking. *Con*vergent thinking involves the search for the single correct answer to a problem. *Di*vergent thinking looks for a variety of acceptable answers to a problem.) The tests Guilford has used in his studies of the intellect suggest the kinds of activities we can use in the classroom to give students practice in creative thought.

To test for fluency, Guilford asks people to do such things as name everything they can think of that's yellow and grows on a tree or tell what all the results would be if automobiles were no longer allowed in this country. The point behind these fluency exercises is to get a great outpouring of ideas.

To test for flexibility, Guilford calls on people to search for possibilities that don't ordinarily suggest themselves. For example, one might be asked to think of ten different uses for a fish bone, or all the things a garden spade could be used for besides digging.

Gordon, in the approach he calls synectics, suggests a three-phase process for training people to think creatively. The three phases are as follows:

1. *Personal analogy.* The individual identifies with an item in a problem situation to be solved. Suppose you wanted to improve a can opener. You could begin by thinking of yourself as the can opener, telling how you move, how you cut the metal, how you feel, and what you like and dislike most about the process.
2. *Direct analogy.* Individuals practice inventing relationships between two items not ordinarily considered together. For example, think of all the ways in which a can opener and a feather duster are (or could be) alike.
3. *Compressed conflict.* The individual is directed to think of opposite words that could characterize the item. Examples for our can opener would be soft cutting or stationary turning.

Osborn suggests using checklists in thinking about ways of solving a problem. Suppose the problem is still how to improve a can opener. A suitable checklist might be as follows:

Can you change its shape, color, odor, texture?
Can you rearrange its parts?
Can you make it bigger, stronger, thicker, more durable?
Can you make it smaller, lighter, softer, shorter?
Can you combine or blend it with something else?

These examples suggested by Guilford, Gordon, and Osborn give only the briefest introduction to the fascinating world of creative production. You should read their works to get a better feel for what it is they suggest.

These ideas, briefly as they are listed here, give us fairly good direction in using a synectics strategy in teaching. Again, the basic idea is that we all have creative ability to make modifications, to put things together in new ways, and to find novel answers to problems. We all can improve that ability. The way to improve is to practice using some of the techniques that people like Guilford, Gordon, and Osborn have described for us.

Using the synectics strategy suggests that we infuse our teaching methods with questions and problems that can have multiple correct answers and that we provide practice for students in seeking answers to those questions and problems.

One way we can make this provision is by setting aside small blocks of class time devoted to this purpose. During this time students might be asked to brainstorm solutions to questions such as the following:

Farmer Smith has two levels of terrain on his farm. One level is low and rocky, very difficult to farm. A small stream runs part of the year through this low terrain. The other level is, on the average, 100 feet higher than the lower level. The soil is deep and free from rocks, but very dry. The rainfall is not sufficient for growing crops. The climate is suitable for growing vegetables that require a great deal of water. What can Farmer Smith do to increase his agricultural production, while keeping expenses within reasonable limits? Once a solution is agreed to, spell out the details necessary to make it work.

At other times, very brief exercises can be included along with subject matter being learned to give practice in fluency, flexibility, elaboration, and analogous thinking.

For fluency, as part of word study, students could think of all the different meanings for the word "run." (There are at least seventy-five meanings.) For flexibility, they could think of unusual uses for a history book. For elaboration, they could list all the steps necessary for growing and caring for a peach tree. For analogous thinking, they could slip into the role of an internal combustion engine, experiencing all its functions with an ultimate eye to making it more efficient and pollution free.

The *teacher's* role in using the synectics strategy is to provide numerous opportunities, both formal and informal, for *students* to practice exercises believed to increase productive thought. These activities can be done as contests, rewards, or extra credit activities.

Why not take a moment to brainstorm other possibilities. Use fluency and flexibility. Develop a checklist. Elaborate details of your plan.

See?

Now build this strategy into methods of teaching you intend to use. It fits several of them.

Values clarification

Just for the heck of it (well, true, there's more to it than that) do this exercise: As quickly as you can, list twenty things you truly love to do. No one else need see your list, so you can be completely candid. When you have listed twenty items, go over them to code (1) those that involve more than casual risk, (2) those that your parents would have been most pleased about, (3) those that best allow you to express your identity, and (4) those that will be least likely to remain on your list 10 years from now.

This activity is typical of a number of exercises that have been developed to help people clarify their values. Note the word "clarify." This indicates that the values are already there, inside you. You may not be fully aware of what your values are. Most school students are only dimly aware of them. Yet our values, conscious or unconscious, guide our lives. We act on the basis of what we consider important. By clarifying our values to ourselves, we have a better understanding of why we do what we do. And we have a better sense of direction in our lives, knowing that our values are our gyroscope and rudder.

Some of the most useful procedures for helping students clarify their values come from the work of Raths (1963); Raths, Harmin, and Simon (1966); Simon, Howe, and Kirschenbaum (1972); and Clegg and Hills (1968).

Simon et al. produced a book entitled *Values Clarification,* consisting of seventy-nine activities that help students clarify their values. An example of these activities is one called "personal coat of arms." Students begin by drawing a large shield on a sheet of paper. They divide the shield into six areas by drawing one verticle and two horizontal lines across it. In the first area they draw two pictures; one indicates something they are good at and the other something they would like to be good at. In the second area they draw a picture showing something they feel too strongly about to ever give up. The third area is devoted to a picture of something that is very important to every member of their family. The fourth area shows a picture of what they would be if they could be anything in the world. The fifth area contains a picture showing something that they wish every person in the world would believe. The sixth area includes four words they wish people would say about them behind their backs.

Raths et al., in their book *Values and Teaching,* describe verbal clarifying procedures that teachers can use to help students. They include such comments as the following:

(Summarize student's assertion.) Is that what you mean?
Can you give me an example?
Where do you think your idea comes from?
Should everyone think as you do?

Accepting comments can include the following:

I see what you mean.
I think I understand better now.

These verbal clarifying and accepting procedures are intended to help students choose, prize their choices, and act on the basis of their choices. They choose freely, from among a range of possibilities, the position they take on value issues. They show that they prize their choice by being willing to affirm it publicly. They show their willingness to act on the basis of their choice by doing so repeatedly.

Clegg and Hills describe a group procedure for helping students clarify their value positions when confronting social issues. First, the students break the issue down into opposing points of view. Second, they consider the points, one at a time. Third, they develop a list of alternatives for dealing with each of the opposing points identified. Fourth, they explore the consequences of each alternative. Fifth, each person individually identifies the alternative that seems most desirable. Sixth, each person expresses the reason for the choice made.

The *teacher's* role in values clarification is both formal and informal. The formal aspect sets up issues or activities designed for the express purpose of providing practice in clarification. Suitable procedures are used in conjunction with the activity.

The informal aspect occurs continually. As students express opinions or show preferences, the teacher uses questions and acceptances that help students put their convictions into words, then decide whether they can publicly affirm and act on these convictions. In this role, teachers must be very careful that their questions are not seen as rejections of the student's point of view, but are seen as requests for further enlightenment. The teacher is actually learning students' perceptions, feelings, and conclusions.

Students do not play a special role in the values clarification strategy. They simply respond actively as called for in the instructional situation.

This strategy fits in very well with methods of

teaching such as facilitation, group process, and inquiry/discovery. It is useful in the development of self-concept and in student self-actualization.

Classroom meetings

If an ounce of prevention is worth a pound of cure, classroom meetings will surely lighten the load teachers have to bear. Developed and advocated by William Glasser (1969), the classroom meeting strategy makes total class meetings a regularly scheduled part of the curriculum. Their purpose is to provide a setting within which students feel free to air concerns that affect their well-being in school. Limits are not placed on the types of concerns that can be discussed. They can be social, interpersonal, or academic. They can be matters that are occurring in or outside school. Whatever the concerns, classroom meetings can help solve them before they become serious.

So that the topics discussed by the group will have common themes, Glasser suggests alternating three different types of meetings:

1. *Social problem–solving meetings,* which concern themselves with problems of interpersonal relationships: bullying, loneliness, getting along with friends, and so forth. The purpose of this type of meeting is to find constructive, positive solutions to the problems discussed. Fault finding and excuse making are not accepted.
2. *Open-ended meetings,* in which students discuss matters important in their lives. There are no restrictions on topics. No solutions or factual answers are necessarily sought. This meeting is an open forum, where students can express their opinions, free from judgmental pressures. The teacher's task is to stimulate thought.
3. *Educational diagnostic meetings,* whose main purpose is to explore difficulties students might be encountering in learning their academic subject matter. The teacher, again, does not judge or evaluate what students say in these meetings. The purpose is to find out what they have learned, what they have not learned, and what obstacles are interfering with their learning.

All three types of meetings are conducted in more or less the same way. Preferably, the students sit in a circle with the teacher so that everyone can speak face to face. The tone is kept as positive as possible. The purpose of the meetings is not to find fault or complain. Rather, it is to state opinions openly, without fear of evaluation or retribution and, when appropriate, to seek positive solutions to problems.

The opportunity to communicate in this fashion does more than solve immediate problems. It also contributes toward a feeling of individual worth, so strongly emphasized by Glasser. If you read his book *Schools Without Failure* (1969), you will find not only detailed descriptions of the classroom meeting strategy, but also descriptions of how he helps students take positive directions in solving their problems (reality therapy) and how he would restructure the grading system in schools so that students would not consider themselves failures. All three of these ideas contribute to individual feelings of personal worthiness, which for Glasser is the key ingredient for successful functioning.

Critics of classroom meetings question their overall usefulness. They cannot be used effectively in primary grades. They consume a good deal of time that could be spent on learning subject matter. They are sometimes preferred by students not for their value, but because it is more fun to air dirty linen than it is to learn mathematics. They too often turn into gripe sessions that in their negativeness do more harm than good.

Glasser counters with impressive notations of the effectiveness of classroom meetings when they are carried out properly. He often demonstrates the techniques with students he has never before seen. The classroom meetings seem especially apropos for older students whose lives contain an overabundance of personal and social problems.

The *teacher's* role in classroom meetings is to first establish a warm, nonjudgmental atmosphere for the group. This is done through friendliness, humor, relaxation, and evident concern about matters of importance to the students. Second, the teacher starts the discussion, either by introducing a question or calling for student contributions. Third, the teacher helps students keep on a positive, constructive tack. Fourth, the teacher helps see that students consider a number of alternative opinions or problem solutions. And finally, the teacher encourages students to make a personal commitment to a course of action, based on opinions or solutions suggested by the group.

Students' roles are to participate actively; maintain a purposeful, constructive attitude; and attempt to identify personal courses of action based on the information forwarded in the discussions.

The *outcomes,* when all goes as intended, are increased student confidence and direction in dealing with problems, improved communication and relationships with other students in the group, and a greater feeling of self-worth.

Reality approach

A person functions at any time feeling either that he is a success and enjoying the psychological comfort of success or that he is a failure and desperately trying to avoid the attendant psychological discomforts. (Glasser, 1969, p. 15)

So says William Glasser, whose suggestions for classroom meetings formed the basis for the teaching strategy we just considered. Glasser has stressed that it is necessary for students to feel self-worth in order to succeed in school. The classroom meetings strategy was one way to help students develop and sustain such feelings of worthiness.

Glasser gives us a second strategy that can help our teaching fully as much as the classroom meeting. This strategy is one we will call "reality approach." It comes from the work Glasser has done in reality therapy, his method for helping people who, unable to find paths to a success identity, suffer from intense frustration and/or withdrawal.

What can we do to help students avoid such suffering and withdrawal? Glasser says "we must work to make them understand that *they are responsible* for fulfilling their needs, for behaving so that they can gain a successful identity. No one can do it for them" (Glasser, 1969, p. 16).

Glasser goes on to say that deviant behavior among students comes not from "mental illness," but simply from the students' making bad choices of behavior. To correct their problem behavior, they must be helped to make better, more responsible choices. They can make these better choices once they have become emotionally involved with people (teachers, in this case) who can and do make such choices.

Glasser doesn't leave matters at this theoretical level. He goes on to lay out clearly defined procedures for helping students make good behavior choices.

When the *teacher* sees a student misbehave in class, the first thing to do is ask "What are you do-

ing?" If this is asked calmly and warmly, the student will usually answer truthfully. The teacher then asks the student whether that behavior is helping either that student, the class, or the school.

If the *student* answers no, then the teacher asks the student what he or she could do differently that would help. The student can usually name a more suitable behavior. The teacher can smile and thank the student for thinking of it. If the student can't name a more suitable behavior, the teacher needs to have some alternatives in mind, from which the student can select. This helps students plan more suitable courses of behavior.

Once students have made a value judgment about a better kind of behavior, teachers must help them build a commitment to that behavior. That is done by refusing to accept excuses of any sort from the student who does not stick by the behavior chosen. Rather than accept excuses, the teacher again helps the student identify an appropriate behavior and makes it plain that the student is fully expected to stand by the choices made.

If you have not read *Schools Without Failure* (Glasser, 1969), try to make it a point to do so. There is much meat there for teachers to get their teeth into, much to help them in dealing with classroom behaviors that are disruptive and nonproductive. You will find many comments there that are balm for the perennial wounds of teachers, comments such as the following:

Love and self-worth are the two pathways that lead to success identity. (p. 14)

There are only two kinds of true failure: failure to love and failure to achieve self-worth. (p. 12)

Students must see they are responsible for their own behavior. Those who can't learn (with our help) to accept this responsibility will continue to fail, no matter how much we improve the schools. (p. 16)

Bad behavior is nothing more than making bad choices. It is corrected by making good choices. (p. 19)

Students who continue to make bad choices should suffer the reasonable consequences of those choices. (p. 21)

Teachers should never give up trying to help students make better choices. Still, the choice is ultimately the student's responsibility. (p. 21)

Teachers who care about their students accept no excuses when the students do not abide by their commitments. They work again and again to help students make value judgments and commitments. (pp. 23-24)

The reality strategy plays a strong role in helping students of all levels, kindergarten through university, to learn to choose appropriate behaviors, act consistently in accordance with those choices, and accept the natural consequences they bring. This approach teaches rational choice making and responsibility. It is neither an imposition of adult standards nor a devious means of controlling behavior. It is a completely aboveboard, conscious procedure, within which students make reasoned choices and learn to live by those choices.

Acceptance

Everything that follows in this section rests on one fundamental notion: It is possible to accept an individual as a person of worth, while not accepting some of the behaviors that person displays.

A great deal of conjecture, opinion, and research has, during the past 15 years, grown up around the notion of teacher acceptance, as opposed to rejection, of students. The sum of this conjecture, opinion, and research seems to say that students who feel accepted by their teachers, when compared with those who do not, communicate more freely, show greater self-direction, like school better, and achieve more in academic areas.

Acceptance can fall into different categories. There is acceptance of the sort that occurs in verbal exchanges between teacher and student. This comes when the teacher says such things as "okay, fine, good thinking, I see what you mean." This sort of acceptance has been emphasized in the work of Ned Flanders (1970) and his followers in interaction analysis; by Thomas Gordon (1974) in his work in teacher effectiveness training; by Haim Ginott (1972), explained in his book *Teacher and Child;* and by William Glasser (1969) in his work with classroom meetings. Acceptance of this sort has been shown to increase the amount of student verbal interaction and is thought to increase self-concept and feeling of worth.

Another kind of acceptance occurs on a more personal level, where teachers show through their friendliness and continual willingness to help that they accept the student as a person of worth. At the same time the teacher may be unaccepting of the student's behavior. Such is the case in the views forwarded by Glasser (1969) in his reality approach to building success identity, by Berne (1964) and Harris (1967) in their considerations of

transactional analysis, and by Rogers (1969) in his considerations of the facilitative method of teaching.

Yet another kind of acceptance is shown through nonpunitive uses of behavior modification. Students are rewarded, or not, strictly on the basis of the behaviors they exhibit. No character analyses are performed, no "bad genes" explanations are advanced. Acceptable behavior is reinforced, often with a mention of exactly what the behavior is and why it is good. Bad behavior is not reinforced. It is ignored, if innocuous, or restrained, if destructive.

We have already considered Glasser's ideas of acceptance in the reality strategy. We have also considered the behavior modifier's ideas of paying attention only to the behavior, not to the character of the student. Let's give brief attention, then, to the ideas expressed by Ginott, Gordon, and Berne.

Haim Ginott is one of those gifted writers whose works make sense to professionals and laymen alike. His book *Teacher and Child* (1972) is typical. Widely read and lauded by parents, educators, and psychologists, it describes how to use the language of acceptance when working with learners. Ginott's point of view is forecast in an excerpt included in the preface to his book:

I have come to a frightening conclusion. I am the decisive element in the classroom. It is my personal approach that creates the climate. It is my daily mood that makes the weather. As a teacher I possess tremendous power to make a child's life miserable or joyous. I can be a tool of torture or an instrument of inspiration. I can humiliate or humor, hurt or heal. In all situations it is my response that decides whether a crisis will be escalated or de-escalated, and a child humanized or de-humanized.

Using language to humanize or dehumanize—that is the issue with which Ginott deals. But how does one use this language of acceptance, this humanizing language? The answer boils down to the crucial division between teachers at their best and teachers at their worst.

Teachers at their best, says Ginott (1972, p. 34), "recognize this core truth: Learning is always in the present tense, and it is always personal." Learning is what is happening right now, at this moment, to the student. This learning is personal for the student. When teachers communicate during this learning moment, they may address the learning situation, including what the learner is doing, or they may judge the learner's character and personality. When they address the situation, they show themselves at their best. When they judge the learner's character, they show themselves at their worst. This division marks the "difference between effective and ineffective communication" (p. 70). The following example illustrates Ginott's point:

Student interrupts teacher.

Teacher (at best): I would like to finish what I was saying.

Teacher (at worst): You're very rude to interrupt.

Ginott (1972, p. 81) continually urges us to be wary of talking with students in ways that do the following:

Dispute their feelings
Deride their taste
Denigrate their opinions
Derogate their character
Degrade their person

This is only the tiniest glimpse of Ginott's marvelous insights into communicating with learners in accepting ways. Find yourself a copy of *Teacher and Child*. If you are serious about working with learners, irrespective of age or grade level, one thing is certain: You will find Ginott's ideas intriguing and helpful.

Following a vein similar to Ginott's, Thomas Gordon developed a communication approach that teachers can use to improve interaction with students. Gordon's techniques, presented in his book *Teacher Effectiveness Training* (1974), suggest ways of helping students to open up, express themselves, and work through their own problems.

Gordon emphasizes techniques of passive and active listening, use of I-messages instead of you-messages, avoidance of the "typical twelve" roadblocks to communication, and adherence to the "no-lose" method of resolving conflicts.

Passive listening techniques the teacher can use to aid communication include the following:

1. *Silence:* The teacher looks at the student, obviously pays attention, but does not interrupt or comment.
2. *Acknowledgment:* As the student talks, the teacher leans forward, nods, smiles, etc., showing attention and willingness for the conversation to continue.
3. *Door openers:* The teacher makes comments that help the hesitant student get started. Examples of door openers are "Sounds like you're upset" and "Would you like to tell me more about it?"

Active listening techniques go a step further. They reflect back opinions and feelings students express. They are always accepting and nonjudgmental. They do not advise or commiserate. They simply summarize what students say. In this way active listening is the same as nondirective or client-centered techniques that counselors, psychologists, and psychotherapists use to help their clients express feelings and deal with them.

As teachers talk with students, they make use of I-messages and astutely avoid you-messages. I-messages tell the student how I (the teacher) feel about a situation. You-messages attack the student. Thus when a student is boisterously disruptive, the teacher should say: "I'm having trouble with my work because of the noise" (I-message). The teacher should not say: "You are ruining things in here for everyone" (you-message).

Gordon lists and describes twelve kinds of teacher talk that he believes inhibit effective communication with students. Often referred to as the "typical twelve" or the "dirty dozen," they include such categories of talk as ordering, warning, exhorting, advising, lecturing, judging, praising, name calling, interpreting, reassuring, probing, and withdrawing. Although some of these kinds of talk may be sought by students on occasion, they almost invariably reduce communication and thus inhibit the likelihood of solving problems. Worse yet, they can cause students to feel inferior, feel guilty, hide their feelings, or even counterattack.

When it comes to conflict resolution, Gordon advocates a no-lose approach. This approach settles conflicts so that neither disputant comes out the loser. The solution is satisfactory to both. The no-lose procedure includes the following six steps:

1. Clarifying the problem
2. Jointly suggesting possible solutions
3. Evaluating the suggestions, eliminating any that are unacceptable to either side
4. Deciding on one of the solutions that is acceptable to both
5. Deciding exactly how to put the solution into effect

6. Evaluating the success of the solution, and if it fails, seeking another one

Eric Berne (1964) and Thomas Harris (1967) have looked at communication and the language of acceptance from another perspective.

Berne, in his immensely popular book *Games People Play* (1964), wrote of three ego states people use when talking with others. These ego states are parent, adult, and child. Each conversant uses one or more of these three states during verbal interaction.

When using the *parent* ego state, people think, act, and talk as their parents did to them when they were children. They admonish and control.

When using the *adult* ego state, people appraise situations objectively and relatively dispassionately, taking into account reasonable possibilities and probabilities.

When using the *child* ego state, people feel, think, and act as they did when they were young children. This state remains active in us throughout our lives.

Berne described "games" that people play when they are using these various ego states. He labels games and participants and describes the typical behavioral patterns that accompany them.

Harris continued this idea on ego states and communication in his book *I'm O.K.–You're O.K.* (1967). He wrote of the following four states of interpersonal communicative relationships that normally occur:

I'm not OK—You're OK
I'm not OK—You're not OK
I'm OK—You're not OK
I'm OK—You're OK

The most effective communication comes with the fourth state, I'm OK—You're OK. In this state, people are accepting of themselves and of others. To reach this state, Harris says we must learn to use our adult ego states most of the time. We learn to use the adult ego state by doing the following:

1. Knowing our typical child ego behaviors—our fears, delights, and vulnerabilities
2. Knowing our typical parent ego behaviors—our fixed positions and the ways we control and admonish
3. Clarifying our system of values (This information is necessary for the adult ego state to function.)

4. Thinking before speaking in conflict situations. (This avoids the immediate parent or child outburst and allows time for the adult to compute an appropriate response.)

STRATEGIES THAT COMPLEMENT METHODS

In this chapter we have examined thirteen strategies of teaching that are known to affect learning. These strategies all fit into and enhance the effectiveness of one or more of the eleven teaching methods described in the previous chapter, as the following list illustrates:

METHOD	ENHANCING STRATEGIES
Diagnostic-prescriptive teaching	Mastery learning, behavior modification, precision teaching, engineered environments, individualized instruction, great expectations
Competency-based education	Mastery learning, behavior modification, engineered environments, advance organization, individualized instruction, great expectations
Read-review-recite	Mastery learning, behavior modification, precision teaching, advance organization, questioning, great expectations, classroom meetings, reality approach, acceptance
Expository teaching	Mastery learning, behavior modification, precision teaching, advance organization, questioning, great expectations, classroom meetings, reality approach, acceptance
Simulations	Advance organization, engineered environments, questioning, great expectations, synectics, classroom meetings
Modeling	Mastery learning, behavior modification, advance organization, great expectations
Projects	Individualized instruction, great expectations, synectics, values clarification, classroom meetings, reality approach, acceptance
Group process	Questioning, great expectations, synectics, values clarification, classroom meetings, reality approach, acceptance
Inquiry/discovery	Individualized instruction, questioning, great expectations, synectics, classroom meetings, acceptance

| Facilitation | Individualized instruction, questioning, great expectations, synectics, values clarification, classroom meetings, reality approach, acceptance |
| Open experience | Individualized instruction, great expectations, values clarification, classroom meetings, reality approach, acceptance |

To this point you have acquainted yourself with eleven methods and thirteen strategies of teaching. You have seen how different strategies complement and enhance each of the methods. Earlier you saw the contributions that each of the various methods and strategies could make toward attainment of established goals and objectives of education.

Now two important tasks remain for you. First, you need to become able to select and use combinations of methods, together with their complementary strategies. Your choices are guided by objectives, subject matter, ages of students, and instructional materials. One method alone will not suffice for most classrooms. Basic knowledge and skills learning calls for one type of method, exploration and creativity for another, aesthetics and personality development for yet another. You are better prepared now to make such choices wisely. Second, you must give attention to the kinds of learning environments that best allow use of the methods and strategies you select. These environments have physical and psychosocial aspects. You probably have fairly good conceptions of what these environments should be. The chapter that follows will provide additional information about learning environments.

SUGGESTED ACTIVITIES FOR FURTHER UNDERSTANDING

1. For each of the strategies described in this chapter, make a three-column list. List the advantages of this particular strategy in one column and the disadvantages in another. In the third column list the subjects and/or skills that can most effectively be taught with this strategy.
2. Divide into groups, with each group selecting two or three strategies of teaching. Devise original ways to demonstrate the strategies to other members of the class. Be sure you convey what the strategy is like, what it is good for, and how it is used.

REFERENCES

Ausubel, D. Use of advance organizers in the learning and retention of meaningful material, *Journal of Educational Psychology*, 1960, *51*, 267-272.

Baker, H., and Crist, J. Teacher expectancies: a review of the literature. In J. Elashoff and R. Snow (Eds.), *Pygmalion re-considered*. Worthington, Ohio: Charles A. Jones Publishing Co., 1971.

Berne, E. *Games people play*. New York: Grove Press, Inc., 1964.

Block, J. *Mastery learning: theory and practice*. New York: Holt, Rinehart & Winston, Inc., 1971.

Block, J., and Anderson, L. *Mastery learning and classroom instruction*. New York: Macmillan Publishing Co., Inc., 1975.

Brophy, J., and Evertson, C. *Learning from teaching: a developmental perspective*. Boston: Allyn & Bacon, Inc., 1976.

Charles, C. *Educational psychology: the instructional endeavor* (2nd ed.). St. Louis: The C. V. Mosby Co., 1976a.

Charles, C. *Individualizing instruction*. St. Louis: The C. V. Mosby Co., 1976b.

Clegg, A., and Hills, J. A strategy for exploring values and valuing in the social studies. *The College of Education Record*, 1968, *34*, 67-68.

Elashoff, J., and Snow, R. *Pygmalion reconsidered*. Worthington, Ohio: Charles A. Jones Publishing Co., 1971.

Flanders, N. *Analyzing teacher behavior*. Reading, Mass.: Addison-Wesley Publishing Co., 1970.

Ginott, H. *Teacher and child*. New York: Macmillan Publishing Co., Inc., 1972.

Glasser, W. *Schools without failure*. New York: Harper & Row, Publishers, 1969.

Gordon, T. *Teacher effectiveness training*. New York: Peter H. Wyden/Publisher, 1974.

Gordon W. *Synectics*. New York: Harper & Row, Publishers, 1961.

Guilford, J. Three faces of intellect. *American Psychologist*, 1959, *14*, 469-479.

Harris, T. *I'm O.K.—You're O.K.* New York: Harper & Row, Publishers, 1967.

Hunter, M. *Reinforcement*. El Segundo, Calif.: TIP Publications, 1968.

Naisworth, J., et al. *Student motivation and classroom management*. Lemont, Pa.: Behavior Technics, Inc., 1969.

Osborn, A. *Applied imagination*. New York: Charles Scribner's Sons, 1963.

Precision teaching in perspective: an interview with Ogden R. Lindsley. *Teaching Exceptional Children*, 1971, *3*, 114-119.

Premack, D. Reinforcement theory. In D. Levine (Ed.). *Nebraska Symposium on Motivation*. Lincoln: University of Nebraska Press, 1965.

Raths, L. Clarifying values. In R. Fliming (Ed.), *Curriculum for today's boys and girls*. Columbus, Ohio: Charles E. Merrill Publishing Co., 1963.

Raths, L., Harmin, M., and Simon, S. *Values and teaching*. Columbus, Ohio: Charles E. Merrill Publishing Co., 1966.

Rogers, C. *Freedom to learn*. Columbus, Ohio: Charles E. Merrill Publishing Co., 1969.

Rosenthal, R., and Jacobson, L. *Pygmalion in the classroom*. New York: Holt, Rinehart & Winston, Inc., 1968.

Sanders, N. *Classroom questions: what kinds?* New York: Harper & Row, Publishers, 1966.

Sapp, A. Succeeding with success environment. *American Education*, 1973, *9*, 4-10.

Simon, S., Howe, L., and Kirschenbaum, H. *Values clarification: a handbook of practical suggestions for teachers and students*. New York: Hart Publishing Co., Inc., 1972.

13 ENVIRONMENTS THAT NURTURE LEARNING

If you had been immersed (swamped? drowned?) in American education as long as we have, you would find yourself both perplexed and astonished at the progress that has occurred in teaching. You would be perplexed because it seems we are so slow in putting into practice the new knowledge we have. But you would also be astonished at the remarkable progress that has occurred in teaching during the past decade. This progress has occurred not only in materials, organ-

ization, and techniques of instructing, but in ways of organizing and providing quality learning environments as well.

You already know, if you have read Chapter 10, that we have recently gained control over new techniques that give us remarkable teaching power. Each of these techniques calls for its own matching learning environment. These desirable environments have numerous traits in common.

This chapter focuses on learning environments—their selection, preparation, maintenance, and management. It suggests suitable environments for primary, intermediate, and secondary levels. It gives attention to the special requirements of various teaching methods and strategies. It considers physical, intellectual, and interpersonal factors. It . . . well, let's move into it and see.

CONTRASTS

Every so often I think, and write, about a most remarkable experience I had in 1941, when I was in the fifth grade. (See, I said it had been a long time.) My teacher was Miss Osborne. Oh, Miss Osborne, wonderful woman, I wish you would read this page and let your lost self be known to me.

In that fifth grade, I had my first, and for several years my only, experience as a learner in a quality, I mean *quality*, learning environment. Did we sit in rows of desks in that room? Yes, sometimes. But we also had some chairs that we moved around however we wanted. Did we remain quiet as mice and listen to Miss Osborne? Yes, a good deal of the time. She expected, I mean *expected*, us to listen quietly when she spoke. But we also had great discussions, and we role played, and wrote and performed and played and sang. Was Miss Osborne a stern task mistress? Yes, in some ways. At least she got across the idea that learning was serious business. Of course, it could be fun and should be fun as often as possible, but when you got right down to it, we were there first and foremost to learn. She made us know that, and we felt good and secure because we knew she would do everything she could to help us. Did Miss Osborne keep good discipline? She surely did. The best. She even insisted on good manners. She could not abide unruliness, sarcasm, disrespect, or cruelty in any form. She made that plain right off the bat. She always, herself, modeled the greatest concern and the finest golden-rule manners, all within her marvelous good humor. But if you got out of line, you could be certain of her wrath, or at least reprimand and disappointment. That last was hard to take, hardest of all.

I have also written of my sixth-grade year, in the same school. But I have not written much, nor even thought about it much. That is because I remember so little of it. I do not remember the teacher's name, nor her appearance. I do not remember anything we did in that room, except sit in rows of desks and take spelling tests. I'm sure Miss/Mrs. ??? conducted classes of some sort. There was no chaos; I would have remembered that. There was no severe punishment; I would have remembered that. There was no evident loving care and warmth, no excitement, no lovely projects, no thrilling undertakings, no eye-opening field trips, no tingling intellectual stimulation; I would have remembered those things. I suppose there was mainly colossal boredom. I believe I would have forgotten that.

ENVIRONMENT

Webster's New Collegiate Dictionary defines environment as "the aggregate of all the external conditions and influences affecting the life and development of an organism." That, of course, is the meaning of environment in the general sense—external conditions and influences. What we want to get at in this chapter is the in-the-classroom conditions and influences that affect human beings. Moreover, we want to identify the specific conditions and influences that have a positive, enhancing effect on learning.

What you have to recognize first is that there is no "off-on" switch as far as environments and learning are concerned. That is, there is no set of classroom factors that will automatically ensure learning, nor any set of classroom factors that will

completely shut off learning. You can learn in conditions of great physical discomfort, even pain. You can learn with people yelling at you, threatening you, hitting you, or giving you hateful, icy stares. You can learn without color, movement, excitement, or your doing much of anything. So you see, it's not yes-no, on-off.

What it is is a matter of degree and a matter of chance. The chances are, under classroom conditions, you can learn more if you are fairly comfortable than if you are miserable. The chances are you will learn more through an organized teaching approach than through chaos; more through teacher encouragement and positive guidance than through sarcasm and humiliation; more through stimulation and excitement than through indifference; more through active doing than through passive listening. The point is, if you are a teacher or a learner, you will want as many odds in your favor as possible.

ENVIRONMENTS IN GENERAL

Several principles of learning are related closely to learning environments. Principles are generalized statements that have stood the tests of time and circumstance. Remember, these principles—or any other principles for that matter—don't always hold true. They vary in accordance with topics, situations, personalities, and so forth. But the principles that follow generally yield results that are hoped for. You can usually count on them, and you can be sure you are doing nothing damaging to learning when you use them.

Generally speaking, classroom environments produce more learning and/or better attitudes and self-concepts when they do the following:

Provide physical comfort for learners
Are aesthetically pleasing
Provide purposeful approaches to learning
Have orderly arrangements of materials and activities
Provide interest, excitement, and stimulation
Allow movement and manipulation of materials
Provide sufficient flexibility for individual needs and preferences
Emphasize golden-rule interpersonal relationships
Are warm, supportive, and nurturant
Show genuine concern for learners and learning

You can see that some of these principles have to do with *physical* aspects of the environment: space, light, heat, seating, color, aesthetics, arrangements of materials. Other principles have to do with *intellectual/activity* aspects of the environment: interest, excitement, involvement, routine, flexibility, purposefulness. Yet other principles have to do with *interpersonal* aspects of the environment: support, warmth, concern, consideration for others. These three groups of principles work in concert with each other. No one of them will make or break the learning process. Yet each of them can help increase the ease, speed, and permanence of student learning.

Classrooms as environments

The most common learning environment in school is the classroom. Obviously classrooms are not the only learning environments provided by schools. There are gymnasiums, playgrounds, libraries, shops, athletic fields and courts, agricultural plots, and laboratories of many sorts. There are auditoriums for plays, concerts, and other performances. There are halls for exhibitions of art. These environments do not constitute special cases. What can be said about classroom environments goes for them as well.

Classrooms have three factors whose interplay produces significant differences in environment. These factors are (1) physical elements, including space, furniture, and instructional materials; (2) the teacher, who sets much of the intellectual and emotional tone of the classroom; and (3) the students, who are active, not passive, in influencing the environment. These three factors combine to determine, to a large extent, whether schooling will be interesting and valuable, relatively pointless, or, in extreme cases, detrimental to students.

The physical elements. The first factor—physical elements—has been hammered, chewed, beautified, and turned around and inside out in attempts to improve the learning environment for students. Recent years have seen the introduction of an amazing array of attractive and efficient instructional materials to enhance student learning. This physical innovation has been accepted everywhere.

Still in the experimental stage are manipulations in the structure and physical organization of the classroom. Currently, open space classrooms are being tried across the nation. "Open space" refers to schools built without the interior walls that normally separate one classroom from another. Students work in very large areas, under a common roof, in small to large groupings. The open space concept facilitates flexible grouping, team teach-

ing, and sharing of materials. On the negative side, some noise spills from one area to another. There are distractions related to movement. Also, groups throughout the open space must all do quiet activities at the same time and noisy activities at the same time. You cannot have one group singing while an adjacent group is reading.

Another innovation is "open education." Not to be confused with open space (actually, open space is somewhat detrimental to open education), open education refers to an instructional approach wherein students assume much greater responsibility than normal for directing their own learning. To make this self-direction possible, open education classrooms are equipped with an unusually large array of materials and activities that students can select and pursue on their own. Such classrooms appear much richer in instructional materials than standard classrooms. However, they also tend to appear disorganized and chaotic, and although some students flower in this environment, others appear to be lost and drifting a good deal of the time.

The teacher. The teacher's personality and philosophy of teaching strongly influence the emotional nature of the learning environment. That students learn better in a warm, supportive, facilitative environment is increasingly becoming a tenet of American education. Much work and progress have occurred in recent years in identifying effective means of communicating with students, in helping them select and self-direct their learning, and in providing useful feedback that promotes their academic and personal growth.

Examples of this person-centered thrust are legion. Notable techniques include interaction analysis (Flanders, 1965), teacher effectiveness training (Gordon, 1970), behavior modification (Skinner, 1968), facilitative teaching (Rogers, 1969), values clarification (Simon, Howe, and Kirschenbaum, 1972), nonpunitive communication (Ginott, 1971), and classroom meetings (Glasser, 1969). Underlying these techniques is the notion that students progress most rapidly in the most desirable directions when they see themselves as successful, feel good about their accomplishments, have a hand in deciding some of their own destiny, can express themselves openly, and can relate in meaningful ways with other people, especially their teachers.

Teachers, far better than before, can now use communication techniques to draw out the best in their students, to encourage and guide them, and to establish supportive environments that allow, even encourage, the making of mistakes without fear of punishment, ridicule, or being made to feel inferior. These developments in the interpersonal realm have resulted in learning environments remarkably different from those supplied by earlier stern masters, canes ready in hands, whose chief interpersonal stratagem was to scare the bejabbers out of students as a means of motivating them to learn. Like it or not (most of us do), finesse has replaced fear in the teacher's instructional repertoire.

The students. Largely overlooked nowadays is the role that students must play in establishing and maintaining effective learning environments. When teachers gave up the rod in favor of gentle persuasion, the idea that students had a responsibility, too, fell between the cracks and out of sight. We stressed motivation, organization, excitement, good manners, and so on and so forth to the point that we came to believe that if, despite all that, the student horses didn't drink, it was because of an unforgivable sin committed by the teacher.

Well, students have their responsibilities, too. Just as the teacher must furnish organization, materials, guidance, and support, so must the students bring their contributions to the instructional broth. They must see that their role is a simple, but highly important one. They must be serious, in a good-humored way, about their learning. They must recognize that they are in school first and foremost to learn, not to pit themselves against teacher and school in a crazy *Catch-22* contest of wits. Furthermore, they must contribute to a climate of cooperation and helpfulness within the class. They must practice the golden rule.

Many students do not see themselves in this light. The worst among us think of themselves as being made to go to school, of teachers out of spite forcing onerous tasks on them. They reluctantly go along with the game, all the while grumbling and plotting ways of getting out of work.

To correct this situation, the entire school must stress contributions of students, teachers, parents, administrators, and support staff to the educational enterprise. Good communication with parents helps establish this climate for learners. So does good communication with the students themselves. The notion of everybody in the school pulling in the same direction should not be astonishing; it should be expected. To get that idea across to everyone takes some doing, but it is well worth the effort.

Environments by levels

The best kindergarten classrooms don't look at all like the best university lecture halls. The best third-grade teachers use an entirely different style of talk with their students than do high school physics teachers. First-grade teachers routinely caress, hug, and kiss their students. College teachers do that only occasionally. High school teachers rarely do so, unless they want to get into a heap of trouble.

It goes without saying that all three aspects of learning environments—the physical, the intellectual/activity, and the interpersonal—must vary in accordance with the maturity levels of students. Yet if you will stop and think, you can see that the underlying principles are the same at all levels. Only the specifics of application are different.

For example, all students need some movement and active involvement with materials and other people. Young children simply need more of it than older people do. All students need some excitement and sense of purpose running through what they are learning. Teachers simply provide excitement and purpose differently for sixth graders than for graduate students. All students seek warmth, support, and help. Older people seek it in different forms than do young children, but we all want it in one guise or another.

Let us see how the several aspects of learning environments are varied to fit the maturity levels of learners.

Primary classrooms. Kindergarten through grade three is usually considered primary level. Students in this age range have a great many social and intellectual traits in common. Although second- and third-grade children are generally capable of performing considerably more advanced intellectual tasks than are kindergartners and first graders, they all seek and give affection with little self-consciousness or embarrassment. They all require much physical movement and frequent changes of activity.

For these reasons, the primary curriculum and corresponding learning environments provide many different activities each day. The activities are changed frequently. Kindergarten children seldom remain engaged in any school activity for more than 20 minutes at a stretch. Then they must switch to something else. They automatically look for things to do with their hands. They must move their bodies. They want to color, cut, and paste, and they want to sing, play, and hear stories.

The kindergarten learning environment is set accordingly. The classroom is typically quite large. It includes areas for noisy and quiet activities. It has carpeted areas for students to sit, roll, lie, and tumble about on the floor. It has tables and chairs instead of individual desks. It contains a rich variety of toy, painting, and craft corners. It has its own special outside play area. Physically, emphasis is put on objects, color, and movement. Intellectually, emphasis is put on routine, order, listening, language skills, and mathematics readiness. Interpersonal relations are heavily stressed, including good manners, sharing, cooperation, and taking turns. Children respond readily to social reinforcement. They seek overt affection from the teacher, and they return it in copious quantities.

Although kindergarten environments are special to themselves, classrooms for first, second, and third graders are usually like those for any other elementary grade. They do not usually have the space that kindergarten rooms have. The students are expected to sit in their chairs more and on the floor less. The students are becoming able to do intellectual tasks—those involving conservation, as described by Piaget—that are beyond the capabilities of kindergarten children. However, although larger, stronger, more capable, and more self-directing, these primary-grade students retain many traits common to kindergartners. They, too, require frequent changes of activity. They must be physically active. They are unabashed in their singing and giving and receiving affection.

Classrooms for these children are rich in materials, interest centers, and crafts centers. Intellectually, this is a great time for growth in reading and other language skills. Mathematics presents a problem for many first- and second-grade children until they become able to conserve number. Then

they can make great strides, but until that time, counting, manipulating, and other readiness skills are stressed.

These children still respond readily to social reinforcement. They seek direct affection and approval from the teacher. They want to be touched, patted, and hugged. They don't want to wait for attention. They want the teacher's approval right now.

Intermediate classrooms. Along about the fourth grade, students begin to change more noticeably, especially in their social behavior. They suddenly begin to seem more grown up, more able to take care of themselves. They can do a great deal of the class work on their own, without constant teacher direction. They retain much of their affectionate spontaneity, but they are becoming less open about seeking attention from the teacher. This trend sets a pattern that will last for many years to come.

These changes that occur between third and fourth grade are subtle ones. Still, they are clear cut enough to cause educators to consider movement into fourth grade a rather distinct phase in the

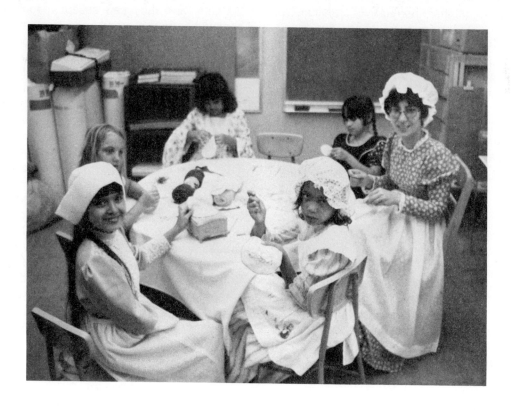

educational progression. They typically refer to grades four, five, and six as intermediate grades. The curriculum for the intermediate grades is given increased amounts of abstract work and problem solving. The learning environment reflects these changes. Intermediate classrooms typically contain smaller quantities and varieties of activities and materials. Students concentrate for longer periods of time on discrete subjects. They can now work for 45 minutes or longer on a given topic, provided it contains an occasional change of pace. For example, fourth graders can easily devote up to a full hour at a time working in a social studies project, if it is subdivided into some reading, some writing, some group discussion, and some work with the hands. They can also work for some time on mathematics and can read silently for extended periods. Thus the intermediate classroom, although still rich in materials and activities, typically appears somewhat less decorated than the primary classroom.

The teacher's role in the intermediate environment differs a bit from the role at the primary level. The end objective is still to provide a warm, accepting, nurturant emotional climate. However, the techniques used to provide that climate now change. The mother hen–chicks relationship, where the teacher cleans runny noses, ties shoes, and herds the chicks around, gives way to a more adult-adult relationship between teacher and student. This means that the teacher uses a different way of talking and acting. Adult-type humor becomes successful: students understand jokes, puns, and plays on words. The teacher can now talk with students in reasoning ways. Students see logic and have a growing sense of morality, justice, and fair play. The teacher can be more businesslike. Work assignments can be made in straightforward ways, without so much reliance on teacher enthusiasm to motivate students.

The teacher in intermediate grades shows concern and care for students not so much through hugging and caressing as through talking with them about their concerns. The teacher accepts sincere worries and opinions, even though they may seem pointless to the adult eye. Help is always offered for dealing with both personal and academic concerns. Often that help is nothing more than listening to a child's point of view. There aren't too many of us who are willing

to, or capable of, doing that. In academic areas, great patience, tolerance, and willingness to go over material time after time produce the social and intellectual climate that best facilitates student growth.

Take a word of caution here, however. Do not make the mistake of confusing "acceptance" with "anything goes." Ultimately the teacher sets the limits of proper classroom behavior and enforces those limits. Teachers don't help students by knuckling under to unreasonable requests, nor by excusing inappropriate behavior such as cruel teasing, bullying, boisterousness, or continued goofing off. Beginning teachers sometimes think they can gain student good will by being a buddy—just one of the gang—and going along with whatever comes up. They quickly find they have made a grave mistake and one that is very hard to undo. Teachers should be friendly to students. But they must be adult friends. They cannot be children. They must help. They must be concerned. But they must also be the classroom conscience and the figure of authority.

Students at the intermediate level can greatly increase their contribution to the learning environment. Now they can fully understand their roles as learners, and they can accept responsibility for contributing to the orderly and mannerly environment that helps produce the most rapid learning, both in academic and personal areas. Again, establishing and maintaining the notion of student responsibility falls to the teacher. But students can function as partners in this process. Class discussions related to this topic can be very fruitful. These discussions must be given the slant of a group decision about what is best for the class. They will not work well if they are given by the teacher as commandments from on high.

Junior high classrooms. The majority of junior high schools across the country consist of grades seven, eight, and nine. A great many include only grades seven and eight. Increasingly, we see the appearance of "middle schools" that include grades six, seven, and eight. Regardless of the breaking point, the junior high years present some of schooling's greatest challenges (a polite way of saying difficulties) for students and teachers alike.

At around age 12 or 13 years, our lovely innocent elementary schoolchildren begin getting knocked about by abrupt physical changes and new social pressures. Everything suddenly looks different to them. (And they certainly look different to us.) Their bodies change, with new hair, lumps, curves, and proportions. Their facial skin is bedeviled with oil and zits. Dark, mysterious processes begin occurring in the reproductive regions, bringing on great concern, dismay, and excitement.

In the social realm, peer concern and pressure reach their zenith. The peer code strictly dictates appropriate styles of dress, hair, language, and demeanor. Intermingled with this process is the first stage of a cutting phenomenon, psychological weaning. Kids begin the painful separation, which will take years to complete, from physical, emotional, moral, and ultimately financial dependence on parents. The first breaks show up in rejection of adult dress styles and in defiance of parental authority. The kids, who of course still love their parents, begin to act as though they detested them. The parents, who of course still love their kids, react in a state of continual exasperation.

As if these physical and sociological changes were not enough for junior high students to cope with, we smilingly stick them into new and strange learning environments. Their elementary classrooms were probably lovely places, reserved for them alone, with one concerned teacher they could see all day long. Familiar materials lay all about. There was security and psychological support. Now junior high switches all the signals on them. They have to change classrooms several times a day. They face a number of different teachers, with different teaching styles and sets of expectations. The rooms are stark, compared to elementary classrooms. Because different classes and different teachers use the rooms during the day, materials can't be left sitting out.

What's more, when the students enter junior high, they shrink from big frog in the elementary pond to tadpole in the junior high—from top to bottom on the totem pole.

If this gives you the idea that it is difficult to conduct school during the junior high years, you're getting the message. How can these adolescents think of themselves first and foremost as learners of mathematics, English, and history, when they have so much on their minds about bodies, peers, infatuations, fusses with parents, pop culture,

overwhelming insecurity, and the magical world out there awaiting?

Yet the junior high schools do hold classes. Teachers do teach. Students do learn. And through it all, most stay on the conveyor into and through high school. But in junior high some fall off, and many get turned off.

Junior high teachers who do their jobs well are among the most talented, specialized teachers we have. Their best talents and specializations are not found in subject matter. Instead, they are found in the ways they relate personally to their students. Their overriding talent, if they are good, is the provision of a classroom environment within which their troubled, harried, and confused students are helped to learn.

Honestly, the situation is not as bleak as these words make it appear. Junior high students do have a number of things going for them to help in school. They are peaking in terms of learning ability. Their mental wheels run quickly, although they do need good pilots to help steer. For another thing, many of these students are developing special interests, perhaps new, perhaps carried over from elementary school, that can consume attention and siphon off frustration. Also, as they begin making the psychological break from their parents, they look for other adult models to emulate or identify with. Such models can come—and, in fact, often do—in the form of teachers, and to please these idealized persons, students will work hard and long.

Enough about the trials and tribulations that beset junior high scholars. The best learning environments for them provide physical work and discussion space, with necessary basic materials, such as reference materials and apparatus, stored or shelved, ready at hand. These materials, so necessary to speed learning, should be quickly replaceable in their storage areas so the room can be readied at the end of each period. There are ways to provide such materials in junior high classrooms, and teachers are remiss when they do not provide them.

Teachers, as has been hinted, make or break the junior high learning environments through their personal actions. They must talk much and frequently with their students, using clarifying and accepting comments instead of stooping to moralizing or giving unasked-for advice. They must maintain an uncommon sense of humor. They must be relaxed and flexible. Still, they must repeatedly show that they mean business about the subjects they teach. The subject cannot be the end-all of everything, but it must have high priority. Then the teacher must work hard to help students understand what they are being helped to learn and why. Quality feedback has to be a part of this process, where teachers not only point out what students do wrong, but give them clear, positive guidance in how to do it right.

Junior high students will find increasing difficulty in fulfilling their roles as learners and climate facilitators. Again, they have so many other things on their minds, much very powerful emotional stuff, that they have trouble engaging intellectually with what the teacher wants them to learn. To counteract this condition requires an additional effort on the part of their teachers. Not only must student responsibilities be discussed frequently, but exceptional care must be put into organizing the subject matter for students. The material must be clear. Its worth must be evident. Its progression must be easy to follow. These conditions will help students keep to their primary in-school duty, which is to learn.

High school classrooms. The high school years mark a return toward, if not complete attainment of, the relative tranquility of the elementary school years. A goodly percentage of the junior high ugly ducklings have evolved, amazingly enough, into swans, or at least into handsome ducks. They have reached a stage of truce with their bodies—a fifty-fifty stand off, in which the bodies are more or less accepted, even though they still engender misconceptions, misgivings, and miseries. Their intellects have continued to mature, and their reasoning ability is often equal to that of their teachers, although not as seasoned. They are fully as capable of abstract thought as adults. Their individualities have begun emerging clearly from the sea of junior high conformity. Their special talents and abilities have commenced to bloom. They are still greatly concerned with sex, cars, and pop music, and they still bend to the breeze of peer pressure. But they do have new minds of their own, often quite reasonable ones. These minds have begun thinking of work, social justice, politics, life after school, what's valuable in life, what life is about, and so forth.

Physical learning environments for high school students are quite similar to those for junior high students. The materials, equipment, laboratories, and other special facilities are more sophisticated. They permit greater depth of study and exploration. But the basic classroom is little more than walls, windows, desks, chalkboard, bulletin board, projection screen, and perhaps a few pieces of material related to the subject being taught. In noticeable contrast to the classrooms stand the athletic facilities, laboratories, and shops. Here you see great provision for sophisticated specialization. Unlike the humdrum classrooms, the specialized areas in high school are replete with the finest equipment, much of it so elaborate as to be unrecognizable to high school students of a few years past.

High school teachers are not greatly different from college teachers in basic approach. Their subject areas sit foremost in their minds. Because high school students have regained an ability to focus much of their energies on these topics, they are able to function well. They often identify with their teachers, even hang ferocious crushes on them, and emulate much of what they do. They seek personal relationships with the teachers they admire, and for that matter they will often place a teacher at or near the top of their list of most admired persons.

The best teachers, as is the case at all levels, provide an accepting, secure atmosphere for learning. They can make great use of humor.

Anecdotes help hold attention and get across points. They help students most by giving clear models of what they expect to be learned and by providing sound, clear suggestions for correcting errors that students make.

High school students, better than any others in public school (except perhaps fifth and sixth graders), can contribute significantly to the environment of the classroom. They can accept the notions that they are in school mainly to learn and that they have responsibilities to make learning easier for everyone around them. This is not to imply that they never misbehave, show reticence, or act defiant. It is simply to say that they can understand their principal roles and can accept their responsibilities within them. Their senses of humor, reason, idealism, and fair play make them fairly easy to work with and refreshingly pleasant to be around.

TEACHING METHODS AND LEARNING ENVIRONMENTS

To this point we have considered learning environments mainly in the light of notable differences that occur in students at different stages of development. We noted these student characteristics with an eye to the physical, intellectual/activity, and interpersonal environments that best seem to allow learning to occur. In addition, we identified some of the inputs teachers and students could make to further the quality of the learning environments.

In this section we will examine the relationship between various teaching methods and the environments they call for (or produce, as the case might be) to enhance learning opportunities for students.

If you have read Chapters 11 and 12, you might recall the detailed descriptions of eleven separate methods of teaching plus thirteen specific strategies. These descriptions specified what ends, or objectives, were being sought through the use of each method, how the instruction was organized and presented, what teacher and students did, and how the effectiveness of teaching and learning was assessed. These methods were as follows:

1. Diagnostic-prescriptive teaching
2. Competency-based education
3. Read-review-recite
4. Expository teaching

5. Simulations
6. Modeling
7. Projects
8. Group process
9. Inquiry/discovery
10. Facilitation
11. Open experience

These methods overlap in some ways. In other ways they differ considerably. These differences are most notable in the ends they seek and in the instructional procedures they use. Because they differ so much in some ways, they require learning environments especially attuned to them. Thus quality learning environments are influenced not only by traits of teachers and students, but also by the teaching method being used. Let's see what sort of environment each of these methods requires.

Diagnostic-prescriptive teaching

Diagnostic-prescriptive teaching (DPT) is a highly structured method that focuses on the attainment of clearly specified objectives. It begins with a master list of behavioral objectives. Diagnostic tests are constructed whose items are keyed to the master objectives. Students are given the tests, which, when checked, provide a diagnosis of student strengths and weaknesses. For each weakness so identified, the student is given a prescription to complete. Prescriptions, too, are keyed to the list of master objectives. When the prescribed activities are completed, students should be able to pass a criterion test, which determines whether the students can now reach objectives they previously could not.

DPT can be used successfully for the teaching of fundamental knowledge and skills at any level, kindergarten through graduate school. It can be used within a variety of classroom environments. Physically, it requires the following:

1. Depository of diagnostic and criterion tests
2. Files of prescribed activities
3. Resource materials called for in the prescriptions
4. Work space for completing prescribed activities
5. Suitable areas for students to complete diagnostic and criterion tests

The intellectual, social, and emotional requisites for DPT environments are relatively few. Intellectually, students must comprehend the procedures being used. From third grade on, they can follow through the processes with little help from the teacher. Socially, the work space is usually located in one area, but students either work individually or in very small groups. The teacher administers diagnostic and criterion tests, keeps records, helps with difficulties in the prescriptions, and sometimes teaches small group lessons to get across key, although difficult, points.

DPT is a straightforward, businesslike approach to teaching and learning. It lets *students* know exactly what to do and how to do it. It lets *teachers* know exactly where each student is working and what has been accomplished. It is a bit cut and dried. Students tend to tire of it quickly, preferring to work, talk, and interact with other students. If a quality emotional environment is to be maintained for DPT, the teacher must enliven matters before and after the DPT work sessions, while the sessions themselves are kept fairly short, to the point, and free from distractions.

Competency-based education

Competency-based education is similar to DPT in that it revolves around objectives carefully specified in advance. In essence, it stresses the development of student ability to do something well that they could not do before. This student ability to *do* is the proof of the competency pudding.

Competency-based education does not require a rigidly prescribed structure, as does DPT. It can take various forms, usually involving a combination of individualized instruction and mastery learning. This combination fits well into instructional modules, which are units of work carefully organized around a given topic. The modules contain objectives, pretests, multiple instructional activities from which students may select for reaching the stated objectives, and posttests, which are criterion measures. Students work through the modules alone or in very small groups.

Competency-based learning, when occurring through modules, does require special arrangements of the physical environment. Support materials for the activity options must be kept in a place conveniently available to students. Also, there must be private spaces provided in which to use the materials. This is especially so where audiovisual media are involved.

But more than this, competency-based educa-

tion is a state of mind that exists within *teacher* and *student* alike. The goal is ability to do something new in a competent way. This goal requires an intellectual determination to succeed and a facilitative stance by the teacher. The teacher is the judge of what constitutes competency and what does not, as well as the organizer and taskmaster who sees to it that students reach competency levels. This design requires a highly communicative interpersonal environment, where students and teacher exchange ideas and exhibit and monitor performances. The teacher must be alert to student errors, so as to provide corrective feedback immediately.

Like DPT, competency-based education is a straightforward, disciplined approach. It wastes little time on exploration and none on frivolity.

Read-review-recite

By far the most common teaching method at all levels of schooling beyond primary grades is one we call, for want of a more compelling name, the read-review-recite method. This method begins with a reading assignment, usually in the textbook being used in the subject. After reading the assignment, students review the material, usually by completing work sheets or answering related questions. Finally, they recite what they have learned. Formerly, that recitation was given orally, with trembling student standing alongside desk fervently hoping to be able to answer questions thrown forth by the teacher. Nowadays, it is more commonly done in the form of written tests, written compositions, or oral reports.

There is a current tendency to disparage this method of teaching. In truth it is not overly imaginative. But we should be cautious about throwing it out completely. The method has been used successfully at most levels, and it has stood the tests of time, convenience, and effectiveness.

The physical environment best suited to this method is one we might call the standard classroom format. *Students* must have available the basic materials to be read and used in review. A quiet work area is necessary. The *teacher* contributes little that is special, being required only to make assignments, supervise reading and review, and monitor recitation. This procedure is easy for teachers, and it can be used with pleasure if great good humor is provided by the teacher and if provisions are made for student interchange of ideas following recitation.

Expository teaching

The term "expository" refers to making things clear and understandable. The expository method of teaching, usually seen in the form of lectures and demonstrations, closely rivals read-review-recite as the most popular method of teaching. This method, usually considered the forte of the secondary and college teacher, places the teacher in virtual complete control of the learning situation. If lecture is used, nothing is required in the physical environment, although lectures are usually improved greatly when they incorporate media such as slides, transparencies, charts, and models.

Since the *teacher* so controls the lecture situation and since *student* participation is more passive than active, the teacher must manipulate the interpersonal aspect of the learning environment. This manipulation is best done by combining the clearest explanation of the material being presented with a deft use of humor, anecdote, and example. The teacher must command and hold attention. Unless the material is unusually engaging in itself, the teacher will need to rely on some of the devices used by performing artists. One such device is modulation of the voice, playing it like an instrument, varying pitch and volume, adding notes of suspense and excitement, and using pauses to produce student anticipation.

Another device is the use of facial expressions and gestures, coordinated with the verbal presentation being made. Still others include asking questions in an affected voice and then answering them and speaking the parts of two or more imaginary discussants.

When demonstrations are used in expository teaching, theatrics can be reduced. The physical environment, of necessity, will contain materials and/or performances to attract and hold students' attention.

Simulations

Simulations are recreations of lifelike situations in the classroom. They are as true to life as the average soap opera or more so, although they are usually not quite as racy. For students they have all the appeal of *Gilligan's Island,* plus the added bonus of active participation in the adventure.

Simulations more and more are coming into vogue in teaching. They lend themselves unusually well to the study of realistic topics in social science. They involve all members of the class, and their motivational appeal is very high.

The key elements in the learning environment for simulations are social. *Student* input into this social realm is very important. The simulation goes, or not, because of student involvement. Here students have a chance not only to learn easily, but also to contribute strongly to helping others learn. They are encouraged to do this by working together toward a common goal. Each person has to make a contribution or else the simulation will will not succeed. This sense of purposeful working together energizes the learning climate.

The *teacher's* input into the learning environment, once past the initial stages, is no greater than the students'. The teacher selects and organizes the intellectual/activity aspect of the simulation, introduces it, and watches over it as it is carried out. The teacher smooths difficulties that might be encountered and often acts as referee when disputes arise. The introduction, especially the first time a simulation is used, is crucial. It sets the intellectual tone for what's to come, and it determines the eagerness with which students enter into the simulation.

The physical environment need only contain appropriate work space plus materials that students use. Both space and materials requirements are determined by the activities.

Modeling

Modeling is a teaching method that is rapidly gaining wide attention. It is a procedure of teaching through example and learning through imitation. As a process, it is very compact. The teacher or some other model demonstrates a behavior, process, or concept. Students observe attentively. In this simple way they become able to reproduce, through imitative learning, what they have seen the model demonstrate. Technically, there is more to modeling than first meets the eye. All in all, though, teaching through modeling is a highly practical, efficient, and effective way to speed student learning.

The physical learning environment required for modeling is not at all complicated. There must be a suitable place for the model to present the behavior, process, or concept. Necessary props must be ready at hand. Students must be arranged so all can see and hear. Later, space and conditions must be provided for the students to reenact, to practice, what they have observed.

The *teacher* sets the stage for modeling, explains its rationale, indicates specifically what is to be learned, helps focus attention on the modeled event, and provides corrective feedback when students reenact what they have observed.

Students make few contributions to the environment. They have only to take the matter seriously and pay attention. Although all the class members observe together, and perhaps practice reenactment together, their roles are more or less individual ones. Cooperation, esprit de corps, etc., are not essential, although naturally a pleasant group feeling makes the process more enjoyable for everyone.

Projects

The project method was one of the truly innovative teaching practices to emerge in the early part of this century. You have to conjure up visions of the past to see how revolutionary it was. Think first of the old-time classroom with knickered and aproned students working diligently in their rows of desks. The teacher stands before them, perhaps behind a lectern on a raised platform, lecturing, questioning, and reprimanding.

In contrast, think of a procedure, new to the school scene, where students assume the responsibility for carrying out an important task, perhaps working alone or (heavens!) together with other students, deciding on procedures, sharing the work load, completing the task, and preparing some sort of report or summary. Such initiative that would require! Such organization! Such cooperation! Such responsibility! See what they were getting at? The project method puts much of the responsibility for learning directly in the students' laps.

The project method is still very popular, probably more popular than ever. It surely helps students learn how to learn on their own. The main complaint about it is that it takes much time and students don't cover enough material in the subject area. That complaint is valid for breadth of knowledge, but it doesn't hold water for objectives that have to do with initiative, responsibility, and orga-

nization. There is no shortcut to those pots of gold.

The physical environment for project work is very important. Naturally there must be suitable work space in the classroom. Naturally there must be a wealth of reference materials for students to use. Provisions must be made for bringing into the classroom an unimaginable variety of materials, objects, and even resource people. And if this were not enough, arrangements may have to be made for students to go outside the classroom or school to secure information and materials for their projects.

The physical environment of the classroom thus becomes a laboratory or workshop. Materials lie about (not in complete disarray, one hopes). Students move about (not frolicking, one insists). They talk with each other about their work (not wildly boisterously; that is forbidden).

The intellectual/activity aspect of the environment speaks for itself. This is the pièce de resistance of the project approach.

The interpersonal aspect of the environment must receive continual attention from teacher and students. Whenever students work together, the likelihood of nonproductive socialization looms large. Squabbles love to pop up. The teacher has to monitor activities closely, keep students on a productive track, nip quarrels in the bud. This is done not so much by forbidding and punishing as by helping resolve conflicts before they reach the destructive level. *Students* can help greatly in this regard. When old enough to use the project method (usually beginning in fourth grade), they are old enough to develop responsibility for their individual and group behavior.

Teaching through the project method is not a lark. It is hard work for teachers. But all who try it (well, almost all) will tell you that it makes work more interesting for them and that it makes a significant contribution to the quality of the educational experience for their students.

Group process

The group process method of teaching has as its primary goal the development of effective social and democratic styles of behavior. That is, the emphasis is put on teaching people how to work together effectively for both individual and group good.

Whereas the project method focused first on the

academic and secondarily on the social, the group process method does the reverse. It stresses the skills of working together in large and small groups. It develops leadership and cooperative qualities. It advocates democratic rule, which ultimately means majority rule. Throughout the process, the give-and-take of ideas is stressed. Rational dissention is encouraged. Opposition is considered a natural part of the process. Conflicts occur, and part of the method deals with their resolution. Throughout, a rational, reasonable attitude is encouraged, and input is sought from all quarters before decisions are made.

This method has heretofore been difficult to use in the classroom on a formal basis. Simulations have made it much easier, however, because they provide the necessary structure, incentives, and ground rules to make group process effective.

Even though *students* have a central role in group process, the *teacher* is crucial. Group process is delicate. With too little fire in the material being considered, nothing happens. With too much, the kettle boils over, and it can burn students and even splash as far away as home, scorching parents who may react with shouts of outrage.

Thus the interpersonal learning environment must be cared for tenderly. Teacher and students alike must continually remind themselves of what the objectives are, and they must cover ground rules frequently. The teacher must inject humor when feelings run high, fan the fevers that rise, and throw on fuel when the coals burn low.

The physical environment for group process is inconsequential. Any place will do. The intellectual/activity environment may include anything (anything the community considers suitable—be careful) that will stir controversy or engender enthusiastic investigation. The crux is the interpersonal environment. Teacher and students alike must work hard to maintain it.

Inquiry/discovery

The inquiry/discovery method of teaching calls on students to use investigative procedures to obtain information and make observations, then organize their observations and thoughts and make sense of them. What results from this "making sense" is discovery, the ascertainment of a concept, insight, or idea new to the student.

Discovery sounds a bit pompous to some. It seems to imply uncovering something grand, such as the source of the Nile or the moons of Jupiter. In education we give the term a much more modest connotation. Discovery simply means finding out things for oneself, not just memorizing what someone else has said or written. It means getting information to fall together so that, for the first time for the learner, it makes sense.

Discovery has been strongly emphasized in some of the newer curricula, especially in the physical and social sciences where careful observation of natural phenomena is stressed. The object of such observation is to find out as much as possible, directly through the senses, and then see what interpretations can be made from these observations.

Given the information, for example, that ducklings just hatched from the egg will follow the mother duck, one might hypothesize that ducklings have an inborn ability to recognize members of their own species. But is this really the case? What do ducklings hatched in an incubator do? What about single ducklings raised in isolation and fed by a man? Will they later flock with other ducks? Inquiry leads one into a search for answers to such questions. The information uncovered enables the student to test the validity of the original hypothesis.

In natural science, students might be encouraged to observe a classroom aquarium at length to find out as much as possible about the life and environments within it. Or they might be sent outside to the lawn to find out as much as they can about grass, how the plant is structured, what seems to nourish it, and so forth.

Observation needn't be restricted to natural phenomena. In social science, for example, the students might read about child-rearing practices among the Eskimos, Navajos, Fiji Islanders, Japanese, and Western Europeans, the objective being to identify—discover—what seem to be common or necessary practices in bringing up human children. As you might imagine, such discoveries, particularly in areas of ethnic group behavior, can be startlingly enlightening.

The physical environment that promotes inquiry/discovery contains a wealth of materials and objects. It extends into the school library, into the out-of-doors, and into the larger community. It is limited only by the imagination, tempered by realistic practicality.

The intellectual/activity environment is one of questioning, searching, and hypothesizing. It must be structured somewhat by the teacher. Students must have a place to start and some idea of how to proceed in their investigations.

The interpersonal environment has secondary importance in inquiry/discovery. *Students* may want to work together, and they will want to share their ideas. The *teacher* provides latitude and encouragement and helps students when they run up against obstacles they can't overcome.

Facilitation

One of the newest and most important teaching methods to appear on the educational scene is one Carl Rogers calls facilitation. To comprehend what facilitation means, we can see how Rogers compared traditional teaching with facilitative teaching. In a nutshell, he saw traditional teaching as entailing the teacher selecting the content to be learned, establishing the objectives to be reached, deciding on instructional procedures, activities, and materials to be used, and specifying how the results would be evaluated.

Facilitative teaching, on the other hand, entails the following: The teacher, in talking with students, helps them clarify (within certain limits, of course) what it is they want to learn, how they want to learn it, and how they want to be checked on it at the end, if indeed they want to be checked at all. Once these questions are answered, the teacher functions as a facilitator of learning, helping students find necessary resources and information, helping them with procedures when necessary, and supporting their productive efforts, even when they don't appear to be fully efficient. Advice is given only when students ask for it. Evaluation, too, comes only when asked for. This procedure puts students in charge of their own learning. The teacher becomes a helper and guide.

The physical environment necessary for facilitative teaching is only vaguely specifiable. Naturally there must be work space. Logically materials will be brought into the classroom. The environment will have to extend out from the classroom to multiple sources of information.

It is in the intellectual/activity and the interpersonal aspects of the learning environment that the *teacher* makes the greatest contribution. Intellectually, a climate of searching, questioning, and productive effort must be maintained. The teacher must delicately keep students on task and progressing, while at the same time allowing them to move into intriguing alleys that turn up unexpectedly. Also, the teacher must be sensitive to students' individual styles and the rates at which they work best.

Interpersonally, the key lies between teacher and individual students. A climate of individual trust and helpfulness must be established and maintained. The security that comes with this trust reduces the destructive anxiety that often hampers learning. The trust also allows teacher and student to speak honestly to each other. If either is dissatisfied with the way learning is occurring, they are expected to say so, in ways as nonthreatening as possible, so that the problem can be resolved in a manner acceptable to both.

Open experience

Going hand in hand with facilitation is a method of instruction called open experience. Open experience makes a number of learning options available to students. As students choose which activities they will pursue, they assume, at the same time, responsibility for organizing and directing their own learning. They also take on the responsibility for conducting themselves in a proper manner, so that they do not interfere with other students' opportunities to learn.

Open education combines a richly equipped learning environment with facilitative teaching. Teacher and students share the task of bringing into the classroom the materials they will use. They may bring in books, magazines, educational games, models, art materials, small electric and gasoline motors—whatever they think they would like to learn about. These materials are placed in convenient work areas around the room. *Students* decide which things they will work on. Then, for a certain amount of each period or day, they work on their own without direction from the teacher.

Yet, the *teacher* is present, watchful, and in charge. Order must be maintained, and that is the teacher's job. The job is not difficult. Discipline problems usually fade in open experience, when students have activities in which they truly want to engage.

The teacher contributes to the interpersonal environment by acting as facilitator, helping when asked, and showing interest in what the students are doing. Students contribute by conducting themselves in productive and nondisruptive ways. Students like open experience. They will usually show their best behavior so that the opportunity for it will not be taken away.

TEACHING STRATEGIES AND LEARNING ENVIRONMENTS

Perhaps you recall that Chapter 12 described strategies of teaching. The distinction made between teaching method and teaching strategy was as follows: Teaching method is a large-scale, overarching way of organizing the teaching-learning process. It includes ways of presenting subject matter, ways of arranging the learning environment, and ways of working with students. Teaching strategy, on the other hand, is a small-scale technique intended to produce a specific effect in the learning environment and, hence, in student behavior.

Teaching strategies fit into various aspects of the methods-environments relationships we have just considered. The various strategies elaborated in Chapter 12 will not be repeated here in detail. But mention will be made of them to show how they, too, relate to teaching method and learning environment.

To keep straight the relationship between strategies and environments, remember this: Strategies fit within, and contribute to, methods of teaching. Methods, in turn, suggest the types of environment that best enhance particular approaches to teaching and learning.

Mastery learning

Mastery learning is a strategy that is very helpful in competency-based education. It also fits in with other structured approaches, such as modeling and diagnostic-prescriptive teaching. Mastery learning is based on the idea that you can bring every student, not just a few of them, up to true mastery level in any subject. Considerable experimental evidence supports this contention. The strategy involves varying the amounts of instructional time available to each student, with the realization that it will take some students longer than others to reach mastery level. Combined with time

variations are provisions for teachers to monitor student progress and provide immediate corrective feedback when necessary.

Behavior modification

Behavior modification is one of the most powerful teaching strategies, and now one of the most widely used, to come out of the second half of the twentieth century. Based on principles of reinforcement, as clarified by B. F. Skinner, behavior modification uses an organized system of rewards, both social and tangible, to shape students' behavior in desirable directions. This behavior is not confined to comportment, but extends to all areas of intellectual, social, and emotional activity.

Precision teaching

Precision teaching is a refinement, or at least a special application, of behavior modification. When using it, students are responsible for charting their own performance over a period of time. Since the chart shows graphic evidence of progress (as well as the opposite), students are highly motivated to improve. Precision teaching is known to fit well with mastery learning, diagnostic-prescriptive teaching, and other structured approaches. There is good reason to believe that it will serve well as a motivator in any method of teaching.

Engineered environments

The term "engineered environments" is a catch-all for a strategy that has appeared under a number of different labels. Basically this strategy serves in the acquisition of subject matter, and it makes up part of the intellectual/activity environment. It fits best into methods with higher degrees of structure. The subject matter is broken into small steps, as in programmed learning. Procedures are used to ensure that students work at levels commensurate with their individual abilities. An organized system of social and/or tangible reinforcement is employed to motivate and speed student learning. This strategy has been shown to produce remarkable teaching gains, especially in remedial classes in language and mathematics.

Advance organization

Advance organization is a strategy for helping students acquire and retain subject matter being presented to them. It is, all in all, a device for adding meaning to what students are about to learn. The organizer consists of a framework, a sort of word skeleton, that summarizes what students are to learn. This skeleton gives an understandable preview of what's to come, and it provides pegs onto which specific information can be hung as it is learned. Advance organization facilitates acquisition of material, enables students to make sense of it, and enables later recall. Clearly, it contributes mostly to the intellectual/activity aspect of the learning environment. Because it is prepared by the teacher, it fits in with more structured environments and is especially useful in expository and read-review-recite methods.

Individualized instruction

Individualized instruction is a strategy that attempts to provide instruction best fitted to the needs, interests, and learning styles of individual students. Often considered a separate method of teaching, individualized instruction can be provided in forms that vary from highly structured, such as diagnostic-prescriptive teaching, to only slightly structured, such as open experience. In essence, individualized instruction provides variations suited to individual students in one or more of the following areas: subject matter content, objectives, learning activities, or time allotments. This strategy can be incorporated into any teaching method and can function compatibly with most other teaching strategies.

Questioning

Questioning is a strategy that has received much attention in the past decade. We have learned how to use questions to improve the intellectual quality of the learning environment. It has been established that different types of questions can cause the students to use different types of intellectual processes. The thrust has been to move teaching beyond a concentration on factual information to greater attention on analytical, creative, and evaluative thought processes.

Great expectations

Great expectations is a label we can use to refer to a strategy that contributes markedly to both the intellectual/activity and the interpersonal aspects of the learning environment. Research has shown that some students will achieve more and conduct themselves in a more exemplary way when teachers hold high expectations for them and, in addition, behave as though they truly consider their students intelligent, capable, and fully able to measure up to the expectations. This strategy can be employed in conjunction with any teaching method, and it is compatible with all other teaching strategies.

Synectics

Synectics is a technical name used to refer to what we usually call creative thinking. As a strategy of teaching, its purpose is to increase students' flow of novel ideas. This quality places synectics in the intellectual/activity aspect of the learning environment. Synectics is based on the belief that creative production is a capability we all have; one that can be learned; and one that, when developed, can markedly increase our productive intelligence. It can be used to advantage in methods of teaching that have moderate to low structure, such as simulations and inquiry/discovery.

Values clarification

Values clarification is a recently developed strategy that helps students clarify for themselves what it is they consider important in their lives. This strategy, which calls on students to choose freely from alternatives, affirm those choices, and then act on them, contributes to both the intellectual/activity and the interpersonal aspects of the learning environment. It can form an important part of some of the more open methods of teaching, such as inquiry, facilitation, and open experience.

Classroom meetings

Classroom meetings is the name used by Glasser for the group communications sessions he advocates as a regular part of the school curriculum. These meetings are intended to help students resolve problems encountered with academic work, with other people, or with life in general. These discussions can help relieve tension and reduce frustration, thereby heading off a multitude of other in-class problems. This strategy fits well into the group process method, as well as into facilitation and open education. It contributes greatly to the quality of the interpersonal learning environment.

Reality approach

Reality approach is a strategy that is especially effective in working with students of all ages. Among other things it helps students learn how to resolve interpersonal conflicts in positive ways, while protecting the egos of everyone involved. This strategy can contribute importantly to the interpersonal learning environment. It fits well into group process, simulation, and facilitation methods of teaching.

Acceptance

Acceptance is a strategy that has been elaborated and popularized by Thomas Gordon, Haim Ginott, Eric Berne, and Ned Flanders. It holds that student achievement, comportment, and interpersonal relations are enhanced through warm, accepting learning environments. The strategy of acceptance shows students that they are competent and worthy as individuals. Acceptance does not mean that teachers condone inappropriate acts. The strategy shows teachers how to reject destructive acts while still accepting the student as a person. This strategy contributes to the interpersonal aspect of the learning environment and fits well into teaching methods such as group process, inquiry, facilitation, and open education.

FIVE LEARNING ENVIRONMENTS

By this time your diligent reading has likely had one of two effects on you: either it has left you dozing or it has set your head to humming with an overabundance of information about learning environments. Hopefully, you suffer from the latter condition. If you are asleep, there is no way these lines of print can wake you. But if your brain sits alertly jumbled, the following paragraphs will straighten it out.

Classroom learning environments can be separated into five types. Can you believe that, after all we've been through so far? Well, it's true. You take all those factors of physical environment, intellectual/activity environment, and interpersonal environment, stir them together with the eleven different methods of teaching, then fold in thirteen teaching strategies. When thoroughly mixed you shake them out, and lo and behold you have five pies, each as delicious as the other, according to your taste. The five pies—well, really classroom environments; let's be serious—are as follows:

1. The standard environment
2. The engineered environment
3. The open space environment
4. The open experience environment
5. The combination environment

Each of these types of classroom environment has its strengths and weaknesses, advantages and disadvantages. Which is best, you ask? Why, there is no best. Teachers' philosophies of teaching and their personality traits differ largely. Their preferences for learning environments vary accordingly. The same holds true for students. Their personalities and learning styles vary, and the environment that best suits one may not be worth beans for another. Subject matter influences the situation, too. The environment that is best for learning basic knowledge and skills does not work so well for creativity and group processes.

Let's see what each type of learning environment is and is not good for.

The standard environment

We will use the name "standard" to refer to the classroom environment most familiar to us. This environment is usually called "traditional," but for some reason that name is beginning to take on a slightly tainted connotation. That's why we will use the name "standard."

The standard classroom environment is set largely by the teacher, who does the planning, makes the assignments, monitors student work, and evaluates student progress. The predominant teaching methods are read-review-recite, expository, and perhaps some projects.

The physical environment consists of an orderly arrangement of desks or tables, with instructional materials and reference books located in the room. Basic textbooks predominate over other kinds of reading material. There may be one or two interest centers in elementary rooms and some charts posted in secondary rooms.

The intellectual/activity environment focuses primarily on the learning of knowledge and skills. It is not rigorously structured, but neither is it loose or student centered. Reading, writing, and taking tests are the main student activities, except at the primary grade level where the oral language component—reading, reading readiness, discussions, etc.—receives greatest attention.

The interpersonal environment is warm and supportive, but the teacher is definitely in control and lets that fact be known continually. The teacher behaves in a fairly authoritarian way, demanding much of the students, supporting them when they do "right," but calling them to task in no uncertain terms when they step over the firm boundaries of acceptable behavior.

Strategies often used in standard classrooms include advance organization, questioning, and behavior modification. This environment has been, and is, a good reliable standby, tried and true. It serves well for the majority of teachers and students.

The engineered environment

The engineered classroom environment is new on the scene. It employs highly effective teaching and student control techniques drawn from behavioral psychology. It is lean, goal directed, and businesslike, without frills or marshmallow creme. It has accomplished wondrous results in subjects where basic essential knowledge is the main objective—subjects such as reading, grammar, and mathematics.

This environment focuses directly on subject matter. It does not pretend to be useful for developing interpersonal relations or creativity. The subject matter is broken into small pieces that follow each other in orderly progression. Students are placed individually into material at appropriate levels of difficulty. They are motivated and guided through use of a scientific system of incentives and rewards, the best of behavior modification.

The physical environment in the engineered classroom is clean, orderly, and uncluttered. All necessary materials are present. Superfluous or distracting items are eliminated.

The intellectual/activity aspect of the environment focuses directly on the acquisition and comprehension of information and sometimes on the application of that information. Activities are mainly confined to text and reference material directly related to the behavioral objectives.

The interpersonal aspect of the environment receives little special attention. The teacher, calm, professional, and efficient, dispenses rewards for desired behavior. The rewards are made so attractive that students work eagerly to attain them. Little attempt is made to establish interpersonal relationships or to further student development in the af-

fective areas of feelings, attitudes, and values.

Teaching methods most effective for engineered classrooms are diagnostic-prescriptive teaching, competency-based education, and expository teaching. Strategies commonly used include mastery learning, behavior modification, individualized instruction, and advance organization.

The open space environment

Many people think open space is a new, avant-garde method or strategy of teaching. It comes as a real surprise to them to find that the open space environment can be highly structured, as in engineered classrooms; can have low structure, as in open experience; or can, as is most often the case, be simply a standard classroom without walls around it. In fact, this lack of interior walls is the only thing about open space environments that is necessarily special.

Then why, you ask, is open space listed here as one of the fabulous five classroom environments prominent on the educational scene? Answer: because it *can* have some special attributes that are difficult to have in self-contained classrooms that have walls around them. These special things are three in number: (1) team teaching becomes much easier to accomplish, since several teachers are together within sight and earshot of each other; (2) flexible grouping, which is almost impossible in schools with self-contained classrooms, is very easy to accomplish, since a large number of students are located in proximity: they have only to move their chairs and you can have a large group with one teacher and several small groups, each with a teacher; and (3) joint use of library, references, and audiovisual media becomes much easier, since those things, too, are located in the large open space.

Theoretically, it is possible to use any method of teaching or any teaching strategy in open space environments. Let's emphasize the word theoretically, however. Why? Since people are not separated by walls, distracting noise can be a serious problem in open space. That means that teachers must plan together, so as to coordinate the kinds of activities they will have during the day. This fact cuts down greatly on flexibility. Methods such as group process, simulations, and open experience are difficult to use, unless all teachers in the space use them at the same time.

The open experience environment

Open experience has already been discussed as a method of teaching. The method and the environment both have the same name, and each serves to explain the other. Both stress choice, freedom, responsibility, and self-direction.

You will recall that the open experience environment has the following characteristics:

Physical: Richly equipped with materials and activities among which students choose. Appears somewhat cluttered. Can get out of hand if students don't assume responsibilities for self-control and for contributing to the interpersonal relations aspect of the environment.

Intellectual/activity: Highly active, with total involvement of students in, hopefully, purposeful activities. Knowledge, attitude, and feeling objectives are stressed equally. Major objectives also include self-direction and responsibility.

Interpersonal: Very important in the open experience environment. Students must learn to work together, share, cooperate, and not get in each others' way, physically or emotionally. Relationships between teacher and student have crucial importance.

Open experience is the name of the teaching method as well as the environment. You remember that it incorporates other methods such as facilitation and inquiry. Teaching strategies often used in open experience include values clarification, classroom meetings, and acceptance.

The combination environment

You have seen how the first four of our fabulous environments overlap each other. They all combine some elements found in other environments. Still, those environments are more than moderately different from each other in their major goals and in their organization, materials, activities, and personal relationships.

It may have occurred to you that practically every one of those different environments' major goals is important. Who would argue against the importance of subject matter knowledge, gained quickly, efficiently, and pleasantly? Who would argue against the importance of personal development, the bringing to flower of our own individual interests, abilities, and potentials? Who would argue against the importance of interpersonal relations, the learning to live harmoniously, to cooperate, and to function democratically? Hardly anyone.

The standard classroom, that comfortable old shoe, gets at bits of all these different goals. However, it doesn't do so as efficiently as it could, because it is not set up to use newer techniques whose effectiveness in meeting various objectives has been so well documented. Thus many teachers are learning how to put together what we can call "combination learning environments." These environments use newer, more efficient techniques for teaching subject matter, for developing the self, and for developing democratic skills. They are excellent for moving toward some of the same ends that the standard environment seeks with less efficiency. They will probably become the new standard environment.

The combination environment will devote some time to the learning and use of subject matter information, recognizing that knowledge is essential for other intellectual endeavors, such as creative production, logical thinking, problem solving, and making wise judgments.

It will devote some time to group processes, recognizing that we all function in a social milieu and that we must work with others for both the common good and our own self-interest.

It will devote some time to open experience, recognizing that each of us needs to learn how to make decisions, follow through on commitments, and take responsibility for ourselves.

Some of the class activities will be done in larger groups, because we need to learn to give and take effectively and because we enjoy and benefit from the interaction with others.

Some of the class activities will be done individually or in very small groups, because we each have our own preferred style of learning, our own interests and abilities, and our inward desire to see what we can make of our individual talents.

Some of the class time will be devoted to reading, because we all need to be able to read fluently, with understanding and pleasure.

Some of the class time will be devoted to talking, part of which will be making clear, persuasive reports and arguments before the class and part of which will be informal discussions about topics of current interest to the group. We all need to learn to express ourselves orally. The same goes for expressing ourselves in writing.

And finally, a good part of the time will be spent in having students use what they know to solve realistic problems. Problem-solving ability ranks high on the list of priorities for education.

The teacher will use methods and strategies appropriate to each segment of this combination environment. Diagnostic-prescriptive teaching, mastery learning, and behavior modification will be stressed in an engineered-type environment to bring about the most rapid learning of information. This will be enlivened with occasional demonstrations and talks by the teacher. Simulations will be combined with group processes to produce meaningful interactions among students. A variety of social and cognitive skills will be taught through polished modeling techniques. Students will practice learning how to learn through projects and inquiry/discovery. Questioning will guide students, draw them out, and cause them to use various levels of the intellect. Interpersonal relations will be strengthened through communication and trust. The teacher will hold high expectations for all students and will accept them as persons even while urging them on and not accepting inappropriate behavior or substandard performance.

Utopian? An impossible dream? Not at all. We have the techniques. We can apply and manage them all. It takes only effort. One day this combination environment, this new standard classroom, will be the rule, not the exception.

BUILDING YOUR ENVIRONMENT

And now to the final point of all the observations made in this chapter. The point is twofold: (1) that most of the hundreds of thousands of classroom environments in schools today happen approximately 25% by design and 75% by chance and (2) that the reverse should and can be true: at least 75% of all that goes into the learning environment should be there by design, not happenstance.*

Why does this 25-75 condition exist? What can be done to improve it? To conclude this chapter, we will consider answers to both these questions.

To the first question, the answer is that learning environments occur largely by happenstance for the following reasons:

1. The techniques, methods, and strategies for accomplishing most of the highly desired ends of education have only recently been refined to the point that teachers can pinpoint accurately what they want to accomplish and how, exactly, they can accomplish it.

Your immediate reaction to this statement may be a vehement, "But no, I've had some fantastic teachers!"

Today, tens of thousands of marvelous instructors hold forth mightily in their classrooms. We have all had the fortune to work with some of them. But we have all had some duds, too. The great teachers hit on their techniques through imitating other great teachers. Then they slipped some of their own insight and inventiveness into the mix. For most of them teaching is mainly—almost exclusively—a form of art.

The advantage we have today is that although teaching remains partly an art, it can have a solid technical basis that it has heretofore lacked. Teachers who previously directed only the first violins in their orchestras can now move the full complement of instruments, including the bassoons and piccolos.

2. The newer materials, methods, and strategies from which teachers can build marvelous learning environments have been with us for several years, some for as long as 20 years or more. Still, they are slow to move, en force, into the instructional picture. This phenomenon is known as institutional lag. We always seem to maintain an unseemly gap between what we know how to do and what we do.

It is a curious fact that teacher training programs across the country, for the most part, do not teach their students how to use the new methods and strategies we have at hand. These things may be mentioned or read about, but they are not practiced. And if not practiced in training, they will seldom be used in teaching.

3. An outdated rhetoric still divides educators, preventing their using the full complement of techniques at their disposal. This rhetoric zings back and forth between behaviorists and humanists. Behaviorists believe in getting down to the business of learning facts, concepts, and skills. They urge the use of behavioral objectives, mastery learning, behavior modification—in short, a behaviorally engineered learning environment. Humanists, on the other hand, believe that the prime purpose of education is to bring to flower the uniquely human and personal qualities each of us carries inside. They

---

*These percentages have not been established through formal procedures. They are the considered opinion of the authors, nothing more.

stress the development of the total person, emphasizing creative talents, values, attitudes, feelings, freedom, and responsibility. They believe these qualities can only be developed through open environments, less structured and less authoritarian than the norm, held together by bonds of warmth, support, and trust.

The rhetoric between behaviorists and humanists was once useful. It clarified what each group was getting at. It caused each to develop and streamline techniques and to put them to the test of practice.

But the argument no longer helps. It only hinders. Teachers can, and given the chance will, use the techniques from both camps. Both positions have much to commend them. Both get at important areas of human learning. Both furnish techniques that are practical and usable.

4. Teachers' careers often span 40 or even 50 years. It would be a full-time job just keeping up with advances now occurring in the areas of teaching and learning. But teachers already have full-time jobs—full-time and more. This doesn't leave time for them to undergo training in newer ways. The changes they do make usually occur in small bits and pieces, in truth as newer instructional materials force different ways of working with learners.

Understand, this comment in no way puts the knock on teachers. People who have never taught cannot comprehend what full, harried professional lives teachers lead. What is surprising is that so many of them do, in fact, learn to use newer techniques. That they find time and energy to do so speaks awfully well for their professionalism and dedication. But the majority is slow to change. Some are slow as molasses in January. They just won't give up ways that are comfortable and satisfactory merely because somebody out there claims they can do better than "just satisfactory."

To answer the second question (What can be done to improve, to move toward planned, rather than chance, learning environments?), let's begin with you—young, fresh, enthusiastic, full of energy. Later, we will find ways to ease the burdens of teachers already overworked on their jobs. Okay, here's what you do:

1. Look at some lists of educational goals and objectives. Start with the Seven Cardinal Principles, listed in Chapter 11. Then move to the *Taxon-*

omy of Educational Objectives: Cognitive Domain (Bloom, 1956). It will be quite enlightening. On the way, take a look at the *Taxonomy of Educational Objectives: Affective Domain* (Krathwohl, 1964), but don't expect too much help from it. For the affective objectives, you can't do better than to read the 1962 Association for Supervision and Curriculum Development (ASCD) yearbook entitled *Perceiving, Behaving, Becoming* (Combs, 1962).

Don't spend too much time looking at these lists of objectives. Dwell on them just long enough to get a feel for the various areas of human learning they aim at.

2. Read a good résumé of what behaviorism is about, what behaviorists would like to accomplish in education, and how they would accomplish it. Try Chapters 1 and 3 in *Educational Psychology: The Instructional Endeavor* (Charles, 1976a). Try to find out what B. F. Skinner has been saying about learning and teaching. Refer back in this chapter to teaching methods and strategies that focus on mastery learning, behavior modification, and engineered classrooms. Refer to Chapter 11 for a more detailed description of behavioristic objectives and teaching procedures.

3. Do the same thing for humanism that you did for behaviorism. Check Chapters 2 and 3 in *Educational Psychology: The Instructional Endeavor,* (Charles, 1976a). Read through *Perceiving, Behaving, Becoming* (Combs, 1962), the 1962 yearbook of ASCD. Particularly know what Carl Rogers has been saying about learning and teaching. Review the humanistic teaching objectives, as well as the procedures such as facilitation, open experience, and acceptance.

4. Decide on relative amounts of emphasis you would put on subject matter, interpersonal relations, group processes, creative production, and individual growth. Your preferences will show much about your philosophy of education.

5. Identify, for the preferences you have specified, the following:

a. The physical environment necessary for each—the objects, materials, space, work areas, and organization

b. General types of intellectual activities that would lead to maximum student development in the areas you specified in step 4

c. Aspects of the teacher-student relationship you think would best contribute to a supportive, facilitative learning environment for students

6. Home in on specific teaching methods and strategies that fit into the general framework you established in steps 4 and 5. Numerous methods and strategies were discussed earlier in this chapter, along with the specific contributions they make to the physical, intellectual, and interpersonal aspects of learning environments.

Now let us *urge* you to do—really *do*—the exercises you have just read. Do them as individual assignments or class projects, or do them just to show your determination to become skilled in teaching based on rational knowledge, skill, and preference rather than on happenstance.

SUGGESTED ACTIVITIES FOR FURTHER UNDERSTANDING

1. Compare and contrast ideal learning environments for primary children and high school students. Give attention to physical qualities, teacher personality, communication techniques, instructional materials, and responsibilities students can assume for improving the environment.
2. Assign class members responsibility for visiting classrooms where different teaching methods are being used. While there, they should observe the physical and social environments and report to the class on how methods and environments complement each other.
3. Select a grade level and/or subject you would like to teach. Describe the environment, physical and psychosocial, that would best facilitate student learning within the method and strategies you would use.

REFERENCES

Bandura, A. Social learning through imitation. In M. Jones (Ed.). *Nebraska Symposium on Motivation*. Lincoln: University of Nebraska Press, 1962.

Block, J. *Mastery learning: theory and practice,* New York: Holt, Rinehart & Winston, Inc., 1971.

Bloom, B. (Ed.). *Taxonomy of educational objectives. Handbook I: cognitive domain*. New York: David McKay Co., Inc., 1956.

Bruner, J. *Toward a theory of instruction*. New York: W. W. Norton & Co., Inc., 1966.

Charles, C. *Educational psychology: the instructional endeavor* (2nd ed.). St. Louis: The C. V. Mosby Co., 1976a.

Charles, C. *Individualizing instruction*. St. Louis: The C. V. Mosby Co., 1976b.

Combs, A. (Chairman Association for Supervision and Curriculum Development Yearbook Committee). *Perceiving, behaving, becoming*. Washington, D.C.: National Education Association, 1962.

Conant, J. *The American high school today*. New York: McGraw-Hill Book Co., 1961.

Flanders, N. *Teacher influence, pupil attitudes, and achievement*. (Cooperative Research Monograph, No. 12). Washington, D.C.: U.S. Government Printing Office, 1965.

Ginott, H. *Teacher and child*. New York: Macmillan Publishing Co., Inc., 1971.

Glasser, W. *Schools without failure*. New York: Harper & Row, Publishers, 1969.

Gordon, A. *Games for growth*. Palo Alto, Calif.: Science Research Associates, Inc., 1970.

Gordon, T. *Teacher effectiveness training*. New York: Peter H. Wyden/Publisher, 1974.

Kohl, H. The open classroom. *New York Review,* 1969.

Krathwohl, D. (Ed.). *Taxonomy of educational objectives. Handbook II: affective domain*. New York: David McKay Co., Inc., 1964.

Rogers, C. *Freedom to learn*. Columbus, Ohio: Charles E. Merrill Publishing Co., 1969.

Simon, S., Howe, L., and Kirschenbaum, H. *Values clarification*. New York: Hart Publishing Co., Inc., 1972.

Skinner, B. F. *The technology of teaching*. New York: Appleton-Century-Crofts, 1968.

CLASSROOM QUESTIONING AS COOPERATIVE DRAMA 14

When you teach, you talk a lot.

Sometimes you tell about things: "When I was a child . . ." "The Lapps are nomads of the North." "The diameter of a circle is the distance through it at its widest point."

Sometimes you give orders: "Let's settle down now." "Take out your books." "Do the exercise at the top of page 97." "Draw a picture showing what you like to do best."

Sometimes you make comments: "Things in this classroom are not going as they should." "That is the correct answer." "What a beautifully drawn picture!"

And you ask questions: "Where is Gabon?" "What do you think would happen if the sun failed to come up one morning?" "Who remembered to bring their trip permission slips back this morning?"

Whenever we discuss classroom questioning, we talk about what you do with words to facilitate learning. Questions are just a part of it.

When you teach, you have to talk for two good reasons. One reason is that you are the responsible leader in the classroom. You have to keep things going and under control. The other reason is that you have to transfer points of learning from your head and other sources into the learners' heads. The problem is that often the points are more important to you than they are to the learners. If you do not use words well, the points may not be transferred.

The bulk of this discussion will be centered on the ways to use words to help learners learn.

Most of us admit a kinship with actors and actresses. Sometimes we misinterpret the kinship to the point of regarding the classroom as *our* stage and the learners as *our* audience. A better way of interpreting the kinship is to regard the

classroom as a stage shared by you and the learners. All of you together produce cooperative dramas. What about the audience? All of you are that, too, to celebrate over the "raves" and to agonize over the "flops."

You have some important roles. You are the stage manager, the director, sometimes the star, and always the playwright collaborator. Let us look into these roles in some detail.

SETTING THE STAGE

You know much about setting the stage already. We shall just review a point or two.

The stage has to be set to accommodate everyone's sociopsychological needs. This means that you have to get along with your learners, they have to get along with you, and they have to get along with each other. Without this setting, no dramas can occur. There may be some great monologues, speeches, harangues, and exhibitions of violence, but no dramas.

The stage also has to be set to accommodate communication among the cast. They cannot communicate well if the properties are arranged in such a way that they must peek around backs and heads to see and speak to each other. Chairs arranged in circles and open U's will encourage communication, but not always if the same people face each other during each production. Periodically you will need to arrange different positions for the members of the cast.

From time to time you will want the stage set in such a way that the learners have the stellar roles. This means that they will lead and conduct their own "buzzing," "brainstorming," and small group discussions. Arrangements of small circles of chairs or cafe settings with tables and chairs will enhance communication.

Of course, you don't have to move all the furniture yourself. Learners like to be stagehands.

BEING AN EFFECTIVE DIRECTOR

The main job of the director is to help the actors make the most of their roles. You have to be sure they know when they are on stage and in their role. You will have to establish a cue system and develop effective ways of responding to their interpretations.

On stage!

Learners have to know when they are on stage. The traditional way is to call on them when they raise their hands. This system is bearable when the learners raise their hands quietly, hold them steadily aloft until someone is called on, and then drop them. We can thank unsung kindergarten teachers who work hard to teach them to do this.

For some of us, hand raising does not work very well. When we ask a question, we are met by such a flutter of hands, panting, and sputtering of our name, that we must quickly choose someone before all become airborne. After the unchosen drop hands and groan, the respondent answers.

Some of us can live with this. Others try to find another way. Here are some of the practices they try:

1. Instead of raising their hands, the learners sit very still and make fixed eye contact with the teacher. This works very well except with some young learners. So anxious are they to give the answer that they noisily assume what appears to be a catatonic trance. We know that it is not a trance because they are constantly emitting grunts because of energy exerted in maintaining their unusual, uncomfortable position.

2. Instead of raising their hands, the learners sit very still and lift their thumbs. This works well with most learners in grade four and below.

3. The teacher presents the issue to the learners. He or she simply remarks that hand raising just does not appear to work very well and then asks for their ideas. To reduce the hand waving, the learners are formed into small impromptu groups to develop suggestions. After discussion, each group reports what they recommend. Suggestions are listed on the chalkboard. Students vote on those they think most workable. Again in groups, they discuss the feasibility of those they selected. With a minimum of hand raising, they decide on the new cue system. They are invited to monitor its use.

This third practice is workable, but it also suggests two other possibilities. The first is that when you have a problem in classroom administration, you can use cooperative drama to find a solution, that is, you can invite the learners to join in decision making. The second possibility is to avoid asking batteries of questions having short answers and to replace them with cue systems. You need only provide forewarning. Here are a few examples:

"When you finish listening to the tape, I am going to give each of you a slip of paper containing a true-false statement. Then you will read the statement, tell whether it is true or false, and see whether the rest of the group agrees with you."

"As soon as all of you have finished reading the chapter, I am going to ask each of you to tell the most important fact you learned."

"You have been formed into groups of three to view the film. As soon as the film is over, you are to discuss among yourselves to decide the three most important facts you saw in the film and arrange them in order of importance. Decide who among you is to report the ideas. Then I'll ask the reporter in each group to tell what was decided."

Directions such as these inform the learners about what to expect. All students know the requirements. All know they will have a turn to respond. When that moment arrives, you have only to ask for responses. No hand raising is necessary. Of course, if you start by asking, "Who would like to be first?" or "Who is ready?" you're back where you started.

If you are addicted to having learners raise their hands, but would like to make it more bearable for yourself, here is something to try: When a cluster of hands rises, say, "I am going to ask John to answer, but I want the rest of you to listen carefully. When he finishes giving the answer, I'll ask each of you who raised a hand whether you agree with his answer." Such a practice helps learners become responsible hand raisers. To raise a hand means to make a commitment and follow through on it.

"OK!" "Well, . . ."

When the learners have the go-ahead to speak, they are center stage. They are about to give a performance. They are in a vulnerable position. Theirs may be success to enjoy or failure to suffer; they are rarely sure which it will be. We must support them when they falter, catch them when they fall, and reward them when they succeed. Let us consider reward first.

Some of us get so caught up in the excitement of hurling questions and hearing correct answers

that we forget about the learners. Our accepting nod, our barked "OK," our quick blink of the eye, or our immediate utterance of another question will be sufficient reward for those learners who find the whole business just as exciting as we do. But not all our learners are like that. Some will not volunteer unless they are very sure their response is correct, and when they do, we must let them know that their participation is worthwhile. We let them know that the limelight is really shining on them when we say things like the following:

"Thank you, Joe. An important fact."

"Thelma, you stated that well. Thank you."

"I knew you knew the answer, Jim. We can always rely on you."

"Very good, Betsy. You always seem to come through on the hard ones."

Spoken sincerely and punctuated with a smile, these help hesitant learners build confidence.

And, finally, there are those learners who are so painfully shy or who just cannot mention facts and ideas quickly. Once in a while, driven by a force that makes them want to belong and to be a part of things, they volunteer and answer. When this happens, you may be so relieved and at the same time so heartened that you will want to gush sweet phrases in celebration. Gush if you must, but if you can, try to say something like this:

"We needed your answer, Pennie. Thank you."

"Bob, your answer helps us. Thanks."

"Good, Elsie, we appreciate your help."

"A good answer, Dave, and in a moment you will see how important it is to all of us."

And then, as soon as you can after the question-and-answer period, contact the learners to tell them how much you appreciated having them participate. A slowly widening grin and a face glowing with self-satisfaction is the reward you get for taking the time to bestow eagerly desired and needed recognition.

Now to the other side of the coin. Let us consider what we can do when students are on the brink of failure. They give answers that are *not what we expected*. If you can regard learners' responses as being either *what you expect* or *not what you expect*, instead of *right* or *wrong*, you have an attitude that will help you maintain interest in responding. We can use an old standard question to illustrate what you might do:

Teacher: Who discovered America? Dan?
Dan: Leif Ericson.
Teacher: Well, Dan, some people think Leif Ericson did. But do you remember what we learned about what kind of people the Norsemen were?
Dan: They really liked to fight.
Teacher: True. Do you suppose that they went back to Europe and told the English, the French, the Spanish, and the Dutch all about their discovery?
Dan: Not if they fought everybody.
Teacher: That is true. Now can you remember who then discovered America and after whose voyages the Spanish, the English, and the Dutch came to explore the newly found land?
Dan: Sure, it was Columbus.

This is what the teacher did: First, he indicated what part of the learner's answer was correct; second, he helped him to surface more information; third, he asked his question in a more precise way. Maybe that was the way he should have asked the question in the first place. At any rate, the learner's willingness to respond remained undiminished, although he would have preferred having the correct answer in his first response. Let us consider another possibility:

Teacher: Who discovered America? Anne?
Anne: George Washington?
Teacher: He was an American leader whom we shall be studying about before the year is out. We are thinking about someone who lived much earlier. He was trying to find a new route to Asia, but he discovered something along the way.
Anne: That was Columbus.

In this case, the teacher first told the learner the question that she had answered and then gave a few more clues to the desired answer. The first action is more important, because it told the learner what she did know.

Here is a different example:

Teacher: Who discovered America? Steve?
Steve: Ponce de Leon.
Teacher: I noticed that you were viewing a filmstrip about him yesterday. Did you like it?
Steve: Sure. Ponce de Leon had the funny idea that he would find a fountain of youth in America. He really needed it because he was old. If he could find it, he would drink from it or take a bath in its water and become young again.

Teacher: That is interesting. Have any of the rest of you learned more about Ponce de Leon? Yes, Alec?

What happened to Columbus? Let's just say the teacher thinks Steve is more important than Columbus. Steve, you see, is one of those learners who rarely participates in discussions or question-and-answer sessions. This is the first time he has volunteered to answer any question. Therefore it is more important for him to be able to share something he knows than it is for the whole class to discuss the exploits of Columbus.

There is another situation that is irksome to most teachers:

Teacher: Who discovered America? Eric?
Eric: Ulp! I just forgot.
Teacher: We were talking about who discovered America.
Eric: Oh! That was Columbus.

The irksome part is that the learner wants to give an answer, but when he is given the opportunity, he says he forgot. He is often left to stew in his own embarrassment. But there is something fair about what this teacher did. She merely asked the question again. As you can see, there is usually something salvageable from a learner's response. For the learner's sake, it is worth salvaging.

To ensure that learners' responses are satisfactory to themselves as well as to you and to ensure that the entire drama is played to its hoped-for end, you will have to give some special kinds of direction. We shall listen to a question-and-answer session and comment on what the teacher does as we go along.

This is the scene: The learners are a few days into the study of Balinese culture as a basis for future comparisons with other cultures to discover their diversity. They know where Bali is, that it is a part of Indonesia, that the people live mostly in agricultural villages where the main crop is rice, and that the people have certain physical characteristics and dress in a particular way. Today's lesson focuses on the people's religious practices. The learners have just finished reading a chapter in their textbooks. They are somewhat edgy because this is the last day of school before spring vacation. The discussion is not likely to move along smoothly.

Teacher: I am sure you found this chapter to be fascinating reading. What do you think was the most interesting fact you discovered? Alma?

Alma: That tooth filing! It makes my teeth ache just to think about it. And without any of that stuff to kill the pain!

Teacher: You mean novocaine?

Alma: Yes, without novocaine.

The teacher has just supplied a word that the learner could not remember. The rest of the learners will probably use this word again as they talk about the tooth filing ceremony. The use of the word will sharpen the discussion.

Teacher: Yes, Carl?

Carl: What is novocaine made from? Is it made from opium?

Teacher: No, it's made from cocaine, a drug manufactured from dried coca leaves. But let's get back to the Balinese people.

At this point the teacher gave a definition of a word. If she had not known it, she might have suggested that Carl find out for himself. Then she brought the discussion back to the point.

Teacher: Bob?

Bob: That tooth filing ceremony seems pretty important. The people believe that if they have pointed teeth, the spirits will think they are devils, and they won't come back to the village any more.

Teacher: Yes, Dave?

Dave: I guess old Denny must be a devil. He has pointed teeth.

Denny: My teeth are no more pointed than yours!

Dave: Oh, yes they are. I'll bet you could use them to . . .

Teacher: Enough of that! Personal remarks like that have no place here, Dave. You know that. Now back to the Balinese.

The teacher had to stop an argument. Allowed to continue, it could end in a disruptive spectacle.

Teacher: Bob told us that if a person did not have his teeth filed, people would think he was a devil. That is right. But is it true that if they looked like devils, they would scare the spirits away?

Bob: I'm sure of that.

Teacher: Elsa?

Elsa: I don't agree with Bob. I think that if a person looks like the devil, she won't be able to get into heaven.

Bob: It's nothing like that.

Teacher: Let's look in the book again to make sure.

Here the teacher has served as an arbiter. She could have sided with either learner, but she decided to arbitrate by having them consult their resource again. Elsa's answer was correct.

Teacher: Now, about this tooth filing. Did anyone notice when it occurs during a person's life? Ed?

Ed: It's when they are young. Maybe somewhere close to our age.

Teacher: True. Was there any reason given for that? Ellen?

Ellen: Because it shows that a person is grown up enough to marry. They marry earlier in Bali than we do.

Teacher: That's right. Do we have any special ceremonies that show us that we are growing up? Bob?

Bob: We are confirmed at our church. That means that we can be full members of the church and that we know what our religion is about.

Teacher: That's a good example. It happens in many churches, but not all. Can anyone think of another example? Dave?

Dave: Well, it's not connected with any church, but I think most of us think that getting a driver's license is pretty important.

Teacher: Another good example. Are all of you looking forward to getting a driver's license?

Chorus: You bet! I can hardly wait! Wow!

Teacher: I think that's probably the way Balinese boys and girls feel about getting their teeth filed.

The teacher asked for examples. This was a good way to help the learners understand how a particular ceremony affected the lives of people. The teacher continues.

Teacher: Although it is a religious ceremony, it is also quite expensive for the family. What if a person's family just could not afford it? What difference would that make in the person's life? Jane?

Jane: It would be terrible. She would not be able to go to heaven, and maybe no one would want to marry her or have anything to do with her because they thought she was a devil.

To guide the learners more deeply into meaning, the teacher has asked them to consider an implication. She goes on.

Teacher: So far, then, we can see that the tooth-filing ceremony has an effect on a person's religious life as well as on life as a person in the community. Did you discover any other interesting facts about Balinese religious life?

At this point the teacher makes a summary of what has been established so far. She could have asked a learner to do it, but to save time she has done it herself. You will often find yourself in a similar position.

How well you can make selective responses to your learners and monitor a question-and-answer session will determine your effectiveness as a director. Being an effective director will often determine what happens to your questions.

WHEN TO STAR

Earlier it was stated that you could sometimes be the star. After all, with such important jobs as being the stage manager and the director, it seems too much for you to be the star, too—the person whose name is put up in lights on the marquee and printed in large letters in the theatrical advertisement. You could be accused of hogging the whole show for yourself. But there are times when it is the best thing ever to happen.

These times occur when there is no one better qualified than you to fill the role. Let's suppose you are an avid backpacker. What do your learners know about it? No more, perhaps, than they see on television. And in all likelihood they are not going to come clamoring to you to tell them all about it or to show them how to do it. What is more, it is not listed anywhere in the curriculum. But there is a place for your expertise as a backpacker.

Your learners know you within a particular frame —the four walls of your classroom, a voice that goes all the time, a creature who always has a cloud of chalk dust over its head. If you are strict or kind or whatever, that is the way teachers are supposed to be. But you are a unique person. Your learners need to see that, too.

So take all that gear to school with you one day. Display it all over the place—your packboard, your boots, your sleeping bag, the kinds of food you take with you, and all the rest of it. Then be a star! Tell the learners all about it. See how much of the stuff they can identify, and tell them about all the rest. Spin a yarn or two about weathering a mountain storm or spraining an ankle. Then encourage them to ask questions about your delightful avocation. They will see you as a very special, different person.

Not all of us are backpackers, sky divers, skiers, or bullfighters, but all of us have something we especially like to do. It may be writing poetry, photographing, painting, needlepoint, rug braiding, or macramé. When our learners see us immersed in it, they see something they have never seen before.

Sometimes being the star in this way brings unexpected returns. Some learners may want to know much more. Sometimes a reticent learner has a similar interest, discovering in you a kindred spirit with whom to relate. School becomes a better place.

In a way you always have a special stellar role. Even when playing a bit part, you give a memorable performance while maintaining personal integrity and giving support to the younger players.

BEING THE COLLABORATING PLAYWRIGHT

Being a collaborating playwright is a heavy responsibility. You have to select the themes and plots (the specific elements to be learned) to develop with your younger collaborators. Most of the play is collaborative product. But there is one part you must develop yourself. That is the prologue.

Creating an effective prologue

Shakespeare wrote incisive prologues that readied us for the dramas that ensued. Teachers need them but don't write them. They cultivate them through what they say and do at the beginning of classes and lessons.

If you are teaching a subject to several different classes of learners each day, an effective prologue is a few pleasant expressions. If you have to go from classroom to classroom or area to area, try to be there before most of the learners arrive. Try to catch each person's eye as he or she arrives and acknowledge his or her presence with a smile and a nod of the head. Perhaps a quickly mouthed "Hi!" and a hand gesture of greeting will be appropriate. This will not be hard to do because the first place learners look on entering an instructional area is at the teacher's station. Your being there and your acknowledgment of their presence help them remember where they are and what they should be doing.

When all are there and seated, say something pleasant, like one of the following:

"Good morning, class. It's nice to see you again."
"I could see by the way you came in today that we are going to be able to do a lot today."
"Things went so well yesterday that I could hardly wait to see you again today."
"From the way you look, I would say that things are going well with you today."

Perhaps you would like to start a brief conversation:

"Today is such a beautiful day. What do you like to do on a day like this?"
"What do you think about last night's game?"

"Right now I'd like to be at the seashore. Where would you like to be?"
"Did anyone watch the news last night? Did you hear that report about the new park at the other end of town? What do you think about that?"

If you don't understand the reason for prologues similar to these, just compare them with the following teachers' prologues:

A steely-eyed glare. Nothing said.
Staring intently out of the window or leafing through a book. Nothing said.
Hustling and bustling about trying to gather materials left from the last class and getting others ready to use in this class. Nothing said.
"Hey, you birds, where do you think you are? At a party?"

You can see that a prologue couched in positive terms can make a difference in how learners feel about what is going to follow. This same positive spirit fits elementary teaching, where teacher and learners remain together during the day. That situation restricts the prologues we can use with learners. Of course, when they arrive in the morning, we can give them the same pleasant greeting and friendly comments. At other times during the day, we might make comments like these:

"You did so well in coming to reading circle today."
"It's really nice to work with people who can change from one place to another so quickly and quietly."
"Today you came over here so nicely that not one other person was disturbed. I really appreciate that."
"It is not always easy to move around our crowded classroom, but you did it beautifully."

If the learners do not change their stations for a new lesson, you might say:

"Let's take out our math books now." (Pause.) "If I hadn't been watching you, I would not have known that you had taken them out."
"Clear your desks now. And everyone is ready. So many sparkling eyes looking at me!"
"Everyone will need a sharpened pencil and a sheet of lined paper. Very good!"
"It is time for social studies. You did very well in getting ready. You're getting better and better at it."

And, then, in most cases, each of us cultivates a mannerism that signals the beginning of a lesson. Some teachers walk to the chalkboard and pick up a piece of chalk, open the textbook to the correct page, dab at their nose with a tissue, or pull an earlobe. Sometimes they clear their throats noisily. Usually this is followed by a little introductory statement, for example, the following:

"Now let's see. It is fractions today."
"And now something more about noun phrases."
"Yesterday we saw how ancient Rome reached its zenith of power. Today we shall see how that power began to disintegrate."
"Today we are going to learn something about the traffic problems in a large city."

As you can see, the prologue turns the learners' heads gently toward the lesson. It seems such a small thing, but a lesson begun with a fumbling prologue or none at all is the nail falling from the horseshoe before the battle ever starts.

• • •

The drama that you develop with your students usually has three acts. The structure and purpose of each act differ from regular dramas. Here is a brief outline of them:

Act I: The lesson opener dealing primarily with knowledge background
Act II: The dynamic part of the lesson in which new knowledge is discovered
Act III: The lesson end in which the point of the lesson is made

You can only compose a part of each act. That part consists of the questions you develop. The other part of the act is composed by the learners as they respond to your questions.

Creating the first act

The first act begins to germinate in your mind as you consider the point of the lesson. This is expressed in the target objective. It is *the concept to be extended by the lesson,* such as free enterprise, family, tribe, community, government, Asia, Oklahoma, triangle, diameter, major key, the body block, or whatever, *and the definition of how far it will be extended.* Only the concept is important to the first act. We use it to compose questions we want to ask. To show you how this works, here are some target objectives, after each of which is given a list of questions that we might ask to open the first lesson:

Target objective: The learners will be able to draw three artifacts used by the Cheyenne Indians in their everyday life on the plains.

a. What do you know about the Cheyenne Indians?
b. What did we learn about the Cheyenne Indians yesterday?
c. Imagine that a Cheyenne Indian of the covered wagon days stepped right now into this classroom. What do you think he or she would look like?
d. Who are the Cheyenne Indians?
e. Have any of you ever seen the Plains Indians as they were during covered wagon days in movies or on television? Tell us what you saw.

Target objective: The learners will be able to write a paragraph identifying the main character, the problem, and the solution to the problem in the story "Tom Sawyer Whitewashes the Fence."

a. What do you know about the people, or characters, in stories?
b. What did we learn about the main character yesterday?
c. Imagine you are developing a main character for a story. What kinds of traits will you give that person?
d. Who is the main character in a story?
e. Were you ever a main character in a play? Tell us what it was like.

Target objective: The learners will be able to write all the determiners they can find in a given paragraph and divide them into three groups: definite, indefinite, and number.

a. What do you know about words like these: the, a, some, one, this, and four?
b. What did we learn about determiners yesterday?
c. Imagine that our language contained only nouns, pronouns, adjectives, and adverbs. How do you suppose we would make sentences? What would they sound like?
d. What are determiners?
e. Have you ever seen a talking robot on television or in the movies? Tell us how it talked (presumably, without determiners).

Target objective: The learners will be able to compute the areas of five triangles having different dimensions.

a. What do you know about triangles?
b. What did we learn about triangles yesterday?
c. Imagine that the lots for peoples' houses were all shaped like triangles. Do you think that a street would look different? In what way?
d. What are triangles?
e. How many different kinds of triangles have you seen? Show us what they were like.

Each of the target objectives is followed by five different questions. As you go back over the questions, you will probably note that they are listed in the same order. By quickly classifying them, we can develop an acronym to help you remember what they are:

P = Preassessment question, which invites learners to tell what they know about the concept involved in the lesson

R = Review question, which encourages the learners to recall what they had learned during a previous lesson

I = Imagination question, which prompts learners to seek in their backgrounds for possible pertinent facts

D = Definition question, which has learners probing in their background to try to tell what something is

E = Experience question, which has learners trying to determine some contact with the concept

PRIDE helps you to remember the possibilities for the kinds of questions you can ask to prompt learners to retrieve facts about a concept. As learners respond to any of these questions, they establish concepts that will be extended in the rest of the lesson.

When writing act I, or developing the questions to ask during the act, follow this simple rule: *Use at least one.*

Indiscriminate use of or trying to use too many PRIDE questions can waste learners' time or get them off to a poor start. Here are a few guidelines:

1. The preassessment question is usually a good choice to use in the beginning lesson of a series of lessons.
2. The review question is likely to be the question you use most frequently. Of course, you cannot use it until the students have learned something. Usually you will get better responses to this question when you help your learners recall. Often the product or exercise completed the previous day can be discussed to conduct the review.
3. The imagination question generates a lot of fun, but only when the learners know sufficient facts.
4. The definition question is the toughest question. A good way to have your learner focus on a definition is to give them a list of two or three and have them decide which is best.
5. The experience question stimulates much thought and expression. It is particularly effec-

tive with young learners. However, if your time is limited, use it sparingly.

So much, then, for act I. Your creation may be no more than a single question. But that is enough as you encourage your learners to respond. As they do, they will complete the act.

Creating the second act

Instructional activities help students acquire information, learn and try skills, and explore for values. The questions you develop will guide them into and through activities. Sometimes this act is a humdrum affair, a point-by-point progression. There is little you can do about it. Some learning is that way. In other cases, this act can generate excitement and rapid movement. This will most likely happen as you teach health study, literature, science, and social studies. Let us deal with the humdrum acts first.

We shall focus first on a lesson on computing the areas of triangles. We can use the same target objective offered in the section dealing with creating the first act.

The first thing you will have to do is decide what instructional materials you are going to use. These may include pages in textbooks, "geoboards" (a special board laid out in squares, with nails, on which you make geometric figures with a rubber band), or something you have devised yourself. Let us suppose that you choose to devise a sheet of paper containing five rectangles of different dimensions. You distribute these sheets to the class. The following demands show how this part of the lesson is to progress:

"What are the geometric shapes shown on your paper?"

"Using your pencil and ruler, draw a line slanted across each shape from corner to corner."

"What do you see on either side of each line you have drawn?"

"What is the area of each geometric shape on your paper?"

"What would be the area, then, of a single triangle within each shape?"

"If the area of each triangle is half the area of each shape, how would we compute it?"

"What would be the area of a triangle with a width of 10 feet and a height of 15 feet?"

"What would be the area of a triangle with a width of 10 feet and a height of 10 feet?"

"What would be the area of a triangle with a width of 16 feet and a height of 7 feet?"

As you can see, our questions guided the learners step by step through the process of discovering how the area of a triangle is computed and then computing some areas.

This is not a very exciting second act, but it is an effective one. Of course, one reason for its humdrum aspect is that the learners' responses are strongly restricted.

Now let us see what can happen in social studies. Let us use the target objective about the Cheyenne Indians. Our learning materials are a filmstrip showing the daily life of the Cheyenne Indians when they lived on the plains and a chart containing pictures of an automobile, a match, a refrigerator, a telephone, and a pair of shoes. Here are the questions we might use:

(Show the chart.) "Which of these things do you think the Cheyenne Indians had when they lived on the plains long ago?"

"What do you think they might have used instead of these things?" (List them on the chalkboard as given.)

"Which of the things in the list are you surest of? Why?"

"Let's view this filmstrip to see how right we are."

As you can see in this example, the learners are much less restricted. Notice how the second question is asked. It has a "thinking" verb in it. The question is "open" because it prompts learners to tell what they think. Just about any response will be accurate in terms of how reasonable it appears to the learner.

The third question prompts more discussion as the learners consider the items in their list, select those items of which they are surest, and give reasons for their choice.

Another teacher wanting learners to meet the same target objective has decided to use the same filmstrip, but does not have the chart. Instead, he has a question sheet containing the following:

1. What did the Cheyenne Indians use for transportation?
2. What did they use for communication over long distances?
3. How did they store food?
4. How did they get fire?
5. How did they get their clothing?

He distributes the question sheet and says, "After you see the filmstrip I want you to write the answers to these questions in complete sentences. Will someone please turn off the lights? Pay close attention to the filmstrip."

If you were a learner, which of these second acts would you prefer? Enough said.

At any rate, we can see that the questions for the second act may guide learners step by step or may open up ideas for discussion.

Sometimes when people are disappointed with the second act of a play they leave the theater before the third act begins. Other people remain in their seats hoping there will be some redemptive qualities shown in the third act.

Creating the third act

The purpose of the third act is to lead the learners to the point of the play. Earlier the point was identified as the concept as well as its extension. In the first act the concept was established, in the second act activities for its extension were provided, and in the third act the point will be made.

Let us again return to the lesson about triangles. Since there is a textbook, the teacher could use questions (or demands) such as the following:

"Do the exercise at the bottom of page 135."
"Let's go over our answers together."

Not a very exciting third act. The learners just do the exercises. Whatever excitement there is occurs when the teacher asks the second question when the exercise is completed. The learners will be discussing their answers and, hopefully, asking questions about anything that gave them difficulty.

Another teacher decides not to use a textbook. His questions are as follows:

"Draw five different triangles with your rulers. Be sure that the width and height are expressed in even inches, no fractions. Then compute the area for each."

"When you are finished, bring your work to me, and we'll go over it together."

In some ways this is more exciting. The learner draws his own triangles and discusses them with the teacher.

Let us now consider the lesson about the Cheyenne Indians. If you remember, two second acts were designed for this lesson. One was dull, the other more exciting. Let's deal with the exciting one first. The learners, aided by a chart, had made some best guesses about items used by the Cheyenne Indians in their daily life. The third act helps them validate their guesses after viewing the filmstrip:

(Indicate the list.) "This is what you thought earlier. What do you think now?"
"Draw three of the things that the Cheyenne Indians used in their everyday life."

The first question generates much discussion as the learners check the list against their findings. The second question brings them to the target objective.

The other second act for this lesson had the teacher handing the learners a set of questions about the Indians. They answered them in complete sentences after viewing the filmstrip. Here is the third act for that lesson:

"Who will read their answer to the first question? Does everyone agree?"
"Who will read their answer to the second question? Does everyone agree with that?"
(Repeat with each question through question 5.)
"Draw three of the things that the Cheyenne Indians used in their everyday life."

There is a redemptive feature in this third act. The learners share their answers and discuss their accuracy.

Apparently the teacher who used this third act found that his learners had moved so expeditiously through their activities that there was a lot of time left before the next class. He added these questions:

"Let's take a look at the pictures you have drawn."
"Let's suppose that the United States government had made and kept a treaty with the Cheyenne Indians to permit them to keep this section of land (the Plains) to live on and use as they wished. Do you think the Cheyennes would be living there in the same way they did more than a hundred years ago? Why do you think so?"

These last two questions have completely redeemed the third act, if not the whole play. Sharing and discussing the pictures generates some good discussion. The second question stimulates a lively discussion.

If the teacher knew about such questions, why didn't he incorporate them in his original third act? That is hard to answer. Perhaps what he has done with this third act is a matter of luck. This teacher could also be a very methodical person who wants to be certain that learners have some hard facts to use during discussion. The last question he asked could have been lifted from tomorrow's lesson. Perhaps he is a timid person who fears grand themes and great questions.

GRAND THEMES AND GREAT QUESTIONS

Aside from certain technicalities in composition, the quality of a great cooperative drama rests on the greatness of the theme it treats. Frequently teachers are just not aware of these themes. For this reason they are forever bound within the dull confines of dull dramas.

As mentioned, dramas consisting only of factual questions are colorless. This is not to say that factual questions are worthless; at times they are vital. Students from kindergarten through grade five need to have the facts before them or fresh in their minds before they can use them for productive thought. This helps with older learners, too. Factual questions should be followed with *questions of higher order*, which are questions that prompt thinking. *Recalling* or finding facts is a low order of thinking, but the questions we use to elicit the facts from recall can make a difference. For example, the question "What facts can you remember about the different things the Cheyenne Indians used in their daily life?" requires more thinking than the following:

1. What did the Cheyenne Indians use for transportation?
2. What did they use for communication over long distances?
3. How did they store food?
4. How did they get fire?
5. How did they get their clothing?

If our intent had been just to have the learners recall the facts, our target objective could have been either of the following:

Target objective 1: The learners will be able to pass a ten-item multiple choice written test about the items that the Cheyenne Indians use in their daily life.
Target objective 2: The learners will be able to write a paragraph telling what the Cheyenne Indians used for transportation, communication, acquiring fire, and obtaining food and clothing.

When we express the target objective, we also indicate the greatness of our theme.

Somewhat higher than the recall question in the order of questions is the *shift-of-medium* question. It requires the respondent to express the facts just experienced in his own medium—his own words, his own drawing, his own model, his own diagram, etc. The kind of product demanded can make a difference:

"Draw a picture of three things used by the Cheyenne Indians in their daily life."

or

"Draw a picture showing a Cheyenne family going about its daily life."

A response to the second question requires more thinking as well as better developed drawing skills. Our target objective might have been expressed in this way:

Target objective: The learners will be able to draw a picture showing a Cheyenne family going about its daily life.

At the next higher level in the order of thinking, we find the *comprehension* question. It prompts the learner to develop meaning from a set of facts. It is a form of inductive thinking; an example would be "How did the Cheyenne Indians use their immediate environment to obtain what they needed for everyday life?" The learners would most likely respond by saying, "The Cheyennes used the animals in their natural environment, particularly the buffalo and the horse, to obtain what they needed." A more difficult comprehension question, in which the learners respond with their own generalization, may be, "Considering all the facts we know, what can we say about how the Cheyenne Indians obtained what they needed for daily life?"

With young learners in grade five and below, we might want to use a question in which they choose the correct response, such as "Would you say that the Cheyenne Indians got most of what they needed by trading things they made with other people or by making use of what they found around them?"

Planning to use either of the first two questions, our target objective might be expressed in this way:

Target objective: The learners will be able to write (decide in a group discussion) a statement about how the Cheyennes used their natural environment to obtain what they needed to live.

And for the last question:

Target objective: The learners will be able to select and write (recite) a statement about how the Cheyennes used their natural environment to obtain what they needed to live.

Yet higher in the order of questions are the *generalization-centered* questions. These questions prompt comparison, validation, drawing implications, or giving examples. Here is a list of target objectives about the Cheyenne Indians and an example of the kind of questions we would ask to prompt the learners to do these kinds of thinking activities:

Target objective: The learners will be able to make a chart showing the similarities and differences between the ways the Cheyenne Indians used to live and the ways they live now.

Generalization question: "Make a chart showing the differences between the ways the Cheyennes used to live and the ways they live now."

Objective: The learners will be able to write a set of notes giving proof that the Cheyennes depended largely on their natural environment for what they needed.

Generalization question: "As you read this selection, write notes on the facts you find that show that the Cheyennes depended largely on their natural environment for what they needed."

Objective: The learners will be able to discuss what might have happened to the Cheyenne way of life if they had been permitted to keep and use land.

Generalization question: "Let's suppose that the United States government had made and kept a treaty with the Cheyenne Indians to permit them to keep land to live on and use as they wished. Do you think the Cheyennes would be living there in the same way they did more than a hundred years ago? Why do you think so?"

Objective: In a class discussion, the learners will be able to give examples of the ways that people might follow today to make as good a use of their natural environment as the Cheyennes did.

Generalization question: "If we used the ways of the Cheyennes as a model today, how might we make better use of our natural environment? Give some examples."

Generalization-centered questions, besides being suitable for use in target objectives, also serve well as impromptu questions asked when the learners appear to need more proof. They often take beginning forms similar to the following:

"Is ___ the same or different from ___ ?"

"Let's look in some sources to find out whether . . ."

"Let's try that experiment again to see . . ."

"What would happen if . . . ?"

"What do you think would happen if . . . ?"

"Can you give an example . . . ?"

The next questions in the hierarchy of thinking are the *analysis* questions, which prompt learners to classify. These questions usually occur in the following predictable order:

"Name all the different kinds of things you think the Cheyenne Indians used in their daily lives 200 years ago."

"Separate all the things you have named into groups."

"Looking at all this information, how would you describe the Cheyennes' way of living 200 years ago?"

The target objective for such a series of questions might be as follows:

Target objective: The learners will be able to express what they think were the different ways of living of the Cheyennes 200 years ago, group and label the different ways, and generalize from their information.

Here is another model:

"What is the hard thing to explain about this situation?"

"What do you think would be a good explanation of it?"

"Which of your explanations do you think is best? Why?"

"What will we have to know before we can decide whether your explanation is best?"

Usually these four questions are about all that can be answered within an instructional period. Here is the target objective that would be used:

Target objective: The learners will be able to define a problem, hypothesize several solutions, choose the most reasonable solution, and decide what questions will have to be answered to prove the solution is best.

After the questions have been answered, the series of questions takes up again:

"What did you find out?"

"Judging your originally chosen solution against your information, do you think it is a good solution? Why?"

You may stimulate the use of analysis questions by asking questions like these at the beginning of the second act:

"Two hundred years ago the Cheyenne Indians were a proud, strong people living on the Great Plains. They were able to take care of their every daily need. Today they are a small number of people living on reservations. Many must depend on the government for the things they need. What is the difficult thing to explain here?"

or

"Two hundred years ago a Cheyenne Indian man would own a string of horses, his weapons, and his clothes. Today a Cheyenne Indian might own a truck and an automobile, a house, and a farm as well as the tools to work it. But such a Cheyenne may complain and say that life for the Cheyenne Indian is not as good as it used to be. What is the difficult thing to understand about what he says?"

You can see that the analysis questions are most frequently used in health study, science, and social studies.

As we near the top of the question hierarchy we find *application* questions, which invite learners to look for and solve problems. Both in the seeking and the solving, they apply information and skills already learned. Here is a target objective about the Cheyenne Indians and some examples of questions the teacher might ask:

Target objective: The learners will explore for alternative solutions to the problems of the Cheyenne Indians today.

Application questions: "What are some of the problems you think the Cheyenne Indians have today? How do you think they might solve them?"

"What do you think is the Cheyenne Indians' greatest problem today? How do you think they might solve it?"

"Suppose you are a Cheyenne person of your own age trying to decide about a future occupation. What problems do you think you might have? How might you solve them?"

"An old Cheyenne man is trying to advise his favorite grandson about what he should do with his life. The young Cheyenne wants to leave the reservation to become a doctor. The old man wants him to stay on the reservation to help run the farm. How do you think the old man might feel? What do you think he might say? How might the young man feel? What might he say?"

At this point we may also consider briefly the kinds of problems that learners might solve using their knowledge about the area of triangles. A question prompting them to apply their knowledge would take a form similar to the following:

"Bob, Bill, and Joe have just finished building their sailboats. They are now ready to make the sails for each of the three boats. The sails are right triangles 6 feet wide and 8 feet tall. The sail cloth is 6 feet wide. How much will they need to buy to make sails for all three boats?"

Often a practical problem works well:

"You have decided that you want to make school pennants to sell at the next game. If you want to make 100 pennants, each an isosceles triangle 9 by 24 inches, how many yards of felt 36 inches wide will you have to buy?"

Perhaps the most stimulating question we can ask is the *synthesis* question. It prompts learners to create. As far as we are concerned, the only deterrent to the kind of question we ask is our learners' level of skills. We specify a kind of product or performance in the target objective, as follows:

Target objective: The learners will be able to write an original story about a Cheyenne family that decides to move to Chicago.

And the prompting question (or demand) is as follows:

"Write a story about a Cheyenne family that moves to Chicago to seek a better life."

There is scarcely a study area in the curriculum that cannot be used to stimulate creativity, as shown in the following questions:

"Invent a form of handwriting that you think would be suitable for use on formal invitations."
"Develop an original system of spelling to simplify English spelling."
"Using triangles of all shapes and sizes, design a wall frieze."
"Using noun phrases and one kernel sentence, write a poem about a spring day in the country."
"Develop a set of rules that you think an absolute monarch could follow to maintain his throne."
"Invent a new game for two teams of three people. It may involve the use of a ball. It should provide a lot of exercise."
"Invent a new language that makes no use of tense."

And finally we reach the pinnacle of questioning: the *evaluation* question. This prompts learners to make judgments about what one should do or feel. The target objective does not specify any alternative as being the best. Here is an example:

Target objective: The learners will make judgments about the most suitable ways they can show respect for the Cheyenne Indians today.

And here is a way to ask an evaluation question:

"The Cheyenne Indians, like other American Indian tribes, sometimes feel they are not respected in this country. What do you think we might do to make them feel respected? Why do you think we should do that?"

Because the response to the evaluation question requires that a criterion be given for a suggested alternative, the follow-up "why?" is required.

Often the evaluation question is used to develop appropriate choices in literature, art, and music, as follows:

"Of all the stories we have read this week, which do you think is the best? Why do you think so?"
"Of the two songs that we have just learned, which do you think is the better song? Why do you think that is the better song?"
"Degas, Renoir, Gauguin, Manet, Van Gogh, and Monet are all impressionists. Which of these do you think best represents the spirit of impressionism? Why do you say _____ ?"

Sometimes a strong statement of opinion prompts an evaluation question:

"This cartoonist believes the courts should protect the rights of a journalist to keep his sources secret. Do you agree with the cartoonist? Why (or why not)?"
"This editor believes the death penalty should be instituted in every state for every crime in which a person is killed or threatened with death. Do you have the same opinion as the editor? Why do you take that stand?"
"That commercial suggests you will be more beautiful and popular if you use that shampoo. Do you think you ought to go out and buy some? Why (or why not)?"

As you can see, the grand theme offers many opportunities for great questions. A question is great to the extent that it prompts discussion, or thought, or both. Evaluation, the grandest of all, is the epilogue of the best of cooperative dramas. It leaves learners with something to think about for a long time.

•   •   •

After this discussion about questions, you probably have a big question to ask, "Do I have to compose all the questions that I am going to ask?" No, you don't have to. As a matter of fact, neither you nor anyone else can compose all the questions you need to ask. You compose only those that you know you will need to guide your lesson from the prologue through the final act. That is one reason we used the term *"cooperative drama"* throughout this chapter. You have to allow opportunities for the learners to compose the rest of the drama. How successful you are with cooperative dramas will depend on your skills as the director.

Perhaps you have also made a discovery about something you would like to try when you teach. That is to develop your lesson plans in the form of questions. That's not a bad idea. Many teachers do it that way.

SUMMARY

Classroom questioning refers to the ways teachers use words in the classroom to guide learners as they learn. Statements, demands, comments, and questions are included.

Developing classroom questions and providing for their responses is the teacher's part in composing the cooperative dramas that facilitate learning.

As the stage manager, the teacher ensures that the instructional setting accommodates the sociopsychological and communication needs of the learners.

As the director, the teacher helps the learners to get the most they can from being respondents. This includes developing a signal system for the learners to use when they wish to make a response and giving them support when they make responses.

The teacher's role as a star is appropriate when he or she has a special skill or interest to share with learners.

As the senior playwright, the teacher composes the questions necessary to bring the learners to an instructional objective. The first task is to create a prologue that makes the learners feel favorable toward themselves and the teacher in the learning situation. The first act guides the learners in establishing a concept basic to the main part of the lesson. They establish it through exploring within their own background. The second act provides for learners to acquire information, to learn and try skills, or to explore for values. In some study areas, such as phonics, vocabulary recognition, grammar, and mathematics facts and basic operations, the second act is often a humdrum affair. In such study areas as literature, health study, science, and social studies, the second act may be more dynamic. The third act brings the learners to the point of the lesson.

The greater the theme or order of thinking possible in a lesson, the greater the depth and breadth of the questions that can be asked. The themes include recall; shift of medium; comprehension; generalization, involving validation, implication, comparison, and examples; analysis, application, synthesis (creating), and evaluation.

SUGGESTED ACTIVITIES FOR FURTHER UNDERSTANDING

1. Describe the purpose of questions, demands, and comments in each part of the cooperative drama.
2. Describe the roles of the teacher as a stage manager, director, star, and collaborating playwright in cooperative drama.
3. If, as a learner, you were allowed to choose your own teacher, which of the teacher's roles related to cooperative drama would you consider most important? Why? Share and discuss what you think with a classmate.
4. You have a friend who is a teacher. You have visited his classroom, and you were surprised to learn that this witty, intelligent man was very terse and businesslike toward his students. One day when he was your houseguest he began to complain bitterly, "Those confounded kids! I can never get started on time because they come straggling in, and when the bell rings at the end of the period, they are instantly gone!" What is your friend's problem? What solution might you suggest to him? This would be a good situation to discuss with your classmates.
5. Design for yourself a card or plaque entitled "Directions for the Director." Develop at least five positive rules you think would help you or any other teacher to be an effective director of cooperative drama. Write or print them on your card or plaque and share the result with some classmates.
6. Admittedly, the cooperative drama between a teacher and an individual learner is restricted in many ways in a classroom in which an individualized curriculum is being followed. What do you think a teacher should do to maintain effective cooperative drama in such a classroom? Why do you think so? Share your responses with a classmate or two.

For practice

7. Arrange to observe in an elementary or secondary classroom. As you observe, note how the teacher follows the roles of stage manager, director, star, and collaborating playwright.
8. Arrange for two observations in an elementary or secondary school. One observation should occur in a classroom when social studies or literature is being taught. The other should occur when mathematics is the subject at hand. Observe the teachers to see how they follow their roles as stage manager, director, star, and collaborating playwright. Compare the performances of the two teachers to see if the subject being taught appears to make a difference in their roles.

9. Choosing a study area or subject at any grade level you wish, select some instructional material(s), and develop the questions and demands you would use during a lesson. Start with the statement of the point of the lesson in a target objective, then provide for a prologue and three acts.

10. Choosing health study, literature, science, or social studies at any grade level you wish, select some instructional materials and develop two sets of questions and demands that you could use to teach a lesson. Develop your first set of questions to restrict your learners' role in cooperative drama and your second set to enlarge the learners' role. The point of each lesson (they may be the same) should be stated in a target objective, and provisions should be made for a prologue and three acts.

For performance

11. In your assigned laboratory or classroom, arrange to teach a lesson in literature, health study, science, or social studies. Using the instructional material available in the classroom, develop the questions and demands you will need to teach the lesson to meet a target objective. If possible, audiotape your performance. Because learners are sometimes puzzled by a teacher's using a tape recorder for personal purposes, inform them that you are using it to see how well you can teach.

12. Do the same as in the preceding activity, but ask a classmate to come observe you. The classmate should observe you to see how you follow your roles as stage manager, director, star, and collaborating playwright. Afterward, discuss your performance with your observer.

REFERENCES

Bany, M. E., and L. V. Johnson. *Educational social psychology*. New York: Macmillan Publishing Co., Inc., 1975.

Beyer, B. K. *Inquiry in the social studies classroom*. Columbus, Ohio: Charles E. Merrill Publishing Co., 1971.

Carin, A. A., and R. B. Sund. *Developing questioning techniques*. Columbus, Ohio: Charles E. Merrill Publishing Co., 1971.

Hennings, D. G. *Mastering classroom communication*. Pacific Palisades, Calif.: Goodyear Publishing Co., Inc., 1975.

Sanders, N. M. *Classroom questions*. New York: Harper & Row, Publishers, 1966.

Servey, R. E. *Teacher talk: the knack of asking questions*. Belmont, Calif.: Fearon Publishers, 1974.

THE MANAGEMENT OF LEARNING

PART FOUR

Odd as it seems, teachers do not live or die by their knowledge, their determination, or their wardrobe. They live or die by their ability to manage student learning and especially to control and guide student behavior in positive ways.

Part IV consists of four chapters that deal with diagnosis and planning, accountability, control and guidance, and communication. Each of these topics has its accompanying objectives and skills. There are specific techniques for diagnosing, for establishing good objectives, for planning lessons and units of work, for assessing and evaluating student behavior, and for shaping it in worthwhile directions. There are specific techniques for talking with students to communicate, encourage, support, and dissuade.

These techniques receive direct attention in the four chapters, the titles of which are as follows:

DIAGNOSING
DISCOVERING WHERE TO BEGIN 15

Diagnosis, prognosis, and prescription are events that have to do with planning instruction. They are closely related. When you speak of one, you speak of the others in some way. Here we will separate them and consider each in its turn. We will concentrate on diagnosis in this chapter. Diagnosis tells us where to begin in teaching. In the next chapter we will turn to prognosis, prescription, and evaluation.

Diagnosis, prognosis, and prescription occur within areas of knowledge. Teachers usually perform them. This means they need to know their

areas of knowledge just as golfers need to know the courses on which they are playing. For this reason we shall quickly review areas of knowledge.

To help you anticipate what the chapter offers, here are a few questions for you to think about. Jot down your responses to the following on a piece of notepaper:

1. In what areas of knowledge do you think an elementary teacher needs to be proficient? How proficient? Why?
2. In what areas of knowledge do you think a high school science or health teacher should be proficient? How proficient? Why?
3. If you were going to diagnose the ability of a third-grade child in spelling, what do you think would be the best way of going about it?
4. If you were an English teacher in a senior high school, what skills would you expect the entering sophomores to have?

Put your notepaper aside. You will review it later to see how much you have gleaned from reading the chapter.

DIAGNOSIS, PROGNOSIS, AND PRESCRIPTION: A PREVIEW

Physicians have long used the terms "diagnosis," "prognosis," and "prescription" to describe basic events in the art of healing. Recently professional educators have begun to use the terms "diagnosis" and "prescription" to describe basic events in the art of teaching.

Diagnosis means determining how much an individual, group, or class of learners knows. This serves as a basis for deciding what needs to be learned or whether there is sufficient background to support further learning. Background may include level of interest as well as extent of knowledge.

Prescription means deciding which learning activities to use. The number, suitability, variety, and sequence of activities are involved in making this decision.

Why haven't professional educators adopted *prognosis* as an event in the art of teaching? It's not because they haven't tried. The *behavioral objective,* a precise statement of what learners should be able to do after receiving instruction, surfaced as an instructional innovation more than a decade ago. It was a prognostic statement.

Unfortunately, more attention was given to how the objective should be stated than to *why* it should be stated. And why? Because the innovators forgot, neglected, or perhaps didn't realize that prognoses rest on diagnoses and prescriptions.

We are past that now. We can now make prognostic statements about what learners will be able to do provided we have made adequate diagnoses and prescriptions. Of course, we have to monitor the prescriptions carefully. Our science is not as exact as that of medicine. And normal learners are not so irked by ignorance as sick people are by misery.

As we try to diagnose, prognose, and prescribe for learning, we must be able to grasp what a study area really is, how it is organized, and how it is related to other study areas. Without this grasp, we cannot understand the purpose of our diagnostic tools and techniques. The results will be meaningless. And prognostication and prescription will be impossible. So let's make a brief exploration of study areas.

AN EXPLORATION OF KNOWLEDGE

One way to make this exploration is to follow the possible development of a concept from the moment it is first perceived or sensed until its growing edge reaches an area of sophisticated values. Our sample concept will be *fan.*

On the left of the page, a description of a level of development will be given. On the right, some implications for diagnosing, prognosticating, and prescribing will be offered.

Perceptual level

We begin with a fan as a perceived object. At the perceptual level we represent the fan as follows:

Description

Implications

At this level the fan is a thing. It is different from the man, woman, bottle, rattle, and teddy bear. Unlike the man and woman, it will not come when you make a noise. Nor can it pick you up, play with you, hug you, feed you, change your clothes, and put you down. But like the bottle, rattle, and teddy bear, it can be picked up and tasted. Like all the other things, it can be seen, heard, and smelled. It exists only when you can directly perceive it through your senses. And so it remains until a symbol for it surfaces from your conscious experience.

This is the foundational level of learning. If your family uses a fan in your presence, you will have a knowledge of many of its attributes. However, if you have never seen a fan in use and knowledge of a fan is essential to further study, the teacher will discover this through diagnosis. You cannot identify a fan or talk about or demonstrate its use. The teacher will prognose for you a knowledge of the attributes of a fan and will prescribe perceptual activities for you.

A similar event may occur if the teacher discovers that you do not know all the attributes essential to further study.

At a later level of development, the teacher will use language as a medium of perception.

First symbol level

The first symbol level occurs when you are able to say the word *fan*. Rather than describe all the oral gymnastics necessary to its intelligible utterance, we shall represent it as /f/a/n/.

Description	Implications
At this level you can assume some control over a fan. You can point to it and say "/F/a/n/!" This may mean that you are showing off what you know. Your performance causes anyone who hears it to smile and make positive, pleasant noises to you. Later they may say, "Yes, it is a fan."	This is the beginning of symbol learning and use. When diagnosing your speech, your teacher may discover that you cannot say /f/a/n/ intelligibly. Maybe you have trouble with /f/'s or /n/'s. The teacher will prognose a correct pronunciation of these sounds. Using a real fan and pictures of a fan, the teacher will say it, and you will try to repeat it over and over again.
But let us suppose you want the fan, and it is out of your reach. You point to it and say, "/F/a/n/." You repeat this until you obtain it or are discouraged from asking for it.	When you learn a foreign language, you may find yourself experiencing similar activities.
Or someone may use /f/a/n/ to control you. "Give me the /f/a/n/," "Put the /f/a/n/ down," "Bring Mamma's /f/a/n/." In the last case, the fan may not be in the immediate vicinity, but you know where it is.	

Second symbol level

At the second symbol level /f/a/n/ becomes a part of the language system. Using this system, people can tell you about fans you have never seen and perhaps may never see, and you can tell others about fans you have seen and used, fans you presently use, and fans you would like to see and use. Your capacity for learning increases immeasurably.

Description	Implications
When /f/a/n/ enters your language system, you will hear and say it in patterns such as these: The /f/a/n/ is new. She has a /f/a/n/. The side of the /f/a/n/ is torn. The /f/a/n/'s handle is broken. The /f/a/n/ stencil is fun to use. I /f/a/n/ myself. It is shaped like a /f/a/n/. The river /f/a/n/ned out across the plain. An electric /f/a/n/ can move air. And you will probably learn that a football /f/a/n/ is not used to cool hot footballs. A beginning for the mathematical system occurs with such expressions as these: You have *more* fans than I. My fan is *smaller* than yours. *One* fan for me and *one* for you.	At this point the teacher's purpose is to ensure that you understand and that you are understood. To diagnose how well you understand, the teacher listens to what you say after hearing something or tests you. If the results are negative, he or she may prescribe perceptual experiences or repeated activities with language patterns. To diagnose how well you make yourself understood, the teacher listens to you. If your patterns are not those generally used in your language, he or she may prescribe repeated activities with language patterns.

Third symbol level

At the third symbol level you learn how symbols operate within their various systems and how the systems are interrelated. The systematic uses of symbols may be defined as *skills*.

Description	Implications

Description

Semantically entered into your language, *fan* now becomes a useful abstraction in language-related systems.

Phonological system. You acquire skill in decoding combinations of visual letters into words. Learning *fan, Fan, FAN* may be generalized into the sound of initial *f,* medial *a,* and terminal *n* to be used in identifying other words as spoken or seen.

Orthographical system. You gain skill in spelling words. You can recognize the letters *f-a-n* in such words as *fang, fancy, fantasy,* etc.

Graphological system. You show skill in making the necessary combinations of curved and straight lines to write *fan* and perhaps to draw a fan.

Grammar system. You acquire skill in identifying and constructing sentences. When combined with the phonological system, it results in your being able to comprehend the sentences you hear or see. When also combined with orthographical and graphological systems, you are able to use it to compose and write sentences. All this, of course, is possible as it relates to *fan.*

Rhetorical system. Your skills include organizing sentences into paragraphs and paragraphs into longer communicative sequences about *fans*. When you can combine this system with the phonological and grammar systems, you can comprehend extended discourse or discussion. You may participate in the discussion. When you also combine this system with the orthographical and graphological systems, you can compose facsimilies of poems, plays, stories, speeches, posters, and advertisements about *fans*.

Mathematical system. You show skill in using number operations in quantitative situations. When you know the mathematical system, you can add, subtract, multiply, and divide fans as well as their parts and compute ratios, percentages, areas, and perimeters of fans with all the dimensions known or some unknown. And, of course, you will be able to compute the costs of buying, selling, building, and operating fans.

Implications

Diagnosis within this level may require the teacher to examine the results of a trial performance* within a system. Prognosis and prescription may be centered at the perceptual level, at any of the earlier levels, or at an operation within a skill sequence.

When diagnosis occurs within combined systems, a trial performance is required. Prognosis and prescription may be centered at the perceptual level, at any of the earlier levels, or at an operation within an identified system.

When teaching within this level, the teacher may guide learning along an analytical path: each symbol and operation is taught in order of complexity.

Alternatively the teacher may teach skills as concepts. The learners see the skill in operation or its result, and then they are guided in learning what they need to do to make it work for them. For example, your teacher may read you a story about a fan to help you see what a story is as a literary concept. Then you may try to write a story to see how well you can mirror the concept. If the story does not mirror the concept, you discuss what might be done to meet this objective. Continued evaluated trials will eventually bring you to the point that you can write a story.

Repetition has a place at this level. This is particularly true with phonological, orthographical, graphological, and grammar systems and learning the number facts in mathematical systems.

Trial performances also have a place. This is particularly true when language-related systems are combined with rhetorical systems and when mathematical systems are used at a simulated utility level.

Each system is characterized by attributes useful in planning as the teacher diagnoses, prognosticates, and prescribes. These attributes include the following:

1. Each may be organized on a simple-to-abstract continuum.
2. Each involves a sequence of easy operations before difficult operations.
3. Effective use of each requires a solid background in symbols.
4. When several are combined, the inadequate use of one may adversely influence the efficient use of the others.

---

*A trial performance occurs when the learner is asked to do something demanding a skill. When he or she tries to perform, the extent of skill will be demonstrated.

Fourth symbol level

At the fourth symbol level you use your previously learned symbol skills to discover generalizations, principles, laws, and criteria of wide application in coping with your personal, social, and physical environment. You learn precision in making statements and become skilled in reasoning.

Description	Implications

Verbal system. Here you discover the criteria to use when you view, listen to, read, compose, or participate in some way in an enterprise involving persuasive messages (such as political speeches, sermons, editorials, or commercials), debates, essays, articles, chapters, stories, novels, plays, and poems as they relate to *fans.*

Nonverbal system. Here you discover the criteria to use when you listen to, play, compose, or sing music; draw, paint, sculpt, or design; read or draw cartoons—all as related to *fans.*

Science system. Here you discover tentative laws, principles, models, and rules of classification in the life sciences (zoology, botany, biology, physiology, etc.), physical sciences (chemistry, geology, physics, etc.), and social sciences (economics, political science, sociology, etc.). All this will have to do with *fans.*

Statistical system. Here you master the reasoning and principles needed to solve problems about relationships and probable interrelationships among matter, time, space, and function as they relate to *fans.* You discover how to predict the average life span of a fan made of certain materials and operated a certain amount of time each day or at what level of confidence a certain fan part will be able to withstand certain operational stresses. Alternatively you may be investigating the effect of fans on controlling the temperature in a hospital room, the amount of air fanned through a particular duct, or the use of a fan to communicate interpersonal messages as seen in some societies.

When the teacher diagnoses for effective use of verbal and nonverbal systems, he or she looks first at the criteria discovered and then for the reasons supporting the criteria. The reasons are more important than the criteria. If the reasoning is not based on logical findings in fact or experience, the teacher diagnoses for efficiency in inquiry procedure. The following points are noted:
1. Was the purpose clearly understood?
2. Was all the pertinent information taken into account?
3. Was the information organized intelligibly?
4. Was the line of reasoning logical?

If 1, 2, or 3 shows an inadequacy, the teacher diagnoses at earlier levels to see whether any of the necessary, pertinent skills are deficient. If the findings show deficiency, diagnosis may have to reach into any or all of the earlier levels. Prescription may begin as low as level 1.

Much the same is true when diagnosing at this level in the science system. Instead of criteria, the learners are seeking for laws, principles, models, and rules for classification.

When diagnosing for the efficient use of the statistical system, the teacher looks for clarity of purpose, appropriate selection or development of formulas, and accuracy of computation. If deficiencies are found, the relationship or interrelationship may be simplified, practice may be given in formula selection or development, or practice may be given in the use of the basic mathematical system. In the last case, diagnosis and prescription may occur at earlier levels.

Each area at this level is characterized by a specific vocabulary. Diagnosis revealing a need for vocabulary may indicate the necessity for diagnosis at earlier levels. Prescriptions may begin as low as level 1.

Fifth symbol level

At the fifth symbol level, you are an independent learner. You are discovering and, in so doing, generating knowledge about yourself, others, and your environment. It may be knowledge of significance to others as well as to yourself.

Description

Verbal discovery. You may be reading novels, stories, plays, essays, or poems or viewing plays, all about *fans*. In so doing you decide what you want to know or express about fans. Or you may be attempting to create a novel, story, play, essay, or poem about a *fan*.

Nonverbal discovery. Focusing on *fans,* you may be viewing drawings, paintings, designs, sculptures, and the like, or you may be listening to songs, operas, symphonies and the like. Again you discover what more you would like to know about fans. Additionally, you may be attempting to create a piece of art or music about a fan.

Scientific discovery. You may be searching for a new material for a fan, a new way to use energy to operate a fan, or the number of revolutions required to circulate air in a given space. You may express the results statistically. Alternatively you may be tracing the history of a fan, its uses in recently discovered culture, the effect of hiding one's face behind a fan, etc.

Implications

When learning at this level, the learner participates directly in diagnosing his or her own learning needs, prognosing a desired result, and prescribing what he or she is to do.

The teacher counsels by helping the learner discover an interest within the capacity of his or her skills and experience.

The teacher simulates the role of the greater universe as the recipient of the learner's discovery.

Valuing

From the moment of your first perception you have preferred certain qualities, objects, and behaviors above others.

At symbol level one you may have chosen a red fan because redness appeals to you.

At symbol level two you may have chosen a fan as a preferred way of cooling yourself.

At symbol level three you may have chosen a fan as something to represent in a geometric design or a topic for a practice paragraph.

At symbol level four you may have discovered that a truly fine Japanese fan must show certain qualities of craftsmanship in the choice of materials, construction, and decoration.

At symbol level five you may have experimented with making fans to the point of discovering new criteria that will influence your choice of fans in the future and perhaps will influence the choices of others who use fans.

In the following description we shall treat valuing at its ultimate stage. Sometimes this is called *evaluation*. It involves critical thinking in which judgments are made and criteria are offered to support them.

Description	Implications
System valuing. The rules and intuitions developed through the mastery and use of any of the systems serve as a basis for valuing. For example, if you master the rules of spelling and can furnish exceptions to its rules, you will value accurate spelling. You will judge others' writing by the accuracy of their spelling.	At this point the teacher diagnoses your attitudes and values as well as your product or performance. He or she looks for your interest, concern, and attitude in the light of your spelling performance. If your performance is weak, the teacher may diagnose further to see where your interests lie and then prescribe activities for you within that area. If your performance is strong, the teacher may prescribe more advanced work for you.
If by mistake you spell *fan* as *phenn,* you immediately correct it and do all you can to conceal the fact that you misspelled it.	If the teacher believes your weakness is the result of lack of skill and understanding, he or she may prescribe easier learning activities.
If you were reading a piece of literature in which *fan* appeared as *fhanne,* perhaps you would be moved to express your dismay in a letter to the publisher.	With regard to personal valuing the teacher is diagnosing you as a person—your concept of yourself or others. If negative, injurious attitudes and actions are apparent, he or she may prescribe situations to help you practice positive, healthy alternatives. For example, if you cannot work cooperatively with others in a small group, the prescription may have you working only with people you like at tasks requiring cooperation and offering the promise of mutual satisfaction.
Personal valuing. Here you would be dealing with morality. You would be concerned about how you use and care for a *fan* and how others do the same. You would be concerned about what was safe, honest, respectable, etc.	Additionally the teacher may prescribe alternatives suggested in class discussions, values clarification, role playing, or simulation.

Admittedly, this has been a quick, steep climb. But look where you have been!

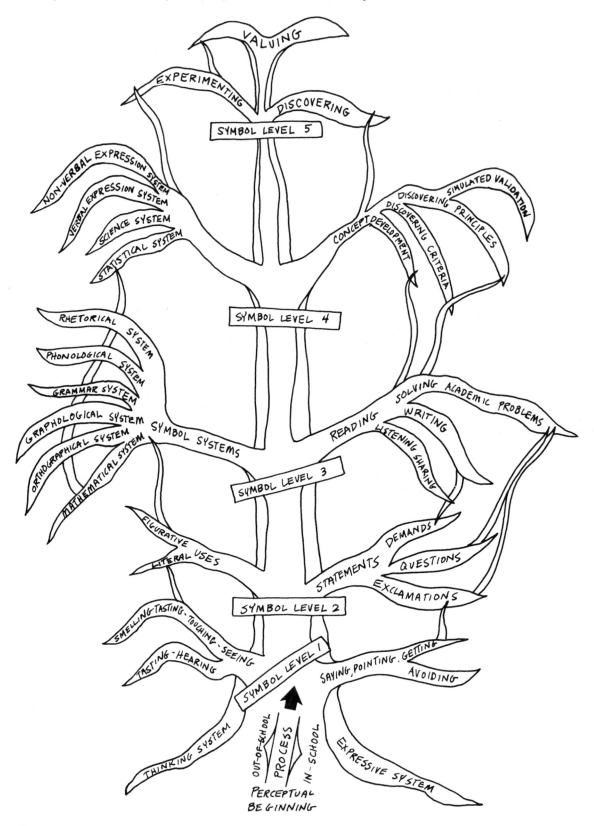

Résumé

Now let's try to see what all this means to us as teachers if we are to diagnose, prognose, and prescribe.

First, we have to know many things, not so much as evidenced by successfully completing college or university courses, but more in the sense of how things are put together and interrelated and how they are related to human experience. These things must be seen from the students' developmental level.

Second, the higher the diagnostic level, the more likely it is that some students will need to work at lower levels.

Third, various areas of knowledge are quite interrelated, particularly from symbol level three upward. Instructional activities will require learners to use all the symbol levels. The difference between the kindergartner and the high school senior, or the university graduate student for that matter, lies in the level of sophistication at which each may operate. We diagnose, prognose, and prescribe within levels of expectancy.

Fourth, mastery should be thought of as adequate performance for moving ahead. Total mastery is a fool's criterion that, when rigorously applied, destroys interest in learning.

• • •

The remainder of this chapter will deal with diagnostic tools commonly available. Prognosis and prescription will be discussed in the next chapter.

OUR DIAGNOSTIC TOOLS

When we diagnose, we are looking for the learners' level of operation, skill, or retention in a given topic. It is a positive venture. We are trying to determine where the students are in their learning. We are trying to establish a baseline from which they can move ahead. We are making no evaluations about where learners ought to be. Our guiding question is "What do the learners know?"

Our diagnostic tools are three in number: observations of performances, product analyses, and tests. Depending on conditions, we may use any one of these or any combination.

We diagnose within expected levels. For example, when we diagnose reading skills of first-grade students, expected levels are as follows:
1. The levels at which children commonly function in first grade: prekindergarten, kindergarten, first grade, second grade, and third grade.
2. The skills in which first graders have already received some instruction: alphabet recognition, maintaining reading direction (left to right, top to bottom), word recognition skills, responding to sentences, retention of facts, making inferences, and determining the meaning of words.
3. The range of first graders' attitudes toward reading and learning to read: very negative to very positive

As you can see, our field of expectancy excludes abilities beyond those associated with third grade. Such skills as skimming, changing the rate of reading to meet particular purposes, using references, performing interpretive oral reading, and doing critical reading are quite beyond what might be expected of children in first grade.

If we were diagnosing the level of reading skills of a high school senior or college sophomore, we would exclude the levels below grade seven or eight. This means that we would not diagnose for skill in recognizing words.

Of course, if our high school senior or college sophomore were performing at levels below grade seven, we would diagnose within levels associated with lower grades, and we would most certainly be diagnosing word recognition skills.

Expectancy, then, determines the scope of our diagnosis.

And now to the tools.

Observations of performances

As an observer, you wish to record what is pertinent to the performance you are diagnosing. For your observation to be valid, you must have clearly in mind what you are looking for. For example, if you were observing a first grader to determine oral language skills, you would keep a checklist with the following points:
The speaker
1. Stands straight and tall
2. Looks at the audience
3. Speaks clearly
4. Speaks loudly enough for everyone to hear
This list of behaviors can be communicated directly to first graders. You might have these behaviors written on a large chart, with sketches to show what speakers are supposed to do. The

chart can be a learning device. Each morning before sharing, attention is focused on the chart and the learners are reminded of what is expected of them. They can evaluate each other's performance.

You can use these behaviors as a base from which to observe if you wish. But if someone sees you using it in this way, they will conclude that you don't know much about guiding children in oral language. It would be better for you to use a list of behaviors like the following:

The speaker

1. Speaks loudly enough to be heard by everyone
2. Speaks distinctly
3. Maintains eye contact with the audience
4. Exercises breath control
5. Uses variety in pitch and intonation
6. Speaks fluently
7. Speaks in complete sentences
8. Maintains the point of discussion

Having these ideas in mind, you might observe Jerry carefully as he tells the class about some rocks he picked up on the way to school. You might write an anecdotal record that looks like this:

During sharing this morning Jerry told the class about some rocks he found on the way to school. From the back of the classroom, I could recognize every word he spoke. The whole time he spoke he kept his eyes on the rock he was sharing. He spoke rapidly in short bursts of monotone speech, inhaling quickly and audibly after each burst. Sentences were broken and strung together. His whole talk was centered on his rocks.

This anecdotal record shows that you were aware of all the behaviors on the list. You recorded what you saw and heard that was significant to speechmaking in first grade. There was direct correspondence between what you wrote and what was included on the list of behaviors.

Perhaps you do not want to rely so heavily on your memory. You use an observation sheet as a record. You observe Jerry for the first 5 seconds out of every 15. During that 5 seconds you mark a tally after each behavior. Your observation record might look like this:

Name _____ Date _____ Activity _____

Behavior	First observation	Second observation	Third observation	Fourth observation
1. Speaks loudly enough to be heard by everyone	/	/	/	/
2. Speaks distinctly	/	/	/	/
3. Maintains eye contact with the audience				
4. Exercises breath control	/	/	/	/
5. Uses variety in pitch and intonation				
6. Speaks fluently	/	/	/	/
7. Speaks in complete sentences				
8. Maintains the point of discussion	/	/	/	/

The entries on the observation sheet tell what Jerry can do when he is making a talk during sharing time. The behaviors after which there are no tallies are those in which Jerry will need prescriptions.

When Jerry's personal file folder is filled to overflowing, you decide that there must be a better kind of observation record. So you devise one like this:

Names of pupils

Behavior	Observation										
1. Speaks loudly enough	1										
	2										
	3										
2. Speaks distinctly	1										
	2										
	3										
3. Maintains eye contact	1										
	2										
	3										
4. Uses breath control	1										
	2										
	3										
5. Varies pitch and intonation	1										
	2										
	3										
6. Speaks fluently	1										
	2										
	3										
7. Speaks in complete sentences	1										
	2										
	3										
8. Maintains the point of discussion	1										
	2										
	3										

Now you have an observation sheet you can use with an entire group, and with several such sheets you can have an observation record of the entire class. As previously, open parts on the record show where the needs lie.

What is convenient about this kind of record sheet is that it can help you group learners for instruction. If most of the instruction is at the class level, it will help you decide which areas of need will have to be emphasized.

Let's see now what behaviors we might expect from a learner in sixth grade:

The speaker

1. Speaks loudly enough to be heard by everyone
2. Speaks distinctly
3. Exercises breath control
4. Maintains eye contact with the audience
5. Uses body language to convey ideas
6. Uses variety in pitch and intonation
7. Speaks fluently
8. Speaks in complete sentences
9. Maintains the point of discussion
10. Introduces the point of the topic
11. Offers enough facts and ideas about the topic
12. Brings the talk to a logical close
13. Holds the audience

The scope of expectancy widens. For a high school senior, we would widen it still further, by adding the following:

14. Makes logical transitions from point to point
15. Offers reasonable arguments
16. Quotes reliable authority
17. Offers a reasonable conclusion
18. Offers reasonable recommendations

You are probably asking: with so many behaviors, won't it be difficult to prepare an observation record for an entire class. The answer is "Yes," unless you can manage to mark tiny marks on huge sheets of paper. The likelihood is that you will want to consult with learners individually. Besides, their performances will be fewer. The individual observation sheet will serve adequately at this level of learning.

Generally observation lets us diagnose learning in which students are called on to perform. There may be no tangible product to examine, or the product may be of such insignificance that it is useless for diagnostic purposes. For example, a group of fifth graders may have worked together to produce a relief map of North America. The map may be a complete mess, but they are proud of it. The instructional purpose, however, was to teach them to work together.

Here are the behaviors you would look for:

The group

1. Decides on a way to select a leader
2. Selects a leader
3. Develops cohesiveness
4. Develops concern for the task
5. Completes the task

The leader

1. Asks for ideas or suggestions
2. Ensures that ideas and suggestions are listened to
3. Listens to ideas or suggestions
4. Brings the group to decisions
5. Assigns tasks
6. Coordinates tasks
7. Provides help where it is needed
8. Encourages work
9. Serves as the group's spokesperson
10. Helps resolve conflicts

Each group member

1. Gives suggestions or ideas
2. Listens to suggestions or ideas
3. Gives reactions to suggestions or ideas
4. Accepts decisions
5. Accepts a task
6. Completes an assigned task
7. Helps others when he or she finishes a task
8. Encourages the work of others

Your major concern is that the learners develop skills in decision making and completing tasks in which all the members are involved. You observe to diagnose for the occurrence of these behaviors.

What about the messy relief map? Instant diagnosis reveals simply that the learners were inexperienced in the use of the medium from which the map was made.

When the performance is controlled, as it may be for a choreographed dance, a designed game play, playing or singing a given piece, or word recognition in a given selection, the choreographed dance, the play design, the musical piece, or the selection to be read becomes the record sheet. The inaccuracies of performance are noted on the record sheet as the learner performs. The boxed material on p. 297 is an example of an oral reading

The candles flickered in their ~~sconces~~ *cones* on the drafty castle walls. (The) flames from the huge logs in the

x
cavernous fireplace cast on the walls an everchanging ˣˣmural of the shadows of those standing or sitting

hot   *s*
near the͜fire. The lord͜of the castle and his family were seated in chairs drawn close to the fire. The men-at-

stuff
arms, servants, and a few families of ~~serfs~~ were seated in a wide circle on the rush-strewn floor. All eyes

ˣˣ
were fixed on the troubadour.

He (had) just finished tuning his lute. His hand swept across the strings once. Even the crackling ˣembers in

the fire seemed to muffle their little explosions. Then he began what all were hoping to hear—the Song of

Roland.

company   x
His fingers played lightly over the lute strings as ~~accompaniment~~ to his recitation. A light strum signaled

x   ˣ ˣ
the end of each spoken line. When he came to the refrain, he played a wild melody and sang in falsetto.

And he sang no more than a word or two before his audience joined the singing.

CODE:
Omitted words or letters are circled.
Inserted words or letters are written in and a caret used to indicate the point of insertion.
Mispronounced words or letters have a line drawn through them, and the mispronunciation is written above.
Repeated words or phrases are underlined.
A 2-second hesitation before a word is noted with an X above the word.
A word pronounced by the observer for the learner is noted with an XX above the word.

test on which the observer has recorded the incorrect behaviors.

Other performances where diagnosis is done through observation include the following:

Discussion skills
Skills in dramatics
Skills in interpretive oral reading
Debate skills
Social interaction skills
Role-playing skills
Science laboratory skills
Group or class inquiry skills
Study skills

Observation may also be used to diagnose the ability to retain and use facts and ideas. The observer convenes a group of five to seven students, gives them a topic or issue that they have re-cently studied, and sits to one side to listen to the discussion. As each learner speaks, the observer records the response in a code similar to the following:

/ = Additional fact given or a strong expression of agreement
+ = Additional facet or example given
X = Important definition, principle, rule, reason, implication, or application given and justified

Observation may be used in this way to diagnose retention and use of facts and ideas in health study, literature study, science, and social science.

Often observation is used at the beginning of a unit or lesson to see whether the learners have sufficient background for new learning. The teacher may ask for a definition, explanation, or review of experience to prompt a discussion. Student responses reveal the background of the individual, group, or class.

Observation is a fine diagnostic tool, but it is often difficult to use because it focuses so narrowly on the individual learner. When working with an entire class, the teacher will have a very hard time directing activities and diagnosing at the same time. Here is a way to cope with this problem:

1. Organize an observation schedule. Decide on the three to five individuals to be observed during an instructional period. Observe each set of learners in turn until the whole class has been observed.
2. Use simple observation sheets on which you merely place a check after the behavior observed. During the instructional period pay special attention to the individuals being observed. As soon as possible, complete the observation record for each individual observed. If you cannot recall what a particular individual did, add that name to the next day's observation schedule.

Another way of coping with the problem is to observe carefully only those learners who are obviously having difficulties.

If you want to use observation but are not sure what to look for, here is what you can do:

1. Consult a textbook on how to teach that particular subject.
2. Make a performance analysis of several learners who perform well. Note the specific behaviors they exhibit. Use the behaviors when developing an observation record sheet.
3. Get together with colleagues who want to use observation in the same study area. Discuss which behaviors are involved. This procedure often results in a very useful set of observable behaviors.
4. Involve your students in a discussion about what behaviors they would like to see. This helps their interest in the performance and provides you with a set of useful behaviors. This also helps you consult with individual students. Both of you know what to look for. The student can also contribute to the prognosis and prescription.

Which procedure is best? Use the one that fits your needs and style. Simply remember that the result will need to be validated from time to time.

Look at some other textbooks, make another performance analysis, or convene your friends or your class again over the same task. Your list of significant, observable behaviors will be refined and improved.

Product analyses

In product analysis, we look at tangible work the students have done. The products include everything from dittoed practice sheets to original paintings. Let us start with the practice sheets and paper-and-pencil exercises.

To begin, we must clarify the difference between diagnosis and checking for accuracy. When we check for accuracy, we are concerned only with the number of correct or incorrect responses. When we diagnose, we are looking for *why* incorrect responses are made. It is crucial to growth that we diagnose whenever errors occur in practice, regardless of whether the student meets the criterion of "passing," "acceptable," "OK, but you can do better," "75%," or whatever. The error patterns will persist and eventually hinder further learning.

An error pattern is simply a repetition of the same incorrect response. Look at second grader Emily's practice in addition:

a.	247	b.	943	c.	441	d.	560
	+268		+742		+238		+830
	516		1785		679		1390

e.	825	f.	732	g.	635
	+774		+946		+254
	1699		1778		889

Examples a and e show that she does not know the addition facts of 8 + 7 and 7 + 8. Examples b and f show that she does not know the addition facts for 9 + 7 and 7 + 9. Her errors are factual errors.

Here is fourth grader Billy's practice in subtraction:

a.	475	b.	789	c.	963	d.	532
	−199		−254		−534		−466
	324		535		431		134

e.	946	f.	999	g.	322
	−625		−567		−177
	321		432		255

Examples a, d, and g show that he does not know how to regroup or "borrow" when subtracting. His errors are operational errors.

Here is ninth grader Jane's practice with the areas of rectangles and triangles:

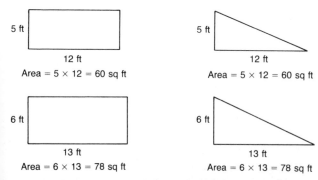

Area = 5 × 12 = 60 sq ft

Area = 5 × 12 = 60 sq ft

Area = 6 × 13 = 78 sq ft

Area = 6 × 13 = 78 sq ft

Jane made errors when she computed the areas of the triangles. She did not reason that triangles and rectangles of similar numerical dimensions could not cover the same amount of area. She made reasoning errors.

Perhaps no other study area shares with mathematics the many possibilities for error patterns, but cursive handwriting is a close second. Patterns may develop around any of the following:

The formation of any letter, lower case or capital
The linking of o, v, and w (bowed letters) with other letters
Maintaining uniform spacing between letters and words
Maintaining uniform alignment of letters
Maintaining uniform slanting of letters

However, practice is usually so painstaking that most learners produce their best handwriting and fewest errors during a handwriting lesson. The error patterns usually emerge when learners are using handwriting to complete a lesson or to compose a paragraph, story, or report. The same is likely to happen with errors in grammar, punctuation, capitalization, and spelling. Analyzing learners' communication products for error patterns is a valid diagnosis procedure.

For example, look at this paragraph:

> The de shak was a rek The dors was hanging from the hinges The windows was broken. We call out. An ole man come throo one the dors he ask what we want. We tole him we wanta drink of water. He point to the well at one side of his house. We got a drink as fast as we cud an run up the rod as fast we cud and hid in the tres to what the ole man. frank and peet and I don't know him. We hope he dont us.

Here are the error patterns:

Handwriting
Poor formation of the *a, d, g, t,* and *w*
W and *o* awkwardly linked with other letters
Irregular spacing between words
Irregular alignment
Irregular slant

Grammatical
Subjects and verbs not always in agreement
Tense not maintained
Ideas not arranged in economic order

Punctuation
Statements not all terminating with periods

Capitalization
Some sentences without a beginning capital
Proper names not capitalized

Spelling
Words containing -*ck*
Words containing vowel digraphs (d*oo*rs, wind*ow*s, tr*ee*s, r*oa*d)
Irregular words (*through, could*)
Words ending in -*ld* (*old, told*)

Admittedly, detecting error patterns can be distasteful, but we cannot deny their existence, no matter how often we say to ourselves, "Nobody's perfect!" Talking them over with students is never pleasant. But there is always hope. "Yes, a lot of errors," we may say. "Which one shall we work on first?" This keeps hope alive.

There is another way of diagnosing written composition to generate hope. It is a word-by-word analysis to determine variety in vocabulary. The boxed material below shows what happens to our illustrative paragraph.

The checks after the words indicate repeated use. The number of words in the paragraph is ninety-two. The number of words in the list is fifty-six. These are the different words used in the paragraph. The ratio of different words (56) to the total number of words (92) is 0.61 (56/92). This can be used as a base number from which the student can improve. It makes communication comfortable. It is a ratio to improve.

It is also possible to determine the ratio of misspelled words to the total number of words used. An X before a word in the list indicates it was misspelled. There are twelve misspelled words. The ratio is 0.21 (12/56). It is a ratio to decrease.

A word-by-word diagnosis such as this need not be made with every composition. Three or four times a school year is quite enough. It is useful only when the learners are able to use a hundred words or more per composition.

Another approach to diagnosis is through the use of a checklist. It is especially useful when you know exactly what you want students to do. For example, when diagnosing drawings, a simple checklist such as this would be helpful:

Name		Date
1. Repetition		
a. Line	_____	
b. Form	_____	
c. Tone	_____	
d. Texture	_____	
2. Rhythm	_____	
3. Balance	_____	
4. Proportion	_____	
5. Emphasis	_____	

the /////	hinges	x through	x told	his	x road	don't
x old //	x windows	one ✓	him ✓	house	again	know
x shack	broken	of //	drink //	got	hid	hope
was ✓✓	we /////	he ✓✓	water	as ✓	in	us
a ////	call	ask	point	fast	x trees	
x wreck	out	what	to ✓	x could	x watch	
x doors ✓	an	want ✓	well	and ///	Frank	
hanging	man ✓		at	run	x Pete	
from	come		side	up	I	

On such a checklist, the teacher places a mark and perhaps a short note describing the need more precisely.

A checklist for a simple report might look like this:

Name _____ Date _____

1. The opening paragraph pre-   _____
   sents the topic or issue.
2. The middle paragraph presents   _____
   facts that develop the topic.
3. The facts are presented in logi-   _____
   cal order.
4. The final paragraph presents a   _____
   logical conclusion.
5. Paragraph structure.   _____
6. Sentence structure.   _____
7. Capitalization.   _____
8. Punctuation.   _____
9. Spelling.   _____
10. Legibility.   _____

As you diagnose, write OK after each item that meets expectancy and a brief note describing the problem after each item where improvement is needed.

As you can see, checklists resemble observation record sheets. They offer these advantages: They serve as records of diagnoses, they pinpoint areas of need, and they do not disturb the integrity of the learner's product. By sharing the diagnosis with the learner, you provide very helpful guidance.

Another form of product analysis occurs when you diagnose a product used as a vehicle to express facts and ideas. For example, you might ask a learner to express some data on a circle graph. The circle may be poorly drawn and the segments erroneously marked, but if each segment is correctly labeled, the graph properly titled, and a conclusion accurately drawn, we may assume that the learner knows how to use a circle graph. This kind of analysis may be used with pictures, sketches, murals, models, posters, creative stories, poems, sculptures, cartoons, or editorials intended to express facts and ideas. Diagnosis first probes into general accuracy of the product and then into number of accurate facts.

Product analysis may also be used to diagnose quality of thinking. For example, if students are asked to draw up a list of rules, guidelines, or principles they think will conserve energy and to rank and justify the entries, quality of thinking is revealed in the list and justification.

Product analysis may be used in this same way to diagnose for quality of thinking in literature study, health study, science, and social studies.

Occasionally product analysis may have us regarding the learner's attitudes and values, which sometimes inhibit learning. Our diagnoses may occur through an interview with the learner or through a learner-completed paper-and-pencil inventory.

Let us suppose we wish to diagnose students' attitudes and values about the kinds of reading they do. One way is to ask the following questions:

"What kinds of stories do you like to read?"
"What kinds of poems do you like to read?"
"What kinds of plays do you like to read?"
"After you read a story, poem, or play, what kinds of things do you like to do to show that you've read it?"
"What kinds of things do you like to read about when you read for information?"
"If you have a choice between reading for fun or for information, which do you prefer to do? Why do you like it better?"
"What would you like to learn how to do better in reading?"
"What things do you like to do more than reading?"

The results will show individuals' attitudes and values about reading as both an activity and as a skill to learn. The interviewer takes notes as the learner responds.

The same questions could be duplicated on paper, and the learner could respond to them in writing. At this point the set of questions becomes an inventory. However, the learner's problems with spelling and handwriting sometimes hinder complete responses.

Using American history as an example, we can compose an inventory in which writing is reduced to a minimum:

1. Mark an X before each of the topics below that you like to study in history:

a. _____ Wars and battles
b. _____ What people used to like to do for fun
   and relaxation

c. _____ What people used to do to make a living

d. _____ What people wore

e. _____ How people celebrated holidays

f. _____ What people grew and made

g. _____ The kind of government people had

h. _____ How people organized themselves to work and play

i. _____ Inventions

j. _____ What kinds of stories, plays, and poems the people wrote and read

k. Other (Write your idea.) _____

_____

2. Mark an X before each of the things below that you like to do to learn about history:

a. _____ Read the history book by yourself

b. _____ Read and discuss the history book with a group of classmates

c. _____ Develop questions in class to be answered by reading the history book and other books

d. _____ Decide on a topic such as farming, manufacturing, communication, etc., find out about it, and write a history about it

e. _____ Act out a situation and find out how people in the past might have acted in the same situation

f. _____ Pretend you are a person living at a certain time, find out as much as you can about him or her, and take that role during class discussions

g. Other (Write your idea.) _____

_____

3. Mark an X before each of the things below that you like to do with the history you learn:

a. _____ Write reports

b. _____ Give oral reports

c. _____ Draw or paint pictures

d. _____ Make models

e. _____ Make posters

f. _____ Draw cartoons

g. _____ Write and give plays

h. _____ Write stories

i. _____ Prepare and present an exhibition

j. _____ Have quiz shows

k. _____ Draw maps

l. _____ Other (Write your idea.) _____

_____

4. What do you like to study better than history? (Write.) _____

The "other" listing at the end of each sublist provides an opportunity to indicate personal choice.

In both the interview and the inventory, the teacher has stayed within the possibilities of the study area. Only promises that can be kept are made.

Knowing learners' attitudes about a study area can be helpful in assisting their learning. When the learners see you using the findings, their responses to the next diagnosis will improve.

Sometimes product analysis and observation are combined. The classic case occurs in handwriting. You may first look at a learner's product to determine whether letters are formed legibly and letter alignment, spacing, and slant are uniform. Then you may make an observation to see whether the learner maintains a handwriting posture, holds the writing tool in a secure but relaxed way, controls the position of the paper with the free hand, and begins strokes at points from which line formation can be constantly monitored.

In this case, the observation not only validates what was seen in the product but also gives insights into reasons for poor performance. Other study areas in which the two diagnostic tools are used together include art, industrial arts, and mathematics. In the case of mathematics, the learner is often asked to talk an operation through as he performs it. This gives clues to errors in thinking.

Like observation, product analysis is a powerful diagnostic tool. The analyst must know the limits of the learners as well as the knowledge structures within the subject. When product analysis is combined with observation, diagnosis may result in the discovery of causes for errors as well as the errors themselves. Observation usually is more positively oriented than product analysis, but both serve to detect needs.

Tests

The terms "tests" and "testing" have unpleasant connotations for most of us. Diagnostic tests and testing need not. Nobody can flunk a diagnostic test. Like observation and product analysis, testing is used to detect needs.

In the previous section the term "inventory" was introduced. In business, to inventory means to count what stock is on hand. In teaching we use the inventory to discover student needs. As we fulfill those needs, students will increase their stock of skills.

In diagnosing needs in reading, teachers often use informal reading inventories. They are called *informal* because they are devised by teachers for their own use. A *formal* test is one that has been standardized, that is, it has been administered to thousands of learners, and norms for it have been established.

An informal reading inventory, which you can make yourself, consists of the following:

1. A set of reading passages is selected from a reading textbook series. A passage is selected from each level of material—preprimer, primer, first grade, second grade, and so forth—until the last book in the series (sixth, seventh, or eighth grade) has been sampled. The selection is taken from the middle of each book.

Passages vary from less than 50 words in primers to about 100 words in more advanced books.

2. A set of questions is developed from each selection. The questions are asked after the student reads to check for comprehension. They require the student to recall facts, draw conclusions, make interpretations, and define words.

3. Record sheets are kept. These sheets contain the selection to be read, duplicated with sufficient space between the lines for noting errors. It also has the questions to be asked. A simple scale is included for interpreting the results.

The boxed material below is an example of a record sheet.

Let us consider the scale at the lower right-hand corner of the record sheet. It indicates three levels: independent, instructional, and frustration. The

---

Name _____   Date _____

Later that afternoon Big Turtle came home. He had been hunting with some of his friends. He proudly showed his mother a handful of brightly colored feathers he had pulled from the birds he had shot. He was in such a good mood that he agreed to help Blue Flower look for a baby parrot. She could hardly wait to get to the forest.

The two crossed the clearing and entered the forest. Because the tree tops were so thick, it was cool and dark under the trees. Big Turtle and Blue Flower looked carefully at the lower branches. They hoped to spot a nest containing little birds.

1. _____ Who are the boy and girl in this story?
2. _____ Where had Big Turtle been?
3. _____ What did he show his mother?
4. _____ What does being in a good mood mean?
5. _____ What did Big Turtle agree to do?
6. _____ How did Blue Flower feel about looking for a baby parrot?
7. _____ Why was it cool and dark under the trees?
8. _____ Where did Big Turtle and Blue Flower hope to find a baby bird?
9. _____ What does *clearing* mean in this story?
10. _____ How well do you think Big Turtle and Blue Flower usually got along?

Silent reading
Lip movements: _____

Eye fixations: _____

Time: _____

Levels	Word recognition	Compre-hension
Independent	0-2	0-2
Instructional	3-6	3-4
Frustration	7-	5-

reading material is at the fourth-grade level. The difficulty for the learner is indicated in the number of errors made under each of the two categories: word recognition and comprehension.

If the learner reads this passage orally and makes no more than two errors in word recognition and comprehension (when asked the questions), he can read fourth-grade material independently.

If the learner makes from three to six errors in word recognition when reading orally and three or four errors in comprehension, this is the instructional level. We can use a book of this level of difficulty for the reading lessons. We can analyze errors to see where help is needed.

If the learner makes seven or more errors in word recognition and five or more errors in comprehension, this level of material is too difficult. We can analyze word recognition errors for clues to needs.

After the passage is read, the diagnostician asks the questions. The accuracy with which the learner responds determines the functional level. An analysis of questions missed indicates comprehension difficulties. Questions 1, 2, 3, 5, 7, and 8 are factual recall questions. Questions 4 and 9 are word meaning questions. Question 6 asks for a conclusion, and question 10 prompts an interpretation. Errors in any of these categories indicate difficulty.

As indicated in the left-hand corner, the inventory may be used for seeing how well the learner reads silently. The diagnostician observes the learner during silent reading. Excessive lip movements are noted, as are the number of eye movements per line. The diagnostician may be using a stopwatch to determine the learner's rate of reading.

If the inventory is to be used for both oral and silent reading, the learner first reads silently (no help is given with difficult words), then responds to the comprehension questions, and finally reads the passage orally. During oral reading, the diagnostician records the errors as they are made. The method of recording was explained in the section on observation.

When a reading inventory is used, the diagnostician has the learner start at a level that can be handled easily. The beginning point is usually about two grade levels below expectancy, that is, a fourth grader would begin the test at second-

grade level. When the learner reaches frustration level, the diagnosis ends.

If you construct a reading inventory, use the following to determine the scale for each passage:

1. The learner's *independent level* requires a very good response—no more than one word recognition error per 100 words and at least 80% accuracy in comprehension.
2. The learner's *instructional level* requires no more than five word recognition errors per 100 words and at least 60% accuracy in comprehension.
3. The learner's *frustration level* is reached when he or she makes more than five word recognition errors per 100 words and achieves less than 60% accuracy in comprehension.

In some cases, the reading inventory indicates a need for further, more detailed diagnosis. This is particularly true in word recognition difficulties. The diagnostician may inventory the learner's skills in word analysis. This inventory may consist of nonsense words grouped for a set of related elements. For example, the following words might be used to see how well the learner responds to single consonants in the final position:

mi*b*, mi*c*, mi*d*, mi*f*, mi*g*, mi*k*, mi*l*, mi*m*, mi*n*, mi*p*, mi*s*, mi*t*, mi*x*, mi*z*

If the difficulty is with consonants generally, the inventory may consist of the various consonants and consonant combinations presented by themselves. The learner performs the oral gymnastics necessary to producing the sounds associated with these letters.

If the learner's difficulty appears to be with comprehension, the diagnostician may use an inventory that consists of short paragraphs, to which the learner responds by recalling facts, drawing conclusions, making interpretations, or defining words.

Inventorying may be used to diagnose learners' needs in a variety of reading skills. Using a table of contents, using an index, using a dictionary, reading maps, and reading the globe are all amenable to this form of diagnosis. When you make an inventory for one of these skills, keep in mind the various stages of difficulty. For example, in preparing an inventory on using the dictionary, you should provide for at least three trials with each of the following:

1. Indicating approximately where in the dictionary a word might be found (beginning, middle, or end)
2. Indicating the guide words between which given words would be found
3. Finding given words in the dictionary
4. Determining the correct pronunciation of the word
5. Choosing the best meaning or definition of a word as used in a sentence or paragraph
6. Using spelling variants to find words

The inventory may also be useful in determining learners' spelling needs. Some spelling textbook series include spelling inventories for your use. However, if you are using graded spelling lists in an individualized spelling program, you construct the inventory by making a test based on the lists. Starting with the easiest list, you choose five words at random from each list. After you administer the test, you examine it carefully to see where a learner begins to make more misspellings than correct spellings. The five words within which the learner first misspells three or more words indicates his or her study list.

Inventories may also be used for diagnosing mathematics skills. Inventories of the basic facts in addition, subtraction, multiplication, and division are easily made. However, these may also be available in your school supply room or materials center. If you wish to inventory your fifth-grade learners' computation skills in subtracting whole numbers, do the following:

1. Carefully determine the levels of difficulty.
   a. Subtracting without having to regroup quantities.
   b. Subtracting when having to regroup quantities in which no zeros are involved.
   c. Subtracting when having to regroup quantities in which zeros are involved.
   d. Mixed practice in which regrouping may or may not be necessary.
2. Determine the scope of difficulty within each level (two- to four-digit quantities, three- to five-digit quantities, or what).
3. Prepare five samples at each level within the scope of the level.

A similar practice would be followed for constructing an inventory in other areas of mathematics.

Perhaps the only times you will have to construct

inventories will be when you have used all the inventories included in your textbook or with your instructional program or when you consider these to be inadequate.

You can probably see that inventories are useful tests for diagnostic purposes, but you may not see them used often. The reason for this is that they are time consuming to construct. If you can persuade your colleagues of their usefulness, they may be willing to work with you to make them.

There are diagnostic tests that may be provided by the school or district in which you work. These include the following:

READING

Diagnostic reading scales. Grades 1-8. G. D. Spache. Monterey, California: California Test Bureau, 1963.
Durrell analysis of reading difficulty. Grades 1-6. D. D. Durrell. New York: Harcourt Brace Jovanovitch, 1955.
Gates-McKillop reading diagnostic tests. Grades 2-6. A. I. Gates and A. S. McKillop. New York: Teachers College Press, Columbia University, 1962.
Gilmore oral reading test. Grades 1-8. J. V. Gilmore and E. C. Gilmore. New York: Harcourt Brace Jovanovitch, 1968.
Silent reading diagnostic tests. Grades 2-6. G. L. Bond, B. Balow, and C. J. Hoyt. Chicago: Lyons and Carnahan, 1970.
Stanford diagnostic reading test. Grades 2-13. B. Karlsen, R. Madden, and E. F. Gardner. New York: Harcourt Brace Jovanovitch, 1966-1974.

MATHEMATICS

Stanford diagnostic arithmetic tests. Grades 2.5-8.5. L. S. Beatty, R. Madden, and E. F. Gardner. New York: Harcourt Brace Jovanovitch, 1965-1968.

In recent years, particularly because of increased interest in individualized instruction, a new kind of diagnostic test has emerged. It is the preassessment test. It is particularly useful in health study, literature, science, and the social sciences. The purposes for its use are to save students time and to alert them to the need for further study.

Here is how it works. The teacher prepares instructional units, modules, or unipaks. The first thing given to students is the preassessment test. Students take it, and the teacher corrects it. Students who pass the test are excused from that unit. Students who fail the test are given specific information about what to study.

The use of the preassessment test is not restricted to individualized study units. It can be used with total class instruction. The learners take the test to see what they already know. The test cannot be flunked. It serves as self-diagnosis. At the close of the unit, the learners are given a postassessment test. They compare the difference between the results of the preassessment and the postassessment tests. They usually make delightful discoveries about how much they have learned.

Perhaps this latest development shows the true meaning of diagnosis. It is preassessment to discover what the learner knows and needs to know. Your decision to observe, analyze products, or give tests will depend both on your preference and on the study area. A paper-and-pencil test on how to write a sonnet does not make much sense. Neither does observing students as they spell. Whatever tool is used, diagnosis is essential to effective instruction and learning. It is the first step in saving time, energy, and effort for both you and the learners.

SUMMARY

Diagnosis determines what learners know and need to know. Prescriptions are activities that help students learn. Prognosis is the instructional objective.

Knowledge grows out of perception. We view it as a tree. The core of the tree is formed by experiences that occur in students' lives, both in and out of school. The left side of the tree is the thinking system, and the right side is the expressing system.

The first branching level is labeled symbol level one. At this level learners are just beginning to explore and cope with their environment. At symbol level two the learners are using language to explore and control their environment. At symbol level three they can use a variety of language-related systems to explore abstractions. At symbol level four they can use a variety of thinking systems to discover laws, principles, concepts, and criteria. At symbol level five they can generate knowledge through experimenting and discovering.

At the crest of the tree learners can think critically to evaluate and make decisions.

Diagnosis is useful at any symbol level. Negative results at any level indicate a lack of background for learning at that level. Diagnoses show where new learning should begin.

Observation is particularly useful for diagnosing performances that leave no product. The observer needs to have a clear idea of the behaviors involved in the performance. Observations may be recorded in anecdotal records or on observation record sheets.

Product analysis is particularly useful when learning generates a tangible product that may be examined closely. The analyst may look for error patterns, for structural aspects, or at the expression of attitudes and values. Records should be kept. Checklists are often useful as records.

Testing involves the use of inventories to assess a skill or the use of preassessment tests to discover what learners know.

When diagnostic results can be shared with learners, the sharing may prompt the learners to become more involved with their learning.

What do you think now?

Now get those notes you made in response to the questions asked at the beginning of this chapter. Are your ideas now about what general knowledge an elementary teacher needs to have the same as those you expressed earlier? If your ideas have changed, in what way or direction? How about what you thought about the high school science or health teacher's need for knowledge? How has that changed, if at all? Hopefully you picked up an idea or two about diagnosing a third-grade child's spelling ability. Better yet, perhaps you have begun to formulate ideas on how to diagnose other abilities. And if you finally decided that sophomores enrolling for the first time in a senior high school would have wide differences in English skills, you are beginning to think in much the same way a competent teacher does.

SUGGESTED ACTIVITIES FOR FURTHER UNDERSTANDING

1. Define each of the following: *diagnosis, prognosis, prescription, symbol level,* and *valuing.* Compare your definitions with those of your classmates, and try to reach an agreement on them.
2. Choose a common object or animal as a working concept and make a knowledge tree showing the various stages of learning related to it. If you wish, make it in the form of a poster.
3. Suppose that a teacher decides to teach a subject without making any diagnosis of what the students know. How do you think this might be done? What do you think will be the ultimate effect of this practice on learning?
4. A teacher has asked the learners to write a paragraph about their summer vacation. When she reads their products, she discovers that most are illegible, and the spelling of what she can read is terrible. What would you do next if you were this teacher?

5. Develop a set of rules you think every teacher should follow when diagnosing. Share your rules with those of your classmates, and try to reach agreement on what the rules should be.
6. Which of the various diagnostic tools do you think is the most useful? Give reasons for your answer. Share your opinion and reasons with your classmates.

For preparation

7. Arrange to visit a classroom in an elementary or secondary school to observe a teacher at work with learners. Try to observe during two lessons in which the entire class or groups are being taught in the elementary school or during two instructional periods in a secondary school. Note the evidence of diagnostic procedures at the opening of each lesson or class session.
8. Arrange to visit an elementary or secondary school in which learning centers are used. Examine the contents of each center, and decide what kinds of diagnostic procedures might have been used to establish the need for the center.
9. Select any instructional textbook in your favorite subject at whatever level you would prefer to teach. If there is a teacher's edition (this is a textbook containing teaching notes) or an instructional manual available, obtain it. Survey what is given to see what suggestions are made for diagnosis and what is provided for diagnostic purposes.
10. Choose an area of learning emphasis within your favorite subject area at the grade level that you would like to teach. Using instructional manuals, teacher's editions, methodology (how-to-teach) textbooks, or instructional guides, prepare at least two diagnostic devices to use to determine learners' needs: a test, an inventory, a product analysis checklist, or an observation record sheet.

For practice

11. Arrange to visit an elementary or secondary classroom when your favorite subject is being taught. Observe and take notes on the learners' performance in class. On the basis of what you find, decide what learning need is most apparent, and develop a diagnostic device you would use to pinpoint the need more precisely. If possible, arrange to use your device with a few learners.
12. In your classroom or assigned laboratory (observation-participation, student teaching, teacher aide), arrange for responsibility to diagnose learners' needs. Develop the devices you will need, and use them with a group of learners. Describe the results as precisely as you can.

REFERENCES

Ashlock, R. B. *Error patterns in computation*. Columbus, Ohio: Charles E. Merrill Publishing Co., 1972.

Burns, P. C. *Diagnostic teaching of the language arts*. Itasca, Ill.: F. E. Peacock Publishers, Inc., 1974.

Ekwall, E. E. *Locating and correcting reading difficulties*. Columbus, Ohio: Charles E. Merrill Publishing Co., 1970.

Nelson, C. H. *Measurement and evaluation in the classroom*. New York: Macmillan Publishing Co., Inc., 1970.

Popham, W. J., and E. L. Baker. *Establishing instructional goals*. Englewood Cliffs, N.J.: Prentice-Hall, Inc., 1970.

Potter, T. C., and Rae, G. *Informal reading diagnosis*. Englewood Cliffs, N.J.: Prentice-Hall, Inc., 1973.

Wolfe, D. M. *Language arts and life patterns* (2nd ed.). Indianapolis: Odyssey Press (Publishing), 1972.

Woods, M. L., and A. J. Moe. *Analytical reading inventory*. Columbus, Ohio: Charles E. Merrill Publishing Co., 1977.

16

THE TOOLS OF ACCOUNTABILITY

This chapter contains a wealth of information on how teachers can be accountable to their students for learning. It deals with diagnosis, prognosis, objectives, planning, sequencing, constructing units, assessment, evaluation, and reporting to students and parents. All these topics have vital importance for teachers who wish to become highly professional.

Because this chapter contains so much information, it is unusually long. Its length may give you difficulty in following the sequence of topics presented. For that reason, we begin with an abstract of the chapter. The abstract presents an overview of the chapter to help you understand what the chapter is about and follow its development.

ABSTRACT

Accountability means *precise responsibility* to someone for something. In teaching we are accountable first to *students* (and then to parents, administrators, and ourselves) for *specific and general learning*.

A *target objective* is a prognostic and assessment tool for accountability. Based on the results of diagnosis, it describes what the learners will be able to do after experiencing a set of prescribed learning activities.

Enabling objectives are the prescriptive tools of accountability. They are instructional activities, carefully selected and sequenced to ensure learning.

Initiators are enabling objectives that help learners prepare for new learning. They call on learners to define concepts, recall experiences, or review previous learning. At least one is required for each target objective.

Explorers are enabling objectives that guide students into new learning through reading, viewing, listening, etc. The number and sequence of explorers are determined by the subject matter and the abilities of the learners.

Integrators are enabling objectives that prompt learners to pull together what they have learned. Integrators may facilitate assessment or evaluation. At least one is required for each target objective.

Initiators, explorers, and integrators are used in *lesson planning*.

Diagnosis, prognosis, prescription, assessment, and evaluation comprise a wheel that must make one full turn for each new learning.

Teacher's *expectancies* for learners are sometimes based on what they themselves remember from being students. More reliable expectancies are based on teaching experiences. To begin to develop expectancies, teachers use open-ended criteria as they consult courses of study, instructional guides, teacher's editions of textbooks, and instructional manuals. As they begin to work with learners, they focus on learners' *attention span* during a variety of activities and on their *limitations* in basic skills.

Sequencing learning activities requires attention to both psychology and logic. The target objective followed by initiators, explorers, and integrators meets the demands for psychological sequencing. *Logical* sequencing often occurs in a linear pattern in which one learning activity leads into or prepares the learners for the next. *Repetitive* sequencing begins with easy activities and moves to more difficult ones. *Nonlinear* sequencing guides learners in looking at various aspects of a concept before generalizing about it.

A *long-range plan* or *unit* is similar to a lesson plan in meeting the demands for psychological sequencing. It is different from a lesson plan in that it is more comprehensive and requires longer to complete. Initiators are used to introduce units; integrators are used to bring learners to the target objective. The new experience part of a unit may consist of explorers, of explorers and integrators, or of miniunits constructed from interim objectives.

Units are modified as they are taught to meet learner needs identified during instruction.

Units ensure *comprehensive learning*. Their use ensures advantages for both teachers and learner, particularly in assessment and evaluation of learning. They serve as guides for making lesson plans.

When teachers *assess* learning, they try to determine how much students have learned. When they *evaluate* it, they judge it against individual learners' capacities or against other learners of the same age or grade. To prepare to assess learning, the teacher gathers preassessment and postassessment results as well as product or performance product samples of work between the preassessment and the postassessment. Rating scales are developed for each subject area to be reported, and a documentation file is made for each learner. The teacher makes a tentative evaluation and invites both the learners and the parents to make evaluations.

If evaluation occurs within humane conditions, the results are noncontroversial, positive, and helpful to all concerned.

Teachers see accountability in two ways. The first is as pressure—pressure from administrators, school boards, legislators, and the public—to do this or that. They regard this pressure as demeaning and threatening to their professional status. They often react in frustrated anger at the mere mention of the word "accountability."

At other times teachers see accountability as the central tenet of their professional code of ethics. This tenet holds that teachers shall be accountable to learners. When they follow this tenet as a guiding principle, they view the learner in three ways: as a person, as a learner, and as a member of society.

What do you think teachers should do to maintain balance in these three views? The purpose of this chapter is to help you refine your response to this question.

• • •

When teachers organize and monitor instruction, they use the tools of accountability to diagnose, prognose, prescribe, assess, and evaluate learning. You already know about the diagnostic tools. In this chapter we shall be dealing with the remaining tools used in the process.

PROGNOSIS, PRESCRIPTION, AND ASSESSMENT: AN OVERVIEW

At this point we are going to examine the tools that good teachers use as they organize for instruction. We shall leave the issues about their use until later.

The target objective: a prognostic and assessment tool

Diagnosis establishes a starting place for the student. Prognosis establishes a goal for the student. The goal, when described in terms of what learners will be able to do when they reach it, is called the *target objective*. Here are a few examples of diagnoses (left-hand column) and related prognoses (right-hand column):

THE LEARNERS NEED TO KNOW:

THE LEARNERS WILL BE ABLE TO:

1 How to recognize the /e/ in words containing the *ea* combination — *Say* /e/ in words containing the *ea* combination *as they occur in a list of mixed words*

2 How to multiply single-digit numbers by 7 — *Multiply* single-digit numbers by 7 *on a written test*

3 How to organize an oral report — *Write a set of notes arranged in sequence that could be used when giving an oral report* about their favorite leisure activity

4 The German vocabulary and phrases necessary to buying gasoline and oil at a service station — *Say in a simulated situation* the German vocabulary and phrases necessary to buying gasoline and oil at a service station

5 How to draw conclusions from written material — *Circle the number of the correct conclusion from a list of four given for each of two paragraphs*

6 The causes of World War I — *Write a list of the causes of World War I on a test*

As you view the column of prognoses, or target objectives, you will note that each tells precisely what the learners will be able to do *after* experiencing a set of learning activities. We use target objectives like these when organizing to teach most of the school subjects. Here we think of the student as a *learner*.

Sometimes we teach things not formally considered school subjects. Then our target objectives are similar to the following:

THE LEARNERS NEED TO KNOW:

THE LEARNERS WILL BE ABLE TO:

1 That a person's aggressive behavior is often harmful to others — *Discuss the consequences of alternatives* to aggressive behavior for controlling others as a result of *participating in a role-playing session*

2 What is possible in watercolor painting for them as persons — *Say what they think* about themselves as painters and as persons *on a self-rating sheet*

As you can see in the target objectives, what the learners will be able to do is open. We use target objectives such as these when what we teach is focused on students as *members of society* (objective one) or as *persons* (objective two).

Let us dwell for a moment on the behaviors described in the target objectives.

1. Each specifies an observable action such as *saying, writing, circling,* or *discussing.* Because *understanding, comprehending, appreciating,* and *being aware of* are not observable actions, we do not use them. Of course, there are many other observable actions such as the following:

drawing	marking an X	jumping
sketching	drawing a line	running
painting	through	dribbling
sculpting	underlining	throwing
cartooning	drawing a line	catching
constructing	from __ to __	sorting
making	crossing out	arranging in
tearing	singing	sequence
cutting	playing an instrument	inserting
composing	reading orally	removing
diagraming	answering orally	rearranging
	reporting orally	transforming
	reciting	

2. The result of each action is indicated as specifically as possible. Frequently the result is an object. When it is, a distinction must be made between the object as something produced for practice or as something produced to express facts, as shown here:

For practice: The learners will be able to paint watercolor pictures *reflecting attention to perspective.*

To express facts: The learners will be able to paint watercolor pictures *showing conditions of travel for a family during the westward movement.*

The first objective focuses on learners' needs to grow as artists, the second on their needs to express factual material.

When the result is a performance, the quality of the performance must be clearly stated, as in the following: *Maintaining constant control of the basketball, the learners will be able to dribble the length of the court.* In this instance, *maintaining constant control* and the *length of the court* are the qualitative aspects of the objective.

Sometimes the action and the result of the performance require a special setting. In this case, the setting and quality of performance must be adequately described, as in the following: *When presented with two lists of eight words each, the learners will be able to draw lines to identify the eight pairs of similar words. When presented with two lists of eight words each* is the setting. *To identify the eight pairs of similar words* is the qualitative aspect.

3. Target objectives indicate the form of assessment to be used to determine whether the students have learned. Actually, then, whenever the learners do the activity described in the target objective, they are being tested, whether or not a paper-and-pencil test is being used. Sometimes a test similar to that used for diagnosis is used. At other times a specially devised test or specially produced artifact is used.

One of the greatest difficulties we have with target objectives is determining the criterion for proof of adequate learning. (Criterion means acceptable level of performance.) Let us try a few different criteria on the same objective to see what happens. Here's how Teacher A writes an objective: *The learners will be able to write reports.* In this case, only the teacher knows what the criterion is. The criterion may be very high or very low, very rigid or very flexible.

Teacher B writes the same objective in this way: *The learners will be able to write reports to the teacher's satisfaction.* This teacher is not saying much more than Teacher A, but he is being straightforward about it. He is saying that he has a criterion and that he is taking responsibility for it. We might suspect that he shades the application of his criterion to meet the capacities of certain learners.

Here is how Teacher C writes the same objective: *At least 75% of the learners will be able to write reports to the teacher's satisfaction.* This makes us wonder what is to happen to the other 25% of the class. Is it the teacher's intent to subject some of the learners to instruction from which they cannot profit? Has he planned failure for these learners?

Let us see how Teacher D writes the objective:

The learners will be able to write reports satisfactory to themselves. Here we wonder what criterion the learners know and the teacher does not.

Teacher E composes his objective in this way: *The learners will be able to write reports in which the topic is established in the first paragraph, the facts pertinent to the topic are presented in the middle paragraphs, and the point of the topic is made in the final paragraph.* Teacher E has a definite criterion. The fact that he has composed this objective and allowed the world to see it means that he intends for every learner to meet it. He has taken into account certain unknowns about himself as a teacher and about his learners. There is a chance that some learners won't meet the criterion, just as not all patients are cured and not all court cases won. The teacher's clear statement of criterion shows confidence in his teaching and in his students as learners.

Enabling objectives: the prescriptive tools

When teachers prescribe, they select and organize learning activities that will help learners reach the target objective. Learners' actions in those activities and the expected results are specified. The prescribed learning activities are called *enabling objectives* because they help learners to learn information, operations, skills, or values. Here are a few examples of enabling objectives:

THE LEARNERS WILL:	THEN THEY WILL BE ABLE TO:
1 View a filmstrip	Name the events in the cheese-making process
2 Perform before a video-tape recorder	Identify the high and low points of their performance
3 Listen to the description of an issue	Discuss it for 5 minutes in impromptu groups to decide possible solutions
4 Participate, either as an observer or a player, in a role-playing session about property rights	Select an alternative behavior for vengeful action

At first glance it is obvious that the actions listed at the left describe the learning activities quite clearly. Why the concern for the result of the activity? There are two reasons. The first reason is that the clearly described result focuses on the purpose for the activity. To ensure that the purpose is met, the teacher must monitor the activity. The second reason is that one activity must often be completed before the ensuing activity can occur. Knowing the result of one activity gives clues to what the next activity must be. Here are examples of how this occurs:

THE LEARNERS WILL: THEN THEY WILL BE ABLE TO:

1 Discuss what they think → Develop a list of duties the duties of a president are

2 Divide the list of duties → Analyze the entries in into groups according to each list to determine a similarity label for the group

3 Examine their orga- → Develop a functional de- nized information finition for the term *"president"*

4 Discuss whether all → Develop a purpose for presidents everywhere further investigation function in the same way

5 Read pages 135-138 in → Recite their findings in re- their textbooks lation to their purpose

In this list of enabling objectives we can see that the result of objective one leads into the learning activity for objective two, the result of objective two leads into the learning activity for objective three, the result of objective three leads into the learning activity for objective four, and the result of objective four leads into the learning activity for objective five. What we see, then, is a progressive ricochet from one enabling objective to another. This may not always be possible to organize, but when it is, it is a sure sign of good sequencing of learning activities.

Another aspect of sequencing is following the psychological organization of learning. We must use three different kinds of enabling objectives to meet the psychological demands for *motivation, new experience,* and *integration of experience* to discover meaning. We call these three kinds of objectives *initiators, explorers,* and *integrators.*

Initiatory enabling objectives: the initiators. The purpose of initiators is to prepare learners for further learning. They do this by helping students recall background information. This background information serves as a base from which learning will proceed. Suppose a class is begin-

ning a study about government. The teacher may use an initiator similar to the following:

THE LEARNERS WILL: THEN THEY WILL BE ABLE TO:

1 Discuss what govern- Develop a definition for it ment is

If the initiator is more imaginative, more interest will be stimulated, as follows:

THE LEARNERS WILL: THEN THEY WILL BE ABLE TO:

1 Listen to a description of Define government as a visitor from outer space they tell the visitor neces- who knows nothing sary information about government, but who needs to know what government is in order to continue living on earth

Sometimes one initiator is enough. At other times more will be needed, as follows:

THE LEARNERS WILL: THEN THEY WILL BE ABLE TO:

1 Name the different lead- Divide the leaders into ers they know about and sublists according to their see them listed similarities

2 Label the lists Integrate the labels to de- velop a definition of what a leader is

3 Decide in groups the Compare ideas about the powers of leaders in gov- powers of leaders in ernment government in order to generate a definition of the term "government"

These initiators are developed in a sequence to provide for greater depth in background, greater learner participation, and more interest.

Remember: Every instructional plan, regardless of length or purpose, requires at least one initiator. Initiators enable learners to prepare for new learning by focusing on a previous, related experience in some way, defining a concept basic to new learning, or reviewing something they learned recently.

Exploratory enabling objectives: the explorers. Explorers are the enabling objectives that provide new learning experiences. If the learning is primarily informational, the activities will help learners acquire information. These activities might include the following:

Listening to the teacher talk
Observing the teacher demonstrate an operation

Doing the operation under the teacher's supervision

Watching a teacher's presentation featuring chalkboard sketches, diagrams, listings, study prints, flannelgraphs, puppet performances, or artifacts of one kind or another

Listening to a resource person

Observing at a site

Reading a textbook, reference book, or trade book

Viewing a film, filmstrip, or videotape

Informational learning is usually more successful for learners if they have a *purpose* for finding information. A purpose helps them choose pertinent facts. It sets limits for what is expected. For these reasons, the first explorer should provide learners with a purpose. Here are examples:

THE LEARNERS WILL:	THEN THEY WILL BE ABLE TO:
1 Review a set of questions offered by the teacher	Identify pertinent information as it occurs
2 Discuss whether all presidents in other countries have the same duties as the president of the United States	Guess whether presidents have the same duties or have different duties

Once the purpose is established, the rest of the explorers have the learners seek information, perhaps like the following:

THE LEARNERS WILL:	THEN THEY WILL BE ABLE TO:
1 Read pages 38-39 in the textbook	Tell about the duties of the presidents of India and France
2 View a filmstrip	Tell about the duties of the president of Israel
3 Read a newspaper article	Tell about the duties of the president of Gabon

At the very least, one explorer must be provided in a lesson to enable learners to acquire information.

When instruction deals with learning an operation in phonics, grammar, or mathematics as a system, the first explorer is frequently an observation of the teacher explaining or demonstrating an operation, as can be seen in the following:

THE LEARNERS WILL:	THEN THEY WILL BE ABLE TO:
1 Observe as the teacher demonstrates how to compute the area of a circle	Try to compute the area of a circle
2 Observe as the teacher demonstrates the possessive transform	Try to transform two kernel sentences, one expressing possession, into a single sentence
3 Observe as the teacher demonstrates what happens when *-ed* or *-ing* is added to a monosyllabic verb ending in a consonant	Try to add *-ed* or *-ing* to monosyllabic verbs ending in a consonant

And sometimes the first explorer has the learners involved more actively, as in the following:

THE LEARNERS WILL:	THEN THEY WILL BE ABLE TO:
1 Draw circles on graph paper	Estimate the areas of circles by counting the squares and partial squares
2 Try to transform two sentences into one	Discover how the possessive transform works
3 Analyze a list of mixed verbs to which *-ed* and *-ing* have been added	Discover that the monosyllabic verbs ending in a consonant double the consonant when *-ed* or *-ing* is added

Chances are that the second set of explorers will better facilitate learning.

When teaching an operation within a system, at least two more explorers are needed—one to lead the learners into some *supervised trials* and the other to provide for *independent practice,* as shown here:

THE LEARNERS WILL:	THEN THEY WILL BE ABLE TO:
1 Compute the areas of circles, each computation checked by the teacher before the next is tried (supervised)	Demonstrate their knowledge of the operation
2 Compute the areas of five circles of different dimensions (independent)	Demonstrate their skill in using the operation

Generally, then, three explorers are needed to ensure learning an operation. These include explorers to *introduce* the operation, for *supervised practice,* and for *independent practice.*

Explorers that facilitate the learning of skills, such as using a dictionary, table of contents, index, card catalog, thesaurus, map, globe, table, chart, or diagram, include all three explorers. Let's use dictionary skills as an example. The operations include using guide words to find the entry word in the dictionary and choosing the best definition for the word. Explorers include the following:

THE LEARNERS WILL:	THEN THEY WILL BE ABLE TO:
1 Examine a dictionary page to find where the guide words occur	Discover that the guide words are the first and last words on the page
2 Try to find guide words between which certain words occur, each pair of guide words being checked before another trial is attempted	Demonstrate their grasp of the use of guide words
3 Find the guide words for the pages on which ten given words will occur	Demonstrate their skill in using guide words to locate entry words

Just about every skill we teach can be broken down into operations that occur in sequence. We have a choice in how the explorers may be organized, either to focus on one operation at a time or on all in sequence. However, when the use of a skill results in a discrete product such as a sentence, paragraph, story, essay, report, poem, picture, cartoon, poster, speech, song, play, or formally recognized game (for example, baseball, football, or basketball), the explorers may focus on examples of the product or performance. To illustrate, here is a set of explorers that might be used to guide students in learning to write paragraphs:

THE LEARNERS WILL:	THEN THEY WILL BE ABLE TO:
1 Compare three paragraphs about the same topic but varying in quality	Identify the best paragraph
2 Compare the best paragraph with the others to determine why it is the best	Generalize that good explanatory paragraphs contain a topic sentence that introduces the main idea, supporting sentences that offer pertinent facts about the main idea, and supporting sentences arranged in logical order
3 Analyze paragraphs for extraneous ideas	Identify extraneous ideas
4 Analyze paragraphs for topic sentences	Identify the paragraphs containing topic sentences
5 Analyze paragraphs for the logical order of supporting ideas	Identify well-ordered paragraphs
6 Rate paragraphs as good or poor on the basis of the criteria developed	Apply the criteria

Of course, a series of lessons would be required for the learners to experience all these explorers.

When we want students to explore *values*, we use enablers that focus on a problem plus some alternative ways of solving it. To consider alternatives, we include in-depth, open-ended discussions, role-playing, simulation, or cataloging and ranking choices. Here is a set of explorers used to treat a value:

THE LEARNERS WILL:	THEN THEY WILL BE ABLE TO:
1 Read an incomplete story	Describe a problem in which the hero's choice is to cheat or to lose
2 Discuss what the hero should do	Produce a list of choices
3 Consider the consequences of each choice	Discover preferred alternatives
4 Read the end of the story	Discover the hero's choice
5 Decide whether other choices might have been better	Clarify the value of honesty

The first explorer in the series enables the learners to define the problem, and the others enable them to suggest, consider, and select alternatives.

As we look back over the explorers we have discussed, we can see that the number and type depend on the knowledge to be learned and the abilities of the learners.

Integrating enabling objectives: the integrators. The integrators enable learners to pull together what they can remember from their explorations. For every target objective there must be at least one integrator. This integrator relates directly to the activity described in the target objective. Here are some examples:

Target objective: The learners will be able to say /e/ in words containing the *ea* combination as they occur in a list of mixed words.

THE LEARNERS WILL:	THEN THEY WILL BE ABLE TO:
1 Try to read a list of mixed words containing the *ea* combination having the sound of /e/	Say the words

Target objective: The learners will be able to multiply single-digit numbers by 7 on a written test.

THE LEARNERS WILL:	THEN THEY WILL BE ABLE TO:
1 Take a written test on the multiplication of single-digit numbers by 7	Demonstrate knowledge of the multiplication facts associated with 7

Target objective: The learners will be able to write a set of notes arranged in sequence that could be used when giving an oral report about their favorite leisure activity.

THE LEARNERS WILL:	THEN THEY WILL BE ABLE TO:
1 Attempt to write a set of notes arranged in sequence that could be used when giving an oral report about their favorite leisure activity	Produce the notes

Target objective: The learners will be able to say in a simulated situation the German words and phrases necessary to buying gasoline and oil at a service station.

THE LEARNERS WILL:	THEN THEY WILL BE ABLE TO:
1 Participate in a simulation of buying gasoline and oil at a German service station	Use the necessary words and phrases

Target objective: The learners will be able to circle the number of the correct conclusion from a list of four given for each of five paragraphs.

THE LEARNERS WILL:	THEN THEY WILL BE ABLE TO:
1 Try an exercise in which they read pairs of paragraphs, read four possibilities for conclusions supported by the facts in each pair, and circle the correct conclusion	Demonstrate their skill in drawing conclusions

Target objective. The learners will be able to write a list of the causes of World War I on a test.

THE LEARNERS WILL:	THEN THEY WILL BE ABLE TO:
1 Take a written test on the causes of World War I	Write a list of the causes

As the teacher examines the results of each integrator, he or she makes an assessment by responding to this question: *Did the learners learn as prognosed in the target behavior?* If all the learners did, that is great. It is almost a miracle. Usually there are a few who do not, and for these the teacher makes a diagnosis to see what additional enabling objectives are needed.

There is one kind of target objective that all the learners meet. This target objective is open, that is, the prognosis is general rather than specific. Here are two examples:

Target objective: The learners will be able to discuss consequences of alternatives to aggressive behavior for controlling others as a result of participating in a role-playing session.

THE LEARNERS WILL:	THEN THEY WILL BE ABLE TO:
1 Discuss the consequences of alternatives to aggressive behavior for controlling others, as identified during a role-playing session	Decide for themselves personally what alternatives are best for them

Target objective: The learners will be able to say on a self-rating sheet what they think about themselves as painters and as persons.

THE LEARNERS WILL:	THEN THEY WILL BE ABLE TO:
1 Say on a self-rating sheet what they think about themselves as painters and as persons	Express what they feel and think about painting as an activity

The integrators used with these target objectives are evaluative integrators. They prompt the learners to make judgments for themselves.

Some teachers use evaluative integrators as a means of helping learners see what they have learned when the target objective prognoses specific learning. Here is a basic model for such integrators:

THE LEARNERS WILL:	THEN THEY WILL BE ABLE TO:
1 Analyze their corrected practice (or test)	Ask questions and evaluate themselves as learners

These integrators help students find the answers to the following important questions: How well did I do? What do I need to do to improve? The use of such integrators lies at the heart of humanistic education, but their use does not ensure humanistic education. If they are used in such a way that they prompt guilt or discouragement, they destroy learners' positive attitudes toward learning and themselves as learners. However, if they are used in a way that generates satisfaction with self and an honest hope for future achievement, they are humanistic tools.

Application

Now let us see what a lesson plan would look like if we were to apply what has been presented so far.

Diagnosis: When given an opportunity to dramatize a story, the learners were unable to do it because they have a limited concept of a story as communicative discourse.

Target objective: After reading the story "All-Star Girl," the learners will be able to write a paragraph telling the name of the main character, what her problem was, and how she solved it.

Materials: A picture of an older girl teaching a younger girl how to make something from pine cones at a summer camp.

The reading textbook, pages 129-136.

Initiator: The learners will view the picture and, as a result, will be able to recall and discuss their own experiences in summer camp.

Explorers:

THE LEARNERS WILL:	THEN THEY WILL BE ABLE TO:
1 Tell what they think is the one good quality a camp counselor should have	Decide on what they think is the one good quality
2 Read the story	Tell whether the heroine of the story has the preferred quality
3 Tell how the heroine used this quality in the story	Reconstruct the story in terms of a main character, her problem, and the solution

Integrators:

THE LEARNERS WILL:	THEN THEY WILL BE ABLE TO:
1 Try independently to write a short paragraph telling who the main character of the story was, what her problem was, and how it was solved	Write a paragraph giving the specified information
2 Read the paragraphs aloud and discuss them	Decide whether or not their paragraphs are correct

This may seem to be a long, detailed plan. It is meant for beginners in teaching. When they develop to the point that they can monitor each activity to produce the desired result, they can use a daily lesson plan like this:

1. Discuss picture.
2. Discuss camp counselor quality.
3. Read story.
4. Discuss main character.
5. Write paragraph.
6. Evaluate paragraph.

This is the kind of plan a seasoned, competent professional uses.

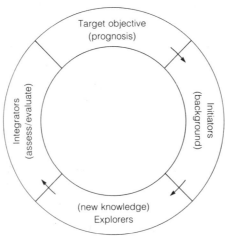

Sequence of learning wheel

As you see, we can express diagnosis, prognosis, prescription, assessment, and evaluation as a wheel that makes a complete turn with each new learning. However, not all learners and classes are the same. Some move rapidly on big wheels; others move slowly on small wheels. The size of the wheels and their speed are partly determined by the learners abilities. We use diagnoses to determine what we can expect. Let us look, then, into the relationship between expectancies, prognosis, and prescription.

EXPECTANCIES: LIMITERS OF PROGNOSIS AND PRESCRIPTION

Most of us have vague notions about what should be learned at various grades in various subjects. These notions remain from our own experiences in school. Poorer teachers use these notions more than any other as a guide for what to diagnose, prognose, and prescribe. As expectancies, they are not reliable. Our experiences may not have been good ones. Our memories are far from perfect. As tempting as it is, avoid using your own experience as a learner as a basis for expectancies. From this point, seek other bases for what you can expect from learners.

Experience as a teacher is the best base. After two or three years of teaching the same subject(s) at the same grade level(s), you will have a reliable set of expectancies as to what learners can do. You will know where to begin to diagnose, the kinds of prognoses you can make, the kinds of learning activities you can prescribe, the order in which they can be prescribed, and about how much time learners will require to meet a target objective.

Let us start by developing our expectancies as open-ended criteria. Try to arrive at generalizations similar to the following basic model:

Many learners in this class can _____ *, but a number of them cannot.*
Many may mean *most,* a *majority,* or a *plurality.*
This class may refer to a group of 8 year olds or 13 year olds, first graders or ninth graders, kindergartners or sophomores, or all the learners I work with between 9:45 AM and 10:40 AM.
Can _____ may mean anything from *look after their own toilet needs* to *write a sonnet.*
A number may be any number less than the plurality.

Once you have developed these criteria for expectancies, keep them open. As you work with each new class of learners, study them carefully to reformulate more precisely your criteria for that particular class.

However, you must start somewhere. Here are steps to help build ideas about expectancies before you ever assume responsibility for a group of learners.

What do the experts say?

Find out what the experts say by examining books, documents, and materials they produce for teachers to use.

1. *The curriculum guide.* This document, prepared by curriculum directors working with experienced teachers, lists goals and objectives for all grades and subjects. The objectives for each area of study are listed by grade level. Sometimes there are entries dealing with the needs of exceptional learners—the gifted, the educable mentally retarded, the educationally handicapped. A review of the document where it treats the area of study and grade level of your concern can give you a general idea as to what is expected of your learners.

2. *The instructional guide.* Prepared by curriculum directors working with experienced teachers, this document focuses on subjects such as mathematics, physical education, or language arts. It lists instructional objectives and suggestions for activities and materials. A review of this document can provide you with excellent ideas about what learners can be expected to do at your grade level.

3. *Teacher's editions and instructional manuals.* To encourage the adoption of their materials, publishers provide teacher's editions of textbooks, containing teaching notes printed on the margins of pages, or separate teaching manuals, suggesting step-by-step teaching procedures. Many teaching packages (usually kits of materials in boxes) are now available with instructional manuals. These materials can give you ideas about the different kinds of learning tasks you can expect learners to do at particular grade levels. If you review an instructional manual, you will need to have the accompanying materials at hand to understand the suggestions. In small districts having limited curriculum

development personnel and facilities, teacher's editions and instructional materials may be your only resources for discovering what the suggested expectancies are.

4. *Materials.* Some publishers produce packets of paper-and-pencil practice sheets, instructional games, or books for students to read independently. Usually these materials are classified in some way according to the age or grade level of the learners for whom they were designed. An afternoon or two spent in a school supply store or instructional center (either school or district) can provide you with some good ideas of what learners might be expected to do.

• • •

A perusal of all the foregoing can give you a good start in developing expectancies for learners. They will put you "in the ball park," but that is the best they can do for you. You could spend a lifetime studying them, and you still would not have developed a set of expectancies that would mirror what you might find with a particular class. That awaits your experience. However, there are a few

Age (years)	Teacher-assisted activities	Independent activities	Group-centered activities
4	5-10 minutes; longer period only when learners can respond actively	3-10 minutes; longer period only with crafts activities	Incapable of doing
5	5-15 minutes; longer period only when learners can observe or listen to something dynamic, such as a film, and can respond actively	5-10 minutes; longer period only with construction or free-play activities	Incapable of doing
6	10-20 minutes; about the same as the preceding otherwise	10-15 minutes; about the same as the preceding otherwise	10-15 minutes, provided the group is no larger than a pair and the group members are good friends
7-8	15-30 minutes; about the same as the preceding otherwise	15-20 minutes; about the same as the preceding otherwise	10-20 minutes, with the same conditions as the preceding; may participate in a group of three to five to discuss a practical problem for 5 minutes
9-10	20-40 minutes; about the same as the preceding otherwise	20-45 minutes; about the same as the preceding otherwise	15-25 minutes, in groups of five to eight members who wish to work in the group and who clearly understand the task
11-12	30-45 minutes; about the same as the preceding otherwise	25-50 minutes; can do independent studies as well as construction tasks; can sustain hard physical activity for 45 minutes	30-45 minutes; same as the preceding otherwise
13 +	35-50 minutes; about the same as the preceding otherwise	Same as the preceding	30-50 minutes; same as the preceding otherwise; however, these learners can often work with peers on an impromptu basis and willingly form into groups

expectancies to which you can be alerted, including attention span, limitations in basic skills, and limitations in thinking skills.

Attention span

By attention span we mean the length of time that learners can spend at an activity. The kind of activity makes a difference. So does the learner's age. In any classroom, the expectancies discussed here will be exceeded or not met from time to time. You should regard them as general tendencies, not absolute laws.

Any time learners are in school they are doing teacher-assisted, independent, or group-centered activities. A teacher-assisted activity is one guided by the teacher holding attention and directing the activity. An independent activity is one the learners do by themselves, such as completing exercises in mathematics or spelling, painting pictures, or writing stories. A group-centered activity has learners in groups discussing issues, making decisions, or doing group projects.

The chart on p. 318 lists what teachers have discovered about attention span from age to age.

The chart supports these conclusions:
1. The younger the learners, the shorter their attention span.
2. The younger the learners, the less capable they are to stay with tasks requiring considerable time.
3. The older the learners, the more capable they are at working for long periods in group-centered activities.
4. The more dynamic the activity, the longer the attention span.

As you begin to plan instruction, use the ideas just given and the specifics listed in the chart as your general guides. Modifications in one direction or the other will establish workable expectancies. However, you may have to temper your modifications with what can be expected from learners in terms of the basic skills they can perform.

Limitations in basic skills

Much of learning, particularly in such study areas as health, literature, mathematics, science, and the social sciences, depends on how well the learners can use such basic skills as reading, handwriting, spelling, composition, listening, observing, grammar, capitalization, punctuation, and computation. What many of us forget is that mastery of some of these skills does not occur for many learners until the final year of high school, if at all. We cannot go into all the details of the expectancies here, but we can cite a few facts that will be useful to you.

We shall restrict our discussion to two general categories: skills of information acquisition and retention, and skills of expressing information.

Skills of information acquisition and retention. In kindergarten and first grade, listening and viewing are the main intake skills. Adequate use of these skills demands that the learners have purposes for which to listen and view. Viewing will have to be carefully guided. If the learners are to retain what they hear or see, they need to be prompted to recall what they have experienced and to use it to make something.

These points are also true of learners in the second and third grades. However, with careful guidance, these learners can read to discover facts. Purposes have to be carefully established, and often the reading can proceed only at a fact-by-fact pace.

Learners in the fourth and fifth grades can read independently to acquire information, but they will also need to have purposes clearly established. The purposes may be broad, such as reading to validate or disprove an idea. The same is true of their use of listening and viewing skills. The retention of facts and ideas still requires an immediate recall activity plus a further discussion or other activity to integrate learning.

Learners in grades six through eight can read independently to acquire and retain information long enough to discuss it. Their performance is usually better if they have class-generated purposes for reading. They can also read maps, globes, graphs, and diagrams and make the interpolations for precise interpretation, or can be taught to do so without much difficulty. The same is true of the retention skills of outlining and notetaking. Listening and viewing still demand class-generated purposes.

Learners in grades nine through eleven can read independently to acquire, retain, and integrate information and can develop their own purposes for reading, listening, and viewing. Otherwise, these learners are similar to learners in grades six through eight.

Learners in grades twelve through thirteen can

usually read independently to acquire, retain, and integrate information but may require special training to develop systematic, purposive reading skills to understand and retain information in abstract areas of knowledge. They are capable of taking selective notes when listening but may need additional training to be able to do this efficiently.

Skills of expressing information. Skills of oral recitation, crude drawing, painting, constructing, and arranging, are the means of expression for learners in kindergarten and first grade. With the assistance of the teacher, these learners can work in groups to generate three to six sentences about a topic. The teacher must record what they say.

These learners may make simple bar graphs and picture graphs showing a one-to-one correspondence, but they need the immediate assistance of the teacher.

With some guidance and instruction, they can become proficient in dramatic play with items they construct, puppets, dolls, figurines, toys, and small-scale furniture, such as houses, crates, and the like. Headgear such as caps, helmets, and headdresses, either made by themselves or provided by the teacher, helps them maintain their roles. Provided a rich background of experience, they can express many ideas effectively.

Learners in grades two and three are much the same as those in kindergarten and grade one, but they can write from one to five sentence independently about a topic when they have a spelling resource immediately available. This resource may be a list of words developed around a topic or the immediate assistance of teacher or aide.

Learners in grades four and five can write extended discourse about a topic or write a story, but paragraphing will be crude or nonexistent. Errors in sentence structure, capitalization, punctuation, usage, and spelling will occur.

Oral recitation can be used to cover a topic, but the teacher's assistance is often required to keep it to the point. The organization of ideas often reflects incompleteness and inadequate sequencing.

Drawing, painting, and constructing are favored activities for expression. Often the learners prefer group-produced products to independently made products.

These learners can make maps to express ideas. They can use simple bar graphs to show relationships, but the number relationships beyond the thousands are usually too difficult for them.

Frequently faulty computation skills will prohibit the use of graphs to express ideas.

Learners in grades six through eight are much the same as fourth and fifth graders in expression skills, with these exceptions: paragraphing, oral recitation, and organization of ideas become more precise; line and circle graphs may be used to express ideas; and these learners show a definite preference for group-produced paintings, murals, models, etc.

Learners in grades nine through eleven can gather information independently and use it to develop written reports, but they will still need teacher assistance with organization and dealing with such details as paragraphing, sentence structure, punctuation, usage, and spelling. With some training they can deal with the simpler aspects of footnoting and bibliography. They can use maps, graphs, and diagrams to express ideas.

Oral recitation skills may be developed to the point that debate, panel and round-table discussions, and speeches may be used as means of conveying ideas.

These learners have few opportunities to use drawing, painting, and construction as expression skills. They tend to regard them as specialized skills.

Learners in grades twelve and thirteen approach the adult level of expression skills. Individuals vary in their ability to cope with spelling and punctuation requirements.

Limitations in thinking skills

Learners usually are not capable of independent reasoning following simple paradigms of logic or scientific inquiry until some time between ages 11 and 15 years, grades five through nine. However, there is much that can be done before this time with teacher assistance.

When dealing with concrete objects, replicas of objects common to their experience, or immediate experiences such as viewing or listening, young learners can be involved in abstract thinking processes. However, they require the assistance of both the teachers and their peers. When guiding groups of young learners, the teacher guides the thinking in a setting of immediacy or recency well within the learners' experience and encourages the *process* of thinking. This means that child logic, not adult logic, holds sway.

Learners in kindergarten can make guesses

about how a story will end, whether or not a certain object can float on water, what people like Eskimos, Pygmies, etc., eat, whether whales are more like goldfish or dogs, and the like. The teacher listens to their opinions and reasons, encourages them to be clear, provides them with some new facts, and has them give opinions and reasons again.

Learners in grades one and two can make independent pictures or sketches of things they know about, such as the supermarket or what families like to do together; group their pictures according to similarities they see; label each group; and develop a group generalization about the represented concept.

Learners in grades three and four depend less on immediacy. They can recall many different things that they have seen or heard. When they are prompted to do so, they can tell about differences they might expect in objects and ideas, group and label them, and generalize from their organized information. They may learn additional facts and judge their generalization against these new facts. After listening to or reading stories they can begin to develop criteria to help them decide whether or not they liked the story.

Learners in grades five through nine may begin to follow paradigms of inquiry under the direct guidance of the teacher. In the earlier stages they will need much help from the teacher in defining the problem and developing the questions to be answered in the inquiry. They will still need the support of their peers at every step along the way. In the later stages (grade nine) they may be able to define a problem, make hypotheses, select a best hypothesis, develop a design for inquiry, investigate, organize their information, state their findings, and judge their hypothesis against their findings—all as an exercise of independent thinking.

Much of what we think has a time and space orientation. Usually learners are not capable of using historical time and geographical or astronomical space meaningfully until grade nine or ten.

. . .

This brief review of expectancies has revealed that growth in the use of basic skills is a long, gradual process.

The expectancies listed here are reasonable and possible. They are reasonable and possible

only, however, if (1) basic skills have been taught systematically and comprehensively, that is, on the basis of need, not whim or preference; in wholes, not in bits and snippets; and to levels of application, not just to practice sheets; and (2) they are assessed from time to time and corrected as needed, not taught once and left to diminish with forgetting.

Now forewarned and somewhat forearmed, you are ready to begin developing your own expectancies.

SEQUENCING LEARNING ACTIVITIES

Because much of the school experience must be carefully organized to ensure systematic and comprehensive learning and the most economic use of learners' time, energy, and effort, we must pay special attention to the ways we sequence the instructional activities. You were exposed to some of these ways in the overview presented earlier in this chapter. We shall now review them and look more deeply into some other aspects of sequencing.

One basic pattern of sequencing that always needs to be followed is the *psychological pattern*. It is explicit in the target objective, initiator(s), explorer(s), and integrator(s) as arranged for a lesson or unit plan. You also saw the ricochet effect of well-organized initiators and explorers, where the result of one activity led into the next. This is a logical pattern we try to follow as often as possible.

When we are sequencing activities for a practical skill, such as how to use a dictionary, index, card catalog, set of tables, and the like, we break the skill down into its *separate operations* we arrange them in chronological order, and we teach each operation separately to an acceptable level of mastery. This pattern of sequencing is particularly suited for use in and beyond grade four.

Our other choice is to present a problem in which the *need* for the skill is obvious and then to guide the learners through all the operations necessary to solving the problem. This pattern is suitable for learners in grades two and three when the skill is being introduced. The teacher guides the learners through each step.

Another sequence introduced earlier focuses on *teaching an operation*. It follows this order: introduction, supervised practice, and independent practice. It ensures effective learning when learners are given independent practice only after they have achieved success during supervised practice. This pattern is basically psychological.

Another pattern introduced earlier deals with learning the skill through making a *product.* We have the learners begin with analyzing products of varying quality to discover the criteria that characterize the product. Then they apply the criteria in a series of activities to help them understand the criteria.

Patterns of sequence for informational learning in health, social studies, and science were also introduced. One pattern began with a *teacher-given purpose,* the other with a *purpose generated through teacher-assisted inquiry.* Learning activities followed for the learners to acquire information and process it.

And finally we noted a sequence to be used when the target objective is *open.* The opening of the sequence has the learners watching a demonstration or considering a problem; then exploring through experimenting, open discussion, or role-playing; and finishing with open-ended evaluative activities.

Now we are going to look into some other aspects of sequencing.

When we are teaching computation facts and skills, phonics, the structural analysis of words, spelling, formal grammar, handwriting, and foreign language vocabulary and grammar patterns, we organize learning activities by placing the same skill in different practice settings. We can use foreign language vocabulary as an example. Look at the explorers in the following lesson plan:

Target objective: On a sheet containing the pictures of ten common foods and beverages, the learners will be able to identify each item in Italian by marking it with a number in the order in which it is recited by the teacher.

Initiator:

THE LEARNERS WILL:

1 Observe the teacher dramatizing an Italian ordering food in a restaurant

THEN THEY WILL BE ABLE TO: Guess what the teacher is doing and anticipate learning to do the same thing

Explorers:

THE LEARNERS WILL:

1 Observe and listen as the teacher points to each item on a chart and says it

THEN THEY WILL BE ABLE TO: Repeat the names of the items

2 Repeat the name of each item three times

Pronounce the name of each item correctly

3 Say the name of each item as the teacher points to it

Identify each item correctly

4 Say *si* when the teacher points to an item and says its name correctly and *no* when an item is named incorrectly

Identify each item correctly

5 Point to an item on the chart when the teacher says a sentence containing its name

Identify the item correctly

6 Take turns saying the items on the chart when a classmate points to them out of order

Identify each item correctly

7 Take turns saying each item on the list in a simple sentence indicating a liking for the item and monitor a classmate's response as he or she tries to point to the item

Identify and say each item correctly in a sentence

Integrator:

THE LEARNERS WILL:

1 Listen as the teacher repeats the name of each item and mark its number on the correct picture on the picture sheet

THEN THEY WILL BE ABLE TO: Identify each item correctly

As you review explorers three through seven, you can see that each new activity has the learners repeat the names of the foods in a slightly different setting. This is a repetitive pattern of sequencing in which the learners deal with the same subject matter during each activity. But each successive activity is different. The best sequence is one in which successive activities reduce the clues to which students respond. Each activity becomes more difficult. Only when the learners are successful with one activity does the teacher guide them to the next.

Sometimes repetition becomes routinized, that is, the same activities are repeated with new content. This frequently occurs when textbooks are closely followed to ensure learning. The materials support the same activities, which always occur in the same order. The following is an example in a spelling textbook:

Target objective: The learners will be able to spell twenty new words on a written test and dictation.

Initiators:

THE LEARNERS WILL:	THEN THEY WILL BE ABLE TO:
1 View a list of twenty words, see how they are used in sentences, and discuss their meaning	Identify the words to be mastered
2 Make a handwritten copy of the words	Experience the details of the organization of the words

Explorers:

THE LEARNERS WILL:	THEN THEY WILL BE ABLE TO:
1 Complete words by writing in the elements that have been omitted	Identify the difficult elements in the words
2 Write an exercise in which long words are broken into root words and affixes	Identify the configuration of certain words
3 Take a self-administered test in which they respond to context clues to write a spelling word from memory	Identify the words they know and those they need to study
4 Practice looking at each word missed in the test, saying it, and writing it	Write each word correctly three times without looking at a model
5 Edit a sample of writing for errors in spelling	Identify each misspelled word and write it correctly

Integrators:

THE LEARNERS WILL:	THEN THEY WILL BE ABLE TO:
1 Take a written test as the words are given orally	Spell the words correctly
2 Take a written dictation containing the words	Spell the words correctly

This is a *long-range plan*. It is designed for a week of instruction in spelling following this schedule:

> Monday: Initiators one and two
> Tuesday: Explorers one and two
> Wednesday: Explorers three and four
> Thursday: Explorer five
> Friday: Integrators one and two

This same schedule is followed, week after week, with the same kind of initiators, explorers, and integrators. Its main advantage is convenience. After being guided through the explorers once or twice, the learners can do these activities by themselves. Its chief disadvantage is that it may not be effective in meeting the needs of all the learners. However, it is a form of repetition frequently followed. You can make it effective by monitoring its results carefully and omitting and replacing the activities that are not contributing to learning.

Most of what has been discussed so far has followed a linear pattern. Sometimes a nonlinear pattern is more suitable. The following is an example:

Target objective: The learners will be able to write an essay about what they believe is the most effective form of government.

Initiators:

THE LEARNERS WILL:	THEN THEY WILL BE ABLE TO:
1 View and discuss a model of the form of their own national government	Describe the purposes of government
2 Discuss what would happen if one branch of government were removed	Describe the functions of the various branches of government

Explorers:

THE LEARNERS WILL:	THEN THEY WILL BE ABLE TO:
1 Discuss how governments in other nations might be different from their own	Hypothesize some differences
2 Compose a set of questions to use to investigate the governments of other nations	Establish a design for their investigation
3 Read about the government of Saudi Arabia	Describe the form of government associated with an absolute monarchy
4 Listen to a presentation by the British Consul	Describe a form of government associated with a constitutional monarchy
5 Read about the German government existing from 1933 to 1945	Describe the form of government associated with a dictatorship
6 View a film on French government	Describe a form of government associated with both a prime minister and a president
7 Read about government in Ecuador	Describe the form of government associated with a junta
8 Interview the Belgian Consul by telephone	Describe the form of government associated with a limited monarchy
9 Read about government in Israel	Describe a form of government managed by political parties

Integrators:

THE LEARNERS WILL:	THEN THEY WILL BE ABLE TO:
1 Work in small groups to design and draw models showing the management of power in the various forms of government	Share and discuss the differences in forms of government
2 Write essays independently to tell what they think is the best form of government and why they think so	Express what they think would be an ideal form of government

This, too, is a *long-range plan*. It would require from ten to fifteen instructional periods to complete.

As we analyze the explorers in the foregoing plan, we can see that it would make no difference how we arranged explorers three through nine. The learners could start investigating any of the forms of government. As you can see, whenever such a sequence is possible, it provides flexibility.

In some ways sequencing and expectancies are related. Through careful sequencing, we can control and build expectancies. Whenever we make an error in sequencing, it is usually because of a miscalculation about expectancies.

LONG-RANGE PLANNING: THE KEY TO COMPREHENSIVE LEARNING

Now that you have been introduced briefly to the *long-range plan,* let us scrutinize it more closely.

Recently during a class discussion about behavioral objectives, a teacher exploded verbally. He swore and then asserted, "Behavioral objectives just won't do it all!"

He was right. He could have pointed out further that they ensure little if anything if they are not part of a comprehensive plan. That is what a long-range plan is.

So far you know this much about a long-range plan:

1. It is similar to a lesson plan in that it is organized to facilitate a prognosis (developed from a diagnosis) stated as a target objective.
2. It contains a sequence of enabling objectives that function to introduce learning (initiators), provide new experience (explorers), and facilitate the integration of learning (integrators).
3. It differs from a lesson plan in that its scope is

broader and it requires more than one instructional period to apply.

What is more, you have a basic idea of a simple pattern for the organization of one type of long-range plan. Here is a diagram of it:

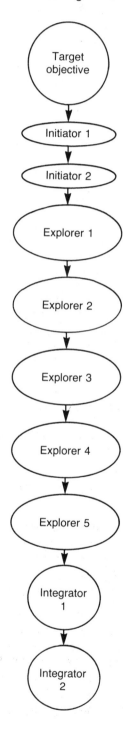

As you can see, the pattern is exactly the same as that for a lesson plan. The basic difference is that the explorers will require more time to complete. You will find this pattern of organization useful when developing long-range plans for nonlinear study in social studies, science, health, and literature and for the operation-by-operation teaching of practical skills, such as dictionary skills, index skills, and so forth.

Now let us examine another comprehensive way in which long-range plans may be organized. And to reduce wordage, we shall refer to the long-range plan as a *unit*. A unit is comprehensive in that it encompasses a manageable segment of learning essential to further learning. It is as much learning as the teacher decides is best for the learners before proceeding any further along a continuum. Here is a target objective from a primary mathematics unit*:

Target objective: The learners will be able to organize and solve problems in situations of subtraction involving minuends of 2 through 5.

We can assume that the learners know at least how to count to 10 and that they can add with the addends 1 through 5. Now they are ready to learn to subtract with the minuends of 2 through 5. The teacher has chosen this manageable segment to complete before further learning is tried. He may have to extend this unit with more learning activities to ensure that his learners can subtract with the specified minuends.

The first entry after the target object is a *unit initiator*:

THE LEARNERS WILL:	THEN THEY WILL BE ABLE TO:
1 Explore freely some situations in which subtraction can be used to solve problems	Apply what they know about counting to solve subtraction problems and create interest in learning about subtraction

The purpose of this initiator is to introduce students to the learning to be covered in the unit.

What follows is a list of enablers, most of which provide new experience for the learners. However, because these enablers are arranged along a continuum, not all are explorers. Some are integrators.

These are necessary to check on progress along the continuum. The number of each of these integrators will be circled:

2	Observe sets of objects on a flannel board in which some of the objects are removed and will help form number names to show what action is taking place	Identify the number of objects in the first set and how many were removed; describe how the minus sign produces the action
3	Form sets with students and move themselves around to correspond with the correct number name	Identify how many students were in the set and how many the minus sign allowed to move away
4	Use markers to make sets and show the action of taking objects away from the sets (five red markers per student)	Give the correct number names they produce
5	Observe objects on a flannel board, sets with objects taken away, and when incomplete number names are given, come up to fill in correct number	Identify the missing number and be able to explain the action taking place in the number name
6	Observe a separating action on a flannel board and perform the action themselves with markers	Build the appropriate number name
⑦	Try independent exercises, page 37-38	Complete the number names for each picture with 90% accuracy
⑧	Evaluate work sheets	Determine how well they did with number names
9	Observe a separating action on a flannel board	Select the correct number name from several choices
10	Use objects to demonstrate given number names on a flannel board	Explain the action the objects take
11	Observe a set and separating action, give a name for the objects left over, for example, $(5 - 3) = 2$, and then consider whether 2 and $(5 - 3)$ name the same number using a flannel board	Explain and demonstrate that 2 and $(5 - 3)$ name the same number

---

*From a unit developed by James S. Smith, POINT V, 1977, San Diego State University, San Diego, Calif.; used by permission.

12	Observe an incomplete number sentence, make appropriate sets, and show the action with markers	Produce the missing number in the sentence	
13	Make flash cards for number names 2 through 5 (300 3 × 4 inch tag board cards, 10 per student)	Make cards for 2 − 1, 3 − 1, 3 − 2, 4 − 1, 4 − 2, 4 − 3, 5 − 1, 5 − 2, 5 − 3, 5 − 4 and practice independently to master them	
14	Play a game in which students hold up a number name equivalent to one the teacher (or another student) is holding up on tag board cards	Find all the different number names equal to a certain number name	
⑮	Try independent exercises, pages 39-40	Complete number sentences with 90% accuracy	
⑯	Evaluate work sheets	Determine how well they completed the number sentences	
17	Play a game with number names in which they hold up equivalent names for a given number using flash cards	Find all the equivalent number names	
18	Observe a joining or separating action and decide what kind of action it is using a flannel board	Recognize whether the action is addition or subtraction and build the appropriate number sentence	
19	Observe an incomplete number sentence and use markers to show action	Complete the missing number in the sentence	
20	Play a game in which they observe a joining or separating action using a flannel board	Select the correct number sentence from several choices	
㉑	Try independent exercises, pages 41-42	Select correct number sentences with 80% accuracy	
㉒	Evaluate work sheets	Determine how well they did in selecting correct number sentences	
23	Complete the missing number at the end of a sentence after watching a separating or joining action on a flannel board	Explain the action and why they chose that number	

24	Observe a number sentence with the number in middle missing and seeing a joining or separating action on a flannel board	Tell whether the action is joining or separating and fill in the missing number	
㉕	Try independent exercises, pages 43-44	Complete the number sentences with 80% accuracy	
㉖	Evaluate work sheets	Determine how well they did in completing number sentences	

Notice that both assessment and evaluative integrators are used. The rest of the enablers in the unit are *unit integrators* and are as follows:

27	Reconsider problem situations in 1	Show they have an understanding of subtraction by solving the problems	
28	Hear orally expressed problems involving subtraction	Write the correct number sentence and answer	
29	Play a game (Around the World) in which they must know the answer to subtraction problems	Demonstrate their mastery of subtraction with numbers 2 through 5	
30	Take a test on subtraction dealing with incomplete number sentences	See how well they have learned to subtract	

As you can see, these unit integrators focus on the learning experienced in the entire unit.

A diagram of the structure of this unit is shown on p. 327.

The preceding plan was organized for five instructional periods. However, if at enabler six the learners are having difficulty, the teacher will insert more enablers to ensure successful learning. Or if the learners were very successful at enabler nineteen, the teacher might decide to omit enabler twenty.

Units are modified in accord with the needs of the learners.

Units following the pattern shown are particularly useful for teaching facts and operations in mathematics, grammar, phonics, and handwriting.

Units may also be comprehensive in that they encompass a body of knowledge that can stand by itself, at least for the time being. This is often true

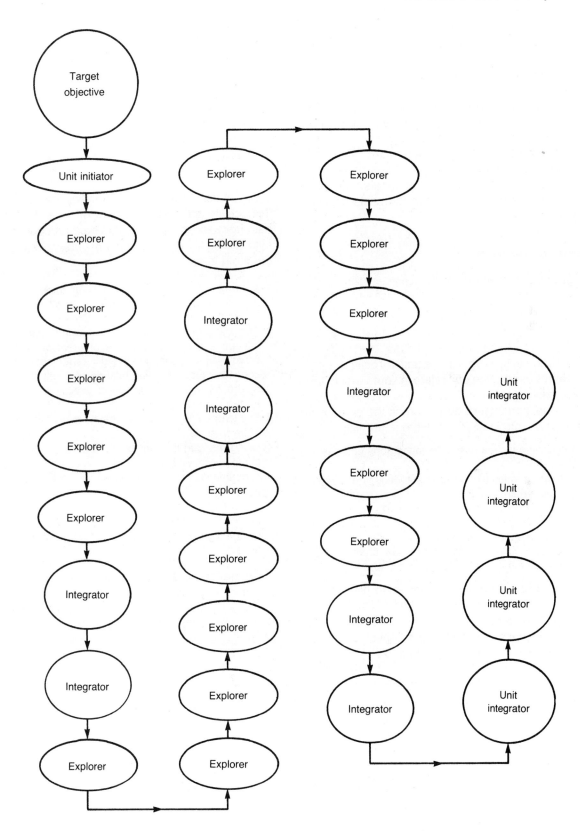

of units in social studies, science, health study, and literature. They are not related, or at best related tenuously, to other units in the subject area.

Our example is a social studies unit that could be taught in grades six, seven, or eight.*

The teacher who constructed this unit had discovered that her learners were deficient in map skills. Before making a prognosis, she reviewed books and other materials about maps, map construction, and map reading. She was particularly interested in the instructional materials she could use with her class. Then she formulated an *organizing idea:*

Unit: Maps as tools

Organizing idea: Maps are flat representations of the earth's surface useful for locating places, finding certain kinds of information about places, and expressing information about places.

This organizing idea describes the body of knowledge to be taught in the unit. All activities and materials used in the unit relate in some way to this organizing idea.

Her next procedure was to break the organizing idea down into main ideas. Here is her list:

1 Physical maps represent the topography of areas on the earth.
2 Latitude and longitude represent location and direction on a map.
3 The scale on a map indicates size and distance.
4 Rainfall, climate, and temperature maps represent the climatic features of an area.
5 Political, economic, population, and product maps represent the uses that people make of areas.

These main ideas are manageable divisions of the body of knowledge to be studied. They are arranged in the order in which they will be studied.

The teacher's next task was to develop instructional objectives guided by the organizing idea and main ideas and based on what she can expect from her learners. This is what she knows about them:

They are skillful in using tables of contents and indexes in textbooks and reference books. They are capable

---

*Adapted from a unit developed by Theresa Reilly, POINT V, 1977, San Diego State University, San Diego, Calif.; used by permission.

of completing individual projects involving the use of paper, cardboard, and paint. Their attention span is the optimum expected for learners of their age.

Bearing these expectancies in mind, the teacher composes a target objective from the organizing idea:

Target objective: The learners will be able to construct a series of maps offering information about a country from which some of their ancestors came.

She is certain that her learners will be able to do this activity and that its product will be sufficient to help her assess learning. The next procedure she follows is to develop *interim objectives* from the main ideas:

1 Viewing a physical map of North America, the learners will be able to label an outline map with at least 12 different topographical features.
2 The learners will be able to record the approximate latitude and longitude of five different places on a world map or globe, find five different places and record their location using latitude and longitude, and record the general direction of five different places from a central point.
3 The learners will be able to draw a map of their classroom to scale.
4 Using maps in their textbooks and reference books, the learners will be able to make a chart showing the comparison of three countries in terms of climatic features.
5 Using maps in their textbooks and reference books, the learners will be able to make a chart showing a comparison of three countries in terms of economic aspects.

As the learners meet each of these interim objectives, they will be acquiring what they need to know to be able to meet the target objective.

The target objective and the interim objectives comprise a skeleton unit to be fleshed out with enabling objectives. The first to be developed are the unit initiators. Because the central concept of this unit is *maps,* the teacher develops initiators to help the learners explore what they already know about maps:

Introduction:

THE LEARNERS WILL:	THEN THEY WILL BE ABLE TO:
1 Read a question written on butcher paper, "What do maps tell us?"	Contribute the uses of maps they know about and see them in a list

2 Find groups of uses that are similar in some way — Develop through discussion a name for each category

3 Analyze the labeled groups to see how they are related — Develop a generalization that defines the uses of maps

She likes to use this sequence of initiators. She could have developed other initiators that would have engaged the learners in a general discussion about what they know about maps, prompted the learners to draw sketch maps of a common area to share, compare, and generalize from, or had them take a preassessment test and discuss the results.

At this point she would also like to give the learners a preview of the final activity specified in the target objective. To accomplish this, she develops the following unit initiators:

4 Consider what features they might put on a map of a country to tell as much as they could about it — View a proposed list and be alert to other features that might be added

5 Tell which countries their ancestors came from — Begin thinking about which country they might choose to map

Now the teacher fleshes out each interim objective with enabling objectives:

INTERIM OBJECTIVE A: Viewing a physical map of North America, the learners will be able to label an outline map with at least twelve different topographical features.

Initiators:

THE LEARNERS WILL:

1 View their hands held flat with palms up — THEN THEY WILL BE ABLE TO: Identify where mountains, valleys, and rivers would be located if their hands were imaginary islands

2 Consider how a mapmaker might show these features — Give their ideas and be alerted to looking for different ways

Explorers:

THE LEARNERS WILL:

1 View a physical map of South America — THEN THEY WILL BE ABLE TO: Use configuration, color, and shading clues to identify islands, oceans, continents, mountains, lakes, rivers, valleys, plains, peninsulas, basins, etc.

2 Work in small groups to compose questions for a game show about topographical features shown on physical maps in their textbooks — Participate in a classroom show to their satisfaction

3 Draw imaginary maps showing topographical features — Identify topographical features through use

4 Draw lines from the labels of topographical features to the features as shown on a black-and-white map — Identify topographical features

5 View their hands held flat, palms upward, and thumbs and fingers spread in any way they want — Describe the topographical features on their hands

Integrator:

THE LEARNERS WILL:

1 View a physical map of North America — THEN THEY WILL BE ABLE TO: Label the topographical features on an outline map

As you can see, the organization of the enabling objectives for a main idea follows the same order as that of a lesson. It might be called a "miniunit within a unit." And now for the rest of the "miniunits":

INTERIM OBJECTIVE B: The learners will be able to record the approximate latitude and longitude of five different places on a world map or globe, find five different places and record their location using latitude and longitude, and record the general direction of five different places from a central point.

Initiators:

THE LEARNERS WILL:

1 Locate the United States and then San Diego on a globe — THEN THEY WILL BE ABLE TO: Experiment with ways of indicating the location of San Diego in the United States

2 Examine the lines drawn on the globe to see how they might be used — Discover the arrangement of the lines and what they are called

Explorers:

THE LEARNERS WILL:

1 Draw and number an east-west, north-south grid across a dittoed picture filled with details — THEN THEY WILL BE ABLE TO: Use the grid to locate items where the latitude and longitude lines intersect

2 Use a world map or globe to locate all the countries lying on a chosen latitude around the earth

3 Do the same as in two, but with a meridian of longitude

4 Compose latitude and longitude readings for various countries and cities around the world

5 Make a rubber band compass

Read the longitude lines that intersect with the latitude line in the center of the country

Read the latitude parallels that intersect with the meridian of longitude in the center of the country
Play a timed game using the readings to discover where places are

Use it on a map to indicate the direction of places from a given central point

Integrator:

THE LEARNERS WILL:

1 Take a written test using the world map in their textbook

THEN THEY WILL BE ABLE TO:

Record the approximate latitude and longitude of five different places, record their location in latitude and longitude, and record the general direction of five different places from a given central point

INTERIM OBJECTIVE C: The learners will be able to draw a map of their classroom to scale.

Initiator:

THE LEARNERS WILL:

1 View a picture of a row of people of varying heights

THEN THEY WILL BE ABLE TO:

Experiment with ways the artist might have indicated the exact height of each person

Explorers:

THE LEARNERS WILL:

1 Find the scale on a classroom map of the United States

2 Make estimates about distances between places on the United States map

3 Find the scale on a globe

4 Find the scale on a map of Africa in their textbooks

THEN THEY WILL BE ABLE TO:

Use a yardstick to measure the distance between various places in the United States
Validate guesses with measurement

Make a measuring tape and use it to measure the distance between various points on the globe
Use the scale to measure the distance between various places in Africa

Integrator:

THE LEARNERS WILL:

1 Measure the floor dimensions of the classroom, the table tops, chair seats, and counter tops, and the top of the teacher's desk

THEN THEY WILL BE ABLE TO:

Determine a suitable scale and use it to draw a map of the classroom on 9 × 12 inch paper.

INTERIM OBJECTIVE D: Using maps in their textbooks and reference books, the learners will be able to make a chart showing the comparison of three different countries in terms of climatic features.

Initiators:

THE LEARNERS WILL:

1 View pictures of banana trees growing in California

2 Share their decisions and decide on those they think are most reasonable

THEN THEY WILL BE ABLE TO:

Join in impromptu groups to discuss why they think the trees rarely grow fully ripened fruit
Validate what they think by consulting an encyclopedia to discover that rainfall and temperature are not adequate

Explorers:

THE LEARNERS WILL:

1 View a world rainfall map

2 View a world temperature map

3 View a world climate map

4 Read in their textbooks

5 Write a paragraph describing ideal climatic conditions and tell why they think the conditions are ideal

THEN THEY WILL BE ABLE TO:

Discover how rainfall is distributed around the earth
Discover differences in temperature around the earth
Discover the various climatic regions and where they are located
Describe the various climatic regions
Apply ideas about climatic features

Integrator:

THE LEARNERS WILL:

1 Locate West Germany, Zaire, and Uruguay on a world political map and on the various climatic maps

THEN THEY WILL BE ABLE TO:

Make a chart comparing the three countries in terms of climatic region, annual rainfall range, and temperature range

INTERIM OBJECTIVE E: Using maps in their textbooks and reference books, the learners will be able to make a chart showing the comparison of three countries in terms of economic aspects.

Initiators:

THE LEARNERS WILL:

1 Compare examples of the maps they have used so far

2 List the symbols for natural items and those items produced by humankind

THEN THEY WILL BE ABLE TO:

Identify the various symbols used on maps

Establish that latitude and longitude lines and boundary lines cannot be seen and that cities, which can be seen, are represented with conventional symbols

Explorers:

THE LEARNERS WILL:

1 View several different kinds of product maps in their textbooks

2 View several population maps in their textbooks and in atlases

3 View road maps and transportation maps in atlases

4 View city maps

5 View land-use maps in their textbooks

6 Draw maps of an imaginary country

THEN THEY WILL BE ABLE TO:

Distinguish between symbols that locate and those that express relative amounts

Discover the conventional ways of symbolizing population

Discover the conventional ways of showing routes

Discover the conventional ways of symbolizing public buildings, parks, golf courses, and bridges

Discover the conventional ways of symbolizing land-use patterns

Use as many of the symbols as possible to express ideas

Integrator:

THE LEARNERS WILL:

1 Use maps in their textbooks, encyclopedia, and atlases to find information about economic aspects in West Germany, Zaire, and Uruguay

THEN THEY WILL BE ABLE TO:

Make a chart comparing the economic aspects of the three countries

So far you have seen the five miniunits developed for this unit. Now the teacher develops the unit integrators:

Unit integrators:

THE LEARNERS WILL:

1 Consider which of their ancestral countries that they want to describe in maps

THEN THEY WILL BE ABLE TO:

Use the maps available in the various classroom sources to construct their maps

2 Share and discuss their maps

3 Rate their own maps

4 Role-play being a representative of the countries about which they have made maps negotiating for trade

Discover how others have used maps

Decide how well they think they have done

Explore the interdependence of nations

As you can see, integrator one brings the learners to the target objective. Integrator two facilitates the learners in making an assessment of what they have done, and integrator three has them evaluating it. Integrator four has the learners seeking for personal meaning in the facts and ideas discovered. Knowing how to use maps as sources of information and as vehicles for expressing ideas would seem reward enough for so much study. However, many teachers believe that the close of each unit dealing with science, social studies, health study, and literature should have learners seeking for meaning at a higher, yet more personal plane.

At the beginning, the term ''unit'' was identified as a comprehensive plan dealing with a single body of knowledge. If nothing more is done with it, the forces of forgetting will soon reduce what the students remember to various amounts of residue. This forgetting can be reduced, however, by providing opportunities for the learners to use the facts, ideas, and skills learned in the unit. In this particular instance, activities for maintaining the knowledge might include making a series of maps as an independent activity, following the fortunes of Zaire, West Germany, and Uruguay as described in newspapers and magazines, and providing for the use of the knowledge in other units.

A diagram of the structure of this unit is shown on p. 332.

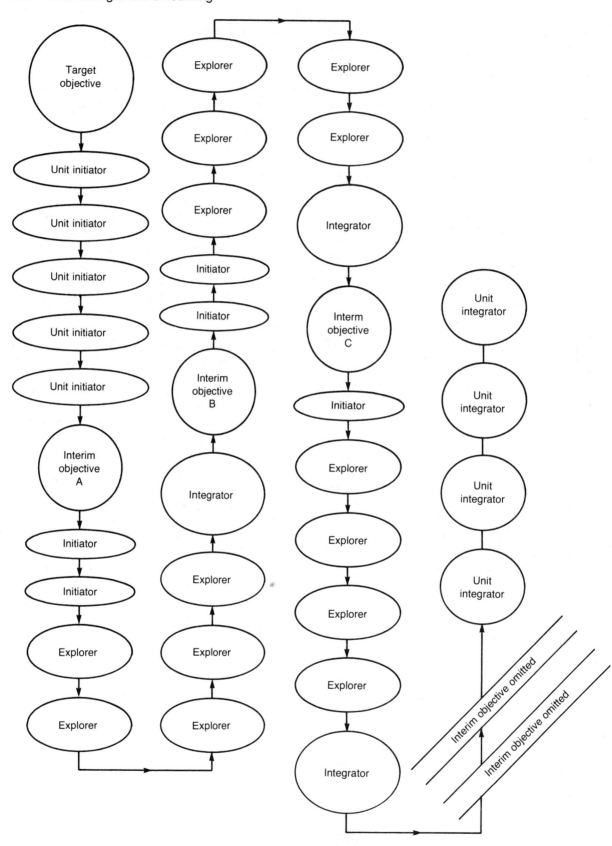

The units we have discussed so far have dealt with specific information. Let us suppose we want to promote creativity. To do this we have to provide the learners with initiators that open their eyes to ways of doing things, explorers that provide opportunities for trying things, and integrators that require assessment and evaluation. Here is an example of such a unit:

Making crayon monofolds*†

Target objective: the learners will discover that creating a crayon monofold is something they like to do that results in a product they like.

Initiators:

THE LEARNERS WILL:	THEN THEY WILL BE ABLE TO:
1 Observe some crayon monofolds made by the teacher	Decide which colors they like most
2 Observe the teacher as he or she demonstrates how to make a crayon monofold	Plan which colors and how much crayon to use or let the project evolve during the making

Explorers:

THE LEARNERS WILL:	THEN THEY WILL BE ABLE TO:
1 Make a crayon monofold on a white card	Experiment with the methods demonstrated by the teacher
2 Make a second crayon monofold using different colors (only for interested learners)	Experiment with skills previously observed and explored

Integrators:

THE LEARNERS WILL:	THEN THEY WILL BE ABLE TO:
1 Confer with the teacher on what they think about their products and how they felt as they made them	Express feelings about the finished product and crayon monofold making
2 Share the completed project with the class (only for interested learners)	Express feelings about the finished product with the group

The "openness" of this unit is indicated in the second explorer, which has learners trying the activity again only if they want to, and in the second

---

*A crayon monofold is a design made by shaving crayon over a card, folding the card over the shavings, and pressing it with a warm iron.

†From a unit developed by Michael Klatt, POINT V, 1977, San Diego State University, San Diego, Calif.; used by permission.

integrator, in which they share the work only if they want to.

The following is a diagram of this unit:

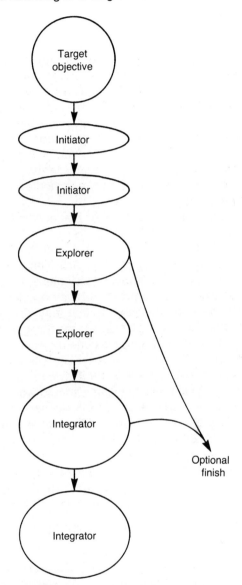

At this point you have probably concluded that constructing units is an arduous, painstaking task. You are right. It is all of that. But let us see what advantages accrue for you and your learners. Let us consider you first.

The first advantage for you is that you know what materials are available; where they are; and, if they are not immediately available, when to make provisions for having them at hand.

The second advantage is that you know what

you are going to be doing with your learners from day to day. Since you know the "territory" to be covered, you will not have to rely on dull routinization of learning activities or pull out your hair in frustration because you cannot think of anything for your learners to do.

The third advantage is that lesson planning becomes simpler. The unit serves as a guide.

The fourth advantage is that you have a basis from which to make assessments and evaluations, which you can share with learners and parents and which help you make your instruction more efficient, effective, and enjoyable. You do not have to rely on a crystal ball or your Madison Avenue skills to survive moments of assessment and evaluation. You are accountable.

And now for the advantages that accrue for your learners.

The first advantage for them is that they have a sufficient number of learning activities to sense their own growth and accomplishment. They can assume some responsibility for their own learning.

The second advantage is that they can anticipate from day to day what they are going to learn. They have an opportunity to generate curiosity and interest.

Their third advantage is that they can have a relaxed, confident teacher with whom to work.

The fourth advantage for the learners is proof that they can and do learn. The teacher can provide it by showing them the difference between what they once knew and what they now know.

Such advantages for teachers and learners make long-range planning worthwhile. And the more you do it, the better you become at it.

ASSESSMENT AS PROOF AND EVALUATION AS JUDGMENT

As we discussed the advantages of long-range planning, ideas about assessment, evaluation, and accountability surfaced. Let us take a closer look at these.

There are few accusations more annoying than that of being unaccountable. Such an accusation implies that the teacher makes poor assessments, establishes inadequate proof of learning, makes poor judgments, or uses inadequate criteria to make judgments. Let us see what teachers can do to establish adequate proof of learning and adequate criteria for making judgments.

When we assess learning, we seek to determine what happened between two points in time. The biggest problem for most of us is documenting where the learning was *at the beginning*. This may mean one of the following three conditions:
1. We made no diagnosis.
2. We made a diagnosis, but it was not carried to a point of utility.
3. We made an adequate diagnosis, but we failed to keep a record of it.

The last is remedial. It is simply a matter of recording the results of the diagnosis or filing the diagnostic materials and results where they can easily be retrieved.

To make an accurate assessment, we often need proof of what occurred during the reporting period. A few of the learners' work samples or products will do. Tests, stories, paragraphs, audiotapes, or whatever they produced to meet the target objectives will serve. A few checklists, anecdotal records, self-rating sheets, and observation records will help.

At the end of a reporting period we may need a comprehensive measurement of some kind to make a more accurate assessment. This is particularly true with reading and mathematics. It is here that inventories are useful. Sometimes the same type of device used for the diagnostic preassessment may be used for the postassessment.

When we have all this documentation before us, we can see how much our learners have learned. What is better, we have something we can show to both the learners and their parents to document that learning has occurred. And, best of all, we have something that all can examine as a basis for making an evaluation, an evaluation that helps us improve instruction.

As stated earlier, evaluation is making judgments against criteria. As teachers, we have two bases for establishing criteria: (1) the learner's capacity to learn and (2) how much other learners of the same age or grade learn.

These criteria become controversial when we try to decide which of the two should receive most emphasis. Too much emphasis on the first is misleading to both the learners and to their parents. Too much emphasis on the second is discouraging to many learners and their parents. To avoid controversy, we try to give equal emphasis to both.

However, equal emphasis to both criteria can

occur only when certain human conditions exist. These include the following:

1. The teacher is a mentally healthy person who regards teaching as a service, not a means of self-therapy.
2. The teacher can regard learners and parents as fellow creatures in this life. Everyone has great hopes and guilts; everyone has successes and failures. All of us are creations of experience. All of us deserve to be heard.

When these conditions exist, the teacher can accept learners as persons, help parents accept learners, guide learners in accepting each other, and give learners the support they need to accept themselves. And it is these very acceptances that evaluation can facilitate.

Evaluation, then, is not a moment of dreaded agony, but an opportunity for growth for both teacher and students.

There are countless moments of evaluation during instructional periods. But these are not the moments we are considering now. They have been thoroughly discussed in other parts of this book. The moment we are considering now occurs when we draw up accounts with learners and parents. Here is how we can prepare for this time:

1. For each subject area develop a rating scale. This may be done with any class set of test scores; study products such as stories, reports, drawings, etc.; checklists; anecdotal records; observation record sheets; or whatever you used for gathering assessment information. Tallying test scores quickly tells you what most of the learners can do, and it identifies those who achieve at lower or higher levels than most. Ranking products, completed exercises, and checklists does the same. Whatever rating scales* you make, keep them easily available for future use.
2. Collate a documentation file for each learner. It should contain the assessment materials you have chosen to use.
3. If you must give a formalized value to what each learner has learned, such as *A, B, C, D, F, 1, 2, 3, 4, 5,* or *Outstanding, Satisfactory,* or *Unsatisfactory,* use your rating scales as a guide. Record these in pencil on a grade or marking sheet.

Now you are ready. At this point you have arrived at a *tentative evaluation.* It is still somewhat open. This allows learners to enter into their own evaluation when you confer with them. Here are some helpful practices:

1. Provide many independent, quiet classroom activities during the day or two when you will conduct evaluation conferences with students.
2. Alert the class to the individual conferences and their purpose. Invite cooperation and understanding.
3. Invite each student in turn to your conference area. Have his or her documentation file arranged in such a way that the conference can begin and end on a positive note, that is, begin and end the conference with an area of strong achievement.
4. Begin the conference with a brief chat about the things that the learner has enjoyed doing or found particularly interesting since the last reporting period. Then with a "let's-see-how-much-you-have-learned" attitude, guide the learner through the documentation file. Encourage comparisons between what was known or done at the beginning and end of the reporting period. This helps the learner see how much was achieved. Ask the learner to comment on the progress.
5. If you must assign a formalized value to learning in each study area, present it in a way that you think the learner can best accept it. Some teachers ask learners what grades they would give themselves. This works well with learners who know they achieve well. It can be agony for those who generally lack confidence or have to work hard to achieve. In these cases, you might as well tell them the value and ask whether they think it is fair. If they are disappointed, use the rating scales to help them see how the grade was determined. Then listen. They may give you clues about their performance that you had missed.

And finally you face the communication with parents. This is usually accomplished through the use of a report card or a conference. If the report card is used, complete it and send it home with the message that parents may confer with you if they have any questions.

---

*Pupils' names on products used as examples on a rating scale should be covered.

If a parent conference is used, you conduct it in ways similar to those you use with learners:

1. Begin the conference with a chat about the learner as a worthwhile person. Comments about anything that he or she does well—mention of leadership qualities, good study habits, affection that other members of the class show toward him or her, and the like—reassures parents.

2. With a "let's-see-how-much-has-been-learned" attitude, guide the parents through the learner's documentation file. Have the file arranged to ensure a positive beginning and end. Share your rating scales and instructional materials with the parents to help them make the evaluation themselves. If you must assign formalized values to learning, share them also.

3. If the parents ask what they can do to help (if there were ways in which the parents could have helped before now, you should have told them long before the moment of evaluation), defend both them and the learner. This may involve urging them to care for the learner as they always have. Again you highlight the good qualities of the learner.

The practices listed here, particularly the preparation and the individual conferences with learners, are time consuming. However, the time cannot be better spent. It ensures our positive accountability to learners and parents.

SUGGESTED ACTIVITIES FOR FURTHER UNDERSTANDING

1. Some teachers do not construct units. They teach from day to day, guiding learners in activities that they themselves find pleasurable or that keep learners quietly occupied. What problems do you think these teachers might have with assessment and evaluation? Discuss what you think with some of your classmates.

2. Make a collage of pictures and captions clipped from magazines and newspapers or make a poster that you think would prompt teachers to take the time necessary to make adequate assessments and evaluations of learning. Share your product with your classmates.

3. Suppose that as a teacher you were given the choice of using or not using formalized value symbols such as A, B, C, D, E or 1, 2, 3, 4, 5. Which choice do you think you should make? Why? Share your thoughts with some of your classmates.

For practice

4. Obtain a course of study, instructional manual, or teacher's edition treating any subject area of your choice. Using any grade level you wish, determine what basic skills and thinking skills the learners would need when entering that grade level to be able to learn effectively.

5. Choosing a science, social studies, health study, literature, or mathematics textbook or other instructional material for learners, select a section from which to develop a unit. Using any diagram presented in this chapter as a guide for structure, develop a unit of instruction.

For performance

6. If you are now working with learners, plan a lesson and teach it. Then evaluate your lesson in terms of how well you judged expectancies, sequenced learning activities, and brought the learners to the target objective.

REFERENCES

Ahmann, J., and Glock, M. *Evaluating pupil growth* (3rd ed.). Boston: Allyn & Bacon, Inc., 1967.

Bloom, B., Hastings, J., and Madhaus, G. *Handbook on formative and summative evaluation of student learning.* New York: McGraw-Hill Book Co., 1971.

Davies, I. *Objectives in curriculum design.* London: McGraw-Hill Book Co. (UK), Ltd., 1976.

Jarolimek, J., and Foster, C. *Teaching and learning in the elementary school.* New York: Macmillan Publishing Co., Inc., 1976.

Kibler, R., Barker, L., and Miles, D. *Behavioral objectives and instruction.* Boston: Allyn & Bacon, Inc., 1970.

Kim, E., and Kellough, R. *A resource guide for secondary school teaching.* New York: Macmillan Publishing Co., Inc., 1974.

McNeil, J. *Designing curriculum: self-instructional modules.* Boston: Little, Brown & Co., 1976.

Nagel, T., and Richman, P. *Competency-based instruction.* Columbus, Ohio: Charles E. Merrill Publishing Co., 1972.

Popham, W., and Baker, E. *Planning an instructional Sequence.* Englewood Cliffs, N.J.: Prentice-Hall, Inc., 1970.

BEHAVIOR 17
ITS NURTURANCE AND GUIDANCE

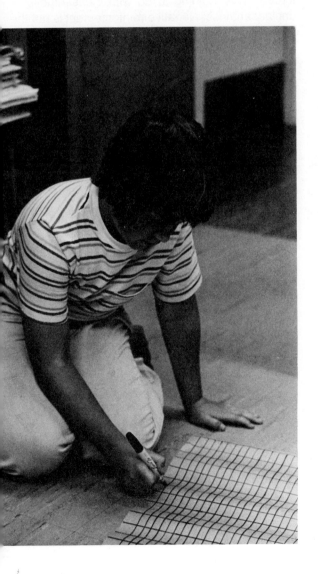

Learning is defined as changes in behavior that result from experience.

Teaching can be viewed as providing experiences carefully selected and presented so as to produce desired learning—desired changes in student behavior.

Behavior refers to all acts that people perform. It is not limited to comportment, which refers to the manners one shows in social settings, but refers as well to knowledge, skills, and values that accrue through learning. Teachers are concerned with student behavior in both these senses. They want students to become able to add, read, speak Spanish, operate a lathe, kick field goals, and live by the golden rule. They also want them to use good manners in the classroom and attend persistently to the learning tasks.

This chapter has to do with nurturing and guiding student behavior. It goes into much detail about two topics—behavior modification and discipline—treated in separate sections. Each section presents a little bit of theory and a great number of practical suggestions.

BEHAVIOR MODIFICATION
The idea: something old and something new

Behavior modification is a popular form of classroom management. The reason is simple: behavior modification works. Teachers are practical people, and they prefer practical management skills that get results. Teachers also want to use techniques that are positive, humane, and constructive to students' self-concept. Behavior modification fits this picture.

Behavior modification is a relatively new management skill. But its underlying principles are as old as human nature itself. There is hardly any secret to it. People always tend to repeat behaviors (and situations) that have resulted in pleasant consequences. Conversely, people tend to avoid behaviors and situations that have resulted in unpleasant consequences. In 1905 the American psychologist Edward L. Thorndike gave this age-old phenomenon a scientific foundation and a name. Thorndike called it "the law of effect." To paraphrase the law of effect, the strength of an act (behavior) may be altered by its consequences. Thorndike's many experiments proved that reward is more effective than punishment in getting someone to learn. When something rewarding follows a behavior, that behavior is more likely to be repeated. And something else happens when a behavior is rewarded: the learner begins to value the behavior and the conditions associated with it. On the other hand, punishing an act does not guarantee that it will not be repeated. Punishment creates more problems than it solves. It gives rise to a pantheon of ugly side effects in learning.

Behavior modification as it is practiced today is based on the reinforcement theory of B. F. Skinner. Skinner's influence on contemporary education is profound. In the 1930's and 1940's Skinner rejected the popular psychological theories, which held that the reactions of animals (including humans) depended on a stimulus. Skinner believed that given stimuli could indeed cause an organism to respond, move, do things. But this explanation of behavior was not complete enough. In his years of careful experimentation Skinner discovered that animals often did things when there were no discernible stimuli present. It was obvious to him that two distinct types of responses occurred in normal behavior. Skinner called the first type the "elicited responses"—responses called forth by a stimulus. He called the second type "emitted responses" or "operants"—responses shown when organisms take the initiative and operate on their environment.

According to Skinner, most human behavior is of the operant type. But an interesting thing happens when animals and people operate on their environment. Skinner discovered that the consequences that follow an emitted response can affect the probability of future responses. If an organism emits a behavior and that behavior is rewarded in some way, the behavior is likely to be repeated. You say that Thorndike expressed this idea in his law of effect, and you are right. But the genius of

Skinner's reinforcement theory lies in the notion that operant behaviors can be *shaped* by their consequences.

Skinner used the term *"reinforcer"* to refer to any object, movement, or situation that increased the likelihood that an organism would repeat an act. He identified two kinds of *reinforcers: positive* and *negative*. Both positive and negative reinforcers increase the probability of responses. Positive reinforcement does this by adding or giving something that is reinforcing. Negative reinforcement does this by removing unpleasant or aversive things from the environment, thus increasing the probability of the behavior being repeated. (It should be noted that positive and negative reinforcers have nothing to do with pleasantness or unpleasantness. Negative reinforcement is not the

---

REINFORCEMENT: The terms used

reinforcer A stimulus whose provision or removal, after an organism performs an act, increases the likelihood of the organism's repeating that act.

reinforcement The process of providing reinforcers.

  positive reinforcement The provision of reinforcing stimuli.

  negative reinforcement The removal of aversive stimuli.

extinction The discontinuance of behavior. By systematically ignoring inappropriate behaviors and reinforcing appropriate behavior, most counterproductive behaviors will be extinguished. When ignoring does not produce results, punishment may bring about extinction.

punishment The supplying of aversive stimuli following performance of an act. Punishment is often confused with negative reinforcement. The two are not the same.

shaping The progressive step-by-step changing of behavior through reinforcement.

contingency management The systematic use of reinforcement to shape behavior in desired directions.

behavior modification The process of shaping the behavior of school students through use of contingency management.

same thing as punishment. But many educators fail to make this distinction and commonly use the term "negative reinforcement" when they mean to say "punishment.")

Shaping operant behavior is a simple matter. You wait for the organism to emit a response that you consider desirable. When it emits that response, you reinforce it. Laboratory animals are easily reinforced by food. Humans are reinforced by praise, affection, privileges, status, and all sorts of tangible things such as food, trinkets, gifts, and money. Behavior is shaped when selective reinforcement is given to behaviors that move in the direction of, or build toward, the total desired end behavior. In other words, behavior is shaped by reinforcing successive approximations or steps (no matter how small) that result in movement toward a behavioral goal. When systematically used, this procedure is known as *contingency management* or *operant conditioning*. Skinner has demonstrated, often before students' eyes, how quickly and easily the behaviors of various animals—rats, pigeons, and humans—can be shaped. Contingency management is a simple procedure that has proved powerful in application. It has revolutionized educational psychology, not just at the theoretical level. It has been widely used by teachers since the later 1960's to (1) prevent behavior problems, (2) maintain rules and standards, (3) correct problem behavior, (4) develop positive attitudes toward school subjects, (5) correct deficiencies in learning, (6) increase rates of learning and (7) improve self-image. Impossible you say? Well, let's take a look and see how it's done.

The basic strategy of RIP

> There once lived a teacher distraught,
> Who cried, "My kids won't do what they ought!"
> She then took a tip,
> Used a technique called RIP
> And now she has all of them taught.

Ask any group of teachers, beginners or old timers, "What is your biggest and most persistent concern in teaching?" Their answer is predictable: "Behavior problems." It is true. Teachers spend a great deal of their precious time attending to student misbehavior. Unfortunately much of this teacher effort is ineffective. It is ineffective because too many teachers forget that they have to accentuate the positive in order to eliminate the negative. About 80% of the typical classroom behavior problems can be prevented. Most of those that are not prevented can be corrected. What it takes is a positive attitude toward students and a willingness to use RIP—a basic strategy of behavior modification (Madison, Becker, and Thomas, 1968).

RIP stands for "rules-ignore-praise." These three words are the keys to a tried-and-proved strategy of solving problem behavior, and they name the three steps in the RIP strategy. Let's take a closer look.

Rules. Establish rules for appropriate classroom behavior. Teachers can make rules, but it usually works better if the students have a hand in establishing them. Student involvement in rule making adds the dimension of self-direction and personal responsibility. Cooperatively established rules are more likely to be adhered to by their authors. Classroom rules should be few in number, stated in positive terms, and easy to remember. They should be reviewed and emphasized often. Some examples might be as follows:

> We raise our hand if we wish to speak.
> We walk in the corridors.
> We work without talking in study hall.
> We take our seats when we enter the room.

The key purpose of the rules phase is to identify the specific behaviors you want the students to learn.

Ignore. Ignore behavior that violates established classroom rules. This may sound preposterous. Ignoring misbehavior runs counter to the way most people have been brought up. Remember the old saying, "Spare the rod and spoil the child"? Most people believe that a teacher or parent should be quick to follow any misbehavior with appropriate disciplinary action. Unfortunately this old scheme is not supported by reinforcement theory. It is not as effective as positive reinforcement. And, worse yet, it has potential side effects that destroy initiative, self-image, trust, and love.

You have to learn to ignore—to pay no attention at all to—students who violate the rules. It may seem difficult to do, but it is an essential part of the RIP strategy. If students become too disruptive, you have to stop classwork, state that class rules are being broken (without naming the violators), and review the rules with the class. (Only in situations where personal injury, property damage, and total disruption are occurring or appear imminent should a teacher step in with direct intervention: ordering, reprimanding, and punishing a student.) Ignoring misbehavior is something that the students should learn to do along with the teacher. No one likes a tattletale or a busybody. It is a fringe benefit of RIP that tattling and minding another's business tend to disappear when misbehavior is ignored by the teacher. The key purpose of the ignore phase is to extinguish behaviors you do not want repeated.

Praise. Praise behaviors that correspond to classroom rules. Catch students being good. When the teacher follows appropriate or on-task behavior with an immediate positive reinforcer such as praise, it strengthens the desired behavior. For example, a class may have the rule: "We take our seats when we enter the room." Children who do not sit down immediately after entering the classroom are ignored by the teacher. Children who sit down immediately are "caught" and rewarded by the teacher who says, "I can tell who is ready to work because they are sitting at their desks." The teacher is quick to reward model behavior. What about the student who has been a rule violator? Make a special attempt to reward any tendency of that student to approximate the desired behavior. Don't wait for the complete behavior to manifest itself. John may rarely go to his seat after he enters the classroom. The teacher will ignore his wandering around. But just let John get next to his own desk and the teacher will say, "I like the way John is getting ready to sit down." When John sits down, he will be further rewarded, "John is really ready to work!" The teacher is shaping John's behavior by rewarding any movement, accidental or intentional, that John makes toward obeying a classroom rule.

Why is each phase of the RIP strategy essential? For one thing, the establishment of rules does not ensure that desired behavior will automatically follow. But rules are a starting point. Rules provide guidelines for behavior. People, young and old, feel more comfortable if they know the rules and standards that govern a given situation. If rules are not made known, they may be broken in total innocence—sometimes to the embarrassment of the violators. If rules are not established, there are no standards by which to judge behavior. Without

standards, identification of right-wrong, good-bad, and acceptable-unacceptable is a highly subjective matter. Without standards, enforcement is arbitrary and difficult. Without standards, rewards and punishment have no reasonable basis. Establishing rules is the first step. But the rules need the support of positive reinforcement.

Ignoring misbehavior is important because we do not want to draw attention to it. It should come as no surprise that certain forms of misbehavior can be very rewarding. Making a friend laugh out loud in a quiet work period might be rewarding enough for the normally well-behaved child to risk teacher disapproval.

For some young people, misbehavior is a purposeful attention-getting device. Many students are not able to gain teacher or peer approval for academic or social skills. The truth is they might not have been given the chance. Labeled as failures or nonachievers, they easily turn to misbehaving, which is sure to put them in the spotlight. They are like Arnold, a seventh-grade boy. Arnold's mathematics teacher, Mr. Steward, would complain that Arnold constantly required reprimands for rule infractions and goofing off. With the baleful look of a depressed beagle, Mr. Steward would say, "I'm after Arnold all the time—why doesn't he ever learn?" The fact is that Arnold learned very well. He learned that he could not get Mr. Steward's attention by being successful in mathematics (Mr. Steward favored his high achievers). But Arnold could get his teacher's attention quite easily by clowning and disrupting the class. Mr. Steward didn't realize it, but he was reinforcing Arnold every time he reprimanded the boy. Mr. Steward should have ignored Arnold's clowning and worked to find reasons to praise the boy's meager efforts in mathematics. We know that ignoring is not sufficient by itself to bring about extinction of inappropriate behavior. One must, at the same time, praise desirable behavior.

When model behavior is exhibited, praise it.

Desired behavior must not be taken for granted. Unfortunately, desired behavior is often taken for granted. We have a traditional belief that has not served us well. Sometimes we hear people express it this way: "No one ought to get rewards for doing the right thing. It's a moral obligation to do right." The facts are that good behaviors, even

SOME BASICS OF BEHAVIOR MODIFICATION

Focus on the *behavior*
of the learner.

The learner's personal history, mental state, and so forth may be important, but they are hard to identify and even harder to do anything about.

Identify the kinds of behaviors that are *appropriate* for given situations. You develop classroom rules. You specify behavioral objectives.

Use *positive* reinforcers to *shape* desired behaviors. Reward even the slightest behavior if it shows movement in the direction of the total desired behavior.

Extinguish undesirable behaviors by (1) ignoring them and allowing them to go unrewarded or (2) if ignoring won't work, by direct intervention or punishment.

Maintain desirable behaviors by occasionally rewarding them on a random basis.

moral obligations, are learned and strengthened when they are rewarded. There is danger in ignoring desirable behavior and allowing it to go unrewarded. Behavior that goes unrewarded loses its strength. Eventually it may vanish or occur only on rare occasions.

What's wrong with punishment? We have seen that ignoring misbehavior helps extinguish it. We have learned that it is helpful if the class participates in ignoring behavior because attention from classmates is just as much, if not more, reinforcing as attention from the teacher. It is relatively easy to practice ignoring simple misbehaviors and errors in learning class routines and subject matter. But the most difficult part of contingency management for teachers is ignoring serious misbehaviors. Sometimes it just cannot be done. The teacher needs to intervene.

Punishment can take many different forms, from the mild tongue lashing to the principal's paddle. At the mild end of the scale, punishment consists of communication (usually one way) between the teacher and child. Typically the teacher sends a solution message to the student. He may firmly give whispered advice: "You may not do that in this room." He may order: "Put down that bat this minute!" He may direct: "I don't want to see you socializing until you've cleaned up the mess you made." Reprimands don't have to be mild. But they should not degenerate into vicious verbal attacks. Teachers should avoid reprimands that are essentially judgmental and convey put-down messages. Statements such as "What you need is a good whipping!" or "You have the nastiest mouth in this room!" directly criticize the child rather than focus on the misbehavior. There is nothing constructive about judgmental and put-down messages. They are a psychologically damaging attack on the person.

Isolation of a disruptive student is a common form of discipline. It appeals to teachers if for no other reason than it buys some time free of trouble. Isolation is a reasonably humane form of discipline, and it is seldom rewarding to the student. Isolation is, nonetheless, punishment. Like other forms of punishment it seldom helps the learner improve behavior.

Punishment should be used only as a last resort. As we noted earlier, it creates more problems than it solves. It may produce some short-term beneficial effects, but in the long run, it's a bad investment. Here's why:

1. It produces anxiety, together with escape and avoidance behaviors. Students learn to fear and dislike school situations and subjects in which they have experienced a great deal of punishment.
2. Lying, stealing, and cheating are common behavior patterns that students develop in order to avoid punishment.
3. Hostility, aggression, and hangdog submission can result from severe punishment, especially if it is continually applied.
4. Punishment often produces feelings of guilt, inadequacy, and a loss of self-esteem.
5. Punishment administered by adults sets up models of aggressive behavior for the young. Children of punitive parents tend to be punitive toward other children, and when they reach adulthood, they tend to be punitive toward their own children. It has been reported that most cases of severe child abuse involve parents who were themselves abused as children.
6. Punishment may prevent the development of a loving relationship between adult and learner, although this is not necessarily the case if the learner believes the punishment is deserved and just.

Above and beyond RIP: higher strategies

So far we have looked at RIP, the basic strategy of rules-ignore-praise. Practically all school applications of behavior modification are based on the RIP design. But praise is not the only useful reinforcer. The use of other reinforcers leads us to some more sophisticated strategies. We could say that they all follow an RIR pattern: reward—ignore—reinforce.

Reinforcement is a powerful factor in learning. People will work hard for payoffs of some kind. Most payoffs fit categories that parallel a hierarchy of human needs. Maslow's hierarchy of universal human needs serves as an example:

Food Water Sex
Safety Shelter
Recognition Praise
Knowledge Understanding

This list represents things that are *primary reinforcers*. They have *intrinsic value* to human beings. We know people normally work hard to attain these things. A day of careful observation around a school will demonstrate how students will work for affection, belonging, recognition, and praise. But reinforcement is not all that simple, because there are many *secondary reinforcers* that motivate human beings. Secondary reinforcers are objects or acts that have been associated with primary reinforcers and have taken on value. The infant likes its bottle even when there is no milk in it. The gambler likes a roll of $10 bills even if there is no place to wager it. The student values a smile from his teacher even though no words of praise are spoken.

Some secondary reinforcers are almost universal. But their value is nonetheless learned. So individual differences in experience determine the strength of secondary reinforcers. Take the student with a history of failure in sports but success in electronics. He will be more motivated to attain the status position of "media technician" than he will to become "chairman of sports activity week." This is important to teachers. One of the first and most crucial aspects of applying reinforcement theory is to identify reinforcers that will have strength as rewards. The value and strength of a given reinforcer can vary from individual to individual and from group to group.

The choice and strength of reinforcers also depend on the age of the student. This fact has strong implications for those planning to implement reinforcement programs. As students grow older, they look more and more to their peer group for approval. They begin to value what their peers value. This does not mean that upper-grade students don't seek approval from teachers and other adults. They do, but in different ways. What works as a reinforcer in first grade will often not work in twelfth grade. Take the business of getting a student to stay on task during a work period. The first-grade teacher can produce great effects with simple praise, "I like the way Bob, Joanne, Chris, and Martha are working." First graders are generally eager to please their teacher and will be rewarded by her direct praise. The same comment to an eighth-grade class would undoubtedly produce derisive laughter, mimicking, and embarrassment for the students singled out for teacher praise. An eighth-grade teacher would reward students with reinforcers that have peer status.

We can define three categories of reinforcers that function in the school setting. They are *social reinforcers,* both verbal and nonverbal; *concrete reinforcers,* including food, tangibles and play materials, tokens, and certificates; and *activity reinforcers,* that is, activities, privileges, and status positions. The following list identifies some specific reinforcers:

Social reinforcers

Verbal reinforcers (praising words and comments)
For children and adolescents:

OK	Fine answer	Exactly
Wow!	Nice going	Thank you
Good job	Great	Right
Tremendous	Good thinking	Beautiful
Excellent	That's clever	Good for you
That's interesting.		Let's give John a hand.
You're on the ball.		That was very kind of
Would you share this?		you.
You should show this		You really have the idea.
to your parents.		I like that.

For children only:

Good helper	Big boy	Big girl
Sharp eyes	Sharp ears	Super worker
Good quiet worker	Nice picture	

I like the way John is working.
Mary is going to finish on time.
You people are working like sixth graders (to a class of fourth graders).
I like the way Larry is sitting up tall.
You are really paying attention.

Non-verbal reinforcers (Facial expressions, gestures, nearness, and physical contact)
For children and adolescents:

Facial expressions and gestures:

Smiling	Winking	Nodding
Laugh with	Looking	approval
eye contact	interested	Thumbs up
Circle thumb and forefinger (A-OK)		

Nearness:

Sit near	Lean over	Give assistance
Be near	Eat with	to
Play with	Go out to	Walk with
	recess with	

Physical contact:

Touch	Pat on back	Shake hand
	or shoulder	

For children only:

Physical contact:
Hug	Hold hands	Hold on lap
Pat on head	Stroke	Kiss
Walk arm over shoulder		Tickle

For adolescents:

Physical contact:
Teacher discretion is advised.
Teacher behavior can be misinterpreted by students and parents.

Concrete reinforcers

Food

For children and adolescents:

Apples	Candy bars	Peanuts
Cookies	Dried fruits	Bananas
Soft drinks	Oranges	Ice cream
Cracker Jack	Popsicles	Raisins
Doughnuts	Popcorn	Gum
Hot dogs	Hamburgers	M & M's
Jelly beans	Chocolate	Beef jerky
Hot chocolate	kisses	

For children only:

| Candied cereal | Lollipops | Minimarsh-mallows |

For adolescents:

| Chips and dips | Herb tea | A free meal |

Tangibles and play materials

For children and adolescents:

Records	Toys	Figurines
Comic books	Puzzles	Dolls
Playing cards	Notebooks	Books
Games	Sports equip-	Key chains
Pens	ment	Pencils
Real money	Magic Markers	Model kits
Art print	Toothbrushes	Combs

For children only:

Clay	Crayons	Jacks
Coloring books	Marbles	Blocks
Balloons	Toy animals	Picture
Legos	Toy cars	books
Badges	Toy soldiers	Noisemakers
Kites		

For adolescents:

School decals	Address books	Tickets to
Tickets to sports	Cassette tapes	concert
event	Paperback	School
School pen-	books	T-shirts
nants	Motorcycle	Calendars
Tickets to movie	magazines	Fan maga-
Hot rod maga-	Jewelry	zines
zines	Stationery	Posters
Cosmetics		

Tokens

For children and adolescents:

Points tallied on chart	Tickets
Points tallied on chalkboard	Coupons
Punches on card	Plastic tokens
Stamps in a book	Golf counters
Class money	

Bonus points stamped or written on schoolwork (to be torn off and redeemed by students)

For children only:

"Happy face"	Tags that go	Play money
marks	on a ring	Rubber stamp
Gold stars	Pennies	marks
Snoopy stickers	Beads	

Praise cards (read "good worker," "good helper," etc.)

For adolescents:

Checks to be drawn on class bank

Certificates

For children and adolescents:
Certificates of:

Academic achievement
Improvement
Specified academic improvement
Special recognition
Check-out mastery for audiovisual equipment

Complimentary letters to parents:

Good attendance
For specified behavior
Good citizenship
Thanks
Specified skill mastery

For children only:
Certificates for being:

"Good listener"
"Quiet worker"
"Good helper"
Special badge to wear in class or home

For adolescents:

Letter of recommendation for a job
Letter of advocacy
Letter of thanks

Activity reinforcers

Individual

For children and youth:

Playing a game	Free reading	Being group
Getting to sit	Going to the	leader
where you want	library	Being on safe-
Choosing the	Being hall	ty patrol
game	monitor	Going first
Being in a skit		
Having extra time	Being team	Having free
at lunch	captain	choice
Taking care of the		Going to an assembly
class pet		program
Helping set up		Tutoring younger stu-
equipment		dents
Working at a		Decorating classroom
learning center		Being class officer
Having dinner with		Visiting the teacher's
the teacher		home
Being ball monitor		

Taking the class pet home for the weekend
Being called on to answer first
Working on special projects or hobbies

For children only:

Sitting near the	Being teacher's
teacher	helper
Leading the flag	Choosing songs to
salute	sing
Getting to draw a	Being paper monitor
picture	Getting to share first
Helping clean up	
Reading or performing for the principal	

Bringing a pet or toy to school
"Snoopy" or other pet toy gets to sit at your table
Having your art or classwork displayed in the hall

For adolescents:

Being excused	Getting to "cut" class
from a test	Choosing alternate
Studying with a	assignments
friend	Demonstrating spe-
Being class repre-	cial skills
sentative	Having a teacher
Making your own	sponsor you
work schedule	

Having a teacher write a complimentary letter to
your parents
Having your picture in the office as "student of the
week"

Group

For children and adolescents:

Getting a free pe-	Watching television
riod	Listening to music
Putting on a show for	Going on a field trip
another class	Playing games in
Seeing a film	class
Having a party	Having class out-
Going out to re-	doors
cess early	Competing with another
Having a longer or extra	class
recess	

Having a class art display in the hall or library

For children only:

Putting on a puppet show
Having a policeman or fireman visit
Being entertained by older students
Being cafeteria helpers
Being hall and yard monitors

For adolescents:

Having a rap session
Changing the "due date" for an assignment
Getting to go home early—having class cancelled
for the day
Having the teacher entertain in class
Being treated to a party or outing by the teacher
Choosing and working on a class project
Having a social affair during class time

A taxonomy of behavior modification in the classroom

From what you have seen so far, you can recognize that behavior modification serves two purposes: *management of behavior* and *facilitation of learning*. Behavior modification can help prevent problems and support appropriate, on-task behaviors. This is the *maintenance function* of behavior modification. When problems arise, they can be effectively controlled or eliminated. This is the *corrective function* of behavior modification. Academic performance can also be improved when behavior modification is used to increase rates of learning and change attitudes about learning. Here it serves a *facilitative function*.

You know, too, that behavior modification can be quite simple or quite complex. It can be manipulative or contractual. The taxonomy and examples listed here will give some idea of the various levels and uses of behavior modification in the classroom.

Informal maintenance: individual and group

Problem: No problems identified
Objective: No specific objective. Mrs. Dalton works at maintaining a positive classroom climate and preventing behavior problems through positive reinforcement.
Examples: Mrs. Dalton uses both verbal and nonverbal social reinforcers. She often says "great," "very fine," "good going," or smiles and pats shoulders right after any student exhibits desirable behavior or finishes a problem.
Program: Informal, that is, no program involved. Mrs. Dalton uses social reinforcers only. She ignores inappropriate behavior. She catches students being good.
Outcome: Mrs. Dalton's class members tend to do their work without fussing. They like her room. Mrs. Dalton accentuates the positive and eliminates the negative.

Informal facilitation: individual and group

The previous example illustrates informal facilitation as well. During all academic work periods, Mrs. Dalton uses praise and nonverbal social reinforcers to reward on-task behavior and progress. She is careful to praise even the smallest achievement made by a slow learner. No student in her classroom escapes her positive recognition. The students in Mrs. Dalton's class feel good about themselves. They have a positive attitude about their schoolwork. As a result, even those who have learning difficulties make progress with Mrs. Dalton.

Informal correction: individual

Problem: Mr. Stanton has trouble with Herbie, who rarely starts to work without a "reminder."

Objective: To get Herbie to go to work without having to be reminded.
Example: Mr. Stanton says "I like the way Herbie is going to work" the minute he sees Herbie attending to his assignment.
Program: Informal rewarding of successive approximations of self-starting behavior; only social reinforcers or simple concrete reinforcers are used. Mr. Stanton tries to "catch" Herbie working. He rewards as much as possible any on-task behavior that Herbie exhibits.
Outcome: Herbie tends to get to work without wasting time. After some time, Herbie's on-task behavior is strong enough that it requires only occasional praise to be maintained.

Informal correction: group

Problem: Miss Harrison's seventh-grade English class is disrupted by four girls who are combing their hair, admiring themselves with pocket mirrors, and whispering about fashions.
Objective: To get the girls working on their assignment and to stop their disruptive, off-task behavior.
Example: Miss Harrison ignores the girls but walks around the classroom nodding approval and looking interested in those students who are working quietly.
Program: Miss Harrison uses the rules-ignore-praise design. She has rules established in her classroom. When rules are broken, she ignores the misbehavior. Instead she uses social reinforcers to reward the students who are exhibiting appropriate behavior. In this way she doesn't call attention to the misbehaving students. She knows that in many cases students find reprimands rewarding and seek attention by misbehaving.
Outcome: The four girls put away their combs and mirrors and get to work.

Systematic maintenance: individual and group

Problem: No problems identified.
Objective: To maintain group performance in accordance with established classroom rules and to minimize problem behavior and keep learners on-task.
Example: Miss Willette rewards students with social reinforcers and points or tokens when their performance is related to established classroom rules and behavioral objectives.
Program: Classroom standards and objectives are cooperatively established. The rules-ignore-praise design is followed. Children earn tokens or points, which can be cashed in for material rewards, privileges, or

activities. The payoff can also be on a group basis, such as a field trip or a Friday afternoon party if a certain level of performance has been maintained.

Outcome: Miss Willette's class members stay on-task and enjoy working in her class.

Systematic correction: individual

Problem: Ms. Larsen wants "hyperactive" Mary Margaret to work at her seat. Mary Margaret's typical behavior is that of wandering around the room bothering other students despite warnings and punishment.

Objective: To get Mary Margaret to work at her seat for periods of at least 15 minutes at a time.

Example: Ms. Larsen provides Mary Margaret with a stamp book with places for ten stamps to a page. She tells Mary Margaret how she will earn stamps for good work habits and what she can "buy" with completed pages.

Program: An individualized token reward system. At first the child is given a token (stamp) for any momentary attention to her work. Her behavior is *shaped* in the direction of working longer periods of time by immediately rewarding a longer period of attention. Behavior is maintained by an unpredictable intermittent schedule of reward. Each time Ms. Larsen gives Mary Margaret a token or payoff, she praises so as to associate praise with desired behavior and strengthen praise as a reinforcer for the child. Ms. Larsen has selected various activities and privileges that appeal to Mary Margaret as payoffs that can be bought with the tokens. Payoffs carry different point values according to desirability or time involved. Some payoffs are "cheap." Mary Margaret was able to turn in her first ten-stamp page for a payoff of 15 minutes of free play with dolls, toys, or games. After experiencing quick, inexpensive payoffs, the child may begin to "bank" her stamps for a privilege that costs 10 completed pages or 100 stamps.

Outcome: Mary Margaret's behavior will be shaped so that she eventually will work for 15-minute periods, perhaps even longer, for only an occasional verbal or token reward.

Systematic correction: group

The preceding example gives a basic technique for systematic correction of group misbehavior as well. One or a number of desired group behaviors may be tied to a reward system. Charting or other record keeping may be necessary. Payoffs may be made on an individual or group basis. If payoffs are made on a group performance basis, individual deviant behavior may cost the group a loss of reward. In this case, behavior modification can bring about peer or social pressure. It can also bring about cooperation.

Systematic facilitation: individual and group

Programs of behavior modification are established to reward on-task behavior, willingness to try, and improvement in academic performance.

Complete contingency management: group

Known as the *consequence-managed classroom* (CMC), or the *token economy system,* this approach involves the earning of tokens and rewards for all behavior and academic activities. Complete contingency management requires a high degree of organization, but it can be plenty of fun for the teacher and students involved.

Program steps for initiating a CMC:
  a. The program begins with a new semester.
  b. It is cleared with school administrators.
  c. Tokens are made or selected. Often there are academic tokens and behavior tokens.
  d. Rules are established for the earning, care, and redemption of tokens, for example, "Tokens are not to be traded with other students."
  e. The token economy system is explained to the class. (An informative letter to parents is also a good idea.)
  f. The class can suggest rewards or payoffs.
  g. Token values are assigned to rewards.
  h. Arrangements are made with other school personnel—librarian, cafeteria manager, etc.—for handling outside-of-class payoffs.
  i. Reward system is charted with token values indicated.
  j. Redemption times and "token time" free periods are planned.
  k. Necessary charting of individual academic progress is planned for academic token rewarding.
  l. Behavioral tokens are awarded according to teacher judgment of individuals or groups.

buy it — you'll like it

THE TOKEN SYSTEM DESIGN*

Rules for establishing the system:
1. Select tokens that are easily given (paper, points, poker chips, marks, pennies, marbles).
2. Select a variety of reinforcers or rewarding activities for which the tokens can be traded.
3. Remember to reinforce a lot in the beginning and gradually reinforce less.
4. Finally, remember to praise when you give out tokens.

Procedures for operation:
1. Explain how the system is to operate to the student or class, and allow some participation by the student or class in the final design.
2. Keep records or a chart of who earns what, so that an evaluation can be made of whether or not the system is working.
3. Start out by attempting to reinforce every new successful response and slowly work to an unpredictable intermittent schedule of reinforcement.
4. To reduce the need for special reinforcement systems in the future, always pair the giving of tokens and payoffs with praise comments. This will help make praise more reinforcing for the students.

*Modified from Becker, W. C., Englemann, S., and Thomas, D. R. *Teaching: a course in applied psychology.* Chicago: Science Research Associates Inc., 1971.

TOKEN REINFORCEMENT IDEAS
1. Buy play money and overprint the bills with the words "class money" or "Driffle Dollars," etc, using an inexpensive stamp set. You can also write over the bills with felt pens.
2. Print your own class money on the duplicator. Be as plain or fancy as you like. Use different colors for different denominations. Try making eight 4 × 2 inch bills on each sheet. Cut with a cutter.
3. Make wooden nickels (coins) by sawing off quarter-inch sections from 1-inch diameter (or larger) wooden doweling. Wooden doweling is inexpensive at lumber yards and popular builder supply stores. The sawing goes quicker if you have access to an electric table or band saw. Making the coins can be a good project for students. Coins can be dyed different colors to indicate denominations.
4. For primary grades, duplicate shapes of kites or balloons of 3- to 4-inch size. On different colored ones, print comments like "Neat desk," "Good job," "Quiet worker," "Good helper," "Quiet mover," or "Ready fast." These can be given following desired behavior. The child can trade these praise cards for privilege (activity) cards, which read "First to lunch," "Free reading," "First to recess," "Magic hat," "You may paint," "Take a ball for 3 days," "Free period," etc. A posted pocket chart containing these cards and their respective token values will add to motivation.

5. Print checks and deposit slips on the duplicator. A banking system can be used effectively in the classroom for contingency management, plus it teaches arithmetic and practical life skills. This idea works well with students in grades five and up. Each student has a checkbook with checks and deposit slips. The teacher also has a checkbook. The students are reinforced with checks written by the teacher for specified amounts of money for certain behaviors. Banking is done at prescribed times during the day or week. Depending on the program, the students can buy privileges, trinkets, or educational book club selections. A further extension of the banking system is the microeconomy system, where students buy and sell their individual and group products and services.

6. Design, duplicate, and cut out tally cards or punch-out tickets. Students are given the cards on Monday morning. They must keep the cards in view on their desks. They receive punches on their cards for desired behavior. The cards can be redeemed at the end of the week for prizes or certificates.

7. Make simple rubber stamps from pink pencil erasers. Miniature stamps can be made by carving the eraser on the end of a pencil. The teacher can circulate during the work period with stamps and ink pad. A stamp can be made directly on the corner of the student's work. Students are allowed to tear off the stamped impressions and "bank" them for redemption at specified times. Teachers can also use this system when grading papers.

Remember: *Tokens can lose their effectiveness after a period of time. When this happens, you may need to design new tokens, new payoffs, or a new program.*

Remember: *Tokens or rewards should not be taken away or revoked once they are earned. Contingency management should be positive, not punitive.*

At the end of the book, you will find patterns for contracts, reinforcers, and self-evaluation forms that are useful in behavior modification.

FOUR EFFECTIVE REINFORCEMENT SYSTEMS*

candy system M & M's make handy reinforcers because they are small, relatively neat, and popular with students. They work very well in behavior-shaping episodes where frequent reinforcement is supplied for very small steps. This system has been used experimentally in various ways: for teaching young children to tie their shoe laces and for teaching lisping students to pronounce "s's" correctly. Hard candy and gum also serve well. (One teacher of mentally retarded children bought a second-hand glass globe dispenser such as those used to sell penny gum balls. He filled it with M & M's and let his students earn pennies that they could then use in the dispenser to get candy.)

point system Students can earn points for good behavior, work accomplished, progress, improvement, initiative, or whatever. Points can be accumulated, kept track of on a master chart, and cashed in for such things as privileges, candy, or prizes.

token system The token system uses tokens instead of points. Tokens, plastic disks, fake coins, and so on are given as reinforcers for desired behavior. These objects can be assigned different values. For example, five green disks can be exchanged for one red disk. Ultimately, the disks should be exchangeable for something like toys or prizes. However, the disks often become sufficient in themselves; students will work to earn them without a thought of cashing them in.

toy money system Toy money such as the bills that come with Monopoly games can be used to "pay" students for making desired responses. The different values are shown on the money, and the bills can be accumulated, traded, and used to buy candy, materials, and so on.

*From Charles, C. M. *Educational psychology: the instructional endeavor* (2nd ed.). St. Louis: The C. V. Mosby Co., 1976.

and if
it doesn't work

Don't give up

Why resort to:

NAGGING • YELLING

BITCHING

CRYING • GROANING • HITTING

THREATENING

INSULTING • NAME-CALLING • GRADING DOWN

REJECTING • EJECTING

POLICING

and all those memorable qualities of
teachers you'd like to forget!

Behavioral analysis: from plan to action

Behavior modification has become even more beneficial with the advent of a technique called *behavioral analysis* (MacMillan, 1973). Behavioral analysis involves the skills of observation study and the strategy of reinforcement theory. More importantly, behavioral analysis looks at a behavior problem in its total context. Basically, behavioral analysis is a double-barreled approach to the solution of behavior problems. It combines contingency management with a concern for contributing factors.

As we might expect, the problem behavior and its consequences are analyzed to determine what is reinforcing the behavior. This is done over a period of time and requires some careful documentation. A desirable behavior is selected to take the place of the problem behavior. This compares with traditional behavior modification approaches, which focus *only* on the behavior and its consequences. The traditional approaches do not concern themselves with causal factors, psychological predispositions, or personal histories of the learner. Behavioral analysis parts company with the traditional approaches by being concerned with what goes on *before* as well as what goes on *after* the act. Behavioral analysis requires the planner to look for antecedents—factors that are contributors to the behavior. There is good reason for this. Although we cannot do much about a learner's personal history or home life, we can often manipulate environmental factors in the classroom that elicit undesirable behavior or contribute to it. Sometimes our best efforts at contingency management fail to produce results because something in the environment—some antecedent of the behavior—is effectively controlling the behavior.

SOLVING A BEHAVIOR PROBLEM: What you need to do

Old behavior	Identify consequences	Change consequences	New behavior

Old behavior

Behavior is inappropriate disruptive dangerous, etc. off-task

Sally H.
hits other child during math

doesn't like math
some other kids
herself

Identify consequences

What happens afterward?
Are the consequences aversive or rewarding?
Examples:
Other child hits back
Group work is disrupted and other children are involved
Other children tattle
Teacher verbally punishes
Child gets attention
Child gets change of task

Identify antecedents

What goes on before?
What is the total context?
Ask yourself who, what, where, when, and how.
Examples:
Home problems generate displaced aggression
History of failure pattern with subjects
Fear of environment or task avoidance
Starved for attention
Need for exercise
Need for food, rest
Seated by friend or foe
Victim initiates problem
Group dynamics elicits problem
Medication not taken
Success in obtaining relief through inappropriate behavior

↑ STRATEGY

Change consequences

(Scheduled reinforcement; contingency management)
Establish classroom rules
Ignore inappropriate behavior (hitting)
Reward appropriate behavior with tokens, points, praise, nonverbal social reinforcers, privileges, activities, goods, etc.
Establish a system of rewards to shape "nonhitting" behavior
Establish a reward system for academic achievement

Change environmental variables

Manipulate classroom variables affecting behavior
What kids are involved?
What was dispute over?
Where did it take place?
When did it happen?
How did it happen?
Set realistic behavioral objectives
Individualize instruction
Provide acceptable alternatives
Change schedule
Provide snack break, rest area
Change seating
Change traffic patterns
Isolate work area
Change grouping
Parent conference
Need for social worker
School nurse conference

↑ STRATEGY

New behavior

Behavior is appropriate and on-task

Sally H.
likes math better
likes other children better
likes teacher better

because she experiences rewards and success with work

Sally gains a better self-image

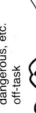

One teacher planned a reinforcement program for a fifth-grade boy who made groaning sounds during quiet work periods. The teacher could not extinguish the groans even though she provided some excellent reinforcement when she caught the boy working quietly. Then one day she discovered what was causing her program to fail. A youngster seated immediately behind the boy would occasionally jab him in the back with the sharp end of a pencil! The boy had good reason to groan. He had been so intimidated by the youngster behind him that he had not given the teacher any clues to the source of his discomfort. In this case there was an easy solution. The pencil-jabbing bully was removed to an isolated seat. The teacher then turned her attention to him and began a program to extinguish his aggressive, hurtful behaviors and shape behaviors of kindness, courtesy, and cooperation. Behavioral analysis does not always lead to simple solutions, but it does bring about a better solution.

There are four steps to take in employing behavioral analysis:

1. *Select the specific behavior to be modified*

CONTRACT FOR USING REINFORCEMENT THEORY IN THE CLASSROOM

Name _____   Date _____

Directions: The contract below will result in a reinforcement program of 2 weeks with subject(s) chosen in cooperation with the classroom teacher. Criterion performance will be a report of at least two pages that is acceptable to your instructor. The report must contain (1) final results or a description on each of the five items below, (2) a description of your reinforcement program with sketches of any materials prepared, and (3) a written evaluation of your project by your cooperating teacher.

1. Describe in general terms the student(s) whose behavior you wish to modify.

2. What undesirable or inappropriate behavior do you wish to extinguish or modify? Using observation periods over 5 consecutive teaching days, totaling at least 2 hours, make a frequency count of the undesirable behavior. Identify the desirable or appropriate behavior you want the student(s) to develop.

3. Describe *carefully* the antecedents and the consequences of the undesirable behavior. What antecedent and/or environmental factors related to the behavior are within your realm to change?

4. What strategy will you use to reinforce appropriate behavior? (Attach additional pages for illustration of your program.)

5. What specifically is the desired level of behavior of the student(s) that will demonstrate *your* competence in applying reinforcement theory? Evaluate the status of the student's behavior *after your program* by using an observation period and frequency count equal to your preprogram assessment.

Instructor's OK _____

(*target behavior*). Identify the undesirable, or inappropriate, behavior you want to extinguish. There may be wide array of problem behaviors that need to be extinguished, but select only one. Identify a desirable or appropriate behavior to take the place of the target behavior. (It is possible to help students select their own targets for change or improvement.)

2. *Assess the target behavior, its antecedents, and its consequences.* Record the frequency with which the target behavior occurs. Find out what is maintaining the behavior. What are the antecedents of the behavior: its possible causes, the time and conditions of occurrence, the persons involved, etc.? What are the consequences of the behavior: its rewards for the student(s), its effect on others, its effect on the environment? This is a "no-action" observational assessment to determine what might be causing the behavior and what might be rewarding it.

3. *Plan a strategy and implement a program for change.* Determine the strengths and interests of the student(s). Determine what kinds of reinforcers will be rewarding to the student(s). Identify the model(s) of desired behavior. Will a simple rules-ignore-praise strategy be enough to extinguish undesirable behavior? Are concrete and/or activity reinforcers needed? Determine when the payoffs are to be given. Determine what kinds of record keeping will be necessary. It may be helpful to decide on starting and finishing dates for the program. The goal date may become a motivating factor in the program for change.

4. *Assess the results of the reinforcement program.* To what degree were undesirable or inappropriate behaviors modified or extinguished by the date of program termination? (Record frequency of target behavior at end of program to compare with preprogram level. To what degree was desirable behavior developed? How can new behaviors be maintained? What aspects of the strategy were effective/ineffective with the student [s]?)

The boxed material on p. 351 shows you a plan that can be used to guide a program of reinforcement theory based on behavioral analysis. The plan has been used with a good deal of success by students of educational psychol-

ogy, student teachers, and classroom teachers.

Let's take a look at some examples of programs that were carried out by Project POINT students at San Diego State University. The three reports that follow resulted from elementary student teachers' use of the contract for using reinforcement theory (p. 352). A last testimonial as to the programs' effectiveness is offered after these reports.

Debbie: Excessive talking*

Debbie is a tall, blond, blue-eyed, delightful fourth grader. She is 9 years old and tells me she has to put up with an 11-year-old brother. She enjoys everything from needlework and oil painting to playing baseball and riding horses. Debbie has a number of pets, including three horses and eleven chickens. With all her interests and activities Debbie has quite a bit to talk about. And this was Debbie's problem—excessive talking. I wanted Debbie to learn when the appropriate times were for talking and when it was best to keep quiet.

My observations revealed her talking as follows:

Day	Time	Talking
1	9:00 to 9:30	||||| ||||| ||||
	9:35 to 9:45	||||| |||||
2	8:25 to 9:00	|||
	9:10 to 9:15	||||| |||||
3	8:55 to 9:00	||||| ||||| ||||| ||||
4	9:10 to 9:25	||||| ||||| ||
5	8:40 to 9:00	||||| ||||| ||||| ||||| ||||| |||

For the most part, Debbie talked during long stretches of study periods, periods with small chances of student contribution. She talked during television programs, filmstrips, and records, in addition to some teacher lessons. Debbie also talked while directions were being given. Debbie has been reprimanded for not listening and for being impolite and told that if she would listen more she would have to ask fewer questions. Debbie has missed out on free time in order to complete work not finished because of talking.

There wasn't much I could do about environmental factors relating to Debbie's behavior. Mrs. Smith has a fairly talkative class so she finds it necessary to rearrange the desks every few weeks. The only thing I could control was the amount of time I spent talking or listening to Debbie. I tried to be available before school and dur-

*Courtesy Beth Farmer, San Diego State University.

FINAL REWARD

This is to recognize Debbie's outstanding contribution to the lowering of the noise level in room B.

Congratulations!!

CONTRACT

I, <u>Debbie Jones</u> agree to try my best to abide by the rules below.

　　1. Talk at appropriate times, e.g., at recess, free time or when called on.
　　2. Refrain from speaking during films, quiet time, when others are speaking or whenever it is appropriate.

In doing this I will be assisted by <u>Beth Farmer</u>.

　　　　　　　　x <u>*Debbie Jones*</u>
　　　　　　　　x <u>*Beth Farmer*</u>

ing breaks to listen to Debbie. Also, during class I tried to call on her as much as possible when she raised her hand. If she spoke out of turn, I tried to ignore her comment.

My strategy involved the use of a contract that Debbie and I signed. Each of us kept a copy. I told her that Mrs. Smith and I thought she was a very good student. I then told her that if she could cut down on her talking, she would be an even better student. I gave Debbie a book of blank pages. Each page was dated and every time I caught her being good I gave her a flower sticker to put on the appropriate page. After 5 days, she brought a picture from home, and together we glued it on a special page in her book. This page was for her 5-day reward. The next 5 days we continued with the flower stickers, until the end of the 2-week period. I told Debbie if she brought in another picture I would decoupage it for her. She still hadn't brought it in a week later, so I made a certificate Debbie could take home. Debbie previously told me that her mom was always getting upset with her because of talking too much in class. Teachers had mentioned it to her several times before. I thought that if I gave Debbie a certificate, it would reinforce her at school as well as at home when she showed it to her parents. If she ever does bring in a picture I will decoupage it for her as additional reinforcement.

At the end of the program I again observed Debbie with the following results:

Day	Time	Talking
1	8:30 to 9:15	////
2	8:45 to 9:15	/
3	8:50 to 9:30	////
4	8:30 to 8:40	//
5	8:30 to 8:40	—

As you can see there was tremendous improvement. These observations were in the same settings as before: television programs, long uninterrupted study periods,

and so on. I am quite pleased with this behavior modification program and hope the results continue.

Learning multiplication facts the behavior mod way*

During the first weeks of school, the whole class was tested on their knowledge of the multiplication tables. Based on the results of these tests the classroom teacher and I chose five children who performed extremely low in comparison with the others.

The undesirable behavior was a low level of skill with the basic multiplication facts. The children's scores on ten separate tests were as shown below (figures indicate number they got wrong).

For most of the children there was a combination of reasons for their low scores. In some cases the testing situation itself was hindering them. Some seemed to draw a blank and wouldn't even attempt to answer many of the problems. The feeling of failure when the others around were marking their answers quickly intensified their frustration. The lack of motivation involved in such a diagnostic test could also be a factor. The children were instructed to do the problems as rapidly as possible, and this also increased the pressure. As a result, the students received low scores on the tests. There was a lack of reinforcement for those they did answer correctly because only those who got 100% were put on a chart called "math masters." The failure to achieve a high score brought punishment from those around them who scored high and then asked, "What did you get?" The overall result was a lack of achievement and a feeling of failure.

To change these factors, the children were placed in a small-group situation and given reinforcement for the things they did correctly. In this group the pressure of testing was removed, as was the competition from the high scorers. The subject matter was made more interesting. The children were rewarded for effort and participation as well as for small successes.

*Courtesy Jane Voelker, San Diego State University.

Students	Test number 1	2	3	4	5	6	7	8	9	10
Roni Sue	0	1	4	3	1	3	4	4	1	2
Jeff	0	2	2	2	2	2	1	0	2	3
Andy	0	0	6	1	1	5	2	5	3	0
Sheri	0	2	6	6	4	9	8	7	8	2
Shelly	9	6	5	0	0	4	6	4	5	10

The reinforcement system used a small coupon book. The first section of the book contained "effort coupons." Each day that the students put out good effort, a coupon in their book was signed.

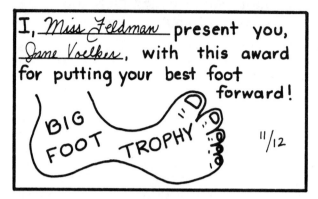

The second section in their book held "mastery coupons," one for each multiplication table, 1's through 12's. Each coupon was divided into three sections: one for the 1's through 4's, one for the 5's through 8's, and one for the 9's through 12's. If the first four facts of a group were mastered, I stamped the section with a "happy face." If the next four as well as the preceding ones were mastered, a star was placed in the second section. If the last four were mastered along with all the others, a sticker was placed in the third section.

Mastery was determined by means of a paper-and-pencil test, with problems given orally. The children volunteered to take the tests when they believed they were ready for them. I had a sign-up sheet for this purpose. As soon as all twelve tables were mastered, the child received a certificate. About halfway through the program I decided the children needed help in pacing themselves. To meet this need, I conferred individually with each child and set a goal for the end of each week. The contract was signed by the student and myself and then taken home for their parents' signatures. When returned, we posted the contracts at our meeting place as a reminder of their goals. Students who reached their goals became eligible for a party on the last day.

My program of behavior modification has been successful. By the end of 2 weeks, all the children except one had learned all their multiplication facts. For the next 2 weeks I continued to work with the group on something else, and the coupon and certificate system was discontinued. To see if the children had retained what they had learned even after reinforcement had been stopped, I gave them a surprise test covering all the multiplication facts 2 weeks after the program was over. Their scores, given here, seem to indicate that I have been successful in changing their behavior:

Students	Number missed	
	Before	After
Roni Sue	23	0
Jeff	23	2
Andy	16	0
Sheri	52	3
Shelly	49	2

Jerry: Hand raising*

Meet Jerry, the subject of a 2-week behavior modification program designed to encourage hand raising and to discourage blurting out responses. Contrary to my first impression of Jerry, he is an immature 5-year-old boy who is slow to respond in a structured learning situation. He frequently acts silly and shows outbursts of temper if someone displeases him. Evidently he was totally unprepared for the demands of a classroom. He shows little respect for authority, has an extremely short attention span, and has a very vague concept of sharing. He does seem to have a sense for rules, especially when someone else violates them. He has had trouble relating to his kindergarten peers, partially because of his tattletale nature. Jerry is rather easily frustrated. It takes little encouragement for him to push or kick another child.

It seems obvious that Jerry has several behavior problems in the classroom. I decided to focus on one that was particularly disturbing to the teachers and other students in the class. Jerry is a very verbal little boy. He has much to say about everything. Unfortunately, his constant talking caused frustration for all concerned. His blurted-out responses never met with anything better than a disapproving look or a blatant admonishment. Thus although Jerry frequently knew the correct answer, he was not gaining approval or positive reinforcement. I chose to try to replace this inappropriate behavior with a more acceptable alternative—raising his hand and waiting to be called on before speaking. If successful, I be-

---
*Courtesy Janice Hartley, San Diego State University.

lieved that Jerry would benefit from the program and so would his classmates and teachers. Jerry would be rewarded for his contribution to the class, and others would have a chance to participate as well.

For my project I used positive reinforcement in the forms of (1) a chart to be filled with stars, (2) lemon drops, and (3) trips to the Brave Center, a "discovery room" used for reinforcement in the school. Each day Jerry would receive stars as a reward for raising his hand and waiting quietly to be called on. After several stars had been earned, he was given a lemon drop. When even more progress was made, he received a trip to the Brave Center. Initially stars were given out rather generously. Close approximations to the desired behavior were rewarded. As Jerry began to learn the new response, he had to work slightly harder for his reward. Throughout the project social reinforcers were used abundantly for further encouragement.

Observing Jerry for 20 minutes on each of 5 consecutive days, I found that he spoke out an average of twelve times per period and almost never raised his hand. I hoped to eliminate 80% of this behavior by the end of my 2-week program. I realize now that I set my goals a bit high. After the project Jerry showed a significant in-

crease in the amount of hand raising he did. However, he still blurted out responses on an average of five times per 20-minute period. The outbursts were frequently accompanied by a raised hand, evidence of my hours of reinforcement. Unfortunately, he hadn't completely integrated the concepts "raise hand" and "lock lips" to the point where he could use them concurrently.

Although I didn't reach my 80% mark, I am still pleased with the results. I saw much improvement in a nearly hopeless case. I am certain that had some of the "technical difficulties" been alleviated, a much more dramatic behavior change would have taken place. Behavior modification is a positive, optimistic approach to classroom control. If used wisely, it can enhance self-concept, rather than degrade; it can replace inappropriate behavior with suitable alternatives, without harsh punishment; and it can create an environment primed for learning, without an ominous fear of "teacher wrath" for misbehavior. I feel very comfortable using behavior modification and am encouraged by the results I have obtained in using it—both intensively with Jerry and more informally with other groups of children. My project with Jerry was an eye-opening endeavor. I enjoyed it, and, by the look on his face, I'm sure Jerry did, too.

I raise my hand.

The reading group*

At first I had some problems with discipline in this group of eleven third-grade readers. They would come in noisily, interrupt each other, poke, and generally act in a manner that did not blend well with the learning of reading (or anything else!). Occasionally they still have a bad day. But I think my efforts to "keep things moving" as well as to use behavior modification have enabled the group to get things done. Some of the rewards I have used are being allowed to play a (learning) game if they read quietly and come in orderly, getting candy kisses on certain days that are "extra special good," and, for children who have improved, receiving verbal encouragement. For the last 2 weeks, I started something new, also. We now elect a "Reader of the Week" every Friday. I made a "pin" (looks like a first-place ribbon from the fair), which the last week's winner pins on the new winner. I made a ditto with each child's name on it, and the class voted for who was most helpful to the teacher, most helpful to other students, most improved or improving reader, most cooperative, etc. We put this list of things on the board each Friday before the kids vote, and I remind them of it all week and say, "Susan is so quiet; maybe she'll be the "Reader of the Week.'" It's really fun, and the children enjoy voting and getting to choose.

Ralph, our first "Reader of the Week," really needed that title. I think it's helped him realize that he *is* a good person and reader, and he is still working at it. Scott, our second "Reader of the Week," is truly a top student and top citizen. He is very self-confident and really deserves the award. I sometimes think that kids like Scott, who are so "up there" and successful in their work, are overlooked because of the need for the teacher to spend more time "noticing" and working with the children who achieve less.

David, a very poor reader in the group, is afraid when I call on him to read. Yesterday morning and this morning, I called him in a little before the group to "rehearse" a part of the reading. He did *very* well. I was surprised. His ability is there, he just needed to *feel* himself doing well in front of the group. So when he read, he was successful, knew all the words, and read with meaning. I was proud. So was he.

Behavior modification is great. I really believe in it. For a good percentage of the kids, it's super. Some children need punishment once in awhile, but as a rule, I *believe* in positive reinforcement. My master teacher uses it as well, and she is a success. It's really helped me and will help my future students as well!

---

*Courtesy Sandra Good, San Diego State University.

DISCIPLINE

Good discipline is a series of small victories in which a teacher, through small decencies, reaches a child's heart. (Haim Ginott, 1972)

By any other name

Discipline is probably the most worrisome word in teaching. We try to shunt it aside, to cover it up with labels, metaphors, and glossy titles—"iron hand in the velvet glove," "classroom control," "behavior modification," "learning management" —anything but the word "discipline." Teachers know you can't run a successful classroom without it. Yet they are reluctant to use it. Parents shudder when they remember ruler-wielding teachers and time spent in the corner. Yet they queue up to enroll their children in schools that boast "old-fashioned discipline."

If discipline is an enigma, "good discipline" is even more so. When Ginott refers to a series of small victories, he tells it like it is. Discipline is not a one-shot deal. It is a nonending process that continues hour after hour, day after day. It is not a hopeless task, not at all. But to be successful at discipline you must show two things: persistence and skill. You furnish the persistence; these pages will give you the stuff from which to build your skills.

But you must remember this: *Nothing* is a magic panacea. The technique that worked so well yesterday may fall flat on its face today. Once you have developed your discipline techniques, use your common sense, and be ever aware of the moods and atmosphere of your class.

We will soon see how you do these things. But first, just what is it that students do that causes all this concern over discipline? That may seem like a foolish question. They misbehave, right? But what is misbehavior, and how does it differ from good behavior?

Ritholz (1959) investigated this matter and made some interesting findings. Teachers see the following kinds of behaviors as most serious among students: sexual activity, stealing, truancy, cruelty, impertinence, and disobedience. You will be interested to know that mental health professionals have a different list of most serious behaviors. Their list includes withdrawing, suspiciousness, depression, resentfulness, and cruelty. You can see that only cruelty was included by both teachers and mental health professionals.

This shows you that the major behavior problems for teachers are those in which students disrupt the class, that is, attract attention of the group away from the lesson and toward the student behavior. In addition to disruptive behavior, inattention also distresses teachers.

The following categories of misbehavior show at a glance which types of acts bother teachers most (Charles, 1976). The prevention and redirection of such acts are what teachers hope to achieve through good discipline.

Now the question is, how do we prevent such behaviors? And once they occur, how do we deal with them? Finding answers to these two questions is what this section on discipline is all about.

STUDENT MISBEHAVIORS*

Categories	Examples of specific acts
Inattention	Daydreaming; staring out window; squirming; reading something else; doodling; playing with object on desk
Talking	Whispering; interrupting; reading out loud; talking to neighbor or across room; mumbling and humming to self
Unruliness	Shoving; stomping feet; moving chairs; moving around room; laughing; calling out; making faces; jumping out of seats
Aggression	Fighting; kicking; calling names; throwing things; sassing; bullying
Attention-seeking	Showing off; clowning; teasing; aggravating others; tattling
Defiance	Refusal to obey; refusal to talk or move; talking back; doing the opposite of directions; writing hate notes
Dishonesty	Cheating on assignments, tests, and games; lying with intent to deceive; stealing

---

*From Charles, C. M. *Educational psychology: the instructional endeavor* (2nd ed.). St. Louis: The C. V. Mosby Co., 1976.

Consulting authorities

You have already examined behavior modification. You have seen how it is used, and you know about its powerful effects in controlling student behavior. Now, to continue the process of building control skills, we will consider what leading authorities in the area of discipline have to say. The authorities whose ideas we will examine include Fritz Redl and William Wattenberg, Jacob Kounin, William Glasser, Haim Ginott, Rudolf Dreikers, and Michael Mahoney and Carl Thoresen.

Redl and Wattenberg. In 1959 Redl and Wattenberg published a book entitled *Mental Hygiene in Teaching*. One chapter in the book was entitled "Influence Techniques." In that chapter they laid out suggestions for classroom control that remain among the best available to teachers. Their suggestions are practical and down to earth, qualities dear to the hearts of teachers.

Redl and Wattenberg group their suggestions into four categories of what they call "influence techniques." These categories are (1) supporting self-control, (2) task assistance, (3) reality and value appraisals, and (4) invoking the pleasure-pain principle.

SUPPORTING SELF-CONTROL. Supporting self-control includes such things as the following:
1. *Signals,* used by the teacher to help students tend to business. Such signals might be head movements, eye contact, facial expression, hand movements, silence, bells, flicking the lights, and placing symbols on the chalkboard.
2. *Proximity,* which is nothing more than physical nearness to students who show signs of wanting to misbehave.
3. *Humor,* which does so much to relieve tension and is one of the traits students appreciate most in teachers.
4. *Interest boosting,* interjecting appropriate words, acts, expressions, etc. to increase student interest that has begun to lag.

TASK ASSISTANCE. Task assistance involves providing help to students who have reached difficult or frustrating obstacles in their work. Redl and Wattenberg use the following terms:
1. *Hurdle help,* providing helpful hints and clues at difficult points in the activity.
2. *Restructuring,* making adjustments in classwork when it is evident that students are having undue difficulty.

REALITY AND VALUE APPRAISALS. Reality and value appraisals are where teachers point out realities, dangers, and consequences of student misbehavior that has begun to occur. Teachers should also give constructive suggestions about more productive ways of behaving, and they can reflect student feelings in encouraging ways: "I know how tired you are. Five more minutes of good effort, and we will have it done."

INVOKING THE PLEASURE-PAIN PRINCIPLE. Invoking the pleasure-pain principle is a way of making misbehavior consequences more painful than pleasurable. These consequences may be grouped into categories, as follows, from most to least pleasant:

1. *Reward,* which is given to students who are not misbehaving. This technique is familiar to you from what you know about behavior modification.
2. *Threats,* those admonitions and forewarnings of dire results. Take care. If you make them, you may be faced with carrying them out. So be careful what you say.
3. *Deprivation,* taking away student privileges as a consequence of their misbehavior.
4. *Restitution,* making up for what was done; making right what was done wrong; replacing what was destroyed.
5. *Corporal punishment,* which was reaffirmed as constitutional by the United States Supreme Court in 1977, much to the relief of teachers. Corporal punishment is seldom used these days. It is not humane, and it leaves bad side effects. Still, most teachers like for their students to know that the possibility clearly exists.

Kounin. In the most significant research we have in discipline, Jacob Kounin and his associates visited many classrooms, observed the misbehaviors that occurred there, noted the control technique used, and gave special attention to what the student, the teacher, and the other class members did. Kounin reported their findings, gathered over several years' time, in his book *Discipline and Group Management in Classrooms* (1970).

Kounin found that teachers could employ certain techniques that markedly reduced the incidence of misbehavior. These techniques he called (1) "withitness," (2) overlapping, (3) momentum, (4) smoothness, and (5) group alerting.

WITHITNESS. Withitness is a technique of continual alertness, of knowing what goes on every moment, at every place, with every student. The teacher is, in short, "with it"—hence the label. This alertness helps you spot situations that might lead to misbehavior, identify exactly who is misbehaving and what they are doing, time your interventions to nip the misbehavior in the bud, and make the corrections that are most appropriate for the situation.

OVERLAPPING. Overlapping refers to the technique of attending to two or more behavior problems at the same time without becoming confused. Skilled elementary teachers are usually adept in this technique. They work with one group of readers, for example, and, while attending to every utterance, they simultaneously monitor the work of all the other students in the room, giving a word here, a glance there, as needed to correct deviant behavior.

MOMENTUM. Momentum means maintaining the tempo of the classroom so that slack periods will not occur. This does not mean that everything must always go pell-mell, with staccato beat. There need to be times of calm. But the calm should be purposeful. The students must know what they are expected to do, even when it is silent reading, listening, reflecting, or just resting.

SMOOTHNESS. Smoothness refers to flow, especially from one activity to another. Smoothness does not allow abrupt changes, with their distractions and confusion. Students know what they are expected to do during transitions. Materials are ready for them. Simple directions are posted or given in advance.

GROUP ALERTING. Group alerting means managing teaching and learning in such a way that all students are kept alert through involvement. The teacher calls on all students to participate and uses suspense and dramatic devices to hold attention. Misbehavior does not occur when students are attentive to the instructional task at hand.

RIPPLE EFFECT. Within this research, Kounin observed an interesting phenomenon he called the "ripple effect." He found that what teachers did and said when correcting one student spread throughout the class, significantly reducing misbehavior from other students. Teachers have long known that correcting one student serves as an example for others by making them afraid, it was supposed, of the consequences if they misbehaved.

Kounin clarified the ripple effect by showing that the effective part for most classroom situations was the suggestion for the correct behavior to replace the misbehavior. For example, yelling "Stop that!" to a pair of students who are talking has short-lived effects on the other members of the class. But if the teacher says "Please stop talking and finish your problems. We only have a few minutes left," the other class members can be seen to renew their efforts to complete the work.

Thus correcting one student can affect the behavior of the others. That effect is increased when the correction reemphasizes clearly what it is the students are supposed to be doing. Simple scolding has less ripple effect.

Glasser. You will find repeated reference in this book to William Glasser. He has contributed much to our knowledge of working with students. One of his most important contributions is in the area of discipline. There he stresses the positive effect of his reality principle on student behavior, and he clarifies exactly how it should be applied (Glasser, 1969).

The reality principle can be understood in this way: Student behavior is reality. We don't need to try to find excuses for that behavior. It results from bad choices made by the student. Yet every class provides an abundance of good choice options. The student can choose to behave properly, and that is ultimately the student's responsibility. Teachers can help students make better choices, and that is the teacher's responsibility. The key question for misbehaving students is this: Forget the past; what are you going to do about your behavior *now*?

In order to put this reality strategy into effect, Glasser reminds us first that schools must be a good place for students. In short, the classroom must provide desirable behavioral options that students can choose. If this essential quality is established, then four other elements should be present:

1. Students must know the rules. They must be fully informed of expectations and restrictions on their behavior. They must know where the boundaries lie.
2. Students should generally agree with the rules. Rules are welcomed when they make sense and when it is evident that they are there to assist learning, good manners, and safety.
3. Students should participate in the continual process of making and remaking class rules. As conditions change, the rules may need to change. When students participate in the process, they understand the rules, accept them, and are more likely to abide by them.
4. Students should know the consequences of breaking the rules. If they have input in deciding what these consequences should be, they will be less likely to break rules and more willing to accept consequences when they do.

Now that the rules are established, the boundaries drawn, and the consequences formulated, it is possible to apply the reality principle to classroom control. Glasser outlines the steps as follows:

1. When a student misbehaves, calmly (not accusingly) ask "What are you doing?" If the student replies "Nothing," be persistent. "You are doing something. What is it?" This step *identifies* the behavior.
2. When the student states the behavior, relate the behavior to the class rules or to individual or class benefit. "Is that in keeping with our rule about _____?" or "Is that helping the class in any way?" This step requires the student to make a *value judgment* about the behavior.
3. If the student acknowledges that the behavior is inappropriate, ask "What can you do that will _____ (abide by the rules or help the class)?" This step helps the student make a commitment to a more appropriate behavior.
4. If the student remains satisfied with the inappropriate behavior, then reasonable consequences, those decided on and accepted previously, must be suffered.

This reality approach is no cure-all. No procedure is. But when consistently used, it shows students that good behavior is possible and desirable, and it helps them make decisions that lead to their experiencing success in the classroom.

Ginott. Haim Ginott has written very instructive ideas for teachers. These ideas are presented in his book *Teacher and Child* (1972), and you will see repeated references to his work.

We began the chapter with Ginott's observation that good discipline is a series of little victories by which the teacher gains student trust. For Ginott, this means finding suitable alternatives to punishment. Punishment generates hate and lowers self-esteem. Whatever does these things must be avoided. Whatever creates self-esteem must be emphasized.

How is self-esteem engendered even when a student is being punished? Ginott has a number of practical suggestions. You need to read his chapter entitled "Discipline" to capture the full range of his ideas. We will note a few of them here, just enough for you to get the flavor of what he advocates.

Discipline is not a matter of finding and applying the right punishment to fit the crime. It is a matter of teaching students to avoid violence and respect the rights of others. It rests on trust.

To correct students in nonpunitive ways, Ginott writes about such topics as prevention, laconic language, long words, being sorry, avoiding trivia, handling angry moments, student decisions, encouraging cooperation, putting complaints into writing, saving face, and siding with the hidden asset. Let's see what he means.

PREVENTION. Misbehavior and punishment do not cancel each other out. To the contrary, they reinforce each other. For that reason alone, teachers should continually strive to prevent misbehavior, rather than cure it later.

LACONIC LANGUAGE. The term "laconic" means sparing of words. When students misbehave, it does no good to berate them endlessly. In fact, that is harmful. Instead of making speeches, Ginott says, teachers should settle things with a few words: "No hitting. It is harmful, and it is against the values of this class."

LONG WORDS. Unfamiliar words have a strong effect on learners. On seeing gross misbehavior the teacher might say, "I am appalled. I am aghast. I am dismayed. I am chagrined."

BEING SORRY. When students say "I am sorry," Ginott reminds them that "Being sorry means you intend to behave in another way, that you are making an inner decision to do so."

AVOIDING TRIVIA. When trivial matters arise, such as disputes over ownership of a pencil, the teacher steps in, provides pencils for both, and tells the disputants to settle the matter after class. This procedure prevents the barrage of claims, accusations, and counteraccusations, and it lets the class get back to work at once.

HANDLING ANGRY MOMENTS. Ginott suggests that the teacher, when seeing a very angry student, ask the student to tell about it. If violence is imminent, the teacher says "I can see how angry you are.

Find some other way to settle your difficulty. We have too much violence as it is."

STUDENT DECISIONS. When students are misbehaving, the teacher can offer options, such as the students staying with the group if the misbehavior stops or sitting alone if it continues. Then if the students persist in the misbehavior, the teacher says "I see you have made your decision to sit alone." The teacher must enforce that decision, not back away from it, if this procedure is to be effective.

ENCOURAGING COOPERATION. Students are often receptive when teachers ask privately for their cooperation. They like to receive letters, either in school or at home, asking for assistance. The requests and letters do not reprimand. They are straightforward in their solicitation.

PUTTING COMPLAINTS IN WRITING. When students bring disputes to the teacher, or when one tells on another, the teacher can save time and help resolve the incident by asking that the complaint be written out to be read later when there is more time for it.

SAVING FACE. If self-esteem is to be preserved, students must be helped to save face when corrected. This means positive correction, private talks, and confidence shown in the student's intention to behave more acceptably.

SIDING WITH THE HIDDEN ASSET. The teacher's hidden asset is this: Always convey the message to students that you want to be helpful. "How can I be helpful right now?" This disarms students, calms them, shows that you care about them, and builds the trust that undergirds positive relations.

Dreikers. Rudolf Dreikers (1968) developed a cogent explanation of why students misbehave and what teachers can do to help them behave acceptably. He recognized that students often misbehave deliberately. They do so because something has thwarted their natural desire to belong. This frustration turns them toward a "mistaken goal," one that they hope will draw attention, give them power, or let them gain revenge.

Every person, says Dreikers, wants deeply to belong, to belong to family, peers, class, other groups, or society. To belong is to feel accepted, comfortable, wanted, and valued.

But many people never feel this sense of belonging. The resultant discouragement and frustration cause them to seek substitutes for belonging. The substitutes, usually attention, power, revenge, and withdrawal, are sought in order to provide the individual either status or grim satisfaction.

In the classroom the teacher becomes the natural object of frustrated students, the target and brunt of misbehavior as students seek their mistaken goals.

Dreikers identified four of these mistaken goals: attention, power, revenge, and seclusion, or desire to be left alone. The student seeks them in sequential order. If the first is not available, the second is sought, and so on to the third and fourth. Thus assuming that belongingness is not achieved, the pattern of misbehaviors will progress through this sequence:

Belongingness not felt → Attention →
Power → Revenge → Seclusion

Let us see what students do at each of these mistaken goal levels.

ATTENTION. Attention is sought mostly from the teacher. This is done by disrupting routines, asking for special favors, and continually calling attention to oneself when the teacher wants to give attention to the group. Attention is also sought from class members. This is done by openly showing disrespect for the teacher and by doing acts behind the teacher's back that the class thinks are funny. If sufficient attention does not result, the individual turns to the next level, power.

POWER. Power is sought in contests of will between student and teacher. This power struggle virtually ruins the student's chances for acceptance by the teacher. But it does bring considerable attention from both teacher and peers. Most students ultimately lose when they set their wills against the teacher's. This causes them to turn to the next level of mistaken goals, revenge.

REVENGE. Revenge, especially in the form of hurting the teacher, provides the student with some measure of significance. However, revenge invariably brings hostility in response. The relationship is bound to deteriorate even further. As it does, the individual withdraws to the final level, desire to be left alone.

DESIRE TO BE LEFT ALONE. Seclusion shows deep discouragement. For the student, it is the most serious response. It prohibits successful interac-

tions with others, and it is very hard to overcome.

PLAN OF ACTION. What can teachers do with respect to student belongingness and mistaken goals? Dreikers developed the following well-organized plan for teachers to follow:

1. *Observe* the student's behavior to see which of the mistaken goal levels is involved.
2. *Refrain* from giving the response the student is seeking. Don't fall into the trap.
3. *Confront* the student with the hidden purpose of the misbehavior.
4. *Take the initiative* by beginning an active program to help the student reach the true goal, belonging. Here is how teachers can go about putting Dreikers' suggestions into effect:
   a. *Attention*. When the student seeks attention through misbehavior, the teacher usually gives negative attention in return. This attention, although negative, is what the student is seeking. It reinforces the misbehavior. Instead of reacting negatively, the teacher should simply say "Why do you think you are doing that? Could it be that you want to keep me busy?" or "Could it be that you want me to pay attention to you?"
   b. *Power*. Challenges to their authority can be very threatening to teachers, who usually react by imposing their will on the misbehaving student. This often increases the misbehavior. Instead, teachers can ask "Why are you doing that? Could it be that you want to show that nobody can make you do anything?"
   c. *Revenge*. When the student misbehaves seriously to get even with the teacher, the teacher's usual reaction is to retaliate. This retaliation destroys the remaining vestiges of personal relationship, and it may provoke more violent misbehavior. Instead of retaliating, teachers should say "Why are you doing that? Could it be that you want to hurt me? That you want to punish me?"
   d. *Seclusion*. All else having failed, the student gives up. No further attempts are made to gain the sense of belongingness. The teacher's efforts to help have no effect. This leaves the teacher wanting to say "Okay, then, just sit there." Instead, the teacher should say "Why are you just sitting here?

Could it be that you want me to leave you alone?"

These responses have three positive effects. First, they offer the possibility for genuine communication, which is always shut off by negative teacher reactions. Second, they improve student behavior. They remove much of the provocation, and the game is no longer satisfying. Third, they take the initiative away from the student, allowing the teacher to implement a positive program for helping the student achieve belongingness.

Belongingness comes with affection, security, achievement, and recognition. These are conditions the caring teacher will now try to provide for the student. They are provided through the use of encouragement and logical consequences.

Praise is given when students are successful. Encouragement is given when they are unsuccessful. Most students, especially those who misbehave, need encouragement more than they need praise. Encouragement is given by the following acts:

1. Helping students see their own strengths and then building on them
2. Enlisting peer-group influences to help all students feel accepted and worthwhile

Logical consequences are used instead of punishment when students do misbehave. Misbehavior should have its consequences, but they needn't be arbitrary expressions of teacher authority and power. Instead, the consequences can be decided on in advance by class members and teacher together. They are invoked when the student chooses to behave in ways that produce them, instead of in acceptable ways that bring praise and encouragement. Their invocation is done without teacher anger or rancor. The teacher can say "You have chosen to _____ (consequence behavior)." The teacher must now enforce compliance with the consequences.

Mahoney and Thoresen. To this point we have considered plans in which teachers play the dominant role in controlling student behavior. Yet ultimately we hope that all individuals will become able to control their own behavior, to attain that nirvana called self-discipline.

Michael Mahoney and Carol Thoresen (1972) are convinced that all people can learn self-control of behavior, that they can train themselves to act in ways they consider desirable. When this notion of self-control is applied to classroom behavior, it means that students abide by the class rules and work productively, even when the teacher is not directing them.

Mahoney and Thoresen developed a three-part strategy that people, including students at all levels, can employ to develop self-control. Older people can teach the strategy to themselves. Younger students need help from the teacher until their self-directing behavior becomes established. The three parts are self-observation, environmental planning, and behavioral programming. These terms sound imposing. Here is what they mean:

1. *Self-observation* refers merely to a particular behavior that you want to change in yourself. It can be anything that can be observed and counted as it occurs.
2. *Environmental planning* refers to making changes in the environment that will assist improvement in the desired behavior. These changes can be removal of distracting elements and addition of supportive elements.
3. *Behavioral programming* refers to setting up a system of rewards and punishments that students apply to themselves in accord with their good and bad behavior.

This self-control strategy deserves much attention from teachers. They can discuss the strategy with their students and apply it to varieties of class experiences. Kindergarten children can use it to improve their ability to stay in their chairs. After a predetermined length of time, measured by the teacher, the children can reward themselves by eating a marshmallow or cracker. Sixth graders can use it to assist task completion. If a certain number of mathematics problems are completed in the allotted time, students can reward themselves with games or free time. Junior school students can use it to increase their social interactive behavior. Each day they can give a certain number of genuine compliments to students who are not among their close friends. They can reward themselves with extra listening to their favorite music.

Remember that the behavior to be modified must be observable and it must be quantifiable in some way—minutes spent, number of times done, amount accomplished, and so forth. Keeping track of improvements is usually reward enough in itself, and students tend to forget about the extra ice cream they promised themselves. Virtue and accomplishment do, in fact, become their own rewards.

Systematic application of discipline

You must certainly be impressed with the observations, suggestions, and techniques made by authorities whose work we have examined. Their ideas are so many, however, that you may be left with more questions about discipline that you had before you read them. Should you adopt a single strategy of discipline? If so, fine techniques from other strategies will have to be left out. Should you, then, try to build your own system of discipline, so you can incorporate your preferences from the various strategies? If so, you will need to put those ideas together in a systematic way.

Most teachers prefer to use their own system of discipline, made to match their own personalities and the characteristics of the students they teach. The purpose of this section is to help you begin to organize ideas about discipline in a way that makes sense to you. In this organization you will want to give attention to the points stressed by the authorities, namely, how to prevent misbehavior from occurring, what to do about it when it does occur, and how to help students develop within themselves their own sense of self-control.

You may find it helpful to think in terms of preventive discipline, supportive discipline, and corrective discipline. In a nutshell, here are points to which you should give attention:

1. *Preventive discipline:* removing the causes
    a. Good planning, with established routines that run like clockwork
    b. Established guidelines and expectations for in-class behavior
    c. A clear sense of purpose and direction in student learning activities that are worthwhile and interesting
    d. Advance planning for special events and unexpected occurrences
2. *Supportive discipline:* helping them along
    a. Continual use of the best communication skills
    b. Continual use of reinforcement for appropriate behavior
    c. Continual use of encouragement
    d. Continual acceptance and guidance
    e. Continual focus on the situation rather than the student's personality

    f. Development of student self-discipline
    g. Physical presence, eye contact, total awareness
    h. Immediate problem response
3. *Corrective discipline:* suppressing and redirecting
    a. Ripple effect, correction with direction
    b. Reality principle, making better choices
    c. Mistaken goal confrontation, seizing the initiative to provide encouragement
    d. Use of logical consequences, rather than authoritarian punishment
    e. Immediate suppression of mimicry and cruelty, using I-messages rather than you-messages
    f. Use of restitution, deprivation, and isolation
    g. Calling in administrator and parent assistance

Let us examine each of these three categories in a bit more detail. Presented here is a general overview of expected teacher actions, how students may respond, and a few helpful hints, illustrated through brief scenarios of actual classroom situations.

Preventive discipline. What you do, or don't do, before students enter the picture can make or break the problems you will encounter later. Remember to do the following:

1. Establish, with class participation, the rules and standards for the class, how they will be enforced, and what the consequences will be when they are broken. Be sure the students consider the rules fair and that they realize they serve the good of the entire class. Be sure they realize that they can choose to abide by them or not, but if they do not, you will enforce the consequences.
2. Treat your students with courtesy. Because we are bigger, older, and sometimes smarter than they, we often order them about in tones we wouldn't use with our worst enemy. If you address your students in a voice that says "I guess this is all I can expect from the likes of you!" they will do their best to live up to your low expectations. The short-range goal of classroom manners is to create a climate in your room that is favorable for learning. The long-range goal is to teach students the necessary "niceties"—courtesy, respect, understanding, and tolerance—that make living and interacting

with other people pleasant. Yelling, being rude, and being unfair do not help attain either of these goals.

3. Identify chronic misbehaviors in specific terms. Determine their causes, and then do what you can do to remove these causes. Sound like a tall order? It is, and it isn't. For instance, "Johnny's always goofing off. What can I do?"

First: What do you mean by goofing off?

"Well, he's not in his seat when he's supposed to be, he's talking to everyone else, he's not listening to me."

Second: When does he do this?

"All the time! Well . . . most often when we're handing out reading assignments. The whole class is seated up front, and I have to pass out papers to all the reading groups and . . ."

Third: Does Johnny have something to do or know exactly what he should be doing during this time?

"Not exactly. There are a lot of papers, and all the moving around that has to be done."

Fourth: What can you do to change some of this?

"I could give out the reading assignments while the children are at their seats. And I suppose it would be better if Johnny's group got their papers first, instead of last, so he could start to work right away."

All right: Now we're getting someplace.

In looking for causes of misbehavior, check through each of these areas carefully:

1. *Planning and routine*. Does your day run smoothly, so transition from one activity to the next is done with little fuss? This was Johnny's problem, and it was easily solved. Watch for the times when students are between activities. Establish routines that minimize difficulties. Plan for the times when you have 5 extra minutes with nothing to do; have games, songs, puzzles, anecdotes, or jokes to share that can fill those awkward times. Whole dams have broken because of a single crack. Learn to mend the discipline cracks quickly.

2. *Established guidelines and expectations*. Do students know exactly what the rules are, and what the consequences will be if they are broken? It will not do you any good if only you know how the classroom should be run. For some students, a daily reminder of exact ex-

pectations is needed. "When we go inside, I need to see you take your seats quietly and be ready to listen for your assignments."

3. *Purposeful, worthwhile, interesting activities*. Are the activities for the students worthwhile and interesting, with a firm sense of purpose? The majority of discipline problems spring up when students are forced to work at boring activities, for example, "Copy these definitions ten times," or when the activity lacks direction, for example, "OK, a group of you get together and make up a book report on a book you read." Students cannot be fooled. They will know when you are giving them busywork and when you are not really sure of what you want them to do. They will respond accordingly.

Preventing discipline problems is the easiest way to control behavior. However, you cannot stop there. You need to learn the techniques of supportive discipline.

Supportive discipline. The most carefully laid rules are of no use if students believe there is no need to follow them. You need to establish an atmosphere that says "We all care about whether or not these rules are followed." To do this, let all your actions show a circle of support, as follows:

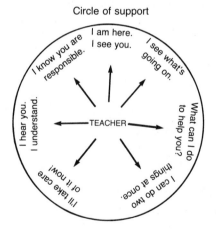

Circle of support

I am here: Just your physical presence helps keep students on task.

I see you: While teaching, correcting papers, or walking around, you catch the eyes of individual students. Let them know you see them as individuals and know what they are doing.

I know what's going on: Popularly called "withitness," this attitude communicates to the students that you know what is happening in every corner of the room, that you cannot be fooled.

What can I do to help you now?: Your desire is always to help. This is your purpose, your professional reason for being. You can do two things at once. Become adept at being everywhere. You can talk to a student privately and still handle the group of gigglers disrupting the class.

I'll take care of it, now!: Students are impatient. They want their problems handled immediately. Except in situations where a cooling-off period is needed, you deal with situations when and where they happen, before they can be blown up out of proportion.

I hear you, I understand you: You accept students' feelings. "I know you're tired, Andrea." You communicate openly about their frustrations. "It is hard to sit still when you feel that way." You guide them into paths that make it easy for them to behave. "If you stand up and stretch for a moment, it will be easier for you to go back to work quietly."

I know you are responsible: This does not mean pointing the finger of blame. You are telling the students that you consider them adult enough to control themselves. They are responsible for their behavior. They make the decision about how they will act. They know what the consequences are for the acts they choose.

All your supportive techniques are aimed at helping students do the best they can do. You are not there to pounce on them, but to help them remember, guide them in the right direction, remove the obstacles that make it difficult for them to follow rules.

Occasionally, however, the best laid plans of mice and men go astray. This is when you step in with your arsenal of corrective techniques.

Corrective discipline. The corrective measures given here are arranged in the order of their impact, of the strength of effect they usually have on students. Learn to use the control appropriate to the misbehavior. Don't chase a fly with an atomic bomb.

A triangle of zips and zaps

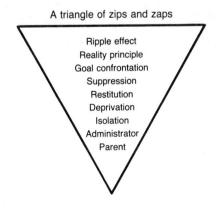

Ripple effect
Reality principle
Goal confrontation
Suppression
Restitution
Deprivation
Isolation
Administrator
Parent

1. Nancy evidently has a secret so exciting she can't wait to tell her friends. While you are teaching the lesson, she is constantly talking, and her friends are beginning to join in the general commotion. Several warning looks shot in her direction have had no effect. You stop, turn to Nancy. "Nancy, this whispering makes it hard for me to teach and hard for others to listen. I must have everyone's attention." Students recognize your displeasure. You have reminded them to listen. The room grows quieter. This correction, which all the other students can hear, quiets both Nancy and the rest of the class. It is called the *ripple effect*.

2. Richard is poking other students, laughing, and talking while the class is at their seats trying to work. You ask, "What are you doing, Richard?" "Nothing. Just talking to my friends." "Is that helping the class?" Richard may reply yes or no. If he says yes, ask him to explain how that is helping the class (or group, or you, or himself). Then ask, "What can you do to help us, Richard?" "Well, I guess I could . . ." He should arrive at the solution to the problem himself. He is responsible for making the choice. Let him know you expect him to stick by his choice. Accept no excuses when he does not. This facilitative approach is called the *reality principle*.

3. Jason has continually talked out and made irrelevant comments during English class. He says, "This assignment is stupid. I'm not going to do it." You ask, "Why do you say that? Is it that you want to show that nobody can make you do anything?" Jason: "No, I just think you are mean to make us do it." You: "Why do you say that? Do you want to hurt me?" Jason: "No." Jason quiets down. You have used the technique called *mistaken goal confrontation*.

4. While working at your desk, you hear Chad taunting Lisa. "You're so dumb, stupid, stupid, stupid." You should make your dismay and your expectations known immediately. "I heard those words. They upset me very much. There is no room for that kind of talk in this class. I do not want to ever hear it again." Children can be cruel to each other, and it is up to you to put a stop to it in your classroom. (A word of caution: Making too much of such an incident can embarrass the victims and cause the tormen-

tors to harrass them even further when you are not around. Handle this situation with tact and firmness.) You need to be alert to and ready to *suppress mimicry and cruelty*.

5. Jimmy is bored with his assignment. Instead of painting his paper, he begins painting the desk. Seeing this, you say, "Desks are not for painting, Jimmy. This needs to be cleaned up, now." Jimmy has created the damage, Jimmy must clean up the damage. When students are asked to make right what they have done wrong, it is an example of *restitution*.

6. Todd, after repeated encouragement, has not completed his writing assignment. You tell him that he has the choice of finishing the assignment during the work time or finishing it by working alone during the upcoming class debate. At the end of the work time, has has only crumpled papers to show. You say, "I see you have made your choice, Todd. You have chosen to use class debate time to finish this assignment." When a student loses a privilege or a preferred activity, it is called *deprivation*.

7. Janet is not having a good day. From the time she entered the room she has done everything but her work and has constantly disrupted the class. Nothing you say affects her. When a disagreement with a classmate turns into a hair-pulling match, you tell her, "Janet, I see that it is very difficult for you to work with the class today. We have a seat in the back; would you sit there, please? You may join us when you and I both feel you can work with the class again." Separating Janet from the rest of the class gives her a chance to calm down and removes her as a stimulant for an entire class problem. In cases such as these, the most effective method is *isolation*.

8. When you have exhausted all other avenues and are still not getting the results you want, you may need to seek *administrator or parent assistance*. Do not turn to parent or administrator for help unless (a) the misbehavior is chronic, and all of your control techniques have failed or (b) the misbehavior is undermining your effectiveness and disrupting the progress of the class.

A final note

Many of the corrective techniques presented here may seem too mild. You may be thinking they will never work. How effective they are depends largely on your delivery. Your voice should be firm and quiet, your face serious. Your whole manner should show that you are displeased with the situation. You do not attack the students, but you show clearly that you will accept nothing less than good manners and compliance with class standards.

As Ginott said, discipline is a series of small victories. There is no one way that works best for everything. You can win the small victories with the techniques described here. To win the students' esteem and respect, you need to combine these techniques with the following:

Concern and caring for the students as people
The expectation that they will do their best
Full encouragement and help with their difficulties
Obvious and ready appreciation for their achievements

SUGGESTED ACTIVITIES FOR FURTHER UNDERSTANDING

1. Write three positively stated classroom rules for a teaching situation. For each of the rules you develop identify (a) five specific related behaviors that you would ignore, (b) five specific behaviors you would positively reinforce, and (c) two behaviors you might punish.

2. For each of the following situations:
   a. Identify the antecedents and consequences of the behavior.
   b. Decide what is reinforcing the behavior.
   c. Decide, on the basis of behavior strength, the appropriateness of extinction by ignoring, punishment, or positive reinforcement.
   d. Devise a strategy to bring about new and appropriate behavior.

   Situation I. John, a physically well-coordinated third grader, "hogs" the game equipment as soon as the bell for recess is sounded. John's classmates are afraid to challenge him. His teacher occasionally lectures him about his behavior. The lectures do not seem to do any good.

   Situation II. When it comes to mathematics, Mary-Jo, a seventh grader of above-average intelligence, won't try. Although she does reasonably well in other work, she turns in blank or barely started papers for mathematics. These papers are always returned with a large red "F." When questioned by her teacher, she says, "I'm dumb in math. I just can't do it. My mom says everybody in our family has trouble in math. She doesn't care if I get a 'D' or an 'F.'"

REFERENCES

Axelrod, S. *Behavior modification for the classroom teacher.* New York: McGraw-Hill Book Co., 1977.

Becker, W. C., Engelmann, S., and Thomas, D. R., *Teaching: a course in applied psychology.* Chicago: Science Research Associates, Inc., 1971.

Charles, C. *Educational psychology: the instructional endeavor* (2nd ed.) St. Louis: The C. V. Mosby Co., 1976.

Dreikers, R. *Psychology in the classroom* (2nd ed.). New York: Harper & Row, Publishers, 1968.

Ginott, H. *Teacher and child.* New York: Macmillan Publishing Co., Inc. 1972.

Glasser, W. *Schools without failure.* New York: Harper & Row, Publishers, 1969.

Gnagey, W. J. *Maintaining discipline in classroom instruction.* New York: Macmillan Publishing Co., Inc., 1975.

Keller, F. S. *Learning: reinforcement theory* (2nd ed.). New York: Random House, Inc., 1969.

Kounin, J. *Discipline and group management in classrooms.* New York: Holt, Rinehart & Winston, Inc., 1970.

MacMillan, D. *Behavior modification in education.* New York: Macmillan Publishing Co., Inc., 1973.

Madison, C. H., Becker, W. C., and Thomas, D. R. Rules, praise, and ignoring: elements of elementary classroom control. *Journal of Applied Behavior Analysis,* 1968, **1**, 139-150.

Mahoney, M., and Thoresen, C. Behavioral self-control—power to the person. *Educational Researcher,* 1972, **1**, 5-7.

Pitts, C. E. (Ed.) *Operant conditioning in the classroom.* New York: Thomas Y. Crowell Co., Inc., 1971.

Redl, F., and Wattenberg, W. *Mental hygiene in teaching.* New York: Harcourt Brace Jovanovich, Inc., 1959.

Ritholz, S. *Children's behavior.* New York: Bookman Associates, 1959.

Weinrich, W. W. *A primer of behavior modification.* Belmont, Calif.: Brooks/Cole Publishing Co., 1970.

18 COMMUNICATION FOR EFFECTIVE RELATIONSHIPS

Of all the skills needed for good teaching, none is more important than the ability to communicate with students. Indeed, communication is essential. If you could not communicate at all, you could not teach. The better you can communicate, the more likely you are to teach well.

Most people think of communication as speaking and writing. These are part of it. You have had courses in how to write and speak clearly, expressively, and convincingly. But when it comes to teaching, there's more to communication—much more. There's listening and acceptance and guidance. There's body language and theatrics. There are ways to enhance communication and ways to stifle it. There are techniques for helping students think and express themselves openly.

These are some of the topics explained in this chapter. Pay attention to them. Discipline makes life tolerable in the classroom, but communication makes it worthwhile. To help you learn important skills of communication, the chapter consists of these parts:

1. *Sending the message,* including explaining, reality communication, and body talk
2. *Seeking the message,* reviewing the rationale and skills of questioning
3. *Exchanging messages,* which deals with the delicate matters of active listening, acceptance, supporting communication, and keeping it parallel, as stressed in teacher effectiveness training, congruent communication, transactional analysis, classroom meetings, and interaction analysis
4. *Using the voice,* as you would play an instrument, to stimulate, soothe, encourage, excite, and enthrall

SENDING THE MESSAGE

Communication means that one person sends a message, and another person receives that message. The communication will be accurate in the degree to which the receiver understands the message, that is, interprets the symbols (words, etc.) so that overall they mean what the sender meant to convey. Communication will be inaccurate in the degree to which the receiver fails to reconstruct the intent of the sender.

When communication is accurate, we say the receiver as "understood." When accuracy is very low or nonexistent, we say the receiver has "not understood."

This looks as though the burden in communication falls on the receiver. When it comes to teaching, the reverse is true. The burden falls to the sender, especially when the sender is the teacher. Receivers have their responsibilities, too. They must pay attention, think, and attempt to capture the sender's message. But teachers must do their utmost to send messages that are very clear, so clear that students will always understand.

To send ultraclear messages, teachers must keep several points in mind. They must use words that all the students know. They must refer to experiences that are recognizable to students. They must speak clearly and distinctly. They must use short, direct sentences. While they do these things, they must continually read the faces of their students. In students' expressions you can see evidence of attention, understanding, or lack thereof.

Explaining

One kind of teacher talk that requires very accurate communication is explanation. When we explain to students, we are attempting to make something very clear, very plain. We want students to understand fully.

Explaining requires, as mentioned earlier, the use of simple sentences. They should be direct and fairly short. The words should be present in the listening vocabularies of the students. The ideas should be sufficiently familiar that students can relate them to ideas already known.

Explanations usually deal with factual information, process, or rationale. Factual information consists of the familiar who, what, when, and where. These elements are ingrained into every news reporter's brain. They are just as important to teachers. Natural and social science are especially filled with this type of factual information.

Process deals with "how to." Explanations of process relate, step by step, how a thing is done, how it works, how it is made. If you want to install a stereo in your car, you will need a process explanation—in common terminology, a set of directions. If these directions use words you know, pictures you recognize, and ideas familiar to you, and if the sentences are straight to the point, you will be able to install the stereo so it will work.

Rationale explanations deal with "why." They make clear the reasons why a thing is done, why it is important. They also make cause-effect relationships clear. When we ask the question "why," we are seeking a cause. Why does lightning make thunder? Be*cause* it expands the air violently, sending powerful sound waves.

Often there will be an interplay of what's, how's, and why's in explanations. Teachers who are explaining weather phenomena, for example, mention facts (what's) such as temperature, humidity, barometric pressure, highs, lows, and fronts. Along with these what's they include how's such as how water gets into the air, how we measure it, how it condenses into drops of rain. They also include why's, such as why our weather pattern moves from west to east, why tornados occur in some places and not in others, why hail sometimes falls during very hot weather.

These explanations are greatly enhanced when accompanied by pictures, models, and other media. Humans are visually oriented. We learn more through sight than through the other senses. But the pictures and models can't teach by themselves. They require the verbal accompaniment, the clear, direct explanations of what, how, and why.

When we assess the effectiveness of our explanations, we look to the students. First, we read their facial expressions and body movements. These signals tell us whether they are attentive, engrossed, bored, frustrated, or puzzled. This assessment is done while the explanation is being made. It lets teachers know if their explanations are effective, and it guides them in repeating, illustrating, or moving ahead.

A second assessment is done after the explanation is completed. This assessment may ask students to explain what they have learned; apply the learning to problem solution; build on the learning in creative, productive ways; or search for analogous situations. Most commonly, we ask students to repeat, using their own words, what they just had explained to them. The repetition may be done orally or in writing. The teacher checks the student explanation to see if it matches the message the teacher wanted to convey. If it does not, the material will need to be explained again. Other students who have understood can help with this task.

When it comes to sending messages having to do with knowledge, explaining is an essential skill. All teachers should practice the skills of explaining and of assessing student understanding.

Reality communication

It will become clear to you that not all message sending has to do with facts, processes, and rationales. Some have to do with acceptance, others with rejection, others with guidance.

Much of what we say to students falls into that last category, guidance. That's where we tell them what they can and cannot do. Guidance entails explaining, too. We make plain what students are allowed, and are not allowed, to do. Hopefully, we make plain the why's of these restrictions. But in the case of guidance, the message has to do with proper behavior rather than with the conveyance of knowledge.

Our lives are chock full of commandments, restrictions, and admonitions. As students, we were all filled to the gills with them. There is no point in mentioning such things here, except for one special case. That case is one we shall call "reality communication," after the suggestions on applying reality therapy to the guidance of student behavior. William Glasser (1969) gave us those ideas.

This special instance of guidance communication stresses, encourages, and insists on students' taking positive action in controlling their own behavior—controlling it in this sense: Student behavior in the classroom is a matter of choice. Students choose to act "good" or "bad." Teachers can correct inappropriate (bad) behavior by helping students make better choices. This is, students can choose to behave in acceptable ways. The question is, how do we get students to make such choices?

Here's what Glasser (1969) says about student failure to behave responsibly:

I do not accept the rationalization of failure commonly accepted today, that these young people are products of a social situation that precludes success. Blaming their failure upon their homes, their communities, their culture, their background, their race, or their poverty is a dead end for two reasons: (1) it removes personal responsibility for failure, and (2) it does not recognize that school success is potentially open to all young people. (pp. 4-5)

This passage lays the foundation for the suggestions Glasser makes. First, it places responsibility for success or failure (good or bad behavior) squarely on the shoulders of students. Second, it asserts that success (good behavior) is available to all students. It's there for the taking.

But how do students come to make the choices that lead to success? Glasser suggests these steps, all of which he has validated in his extensive work with students:

1. When students misbehave, get them to make a value judgment about their behavior in terms of its benefits to individuals and to the class. Calmly as, "What are you doing?" Wait for the student to reply. As, "Is that helping your work or the work of the class? Are you satisfied with that behavior?"

2. Students who are satisfied with the undesirable behavior they are showing must suffer the reasonable consequences of the misbehavior. The student must not be excused from these consequences.

3. Be very persistent. Every time a student repeats the misbehavior, ask the same questions. Each time get a value judgment about the behavior from the student. Sooner or later, the student will begin to doubt that the behavior is worthwhile.

4. If the student decides that the behavior is not helpful to self or class, ask, "What could you do that would be more helpful?" Don't suggest solutions. Get the suggestion from the student. This is an important part of the process of making better decisions.

5. Once students identify a better course of behavior, do your best to help them make a commitment to that behavior. Help them with it, show your approval, comment on their ability to stick with their suggestion.

6. When the commitment is broken, accept no excuses from students. Let them suffer the natural consequences. But, again, get them to make a commitment to a better course of action. Continue this process with determination.

Glasser is convinced that this communication procedure will significantly improve the behavior of almost all students who misbehave. He insists that teachers must never accept excuses from students for unacceptable behavior. To do so suggests that the teacher does not really care about either the behavior or the student. But teachers who persist in helping students make better choices and live by those choices foster maturity, respect, love, and successful self-identity.

SOME BODY TALK, BY GAR*

GAR behavior categories	Examples of sounds	Examples of facial expressions	Examples of gestures	Examples of body movements, acts, positions
Guide Focus Demonstrate Direct	Shhh Un-huh (encouraging)		Beckon Cup hand to ear Put finger to lips Motion with hand	Act out Flick lights on and off Help do something Lead by hand Open to right page Point a direction Point to place Set example Show how Show where Walk with
Accept Show interest Encourage Praise	Giggle Laugh with Whistle Mmm (tasty)	Grin Lift eyebrows Smile Wink	Applaud Give OK sign Give "V" sign Nod affirmation Nod agreement Thumbs up	Hug Look attentively Open arms Pat on back or shoulder Shake hands
Reject Ignore Suppress Punish	Clear throat Expell breath in exasperation Groan Moan Laugh at Laugh sarcastically Sigh Sniff	Bite lips Clench jaws Close eyes slowly Give dirty look Furrow forehead Frown Glare Grimace Look bored Look disgusted Lower eyebrows Press lips together Smirk Sneer Squint Stare ahead	Cover ears Point, to blame Shake head no Shake finger Thumbs down	Fold arms, waiting Grab Place hands on hips, waiting Pinch Pull hair Push student aside Shake student Slam book down Swat student Rap ruler Tap foot impatiently Turn away Look away while student is talking

*From Charles, C. M. *Educational psychology: the instructional endeavor* (2nd ed.). St. Louis: The C. V. Mosby Co., 1976.

Body talk

So far we have given all our attention to verbal communication. There is more to communication than words. Often the way we behave says much more than our words. Actions really do speak louder than words, especially when it comes to feelings about topics and people, about whether we like them, accept them, enjoy them, have interest in them, merely tolerate them, or fervently wish they weren't there.

If we don't say these feelings with words, how do we communicate them? We communicate them with our bodies—posture, attention, smiles, nods, frowns, stares, touches, gestures, proximity. In fact, there are a surprisingly large number of different body actions that communicate very powerfully.

The acts that have most importance for teachers are those that communicate guidance, acceptance, and rejection. Typical examples of acts that occur within each of the "guide-accept-reject" (GAR) categories (Charles, 1976) are shown on p. 373.

The odd thing is that while we are fairly conscious of what we say, we hardly know at all what we do with our bodies while talking with others. We seem to be unaware of many of our facial expressions, our eye contact, or our "open" and "closed" arm and leg positions. The same is true, but not to such an extent, for the body language that others use when talking with us. We may gain the distinct impression that a person really likes or dislikes us, accepts or rejects us, values or simply tolerates us, without knowing exactly why we feel that way. Usually it has much to do with the body language they are using.

Because this body language is so powerful, so observable, and yet so inconspicuous, it is important that teachers take special note of it. They should practice observing other speakers to identify physical mannerisms that communicate attitude. They should have videotapes made of themselves so they can see what they do and how they look. They should practice using body language that accepts and guides. They should consciously replace rejecting acts with other acts that accept.

The distressing thing is that even as you read these observations, hopefully agreeing strongly with them, your body language will not change appreciably, not, that is, unless you get together with someone else, or better yet alone in front of a mirror, and actually practice behaviors you would like to exhibit naturally. Just reading about them won't do, because your behaviors won't change much unless you practice the changes.

SEEKING THE MESSAGE

A very important part of the teaching task consists of seeking messages from students, of actually drawing them out. This may seem odd at first glance, because students are almost always sending messages, both to teachers and to other students. Unfortunately, the messages they send usually do not serve the higher goals of education. They can do so, however, given proper encouragement and direction.

Teachers are particularly interested in seeking the following kinds of messages from students:
1. Messages that reveal *understanding* of what was taught
2. Messages that reveal *interests and needs*
3. Messages that reveal *anxieties*
4. Messages that reveal *self-concept*
5. Messages that show evidence of *higher-level thought*

These kinds of messages are important because they furnish useful guidance in teaching. They are so important that teachers use special techniques to solicit them. These techniques are embodied in the various skills of questioning.

Earlier we considered student messages that revealed understanding, misunderstanding, or lack of understanding. To solicit these kinds of messages, teachers simply ask students to repeat, in their own words, that which had been explained to them.

A different sort of questioning technique is used to identify student interests and needs. In the first place, many interests and needs will be evident in what students do, say, talk about, and write about. For needs and values that lie deeper, that may not even be recognized by the students, messages can be drawn out through value clarification techniques, art interpretation exercises, and open-ended problem situations.

Value clarification is a procedure for helping students identify what is truly important to them in their lives (Raths, Harmin, and Simon, 1966). It begins with the teacher listening attentively to what students say, during both class discussions and informal conversations. The teacher then asks nonjudgmental questions that elicit more responses from students. Examples of such questions are as follows:

"Is that what you mean?"
"Where do you think that idea comes from?"
"Have you thought of any other possibilities?"
"Should everyone think that way?"

Such questions, in the way they cause students to reflect on what they have said, help establish in students' minds those things that have deep importance for them. Evidence for such importance comes when students show that they *freely choose,* from among alternatives, the position they have taken; that they *prize* the choice they have made, as shown by their willingness to affirm it publicly; and that they will *act* on the basis of their beliefs.

Raths (1963) suggests that teachers listen for student comments such as "When I get . . . ," "What I like to do . . . ," and "Someday I'm going to. . . ." The teacher can then follow with the clarifying questions listed previously, plus questions such as the following:

For prizing: "Are you glad you feel that way?"
"Do you tell others about it?"
For acting: "Is there anything you can do about that?"
"Will you do it?"
"Have you done it before?"

Another procedure for determining student needs, interests, and feelings is one that involves the interpretation of art. It is used mostly for young children, who naturally have difficulty expressing their deeper concerns and needs. After students have completed drawings or paintings, the teacher simply says "Tell me about your picture." Children's art oftentimes shows aspects of their lives that are especially enjoyable, that provide security, that are the source of fears, and that show bothersome shortcomings. Children who would not otherwise be able to explain what thrills, troubles, or terrifies them can express information that helps teachers better understand their behavior and needs.

At a much more sophisticated level, pictures can be used as projective devices to examine the concerns, anxieties, and phobias of older students. Two of the best-known devices are the Rorschach inkblot test and the thematic apperception test. In the first, inkblots are shown to the individual, who is asked to interpret what they represent. In the

second, a series of pictures are shown. They, too, are interpreted. These devices have no right or wrong answers. Instead, the responses the individual gives are used to interpret deeper aspects of the personality. These two tests may be administered only by highly trained clinicians.

Students' self-concepts are also a matter of concern for teachers. Evidence suggests that one's ability to function well in many different situations is related to self-concept. At the very least, people with strong self-concepts seem happier and more content with life.

You can hardly go up to a student, ask, "what kind of self-concept do you have?" and expect to get a sensible answer. But you can get useful information if you ask students to respond to such questions as the following:

	Good	OK	Bad
1. How well do you like your face?			
Hair?			
Body?			
Clothing?			
2. How do you feel about the way you play games and sports?			
3. How do you feel about the schoolwork you do?			
4. How do you feel about the way other students treat you?			

If you want a more detailed picture, there are several good self-concept scales available. For their sources, prices, merits, and uses, check the current Buros' *Mental Measurements Yearbook* in your college library.

Although questions can be used to solicit much useful information about student interests, attitudes, values, and self-concepts, questioning as a teaching technique has found its greatest applicability in another area. This area is student thought. Questions can be used with great effectiveness to explore thought processes and to guide students toward use of "higher" levels of thought.

What does "higher" thought mean? In this case, it refers to the following levels of cognitive processes (Bloom, 1956):

Evaluation	↑
Synthesis	Higher
Analysis	
Application	Lower
Comprehension	
Knowledge	↓

Benjamin Bloom and his associates, who composed the now famous *Taxonomy of Educational Objectives. Handbook I: Cognitive Domain,* identified these processes as "levels" of objectives. Knowledge is the lowest, in that it requires the least complex thought. Evaluation is the highest, because it depends on all the others and is therefore the most complex.

Throughout history, education has focused mainly on the lowest of these levels, knowledge. Recently, however, educators saw the need to develop higher thinking abilities in students. Norris Sanders (1966) was one of the first to develop types of questions teachers could use to promote higher-level thought. His work was followed by a good deal more along the same lines, Charles (1976), for example, composed thirty-five prototype questions that teachers could use to generate their own questions. He modified Bloom's list of levels so that it included the following: perceiving, relating, reproducing, analyzing, applying, evaluating, and producing. He called them cognitive/psychomotor acts. He identified five categories of information used in schools: objects, symbols, meanings, behaviors, and compositions. The interaction between the seven cognitive/psychomotor acts and the five categories of information produced the thirty-five types of questions, which follow:

Thirty-five sample questions*

The seven cognitive/psychomotor acts and the five information categories can be combined in thirty-five different ways. Below you will see a sample question provided for each of these combinations.

Perceiving
1. *Perceiving objects*
   "Can you point to the largest red block?"
2. *Perceiving symbols*
   "Which symbol stands for sodium?"
3. *Perceiving meanings*
   "Can you raise your hand when you hear the colloquialism that expresses surprise?"
4. *Perceiving behavior*
   "Who noticed what Jack did in the pet shop?"

---

*From Charles, C. M. *Educational psychology: the instructional endeavor* (2nd ed.). St. Louis: The C. V. Mosby Co., 1976.

5. *Perceiving compositions*
   "Does the nursery rhyme 'Little Bo Peep' come first, second, or third on the record?"

Relating
6. *Relating objects*
   "In what ways are a lemon and a grapefruit alike?"
7. *Relating symbols*
   "What do you think the following abbreviations stand for?"
8. *Relating meanings*
   "How are these sayings alike? How are they different? 'Look before you leap' and 'Strike while the iron is hot'?"
9. *Relating behaviors*
   "How does rapid walking affect the heartbeat?"
10. *Relating compositions*
    "Which of these paintings fall in the American Primitive group?"

Reproducing
11. *Reproducing objects*
    "Can you construct a model of the hydrogen atom?"
12. *Reproducing symbols*
    "Can you draw whole, half, quarter, and sixteenth notes?"
13. *Reproducing meanings*
    "Can you tell the fable of the fox and the grapes in your own words?"
14. *Reproducing behaviors*
    "Can you serve the tennis ball the way I showed you?"
15. *Reproducing compositions*
    "Who thinks he can recite the Gettysburg Address?"

Analyzing
16. *Analyzing objects*
    "Where does the spark plug fit in this Wankel engine?"
17. *Analyzing symbols*
    "Can you circle the letters in the Spanish alphabet that don't occur in the English alphabet?"
18. *Analyzing meanings*
    "What are the word origins from which our word 'neology' is derived?"
19. *Analyzing behaviors*
    "Can you summarize the main things an artist does as he prepares his canvas?"
20. *Analyzing compositions*
    "In which part of his poem did Frost hint at a possibility of suicide?"

Applying
21. *Applying objects*
    "How are you supposed to use the grafting compound to seal wounds on the tree?"

22. *Applying symbols*
    "Can you use these pictographs to write a message to a friend?"
23. *Applying meanings*
    "What trend is the food-population ratio likely to follow in Bolivia?"
24. *Applying behaviors*
    "Can you use the scale to play this simple tune?"
25. *Applying compositions*
    "Can you use these articles to illustrate Marcuse's point of view?"

Evaluating

26. *Evaluating objects*
    "Is this cake sweet enough?"
27. *Evaluating symbols*
    "Which of these drawings best represents the spirit of ecology? Why?"
28. *Evaluating meanings*
    "Why do you think the statement 'All change must come in the hearts and minds of men' is valueless for change?"
29. *Evaluating behaviors*
    "Overall, who has had a greater influence on their respective sports—Bill Russell or Arnold Palmer? Why?"
30. *Evaluating compositions*
    "Can you compare Marlowe's and Goethe's delineations of Faust, with emphasis on his believability as a human being?"

Producing

31. *Producing objects*
    "Can you cut a Christmas scene on this linoleum block?"
32. *Producing symbols*
    "What do you think would be a good code mark to represent happiness? Show us."
33. *Producing meanings*
    "How could we go about writing our own mottos?"
34. *Producing behavior*
    "How would you react to a surprise birthday party?"
35. *Producing compositions*
    "What melody can you compose to go with this verse?"

In addition to the types of questions that elicit different messages from students, there are specific skills one may employ to make the questioning more effective. These skills were treated in detail in Chapter 14.

EXCHANGING MESSAGES

There are two types of communication. The first is one-way communication, where the sender transmits a message that, hopefully, the recipient grasps accurately. We have dealt mainly with this type of communication up to this point. A second type is two-way communication. Here both individuals are sending and receiving messages. This communication has the sense of "talking with" instead of "talking to." It is fully as important as one-way communication in teaching. Moreover, it can be used to reach several ends for which one-way communication is not effective. It permits exchange of ideas; it allows discussants to form ideas mutually; it can be used to build effective personal relationships; it can forestall and solve many problems that occur when groups of people work together.

In these pages we will consider five fully developed techniques that can be used to improve the quality of interpersonal communication. These five techniques are teacher effectiveness training, congruent communication, transactional analysis, classroom meetings, and interaction analysis.

Teacher effectiveness training

Teacher effectiveness training is the name chosen for a training program developed by the psychologist Thomas Gordon (1974). The title of this program does not explain its contents. These contents, however, have great importance for teachers. Fortunately, they are taught as skills that are fairly easy to learn. Especially important among these skills are active listening, avoiding roadblocks to communication, and using the "no-lose" approach to the resolution of personal conflicts. These communication skills, when applied in teaching, help students learn faster, and they increase student confidence, self-esteem, and creativity. Let's consider each of them.

Active listening. Active listening is a technique for helping students express themselves freely and openly. It is simple for teachers to do. It requires that they do very little talking (maybe, after all, that's not so simple for teachers!) but that they say and do things that make it possible for students to talk. It does require genuine listening. In addition, teachers must use silence, acknowledgment responses, door openers, and reflective comments as ways to increase student talk.

Silence is just what it implies. The teacher says nothing at all and merely pays attention while the student talks. This attention is shown with the eyes and the face. The attentive silence, without interruptions, communicates interest in and concern for what the student has to say. It makes students feel free to say what's on their minds.

Acknowledgment responses include leaning forward, smiling, nodding, and saying such things as "uh-huh" and "I understand." They reassure students, as they speak, that you are interested in what they are saying, following it, and accepting it as worthwhile. These responses help students continue saying what they have on their minds.

Door openers become useful when students have difficulty in beginning to express themselves, or when they become hesitant. They are statements the teacher makes, always nonevaluative. Examples include the following: "Looks like you are upset about something." "Would you like to tell me more about it?"

As these three techniques help students speak, the teacher can take a more active role. Comments can now become *reflective,* that is, they can reflect back what the student has said. Reflective comments do not evaluate or make suggestions. They only try to help students see more clearly what it is they are saying. Examples might include the following: "It upset you that Bill spoke to you that way." "You felt slighted that you weren't included." "You feel the assignment is too difficult for you to do without help." Remember, these reflective comments must not be the teacher's wise interpretation that is delivered to the student. Instead, they are reflections of what the student has said, bounced back as if from a mirror.

These active listening techniques are very helpful to students. Instead of giving them ready-made solutions, they help them think through their problems and find their own solutions. At the same time they show that the teacher accepts the students and values them.

Avoiding roadblocks. A second emphasis in Gordon's training program has to do with roadblocks that stifle effective communication. There are twelve such roadblocks, and teachers have to learn to avoid them. Some of them include responses that teachers make as a matter of course. These are difficult to change, because they are generally considered good things for teachers to do. Examples include No. 4, "advising, giving suggestions and solutions"; No. 7, "praising, agreeing"; No. 10, "reassuring, sympathizing, consoling, supporting"; and No. 11, "probing, questioning, and interrogating." These roadblocks are difficult for teachers to remove because there are times when each is important. Indeed, praise, agreement, suggestions, support, and questioning all have important roles in some teaching activities. The main thing is to remember that although they are good under some circumstances, they are not good for enhancing communication. To the contrary, they tend to stop student talk instead of encouraging it.

Other categories of teacher talk that stifle communication are easy to correct. They are rarely acceptable. Examples include No. 3, "exhorting, moralizing and preaching"; No. 6, "judging, criticizing, disagreeing, blaming"; No. 8, "name-calling, ridiculing, shaming"; and No. 12, "withdrawing, distracting, humoring, diverting."

The other four roadblocks, although usually expected from teachers, can also be changed fairly easily. They include No. 1, "ordering, commanding, directing"; No. 2, "warning, threatening"; No. 5, "lecturing, giving logical arguments"; and No. 9, "interpreting, analyzing, diagnosing."

Again, to use fruitful comments in teaching that take the place of these roadblocks, you have to practice. The right words will not come automatically until they have been ingrained through repetition.

No-lose approach. A third emphasis in teacher effectiveness training is the "no-lose" method of resolving conflicts. Ordinarily when people come to odds, one ultimately gets the better of the other. When this happens, the consequences can be destructive to the "loser." Gordon stresses an approach to conflict resolution that produces no loser, leaving all egos intact. Here's how you do it:

1. Clarify exactly what the problem is.
2. Jointly suggest several possible solutions.
3. Evaluate each of the suggestions. Eliminate any that produce negative reactions from either disputant.
4. Decide on one of the solutions. The decision is made by consensus, but it is always considered tentative.
5. Decide on details of how to put the solution into effect. Spell them out clearly.
6. As the solution is implemented, continually evaluate it. If it fails, try one of the other suggested solutions.

Congruent communication

Congruent communication, a term developed by Haim Ginott (1972), refers to "communication that is harmonious, authentic; where words fit feelings" (p. 67). It is a process for enhancing personal communication between teachers and students. It stresses "sane" messages, positive ways of expressing anger, ways to invite cooperation, how to accept and acknowledge, why you shouldn't label students, how to correct students, why you shouldn't use sarcasm, and why brevity is effective. By considering each of these points, we can see what Ginott means by congruent communication and why it has proved so effective.

Sane messages. Sane messages show trust in students' inner integrity. They avoid the innuendos that occur so frequently when teachers talk with students, where the students are blamed, shamed, bossed, admonished, accused, ridiculed, belittled, threatened, and bribed. These techniques, says Ginott, brutalize, vulgarize, and dehumanize students.

It is one thing to recognize the defects of such comments. But it is another to make positive changes in them. How does one do this?

Ginott (1972) suggests beginning with this "cardinal principle" of congruent communication: "At their best, teachers address themselves to the (student's) situation. At their worst, they judge his character and personality" (p. 70). In other words, when talking with students, talk to the situation, not to the student's personality. This cardinal principle forms the basis for the other points that Ginott makes about effective communication.

Expressing anger. The cardinal principle enables you to see why Ginott thinks it is good for teachers to express their genuine anger. Most teachers think they should not show anger in the classroom. They believe they have lost control when they do. Not so, says Ginott. Teachers face many situations that provoke anger. They are neither saints nor martyrs. They should not by hypocrites, either. When provoked, annoyed, or angered, they have every right to say so and indeed should say so. But they must address the situation, not the students. They do not shame, bully, or ridicule. Instead, they use I-messages—"I do not like inattention. It makes me feel frustrated and angry." "I am appalled at the noise in this room."

"I feel angry and very bad when I see cruelty and disrespect shown to other people."

Inviting cooperation. Instead of coercing students into compliance with the teacher's wishes, one can use different ways of inviting their cooperation. One way is to give students *choices*. Options can be equally worthwhile, but students can select the one they prefer. This helps them feel they have a say in the conduct of their lives. Another way is to *avoid commands*. Instead of saying "Get to work," say "There is work to be done." This describes the situation, and the solution is obvious. Yet another way of inviting cooperation is to *grant in fantasy* what cannot be granted in reality: "I *wish* there were time for us to hear all the stories." This shows there is not time, and students are more likely to accept it. Finally, *succinct* statements are more likely to bring cooperation than are long-winded admonishments. Simply saying "It's time to clean up" is more effective than covering all the details of what students should do during cleanup time.

Accepting and acknowledging. What teachers say to accept and acknowledge students makes a difference in what students do and how they feel. This calls for effective use of you-statements. These statements are made when the teacher consciously wants to draw attention to the student. They accurately acknowledge the student's state of mind, contribution, expression, evaluation, and so forth. They do not dispute the student's expression, argue with the experience, or attack the personality. "Oh, your dog had puppies, too? You must be excited." (Even though you, the teacher, know that the student doesn't even have a dog.) "You are worried about the play tonight. You must have stage fright, like all good actors do."

Labeling students. Ginott makes a special point of the dangers of labeling students. "Labeling is disabling," he writes. He refers, of course, to negative labels, such as slow, irresponsible, or troublemaker. Students, once labeled, often live up to the labels. At least teachers continue to see them in that same light. Again, one avoids labeling by talking about the situation rather than the individual. You can do this by talking to students as though they were guests in your home. You wouldn't call guests irresponsible if they forgot their raincoats. You might say "It's raining. You will need some protection." Anytime we hang negative labels on students, we run the risk of adding limitations to their personal behavior that might not have been present before, that is, we tend to disable them.

Correcting students. When you want to correct students, says Ginott, direct them. You don't change inappropriate behavior by berating individuals. You do change it by giving them positive suggestions on more appropriate ways of acting. Students do not need negative criticism. They do not need to be told they are lazy, poor workers, or disrespectful. They need to be reminded what to do, how to do it, and when it should be done. You correct by giving attention to the situation, not by launching into the students. Again, it is fine for you to express your concern, dismay, disappointment, or anger. But you tell how you feel—you do not put direct blame on the students. They will get the message well enough, but will avoid most of the personal hurt that often occurs when teachers correct them.

Using sarcasm. Especially, urges Ginott, avoid sarcasm when talking with students. A few teachers can use sarcasm in a spirit of good humor. Once students become fully aware of the teacher's personality, they can usually tell the difference between cut and fun. However, even under the best circumstances there is a chance of hurting feelings with sarcasm. When used seriously, sarcasm does cut, burn, and wound sorely. This inescapable fact causes most authorities to assert that there is no place at all for sarcasm in the classroom.

Brevity. One of the teacher's greatest strengths in communicating with students comes with the insight that brevity is beautiful. Teachers' days are filled with minor mishaps, incidents that for all practical purposes are inconsequential. Someone loses a pencil, a paper gets torn, two students get cross with each other—and on and on through the day. Some teachers use up three fourths of their psychic energy dealing with such incidents. For one reason or another, they interrogate, reprimand, give elaborate directions, and put the students on the spot and keep them there. How much better things go when a new pencil or paper is dispensed without comment, when fussing students are simply separated or asked to write out their versions of the conflict for the teacher to read later. Ginott judges that most of the statements

teachers make at such times are nonproductive, even counterproductive. Most explanations go in one ear and out the other. Most admonitions have no effect other than to hurt. If something must be said, it should be said in the form of positive directions for better behavior stated in terms that are short and to the point.

The one time that brevity doesn't prove effective is when students have strong emotions with which they must deal. In this event, Ginott suggests giving help that is *unhurried*. It does no good to tell students they have nothing to be afraid of, nothing to be angry about, or nothing to feel hurt about. Here the teacher must find time, if possible, to talk about the student's problem, listening actively and reflecting back what the student says. In this way, students will develop the ability, plus the confidence, to begin solving their own problems.

• • •

These paragraphs have illustrated some of the remarkably helpful suggestions that Ginott makes for teacher-student communication. They all rest on these two points: address the situation, not the personality, and speak to the student as you would speak to a guest in your home.

Transactional analysis

In psychology classes you have learned about the ego. Freud considered the ego to be the conscious regulatory state of the mind. He contrasted ego with id, the unconscious, baser level of the mind, and with superego, the level of mind that concerns itself with right and wrong. In that widely known theory of personality, the ego was seen as a single entity. Once emerged, it balanced id and superego, but it remained a relatively unchanging entity.

Eric Berne (1964) considered the ego in a different way. Instead of our having a single ego state that remains constant, we can be seen to function in ways that suggest different states of the ego. These ego states are accompanied by styles of behavior that change from one moment to the next. These behaviors are particularly noticeable in the ways we communicate with each other.

Berne believes that we can employ three such ego states when we communicate. He calls these states "parent," "adult," and "child." Ordinarily we use only one of the three when communicating with a particular person. Moments later, however, we may switch to another state when we begin talking to a different person. Here is how Berne characterizes each state:

Parent: When using this ego state, we think and talk to others as our parents did to us when we were young. That is, we use talk to control, admonish, advise, and correct. What we say reflects the standards of society, the idealized right-or-wrong, either-or, all-or-nothing perspectives that are presented to us as children.

Adult: When using this ego state, we think and talk in reasoned, rational, objective ways. We do not moralize or preach. Neither do we strike servile, bootlicking, dependent stances. We behave dispassionately, coolly. We take in facts, sort them out, and use logic. We consider all the possibilities and probabilities.

Child: When using this ego state, we talk, act, and think as we did when we were children between the ages of 2 and 5 years. We defer to adult or parental authority. We act on impulse. We behave emotionally. This emotional behavior can be seen as spontaneous joy, excitement, and exuberance or as hurt feelings, petulance, and brattiness.

These three ego states can be seen in all individuals—children, adolescents, teachers, and other adults. Even children in primary grades can use their parent and adult ego states. Listen to them at play, and you will see.

Thus all of us, whether communicating with children, adolescents, or adults, make regular use of all three ego states. They are present in all our personalities. Thus when two people communicate, the possible ego state interaction pattern looks like this:

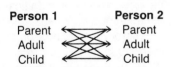

Person 1 — Person 2
Parent — Parent
Adult — Adult
Child — Child

Effective communication can occur if the two people use complementary states, that is, if the directions of communication are parallel, for example, as follows:

Person 1 — Person 2
Parent — Parent
Adult ⟷ Adult
Child — Child

or

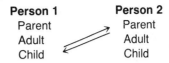

Person 1 — Person 2
Parent → Parent
Adult — Adult
Child ← Child

Three such parallel directions are common when two people communicate. They are parent-child, adult-adult, and child-parent.

But when communication directions are not parallel, when they are crossed, problems can occur. An example of crossed communication is as follows:

Person 1 — Person 2
Parent — Parent
Adult ⟵ Adult
Child ↘ Child

When crossed communication occurs, it tends to be ineffective. Ideas are not exchanged adequately, and at least one of the people will feel awkward and uneasy during the interchange.

Such effects of communication on feelings were the theme of Thomas Harris's book *I'm O. K.—You're O. K.* (1967). Using Berne's concept of ego states, Harris suggested ways to analyze verbal transactions between people. This transactional analysis reveals which ego states are being used when two people communicate. Furthermore, it helps us use ego states that produce the fullest, most effective communication.

Harris describes four postures that pairs of people assume when they communicate. These postures result from, or at least coincide with, ego states used in communication. The four are as follows:

I'm Not OK—You're OK
I'm Not OK—You're Not OK
I'm OK—You're Not OK
I'm OK—You're OK

Harris believes the most effective communication occurs in the fourth posture, I'm OK—You're OK. This posture results when both people use their adult ego states. It permits the greatest degree of openness, and it allows the greatest use of reason. The other three postures restrict reason, replacing it with emotion and impulse. One person, at least, is bound to feel inferior in the dialogue.

Harris makes two suggestions that he believes engender more effective communication. The first is to learn the nature of the three ego states, parent, adult, and child, and how to recognize them.

The second is to learn to maximize use of the adult ego state when talking with others.

With regard to the first suggestion, he urges us to do the following:

1. Recognize that we all have to contend, inside ourselves, with our own three ego states. Each state handles data in its own way. The *parent* is closed to new ideas. It reacts in authoritative ways, taking the "how dare you" and "tsk-tsk" attitude. The *adult* seeks the facts. It processes them with openness and reason. It looks for causes, consequences, and probabilities. The *child* shows the emotions of pleasures, fantasies, and fears. It tends to giggle and whine in hopes of receiving affection. It reacts with stubbornness and tears when it doesn't get its way.

2. When we communicate with others, we should assess our behavior to determine which of the ego states we are using and which the other person is using. This knowledge permits us to switch to the adult, if necessary, and to interpret better the messages the other person is sending.

3. We should make every effort to use our adult state when we talk with others, young or old. Let it be in charge. It is reasonable, open, and nondefensive. It permits change to occur. Parent and child resist change. They are inflexible and tend to maintain the status quo.

With regard to Harris's point about learning to maximize the adult state, he makes these suggestions:

1. Know our child behaviors. They show us our fears, vulnerabilities, and delights, together with our ways of expressing them. Know also our parent behaviors. They show us our fixed positions and our stereotyped ideas, together with our ways of expressing them. Remember, too, that we all have feelings of being "Not O. K."

2. When conflict occurs during communication, we should remember the adage about counting to ten. This delay forestalls child or parent states, which spring forth automatically, and gives time for the adult, which is slower, to emerge and take over.

3. We should be ever sensitive to the child in others. Child behaviors reveal a strong need for acceptance, attention, and affection. When the child is in evidence, give the other person

strokes. This is no disagreeable task. Although we may fear the parent in others, we love the child in them.

4. Remember that we need the parent and child in ourselves. The parent gives us stability and security, something steadfast we can count on. The child gives us wonder and delight. We simply need to curtail the restrictive, destructive qualities present in each of them.

These ideas are basic in transactional analysis: We all have within us, whether we are children, adolescents, or adults, the three ego states: parent, adult, and child. Each state has its own accompaniment of peculiar behaviors. The behaviors of the adult state permit the most effective communication between people. Therefore we should learn to identify the three states and become adept at employing the adult state as much as possible.

Classroom meetings

Earlier we considered the reality approach in sending messages to others, especially insofar as we wished to help students take positive steps toward self-direction, good choices, and success. Those ideas came from the work of William Glasser (1969). This section relates ideas about communication that come from the work of that same man.

In his book *Schools Without Failure,* Glasser devotes much attention to "classroom meetings." These meetings are sessions that occur within the classroom on a regular basis and involve all the students. They provide a means of greatly increasing purposeful communication. Moreover, when properly used, they give students the clear idea that they have, even in school, significant say over the events that influence their lives. Glasser bases the value of classroom meetings on that precise point, that when students believe they have some control over their own destiny, it makes all the difference in how they behave and perform in school.

Toward this end of self-determination, Glasser suggests establishing classroom meetings as a regular part of daily school activities. The meetings ideally alternate among three separate thrusts. These thrusts are shown in the names given to types of meetings, which are as follows:

1. The social problem–solving meeting
2. The open-ended meeting
3. The educational diagnostic meeting

Let's see what Glasser would have us include in each of these three types of meetings.

The social problem–solving meeting. The social problem–solving meeting has as its purpose the search for positive solutions to interpersonal problems that arise in school. These may be individual, class, or school problems. Glasser suggests the following guidelines for this type of meeting:

1. Problems eligible for discussion include those of the school, the class, or any individual member of the class. Problems can be raised by anyone. They can have to do with oneself, parents, students, teachers, administrators, or any school personnel. These problems have to do with people and their relationships. They will usually revolve around personal conflict or unreasonable expectations. They may sometimes have to do with personal feelings of loneliness, rejection, frustration, fear, or anxiety.
2. The discussions have only one purpose: to find solutions to the problem. The purpose must be kept on this positive track if the meeting is to be successful. Students are not allowed to find fault, blame, gripe, or punish. They must constantly direct themselves to the search for positive, constructive means of reconciling the matter of concern.

The open-ended meeting. The open-ended meeting allows students to bring up any topic to which they have strong reactions, topics that puzzle, perplex, interest, delight, motivate, anger, or frustrate. The purpose is to consider, explore, and talk about the topics, not to find solutions to them. These meetings make education relevant to the lives of students, Glasser asserts.

The discussions are carried out in natural, unforced ways. Often they will turn back to subjects in the curriculum. It surprises students to know that old familiar subjects such as sociology, anthropology, biology, communications, art, and music have any relationship at all to pressing day-to-day concerns.

The educational diagnostic meeting. Educational diagnostic meetings have to do with concerns directly related to teaching and learning. The purpose of this type of meeting is to get clear student feedback about class activities, assignments, and instructional procedures. These meetings can show what students consider fun, exciting, challenging, stimulating, and worthwhile. They can also show what students consider dull, boring, frustrating, useless, and irrelevant.

The information that comes from this type of meeting can be used to advantage by the teacher. Topics that seem irrelevant can be explored by the entire class to determine ways they can be instilled with value or else deemphasized. Requirements that produce fear, such as examinations, can be restructured to make them more suitable.

This type of meeting can produce much anxiety in teachers. Most of us have difficulty with them at first. That's because we put ourselves on the line when we teach. What we do in the classroom is an extension of our personalities. Criticism of our procedures seems therefore to be criticism of ourselves.

For these reasons student comments must not take the tone of harsh criticism. They should focus on constructive, positive alternatives to what students find objectionable. Students should recognize that teachers have delicate feelings, but that they do want to make teaching and learning as pleasant and useful as possible. Glasser further suggests the following general ground rules that help classroom meetings be more effective:

1. Students and teacher should sit in a tight circle, so that all participants can see each others' faces.
2. Meetings should be held on a regular basis. They are just as important as any other part of the curriculum.
3. The length of the meetings should be appropriate to the age of the students. Between 10 and 30 minutes is about right for primary children. Older students need at least 30 minutes, but the meetings should not run longer than 45 minutes. Each type of meeting has its own particular purposes and rules. Students must abide by them if the meetings are to be successful.

• • •

In summary, classroom meetings provide very effective means for maximizing communication among students and teacher. When used as suggested, they make education relevant, they help students find solutions to troublesome problems, and they enable teachers to improve the quality and efficiency of their instructional programs.

Interaction analysis

Interaction analysis enables us to do some of the same things that transactional analysis did, only with a completely different slant. It furnishes a tool for analyzing the verbal interaction that occurs in the classroom, and it suggests kinds of teacher talk that assist students in more rapid learning and in developing more positive attitudes toward school, teachers, and themselves.

Interaction analysis grew out of the work of Ned Flanders (1960), who developed the conceptual scheme, clarified procedures and interpretations, and conducted much of the earliest research. This research and development has been continued by some of Flanders' associates, most notably Edmund Amidon (Amidon and Hough, 1967).

When Flanders began his research, he sent trained observers into numbers of classrooms of different levels and different subjects. These observers noted systematically who spoke in the classroom, what they said, how often and how long they spoke, and what sorts of responses followed. When their observations were summarized, some interesting conclusions about classroom communication emerged.

Outstanding among these conclusions was one that Flanders called the "two thirds rule":

Two thirds of the time someone is talking in the classroom.
Two thirds of that time it is the teacher who is talking.
Two thirds of that time the teacher is using "direct" influence.

In a nutshell, this finding shows that the teacher takes the lion's share of time available for classroom communication, leaving very little for each individual student.

Another conclusion had to do with "direct" and "indirect" influence used by the teacher. Flanders described *direct influence* as lecturing, giving directions, disciplining, rejecting students' comments, moralizing, and justifying authority. *Indirect influence* included asking questions and accepting student responses. When the classes of "most direct" teachers were compared with the classes of "most indirect" teachers, it was found that students of indirect teachers tended to score higher on achievement tests and to have more positive attitudes toward school. Later research showed that teachers could learn, through training, to teach in

more indirect ways and that their changes from directness to indirectness would persist over time.

Interaction analysis research does not reveal the optimal level of indirectness. Obviously, complete indirectness—all questioning and accepting—would be a grossly inefficient way of teaching. Evidence does suggest that the most effective teachers tend to be quite indirect in the beginning sequence of lessons. They ask many questions to get a large outpouring of student ideas. In later sequences of a lesson, they become much more direct. They have decided on procedures, and they begin giving directions and corrective feedback to students.

Less effective teachers, on the other hand, are quite direct from beginning to end. They do not draw students out. Instead they only lecture and give directions.

Although these findings are generally true, regard them with caution. Some indirect teachers are not too effective, whereas some direct teachers produce very good student learning. The teacher's personality seems to play a large role. Also, some topics lend themselves to directness, others to indirectness. To illustrate, compare teaching students how to do algebraic factoring with teaching them about what they can do to preserve the environment. You would have great difficulty teaching algebra through questioning and acceptance. Finally, students vary markedly in personality and background. Some students need structure and direct guidance. Others prefer openness and room for exploration and expression. When students are accustomed to the teacher always telling them what to do, they cannot suddenly begin to function well in a much more open atmosphere.

Still, interaction analysis has much to teach us. Far from a mere analytic tool, it shows us the importance of communicating more indirectly with students, that is, of drawing out messages from them. Moreover, it gives us clear directions about what to say to students to show acceptance. If you want to maximize your potential as a teacher, you will want to look further into interaction analysis, find out what it has to teach, and learn to apply its principles in your work with students.

USING THE VOICE

Teachers have a very powerful tool to use in communication, a tool that can excite, soothe, mystify, prod, rally, and heal. You could say they have it right at their fingertips, except that it's in their throat and mouth. This tool, of course, is the voice. It can be extremely effective in communicating, not only because of the words it says, but also because of the tone, lilt, rhythm, volume, pitch, emphasis, and pacing with which it is used. Some teachers play their voices like beautiful instruments. They captivate their students. Others speak in monotones, oblivious to the great potential they are wasting.

We conclude this chapter on skills of communication by giving attention to the voice. We will see how teachers can use it, make it one of their greatest allies. Specifically, mention will be made of modulation, quality, pitch, volume, animation, rhythm, pacing, and drama.

Modulation

Modulation refers to overall control of the voice. The modulated voice reveals conscious control over pitch and volume. Both are continually varied for effect. Its quality is pleasing. It varies tempo and emphasis in accordance with the situation. When we say a person has a well-modulated voice, we mean it is pleasant, even exciting, to listen to. It is always under control, and it is used to the best possible advantage. Modulation, in fact, incorporates all the other voice qualities considered here.

Quality

Voice quality refers to its degree of strength and pleasantness. Good quality includes clarity, smoothness, and resonance. Poor quality includes harshness, whining, and muddiness. Depending on its quality, the voice can soothe, enthrall, irritate, or "turn-off" listeners. The voice is soothing when it is calm, soft, and measured. It enthralls when it resonates and lingers on certain words. It irritates when it is pitched too high, when it grates, when it whines. It turns listeners off when it is monotonous, when it never varies in pitch, volume, or speed.

Pitch

Pitch refers to how high or how low the voice is. Lower-pitched voices are generally more effective than higher-pitched voices. Many beginning teachers, especially women, have voices that are pitched too high. They can, with effort and practice,

lower the pitch. As women grow older, their voices lower naturally.

Whether one has a higher or a lower-pitched voice, the important thing is to learn to vary the pitch. The modulated voice that varies pitch and volume is interesting to listen to. It holds attention. This variation produces special effects of emphasis and meaning, as you can see in these examples:

This
⌐‾‾\ is my pen.

is
This ⌐‾\ my pen.

my
This is ⌐‾\ pen.

pen
This is my ⌐‾\.

Notice the effects when you read the following sentences in two different ways:

(Read flat, without pitch variation.) Where would you go if you were in Bill's place?

(Now read with pitch variations as shown.)
you   you
Where would ⌐‾\ go if ⌐‾\ were in Bill's place?

Volume

Volume refers to how loud or soft the voice is. Voices that are too loud or too soft have undesirable effects on students. Loud voices excite and agitate. They set the head to buzzing. Very soft voices cause some students to strain to hear, particularly those farther away from the teacher. The strain becomes irritating. After a time these students disengage from what the teacher is saying.

It is best to settle on a middle-level volume, one that allows the farthest students to hear without strain, yet does not agitate nearer students.

This middle level makes it possible to vary volume for powerful effects. Sudden increases in volume lay stress and capture immediate attention. Sudden decreases in volume give an air of suspense and mystery. They capture attention, too. Note this example:

(Quiet and suspenseful.) The wolves slipped quietly along the ridge, paused for a moment, then—DOWN THEY CAME.

Animation

Animation refers to liveliness in the voice. An animated voice is peppy. It is rhythmic. It shows variations in pitch, volume, and speed.

Animated voices help make learning exciting. They convey a sense of spirit, fun, happiness. Contrast them with dull, tired-sounding, monotonous voices, and you can see the point.

Remember, though, animation is not always desirable. There are times when you want to sooth students, to calm them. Then you need to use a soft, slower voice. There are times when you want to make yourself understood in no uncertain terms. Then you want to use a strong, measured voice.

The majority of the time, however, animation is useful. It helps keep students in good spirits, it motivates them, and they find it contagious. Again and again you will hear how important it is for teachers to be enthusiastic about what they teach. They don't convey this enthusiasm by saying in wooden voices "I - - - am - - - enthusiastic." They convey it by the lilt and melody in their voices.

Rhythm

Rhythm is closely tied to animation. It is a beat, a variation. To see this point more clearly, read the following sentence in two different ways. First, give equal emphasis to each syllable. Then read it so that the rhythm is evident:

Her voice has a rhythm to it.

Her voice has a rhythm to it.

Rhythm is the opposite of woodenness. It provides the staccato, the allegro, the syncopation. It makes the difference between robot speech and human speech.

Pacing

Pacing refers to the speed with which one talks and to the variations made in that speed. As was the case for pitch and volume, variations in pacing grab student attention and hold it.

Never should you speak so rapidly that students cannot understand. Nor should you speak so slowly that they fall asleep between words. There are times, however, when you can approach these limits. Fast talk conveys excitement and agitation. Bodies resonate to it like guitar strings. Slow talk conveys many different feelings—calm, convic-

tion, no-nonsense, sympathy. Students tune in quickly to these feelings, too.

You can see, again, the point made repeatedly in this section. Vary your pacing. Talk fast when appropriate, and talk slowly when appropriate. Different speeds have different effects. Simply changing speeds draws student attention.

Drama

Someday teachers may receive special training in dramatic arts as a means of improving their effectiveness. In many ways, teaching is a performing art, much akin to acting. For this reason, we would do well to learn what actors know about attracting attention and conveying their messages with effect.

Good teachers often use their voices with dramatic quality and effectiveness. They show an uncanny sense of timing. They build their presentations through a series of climaxes. They introduce problems filled with suspense. They keep students hanging on every word. When their lessons end, students feel a lingering sense of pleasure.

Much of this they accomplish through the way they use their voices. They vary pitch, volume, and pacing to captivate students. They pause at the crucial moment. They play the roles of several people at once, reenacting incidents, arguments, debates, and discussions. They mimic the speech of characters in their dramas. With these techniques, they transcend the confines of the classroom. They move easily through time and space. And their students move with them.

A FINAL WORD

This concludes our brief consideration of some of the more important skills of communication. Two points should be reemphasized. First, communication is the hallmark of effective teaching. True, discipline is absolutely necessary. Planning is highly desirable. Both enable good communication to occur. But it is communication that makes the difference in what students learn. Second, you must realize that simply reading about communication does little to help you. If you truly want to improve your skills, you must practice. There is no shortcut.

SUGGESTED ACTIVITIES FOR FURTHER UNDERSTANDING

1. Divide the class into groups. Assign techniques for exchanging messages, one to each group. The groups pre-

pare various kinds of class presentations that illustrate the basic ideas and strategies involved in the techniques.

2. Practice using the voice techniques described at the end of this chapter. Demonstrate before the class to illustrate special techniques of voice utilization in realistic situations.

REFERENCES

Amidon, E., and Hough, J. *Interaction analysis: theory, research, and application.* Reading, Mass.: Addison-Wesley Publishing Co., Inc., 1967.

Berne, E. *Games people play.* New York: Grove Press, Inc., 1964.

Bloom, B., (Ed.). *Taxonomy of educational objectives. Handbook I: cognitive domain.* New York, David McKay Co., Inc., 1956.

Charles, C. *Educational psychology: the instructional endeavor* (2nd ed.). St. Louis: The C. V. Mosby Co., 1976.

Flanders, N. *Teacher influence, pupil attitudes, and achievement.* Minneapolis: University of Minnesota Press, 1960.

Glasser, W. *Schools without failure.* New York: Harper & Row, Publishers, 1969.

Ginott, H. *Teacher and child.* New York: Macmillan Publishing Co., Inc., 1972.

Gordon, T. *Teacher effectiveness training.* New York: Peter H. Wyden/Publisher, 1974.

Harris, T. *I'm O.K.—You're O.K.* New York: Harper & Row, Publishers, 1967.

Raths, L. Clarifying values. In R. Fliming (Ed.). *Curriculum for today's boys and girls.* Columbus, Ohio: Charles E. Merrill Publishing Co., 1963.

Raths, L., Harmin, M., and Simon, S. *Values and teaching.* Columbus, Ohio: Charles E. Merrill Publishing Co., 1966.

Sanders, N. *Classroom questions: what kinds?* New York: Harper & Row, Publishers, 1966.

PROFESSIONALISM
SKILLS, ETHICS, AND STYLE

PART FIVE

There are levels of professionalism, as there are levels of everything else. Some school people are highly professional, others less so. Professionalism is a conglomerate of many traits and behaviors: communicating, diagnosing, planning, interacting, directing, guiding, facilitating, supporting, encouraging, keeping records, getting along with others, contributing to the fund of knowledge and skills of teaching.

This final section does two things. First, it communicates directly to paraprofessionals and teachers who use them. A number of very definite, practical suggestions are made to help paraprofessionals perform their duties well. Second, it provides a guide to assist the professional growth of teachers, beginning where they enter teacher education; continuing with training experiences, job seeking, and on-the-job learning; and ending with graduate studies and self-actualization in teaching.

The chapter titles are as follows:

PARAPROFESSIONALS IN THE CLASSROOM* 19

para Alongside of
paraprofessional Alongside of the teacher

Teaching has become a most complicated business. Almost gone are the days when one teacher stands before rows and files of students, lecturing brilliantly or bumblingly, while students dutifully transfer into their notebooks every dripping pearl of wisdom. Not gone completely, but steadily vanishing—even, believe it or not, in the university.

Gently shoving these ways aside are newer notions of teaching, notions such as project approaches, individualized instruction, diagnostic-prescriptive teaching, inquiry-discovery, and group process activities. These approaches put the students much more in charge of their own learning. Students thrive on them.

But the newer approaches exact their toll. They demand of the teacher great expenditures of time and energy. Materials must be procured and readied. Groups must be monitored. Individuals must be assisted. Records must be kept. The teacher's presence must be distributed among all. The entire procedure must be managed and orchestrated. An awesome task, is it not?

These newer approaches, with the demands they place on teachers, have made additional help in the classroom a necessity. Many of the classroom jobs need not be performed by a highly trained teacher. They can be done by a perceptive,

*The authors gratefully acknowledge the collaboration of Miss Kathleen McCormick in the preparation of this chapter.

caring adult, one who is willing to learn quickly and who truly wants to help students learn. Such an adult, now called a paraprofessional, can contribute marvelously to the teaching-learning situation by relieving the teacher of many of the more routine duties. The teacher can then spend more time planning, guiding, and interacting with students.

The remainder of this chapter is written directly for people who intend to become paraprofessionals. It lays out the duties and responsibilities typically expected of adults who work alongside of teachers, explaining as many of the whats, hows, and whys as space permits.

YOU ARE NEEDED

Students have many needs. They need to be listened to, talked with, read to, touched, and shown how. Young children ask for these things naturally and eagerly. Older children want these things just as eagerly, but ask for them in different ways. Young or old, most students learn best when they have someone at hand to encourage and assist them.

Teachers have needs, too. They need to have more time, to correct fewer papers, to reach more students, and to be in three places at once. Teachers can teach better when they have beside them another adult who wants to help students learn.

Because of what students need and because of what teachers need, you are needed.

Instructional aide, teacher assistant, volunteer, parent helper, whatever name you may be called, you are a vital part of the classroom. Your functions and duties may be many and varied, but they will all be aimed, in one way or another, at helping students learn.

Your importance to students and their learning cannot be overemphasized. A good deal of money, time, and effort will be spent in putting you into the classroom. If you are a volunteer, hours will be spent seeking and securing you, and you in turn will be spending part of your life in this work. If you are a paid assistant, a portion of the school budget, now so limited, will be set aside for your salary. Administrators, teachers, and students all believe that your presence will make a difference, and they are more than willing to invest time and money in you.

Being important and needed is vital. But it is scarcely enough by itself. You must earn your keep by what you do.

Principals and teachers will make a fuss over you when you first arrive. They will tell you much the same thing you have read here—that you can make an important difference in the learning of the students. But please notice the word *"can."* Although extra help in the classroom is appreciated, the learning improvement that results depends on you. You can affect learners a great deal or very little. It all depends on what skills you contribute to the classroom and what you give of yourself while there.

Where do you learn these skills? When you get to your school you will find everyone very nice, but they will all be so busy. . . . You can guess the rest.

So busy that you hardly even have time to ask the teacher's name. That's not uncommon. When a teacher is nudged, tugged, and beseeched by thirty-five pairs of hands, arms, legs, and eyes, as well as thirty-five voices, it is hard to find time to talk to the new adult. Even the ones who make time to sit down and talk have a way of lapsing into "teacher talk," using words and expressions you just can't figure out. All this will frustrate you. Everyone tells you how much they need you and what a fantastic help you will be, and then no one tells you how.

Well, that's exactly what this chapter is for.

It's about how you, as a paraprofessional, can become a significant influence in the classroom, an influence that will, in turn, help students progress significantly. Toward this end, specific suggestions and techniques are presented for your growth in the following areas:

1. The first day: what to do and who to see
2. The first day: what to look for
3. Duties: the agonies and the ecstasies
4. Skills: jack of all trades
5. The lesson: when your learning begins

Do your best in these areas, and you can be sure of this: You will be well on your way to becoming a crackerjack paraprofessional.

THE FIRST DAY: WHAT TO DO AND WHO TO SEE

Remember what you, as a student, used to do to substitute teachers? Those poor souls didn't know the ropes, and you did your best to make things even harder for them.

As a new aide, volunteer, or assistant, you will face the same situation. The students will know classroom routines and procedures, and you will not. This puts the students at a definite advantage. Most students, whatever their age, will use this advantage as long as they can. It's up to the newcomer—you—to find out what is going on and to put yourself on an even footing with your students. In other words, *how much you learn on the first day will determine how easily the rest of your week, month, and year goes. It is paramount to your survival.*

To survive, here's what you need to do the first day:

1. Look your best. You will feel better about yourself, and students will respond better to you.
2. Arrive half an hour before your job is to start. If your work hours begin in the middle of the day, try to arrange a time to talk with the teacher before you begin, preferably when students are not there and you can both relax.
3. Go to the office and introduce yourself to the secretary, principal, and any other school staff members who might be there. There may be an introductory meeting scheduled for incoming aides. If not, you will need to find out the following information:
   a. What parking space is available to you?
   b. Where do you sign in and out?
   c. Are you allowed a break? If so, may you use the teachers' lounge or is there another place? Are there refreshment funds to which you should contribute?
   d. If you have to be absent, who should you contact? Do you arrange for a substitute or does the school? Are you allowed sick leave? Can you make up the time you are out? This information is important. Don't underestimate your value to the classroom, whether you are paid or a volunteer. If you are absent, someone will need to fill in for you.
   e. Is there an aide coordinator to whom you will be responsible? Where do the funds come from that pay you? Is your job part of a special program that has definite goals and expectations you must live up to? Will you be evaluated during the course of your job?
   f. What room, teacher, and grade level have you been assigned to?

You have seen the secretary, principal, aide coordinator, and various other people. Now it is time to see your teacher and your students. When you see the teacher, do the following:

1. Introduce yourself.
2. Ask if there are any special duties you will assume during the first day, such as cafeteria duty or outside supervision.
3. Ask if the teacher already has in mind what you will be doing—working with slower learners, giving individual tests, correcting papers, keeping records, etc.
4. If the teacher doesn't have your duties in mind, tell about any special talents or interests you have that might be useful in the class.
5. Your teacher will probably volunteer some information about the class, but much of it will come from your own observations. Try to find out the following:
   a. What is the general background of the students? Are there Navy families, so the students move and change schools a great deal? Is it a rural area, with much of the community's social life revolving around the school?
   b. Are there any particular likes and dislikes of this class? Do the students like to discuss? Are they physical in showing affection and quarreling? Is this a class of bright college preparatory students?
   c. What areas or subjects are the students concentrating on?
   d. Is there a wide range of abilities in the room or are most of the students near the same level?

The teacher may also tell you of special cases in the class. If you are to be working in a class of educationally handicapped or mentally gifted students, this information can be very helpful. However, if the information is about a class troublemaker, guard against prejudging the student. Part of your purpose is to give students the opportunity to relate positively to an adult. If you prejudge, you may defeat your own purpose.

There will be hundreds of bits of valuable information the teacher will be able to give you, much of which comes up when situations arise in the classroom. Make an effort to talk with the teacher for a few minutes each day after class; it will give you a chance to ask questions, express concerns, and receive suggestions. For the first day, however, the most important things are to get a picture of your class as a whole and to begin finding a place for yourself in that picture.

In your first meeting with your teacher it is very important to establish good rapport. Show your controlled enthusiasm, your willingness to listen, to learn, and to work. Recognize the fact that although your ideas on education may differ (most people's do), you will be working with and relying on the help of this person every day. An easy working relationship will benefit you, the teacher, and the students.

Speaking of the students . . .

Your teacher will probably introduce you to the class as a whole. It will be up to you to meet the students individually. Make every effort to learn their names on the first day. It is common courtesy to them; no one likes to be "hey you." Also, it makes things much easier for you when you begin working with them. Here are a few tricks that will help you with the name learning:

1. Before class, obtain a copy of the roll sheet and familiarize yourself with the names. Note any that are unusual. Make those the first that you try to connect with faces.
2. Ask the teacher if you can call roll. While you read off names, concentrate. Half the battle of remembering is determination to remember. Repeat the names to yourself while watching the faces. Again look for something unusual in dress or appearance to help you make the right connections.
3. If you work with a small group, ask them to tell you their names in some sort of logical order. Immediately repeat them back in the same order. When asking questions, force yourself to use names.
4. Concentrate on first names only. The last names can come later.

Learning the names will take determination on your part, but the results will put you miles ahead.

THE FIRST DAY: WHAT TO LOOK FOR

You may begin the day by observing or the teacher may put you right to work. In either case, keep your eyes open and watch for signs that will tell you about your class.

These questions will help you focus in on the areas you need to watch so that your first day will be more than just a jumble of vague impressions.

YOU NEED TO FIND OUT

Where are

Student seats?

Special activity areas?

Extra supplies?

Libraries?

Restrooms?

Physical education areas?

Storage spaces?

Work areas for you?

When do

Instruction, class breaks, and free time occur?

Students work in small groups, pairs, independently, as a total class?

Teachers and students ask and answer questions?

Students find out the results of their work?

What are

The textbooks and workbooks?

The games in the class?

The available art materials?

The amounts of noise allowed?

The class rules, and who knows them?

Who does

Opening activities, if any?

Distribution and collection of materials?

Most of the talking and questioning?

What when work is finished?

How

Do students take care of personal needs—water, restroom, hall pass?

Do students get daily supplies?

Do students move from class to class, to recess, to assembly?

Does the teacher get the attention of the total class?

Does the teacher maintain classroom control?

But what if the teacher gives you a group of students to work with on the very first day?

Keep calm. Quickly review the lesson plan the teacher has just handed you. If the instructions are minimal or nonexistent, don't ask the entire class for help. Take one of the students aside and ask what the normal procedure is. On a one-to-one basis, students will be very helpful and will tell you who, when, where, and how.

Because you are new, the students will test you. They will see how far they can go. This presents a real dilemma for paraprofessionals. They are reluctant to reprimand because they want students to like them. It's natural to want to be liked, and it's important to establish good rapport. However, you must not allow the students to run all over you, either. Your best defense, especially when you don't know the teacher's methods of discipline, is shown below.

Despite your best efforts to sort everything out, the first day will be a kaleidoscope of impressions, names, faces, trials, and errors. Don't let the confusion throw you. If you don't understand, ask. Teachers are practical people. They have to be. They will give you practical answers.

Before you go home at the end of the first day:

1. Have a general idea of what your duties will be.
2. Obtain a list of school rules.
3. Have your working conditions and regulations understood.
4. Meet and be learning the names of the following people:
   a. The principal
   b. The school secretary
   c. The paraprofessional coordinator
   d. Your teacher
   e. Your students

Have a good sense of the general routine of the class and the teacher's approach to students and subject matter. On your way home, take time to drive around the school area to get a feeling for the community from which your students come.

If you have managed to do all of this while showing your excitement and enthusiasm for your new job, you will have taken the first steps toward becoming an excellent paraprofessional and a significant part of the classroom.

DUTIES: THE AGONIES AND THE ECSTASIES

Dave was all set to be a teacher assistant. He had more than the necessary qualifications; calm, organized,

---

⟫ THE FOUR-POINT EMERGENCY PLAN ⟪

Like all good emergency plans, this one is practical and sound enough to be built into your everyday routine. In fact, it could well form the basis for your routine.

Point 1: Use positive reinforcement. Catch the students being good and let them know how much you appreciate it. This approach can forestall a number of problems.

Point 2: Nail the first thing that goes wrong, not the third, fourth, or fifth. It is easier to stop the talking, pushing, or goofing off the first time it happens. Act immediately.

Point 3: Let the students know that you're with it, that you know exactly what is going on in the classroom at all times. You have the old eyes in the back of the head, and the Shadow knows.

Point 4: Carry authority in your voice. This doesn't mean you have to yell. You can joke, laugh, give instructions or reprimands, but your voice always carries a note that says "I am in charge." You may be scared stiff, but the students won't know it.

enthusiastic. All his life he'd been told he had a special way with kids. He was eager to interact with his class of high school students, to listen to their problems, to become their buddy and hero.

After the first week on the job, Dave wanted to quit. "All I ever do is check papers, run the ditto machine, and watch detention hall. The students don't know me, and I don't know them. I give them absolutely no help. I'm just here to allow the teacher more free time. This isn't what they hired me for, is it?"

Mrs. Sanchez had volunteered to work in Mrs. Reynold's third-grade classroom at the insistence of her daughter. "All the other mothers do it, Mom. Why don't you?" When she arrived, the teacher greeted her warmly and introduced her to a reading group of seven children, one of whom was her own daughter, Maria. "Mrs. Sanchez is going to help you read today, children. Please be on your best behavior."

The children were not on their best behavior, but they were on everything else, the walls, the floor, the tables, Mrs. Sanchez. They didn't want to settle down, and Mrs. Sanchez couldn't make them. She didn't know their names or the class rules. She didn't know school techniques of discipline. She wasn't sure what the teacher wanted her to do. To make matters worse, her own daughter was impossible. Mrs. Sanchez had never seen her so wild. Mrs. Reynolds had to step in and take over the group.

That night Mrs. Sanchez told her husband, "I never want to go back. I expected to check papers and work with materials in the room. But not to play teacher. It just wasn't fair. I'm not a teacher."

Dave and Mrs. Sanchez, in different situations, faced the same problem: their expectations did not match reality. That's a fact that you, too, will have to live with. Tasks given to paraprofessionals range from one extreme to the other, and the duties change from one day to the next. It will help you to know the types of things you may be asked to do and to have a set of general guidelines on how to do them. Such types and guidelines are discussed here.

We can divide most paraprofessional tasks into five categories: housekeeping, making things, clerical work, supervising, and teaching and tutoring. Most paraprofessionals do some things from each of these areas. In some cases the work is concentrated in one of them. We can see a list of the major tasks in these five categories on p. 397. We might add a few more words about each of these five categories of paraprofessional work.

Housekeeping

Teachers will tell you that an inordinate amount of their time is spent in straightening up. You can't put 30 to 180 active students in a room each day and engage them in diverse activities with diverse materials without making a lot of messes that have to be cleaned up. Much of your paraprofessional time will be spent in housekeeping tasks such as those mentioned before.

But here's a word to the wise. Class monitors can help greatly with these tasks. Use them. Students will feel more a part of their classroom, and your load will be lightened.

Also, remember the adage "a place for everything and everything in its place." Have designated places, clearly labeled, for all equipment, materials, books, and supplies. Make sure your students know where they are. Perpetuate the notion of everyone's being responsible for neatness.

Making things: the bold and the beautiful

Soon after they are born, human beings take delight in objects that move, shake, rattle, and glow with color. That delight never dies. Things that catch the eye, tickle the ear, or intrigue the hand are instant hits with learners of all ages. All people work longer, harder, and with more enthusiasm when their learning tasks and environments are attractive, warm, and colorful.

Attractive materials and activities provide great aids to learning. These aids include motivation, concrete examples, and memory assistance.

Motivation. Motivation is the force that inspires students to learn. When intrigued by a clever illustration, an interesting game, or an exciting filmstrip, they are much more willing to attend to and engage in their lessons.

Concrete examples. Most of us think, most of the time, in terms of concrete objects. The abstract becomes real when we can translate it into concrete terms. Any thinking process taught to students becomes easier to understand when students can manipulate materials, think out loud, or see graphic examples.

Memory assistance. Research has shown that the more senses you involve in learning, the better you remember. There is the following old saying:

I hear, and I forget.
I see, and I remember.
I do, and I understand.

PARAPROFESSIONAL TASKS

Housekeeping
Collect money
Set up student work areas
Mix paints for art
Arrange learning materials
Supervise cleanup
Water plants
Help with refreshments
Dust counter tops
Clean tables
Straighten shelves
Help children with coats
Oversee audiovisual material
Dispense laboratory materials

Clerical work
Keep records
Take roll
Check papers
Operate duplicators
Type
File
Score tests
Requisition supplies
Maintain inventories
Coordinate folders
Do necessary telephoning

Making things
Mount artwork
Decorate bulletin boards
Display student work
Cut, paste, color
Laminate materials
Prepare duplicating materials
Prepare newsletters and bulletins
Arrange learning stations
Help produce assemblies and plays
Prepare charts and transparencies
Organize and arrange displays

Supervision
Direct student movement
Supervise children's games
Serve grounds and cafeteria duty
Manage classroom library
Oversee bus loading and unloading
Direct intramural activities
Sponsor club meetings
Settle student disputes
Accompany students to office
Assist on field trips
Oversee student laboratory work
Supervise afterschool activities

Teaching and tutoring
Work with bright and slow students
Assist students with seat work
Review homework and test papers
Help absentees catch up
Tell stories to children
Give oral tests
Help students find references
Assist in demonstrations
Instruct students in safe use of tools

Supervise reading groups
Distribute and gather materials
Review and evaluate student work
Assist with grammar and spelling
Teach songs and play instruments
Assist in drill work
Check seat work
Put written work on board
Be a good model in every way

Teachers now use incredible varieties of instructional materials to assist learning. Gone forever are the days when a teacher's only instruments were voice and blackboard. Now classrooms are loaded with the following:

Work sheets
Tapes and records
Models
Slides and transparencies
Charts of every type
Maps and globes
Graphs and tables
Laboratory apparatus
Art materials
Learning centers
Flash and drill cards
Musical instruments
Board games
Puppets
Books and magazines
Tokens and certificates
Supplies such as construction paper, scissors, paste, glue, tape, paper clips, paints, colors, marking pens, fabric scraps, stones, travel posters, chip board, tag board, bottles, sticks, straws, towel rolls, egg cartons, boxes, wire, string, ribbon, wrapping paper . . . The list goes on and on.

Some of these items are suited to exploratory and creative activities, whereas others are suited to specific learning tasks. In general, items such as charts, models, dittoes, flash cards, graphs, maps, and board games are used to foster *convergent learning,* where you want students to become able to reproduce in a specific form what they have been taught. These materials are used to introduce, reinforce, and test factual information. Other items, such as musical instruments, art items, library books, learning centers, tape recorders, and cameras are used to foster *divergent thinking,* where you want students to create, to carry on beyond the lesson. They furnish springboards for creative activities.

How does one assemble these things? You begin with available materials, with imagination, and with the needs of the students in mind. Take an egg carton, for example. You can make any of the following:

A multiplication device
A vocabulary device
A holder for clips, staples, and erasers
Minipuppets
Texture and shape games
Word games

The possibilities are endless. There are no restrictions on what you can do, and there is a wide variety of resources available to give you ideas, materials, and how-to's. With this in mind, check the following:

1. Make it a practice to attend workshops available in your school district. In a couple of hours you can see enough ideas to keep you busy for a year.

2. Look at commercial games and objects. Many of them can be adapted to suit classroom situations. Old game boards can be reused with new instructions and cards for years on end.

3. Coloring books, cartoons, and comics can be used to illustrate, decorate, or create bulletin boards. They can be used as is or blown up to larger sizes.

4. Don't limit yourself to any one type of arts and crafts. Try different types of textures, three-dimensional effects, unique lettering, collages of pictures, tissue paper, food containers, and dried leaves and flowers. Marking pens come in all sizes and colors. Don't overlook varieties of chalk, watercolors, tempera paint, block printing, and sponge painting.

5. Comb the local dime stores, thrift stores, Salvation Army stores, novelty shops, and rummage sales. Inexpensive items that seem worthless to other people are treasures to teachers.

6. Check local industries, businesses, shops, supermarkets, liquor stores, and government agencies. They often have free materials for teachers. Look through lumber yards, packing plants, and office supply stores. Write or ask for free documents, posters, leaflets, brochures, pictures, and historical information. Chambers of commerce often have local maps and pictures. Write to companies that furnish school supplies, glue, tape, paper, crayons, paints. Most of these companies have free materials and special projects that can be made with their products.

7. Your teacher, the local library, and the school district library have books that list ideas for making materials in every subject, for every grade. Copy them, and use them as idea starters. Don't reinvent the wheel. Take advantage of other teachers' years of experience.

8. When you go to a great deal of trouble to make something, preserve it. Cover it with clear contact paper or laminate it. These materials can then be cleaned and reused again and again. If your materials have parts, label everything clearly so you can tell what goes with what. Double-check all materials you make to be sure they are free of spelling errors.

How many materials should you use in teaching? Opinions differ greatly. Some teachers think you can never have too many materials. Others believe they should be used sparingly to enhance their novelty and special effect and to prevent their distracting students. Balance your own opinions with those of your teacher.

Clerical work: the fine art of pencil pushing

Remember Dave, the frustrated TA? Part of his frustration had to do with the amount of paperwork he was expected to do. He didn't believe that was what he was hired to do. In a sense he was right. Using paraprofessionals for nothing besides paperwork can be a waste of a valuable resource.

But you must remember that education has undergone drastic changes within the last few years. It used to be that the only paperwork a teacher had to contend with was student-written work and report cards, surely a big enough load in itself. Now, with individualized instruction, federal and state programs, DPT, IGE, ECE (the list seems almost endless), teachers must handle double, triple, quadruple the amount. So much is going on in the classroom that a teacher is forced to put down on paper much of what could formerly be carried in the head. There is simply no other way to keep track of it. It is no wonder that many teachers believe they are losing individual contact with their students and that they eagerly welcome paraprofessionals as people who can help take the load off them.

When you are asked to correct papers, keep records, or maintain files, the teacher is not delegating you to the unimportant. The innumerable charts and folders are necessary. The teacher is

seeking some relief from the load in order to have more time to work with students. Remember, both teachers and students have needs; that's why you are there.

As you approach these clerical molehills (or are they really mountains?), keep these things in mind:

1. If your teacher gives you instructions on how to mark or score a paper, *follow them exactly*. There is a system involved, and you may mess up everything if you deviate from it.

2. If you are in an elementary class, learn the proper way to write and print. Most teachers will have a book of correct printing (manuscript) and handwriting (cursive). Learn these. Your students will imitate you, and they are supposed to learn to write in a certain way.

3. Most school duplicating machines—the ditto, the Thermofax, and the Xerox—are simple and easy to operate. Ask one of the teachers to show you how.

4. If you are asked to make a telephone call for the teacher, use the same courtesy and efficiency you would expect in a business office. Be particularly careful with calls to parents. They associate school calls with trouble. Put them at ease with your voice and manner.

5. In the course of keeping and checking files on various students, you may run across confidential information. As a matter of fact, any information regarding a student's academic progress, social behavior, or home situation is strictly confidential. It should not be repeated to *anyone*. Questions concerning a student should always be referred to the teacher. You say nothing.

It is impossible to give you samples of all the types of charts and records you may be expected to keep. Becoming familiar with the words in the glossary (p. 437) will help you make sense of the various forms that are in use.

Remember, paperwork is a necessary part of the school day. You are doing a service to both students and teacher by helping with it.

Supervision: riding herd

When Alice first began working as a TA, she was assigned to a class of angelic (so she thought) second graders. She watched the teacher work with them, saw how they responded to every suggestion instantly. "Let's line up now, please." Two straight lines formed. "This way, please." Two silent lines moved down the hall. This will be a snap, Alice thought to herself.

The day came when Alice was to lead her little charges outside for physical education. She beamed at them. They beamed at her. She was entranced. They were waiting in ambush. "This way, boys and girls." She started off, confident that they were marching behind her in perfect order. When she turned around, what she saw was perfect chaos. Her pleas fell on deaf ears. Her turn-coat angels, how could they? And how could she have so much trouble just moving thirty kids from one place to another?

Moving a class from one place to another, keeping a class in one place instead of another, cafeteria duty, hall monitoring, restroom overseeing, recess, bus duty—all these things are part of supervision. A paraprofessional, although technically under the direction of the teacher, can and will be left alone with students. As a supervisor of student activity, you are responsible for the safety of the students first, and for calm and order second.

The key to easy, smooth-running supervision is advance preparation. Obviously, both you and the students must be aware of the rules that govern the classroom, cafeteria, and school grounds. Schools usually have printed rules with the do's and don't's clearly explained. Make sure you know them. Even first graders are con artists. It is the teacher's responsibility to inform the students, but it will be your responsibility to enforce the rules.

Students always seek interesting things to do. They imitate each other. They show off. They horse around. Some of the resulting acts are cute. Others are devilish. Most of the problems that arise come from boredom, frustration, and contact with other students. Ways to prevent problems include the following:

1. *Make a game of it*. If children are to walk for short distances in line, tell them that they are on a spy mission or that they are walking past an avalanche. For older students, use competition against other classes or against their own past performance. Learn how to direct stand-in-place calisthenics, finger exercises, and games like Simon Says. This will help you keep students occupied when they have to be held in line.

2. *Spread and separate*. Pushing and shoving usually mean that students are too close together. Keep them an arms' length apart. If you

are playing indoor games, make sure sufficient space is available.

3. *Prevent blowouts*. It is the frustrated student, the one who is left out, who will often cause problems. Set up quick and easy ways to choose sides for games. Help your loners find activities that keep them occupied.

4. *Separate fights immediately*. If a fight breaks out, deal with the situation at once. Don't try to determine the cause; just see that the fight stops. Let the students cool off. Each school has its own policy for handling fights. Know that policy, and follow it to the letter. If in doubt, separate the combatants from other students until the teacher or principal is available.

5. *Discourage tattling*. Every class, particularly elementary ones, is over endowed with tattle-tales. Most teachers try to discourage this behavior. Ignoring it, or asking tattlers to write their stories out on paper for you to read later, will help. Be sure you watch closely enough that you don't have to rely on little Suzy to report to you what little Johnny is doing.

6. *When a student is injured while under your supervision, send for help*. Under no circumstances leave the student unless another adult is there to take your place. Do not administer first aid unless you are qualified and can prove it. Do not try to move the student without trained help. If the injury is minor, send the student, with a companion, to the principal's office.

The most important things to remember about supervision are first, to prevent problems from arising; second, to observe all students closely and diligently while you are in charge; and third, when a problem arises, step in quickly and firmly to correct the situation.

Teaching and tutoring: the heart of the game

Millions of words have been written about teaching. Even the most experienced teachers regularly learn new methods, strategies, and techniques. This learning is a never-ending process. Make it your way of life.

Teaching is not a single act. It is a conglomerate of acts that fit into categories quite different from each other. These categories include planning and preparation, implementation, and evaluation. Each category has numerous subcomponents, as you can see in the following:

Planning and preparation

Assessing needs of students
Selecting content—what is to be taught
Organizing teaching methods and strategies
Preparing the environment
Organizing instructional materials
Arranging management and record keeping procedures

Implementation

Motivating
Introducing the lesson, its contents, and its procedures
Presenting the lesson contents and activities
Facilitating student work and use of materials
Managing assignments, movements, pacing, and record keeping
Closing the lesson at the proper time in the proper way

Evaluation

Assessing student progress
Judging student effort and teaching effectiveness
Recycling, using this information to make instructional improvements

Throughout, good teaching is based on sound principles of learning. These principles were discussed in Chapter 10. You might wish to refer back to them.

You, as a paraprofessional, will be given major responsibilities in some of these aspects of teaching, minor responsibilities in others, and no responsibilities at all in some of them.

Almost certainly, however, there will come a time when you will be asked to perform what most people think of as teaching—presenting material to learners and controlling their work. Usually your teacher will have selected the material and perhaps will have outlined the procedures for presenting it. This leaves you with two major duties: communicating effectively with the students and controlling their behavior. Both duties are to help students engage productively with the learning task. The first duty is difficult. The second is the hardest of all for paraprofessionals. Let's consider each of them briefly.

Communication. The basis of all learning and teaching is communication. You, as the teacher, want to communicate your knowledge of subject matter and learning procedures to the students. The students, as learners, need to communicate their questions, confusions, and difficulties to you. If you are perceptive, you will pick up on students' feelings and assist with anxieties and rough spots.

To do this, you must establish an atmosphere that is open and trusting, learn to do as much listening as talking, and learn to respect the views and ideas of your students.

Communication is truly the essence of good teaching, the inner quality that is said to make the born teacher. However, most good teachers are made, not born, and you can learn to communicate with students far more effectively than you do now.

Good communication has two prime qualities: clarity and openness. It has clarity when it is meaningful, understandable, relevant, and to the point. It has openness when it allows free give and take, with acceptance and without defensiveness. Communication that has these two qualities facilitates learning and builds positive attitudes.

Control. Control, or discipline, is the greatest hurdle teachers must leap. Teachers live or die by their ability to control the class. Paraprofessionals must show that ability, too, if they are ever to have true teaching responsibilities. Work with students is what teaching is all about. To work with them effectively you must keep them on task.

On-task behavior can be maintained through control techniques that fall into three categories: preventive control, supportive control, and corrective control. Specific elements within each category are listed here. You *must* take these ideas to heart, practice them, and make them a natural part of your style if you are to control students effectively.

PREVENTIVE CONTROL: LEAVE NO STONE UNTURNED

1. Plan and organize in detail. Have everything ready, so the activities go like clockwork.
2. Be sure that what you have students do is worthwhile and interesting.
3. Be sure students have a clear sense of purpose and direction.
4. Establish clear expectations and guidelines.
5. Always be ready to use behavior modification techniques.
6. Have quick, interesting backup activities ready in case you have to change plans at the last minute.

SUPPORTIVE CONTROL: A STITCH IN TIME

1. Maintain eye contact with students.
2. Always show that you are "with it"—that you know everything that is going on in the group.
3. Respond immediately the first time misbehavior occurs. Nip it.

4. Remain physically near to the students with whom you are working.
5. Overlap, that is, pay attention to individuals and to the total group simultaneously.
6. Use accepting language. Try not to make students feel rejected.
7. Guide students when they have difficulty. Show them how.
8. Show that you can listen. But don't let students lead you too far from the topic at hand.
9. Be pleasant and friendly, but firm. At the same time, be businesslike and purposeful. Show that you are nice, but that you are very serious about learning.

CORRECTIVE CONTROL: THE MOMENT OF TRUTH

When problems do occur:

1. Use a reality approach. Guide the misbehaving student to selecting a more acceptable behavior and following through with it.
2. Suppress mimicry and cruelty immediately. They are contagious.
3. Use restitution when appropriate; have students repay in good deeds for what they have done wrong.
4. Use deprivation when appropriate; take away rights and privileges as a just consequence of the misbehavior.
5. Use isolation when appropriate; remove the misbehaving student from the group and from the activity.
6. Call for teacher assistance if things get beyond your control.

After you have taught, try to analyze your control techniques. Ask the teacher to observe and make suggestions. Record your lesson, and play it back to see how you talk and sound. If you had difficulties, they may have been caused by the learning tasks, your own traits, or traits of the students that you will want to modify. Let's examine these three possibilities.

THE LEARNING TASKS

You cannot always control the content of the lesson you must teach, but you can control the way it is presented, for how long, in what manner the students must respond, and what you do to liven it up. Use every trick you know to circumvent the following:

1. *Fatigue.* When students become overly tired, they no longer work. They find other, less appropriate things to do.
2. *Boredom.* When activities are not interesting to students, their eyes, minds, hands, and bodies wander elsewhere.

3. *Frustration.* When tasks are too difficult, too long, or too confusing, students throw down pencils; crumple papers; stare off into space; and become restless, upset, grouchy, or belligerent.

When you see signs of fatigue, boredom, or frustration, you know your lesson is no longer getting across to students. Do not doggedly continue on course. The students have already turned you off. This is the time to let them stretch, move about, ask questions. It is also a signal to you to speed up or slow down, shift the focus, tell an anecdote, or change the content of the work.

YOUR OWN TRAITS

Control problems can stem from your own traits, of which you may not be aware. These traits can include the following:

1. *Lack of clarity.* Directions are fuzzy, examples are vague, purpose of the lesson is unclear. Students do not know what to expect or what is expected of them.
2. *Poor voice characteristics.* This includes both the actual quality of the voice—too high, soft, monotonous, grating—and the tone and expression—patronizing, sarcastic, disbelieving, confused, or unsure.
3. *Poor questioning techniques.* Questions seem to grill more than assist. Sufficient time is not allowed for students to answer. You may be answering your own questions, putting down students' answers, not allowing students to speak, or continually asking short, memory-type questions that do not require students to think.
4. *Lack of acceptance.* You may be responding to students with nonattention, vindictiveness, sarcasm, moralizing, or attacks on the character instead of dealing with the situation at hand. You can also hamper student learning with too much kindness if it is oversympathizing, excusing, or meaningless praise. On the surface, this manner seems to be warm and accepting. In reality it communicates that you do not see students as they really are and that they are not free to be themselves in the classroom.

If you find that one of these traits is adding to control problems, work on correcting it in the following ways:

1. If clarity is the problem, give directions that are short and to the point. Speak distinctly and

slowly. Use words all the students understand.

2. If voice quality is the problem, find out how your voice sounds. Then learn to use it as an instrument. Vary its pitch, volume, tone, and speed. Use pauses to draw attention. Replace negative tones with notes of surprise, suspense, drama, delight, trust, and humor.

3. If you are poor at asking questions, practice asking them simply and directly. Give students enough time to answer. Try to use questions that relate the material being learned to students' experiences. Don't reject students or put them down because of the answers they give.

4. If you see that you tend to reject students, practice dealing with the situation, not the student's character. For example, "The beaker spilled. We need to clean it up" is far more effective than "You are so clumsy. Look what you've done. Clean up the mess you made." Let students know you accept them, their feelings, and their problems, even when you do not accept their behavior. Help them face their feelings of anger, frustration, loneliness, and fear by talking with them in accepting ways. Earlier, mention was made of some of the dangers of praise. To make praise useful and meaningful, direct it to specific acts. "You read that passage with excitement and feeling" is much more effective than "You surely are a good reader." Also, be careful of commiserating too much with students. "It must be tough to work at an after-school job and keep up with homework, too. That takes real determination and maturity" is greatly preferable to "You poor thing, what are you going to do! Maybe you had better quit your job."

TRAITS OF THE STUDENTS

Control problems often come from factors that belong to the student. Among these factors are the following:

1. *Ignorance*. The student doesn't know what is expected. There is no intent to misbehave. The rules of proper and improper conduct are not known.

2. *Mimicry*. For some reason students like to imitate each other. Mimicry of undesirable behavior can spread like wildfire, especially if modeled by students with prestige in the class.

3. *Habit*. From other classes, other people, and even from home, students sometimes develop habits of misbehavior. They hold onto acts that have brought them recognition or pleasure— whining, defiance, smart aleck talk, talking out, sarcasm, punching and pinching, or making noises.

4. *Displacement*. Teachers think learning should be the number one priority in school. Students are often afflicted with emotional pressures that interfere with learning and that cause them to disrupt learning for others. Hostility at home breeds hostility at school. Poor self-concept causes withdrawal or physical and verbal bullying.

When you find ignorance, mimicry, habit, and displacement causing students to misbehave, you can do the following:

1. Make sure all students know what is tolerated and what is not tolerated in your classroom. Most of these limits are established by the teacher. You, too, may have your pet peeves. It is reasonable to expect students to refrain from acts, such as sarcastic remarks, that bother you. You have to let them know.

2. When students begin to mimic each other, discuss the problem with them. Tell them the effects mimicry produces and how it interferes with learning. When mimicry begins, use your authority to say "That does not go in this room."

3. Misbehavior that has become habitual is resistant to change. However, habits are learned, and they can be unlearned. Rather, new habits can be learned in their place—habits of courtesy, diligence, friendliness, and so forth. They are learned through example and practice, with reinforcement for desired behavior.

4. There is little you can do to correct unfortunate conditions in students' life outside school. But when they displace stress into disruptive behavior, you will need to employ your best communicative talents. It does the student little good to be punished if fear, hostility, and bad self-concept are causing the problem. Be flexible. Talk individually with students. Allow them to talk about problems occasionally. Again, however, you cannot allow displaced aggression to disrupt learning for the rest of the students in the class.

OTHER CAUSES

To this point we have considered three general causes of student misbehavior: characteristics of the learning tasks, traits of the teacher, and traits of the student. Although the majority of misbehavior causes fall into these three groups, there are still others that do not. Chief among these "other" causes are poor class environment, special events, and the unexpected.

1. *Poor class environment.* This has two aspects —physical and emotional. Poor physical environment includes bad lighting; uncomfortable seating; high noise level; and awkward arrangements of furniture, materials, and work spaces. Poor emotional environment includes barriers between teacher and students, coldness and rejection, punitiveness, sarcasm, cruelty, and intellectual intimidation. In such environments, student work is hampered because students feel threatened, rebuked, ignored, and unimportant. They believe they have no say in their own lives.

2. *Special events.* Special events are those parties, holidays, athletic games, plays, carnivals, and so forth that distract students and keep them in a state of excitement.

3. *The unexpected.* The unexpected includes anything out of the ordinary that happens without warning. A dog runs into the room; a student faints; two students get into a fight; the teacher gets sick; the electrical power goes off. Any of these things make it virtually impossible to continue with the lessons under way. They provide a fertile bed for student misbehavior.

How does one cope with these things? You might try the following:

1. You can do much to improve the classroom environment, whether the problem is physical or emotional. A great deal of information exists to help you do that. Much of it is spread throughout the pages of this book.

2. As far as special events are concerned, anticipate them and use them to advantage. Pay attention to the calendar and to what students are talking about. Plan ahead so you can build meaningful activities around the upcoming event. Almost all events are good for excellent discussions. Many lend themselves to interpretation, analysis, prediction, and debate. Many inspire dramatic representation, music, art, and creative writing. Motivation for these activities already exists. Learn to use it productively.

3. The unexpected, odd as it may seem, can also be anticipated and planned for. Discuss with the students and plan procedures to be used should the teacher have to leave the room. Practice opportunities for students to take charge and conduct themselves in exemplary ways. Stage mock disputes, then have students write about the event as though they were eyewitnesses. The main idea is to expect the unexpected and have a plan to follow.

SKILLS: JACK OF ALL TRADES

Mary was one of twenty-five persons outside the school district office applying for a position as instructional aide. When her name was finally called for the interview, she followed a gentleman into the inner office and nervously seated herself on the edge of a chair. The interviewer chatted with her for a few moments, then got down to his questions.

"Well, Mary, you want to be an instructional aide?"

"Yes, sir. I really enjoy kids."

"Umm . . . mm . . . m, that's important. How do you think you are qualified for this type of work?"

"Well, sir, I really do like kids."

"I see. But what *skills* do you have to bring to this job?"

"Skills? Sir, I really *love* kids."

Mary finally did get the job, although not on the basis of the questions here. The interviewer recognized that Mary was highly qualified and had simply not taken stock of her assets. He asked her to check off her talents on a checklist similar to the one that follows. Although enjoying children and young people is important, there are many other skills you need in order to be a successful paraprofessional.

Which of the hidden talents listed on p. 405 do you have?

You probably didn't realize you were so highly qualified, did you? All these are skills that you have or can reasonably develop. Really look at yourself as an individual; you will no doubt be surprised by all you have to offer your students and your school.

THE LESSON: WHERE YOUR LEARNING BEGINS

Most of us don't remember exactly what it was like to be young students in school. The memo-

SKILLS CHECKLIST

Understands and is able to use

Film projector

Slide projector

Tape recorder

Overhead projector

Record player

Ditto machine

Thermofax copier

Laminating press

Can

Type

Play a musical instrument

Speak a second language

Write legibly and in the proper form

Is interested and experienced in

Art

Choral directing

Drama

Industrial arts

Photography

Recreation

Outdoors/Nature

Sports and coaching

Travel

Has taken classes in

Child development

Cultural/ethnic studies

Counseling

Education

Family studies

Is familiar with education programs in

Early childhood education

Individually guided instruction

Diagnostic-prescriptive teaching

Has experience as a

Camp counselor

Recreational aide

Counselor (adults or children)

Sunday school teacher

Day care center aide

Big brother or sister or volunteer in any
program that specializes in youth

Parent

Personal traits include

Good health

Well-groomed appearance

Even temper

Organized approach

Warm and outgoing nature

Ability to listen

Familiarity with the community

Speech is clear and fluent

Ability to be comfortable with both
adults and children

ries we have are colored with time. We recall recess and sharing, those happy moments when we got gold stars, and those bad moments when we didn't know our 3's on the multiplication test. Some of us can remember straining, pushing, and knotting our hands until knuckles were white and sweat popped up on our foreheads. We were trying to understand what the teacher wanted us to do, what she was getting at. We can remember trying so hard, but we never knew why it was so difficult for us in the first place.

A child having problems in school can't tell you what the trouble is; he doesn't know. He can't say to you, "You see I don't understand the addition facts because I'm not yet ready for them, and you haven't presented them with mnemonic devices to help me learn them by rote." Children are not miniature adults; they perceive and think and understand in completely different terms than do adults. We, as teachers, need to remember this when we become frustrated with a child who doesn't understand what seems perfectly obvious to us.

Because students are so often faced with learning new ideas, mastering new skills, and forming new relationships, it is up to teachers, and their assistants, to make learning as easy and clear as possible.

As a paraprofessional, you will be approaching lessons from two points of view: (1) As an extension of the teacher when you are following ready-made lesson plans and (2) as a teacher when you plan and present instruction.

Let's look at the first view, following the teacher's plans. They may be as follows:

Oral directions: The teacher tells you what to do, what work sheets are needed, what materials you should have, and which students to work with.

Teacher's manual: Usually used in coordination with the pages of a certain textbook, the manual outlines the skill being taught and the pages to be covered, as well as giving ideas and suggestions for teaching the concepts listed. You are to organize them into a coherent lesson.

Written plans: The objectives, steps, materials, and times are written out for you. You simply follow the established plan.

When you receive any one of these plans from your teacher, you need to go through it to do the following:

Identify the objective: What should the students be able to do after completing this lesson? Sometimes it's to simply understand a story and be able to answer comprehension questions about it. At other times the objective is to be able to write spelling words correctly. Sometimes the objective is to be able to compute the area of an isosceles triangle. Know what the target is you're aiming for, and always keep it in mind.

Identify the materials: What things are you going to need to teach this lesson effectively? Will you need to use a chalkboard, chalk, flash cards, illustrations? Will the students need to have their textbooks, papers, pencils, workbooks? Gather all these things together before the lesson starts. Do not jump up in the middle to do so.

Identify the organization: What is the best way for the students to be grouped for the lesson? Should they be at their seats, at the front, along the sides of the room? In the midst of all this, where should you be? Do you need to be near a record player, chalkboard, chart? Will your students need to move around. Is there room to do this? And, very important, can they see and hear you?

Identify the sequence: What's going to happen first, second, and third in your lesson? Will you play the game at the beginning or the end? When will your students do independent work? When will you ask questions? Will you introduce the skill and then read the story or read the story and then talk about the concept? Lessons should have a logical order; they should be broken down in simple steps that proceed from:

Simple to difficult: Give easier problems, examples, concepts, and questions before moving on to more difficult ones.

Concrete to abstract: Use well-known examples, facts, and questions before leading in to an abstract notion.

Identify the time: This is extremely important! You need to find out how much time has been allotted for this lesson (20 minutes) and then decide how much time you can spend on each part (5 minutes introducing skill, 10 minutes independent work, 3 minutes reviewing concept and evaluating the lesson). The extra 2 minutes? That's time for the students to move from the front of the room to their desks and back again. Don't forget to allow for this moving time; it's necessary.

Identify student participation: What are the students going to do to show you they know the material that has been covered? What are they going to write, say, point to, do, think? What practice are they going to have (work sheets, writing, reading, drawing, acting out, relating) with their new skill?

Identify the motivators: What has the teacher included or what will you have to include that will motivate the students to learn? They learn best when what they are learning is important to them. It must matter to them personally, and it should make a difference to them *now, right away,* or *immediately.* Motivators come in a variety of shapes, sizes, colors, and temperaments, just as do students. Certain types of motivators work best with certain people.

You cannot please everyone all the time, but you can provide a mix-and-match grab bag of inspirations within each lesson. Read the ABC's of motivators shown below. Most of these motivators will work with most students most of the time. When you are teaching a lesson, check to see that you have used one or more of these motivators to stir, coax, push, and entice your students to better learning.

THE ABC's OF MOTIVATORS

A **Appealing** materials to move and manipulate.

B **Building** on previous lessons, letting students see how what they know helps them.

C **Contracts,** agreements, written or oral, between teacher and students for work to be done.

D **Development,** showing how the lesson you did in social studies applies to literature; the subjects interrelate.

E **Excitement,** in that the subject itself is an exciting one students are eager to study.

F **Films** that can spark interests.

G **Games** that teach and give practice to various skills.

H **Humor,** a delight in the moment, a wry sense that lets students see the funny side.

I **Interests,** appealing to already established interests of the student.

J **Jobs,** duties, and responsibilities that involve students in the lesson.

K **Kinesthetic awareness,** moving about, touching, handling, manipulating.

L **Listening,** letting students talk, ask questions, and practice the skills of listening.

M **Mnemonics,** memory aids that will help students remember what they learn.

N **Novelty,** the unexpected, the strange, the different; even the ordinary is novel when seen for the first time.

O **Openness** to new directions the lesson may take; being flexible.

P **Praise,** letting students know how well they are doing.

Q **Questions** that stir students' curiosities, ask them to project and think creatively.

R **Rhymes and riddles,** putting facts, dates, and ideas together in unique patterns, arrangements, and ditties.

S **Sensory involvement,** including touch, taste, smell, sight, and hearing in the learning activities.

T **Tests** that help the students know what they are capable of.

U **Unusual and unique** projects that let the students explore.

V **Voice,** your voice, conveying warmth, excitement, suspense, and interest in your subject.

W **Withitness** so that the subject and the way it is presented relate to the contemporary world of the student and day-to-day events.

X **X-amples** that are concrete, bright, inventive, clear, and easy to understand.

Y **You,** for if your students like and enjoy you, they will work to please you.

Z **Unknown factors** of your own personality that you will add to the lesson.

Once you have identified the *objective, materials, organization, sequence, time, student participation,* and *motivators,* you are ready to begin. You're on stage.

While you are teaching, watch yourself and your students for cues as to how the lesson is going. Their faces and actions will tell you to do the following:

1. Speed up.
2. Slow down.
3. Make instructions clear.
4. Go over that again. Give another example.
5. Listen.
6. Get on with it.
7. Change directions.

In teaching, ignoring any of these is one of the seven deadly sins—deadly, because if you ignore your students once you begin to teach, you are defeating your purpose. Be flexible enough that you can react to these changes.

All these hints are to help you deal with a plan that has already been made. If you are responsible for making the lesson plan yourself, you would follow the same steps. Except instead of merely identifying the components from someone else's directions, you must think up the same components on your own. Again you need to determine the *objectives, materials, organization, sequence, time, student participation,* and *motivators.* Once you have these firmly in mind, plug these parts into the *master lesson plan.*

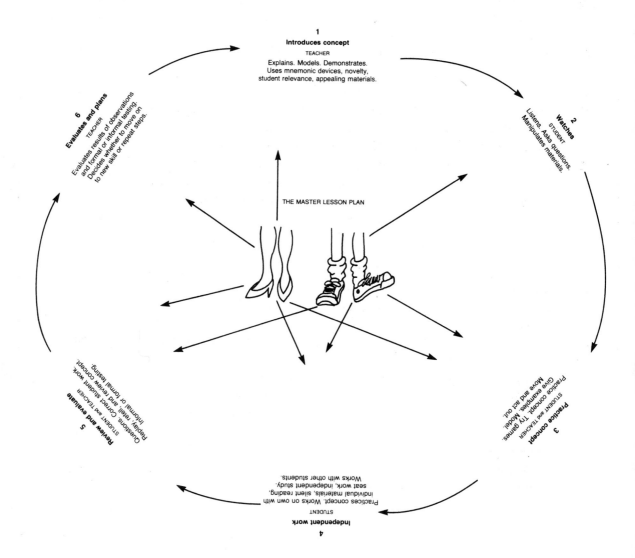

1
Introduces concept
TEACHER
Explains. Models. Demonstrates.
Uses mnemonic devices, novelty,
student relevance, appealing materials.

2
Watches
STUDENT
Listens. Asks questions.
Manipulates materials.

3
Practice concept
STUDENT and TEACHER
Practice concept. Try games. Give examples. Model.
Move and act out.

4
Independent work
STUDENT
Practices concept. Works on own with
individual materials, silent reading,
seat work, independent study.
Works with other students.

5
Review and evaluate
STUDENT and TEACHER
Questions. Correct student work.
Replay, retell, and review concept.
Informal or formal testing.

6
Evaluates and plans
TEACHER
Evaluates results of observations
and formal or informal testing.
Decides whether to move on
to new skill or repeat steps.

THE MASTER LESSON PLAN

The master lesson plan is a foundation for helping you decide who does what, when, and with whom. It can be modified and adapted to almost anything you wish to teach. So let's look at how this plan might work teaching a creative writing lesson to elementary school students. First, identify the following:

Objective: Students will be able to compose a short story concerning George Washington and using at least four of the facts related by the teacher's story.

Materials: Chalk, large manila papers, teacher-made sentence chart, notes, lined paper, pencils, erasers.

Organization: Teacher is in front of the class by chalkboard; students are grouped in a circle.

Sequence: Teacher tells story of George Washington's life and reviews major points with students; students write stories; teacher and students share work.

Time: Altogether, 1 hour (see master lesson plan for details).

Student participation: Students volunteer information and ask questions during storytelling, write own stories, and share their work with class.

Motivators: Watching teacher draw while relating anecdotes about George Washington's life; praise from teacher for student efforts.

The following is an example of the plan in action.

Master lesson plan

1. *Introduction of concept by teacher* (15 minutes). Teacher tells story of George Washington's life while drawing chalk pictures to illustrate the story.
2. *Watching.* Students listen, ask questions, volunteer information, add highlights.
3. *Practicing concept* (7 minutes). Students and teacher go over the main points of the story together, using the teacher-prepared sentence chart, recalling, and adding comments. Teacher states expectations of students' work: neat, in own words, using at least four of the points listed in the sentence chart.
4. *Independent practice* (30 minutes). Students are dismissed to their seats, begin work (materials already at their seats). Teacher circulates to help when needed.
5. *Evaluation and review* (6 minutes). Teacher and students read selected work out loud and offer comments. Students talk about parts they enjoyed most.
6.
7. *Evaluation and planning.* Teacher checks stories and determines whether objectives are accomplished. Teacher decides that students need work in punctuation.

NOTE: Two minutes are allowed for class moving time.

With this plan in hand, your materials available, and your students grouped properly, *you are ready*.

Experience will help you polish and refine your teaching techniques. Watch your teacher, and note discipline, explanations, questions, and expectations. Have your teacher watch you to give helpful suggestions. Most of all, watch your students. What they are able to do, how they react, and what they learn from you are the real measures of your success in teaching.

SUGGESTED ACTIVITIES FOR FURTHER UNDERSTANDING
For aspiring teachers

1. Make a list of what you believe would be the most important information to tell your new aide on the first day of school. You may want to make up a packet of information that could be used by aides.
2. Try writing a lesson plan for a nonteacher. Be careful of the terms you use. Have another student read it to see if he or she could teach from the plan without previous education experience.
3. Choose four different "teacherese" terms, and define them so that they are easily understood. Be careful not to throw in more teacher talk in your definition.
4. Role-play: You have an aide working in your room whose manner with students does not please you. Perhaps the aide is too easy on students, with no standards set or enforced. Or perhaps he is excessively strict and authoritarian. Obviously your teaching styles are not meshing. With another student, enact how you would diplomatically make your views known.

For aspiring paraprofessionals

1. Make a list of what you would want to find out from the teacher *and* what you would want the teacher to know about you on your first day.
2. Practice writing up a lesson plan from a teacher's manual. These manuals give many helpful ideas, but make the plans your own. Discuss your plans in class.
3. Practice memorizing names. In every situation in which you find yourself, work on connecting names and faces. Begin developing your own system in memorization.
4. Role-play: You are an aide in a classroom where you feel terribly dissatisfied with the jobs assigned to you. You may believe your talents are wasted, or you can't control the students, or what you are asked to do is too much for your working day. How would you tactfully inform the teacher of your feelings, and what alternatives could you suggest?

REFERENCES

Charles, C. *Educational psychology: the instructional Endeavor* (2nd ed.). St. Louis: The C. V. Mosby Co., 1976.

Collins, M., and Collins, D. *Survival kit for teachers (and parents)*. Pacific Palisades, Calif.: Goodyear Publishing Co., Inc., 1975.

Ginott, H. *Teacher and child*. New York: Macmillan Publishing Co., Inc., 1971.

Glasser, W. *Schools without failure*. New York: Harper & Row, Publishers, 1969.

Kounin, J. *Discipline and group management in classrooms*. New York: Holt, Rinehart & Winston, Inc., 1970.

Redl, F., and Wattenburg, W. *Mental hygiene in teaching* (2nd ed.). New York: Harcourt Brace Jovanovich, Inc., 1959.

GROWTH OF THE PROFESSIONAL

Sally Smith decided during her junior year in college that she wanted to be a teacher. It's hard to say exactly why she made the decision. Two years earlier she would have scoffed at the idea. But the time was coming when she would be on her own, economically. There were the harsh bills of housing, food, clothing, and car. There was the desire for a job that would pay the bills and at the same time be rewarding, enjoyable, and respectable. Two of her friends had decided to go into teaching. A couple of relatives were teachers, and they seemed to like it. So, more or less by chance, Sally set her sights on a teaching career.

She didn't know much about teaching when she made her decision. She had only the memories of her own years in school. They didn't include much about what teachers did. She had heard her uncle mention the physical education classes he taught. His remarks didn't shed any light at all on teaching English, which was Sally's major. She was about as naive about her chosen profession as anyone could be.

Six years later Sally had become the epitome of the professional teacher. She possessed a formidable range of teaching skills. She provided model learning environments in her classroom. She earned respect from her students and cooperation from their parents. She worked well with her colleagues, using her warm personality to disarm the occasional malcontent who thought she was too lively and hard working, setting a bad example by spending long afternoons at work after the students had left. Why, she even did some occasional work at school on weekends and was forever doing those silly things with kids, like putting on plays, skits, and readers' theater.

Today Sally is admired by colleagues, liked and respected by students, and supported by administrators and parents. She contributes to them with her hard work, enthusiasm, encouragement, and personal commitment. Quite an accomplishment, eh? And all in just 6 years.

Sally's case, while exemplary to be sure, is not all that exceptional. She had the raw stuff—personality, drive, and genuine concern for others—

411

inside her to begin with. She then underwent a series of educational and training experiences that allowed her to refine her talents. These experiences are available to all who wish to become teachers. Some people take full advantage of them. Others do not. But they are there, and they combine with raw talent to produce the growth of the professional.

That growth and the experiences that foster it are what this chapter is about. You can't describe all such experiences in one short chapter. We will consider some of the more significant ones, so that you might set your eye on them and use them to chart the course of your own professional development. These considerations will be presented in the following order:

1. Professionalism: what it means
2. Preservice education and training: honing rough edges
3. Getting your teaching job
4. Quick learning on the job: occupational socialization
5. Professional organizations: what they and you contribute
6. Advanced studies: Self-actualizing in teaching

PROFESSIONALISM: WHAT IT MEANS

You will hear teachers argue about whether teaching is a profession. We won't spend much time on that argument. Here are some descriptions of characteristics of professions. See what you think.

We will begin with Paul Woodring's (1960) observations because they are short and to the point. He says that three qualities separate professions from other vocations:

1. Professions require deep commitment from their members, a commitment that goes far beyond considerations of how much money you can make.
2. Professions rest on an organized body of scholarly or scientific knowledge, whereas other types of occupations do not.
3. Professions involve the careful selection of members and advanced studies of the kind provided in colleges and universities.

Woodring goes on to say that in terms of these criteria, teaching is a profession. But all teachers are not professional. They often lack the necessary commitment and scholarly preparation.

Myron Lieberman (1956) defines a profession in the following terms:

1. It provides a definite, essential social service.
2. It emphasizes intellectual techniques in performing its services.
3. It requires a long period of specialized training.
4. Individual members and the group have a broad range of autonomy.
5. Practitioners accept personal responsibility for their judgments and acts.
6. It emphasizes service more than economic gain.
7. It is self-governing.
8. It has a clear code of ethics for its members.

William Goode (1957) suggests yet another set of criteria for a profession, as follows:

1. Its members clearly identify with the profession.
2. Few members leave the profession. Most remain for their entire careers.
3. Members share values in common.
4. Members' role definitions are standardized.
5. There is a common "language" whose terminology is only partially understood by people outside the profession.
6. The profession has power over its members.
7. Its boundaries are social, not geographical.
8. It reproduces itself through its recruitment and training procedures.

Finally, the National Education Association has published the following list of criteria, stating that a profession:

1. Is essentially intellectual.
2. Requires specialized knowledge.
3. Requires professional preparation.
4. Stresses in-service growth.
5. Is a life career, with permanent membership.
6. Sets its own standards.
7. Advocates service above personal gain.
8. Has its professional organizations.

These descriptions give you an idea about professions in general. But much more important for us, as we consider the growth of the teacher, are these questions: What is a professional teacher? What does a truly professional teacher do? These questions were answered in very general terms in the description of Sally Smith. For your benefit, however, we will take a detailed look at professional growth from the perspective of preparation and skills. This will let us see what abilities and traits highly professional teachers are supposed to have. The remainder of this chapter is devoted to those traits, skills, and behaviors.

PRESERVICE EDUCATION AND TRAINING: HONING ROUGH EDGES

The term "preservice" refers to the time prior to your earning the teaching credential or license. It contrasts with the term "in-service," which refers to the time after you have begun regular teaching. Preservice education occurs primarily at the undergraduate level.

Undergraduate preparation

Colleges and universities differ a good deal in the kind of undergraduate preparation they require of prospective teachers. These differences are the result of differing philosophies of teacher education and variations among states, which issue teaching licenses to the people who teach in their schools. We won't dwell on these differences at this point. Instead we will stress commonalities that you are likely to encounter.

Undergraduate preparation usually consists of two parts: course work in academic subjects that ends in a major and possibly one or more minors and course work in professional education. The education portion is commonly referred to as teacher education or teacher training. It is divided into two major components: class work and student teaching. Although typically done at the undergraduate level, the teacher education program is completed by many students during a year of study at the graduate level.

Majors and minors. The majors and minors required for the teaching credential vary from state to state. Most states require an academic major for high school and junior school teaching. Some require academic majors for elementary teaching, too. Others require a major in "elementary education" instead of one of the academic disciplines.

Where academic majors are required for elementary teaching, students may be encouraged to take a major especially designed for teachers. Such is the case in California, where elementary teacher education students may complete a "liberal studies" major. This major consists of groups of courses from the humanities, English, social science, and science and mathematics that provide the broad background necessary for elementary teaching.

Teacher education. At some point in the undergraduate years, prospective teachers seek admission to programs of teacher education. This admission can occur as early as the sophomore year in some institutions and as late as the graduate year in others. Often the teacher education program will be offered during one's junior and senior years in college.

To qualify for admission, candidates must show that they meet the criteria set up by the college, school, or department that offers the program. These criteria are stated in the college catalog. Often they include grade point average, the completion of a certain amount of college work, documented experience in working with youth, health clearance, and letters of recommendation. In addition, candidates must usually pass oral interviews conducted by program screening committees. These interviews are intended to assess candidates' abilities to see the point, express themselves well, and interact personally with others. They may also probe candidates' commitment to education as a career.

When admission to the program is granted, program advisors map out the total program of studies one must complete to earn the degree, have the proper major and minor, and qualify for a teaching credential issued in that state.

The teacher education program that candidates undertake consists of a combination of education course work and student teaching experience. Sometimes the two are taken at the same time, with attempts to correlate course work with student teaching experience. Otherwise, classes are taken first, and the period of student teaching follows.

EDUCATION COURSES. There are two basic types of education courses: "foundations" courses and "methods" courses.

Foundations courses provide the basic background information for understanding the profession and for understanding how students grow, learn, and behave. Such courses include introduction to education, history of education, philosophy of education, educational sociology, human growth and development, and theories of learning. When you complete them, you will be conversant about what education is supposed to do for whom, how it has developed through history, and what students are like intellectually, physically, socially, and emotionally at different ages.

Methods courses teach you how to teach. There is a methodology that is common to all subjects for all learners. That methodology includes diagnosis, planning, presentation, use of materials, assessment of student progress, and evaluation. In addition, there are specialized methodologies for teaching the various subjects. The materials, activities, and assessment procedures differ from music to history to physical education.

Some programs set up their methods courses to correspond with each subject. Thus they offer methods of teaching English, mathematics, physical education, and so on at the secondary level and methods of teaching reading, arithmetic, art, and so on at the elementary level.

Other programs organize their methods courses in more general ways. They may offer one or two courses in general methods of teaching, with attention to subjects that require special materials or techniques. Alternatively, they may offer methods courses with a skills emphasis. Examples would include skills of classroom management, instructional planning, media utilization, and individualizing instruction.

Although foundations and methods courses are considered very important by university professors, most teacher candidates put far greater stock in student teaching. That's where the action is, and that's where candidates believe they come to know what teaching is really all about.

STUDENT TEACHING. When you begin the part of your program that calls for student teaching, you get the chance to show what you can do with learners. For some students, this is the first return to the classroom since they themselves were students. Increasingly, however, candidates are setting earlier sights on teaching. This gives them a chance to obtain positions as aides or volunteers in schools. There they perform the tasks mentioned in the preceding chapter. Thus they are already familiar with classrooms when they enter student teaching.

For the student teaching experience, you will be placed in a classroom with a highly skilled teacher, a "master teacher." The class will be at the subject and grade level you prefer. You will begin by observing the master teacher work with students. Bit by bit you will assume a teaching role. Perhaps you will start by teaching a short lesson to a small group of students. Before long you will be conducting sizable portions of the instruction, and well

before the end of your experience you will be in charge of the total group most of the time you are there. This process continues for at least one semester. Some programs call for as much as four semesters of student teaching.

To speed your grasp of the myriad aspects of classroom procedure, you may be given an observation guide. This guide draws your careful attention to important aspects of the learning situation. The boxed material on pp. 415–418 is one such guide.

You may also be given a student teaching handbook. Good handbooks answer many questions for you, questions such as the following:

What time do you report? Do you sign in?
How can you meet the secretaries, the custodian, the counselor, the nurse, and other school personnel?
What about dress? This may be a big question in some schools. Just think about what kinds of tasks you will be doing. Sometimes you are supervising and a child is hurt; you need to get somewhere fast. However you feel about personal grooming, it will be to your advantage to appear for your teaching looking clean, pressed, and in good repair.
Do students and teachers use first names or Mr., Miss, Mrs., Ms.?
How about bells? What do they mean?
Where are the restrooms?
Where is the teachers' lounge? May you go there on your break?
What about visitors?
Where do students go for lunch, play, etc.?
Where is the lunchroom?
May a student teacher order supplies? Where is the supply room?
If you have to leave, who checks you out?
How do the children receive permission to leave the classroom? The school?
If you are ill, what do you do?
When do you confer with the master teacher?
When may you expect visits from your university supervisor?
How much responsibility for planning do you assume?
Do you attend faculty meetings and school functions?
How are you to be evaluated?

Name   School assignment   Room

OBSERVATION GUIDE

Expectancy survey

1. What is the organization of the instructional setting to which I have been assigned? (Check the appropriate one.)
   _____ Self-contained classroom
   _____ Loft or open space
   _____ Learning laboratory
   _____ Other (Describe: _____)

2. How are the students organized for learning activities? (Check those appropriate and indicate the subject areas involved.)
   _____ Total class _____
   _____ Ability groups _____
   _____ Interest groups _____
   _____ Discussion groups _____
   _____ Task groups _____
   Individualized
   _____ Independent study _____
   _____ Contract _____
   _____ As assigned to learning center _____
   _____ Learning center as self-choice _____
   _____ Tutorial _____
   _____ Other (Describe: _____)

3. During your observation period (Date: _____ From _____ to _____),
   in what order did instruction in the following subjects occur, and how much time was devoted to each?

Elementary		**Secondary**
Order	**Time**	
_____ Reading	_____	*Directions:* Write in sequence of topics.
_____ Mathematics	_____	
_____ Social studies	_____	
_____ Language arts	_____	
_____ Spelling	_____	
_____ Handwriting	_____	
_____ Science	_____	
_____ Physical education	_____	
_____ Music	_____	
_____ Art	_____	
_____ Other	_____	

4. What materials are permanently kept at the learners' personal study stations or materials depositories?

Continued.

OBSERVATION GUIDE—cont'd

5. What materials are distributed to learners at the beginning of an instructional period and collected when it is over?

6. Where are these materials kept?

7. How are these materials distributed and collected?

8. When the learners are involved in paper-and-pencil tasks, on what do they mark their responses? (Check as appropriate and identify the subject area.)
   Learners' materials
   _____ Workbook pages _____
   _____ Plain paper _____
   Dittoed work sheets
   _____ District-prepared work sheets _____
   _____ Teacher-prepared _____
   _____ Commercially prepared _____
   Other (Describe: _____
   _____)

9. What instructional media appear to be always available?

10. How are bulletin boards and other display areas used? Counter tops?

OBSERVATION GUIDE—cont'd

11. What special areas, if any, are maintained within the classroom?

12. How are learner's basic needs signaled?
    Toilet _____
    Thirst _____
    Broken or dull pencil _____
    No materials _____
13. How long do the learners appear to be able to work independently at a task?

14. What provisions are made for learners who finish early?

15. How long do the learners appear to be able to give the teacher their undivided attention?

16. What means of control does the teacher appear to use? (Check as observed.)
    _____ Reinforced adherence to class standards of behavior
    _____ Preactivity discussion of standards of behavior
    _____ Verbal reinforcement as needed
    _____ Verbal reminders as needed
    _____ Ignoring most inappropriate behavior
    _____ Nonverbal, "body talk" messages successfully transmitted
    _____ Individual counseling
    _____ Exclusion from the group
    _____ Some form of tangible reward (Describe: _____)
17. When the class is released from the classroom to go to recess, lunch, assembly, physical education, etc., what does the teacher do?

Continued.

OBSERVATION GUIDE—cont'd

18. When the class is to enter or reenter the classroom, what does the teacher do?

19. What are the learners expected to do when they enter the classroom?

20. How do the learners signal when they are ready to give a response?

21. How does the teacher obtain total class attention?

22. Do other adults work in the classroom? If so, what are their roles and responsibilities?

From this beginning, you are expected to make immense progress by the end of the student teaching period. Your progress may be guided by a list of expectancies shown in your student teaching handbook. The expectancies may be stated in general or in very specific terms. Here is a list of general expectancies, based on recognized characteristics of good teachers (Hamachek, 1969):

1. *Flexibility*. Can be direct or indirect as the situation demands. Can change directions. Can tolerate and make the most of unforeseen events.
2. *Perceptiveness*. Notes the world from the students' point of view. Recognizes student interests and needs.
3. *Ability*. Personalizes instruction and handles student difficulties tactfully and constructively.
4. *Openness*. Accepts new ideas. Shows willingness to experiment.

5. *Skillfulness*. Asks questions and communicates with students.
6. *Knowledgeability*. Knows about subject matter and its relevance to the students' world.
7. *Provision*. Offers direct study help to students.
8. *Appreciativeness*. Recognizes student problems, efforts, and achievements.
9. *Informality*. Uses conversational tone. Is relaxed. Has sense of humor.

This list of characteristics corresponds closely with what students like in teachers. They want teachers to be warm, friendly, open, tolerant, flexible, and understanding. But they also want them to teach, to know their subjects, and to be able to make them interesting and relevant. Above all, they want them to be fair.

As laudable as these traits and characteristics are, they are not very precise. Stated in these terms, it would be awfully hard for you to assess your progress or for your supervisors to evaluate it. For this reason, you may be expected to show strengths specified in very explicit objectives. Presented here is a detailed list of student teaching objectives adapted from the San Diego State University *Student Teaching Handbook*.

COMPETENCY AREA 1. Using the basic skills of communication

Sample behaviors

  1.1 Handwriting: correct form, legible, good model
  1.2 Language usage: grammar and pronunciation, fluid and correct
  1.3 Voice and speech: pleasant, modulated, well paced
  1.4 Spelling: accurate at chalkboard and on work sheets and evaluations

COMPETENCY AREA 2. Establishing rapport with students

Sample behaviors

  2.1 Teacher-to-student relations: respectful, helpful; maintains identity
  2.2 Learner-to-teacher relations: responsive; seeks out teacher
  2.3 Learner-to-learner relations: respectful, considerate, friendly

COMPETENCY AREA 3. The management of learning

Sample behaviors

  3.1 Communication: clarity, good questioning techniques, suitable responses
  3.2 Planning: short- and long-range plans with suitable form and sequence
  3.3 Guidance: identifies and communicates student needs and progress
  3.4 Management: of small and large group activities
  3.5 Teaching strategies: to meet specific needs in specific topics
  3.6 Discussions: with direction, purpose, participation, and conclusion
  3.7 Motivation: securing and holding student attention throughout lesson
  3.8 Discipline: maintaining standards of behavior appropriate to group

COMPETENCY AREA 4. Developing curriculum

Specific competencies and sample behaviors

  4.1 Maintained: an original and effective physical environment
  4.2 Devised: original and effective instructional materials
  4.3 Developed: original and effective teaching strategies
  4.4 Used: curriculum guides and instructor's manuals effectively
  4.5 Demonstrated: effective use of role-playing, simulations

COMPETENCY AREA 5. Maintaining the learning environment

Specific competencies and sample behaviors

  5.1 Physical: functional, safe, attractive
  5.2 Social: warm, open, accepting, trusting, with high expectations

COMPETENCY AREA 6. Supervising learning

Specific competencies and sample behaviors

  6.1 Identified: special student needs from cumulative data records
  6.2 Determined: student needs from analyses of work and behavior
  6.3 Guided: students in planning individual, group, and class activities
  6.4 Assessed: student progress through objective means

COMPETENCY AREA 7. Accommodating to class and school

Specific competencies and sample behaviors

  7.1 Participated: in school-community activities and meetings
  7.2 Maintained: harmonious relations with all school personnel
  7.3 Showed: willingness to assist beyond required levels

Communicating about learners' progress

Specific competencies and sample behaviors

    8.1 Documented: student progress through records and files of work

    8.2 Communicated: with administrators and parents about student progress

Certification

When you have completed your program of teacher education and have your bachelor's degree with its appropriate major and minor, you may apply for a credential to teach. This process is called teacher certification. It allows you to obtain a license that legitimizes your qualifications and stipulates what you may teach and for how long.

There are two basic types of teaching credentials: elementary and secondary. The elementary credential usually permits you to teach all subjects in kindergarten through grade 6. The secondary credential permits you to teach certain subjects only in grades seven through twelve.

The credential specifies not only what you may teach, but for how long you may teach. Some states require that credentials be renewed every few years. To renew the credential you may have to take college courses to show that you are keeping your knowledge current. Some states issue credentials that never have to be renewed. Teachers have the incentive to take new courses, however, because course work beyond the bachelor's degree level entitles them to salary increases.

Presently each state is responsible for certifying its teachers. Although requirements differ from one state to another, these differences are not significant. Teachers with a credential from one state can be employed in another state. They will be given a period of time during which they must complete the requirements for the credential in the new state.

If you had wanted to teach 100 years ago, you would not have had so many requirements to meet. Of course, you could not have earned much salary, either. Up until the Civil War, local communities or counties hired whomever they wanted for teachers. There was no system of qualification. Often people who had finished sixth grade taught younger students. You had only to finish high school in order to teach high school students.

As the states began supporting public educa-tion, they began taking control of teacher certifica-tion as well. By the early 1900's most states were issuing the teaching credentials. At first they required only that applicants pass a written examination. There were no requirements respecting educational background, except that most teachers were expected to have completed tenth grade. The certificates issued were good for all grade levels and all subjects.

After World War I, insistence grew for better qualified teachers. In 1918 the national teaching force consisted of 600,000 members. One sixth of them had not completed tenth grade, and one half of them had no preparation in how to teach (Hodenfield and Stinnett, 1961). Higher standards began going into effect, but teachers were never overly abundant, and these standards did nothing to increase the supply.

The great depression of the 1930's did, however, result in an overabundance of teachers. States began enacting regulations requiring college degrees for teachers, especially high school teachers.

World War II reversed the trend. As teachers entered the armed forces and the war industries, the teaching ranks were decimated. Teachers had to be found for the classrooms. Anyone who was educated and interested in teaching could find a job. In the middle 1940's it was estimated that 140,000 teachers held emergency, substandard credentials (Hodenfield and Stinnett, 1961).

After the war, things slowly returned to normal, and certification standards began to rise notably. By the middle 1950's most states required bachelor's degrees and teacher training for all who sought teaching jobs. The scarcity of teachers continued, however. Many teachers were employed with "provisional" credentials, which entitled them to teach until they could complete requirements for the standard credential. It was not until the early 1970's that teacher supply exceeded demand.

At present, certification requirements are quite stringent. Some states require a fifth year of college preparation, even for elementary teaching. Academic course requirements have been increased greatly. Faced with a shortage of jobs, teacher education students have begun to outdo themselves, especially in student teaching. They believe they must truly shine if they are to have a chance at getting a job. Without doubt, we now have the most talented and best trained beginning teachers we have ever had.

GETTING YOUR TEACHING JOB

When you begin seeking a job, you have one thing going for you and other things going against you. For you is the fact that you are one of the best prepared teaching candidates ever produced. Against you are the facts that jobs are few and far between and the competition for them is keen.

Facing this situation, you must find ways to present yourself in the strongest, most positive ways possible. This section can help you do that. Here you will find detailed suggestions on résumés and professional dossiers. You will also find suggestions on how to obtain interviews and how to show yourself to best advantage in them.

Résumés

Your résumé presents a clear, concise verbal picture of you on one page or, at most, two pages. If it's any longer, people won't read it. Your task is to show yourself to the best advantage possible in that short space. To see how to do this, let's consider possible contents. Try to include the following information about yourself:

1. Name, address, and telephone number
2. Credential earned
3. Personal data such as age, health, and marital status
4. Professional objective, that is, type of job sought
5. Date available for employment
6. College education
7. Student teaching experience
8. Other teaching experience, such as aide or volunteer
9. Special skills
10. Professional contributions
11. Honors received
12. References, that is, where professional file is available

On the following pages you will see two résumés that include mention of most of these points.

RÉSUMÉ

NAOMI ANN GRANT

4340 Elm Drive

Chula Vista, Calif. 92010

Telephone: (724) 480-1835

PERSONAL	Single 5′4″ 22 years old Excellent health
CREDENTIALS	California Multiple Subjects Credential-Preliminary-May, 1977.
PROFESSIONAL OBJECTIVE	Teacher at the elementary level
DATE AVAILABLE	June, 1977
EDUCATION	B.A., May, 1977, San Diego State University, San Diego, Calif. Major: Liberal studies; social science emphasis. Minor: None required.

Continued.

Naomi Ann Grant—cont'd

STUDENT TEACHING EXPERIENCE	Teacher education received through a four-semester extensive and intensive program with emphasis placed on skills, attitudes, and experiences gained through course work and a total teaching experience. Project POINT.
1/77 to 5/77	Magnolia Elementary School, Cajon Valley Union School District, El Cajon, Calif. *Student teacher.* Taught second-third grade combination in a self-contained classroom. Subjects taught included reading, mathematics, language, art, social studies, music, physical education, and science. Developed an "All-School Sing." Had full responsibility all day.
9/76 to 12/76	Avocado Elementary School, Cajon Valley Union School District, El Cajon, Calif. *Student teacher.* Taught sixth grade in an open-space school. Subjects taught included reading, mathematics, science, social studies, art, physical education, music, and language. Assisted in directing and accompanying the school glee club. Wrote and produced a holiday musical. Had full responsibility all morning.
9/75 to 6/76	John Ballantyne Elementary School, Cajon Valley Union School District, El Cajon, Calif. *Student teacher.* Taught kindergarten–first grade combination under the Early Childhood Education Program. Subjects taught included reading, language, literature, mathematics, spelling, science, music, art, physical education, and drama. Taught small groups first semester and had full responsibility second semester.
PUBLICATIONS	*Learning Centers That Teach,* Co-author. A unique manual that gives detailed explanations on the creative and instructional techniques of designing, making, and implementing learning centers in the classroom.
SPECIAL SKILLS	Music: Vocal—teaching, directing, accompanying. Voice at performance level. Instrumental—piano, guitar, autoharp, and flute at performance level. Related skills: Creative dramatics, pantomime, and choric verse. Critical thinking skills, Piagetian tasks, learning centers, child study skills, classroom management, applying principles of instruction, reading assessment techniques, individualized instruction.
HONORS	Member of Pi Lambda Theta, Educational Honor Society; Dean's List—six semesters; life member of Alpha Gamma Sigma; educational scholarship from Chula Vista Elementary Education Association.
REFERENCES	Confidential career file No. 39 542 is available on request from the San Diego State University Placement Office, 5850 Hardy Avenue, San Diego, Calif. 92115. Telephone: (714) 286-6855. Copies of the file will be furnished on the district's request.

NANCY JOAN ROCHE
Temporary address: *Permanent address:*
3690 Lake Blvd. #4   16852 Street Place
La Mesa, Calif. 92041   Sepulveda, Calif. 91343
(724) 482-8186   (243) 863-5282

PROFESSIONAL OBJECTIVE	Teacher at the junior high level.
CREDENTIAL	California Single Subjects Credential-Preliminary-August, 1977. English and Spanish.
DATE AVAILABLE	August, 1977.
EXPERIENCE: STUDENT TEACHER	Rogers Junior High School, Vista Valley Union School District, English grade 7. Spring, 1977. Master teacher: Bernadine Hollers.
STUDENT TEACHER	Avocado Middle School, Cajon School District, Open Space Experience, English, grades 7-8 gifted. Fall, 1976. Master teacher: Lucinda Gardner.
PROFESSIONAL SKILLS	Secondary reading diagnosis; creative writing; behavior modification techniques; learning centers; Piagetian testing; community study; interaction analysis; individualized instruction; curriculum organization; long-range planning; methods for inquiry; creative dramatics; values clarification; modeling techniques; language laboratory.
EDUCATION	Bachelor of Arts, August, 1977, San Diego State University, San Diego, Calif. Major: Liberal studies Emphasis: Mathematics and science Major GPA: 3.9
PROFESSIONAL ASSOCIATIONS	Student member of California Teacher Association.
HONORS	Dean's List, San Diego State University.
PERSONAL DATA	Birthdate: 6/25/55 Height: 5'5" Weight: 120 lb. Single Excellent health
REFERENCES	Career file No. 10936 is available on request at Career Planning and Placement Center, San Diego State University, San Diego, Calif. 92182 (714) 286-6851.

Your résumé should look attractive but not gaudy. You want its appearance to make an impression. But the impression should be one of neat, tasteful professionalism.

It is worth the investment to have the résumé typed professionally, or even set in print, and then duplicated by a quality process such as photo-offset. Have it done on paper with soft tones, white, off-white, ivory, or light beige. Have envelopes that match. Use black ink in reproducing the résumé. Brown or blue ink may look nice, but be careful that the combination of colors shows subdued taste. Don't use bright colors such as red, pink, or yellow. Have about fifty copies made. The cost is minimal. Have several copies made of a color photograph of yourself, showing tasteful hair and clothing and pleasant expression. Attach it with rubber cement to your résumé. You are not required to do this, and the personnel director may remove it. But it does no harm, and it may do some good.

When your résumé is ready, put one in your dossier, which will be described later. Give a few to friends and relatives. But save the majority to mail to school districts when you request applications for teaching positions.

Letters

Decide on the school districts to which you want to apply. Write a letter to each of them requesting an application form for a teaching position. These letters are not to be form letters that you duplicate like your résumé. They must all be individual, personal letters. Yes, that will require a good deal of typing, but it must be done. Form letters make a bad impression. Type each letter individually, using a format such as that shown on p. 425.

Buy about 100 sheets of the same paper on which your résumé is printed. Type your letters on that paper. Enclose letter and résumé inside the matching envelope. If you use white or off-white paper, you will be able to use white correcting tape when you make typing errors. The corrections will hardly show.

Applications

When you receive application forms, fill them out as soon as possible. Return them with a short cover letter thanking the personnel director and mentioning your availability for an interview.

If you receive no response within 4 weeks, send a brief personal letter inquiring about the status of your application. You may inquire by telephone, too.

Dossier

During your final semester of student teaching, you should put together a professional dossier. This is an attractive, informative set of materials that document graphically your preparatory work, both in student teaching and in college courses. Ideally the dossier should document the experiences, skills, contributions, etc. that you listed in your résumé. It can do this best through photographs, samples of work you produced, and comments written by students, teachers, administrators, and supervisors. Also include a copy of your résumé and a list of professional books you keep in your personal library. Be sure you can comment on any of the books listed in case you are asked about them.

Many students use a three-ring binder for their dossier, with attractive lettering or appliques on the cover. Inside, they use acetate sleeves into which photographs and samples of work can be placed. The photographs should be taken with care. They should show the following:

1. You working with students individually, in small groups, and before the entire class, each with a different topic
2. The class format and space within which you worked—self-contained, open space, open education, laboratory, gymnasium, and so forth
3. Instructional materials you prepared, also showing them being used by students
4. Special events or programs you helped organize and conduct
5. The students at work under your direction

The dossier should also contain sample materials that document the special skills you mentioned in your résumé. Such materials can include sample pages, preferably with a professor's or teacher's laudatory comments written on them.

Finally, the dossier should be arranged tastefully and artistically. Use plenty of color, but don't let it look carnivalesque. Show your spirit, creativity, taste, and organizational skills.

The beauty of the dossier is that it permits you to take the initiative in interviews, as we shall presently see.

Your name
Address
Telephone number
Date

Name
Director of Personnel
(   ) School District
Address

Dear (Name):

   This is a letter of inquiry about possible teaching vacancies in the (   ) School District.

   In (month) of this year, I will complete the professional education program at (name of institution) and I will receive a (type) credential in (level, subject).

   My experience, background, and preparation have allowed me to develop several special strengths that I will bring to teaching. These strengths are mentioned in my professional résumé, which is enclosed. I would very much appreciate your taking a moment to look over the résumé.

   If you anticipate a teaching vacancy for which I am qualified, I'd be pleased to receive an application form. I am available for personal interviews at your convenience. (Or I can arrange to come for a personal interview on one of the following dates: _____.)

   Should you desire further information, please write or telephone. I can usually be be reached by phone after (hour).

                              Sincerely yours,

                              (Signature)
                              Name typed

Interviews

If a district has a vacancy and if they like your résumé and application, they will contact you for a personal interview. Here are three things to remember about interviews:

1. Make a good first impression
2. Feel secure that you can respond to almost any question that is asked
3. Be sure you follow up after the interview

Let's consider each of these points.

First impressions. Remember this: The person who interviews you will be one or two generations removed from your age level. In all likelihood that person will not be looking for somebody who is uh, like, "cool," ya know whadda mean? They will be impressed by punctuality, neatness, poise, smiles, firm handshake, and tasteful appearance. Their first impression of you can make all the difference.

This being the case, find the place of the interview, and be there ahead of time. Don't come rushing in 10 minutes late, flustered, and out of breath. Have your hair arranged neatly. If you have a mustache or beard, trim it a little more than usual. Wear moderately conservative clothing and shoes. Women should wear dresses and nylons; men should wear a jacket and even (yes, ugh) a tie. Shake hands; look the interviewer in the eye; smile; and assume a poised, relaxed manner. Your dossier and advance preparation should make you secure. You can be confident.

Questions. There is no set format for conducting interviews. You may expect almost any question. They may be simple or involved, long or short, theoretical or practical. In the main, however, questions notoriously hit on the following points, for which you should prepare yourself in advance:

Tell me about yourself. Here you are in charge. Mention background, interests, hobbies, family, travels, and education.

Why do you want to go into teaching? Stress the enjoyment and satisfaction of working with students.

What do you have to contribute to teaching? Mention your enthusiasm, genuine concern for others, hard work, and special skills.

How would you handle the following discipline problem? Listen carefully. Let your solution stop the disruption, maintain relationships with student(s), and provide positive guidance for the student(s).

How would you set up your (   ) program? Tell not only how you would, but how you did set it up. Re-

fer to the dossier to show evidence. Here the interviewer will want to look at the pictures and ask about them. You now have much control over the interview.

You can see how the dossier helps. No longer are you on the defensive, wondering with trembling fear what the next question will be. You are showing, explaining, documenting. All this makes a most positive impression on the interviewer.

Meanwhile, be prepared in the following areas, too:

Know the job description, if possible. Show how your qualifications match it.

Really listen to the interviewer's questions and comments. Answer them succinctly and accurately.

Emphasize your qualities of cooperation, creativity, and spirit.

Mention your experiences outside of education. Show that you are curious and well read.

Do not be brash or aggressive in the interview.

If you are hired, the taxpayers will be making an investment of well over half a million dollars in you, even at today's dollar value. They will want to be sure they are getting their money's worth.

Following up. As the interview draws to an end, be sure to ask what the next step should be. The next day, send a personal note to the interviewer expressing thanks for the interest and kindness shown to you. If you do not hear from the district within the time expected, call or write to inquire about your status in their deliberations.

QUICK LEARNING ON THE JOB: OCCUPATIONAL SOCIALIZATION

If you do your part, really beat the bushes far and wide, make favorable impressions, and leave nothing to chance, you will land your job. Now comes the quick learn. Within the first year you are expected to become occupationally socialized.

What this means is that you must learn the modus operandi of your school, including what every member of the clerical, custodial, instructional, and administrative staff does; what you are allowed to do and not do, expected to do and not do; what the students are like; how the coffee fund is handled; who has to take hall, grounds, and cafeteria duty; how records are kept and report cards made—the list goes on and on, seemingly forever.

Your quick learn will be eased considerably if

you read your district handbook and curriculum guide and if you ask questions. Don't worry about appearing ignorant. It makes experienced people feel good when neophytes ask questions.

Handbook

You should receive a copy of the faculty handbook used in your district. If you do not, ask your principal for one. It may be boring and detailed, but read it carefully. It's a summary of the do's and don'ts, can's and can'ts of your district. Between its covers you can expect to see mention of school personnel; school calendar with holidays and important events; daily schedule; rules and regulations concerning absences, accidents, illnesses, buses, and assemblies; attendance regulations; audiovisual holdings and requests; awards and honors; bicycles; cafeteria; classroom management of books, supplies, etc.; communication with parents; conferences; cumulative records; damage to property; discipline policy; entering and departing students; faculty organization and structure; field trip policy; fire drills, individual duties; flag salute; gifts to teachers; homework; library; mail room; payroll; promotion, retention, and dismissal criteria and procedures; tenure; grievance procedures; parties and dances; athletic contests; school psychologist, nurse, and physician; curriculum specialists; speech specialist; counselors; referrals; security; sick leave; student teachers; paraprofessionals; substitute teachers; lesson plan books; supply requisitions and depositories; testing; visitors; and use of the building at night.

Quite a list. And that's just part of it. It doesn't even mention what, where, and how you are supposed to teach.

Curriculum guide

The curriculum contents suggested for your grade and/or subject are specified in the curriculum guide. Obtain one of these. They can save you hours of work and quantities of headaches. They list suggested topics and materials of instruction available in the district. They often include specific objectives for learners and ways of assessing progress.

These guides don't limit your teaching. You are allowed to go above and beyond their suggestions and even around some of them. If you use them,

however, you can be sure that you are presenting a balanced program, one considered excellent by the curriculum experts who composed the guide.

Personal relations

Your success and enjoyment on the job will depend in large measure on how well you get along with others—faculty, administrators, secretaries, and custodians. These relationships grow positively when people show interest and concern for each other. They decline when disagreements are not handled constructively but are allowed to deteriorate into petty bickering, gossiping, and backbiting. Be especially conscious of malicious gossip. Sad but true, negativism is a reality of many faculty lounges. A few pressured teachers relieve their frustrations by running down everyone and everything. Getting caught up in this syndrome of behavior is one of the greatest threats to your professionalism. It can ruin relationships, and it can turn you unwittingly into a negative complainer instead of a positive doer.

People who put down others in derogatory terms do so in an attempt to build themselves up. They think they can make themselves look wiser, more skillful, and more effective as they try to make others appear inferior. Their behavior is reinforced by others who gleefully participate in character assassination.

But they accomplish just the opposite of what they intend. They develop for themselves a reputation of disloyalty and unreliability and are the kind of people you don't want to be close to. Instead of building themselves up, they pull themselves down.

As a beginning teacher, you may be tempted to gain acceptance through gossip. You will most certainly harm yourself if you do. Instead concentrate on the positive. When you think there is reason to say something uncomplimentary about something or someone, quickly ask yourself the following questions:

1. Is it true?
2. Is harm done if I keep quiet about it?
3. Can my saying it have positive effects?

If your answer to any of these three questions is no, hold your tongue. Bite it if you have to. But don't lower yourself, even for an instant, into the morass of destructive negativism.

Code of ethics

One of the characteristics of a profession is that it has a code of behavior by which its members live. Teachers have such codes. One of them was formulated by the National Education Association (1971) and is shown here.

NATIONAL EDUCATION ASSOCIATION
CODE OF ETHICS OF THE EDUCATION PROFESSION*

Preamble

The educator believes in the worth and dignity of man. He recognizes the supreme importance of the pursuit of truth, devotion to excellence, and the nurture of democratic citizenship. He regards as essential to these goals the protection of freedom to learn and to teach and the guarantee of equal educational opportunity for all. The educator accepts his responsibility to practice his profession according to the highest ethical standards.

The educator recognizes the magnitude of the responsibility he has accepted in choosing a career in education, and engages himself, individually and collectively with other educators, to judge his colleagues, and to be judged by them, in accordance with the provisions of this code.

Principle I
Commitment to the student

The educator measures his success by the progress of each student toward realization of his potential as a worthy and effective citizen. The educator therefore works to stimulate the spirit of inquiry, the acquisition of knowledge and understanding, and the thoughtful formulation of worthy goals.

In fulfilling his obligation to the student the educator—

1. Shall not without just cause restrain the student from independent action in his pursuit of learning, and shall not without just cause deny the student access to varying points of view.
2. Shall not deliberately suppress or distort subject matter for which he bears responsibility.
3. Shall make reasonable effort to protect the student from conditions harmful to learning or to health and safety.
4. Shall conduct professional business in such a way that he does not expose the student to unnecessary embarrassment or disparagement.
5. Shall not on the ground of race, color, creed, or national origin exclude any student from participation in or deny him benefits under any program, nor grant any discriminatory consideration or advantage.
6. Shall not use professional relationships with students for private advantage.
7. Shall keep in confidence information that has been obtained in the course of professional service, unless disclosure serves professional purposes or is required by law.
8. Shall not tutor for remuneration students assigned to his classes, unless no other qualified teacher is reasonably available.

Principle II
Commitment to the public

The educator believes that patriotism in its highest form requires dedication to the principles of our democratic heritage. He shares with all other citizens the responsibility for the development of sound public policy and assumes full political and citizenship responsibilities.

*From *National Education Association Handbook, 1971-72.* Washington, D.C.: The Association, 1971.

Principle II—cont'd
Commitment to the public

The educator bears particular responsibility for the development of policy relating to the extension of educational opportunities for all and for interpreting educational programs and policies to the public.

In fulfilling his obligation to the public the educator—

1. Shall not misrepresent an institution or organization with which he is affiliated, and shall take adequate precautions to distinguish between his personal and institutional or organizational views.
2. Shall not knowingly distort or misrepresent the facts concerning educational matters in direct and indirect public expressions.
3. Shall not interfere with a colleague's exercise of political and citizenship rights and responsibilities.
4. Shall not use institutional privileges for private gain or to promote political candidates or partisan political activities.
5. Shall accept no gratuities, gifts, or favors that might impair or appear to impair professional judgment, nor offer any favor, service, or thing of value to obtain special advantage.

Principle III
Commitment to the profession

The educator believes that the quality of the services of the education profession directly influences the nation and its citizens. He therefore exerts every effort to raise professional standards, to improve his service, to promote a climate in which the exercise of professional judgment is encouraged, and to achieve conditions which attract persons worthy of the trust to careers in education. Aware of the value of united effort, he contributes actively to the support, planning and programs of professional organizations.

In fulfilling his obligation to the profession, the educator—

1. Shall not discriminate on grounds of race, color, creed, or national origin for membership in professional organizations, nor interfere with the free participation of colleagues in the affairs of their association.
2. Shall apply for a specific position only when it is known to be vacant, and shall refrain from underbidding or commenting adversely about other candidates.
3. Shall not knowingly withhold information regarding a position from an applicant, or misrepresent an assignment or conditions of employment.
4. Shall give prompt notice to the employing agency of any change in availability of service, and the employing agent shall give prompt notice of change in availability or nature of a position.
5. Shall adhere to the terms of a contract or appointment, unless these terms have been legally terminated, falsely represented, or substantially altered by unilateral action of the employing agency.
6. Shall conduct professional business through channels, when available, that have been jointly approved by the professional organization and the employing agency.
7. Shall not delegate assigned tasks to unqualified personnel.
8. Shall permit no commercial exploitation of his professional position.
9. Shall use time granted for the purpose for which it is intended.

Principle IV
Commitment to professional employment practices

The educator regards the employment agreement as a pledge to be executed both in spirit and in fact in a manner consistent with the highest ideals of professional service. He believes that sound professional personnel relationships with governing boards are built upon personal integrity, dignity, and mutual respect. The educator discourages the practice of his profession by unqualified persons.

In fulfilling his obligation to professional employment practices, the educator—

1. Shall apply for, accept, offer, or assign a position or responsibility on the basis of professional preparation and legal qualifications.

Continued.

Principle IV—cont'd
Commitment to professional employment practices

2. Shall accord just and equitable treatment to all members of the profession in the exercise of their professional rights and responsibilities.
3. Shall not use coercive means or promise special treatment in order to influence professional decisions of colleagues.
4. Shall withhold and safeguard information acquired about colleagues in the course of employment, unless disclosure serves professional purposes.
5. Shall not refuse to participate in a professional inquiry when requested by an appropriate professional association.
6. Shall provide upon the request of the aggrieved party a written statement of specific reason for recommendations that lead to the denial of increments, significant changes in employment, or termination of employment.
7. Shall not misrepresent his professional qualifications.
8. Shall not knowingly distort evaluations of colleagues.

Teacher rights

At the same time that they abide by their code of ethics, teachers should realize that they have definite rights. Supreme Court Justice William O. Douglas once wrote

The Constitution guarantees freedom of expression to everyone in our society. All are entitled to it, and none needs it more than the teacher.

First, then, we should recognize that teachers have the same rights as other citizens. Those rights do not always apply in the classroom, however. For example, a teacher may not use the classroom as a forum for expressing personal political or religious ideologies or for advocating practices contrary to law or the moral standards of the community. Knowledge may not willfully be presented in a distorted way, even though the teacher may stand on a soapbox in the park and say whatever he or she believes to any citizens who will listen.

There are two classes of teacher rights you should recognize. One class consists of civil rights. The other consists of teacher rights under tenure. With regard to civil rights, the American Federation of Teachers has stressed the following points:

AMERICAN FEDERATION OF TEACHERS
BILL OF RIGHTS*

The teacher is entitled to a life of dignity equal to the high standard of service that is justly demanded of that profession. Therefore, we hold these truths to be self-evident:

I

Teachers have the right to think freely and to express themselves openly and without fear. This includes the right to hold views contrary to the majority.

II

They shall be entitled to the free exercise of their religion. No restraint shall be put upon them in the manner, time, or place of their worship.

III

They shall have the right to take part in social, civil, and political affairs. They shall have the right, outside the classroom, to participate in political campaigns and to hold office. They may assemble peaceably and may petition any government agency, including their employers, for a redress of grievances. They shall have the same freedom in all things as other citizens.

IV

The right of teachers to live in places of their own choosing, to be free of restraints in their mode of living, and the use of their leisure time shall not be abridged.

V

Teaching is a profession, the right to practice which is not subject to the surrender of other human rights. No one shall be deprived of professional status, or the right to practice it, or the practice thereof in any particular position, without due process of law.

VI

The right of teachers to be secure in their jobs, free from political influence or public clamor, shall be established by law. The right to teach after qualification in the manner prescribed by law, is a property right, based upon the inalienable rights to life, liberty, and the pursuit of happiness.

VII

In all cases affecting the teacher's employment or professional status a full hearing by an impartial tribunal shall be afforded with the right of full judicial review. No teacher shall be deprived of employment or professional status but for specific causes established by law having a clear relation to the competence or qualification to teach, proved by the weight of the evidence. In all such cases the teacher shall enjoy the right to a speedy and public trial, to be informed of the nature and cause of the accusation; to be confronted with the accusing witnesses, to subpeona witnesses and papers, and the assistance of counsel. No teacher shall be called upon to answer any charge affecting his employment or professional status but upon probable cause, supported by oath or affirmation.

VIII

It shall be the duty of the employer to provide culturally adequate salaries, security in illness and adequate retirement income. The teacher has the right to such a salary as will: (a) Afford a family standard of living comparable to that enjoyed by other professional people in the community; (b) Make possible freely chosen professional study; (c) Afford the opportunity for leisure and recreation common to our heritage.

*Courtesy American Federation of Teachers, Washington, D.C.

Continued.

**AMERICAN FEDERATION OF TEACHERS
BILL OF RIGHTS—cont'd**

IX

No teacher shall be required under penalty of reduction of salary to pursue studies beyond those required to obtain professional status. After serving a reasonable probationary period a teacher shall be entitled to permanent tenure terminable only for just cause. They shall be free as in other professions in the use of their own time. They shall not be required to perform extracurricular work against their will or without added compensation.

X

To equip people for modern life requires the most advanced educational methods. Therefore, the teacher is entitled to good classrooms, adequate teaching materials, teachable class size and administrative protection and assistance in maintaining discipline.

XI

These rights are based upon the proposition that the culture of a people can rise only as its teachers improve. A teaching force accorded the highest possible professional dignity is the surest guarantee that blessings of liberty will be preserved. Therefore, the possession of these rights imposes the challenge to be worthy of their enjoyment.

XII

Since teachers must be free in order to teach freedom, the right to be members of organizations of their own choosing must be guaranteed. In all matters pertaining to their salaries and working conditions they shall be entitled to bargain collectively through representatives of their own choosing. They are entitled to have the schools administered by superintendents, boards or committees which function in a democratic manner.

The other important class of teacher rights comes under the tenure law. Tenure provides employment protection to teachers. It prevents their being summarily dismissed for capricious reasons, and it helps protect their civil rights. Teachers gain tenure status after successful completion of a probationary period in the district, usually with acceptance of the fourth yearly contract.

Tenure does not guarantee permanent employment. If enrollments should drop or if certain programs are cut from the curriculum, it is possible for tenured teachers to be dismissed. Tenured teachers can also be dismissed for good cause, a term that usually includes incompetence, insubordination, or the commission of crimes. Here we get into the legalities of teaching, a matter treated in detail in Chapter 8.

PROFESSIONAL ORGANIZATIONS: WHAT THEY AND YOU CONTRIBUTE

Another characteristic of professions is that they have organizations for the protection and furtherance of member welfare and goals. Teaching has such organizations, and some of them are powerful. They have been responsible for many of the gains teachers have made in salaries, load, teaching conditions, and preservation of civil rights.

National Education Association

The organization most familiar to teachers nationwide is the National Education Association (NEA). Originally founded in 1857 as the National Teachers Association, it merged in 1870 with the National Association of School Superintendents and the American Normal School Association.

Its stated purposes have remained two in number: (1) To elevate the character and advance the interests of the profession of teaching and (2) to promote the cause of education in the United States. In attempting to reach its aims, the NEA is currently stressing the areas of professional excellence, economic security for educators, adequate financing for public education, human and civil rights for all teachers and students, and leadership in solving social problems.

The NEA has close to 1¼ million members. Its income is derived almost entirely from membership dues. Its annual budget of expenditures runs well into the millions of dollars. It finances a number of commissions, among which are the National Commission on Professional Rights and Responsibilities and the National Commission on Teacher Education and Professional Standards. It has its headquarters in Washington, D.C., and has a staff of over 1,000 members. Its annual national conventions draw attendances of 20,000 and more.

The committees and commissions of the NEA develop educational policy with regard to finance, human relations, instruction, professional development, ethics, and teacher rights. The organization also publishes a number of pamphlets and books. Its journal, *Today's Education,* is mailed monthly to members. The journal provides articles on educational issues, teaching methods, instructional aids, and publications of interest to teachers. The NEA also produces films, represents education before Congress and federal agencies, and conducts numerous conventions, workshops, conferences, institutes, and exhibits.

American Federation of Teachers

The second most powerful teachers' organization is the American Federation of Teachers (AFT). Organized in 1916, the AFT is the nation's largest teachers' union. It is affiliated with the AFL-CIO and has about 400,000 members. Although only one third the size of the NEA, it is very powerful, especially in some of our largest cities. Its aims are five in number: (1) To bring about mutual assistance and cooperation among teachers, (2) to obtain for all teachers the civil rights to which they are entitled, (3) to pursue the conditions essential to enabling teachers to perform at the highest level, (4) to promote the democratic processes

that will best enable students to take their places in industrial, social, and political life, and (5) to promote the welfare of the young through better educational opportunity for all.

The AFT maintains national headquarters in Washington, D.C. The offices house the administrative staff and standing departments on finance, organization, law, research, publications, public relations, civil rights, state federations, colleges and universities, and membership. Much of the work at the national level consists of informing, assisting, and coordinating the work of more than 650 local teachers' unions.

The AFT gains tremendous national leverage through its affiliation with the AFL-CIO, which boasts nearly 15 million members nationwide. The alliance is a fortuitous one for education. Organized labor has always supported public education. This support becomes much more telling when delivered politically through the AFT.

Of the benefits the AFT has gained for teachers, foremost has been the clear affirmation of their civil rights. This has helped teachers to function as true professionals, without having to guard their every word and act for fear of reprisal. The next general service the AFT will provide will likely be improved procedures for negotiating teacher salaries, benefits, and working conditions. In some large cities the AFT has replaced the NEA as the organized voice of teachers, a trend that indicates its effectiveness in promoting teacher well-being.

State and local organizations

All states have educational associations for teachers. By and large, these organizations are affiliates of the NEA and the AFT. NEA affiliates have the state name in place of "national"—New Mexico Education Association (NMEA), and so forth—or else the name is similar—California Teachers Association (CTA). AFT affiliates use the same name as their national organization, but AFT power is located more in cities than at the state level.

The state organizations work actively on teachers' behalf in matters of finance, teaching load, and credentials. They attract members through low-cost life, health, liability, and automobile insurance; group purchasing rates; and reduced rates for travel and recreation. They provide legal services for members at low rates or even free.

Local organizations include both NEA and AFT affiliates. Typically these organizations work on behalf of teachers in matters of salary, class size, and fringe benefits. They watch over teacher welfare. When violations of a teacher's rights occur, they come to the teacher's defense, calling in state assistance if necessary.

Costs

In return for the benefits provided by national, state, and local organizations, teachers pay annual dues. If available separately, the dues are quite low for local organizations, fairly high for state organizations, and moderate for national organizations. Members of the AFT have unified membership in the national, state, and local organizations, and that is the predominant pattern for NEA affiliates as well. For membership at all levels, the average teacher can expect to pay dues of between $100 and $175 per year.

Organization membership presents a dilemma. The NEA and AFT and their affiliates work for the welfare of all teachers. Yet only about one half of all teachers are members. This means that those who don't join, and therefore don't pay dues, enjoy benefits resulting from the contributions of those who are members. But membership is a matter of choice and conscience.

ADVANCED STUDIES: SELF-ACTUALIZING IN TEACHING

Up to this point we have examined aspects of professional growth that enable teachers to enjoy security, sense of belonging, and esteem from others. These things enable them to perform their jobs well, even admirably, and to enjoy cooperative fellowship with other professionals. This is the level that we called occupational socialization.

Outstanding professionals continue to grow beyond this point. A fortunate percentage of them move ahead into a level where, to borrow a term from Abraham Maslow, they self-actualize. Self-actualization means becoming the best you can be, where you pursue and develop your special aptitudes to a high degree of refinement, where you become especially helpful, skillful, creative, or productive. The urge to perform in this way lies within many teachers. Few can express it until they are relatively safe, secure, and recognized in their positions. Others, even after becoming

occupationally socialized, never self-actualize. Their psychic energies are drained off by other matters, or they simply may not care enough to put forth the effort required. For those who do, graduate studies provide one of the best avenues to assist their growth. Advanced study provides the stimulation, guidance, psychological support, and, yes, even the requirements and deadlines that help us move ahead. Many teachers take advantage of these factors to develop advanced knowledge, skills, materials, and programs that make significant contributions to students and teachers. The prime motive of self-actualized behavior does not, however, reside in the desire to contribute. Rather, it is a trait of the personality that, when not fulfilled, leaves one feeling dissatisfied.

It is unfortunate for students, in a way, that self-actualizing professionals so often move into positions outside the classroom. The mundane, uninspired teacher seldom moves either upward in capability or out of the classroom. In another sense, however, students still benefit from the work of professionals who no longer teach in the classroom. These professionals move into administrative and supervisory positions. Many become experts in curriculum development. They plan and organize newer programs for students in school. Others become trainers of teachers and so pass their enthusiasm and insights along with the fine new teachers they prepare. And more and more, self-actualizing teachers are remaining in the classroom. Somehow they resist the higher salaries they could earn as administrators, and they remain happily working directly with students.

All this is not to imply that self-actualizing brings no rewards outside itself. As you earn college credits and advanced degrees, your salary goes up accordingly. These credits are usually earned in the universities, but many school districts maintain their own programs of in-service training. They let work taken there count for salary credit, too. Skillful, productive teachers do receive attention, also. Some receive awards, plaques, and certificates for outstanding performance. Some are granted sabbatical leave for further study. Almost all good teachers receive an abundance of recognition from students, parents, and administrators.

Still, the desire to self-actualize operates mostly on its own. It is a desire to test oneself, to push to the limits, to say I gave it my best and this is what resulted. To complete your growth as a professional, you will have to do your utmost to rise to this level.

Complete is the wrong word. Your growth will never stop, hence will never be complete, once you begin to self-actualize. The process is painful and frustrating. When you extend yourself, when you take risks, you are bound to find trials and failures. But the process brings unequaled rewards, as well. It brings exhilaration, fascination, joy in professional living. These emotions are the capstones, the ultimate. They are the finest that teaching has to offer.

SUGGESTED ACTIVITIES FOR FURTHER UNDERSTANDING

1. In small-group discussions, specify characteristics of ideal programs of student teaching or similar laboratory experiences. Include a list of pointers for student teachers to follow in order to make the best impressions possible.
2. Obtain permission to make visits to classrooms in different schools, grades, and subjects. Use an observation guide to record observations. Compare them in class.
3. Invite an experienced master teacher to talk with the class about student teaching and student teachers and to mention duties, roles, and desirable personal skills and traits.
4. Obtain copies of faculty handbooks and curriculum guides. Assign responsibility for making class reports on them.
5. Conduct a class discussion on professional ethics and rights of teachers. Include the rights of students, too. Explore the reasons for codes of ethics and rights.
6. Invite representatives of local NEA and AFT affiliates to present their programs and views to the class.
7. Identify an exceptional teacher, one who is self-actualizing in skills, programs, or materials development. Invite that teacher to discuss his or her work and the motivations that underlie it.

REFERENCES

Goode, W. Community within a community: the professions. *American Sociological Review*, 1957, *22*, 194-200.

Hamachek, D. Characteristics of good teachers and implications for teacher education. *Phi Delta Kappan*, February, 1969, *50*, 341-345.

Hodenfield, G. and Stinnett, T. *The education of teachers*. Englewood Cliffs, N.J.: Prentice-Hall, Inc. 1961.

Lieberman, M. *Education as a profession*. Englewood Cliffs, N.J.: Prentice-Hall, Inc., 1956.

National Education Association Handbook, 1971-71. Washington, D.C.: The Association, 1971.

Woodring, P. Teaching: a unique profession. *CTA Journal*, March, 1960, *56*, 10-12.

GLOSSARY OF TEACHER TALK

ability level The highest level at which a student can function in any area of the curriculum. Teachers need to know it to make their instruction challenging, yet allow for success. Ability level varies greatly from person to person.

abstract A quality applied to ideas or thoughts not represented by specific objects or actions, such as honesty, love, or the theories behind simple processes of addition and division. When teaching abstractions, examples are needed to clarify the idea. Abstract reasoning is the highest level of thinking in Piaget's theory of development.

acceptance Word used in many different philosophies and techniques of education. Basically it is an attitude that says, "I may not always agree with everything you say and do, but I value you as a person. I am genuinely concerned about your development and am here to help." This feeling improves a person's self-concept and may lead to increased academic success.

accountability The responsibility ascribed to educators for student learning. This is a major issue in education today. "If Johnny can't read, why? Who is responsible?"

activity When teachers mention activity, they are not necessarily referring to students jumping up and down. Rather, an activity is any task, game, performance, discussion, etc. that enables the student to become involved, think, move, talk, or do instead of just listening to the teacher talk.

affective domain The area of human events that involves feelings, emotions, attitudes, and values. You deal in the affective domain when you include in your teaching those things that cause students to enjoy and feel good about what they are learning.

assessment Measuring how a student, teacher, or school stands in a particular area of concern. For students: "How much have they learned?" (measured by tests observations, etc.). For teachers: "What do they do when they teach?" (measured by observations, etc.). For schools: "What is the nature of their program?" (measured by observation).

basic skills Awhile back and even today, the basics were defined as the three R's: reading, writing, and arithmetic. Skills are the processes needed to perform addition and subtraction, recognize letters and sounds, write numerals and letters, etc.

behavior modification Behavior is what you can see a student do: work on an assignment, wander around the room, punch Jimmy in the nose. Behavior modification is a technique that changes or modifies this behavior through the use of positive reinforcement. It does not deal with whys and wherefores, but simply increases desirable student acts and decreases undesirable ones.

center A learning or interest center is an area of the classroom equipped with materials, instructions, and tasks related to a particular topic. Centers may be as familiar to you as the traditional library corner or as new as a metrics area. A resource center is usually a location in a school that houses ideas, equipment, and supplies for teachers to use.

cognitive domain All things, especially in learning, that have to do with thought, thinking, and knowledge—the "gray matter" so to speak. The majority of school instruction is aimed at helping students perceive, become aware of, know, understand, create, and make use of knowledge.

community aide An important person in many schools, this aide works to make available the resources of the community (people, money, places of interest) to fill the needs of the school.

competency The demonstrated ability to perform certain acts. Is Susie competent in addition facts? Yes, if she can demonstrate on a test (or verbally or whatever) an acceptable level of accuracy in working addition fact problems.

components Once the key word in electronics, components in education refer to parts of a master plan. A component can be large, as the "parent participation component" of a school plan, or small, as the "activity component" of a daily lesson.

concepts Mental pictures of the relationships and qualities of objects or ideas. Your concept of "kitten" consists of whatever you see in your mind about this animal. Your concept of "kittenish" consists of actions and traits you associate with kittens, yet find in other animals and people, too.

concrete As the name implies, something solid, visible, touchable—the part of learning that can be shown to students. A concrete example of addition is counting out three blocks and five blocks and counting that $3 + 5 = 8$ (which is a numerical abstraction).

conferences Conferences occur when teachers meet with parents, other teachers, principals, or students to discuss matters such as teaching, learning, and misbehavior.

contracts A popular method for making assignments, especially among older students. Teacher and student set up in writing exactly what the student will learn, what activities will be done to reach this learning, and the time that will be allotted for it. Contracts help students take responsibility for their own learning.

convergent Convergent production involves the search for a single correct answer to a question or problem. How much is $2 + 2$? The one possible answer, 4, is reached through convergent production. Convergent contrasts with divergent.

criterion The standard you set, the level you will accept. Criterion-based instruction intends to enable all students to reach the chosen standard.

cumulative Cumulative tests are examinations that cover a buildup of knowledge over a period of time. Cumulative files (affectionately known as "cums") are a compilation of student records that are kept during one's years of schooling.

curriculum The schools' programs for learners, or parts of those programs. We may speak of the elementary curriculum, the secondary curriculum, the English curriculum, and so forth.

development The normal process of human growth, which occurs in steps and stages. Applied to instruction, it refers to a sequence of small steps that occur in a logical pattern.

diagnosis The procedure for identifying strengths, weaknesses, and error patterns. Diagnosis of learning problems looks for the exact cause of failure, not just the failure itself. Can you diagnose the student's difficulty in this problem: $29 + 8 = 217$?

diagnostic-prescriptive teaching (DPT) An individualized method of teaching that *diagnoses* weaknesses, *prescribes* activities to remedy these weaknesses, and *tests* students to check their improvement. Pretests (before instruction) and posttests (after instruction) assess student progress.

divergent Divergent production involves the search for many different correct solutions to a problem. "How would you end this story if you were the author?" (There is no single correct answer.)

dyslexia A learning disability that involves perception problems, making it difficult for the student to recognize the direction and order of symbols, letters, and words. Because of the reading problems this fosters, additional, modified instruction is needed for the student to succeed.

Early Childhood Education (ECE) program A large-scale, funded program that focuses on the education of children from preschool through third grade. To qualify for funding, schools must establish a need and develop a master plan to remedy that need. ECE in California uses parent volunteers, aides, and individualized instruction. Assessment teams monitor the progress.

educationally handicapped (EH) Having a learning disability, manifested in a behavioral or emotional problem that makes normal classroom instruction ineffective for the student. Special classes, teachers, and techniques are used to supplement or substitute for the regular teaching.

evaluation One of those multiple-meaning words. Essentially, it is judging, measuring, and testing to determine the effectiveness, quality, and progress of learning and instruction.

evidence The observable acts or products needed to develop and support a conclusion. Does Donald know his new French words? Yes, he does, based on the evidence of his performance on this week's test.

facilitation Any process that encourages and makes possible a desired outcome. You facilitate student interaction when you arrange desks in semicircles instead of straight rows; you facilitate discussion when you ask intriguing questions; you facilitate independent reading when you supply high-interest books to bored readers.

formal In thinking, the term "formal" refers to operations and processes done at the abstract level (Piaget's theory again). Formal instruction usually means deliberately planned and taught lessons using traditional techniques rather than methods such as discovery or open experience.

frustration A level of difficulty in instruction where learning continues only with extreme effort. What is being presented is beyond the student's abilities, and there is little chance for success.

graphics A poster, picture, film, chart, display, map, or any such material that visually displays the point of a lesson, making it clearer for the learners.

heterogeneous A group or class consisting of students who are very similar in ability or performance; selected.

homogeneous A group or class consisting of students who show normal differences in ability or performance; unselected.

hyperkinetic Refers to students who are overactive and easily distracted, unable to give attention to any one thing for very long. There are many theories as to the cause for this, one being that the student has "overloaded circuits" of sensory stimulation. Normal objects and events of the day prove to be too exciting for the student.

individualized instruction A strong trend in education today, this teaching strategy has given rise to more programs, acronyms, commercial kits, and management systems than you would care to count. Individualized instruction recognizes that every student is different, and it attempts to match instruction to needs, interests, and abilities.

in-service training Classes or training provided by the school district for the benefit of teachers and other school personnel.

instructional programs An overall plan of teaching and learning activities with definite objectives in mind for the students. It may refer to the total curriculum or focus on one particular part of it.

intelligence quotient (IQ) The score a student achieves on a standardized test designed to measure ability to do abstract thinking. Although these scores are fairly good predictors of school success, they are not an end (or dead end) in themselves. They are only one measure of what we call intelligence.

learning disability Difficulties in sensual perception and cognitive processes that make normal classroom instruction ineffective for a given student. Special classes, teachers, and teaching techniques are used to help such students learn.

lesson plans Be they short or long, written in detail or carried in a teacher's head, a lesson plan is a guide for what the teacher will do when instructing students. Important points of the plan include objectives, materials, sequence of teaching steps, and evaluation.

mastery Reaching a set standard; a high level of performance that demonstrates competence in a skill or subject. The standard can be set by the teacher, instructional program, or the students themselves.

maturation The process of maturing. Maturity is judged through students' social, physical, cognitive, and emotional behavior as related to their actual age. An attention span of 15 minutes is mature for a kindergartner, immature for a high school senior.

measurement The processes used to identify precise levels of achievement, capability, or growth. Measurements can be done through observation, testing, analysis of student work, and self-appraisal.

mentally gifted minors (MGM) Students whose school work and test scores have shown they have very high intelligence. Separate classes or supplemental instruction is usually given to help these students develop their full potential.

modules Usually found in individualized instruction plans, they are sometimes called unipaks, packets, units, series, steps, levels, or components. By whatever name, they are a series of instructional units that make up a total plan.

motivation A condition that causes one to act. In learning it is an inclination to become involved in a learning task. In teaching it is what the teacher does to activate students. Teachers often motivate with humor, novelty, visual aides, rewards, threats, and punishment.

norms Summaries of performance in many different areas by a large population of people. Norms reveal what the typical performance is for students at a certain age or grade level. Individual performances can fall below, at, or above what is considered normal for other, similar students.

objective The goal toward which one strives. Objectives may be behavioral—"The student will be able to define ten new words"—or expressive—"The student will be able to listen to Beethoven's symphony with enjoyment."

open education A system of classroom management in which students play responsible roles in selecting, organizing, and carrying out their learning activities.

open space Schools that have no interior walls to separate classrooms. They contrast with self-contained classrooms. "Classrooms" exist in designated areas within a large building where two or more other classes may be meeting.

operation The process of solving a problem in either concrete or abstract terms. Most often used in connection with mathematics, as in subtraction.

parent participation A vital part of many schools' programs today, the idea of parent participation has opened the forbidden classroom door, especially in elementary schools. Parents as paid aides or volunteers now work in the classroom tutoring, working with small groups, making materials, etc. As a result, the home, the student, and the school have now become a more coordinated unit.

percentile A statistic that shows how one stands in relation to other people. If a test score shows that a student is in the 92nd percentile, that student has done as well as, or better than, 92% of the people who took the test.

performance Actions and behavior, as on a test, assignment, or activity, that show a student's accomplishments.

positive reinforcement In layman's terms, supplying rewards after a student shows desirable behavior of any kind. You give positive reinforcement when you smile or say "good job" to a correct response or give a special privilege to the quietest person in the class.

The frequency of this rewarded behavior will then likely increase.

psychomotor domain The area of human events that deals with physical movement and coordination. We work with a student's psychomotor domain during physical education, creative dramatics, athletic events, and so forth.

self-concept The totality of ideas, impressions, and beliefs about oneself. Self-concept is a vital, yet fragile part of the human makeup. How students feel about themselves, and what you can do to improve these feelings, will have a bearing on students' academic success.

self-contained classroom The traditional classroom as most of us know it: four walls and windows, everything needed for a class contained within one room.

socialization The process of learning how to get along with people. Theodore Roosevelt called it "the most important single ingredient in the formula of success." Part of education's job is to teach students how to work within our society. Teachers play an ever-expanding role in instructing students in basic social skills, as well as in helping them formulate their own ethics and value systems.

standardized tests Commercially prepared tests, carefully checked for reliability and validity and accompanied by norms and directions for administration and scoring. This type of test includes achievement tests that measure academic performance, aptitude tests that measure the probability of future success in specific areas, and intelligence tests that measure the ability to solve problems and think abstractly.

teacher-made tests As opposed to standardized tests, these instruments are a labor of love by the teacher to find out how well students have learned what has been so carefully taught. "Essay tests" include items that require long written responses. "Short-answer tests" contain items that require at most one- or two-word responses, as in true-false, completion, multiple-choice and matching tests.

teacher or instructional aide A paraprofessional in the classroom who assists the teacher. Duties range from record keeping and housecleaning, to tutoring, to entire group instruction. These people are especially needed in programs of individualized instruction.

team teaching A way of teaching often used where the physical setup of the classroom lends itself to sharing of facilities and flexible grouping and in which teachers work together to plan and instruct a large group of students. They capitalize on individual skills and strengths to provide students the best teaching they can.

tests Instruments or techniques that require students to work independently to demonstrate proficiency (or lack of it) in given areas.

traditional Word used to describe an array of teachers, books, methods, and materials. It is almost impossible to define because it is relative to the speaker. Traditional usually means a teaching method or philosophy that was popular and in vogue about 10 years before the speaker entered teaching.

transfer A student's ability to take knowledge and competency learned in one situation and use it in a similar, but unfamiliar, situation. Mary, after repeated instructions, has learned and seems to understand how to use the standard ruler for measurement. Given a meter stick, perhaps she will be able to transfer old skills in the measuring process to the new instrument.

verbal Having to do with oral and written language. Most knowledge is transmitted in verbal form, its understanding is demonstrated in verbal form, and its scope is broadened in verbal form. Thus students with strengths in verbal skills (anything having to do with language) will succeed in a wide variety of areas, including social contacts.

ACCOUTREMENTS FOR BEHAVIOR MODIFICATION

EXAMPLES OF PRIVILEGE OR ACTIVITY CARDS THAT CAN BE EARNED. A POINT SYSTEM.

Puppet (Self Selection)

10 pts.

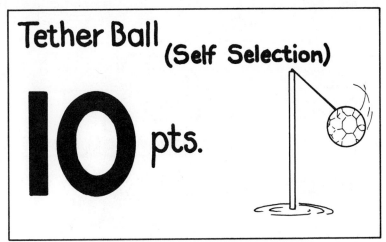

Tether Ball (Self Selection)

10 pts.

Continued.

Cards (Self Selection)

12 pts.

SLINKY (Self Selection)

15 pts.

Good Work Badge (worn all day)

7 pts.

Good Work!

SOME TOKEN IDEAS

"Money" tokens

Continued.

Simple tokens teachers can make

Room 10
Riles School
El Cajon CA

DATE _____

Pay To_____

THE AMOUNT OF_____

_____

for_____

signed_____

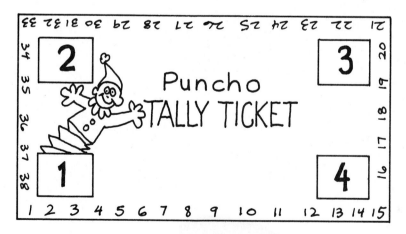

Contract for behavior modification

I've Got An Offer You Can't Refuse

If Jane Voelker can learn up through her sixes by Friday, Oct. 24 and finish the rest **by** Oct 29

Then she may attend the party on Oct. 29

10-20-78 _____
date

_____
student

_____
witness

Miss Feldman
teacher

Self-appraisal form

Take a good look at yourself
Do you like what you see?

Today I feel _____

I am going to try harder to _____

My best trait is _____

If I could change something about myself, I would _____

The last time I helped another person was when _____

_____
date

_____
signature

SELF EVALUATION -- I AM...

a noisy worker	├────┼────┼────┤	a quiet worker
a neat worker	├────┼────┼────┤	a messy worker
an independent worker	├────┼────┼────┤	dependent on others
usually able to finish my work	├────┼────┼────┤	usually behind in my work
friendly and outgoing	├────┼────┼────┤	quiet and reserved

_____
signature

_____
date

ME

Record-keeping chart

DAY	:)	:|	:(	comment
THURSDAY	:)			
FRIDAY	:)			
MONDAY	:)			
TUESDAY	:)			
WEDNESDAY	:)			
THURSDAY	:)			
FRIDAY	:)			

George's Daily Progress

Great Citizenship- <u>one</u> whole week!

Moving along to show that I have mastered the _____'s in multiplication.

_____
name

_____
date   teacher

No "Lion" I've been Trying!

_____participated and showed efforts in class today. Date_____

_____
Teacher

Hurrah!

I have completed my work and have corrected my errors

_____
name

_____
date

_____
Teacher

This is to certify that

_____

Has Won
Student Honor Award
for Class Behavior

Room 4   Riles School

_____
date

Signed _____ Teacher
       _____ Principal

CONGRATULATIONS

You've made it
to the top!

This is to certify that ___Jane Voelker___

has mastered the multiplication facts from _1's_

to _10's_ this _29th_ day of _October_ , in the year _1977_

_____Miss Feldman_____
teacher

_____
witness

INDEX

452